Fourth Edition

Early Childhood Program Management

People and Procedures

Barbara J. Taylor

P9-DML-603

Merrill
Prentice Hall

Upper Saddle River, New Jersey
Columbus, Ohio

·rary of Congress Cataloging-in-Publication Data
ıylor, Barbara J.
    Early childhood program management : people and procedures / Barbara J. Taylor.—
4th ed.
        p. cm.
Includes bibliographical references and index.
ISBN 0-13-032630-5
    1. Day care centers—United States—Administration. I. Title.
HQ778.63 .T39 2002
362.7'12'068—dc21   2001030406

Vice President and Publisher: Jeffery W. Johnston
Executive Editor: Ann Castel Davis
Editorial Assistant: Keli Gemrich
Production Editor: Linda Hillis Bayma
Production Coordination and Text Design: Linda Zuk, WordCrafters Editorial Services, Inc.
Photo Coordinator: Valerie Schultz
Design Coordinator: Diane C. Lorenzo
Cover Designer: Diane Ernsberger
Cover Photo: Supplied by the Author.
Production Manager: Laura Messerly
Director of Marketing: Kevin Flanagan
Marketing Manager: Amy June
Marketing Coordinator: Barbara Koontz

This book was set in Palatino by Carlisle Communications, Ltd. It was printed and bound by R.R. Donnelley & Sons Company. The cover was printed by The Lehigh Press, Inc.

Photo Credits: pp. vii, 138, 362, 428 by Dee R. Taylor; p. 2 by Glen Anderson, Instructional Graphics/Brigham Young University; p. 52 by Todd Yarrington/Merrill; pp. 98, 320 by Anne Vega/Merrill; pp. 164, 250 by Dan Floss/Merrill; pp. 188, 400 by Anthony Magnacca/Merrill; p. 284 by Scott Cunningham/Merrill.

Pearson Education Ltd., *London*
Pearson Education Australia Pty. Limited, *Sydney*
Pearson Education Singapore Pte. Ltd.
Pearson Education North Asia Ltd., *Hong Kong*
Pearson Education Canada Ltd., *Toronto*
Pearson Educación de Mexico, S.A. de C. V.
Pearson Education—Japan, *Tokyo*
Pearson Education Malaysia Pte. Ltd.
Pearson Education, *Upper Saddle River, New Jersey*

10 9 8 7 6 5 4 3 2 1
ISBN 0-13-032630-5

*To my husband and family for their love, encouragement,
endurance, and appreciated contributions to
my personal and professional endeavors*

Preface

By the fact that you are browsing through this text, it is assumed that you plan to operate or own a child care center, want to learn more about the tasks of owning/operating a child care center, are interested in applying at a government (Head Start) program, or are considering preschool teaching in an early childhood education center. You may be saying to yourself, "I enjoy young children, and I want to gain knowledge and experience so I can effectively guide their growth, development, experiences, and attitudes!"

Your next thought may be, "But where do I start? The field is so broad and my influence on young children and families will be so lasting. How do I prepare myself for this tremendous undertaking?" You do it one step at a time! You listen carefully, you read for meaning, you ask questions, you watch others, you are perceptive and teachable. You share your talents and you broaden your interests to what is going on around you and throughout the country that will have a permanent bearing on children and families. What is happening in social/cultural circles? What bills are being proposed and passed in state and federal legislatures that affect families? What are the concerns of child care directors, teachers, staff, and parents, and how can they be resolved? You'll want to ask yourself (and others) this question: "Is early care good for young children?" What about the different types of care for young children—and how can

you make it better and also prepare children for their future experiences? Let it be clearly stated here and throughout the text that there can be no division between "care" and "education" of young children. They are inseparable; for when one is caring for a child, one is also educating the same child, and vice versa.

WHY THIS BOOK?

Today more than ever, the education and care of children is the shared responsibility of parents, educators and other professionals, and the children themselves. The unique pressures of our times demand a cooperative plan, so that all these parties can work together comfortably. In colonial days, parents reared their children in the home, schooled them, and prepared them for careers or occupations through experience or apprenticeship. Travel was limited, families produced their own food and clothing, and printed materials were luxuries. Today the situation is different. Children have many encounters that influence their lives, both outside the home and within it. Public-, private-, and home-schooling options are available to students. Employment opportunities change—jobs once considered stable are phased out and new types of jobs are created. For a variety of reasons (including lack of time, know-how, and patience), parents need or want help with their infants, toddlers, and preschool children, whose needs are different from those of school-age children.

It is often difficult for parents to find the type of substitute care that they desire. However, it is extremely important that during the children's early years both they and their parents interact with individuals who are capable of building self-confidence, satisfaction, happiness, and trust.

This text addresses the need for out-of-home care, the provision of quality care, and the value of a harmonious balance between the two. Throughout the text, the worth of all individuals (whether children or adults) is emphasized, as well as the need to appreciate the significance of building their relationships with others.

Among other inquiries, you'll want to know what this book is all about and how it will help you understand the needs of children and families in our country today. You will wonder how it will help you to be a good teacher, administrator, parent, or advocate for young children, and if choosing this field is wise for you as you learn about the needs of children and others and study related issues. Much of your commitment to children and issues will depend on you. Hopefully, you will take more responsibility in discussing and promoting important issues and possible resolutions—in other words, being an informed voter and supporter of important educational, social, legal, and community issues.

In the earlier chapters the reader becomes acquainted with the past, present, and future needs of children and families (Chapters 1, 2, and 3). Then the discussion turns to the philosophy, organizational structure, and management of personnel, programs, resources, and time (Chapters 4, 5, 6, and 7). The text continues with a discussion of the health of children and staff, environmental hazards, and safety in child care (Chapters 8 and 9).

After providing background in philosophy, management, resources, health, and safety, the text turns to physical considerations: planning space, purchasing equipment, finance, and budgeting (Chapters 10, 11, and 12). The final section of the text is divided into eight appendixes, including Handbook for Parents, Child-Care Applications, Children's Records, Contagious Diseases and Immunizations, First Aid, Job Descriptions and Announcements, Employee Records, and Inventories. The text ends with the glossary and the index. The appendixes, glossary, and index contain valuable and supportive information. They are important and should be consulted frequently.

Goals cannot be achieved without an organized plan. To develop a successful program, each chapter should be considered on its own and then all chapters should be used as an integrated unit.

At the beginning of each chapter is a **Guide for Readers,** which presents a quick chapter overview. A **Chapter Summary** concludes each chapter. Also included in each chapter is a feature called **Participators,** which are actually application exercises or "stimulators" to help the reader focus on particular principles presented in the chapter. A list of references cited appears at the end of each chapter.

For the sake of convenience, masculine and feminine pronouns are used alternately in chapters: "she" in odd-numbered chapters and "he" in even-numbered chapters.

WHO CAN BENEFIT FROM USING THIS TEXT?

This book is designed for training programs at various levels: community and state colleges, universities, private companies, government, and others. It can be used as a self-help aid by individuals preparing for credentialing and by administrators or employees who have no opportunity for other means of instruction (corporate day care, family day care providers, and others).

Parents, lawmakers, and community-minded individuals will find this text helpful in understanding the needs of young children and families in promoting legislation that will build community cohesiveness and strengthen families.

Typical scenes from a child-care center

WHY INTEGRATE HUMAN AND ADMINISTRATIVE NEEDS?

When the child-care needs of parents and children are considered in the context of entrepreneurship, results are more likely to be successful than if the two aspects are considered separately. For example, when parents need child care, they must seek or create solutions. On the other hand, before any child-care business can be successful, it must consider various risk factors, such as location, finance, and need. By working cooperatively, parents and center operators can address their needs and limitations; otherwise parents may have to settle for less than desirable circumstances, and centers may be unsuccessful.

ACKNOWLEDGMENTS

I would like to thank the following reviewers for their assistance and helpful suggestions in the preparation of this text: Toni Campbell, San Jose State University; Jill E. Gelormino, St. Joseph's College (Brooklyn, New York); John R. Hranitz, Bloomsburg University of Pennsylvania; and Herman E. Walston, Kentucky State University.

Discover the Companion Website Accompanying This Book

THE PRENTICE HALL COMPANION WEBSITE: A VIRTUAL LEARNING ENVIRONMENT

Technology is a constantly growing and changing aspect of our field that is creating a need for content and resources. To address this emerging need, Prentice Hall has developed an online learning environment for students and professors alike—Companion Websites—to support our textbooks.

In creating a Companion Website, our goal is to build on and enhance what the textbook already offers. For this reason, the content for each user-friendly website is organized by topic and provides the professor and student with a variety of meaningful resources. Common features of a Companion Website include:

For the Professor—

Every Companion Website integrates **Syllabus Manager**™, an online syllabus creation and management utility.

- **Syllabus Manager**™ provides you, the instructor, with an easy, step-by-step process to create and revise syllabi, with direct links into the Companion Website and other online content without having to learn HTML.

- Students may log on to your syllabus during any study session. All they need to know is the web address for the Companion Website and the password you've assigned to your syllabus.

- After you have created a syllabus using **Syllabus Manager**™, students may enter the syllabus for their course section from any point in the Companion Website.

- Clicking on a date, the student is shown the list of activities for the assignment. The activities for each assignment are linked directly to actual content, saving time for students.

- Adding assignments consists of clicking on the desired due date, then filling in the details of the assignment—name of the assignment, instructions, and whether it is a one-time or repeating assignment.

- In addition, links to other activities can be created easily. If the activity is online, a URL can be entered in the space provided, and it will be linked automatically in the final syllabus.

- Your completed syllabus is hosted on our servers, allowing convenient updates from any computer on the Internet. Changes you make to your syllabus are immediately available to your students at their next logon.

For the Student—

- **Topic Overviews**—outline key concepts in topic areas
- **Web Links**—general websites related to topic areas as well as associations and professional organizations
- **Read About It**—timely articles that enable you to become more aware of important issues in early childhood education
- **Learn by Doing**—put concepts into action, participate in activities, complete lesson plans, examine strategies, and more
- **For Teachers**—access information that you will need to know as an in-service teacher, including information on materials, activities, lessons, curriculum, and state standards

- **Visit a School**—visit a school's website to see concepts, theories, and strategies in action
- **Electronic Bluebook**—send homework or essays directly to your instructor's email with this paperless form
- **Message Board**—serves as a virtual bulletin board to post—or respond to—questions or comments to/from a national audience
- **Chat**—real-time chat with anyone who is using the text anywhere in the country—ideal for discussion and study groups, class projects, etc.

To take advantage of these and other resources, please visit the *Early Childhood Program Management: People and Procedures,* Fourth Edition, Companion Website at

www.prenhall.com/taylor

Contents

Early Childhood Program Management

Chapter 1

The Needs of Children and Families

Guide for Readers

Note to Readers: Due to a lag between collection and dissemination of figures, some statistics represent a trend but not immediate conditions. There may also be a discrepancy between figures due to the date or method of collection.

❖ *Care and education of children has always been a common societal concern. Men and women from various countries and periods of time have been instrumental in the progress and strength of programs for young children (see graphics throughout the chapter).*

❖ *European practices have been influential on American child care and education. The Child Study Movement in the United States brought new ideas and practices regarding the growth, education, and development of our young children.*

❖ *Educational promoters, philanthropists, and "doers of the work" have encouraged and produced important changes in our thinking and actions regarding young children.*

❖ *The current and future needs of young children are changing.*

❖ *One of our current and serious problems regarding young children is "homelessness."*

❖ *There are many theories about the nature of children. Some current programs have developed from modification to earlier programs and research findings.*

❖ *Different families and their children have different needs; however, children learn and develop by following a sequential pattern, by which adults can plan activities and expect realistic actions for the child's present stage.*

❖ *Parents may have unrealistic goals for their children.*

❖ *Other data and statistics of the state of child care and family needs will be used for emphasis throughout the book.*

❖ *Carefully note the figures throughout the text. They will add depth and understanding to the material being discussed.*

❖ *Each chapter has "Facts and Figures." They provide an overview of what has transpired on a particular topic during certain time periods.*

❖ *You will also encounter "Stimulators." Each one is to help you understand principles presented while giving you an opportunity to express your own ideas. Spend time thinking through the implications for your teaching and interaction with young children, supporting staff, and parents. Through these exercises you may be better able to resolve "hands-on" experiences in your daily teaching.*

❖ *At the end of each chapter are a number of "Participators." Carefully read them. Then select and complete those that are of most interest to you or about which you want further information and experience. This is a good way to increase your understanding of early childhood education.*

❖ *The National Association for the Education of Young Children (NAEYC) has a very specific* **Code of Ethical Conduct,** *which will be referred to in various chapters. In essence it states: "Teachers will avoid practices that are harmful, disrespectful, degrading, dangerous, exploitative, intimidating, emotionally damaging, or physically harmful to children" (p. 7). There are ethical responsibilities (ideals and principles) to children, families, coworkers, employers, employees, and community and society.*

Facts and Figures

- "Ten Most Critical Threats to America's Children: Warning Signs for the Next Millennium," a report presented in November 1999 at the National Press Club in Washington identifies these threats to be: abuse and neglect at home, substance abuse, teen pregnancy, inadequate child care, lack of health care, poor schools, dangers in the environment, poverty, absent parents, and crime. Each of the threats is listed with possible solutions.

- In 1990 in the United States, 25 percent of all children were being raised in single-parent homes; 90% of these single parents were women (Children's Defense Fund, 1990).

- At the White House Conference on Children in 1970, child care was voted to be the No. 1 problem facing American children and families. Subsequently, the 1971 Child Development Act was passed, but vetoed by President Richard Nixon. . . . Little action taken at the national level until 1990 when a child-care bill authorizing $750 million was passed, a funding level lower than that proposed in 1971 (Zigler & Gilman, 1993, p. 176).

- U.S. employers have been involved in providing child-care benefits since the Industrial Revolution. The first child-care program in the United States was offered in 1834 by an employer, Robert Owens, in New Harmony, Indiana.

- Michael Lamb and his colleagues (1993), reviewing the nation's child-care settings in 1993, found that low quality of child care may seriously jeopardize children's growth and development. America was particularly concerned about school readiness, so it was ironic that as a nation we had failed to consider the plight of a child who is expected to enter school ready to learn after some 5 years of poor or even destructive child care (Zigler & Gilman, 1993, p. 175).

- In 1993, 54 percent of mothers with children younger than 3, and 74 percent of those with children ages 3 to 5, were in the civilian labor force. And many parents, regardless of whether they require child care because of employment, now want their children to have some kind of preschool experience to help prepare them for school (Children's Defense Fund, 1992).

- The proportion of fathers caring for their preschoolers reached an all time high of 30 percent in 1991; however, subsequent data for 1993 now suggests that this increase was a temporary response to the 1990 to 1991 recession—further suggesting that future researchers should acknowledge fluctuations in the economy when conducting or replicating studies on husband's participation in traditional female tasks (Casper & O'Connell, 1997).

- No further research is needed to demonstrate that high-quality care is good for children and that poor-quality care is destructive (Zigler, 1993, p. 175).

- School systems are a major source of services to children younger than the traditional kindergarten entry age—with both positive (ability to bring the same level of standards they apply to other grades) and negative (inappropriate role for public schools; being slow to meet the full-day needs of families, etc.) outcomes (Clifford et al., 1999, p. 48).

HISTORICAL PERSPECTIVE

The needs of children and families for care inside and outside the home are not new. They may seem more pressing now because *we* live in the now, but for centuries parents have needed and sought child care because of their immediate circumstances—large families, poverty, unwillingness of parents to provide for their children, desertion, and other personal or social reasons.

In ancient Greece, infanticide was practiced, usually on female babies. During the Middle Ages, common methods of infanticide were exposure to the elements, overlaying (suffocation while lying in bed with her parents), opiates, starvation, dunking (in very cold water), and other ways. To curb infanticide, some large cities in Europe established foundling homes, institutions, and hospitals.

Christianity had a strong influence in changing the attitudes toward children, but as late as 1895 missionaries to China often noted infants being thrown into the streets and allowed to die of exposure. Working mothers at the time of the Industrial Revolution practiced "baby farming" by hiring wet nurses (called "angel makers") with the intent of disposing of their infants through death, desertion, or other means.

Each period in history has unique social, economic, political, and personal norms of how children should be treated. It is how these norms are applied individually and collectively that makes a period "good" or "bad" for children. Problems of overpopulation, war, depression, social upheaval, political changes, personal unrest, and economic instability are handled better by some individuals and localities than others. Religious, social, and government agencies are often available for families in dire need.

Although this is not a text on the history of education, some background will shed light on the conditions that determine why children and families need out-of-home care, how it should be organized, and some of the characteristics of good child care.

European Influences on Child Care and Education

In this overview, care and education of young children will be considered collectively—for how can one be separate from the other? When one is caring for children, one is also educating them and vice versa.

Two early advocates of children under the age of 6 were Plato (428–348 B.C.) and Aristotle (384–322 B.C.). Plato was an idealist who wanted to restore moral standards through education. He taught that parents were unfit for child rearing, so this task should be assumed by state nurseries. Aristotle was a realist who observed small children and set guidelines for their upbringing. He also recognized individual talents and skills in young children.

Only 10 European educators making significant contributions to early child care and education will be mentioned in this text. (See Appendix 1A at the end of this chapter.) Each person cited made intriguing personal, political, social, economic, or educational contributions. As you continue your study of this text, it will become apparent why certain early educators are mentioned. These are the individuals who laid the foundation for the program philosophy advocated in this text by emphasizing the importance of early experiences, individual differences, making the setting fit the child, play (re-creation or recreation), sensory learning, respect, recognition, nurturance, choice (interest and/or attention span), developmentally appropriate materials and activities, firsthand opportunities, family involvement, parent education, and so on.

Modern early childhood educators are indebted to Martin Luther for books and music; John Amos Comenius for visual aids, parental involvement, and advocating that *all* children be educated; John Locke for individual differences; Jean Jacques Rousseau for removing pressures from children; Johann Heinrich Pestalozzi for multiage grouping; Robert Owen for infant schools; Friedrich Wilhelm Froebel for the importance of play and teacher training; Margaret

McMillan for open-air nurseries; Maria Montessori for didactic materials; and Jean Piaget for a theory of cognitive development. All of these people have contributed much to make a better world for young children; they have left a great legacy. You will gain information and a new appreciation for these educational forbearers if you carefully study the appendices to this chapter.

American Influence on Child Care and Education

While attention was being given to children in other nations and places, were Americans less concerned? Of course not. Americans visited the schools of Pestalozzi and Froebel, and Owen established an infant school in his American settlement. European educators visited America. There was an active interchange between the two sides of the Atlantic, with some agreement, some disagreement, some new theories, and some revival of old theories. Individuals of different backgrounds and ambitions sought firsthand knowledge through visitations, discussions, experimentation, and information in order to promote interest and support in the new country.

This section consists of four interrelated parts: (1) general influence of the child study movement, (2) promoters of educational philosophy, (3) doers of the work (participators and leaders), and (4) organizations, government, and other support. (See Appendices 1B to 1F at the end of this chapter.)

General Influence of the Child Study Movement (Appendix 1B). Many individuals have influenced or added depth to the care and education of young children.

By the 1830s, the idea of children as miniature adults was fading, and the idea of childhood as a distinct phase was gaining more importance. The dress, treatment, and behavior and work expectations for young children were looked at in a new light. An increased emphasis was placed on the role of mother as educator and caregiver in the home. Of this period Spodek (1988) writes:

The role of women still haunts us. Calls for the development of child care centers are countered by the argument that prematurely wresting young children from the bosom of their families plays havoc with our social, cultural, and economic system. Child care has been accused of destroying family life, and of taking children away from the cozy warm relationships found only in the home. Women are often burdened with guilt for seeking services for their children outside the home just as they were in the pre-Civil War days of "Fireside Education." (p. 12)

For bureaucratic and financial reasons children under six were excluded from the school system (May & Vinovskis, 1977). Children were educated by parents or dame schools, whose main purpose was to teach reading and morals.

Industrialization, child labor, and middle-class moralism eventually led to the birth of the child rescue movement. In America, orphanages were operated as day-care centers for poor children and were custodial in nature. "Actuarial data disclosed a relationship between maternal employment and infant mortality," according to Fein and Clarke-Stewart (1973, p. 14). "In 1854 the first American creche was established in collaboration with the Children's Hospital in New York City (Forest, 1927). The children, whose ages ranged from 15 weeks to 3 years, received regular medical examinations and were under the supervision of experienced nursemaids."

Social institutions were established for relief, rehabilitation, and reconstruction. Day nurseries were classified as "relief." The first settlement house nursery was opened at Hull House in 1898 under the direction of Jane Addams, social worker. The same year, the National Federation of Day Nurseries was founded to call attention to the poor quality of care offered by day nurseries. When working mothers were asked why they were not using the day nurseries (there was a 29 percent vacancy rate), their reasons included inconvenience of location and dislike of care and education their children were receiving (Fein &

Clarke-Stewart, 1973). Beginning with glowing optimism, in ensuing years the goals of the day nursery shifted from "mind to body, to practical habits and skills, to protection rather than change" (p. 18). The introduction of nursery schools, which promoted parent education, programs for and about children, cognitive and emotional development, management of routine functions (sleeping, eating, and eliminating), and importance of play, eventually led to a decline in day nurseries.

Differences between day nurseries and nursery schools were apparent in their purposes and approach. Day nurseries provided a place for children away from home while nursery schools functioned mainly for research and teacher preparation. Day nursery staff were concerned about physical health and survival; nursery school teachers attempted to develop the child's independence, expand the child's expressive abilities, and not impose adult values. "By 1942 the educational and developmental philosophies of the day nursery and the nursery school were indistinguishable (Fleiss, 1962, Appendix A)" (Fein & Clarke-Stewart, 1973, p. 22).

The child study movement began as new ideas were formulated about the growth and development of young children and how they should be treated and taught. For some time, the principles of Froebel had been advocated in a rather strict interpretation. Children were seated most of the time doing Froebel's gifts and occupations. Most educators acknowledged the importance of the early years, but there was no consensus about how this idea was to be interpreted and implemented. Psychoanalysts (like Sigmund Freud) studying disturbed adults turned to their patients' early childhood years, and a rather permissive attitude toward early child rearing evolved.

Parents kept diaries on their children (Gesell, 1939), questionnaires were formulated, intelligence tests were initiated, new teaching methods were advocated, and new ways of observing and recording normative data were implemented. The period of childhood was divided into ages and stages by researchers like Arnold Gesell, Erik

Erikson, Lawrence Kohlberg, and Abraham Maslow, who focused on different aspects of the child (see Figure 1–1). The study of children came to be seen with acceptance and support. Enrollment in nursery schools was encouraged for children's social development.

The Progressive Education Association was formed. Its membership exceeded 5,000 in 1927 and reached a peak of 10,500 in 1938. By 1955, the enthusiasm, the money, and the members were gone; all that remained were the slogans (Cremin, 1957).

Advocates of the progressive philosophy believed that: (1) children have individual needs and differences, (2) teachers must be attentive to children's needs, (3) children learn best when they are interested and highly motivated by the material, (4) rote memory learning is wrong and useless to children, (5) the child's total development includes social, physical, intellectual, and emotional aspects, (6) the best learning occurs from direct contact with and manipulation of materials, and (7) children need information and learning at their own pace (Osborn, 1991).

The compensatory education movement, exemplified by the Head Start Program, has been based on a contrasting belief system, that of optimistic environmentalism. Its basic premise is that intelligence is not a fixed entity, but can be improved by stimulating and systematic programming. David Elkind (1977) cites several reasons for the paradigm shift to environmentalism that occurred in North American education and psychology in the 1960s, the civil rights movement, the Sputnik launching in 1957, the fact that American psychology was inadequate for development of curriculum. . . . Learning theory and maze psychology, heavily based on animal research, provided little inspiration for the new cognitivism. Consequently, American psychology was forced to broaden in the 1960s to include more emphasis on developmental psychology, ego psychology, social psychology, and information processing psychology (Woodill, 1988, p. 21).

The child study movement pushed educators to recognize that children of the poor were in need of better housing, nutrition, child care, edu-

Erikson: Seven psycho-social steps to a healthy personality (1950) (*Young Children*, Sept. 1994)	Trust vs. mistrust (birth to 1 year) Autonomy vs. shame and doubt (ages 1 to 3 years) Initiative vs. guilt (ages 3 to 6 years) Industry vs. inferiority (ages 7 to 11 years) Identity vs. role confusion (adolescence) Generativity vs. stagnation (adulthood) Integrity vs. despair (adulthood)
Gesell: Progress of child in four areas (1923–1945)	Motor characteristics Language Adaptive behavior Personal-social behavior
Kohlberg: Model for moral development (1968)	Obedience and punishment orientation (ages 1 to 3 years) Simple exchange (ages 3 to 5 years) Good child morality (ages 6 to 12 years) Law and order stage (ages 13 to 16 years) Morality of democratic and representative government (ages 16 to 19 years) Morality of individual conscience (ages 19 to 25 years)
Maslow: Hierarchy of needs (1970)	Physiological: hunger, thirst, etc. Safety: to feel secure and safe, out of danger Belongingness and love: to affiliate with others, be accepted and belong Esteem: to achieve, be competent, and gain approval and recognition Self-actualization: to find self-fulfillment and realize one's potential

Figure 1–1 Four well-known classifications frequently cited in early childhood education literature.

cation, parent education, and personal security. As researchers/educators shared information, philanthropists appeared, but came to the aid of far too few of the children. A brief summary of some of the major trends in the child study movement follows. (For more details, see appendices at end of this chapter.)

Promoters of Educational Philosophy. American educators learned of progress in Europe through publications, visits abroad, and demonstrations by foreign educators in this country. (See Appendix 1C.)

During the 1800s education was not universally available throughout the country. Children were being exploited in the workforce. "The first formal playgrounds in America appeared in 1886 at the Boston sandgartens and launched the playground movement" (Osborn, 1991, p. 42). Mothers' groups, called maternal associations, were organized in several cities by ministers' wives and dealt with the religious and moral training of children. The first magazines for parents were published: *Mother's Magazine* in 1832, *Parents' Magazine* in 1840, and *Mother's Assistant* in 1841 (Osborn, 1991).

In an effort to improve the lives of children of mill workers, Robert Owen began a community cooperative in New Harmony, Indiana, with day care and an infant school. He prohibited children from working in the mills until they could at least read and write. Owen's community experiment failed and was abandoned in 1827.

Nearly 50 percent of all factory workers were children. The first child labor law in the United

States was passed in Massachusetts in 1836 but was seldom enforced. It prohibited children from working in factories unless they had attended school for 3 months in the preceding year (Osborn, 1991).

1920s–1930s	Physical development and individual intelligence testing were a major focus. (Binet, Hall, Gesell) Behaviorism—conditioning and behavior shaping. Schedules, impersonal interaction, "make children what you want them to be" (Watson)
1940s–1960	Physical and social-emotional development. Psychoanalytic awareness (Erikson, Freud)
1960s–1970s	Attention to social-emotional development. Increased emphasis on intellectual development (Piaget)
1960s-	Social problems of children—poverty, segregation, prejudice

Parents were the primary educators of their children in early American settlements, teaching the alphabet, writing skills, and reading—mainly for the purpose of reading the Bible. When children were apprenticed out, shop owners and masters were expected to educate the children under their tutorship.

As people moved westward, efforts to establish education for children moved with them, but progress was slow. Some states established departments of education, but they were somewhat ineffective. Classes were often taught by young men with five or six years of education (Osborn, 1991).

Eventually, men in high educational positions in the government gave credibility to the educational movement. Henry Barnard (1890), the first commissioner of education (established by Congress in 1867), reported to Congress on a visit to Froebel's kindergarten exhibit in London in 1854. He became a strong supporter of the movement and later published *Kindergarten and Child Culture*

Papers. The Hon. William Torrey Harris, superintendent of schools in St. Louis and later United States commissioner of education, added his support, which caused educators who had ignored the kindergarten movement to seriously consider its principles. On the urging of Elizabeth Peabody and Susan Blow, Harris agreed to set up a kindergarten in St. Louis and sent Blow to New York for training.

As the child study movement began and different ways of educating children were initiated, some major criticisms began to be raised about the rigidity of Froebel's ideas.

Thousands of people attended the centennial exposition in Philadelphia, and many observed the outstanding exhibit of a daily kindergarten and heard lectures on its philosophy. Because of the popularity of the exhibit, kindergarten classrooms were set up at the Columbian Exposition in Chicago (1893) and Southeastern Exposition in Atlanta (1895) (Osborn, 1991). For details about the individuals mentioned in this section, see Appendix 1B.

Doers of the Work (Participators and Leaders). Doers were the hub of the child study movement. *Strict* interpreters of Froebel's philosophy were trying to convince others to remain pure and true. Believers of Froebel's *intentions* wanted to follow some of the practices, but in moderation. Students in teacher training either accepted Froebel in total or tolerated the teaching and then implemented the program as they saw fit. There were varying degrees of support, many disagreements, diverse practices, and sometimes conflicting temperaments. (See Appendix 1D at end of this chapter.)

Froebel's followers, especially in Germany, were seeking refuge from political unrest and wanted a place to promote their educational beliefs. Many crossed the Atlantic to begin anew in America. They published articles, taught courses, began kindergarten classes, and often spent their own money furthering the cause of education with varying degrees of success.

Nursery school and day-care centers were also undergoing changes as a result of the child study movement, exchange with Europe, growing acceptance of the study of children, social and economic conditions, and less restrictive child-rearing practices.

Other philosophies were attracting attention as well. For example, Maria Montessori's programs were popular in Europe, but Montessori found it difficult to promote her ideas in America because of professional criticism (from William Kilpatrick, 1914, for one) and rejection by some women's organizations. The nursery school program as presented by McMillan (Bradburn, 1976) was in direct contrast to both Froebel and Montessori. Nursery schools, day-care centers, kindergartens—all these different programs were devised for different types of individuals in different circumstances. When a program was transported out of context, issues were raised by critics.

Many of the kindergarten supporters were interested in the social and economic conditions of children in addition to their educational or cognitive conditions. They believed that to care for children is to educate them and to educate children is to care for them.

There are many charming, humanistic, tender, and personal stories about each of these doers. Margaret McMillan felt that clean children could learn better. She got an old tub from the junk yard and painted it white, then instructed her teachers to bathe the children in it. Imagine her surprise when the children stuck to the tub because the paint was still wet. Elizabeth Peabody would sometimes wear her nightgown under her clothes on lecture tours and carry her toothbrush in her pocket to save time and luggage! Imagine attending a Broadway play with Patty Smith Hill when her song "Happy Birthday to You" was sung without permission. She sued, won, and used the money to support her kindergartens for the poor. There are at least five sets of sisters who dedicated their lives to bettering the care and education of young children: Margarethe Meyer Schurz and Bertha Meyer (and even brother Adolph), Margaret and Rachel McMillan, Elizabeth Peabody and Mary Peabody Mann, Kate Douglas Smith Wiggin (Riggs) and Nora Archibald Smith,

and Patty Smith Hill, Mary D. Smith, and Mildred Smith. (See Appendix 1E at end of this chapter.)

As nursery schools expanded and became more popular, a multidisciplinary program evolved—home economics, nursing, medicine, social work, psychology, and education joined forces. Lawrence K. Frank provided leadership for the interdisciplinary approach to the study of children.

Organizations, Government, and Other Support. The War on Poverty has been long and hard. Possibly the most successful impact has been the initiation of Head Start with supporting federal budgets and laws. (See Appendix 1F at end of this chapter.)

Historical Perspective: A Review

Over the years, some significant events have caused people to take another look at how children are treated, taught, and nurtured. Illiteracy, the segregation of children in educational circles, and world events (e.g., the arms race, human rights issues, and social conditions) have influenced the way children are viewed and treated.

In early times children were often considered burdens. Children were abandoned, infanticide was practiced, child labor flourished, and apprenticeships were common. Today we believe that children are our greatest asset and that it is our responsibility to nurture and educate them for their sakes and ours. Children go through childhood but once. We must be advocates for children! We must look on them as our chance for a better and more peaceful world tomorrow.

Looking back and looking forward, we see faults and promises. Research can help us evaluate and plan. We can take advantage of past experiences and findings; we can plan what steps to take and initiate procedures to improve the lot of children (see Bradburn, 1976; Braun & Edwards, 1972; Hymes, 1978, 1991).

Research has shown that intelligence is not fixed as was thought at one time. Environment, opportunities, and experiences influence how well the child's cognitive potential is reached.

Children who experience intellectual stimulation at home tend to do well in school. Studies indicate that 80 percent of intellectual development occurs by age 8 (Bloom, 1964; Hunt, 1961; White, 1985) (see also "Children"). Therefore, most intellectual stimulation occurs within the home. The things children learn early in life, especially from their parents—their first teachers and nurturers—are hard to change later. Parents and early caregivers (inside or outside the home) have a tremendous impact on a child's attitudes and learning.

Social conditions of the child's environment are also important. Children raised with poverty, stress, fear, and/or abuse exert much of their energy trying to *exist* rather than growing, developing, and enjoying life.

Current and Future Needs

Social and economic conditions may fluctuate between poverty and prosperity, but there will always be a need for education and care of children outside the home—for reasons of choice or necessity. (See Chapters 8 and 9.)

Situations of individual families differ greatly. One fifth of all American children are born into

---

Facts and Figures

- Homelessness is on the increase. One study estimated that up to 3 million people in America have not, at some time during any given year, lived in a fixed residence (National Coalition for the Homeless, 1990).

- Families with children constitute more than one third of the homeless population (Children's Defense Fund, 1992; McChesney, 1992; U.S. Conference of Mayors, 1990).

- Children are the fastest growing segment of the homeless population. On any given night, as many as 100,000 children are homeless (National Institute of Medicine, 1988), and children younger than 5 now compose over half the population of children without homes (Klein et al., 1993).

- Three fourths of homeless families are single-parent families, typically headed by women (Bassuk, 1990).

- Some homeless families live in cars, abandoned buildings, tent cities, and public places (Alkers, 1992).

- Up to 600,000 school-age children are homeless at any one time in America. About one third of those children were reported as not attending any school (Freedman, 1990).

The *FYI* report of 1994 (January) by NAEYC included the following information:

- From 1980 to 1990, the number of poor children increased by 28 percent, while the total preschool-age population increased by only 16 percent.

- The number of preschoolers in poverty increased in *all but four states* between 1980 and 1990.

- The number of preschoolers living in single-parent families increased for all categories. However, *60 percent of poor and 30 percent of near-poor children of preschool age live in single-parent families* as compared to the less than 10 percent of the nonpoor preschool population who live in single-parent families.

families with financial strains so severe that they will suffer basic deprivations.

Homeless Children and Families (See also Chapter 3)

As bleak as these numbers appear, the trend continues. A 1993 *Current Population Report* cites *one in four children younger than age 6 living in families with income below the poverty level.* "These statistics are more than information, they reflect real children in our homes and early childhood programs, in our communities and classrooms."

The U.S. General Accounting Office (1993) reports the following:

> About one-fourth of poor preschool-aged children live in rural areas. (p. 26)
>
> Minorities comprised approximately 30% of total preschool-aged population. By contrast, about 60% of poor preschool-aged children were minority. (p. 24)
>
> About 35% of poor and near-poor preschool-aged children participated in preschool, compared with 45% of the nonpoor population. Poor and near-poor 3-year-olds participated in preschool at much lower rates than nonpoor 3-year-olds. (p. 35)

Of great interest and serious concern is the growing number of homeless individuals of all ages in our country. Centers located near homeless shelters have a great opportunity to enhance the lives and welfare of young children. They can contribute measures of safety, security, and stability for these children at a very crucial time in their development. Recall earlier in this chapter where Maslow (1970) identified safety and security as essential in the hierarchy of needs, following shelter, food, and clothing (see Figure 1–1). Erikson's building of trust and autonomy are also important for the homeless child, for "success breeds success as well as feelings of self-worth and accomplishment" (1963).

For someone who feels secure in life, home, relationships, and oneself, it is difficult to understand this role of the homeless person and/or family. For those who are homeless—adult or child—there is little security, predictability, privacy, routine, or relationships on which to rely. In a shelter there may be a place to eat, sleep, and spend at least part of one's time, but things are just not under one's control. Children, unsupervised while parents look for work or housing, may encounter unsanitary conditions, disease, no immunizations or health care, poor nutrition, and their safety may well be in jeopardy.

The following actions or situations may be characteristic of a homeless child:

Insecurity: No place for oneself or belongings; restless. "Even publicly supported shelters can

---

❖ Stimulator

The setting is in the heart of a large, industrial city. You remind yourself that you are in a homeless shelter—evidenced by the many beds, scattered boxes, crowded conditions, and wandering people of all ages—and that you have never seen anything like this before. Several small children are huddled near a parent for comfort, protection, and encouragement. You surmise that the family is here due to unemployment, illness, desertion, or other unfortunate circumstances. As you stand there, your thoughts turn from discomfort to action. You are approached by the director of the center, who says, sincerely, "I hope you have come in response to our plea for volunteers. Our greatest need is for stability and assurance to our preschool children. I do hope you have had some experience with young children." Through your mind flashes several responses that will reassure you: your past experiences, your future goals, your personal qualities, your feelings about families, your sympathy for those less fortunate than you, and so on. Do you focus first on the children, the facility, the responsibility, parents and families, center support? Select a partner or small discussion group and consider the factors and steps necessary in making this a satisfying and rewarding experience for all those involved at the shelter.

be dangerous because their crowded conditions allow crime to thrive" (Eddowes & Hranitz, 1989, p. 198). "Some adults in homeless settings use alcohol and/or drugs, increasing the potential danger to children" (Bassuk, 1990, p. 9).

Eating habits: May eat unusual amounts of food, may need encouragement to eat healthy foods, or may be malnourished.

Space: Personal space for individual and cooperative play, but not so much space that they lose security with belongings and individuals. They like to be within sight of familiar objects and people. However, within the shelter there is no real privacy.

Health and rest: Because of close confinement, limited health standards, and poor diet or eating habits, children may become ill with common or chronic illnesses. Rest will be important. "Lead based paint peeling from old buildings' walls can cause lasting health and developmental problems, such as low energy levels and mental retardation" (Children's Defense Fund, 1992, p. 37). "Exposed electrical wires, broken glass, unscreened windows and crawling insects may also cause injury to the curious child" (Eddowes, 1992, p. 104).

Behavior: "Often adults describe the behavior of homeless children as disruptive and/or scattered. Try to understand that what you or I might ordinarily call disruptive may actually be a request for adult supervision or loving attention—in effect, a request for someone to notice that I am really here and a part of your world" (Boxill, 1994, p. 37).

Hygiene: Many children enjoy games and activities related to hygiene: brushing hair, bathing, washing, or general hygiene. They may prefer activities in the housekeeping corner as a way to make order out of disorder.

Relationships: Children must decide whether or not to risk ties with others that may result in broken bonds. Adults at the shelter (or child-care center if a child is fortunate enough to attend one) can help provide security through relationships.

If the teachers will use the relationship as a way to help children make connections with the constant world that the children have lost, the time in the child care center will be well spent.... But what you can change is to decide that *you* can be the difference.... What happens here is that people care for and about you . . . you find a place to think, ask questions, and see yourself reflected in this place . . . to leave the stress, sadness, and uncertainty of homelessness at our doorstep and find in its place a birth befitting childhood. (Boxill, 1994, p. 35)

Child Care/Schooling for the Homeless Young Child.

In 1987, Congress enacted the Stewart B. McKinney Homeless Act, which provided homeless children with access to free, appropriate public education. The statute directed states with residence requirements to review and undertake steps to revise such laws (proof of residency, immunizations, birth certificates, enrollment of the child by a parent or legal guardian, and other barriers). These provisions made it clear that everything possible should be done to support the educational pursuits of homeless children and youth (Eddowes, 1994; Helm, 1992).

Different types of programs are available throughout the country, but certain features must be incorporated in order to give homeless children a sense of safety and security. Schools can provide bathing facilities, clean clothes, toothbrushes, and nutritious meals. Community agencies can provide health and dental services. A parent education program, whenever possible, will add stability (Eddowes, 1992). Although programs for homeless children vary by funding, staffing, space availability, length of day, and type (child care, drop-in, etc.), each program will play an important part in the child's life.

Participation in schooling programs does make a difference for young children in emergency shelters as evidenced by this report from Koblinsky, Taylor, and Relkin (1990):

Recent research illustrates the potential value of early childhood education for homeless youngsters. In both Baltimore and New York, homeless children who had attended preschool for a minimal length of time (one month in Baltimore, three months in New York) scored significantly higher on a developmental screening measure than homeless children who were not enrolled. In the Baltimore study, the most significant predictor of homeless children's developmental skills was the number of months they had spent in an early childhood program.

Common Behaviors of Homeless Children (see also Chapter 3).   Studies examining the effects of homelessness on young children have documented the poor health status, higher-than-expected rates of developmental delay, and emotional and behavioral problems exhibited by the children (see Molnar et al., 1990; Rafferty & Shinn, 1991). Others report the following:

> Teachers and other professionals also report behavioral problems, including short attention span, withdrawal, aggression, speech delays, sleep disorders, difficulty in organizing behavior (especially during transitions), regressive behaviors, awkward motor behavior, and immature social skills. At the same time, however, they note the children's impressive resilience, adaptability, and flexibility. (Klein et al., 1993, pp. 22–23)
>   . . . homeless children are also likely to lag behind their peers in their cognitive, motor, and social-emotional development. (Koblinsky et al., 1992, p. 25)

Teachers and parents report that many homeless preschoolers are displaying behaviors such as short attention span, aggressive behavior, shyness or withdrawal, speech delay, sleep disorders, regressive behaviors, and immature motor behavior that may jeopardize their learning and social adjustment (Bassuk & Rubin, 1987; Koblinsky et al., 1990).

Also researchers have noted that children who are continually in the presence of others often display either aggressive or withdrawn behaviors (Wolfe, 1978).

Stress in homeless children's lives may cause them to experience fear, sadness, and loneliness (Bassuk & Rubin, 1987).

> Emotional distance between parents and children may contribute to a variety of behavioral problems, including regressive behavior (e.g., thumbsucking and toilet-training accidents), withdrawal, and inappropriate interaction with strange adults. Many homeless preschoolers seek constant attention from teachers, physically clinging to them for support. (Koblinsky et al., 1990)

All homeless children share two commonalities: no permanent residence and poverty. Some other common characteristics include fear, shame of their situation (Tower & White, 1989), distrust, regression/aggression, depression, anxiety, malnutrition, insecurity, and others. But these same characteristics may also appear in children with homes.

Role of the Teacher in Shelters or Child Care. Frequently, children from shelters are in the minority in child-care or public facilities. In addition to the best educational and personal attributes, the teacher of homeless children can help in a number of specific ways:

Teacher-Child Interaction.   The teacher can strive to foster loving, consistent, and secure relationships with the child; interact with individual children or in small groups; value each class member as a worthwhile individual—promoting a sense of self-worth, autonomy, and trust in the physical and social world; offer appropriate choices; help children with simple routines—keep routines and transitions consistent, help children make decisions; help children to adjust to various situations especially at arrival and departure times and schedule changes; help classmates to be accepting and understanding by encouraging friendships and small group activities; recruit children by visiting shelters; help children express feelings and frustration; provide children with personal possessions and private

❖ Stimulator

Make a list of *typical* characteristics/behaviors of preschool children (such as small and large muscle skills, language usage, cooperation, emotional expressions, etc.). When you are satisfied that your list is accurate (but flexible), observe preschool children in a homeless shelter. How are these children similar to other children? How are they different from other children? If you were a permanent preschool teacher in a homeless shelter, how would you select activities for these preschool children (art, building, music, literature, etc.). How do they differ in ideas about: cleanliness (health), manners (social relationships), physical ability (safety), language development (communication), self-expression (emotional release), freedom to choose (independence), and so forth? What is the greatest contribution you could make to *these* children?

OR

If you were asked to do a service project in your community, would you be willing to work with homeless children and families? If so, how would you go about organizing and fulfilling your commitment? Would one (or more) of the following methods appeal to you: (a) providing inservice training; (b) volunteering at a shelter; (c) donating clothing, toys, and so forth; (d) helping them develop an environment that is developmentally appropriate—"with sensitivity, compassion, and understanding . . . for these highly stressed and at-risk children" (Klein et al., 1993, p. 31); (e) making a wide range of developmental levels in curricula (small, easily manageable tasks that can lead to mastery and success in completing tasks); (f) varying the curriculum: indoor/outdoor, quiet/active, private/cooperative; (g) meeting health and nutrition needs through activities and materials—perhaps even offer snacks or meals; (h) encouraging hygiene (opportunities to practice handwashing, bathing, teeth brushing, etc.); (i) devising a method to track children's progress and development; (j) including experiences that these children may not otherwise have (large/small muscle development for strength, balance, coordination, dexterity, etc.); (k) encouraging drama, art, and dance for creativity and to stimulate the senses; exposure to books for language and enjoyment; (m) field trips for life outside the immediate environment; and (n) help children express feelings and frustrations in constructive ways. Using one's imagination while working with the children will help the children have meaningful experiences.

❖ ❖ ❖ ❖

For further readings, see the Bibliography at the end of this chapter.

---

space; avoid forcing children to talk about personal lives, but be willing to discuss fears and frustrations; respond patiently when children are out of control; prepare children for moves (new school, new shelter) when appropriate; reduce burdens on young children (family/sibling problems) when possible.

Teacher-Family Interaction. The teacher can strive to get acquainted with whole families; help parents appreciate, respect, and understand their children; involve parents in children's schooling when possible (using school resources: lending library, toys, hand-outs); help families understand the growth and development of children's mind and body; interpret children's concern and frustrations; encourage parents to respect and love themselves.

Teacher/Community/Environment. The teacher can strive to help others understand the plight of the children and their families; use referrals when appropriate (health, dental, physical, emotional, or other); network with other agencies serving homeless families.

Teachers, Coworkers, and Curriculum. The teacher can strive to help coworker and other classroom personnel to understand the plight of the homeless and help meet their needs.

Mistreated, Abused, or Misbehaving Children

Children and Families in Crisis. (See also Chapters 8 and 9.) Statistics related to problems of children and families have been reported in *Education and Care: Early Childhood Programs and Services for Low-Income Families* (U.S. General Accounting Office, 1999).

In this report, "early childhood care and education" includes care that is provided to low-income children whose parents are out of the home in work activities and who may be in a center or a home, as well as care that is focused on a child's education, such as care provided by preschools and the Head Start program (p. 1).

Recent developments in the 1996 welfare reform legislation require that more welfare families, including those with very young children, find and keep jobs (p. 1).

The federal government invested about $11 billion in fiscal year 1999 on early childhood care and education programs for low-income children through a range of programs, and the states invested almost $4 billion for such programs.

The Department of Health and Human Services (HHS) provides most of the federal support for early childhood care and education, about $8 billion, through the Head Start program and the Child Care and Development Fund (CCDF), which subsidizes the child care expenses of low-income working parents (p. 2).

Although a number of federal and state programs provided significant funds for early childhood care and education, some types of child care were still difficult for low-income families to obtain, including infant and toddler care, care for children who have special needs, such as children with physical disabilities, and care for children during nonstandard hours (evenings and weekends) (p. 3).

The implementation of TANF (Temporary Assistance for Needy Families) has put more low-income children in care outside the home and put them in care earlier in their lives (p. 17).

In 1993, child-care expenses averaged 18 percent of family income, or $215 per month, for poor families paying for care for one or more preschool children while their mother worked. Families with income of less than $14,400 ($1,200 per month), the average share of income devoted to child care was even higher—25 percent or one-fourth of the family income (Census Bureau, SIPP, Fall 1993).

The Cost, Quality and Child Outcomes Study (1995) found that the quality of child-care programs attended by preschool children had a lasting impact on their school performance. According to other research, almost half of the infants and toddlers in child-care centers are in rooms rated at less than minimal quality. When families cannot get help in paying for child care, it is harder for them to find quality care that helps prepare their children for school success (p. 26).

Additional statistics related to problems of children and families have been reported and summarized in *The State of America's Children* (Children's Defense Fund, 1992, pp. 62–63), for example:

- Nearly 3 million children have been reported to protection agencies as victims of neglect, physical abuse, sexual abuse and emotional abuse, and maltreatment—many of them younger than 1 year of age.

- Arrests of youths for violent criminal acts, particularly those that are weapon- and drug-related, increased 24 percent within a 5-year period (1987–1991).

- Infants and very young children in increasing numbers are being cared for in foster homes. Caseworkers are often hampered from giving adequate help and attention to the children; children may be moved frequently and may be unable to bond with a setting or family. Children admitted to private psychiatric hospitals has escalated dramatically.

Other sources, such as the World Summit for Children (reported in a local newspaper in 1994), give equally distressing figures: poor-quality child care, limited nutrition services, no health insurance or immunizations, children underachieving or failing in school, family break-ups, and high injury and accidental death rates.

Other Needs of Children

What about abandoned children or those suffering from learning disabilities stemming from parental substance abuse, chemical dependency, or sheer neglect? What about children who are abused sexually, physically, emotionally, or socially (Meddin & Rosen, 1988)? How will all these children be cared for and educated? Will their problems be more difficult than those of children of so-called normal families? Do parents of children in these categories need to be even more selective in the care of their children? Do directors and teachers in centers need to have more training, be more patient, understanding, and willing to work with a "different" child? What attitudes and values will be conveyed to these children and families? Do we need to pay particular attention to see that children have good role models? It is up to parents and teachers to carefully consider individual circumstances and how best to improve them.

Care outside of the home can no longer be thought of as just a convenience for working parents when so many other children have such great needs. If children are to have any chance to be successful or move toward their potential, they need love, security, and stability in infancy, independence in toddlerhood, and responsibility in preschool years. These opportunities can be provided outside as well as inside the home. However, different families have different expectations of the role of a child-care center. To meet the needs of children and families, the director and employees at the child-care center must know the characteristics and expectations of the individuals they serve. Geographic location, ethnicity, socioeconomic status, and other characteristics will influence the compatibility of center and home. The health, safety, happiness, welfare, and development of the children must be the main focus of any center or group experience, regardless of its philosophy, funding, or management. Parents can be assured that out-of-home care for young children has improved greatly over time because of dedication and legislation. At both state and national levels, licensing is formulated and enforced for the welfare of children, families, and caregivers. Chapters 2 and 3 discuss licensing and ways to select the appropriate center. See also Appendix A, page 451. Parents must know and convey their expectations when selecting a center if they and the center are to function together without friction. Parents will be concerned about the way the policies of the center affect their children (see Chapter 4). Whenever there is disharmony between the home and the child-care center, it is the child who feels the greatest pressure. The way children perceive their experiences determines the effectiveness of the program itself. Activities must address capabilities *without attempting to mold children to the curriculum.*

One Possible Option. Zigler and Gilman (1993) state: "We must also commit ourselves to the proposition that each child who needs it is entitled to good-quality child care. . . . It is time to simplify and to organize a real child care system in America" (p. 176). They propose restructuring the American school, which they call the Schools of the 21st Century ("only 4 years ago, the concept was only an idea; today, examples of these schools are to be found all over America," p. 177), and which would house two separate but allied systems:

1. The traditional formal school (8 A.M. to 3 P.M., 9 months a year)
2. A child-care and family-support system (7 A.M. to 6 P.M., 12 months a year), funded mainly by parents who use the services.

There would be a highly flexible preschool component with developmentally appropriate curriculum, high-quality care for children from age 3 onward for parents who need out-of-home care. A second component includes a before and after school and vacation program, which would be a supervised recreational program. In addition they advocate a three-part outreach program: child care and family support with home visits and consultations, family day care, and an outreach program (referral services). There is a high degree of parental involvement, the belief being that parents are the primary raisers of their children and that the home and school should work together for the best of each child.

One problem still unresolved is the care of infants and toddlers, which requires a high staff-child ratio and typically costing more than $200 a week in many areas of the country (Zigler & Lang, 1991). For low-income working families, the cost of infant care represents a high proportion of family income. The Profile of Child Care Settings, conducted in 1991, found that families with annual incomes below $15,000 who do pay for infant care pay as much as 23 percent of their income for such care (Willer et al., 1991). The National Child Care Survey, conducted in 1990, found that 88 percent of the spaces available in early education and day-care settings, as well as those in regulated family-day-care homes, had been filled (Hofferth et al., 1991).

Zigler and Gilman (1993) say the following:

> America now stands alone among industrialized nations in its failure to enact a paid infant-care leave and other forms of family assistance. Clearly, some means must be found to help families with their child care needs, particularly in the area of infant care. We must find such a means that does not require vast federal and state expense. (p. 177)

There are other possible options about child care; some still in the formative stage. The Zigler and Gilman plan mentioned here has been in operation.

Other needs of children and families, such as disabilities and diversity, will be discussed in Chapter 3. If the National Education Goals were to be operational by the year 2000, groundwork should have been laid by now. Succinctly, the goals read:

- All children ready to learn
- 90 percent graduation rate
- All children competent in core subjects
- First in the world in math and science
- Every adult literate and able to compete in the workforce

- Safe, disciplined, drug-free schools
- Professional development for educators
- Increased parental involvement in learning

CHILDREN

Theories

Theories vary about the nature of children, describing them as good, evil, or blank tablets to be filled with experience. Some concentrate on one aspect of development, for example, cognitive, and some on the total child. Some give specific approaches to child rearing, and others report about curriculum areas. Some educators and center directors have preferences about which theory to follow. Others have an imposed philosophy that they *must* follow. Chapter 4 outlines several theories concerning early childhood education and philosophies for child-care centers. Parents may select group child care from diverse philosophical approaches. Some children thrive on a given program, and other children do not; therefore careful consideration must be taken to see that children and programs are carefully matched.

Piaget

Most centers for young children prefer to establish a philosophical base. The developmental theory of Piaget is used here. His theory that children progress through invariable time and sequence stages is sound, verifiable, and pertinent. His theory has "helped produce programs that emphasize the development of broad intellectual powers rather than the mastery of narrow academic skills" (Leeper et al., 1984, p. 264). Piaget has been acclaimed as an astute observer of children; his developmental philosophy is popular in the United States and other countries. For in-depth study of his philosophy, the total growth pattern of the young child, or other points of view, consult a basic child development text.

Different theorists have interpreted and adopted Piaget's theories. He gave depth and meaning to the active organism position—many of his terms were used to explain the individual's role in his own intellectual growth. Piaget repeatedly uses the terms *assimilation* ("the filtering or modification of the input") and *accommodation* ("the modification of internal schemes to fit reality") or twin processes subsumed under his term *equilibration*, defined as "the search for a better and better equilibrium in the sense of an extended field, in the sense of an increase in the number of possible compositions, and in the sense of a growth in coherence." Piaget ranked it as one of the four factors that explain development. The other factors are maturation, direct physical experience, and social transmission—however, he considered equilibration to be "pedagogically fundamental."

The key to the educative process, according to Piaget, is the interaction between the learner and the environment as the learner integrates new understandings into those already established. "The child is considered active at all levels, a purposer and a constructor of his own knowledge." About Piaget's theory, Weber states:

Continual interaction with materials in the classroom supports the construction of knowledge and meaning for the learner. No cutoff age of six exists for such interaction. Throughout the period of concrete operations—even to the age of eleven or twelve—classrooms need to be workshops where

freedom for use of materials prevails. There is no theoretical support to substantiate diverse classroom organization for four- and five-year-olds as opposed to six- to eight-year-olds. During all the early childhood years the research for meaning is facilitated or impeded by the nature of the environment; opportunities for exploration, discovery, and the integration of learnings are essential. Interaction is not limited by the physical alone. (1984, p. 210)

Piaget's stages of development, beginning at birth and continuing through age 16, have specific characteristics and time periods. Each successive period is built on the success and completeness of the preceding one(s). A brief, modified sketch of Piaget's periods is shown in Figure 1–2.

Sensorimotor Period.   Children's greatest educators are their senses: seeing, touching, tasting, smelling, and hearing. They rely on them to teach, satisfy, and warn. Children pick up objects of varying sizes, shapes, and textures. Objects not of particular interest take on interest if someone handles or moves them. Children touch things without awareness of their value or sentiment. Edibles and nonedibles alike are placed in the mouth for exploration, even if children are told they are harmful or distasteful. Noses are keen to both noxious

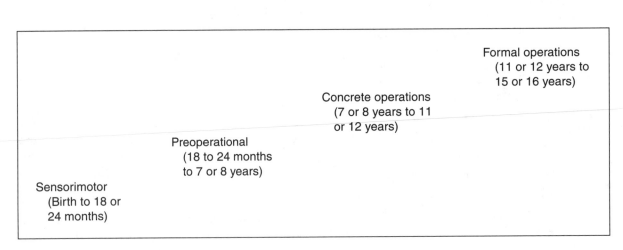

Figure 1–2   Piaget's stages.

and pleasant smells. Although loud noises may startle children, they listen intently and respond enthusiastically. Catchy tunes, repetition, and rhythm are especially enjoyed at this age.

The principal development during this period involves the large muscles that enable children to move around quickly and adeptly as maturation occurs. Children find self-locomotion exciting and rewarding.

Children like to be near other children and adults, but also engage in solitary play. Their activities are limited by skills and experience.

Implications.   The infant/toddler is an inquisitive ball of action who plays alone, but needs constant supervision. The caregiver needs to provide stimuli that will encourage children's use of sensory, motor, mental, and social awareness. More than mere entertainment, children enjoy personal interaction with adults and other children. Provisions must be made to protect each child from harm from materials, individuals, and the environment.

The youngsters' environment should be safe, interesting, stimulating, inviting, and friendly. Daily curriculum should include opportunities to see stimulating items, to touch safe textured objects, to taste flavorful edibles, to smell delectable (nonharmful) odors, and to hear different pleasurable sounds. Activities that exercise the senses and large muscles through play, creative art, music, simple science experiences (water and air), physical exercise and movement, and language arts (simple stories, nursery rhymes, songs) both indoors and outdoors will benefit young children.

Preoperational Period.   During the sensorimotor period, young children frequently mimic others, but in the preoperational period, they model or imitate rather than mimic. For example, toddlers will repeat with precision gestures or acts they have seen, whereas preschool children will pattern but not necessarily duplicate the acts of others, such as pretending to be an animal or another person. Such symbolic thought begins to develop as children increase in ability to think about things that are not immediately present (the past and the future).

Preoperational children are characterized by the following:

- Are egocentric (see things mainly from own viewpoint)
- Center on one idea at a time [e.g., when an item has several characteristics (shape, color, and size), children will consider it as having only one property such as size and ignore or overlook the other characteristics]
- Are animistic (believe everything in the world is alive)
- Function intuitively rather than logically

Unfortunately, many individuals think that children and adults possess the same cognitive structures (Kohlberg, 1968). In fact, adult structures are more complex in thought, ideas, knowledge, memories, problem-solving abilities, and logical thinking, to name a few. Because of this misconception, adult expectations of young children may be unrealistic.

Implications.   Preoperational children are real doers and goers who need many hands-on experiences. The caregiver must carefully select the toys and activities that will further children's self-concept, abilities, interactions, and knowledge in a way that is indicated by the individual child. During this period, children are able to initiate activities and personal interactions but must rely on the caregiver for decisions they cannot make for themselves.

With time, experience, and maturity, sensorimotor children emerge into preoperational children as more social, more competent, more curious, and more energetic beings. Preoperational children want more involvement with peers, situations, and ideas. They are no longer content to play beside other children; they want involvement with them. Geographic interests and association horizons are rapidly expanding.

Preoperational children are still trying to gain control over large muscles. In addition, they are involved with small muscle development (becoming more proficient in the use of fingers and hands). Based on the individual readiness of each child (rather than age or group norms), increased maturation of large and small muscles makes preoperational children ready for more complex exposure to art, math, the sciences, music, physical education, social studies, and language arts than previously. They delight in using both large and small muscles in outdoor and indoor play (climbing and finger plays or table activities). They enjoy hearing stories that arouse curiosity and imagination. Language skills and ability to distinguish reality from fantasy are increasing. Children at this stage are becoming better listeners and, in return, want to be listened to. Their attitudes are shifting from self-centered and narrow to cooperative; their views broaden to include the ideas of others.

During this period, it is important for children to have many hands-on experiences—a reinforcer of the sensorimotor period. Piaget identifies two different types of knowledge children gain when they act on objects: *physical knowledge* and *logicomathematical knowledge*. Williams and Kamii (1986) offer the following explanation:

> *Physical knowledge* is knowledge of objects that can be observed. We acquire physical knowledge by acting on objects—by pushing, poking, and dropping them. . . . *Logicomathematical knowledge* is created when we make relationships between objects, such as when we compare two balls—one red and one blue—and think that they are *different* . . . . The difference exists . . . only in the mind of the person who puts the two balls into this relationship. (p. 23)

Thus, children between 18 months and 8 years gain much when they are permitted to explore objects and ideas through visual, auditory, oral, tactile, and olfactory means.

Concrete Operations Period.   This is a time of symbolic representation. During this stage, children come closer to doing the things most adults expect of them. Initial attempts at symbolic thinking are intuitive and illogical. Children *decenter* their thinking as they practice their new skills; they slowly improve. (Recall that preoperational children *centered* on one characteristic of an ob-

ject. Concrete operational children consider characteristics collectively—an object is blue, triangular, small, and plastic. See Ginsburg and Opper (1969, pp. 151, 168). They begin to think in more abstract ways, but their thought processes may rely on observable events and objects they can manipulate physically. They now can demonstrate and understand such concepts (familiar in Piaget's theory) as *centration-decentration, reversibility* ["the child can combine subclasses of animals into a supraclass and he can reverse the process" (Honstead, 1968, p. 133)], *classification* ["the operations of putting things together, of placing them in classes, of forming hierarchies of classes, and so on" (Ginsburg and Opper, 1969, p. 22)], *seriation* (arranging things in a series by number, time, volume, or length), and other scientific concepts.

Implications.   During this period, children will be noisy and social and will test limits frequently. Teachers will need to access and provide for the interests and abilities of the children by some friendly competition, active games, change from passive classrooms, nourishment, and allowance for solitude.

During this period children like to help establish rules for their own behaviors. They generally follow rules with precision—and expect others to do likewise. Often their standards and punishment are more strict than those of adults. Because of their abilities to think more abstractly, academic learning is on a higher level than it was previously. For example, children may now use math concepts in games (scoring), read books with more printing and fewer visuals, write their own stories, participate in music lessons, engage in sports, or plan and carry out activities in art, science, or dramatic play. They are learning new ways to assemble and use information.

Children in this stage need opportunities to ask and answer questions, to discuss and propose, and to integrate their ideas with those of others. They need and want to discover things on their own with the reassurance of help when and *if* they need it.

Formal Operations Period. Most early childhood texts give little or no attention to Piaget's last stage—formal operations—because it is beyond the period of early childhood. However, to round out Piaget's four periods, and because some centers may employ or have other contact with adolescents (before- and after-school programs), brief information will be given for this period.

During adolescence, individuals are able to think, dissect, speculate, hypothesize, ponder, propose, postulate, and examine abstract concepts, making possibility more important than reality. Adolescents' thoughts are flexible and versatile, so they can reason without becoming confused by unusual results. Their neurological development, social environment, experience, and their own activity contribute to this state (Ginsburg & Opper, 1969). Major acquisitions during this period include the idea "that there are many answers to every question, and many questions about every answer. Ethics, politics, and all social and moral issues become more interesting and involving" (Berger, 1991, p. 55).

Implications. Individuals rely heavily on peer contact, and this contact may result in conflict between peers and adults. Individuals no longer take things at face value. They want to examine possibilities and draw their own conclusions. Science and religion are especially vulnerable topics.

If employing adolescents at the center, the director will need to make clear the expectations, responsibilities, and privileges of employment, and be willing to clarify and examine issues with these employees.

Characteristics of Piaget's Stages. Theories such as Piaget's that advocate the importance of change over time have been labeled *constructivistic.* Lay-Dopyera and Dopyera (1987) state: "Constructivists do not expect that any specific learning (such as letter recognition) or any small modification of behavior (such as frequency of 'attending' behavior) will significantly influence long-term development" (p. 190). They described conditions for young children favored by constructivists to include all kinds of experiences—not limited to academics; long, unstructured periods for children to plan and execute projects of their interest; social interaction for one to try and modify personal views; initial adult input with individual children or small groups; adult interaction with children that requires recall, synthesis, conjecture, and so on; and a constant focus on better conceptualization of the physical and social world (pp. 190–191).

Open education is another term used with a Piaget-type program. Children of various abilities and ages are grouped together. Although the sequence of developmental stages does not vary, growth may be faster or slower during some stages. Also, children of the same chronological age may be at different stages of growth and will frequently revert to earlier patterns for security. The important thing is that each child is actively involved in the process; the children learn by doing. Each individual is important, loved, accepted, and valued.

Implications of Piaget's work for educators include such ideas as differences between adults and children, in that children think differently,

 **Stimulator**

A popular philanthropist in your community has offered to give seed money for a child-care center and after-school program for children whose parents work at a dam construction site. The dam construction will bring the community out of high unemployment. Without this new center, children will receive little or poor care. The only stipulation of the offer is that a committee be formed to study the process of setting up and running the center. Committee members include a retired schoolteacher, a member of the town council, an unemployed farmer, a recent college graduate in early childhood education, and the wife of a local church official.

Imagine yourself as each member of the committee and list your arguments for and against the offer. Then compare your ideas with the text material as you read the following chapters.

need to interact physically and actively with their environment, learn best from moderately novel or different experiences, vary in their rate of development, and need to talk one with another (McCarthy & Houston, 1980).

Other Theories

Other theorists have been popular at various times. Early childhood educators are influenced by current trends, by where and when training was received, and by preference for one theory over another. Some child study theories have been readily accepted and others have been closely scrutinized.

PARENTS

Parents of the enrolled children are a very important component of the center. They should feel that the center is a resource to them in their child-rearing responsibilities—never that the center is usurping their role. They will seek confidence, information, and support from the center, realizing that parenting is a complex and lifelong occupation.

Parents need centers for a variety of reasons. Many one-parent or two-income families depend on out-of-home people to help care for, rear, and educate their young children. Parents who do not work outside the home (stay-at-home parents who work in the home as compared with an office, school, factory, and so on, but do nonetheless important work) may want their children to have opportunities that cannot be provided within the home. Some need a home substitute because of family illness or other extenuating circumstances. Some want their children to have an academic advantage.

In the early sixties, several influential people wrote about the importance of early learning experiences. Bloom (1964) argued "that four-year-olds had attained half of their intellectual ability"; Bruner (1962) hypothesized that one can "teach any child, any subject matter at any age in an intellectually responsible way"; and Hunt (1961) concluded "that intelligence was malleable and not fixed," the view he attributed to professionals

of the time. "But," Elkind asked (1987b), "are these findings true?" Elkind stated: "Bloom was talking about mental test data, not about mental growth." Bruner's hypothesis is true only if persons "either redefine the child or redefine the subject matter." And for Hunt (1961): "No reputable psychologist ever claimed that intelligence was fixed" (pp. 9–10). Hunt (who helped popularize Piaget in the United States) concluded that early deprivation causes deficits in learning, and conversely, that benefits can be expected from early enrichment (Lay-Dopyera & Dopyera, 1987). American educators, theorists, parents, politicians, scientists, and others feared the United States would be left behind other developing countries. They interpreted the research to mean that enriched preschool learning environments would make children smarter and subsequently help them do better in school. Thus, they pushed for a strong academic approach, mainly for highly "disadvantaged" children from poor families. Some supported this increased wave for academics, and others maintained it was not in keeping with the "nature" of children. Elkind (1987b), a child advocate, summarized his viewpoint:

> As in the past, we have not only to assert the values of child-centered early childhood education, but we must also struggle to reveal the concepts of early childhood malleability and competence for what they are, namely distortions of how young children really grow and learn. (p. 11)

Parents seeking child care may be uninformed, misinformed, misguided, or looking for inappropriate or unrealistic care because they are unaware of growth patterns, learning sequences, and characteristics of young children. There are five common misunderstandings that adults have about how children learn. They were identified by Elkind (1977) as follows:

1. Children are most like adults in their thinking and least like them in their feelings. [Elkind states: "In fact, just the reverse is true: *children are most like us in their feelings and least like us in their thoughts*" (1981, p. 187).]

2. Children learn best while sitting still and listening.
3. Children can learn and operate according to rules.
4. *Acceleration* is preferable to *elaboration*.
5. Parents and teachers can raise children's IQs.

Elkind (1981) continues:

In large measure, all of these misunderstandings derive from a contemporary overemphasis on intellectual growth to the exclusion of the personal-social side of development. Although I know it sounds old-fashioned to talk about the whole child and tender loving care, I strongly believe that many problems in child rearing and education could be avoided if concern for a child's achievement as a student were balanced by an equally strong concern for his feelings of self-worth as a person. (pp. 125–126)

Added to the five misconceptions is the unfortunate notion of "hurrying" children—not letting them have time to be children or to live happily and healthily in their current stage of growth. Elkind (1981) reported: "Young children (two to eight years) tend to perceive hurrying as a rejection, as evidence that their parents do not really care about them" (p. 186). In this same publication, Elkind addressed the hurrying of children in two ways: clock hurrying and calendar hurrying:

Clock hurrying occurs when children have to make too many adaptations in too short a time [baby sitter to nursery school to day care center to home]. Calendar hurrying occurs when a child is presented with learning experiences that are inappropriate for his or her stage of development [reading, ballet, make-up, being left alone before age nine, athletics, music lessons]. Both types of hurrying stress children and force them to call up energy reserves that they need for healthy growth and development. (Elkind, 1984, p. 162)

Psychiatrists are reporting frequent aches and pains (stomach, head), problems with eating and sleeping, nervous habits, lack of interest, and low self-image in young children as a result of stress or pressure (Elkind, 1986). Katz (1983) reported that the best learning environment for children is a homey atmosphere in which learning occurs naturally. She presents a recurring theme that children should set their own pace for learning with parents encouraging them. Pressure from parents may lay the groundwork for later tension about schoolwork.

Why do parents hurry their children? Reasons include the following:

1. Head start for the children (ahead of other children)
2. Advantages the parents did not have
3. Vicarious accomplishment through children
4. Evidence of parents' wealth or power

Pushy parents need to know when they are expecting too much and when they are not expecting enough. Elkind (1984) concluded: "One of the most important things is for parents to say 'no' to things they feel are too advanced. Saying 'no' gives kids a sense that their parents care about them enough to take the risk of confrontation" (p. 201).

According to Weikart (1989), there are some hard decisions to make in the future of early childhood programs, about such things as supply and demand, equity of services and costs to parents and providers, curriculum assessment, nurturance, ages of care, and use of research.

Galinsky (1990) summarizes the challenges of the 1990s *for families* to work together as they enjoy, nurture, and guide their children; *for educational institutions* to work cooperatively to meet diverse family needs and to strive for quality in care and equity in compensation; and for *businesses* to understand and be supportive of families and employees. Employers are beginning to explore some options for working mothers of young children such as flexible schedules, job sharing, working at home; benefits such as payment of child care, employer-sponsored on-site child-care centers, more flexibility in parental leaves, and use of sick leave to care for children/elderly. (See also O'Connell and Bloom, 1987.)

Facts and Figures

"In the fall of 1998, about 4 million children were attending kindergarten in the United States, approximately 95 percent of them for the first time. Of the children attending kindergarten, 85 percent were in public school, 15 percent in private school, 55 percent were in full day programs and 45 percent were in part day program" (U.S. Department of Education, Fall 1998).

"Whether or not children succeed in school is in part related to events and experiences that occur prior to their entering kindergarten for the first time. Children's preparedness for school and their later school success are related to multiple aspects of their development. Children's physical well-being, social development, cognitive skills and knowledge and how they approach learning are all factors that contribute to their chance for success in school" (Kagan et al., 1995).

"A complex and continuous collaboration exists between the child and the family; and, the family can provide the resources and support that children require to increase their chances of succeeding in school" (Maccoby, 1992).

Key Findings (U.S. Department of Education NCES Longitudinal Study, Kindergarten Class of 1998–99, Fall 1998)

- *Cognitive Skills and Knowledge:*   In reading, mathematics, and general knowledge, kindergartners (a) who were born in 1992, (b) whose mothers have more education, (c) who come from two-parent families, (d) who primarily speak English in the home, and (e) are white are more likely to score in the highest quartile.

- *Social Skills*   "Are an important part of children's development. . . . Children's social skills may be related to their later academic achievement (Meisels et al., 1996; Schwartz and Walker 1984). Young children construct knowledge by interacting with others and their environment (Bandura 1986). They need interpersonal skills to join, question, and listen to their peers and adults. Teachers rate black children more likely than white and Asian children to exhibit higher levels of problem behaviors (arguing with others, fighting with others, getting angry easily)."

- *Prosocial Behavior*   "Both parents and teachers rate girls as more likely than boys to comfort others often or very often; the older children and those at less risk are more likely to accept ideas of others and to comfort others. As might be expected, children who come from homes where other than English is spoken are less likely to engage in prosocial behaviors."

- *Problem Behavior*   "Teachers are less likely to rate children from households with two parents than children from single-mother families as exhibiting problem behavior. . . . Problem behaviors vary by race/ethnicity. Black children are more likely to be seen as exhibiting higher levels of problem behaviors (arguing with others, fighting with others, getting angry easily)" (p. 29).

- *Motor Skills*   "More girls than boys score in the higher portion of the distribution for both fine and gross motor skills. . . . Children's fine and gross motor skills vary with their age, their mother's education, family composition, and race/ethnicity. Older kindergartners, whose mothers have a higher level of education, who come from a two-parent family, score higher on fine motor skills. . . . Children's gross motor skills vary by their race/ethnicity. Black children are more likely to score in the higher portion of the distribution for gross motor skills than white, Asian or Hispanic children." (p. 37)

- *General Health*   "Only a minority of children are reported as having fair or poor general health. Kindergarten children whose mothers have higher levels of education, come from two-parent families, and have never used public assistance are more likely to be in excellent general health. Children's general health status varies by their race-ethnicity. White children are more likely than black, Hispanic or Asian children to be in excellent health" (p. 40).

- *Developmental Difficulties*   "Only a small percentage of first-time kindergartners are experiencing vision (6 percent) and hearing problems (3 percent). Hyperactivity varies by child's sex, mother's education, welfare receipt and race/ethnicity. More boys than girls are reported as a lot more active. . . . Black children are more frequently reported as a lot more active than white, Asian and Hispanic children. Thirteen percent of parents report their children encounter difficulties in paying attention. Difficulty in paying attention varies by children's sex, mother's education, welfare receipt and race/ethnicity. Boys seem to pay attention less well or much less well to a great extent than girls. . . . Asian children are less likely to experience attention difficulties than white or black children. . . . Articulation of words and ability to communicate varies by children's sex. Boys are more likely than girls to have difficulties in this area" (p. 43).

- *Literacy Environment and Family Interactions*   "The majority of parents report having more than 25 children's books in the home (which varies by maternal education and family receipt of welfare); more than half the parents report having more than five children's records, audiotapes or CDs in the home. Activities such as reading and singing songs vary by maternal education, family type, welfare receipt and race/ethnicity. . . . Children with single mothers, families with receipt of welfare services and black parents are more likely to be sung to every day than those with two parents, families with no receipt of welfare services, and white, Hispanic and Asian parents (respectively)."

- *Child Care*   "About four out of five first-time kindergartners (81 percent) receive care on a regular basis from someone other than their parents the year prior to starting kindergarten. This care is most often provided in a center-based setting (69 percent), followed by care by a relative in a private home (24 percent) and care by a nonrelative in a private home (15 percent). Prior to kindergarten of the children in nonparental care, children whose mothers have higher levels of education are more likely to be in center-based care than children whose mothers have less education. Prior to kindergarten, children from homes where English is not the primary language are less likely to have attended a center-based program the year before kindergarten. Once children enter kindergarten for the first time, about 50 percent of these children receive care before and/or after school from someone other than their parents. As children enter kindergarten, before- and/or after-school care is most often provided in a private home by a relative of the child. Center-based care is the second most frequent type of before- and after-school setting followed by nonrelative care. At kindergarten entry, children whose

(continued)

Facts and Figures (continued)

mothers have less than a high school education are more likely to receive be-
fore- and/or after-school care from a relative than a nonrelative or center-based
provider. In contrast, kindergarteners whose mothers have a college education
are more likely to receive care in a center-based setting than in either of the
two home-based settings. At kindergarten entry, black children are more likely
than white, Asian or Hispanic children to receive before-and/or after-school
care." (p. 57)

Relationships Within and Across Areas of Development

- The children who do well in reading are also likely to do well in mathematics
  and general knowledge.
- Both parents and teachers in the ECLS-K provided information on children's
  social skills.
- Parent perceptions of children's social skills are not directly related to their
  cognitive skills and knowledge. . . . Teacher perceptions of children's other social skills (i.e., accepts peer ideas, comforts others, argues, fights and gets
  angry easily) are only slightly related to children's cognitive *t*-scores.
- Children's fine motor skills relate to their cognitive skills and knowledge.
- Children's gross motor skills relate to mathematics but are not directly related
  to their reading and general knowledge. Neither fine nor gross motor skills
  are directly related to their home literacy environment, their home educational
  activity experiences, or the child-care history.
- Children's approaches to learning were described by both their parents and
  their teachers. Parents' perceptions of children's approaches to learning (i.e.,
  task persistence, eagerness to learn, and creativity) do not directly relate to
  children's cognitive *t*-scores. Teacher perceptions of children's approaches to
  learning (i.e., task persistence, eagerness to learn, and attention) are related
  to children's reading, mathematics, and general knowledge *t*-scores.
- There are small realtionships of children's home literacy environment and
  home educational experiences to their reading, mathematics, and general
  t-scores. The number of children's books in the home related to children's
  general knowledge but not directly to their reading or mathematics knowledge
  and skills. And how frequently a family member reads to the child relates to
  the children's reading and general knowledge, but not directly to their mathematics knowledge and skills. Children's literacy environment and home educational experiences do not directly relate to the child-care history.

Of current and great interest is the report *America's Kindergartners,* an early childhood longitudinal study from the National Center for Education Statistics, U.S. Department of Education, Office of Educational Research and Improvement, NCES 2000-070 (Revised) dated April 2000. While it reports on children older than the focus of this textbook, it has many implications for parents and teachers of preschool children. Here are a few of its findings:

Children entering kindergarten in the United States in the 1990s are different from those who entered kindergarten in prior decades. They come from increasingly diverse racial, ethnic, cultural, social, economic, and language backgrounds. Many kindergartners now come from single-parent families and from step-parent families. They also differ in the level and types of early care and educational experiences that they have had prior to kindergarten (Zill et al., 1995).

Our nation's schools face new opportunities and new challenges. Schools are expected to meet the educational needs of each child regardless of their background and experience. Services, such as meals and before- and after-school child care, that were provided by other institutions in the past are now being provided by schools. Teachers are faced with classrooms of children with increasingly diverse needs. In addition, growing pressure to raise academic standards and to assess all students' progress towards meeting these standards places even more burden on schools and teachers. (p. v)

CHAPTER SUMMARY

1. Readers who note the Facts and Figures, who do some of the Stimulators, and who use the Participators at the end of each chapter will have a better understanding of the field of early childhood education.
2. Statistics show the needs of children and families.
3. Early care and education of children has been a concern for hundreds of years.
4. To get a feel for the current struggles and progress of educating young children, one needs to understand the background and

influence of both European and American educators.
5. The child study movement influenced the care and education of young children.
6. Individuals influencing early childhood education have backgrounds in education, child development, social work, psychology, medicine, and other related disciplines.
7. For over 200 years, intervention and support from political, educational, religious, profit, nonprofit, and other organizations and private individuals have been and are strong advocates for the welfare of children and families.
8. Homelessness for children and families is an ongoing and growing concern.
9. Mistreated, abused, and misbehaving children have special needs.
10. There are many theories about the growth and development of young children. Piaget's stages of development are helpful to explain the child's growth pattern.
11. Parental support is very important in the development of each child.
12. Parents seeking out-of-home care for their children have different expectations and needs.
13. Some adults have misconceptions about the way children learn; these misconceptions may cause adults to have unrealistic expectations about children and their behaviors. During the 1960s, there was a strong push for academic programs for young children; American parents have a tendency to hurry their children.
14. The recent study by a group of government and educational bodies has presented helpful information regarding the skill and behavior development of kindergarten children in the United States.

PARTICIPATORS

These exercises are a very important part of your training. Begin a portfolio (file) and build important experiences. *Start with Chapter 1 and be diligent!*

If you respond to some of the *participators* and *stimulators* in each chapter, you will increase your knowledge and convictions about your important role in working with young children, their parents, your colleagues, the community people, and local and federal legislators.

1. Decide what method would be most useful for *you* to make an ongoing professional file (notebook, folders, card system, computer record, or other). Make preparations so materials can be easily filed as they become available. Some sections may need to be subdivided for easy access.

2. As a brain stimulator, try this one: President Herbert Hoover's White House conference on Child Health and Protection (adopted in 1930) recognized the rights of the child as the first rights of citizenship and pledged: "For *every* child these rights, regardless of race, or color, or situation, wherever he may live under the protection of the American flag."

Right	Right Content
1	Spiritual and moral training
2	Guarding and understanding child's personality as a precious right
3, 7	Harmonious and enriching home environment or nearest substitute
4, 5	Prenatal, natal, and postnatal health protection through adolescence
6	Promotion of health, wholesome physical and mental recreation; safety and protection against accidents
8	A school that is safe, sanitary, and properly equipped; free from hazards; with nursery schools and kindergartens to supplement home care
8, 9	A community that recognizes and plans for child's needs, protection, safety, wholesome play and recreation; provides for child's cultural and social needs
10	Education through discovery and development of child's individual abilities; provides training and vocational guidance for future work and satisfaction
11	Teaching and training for successful parenthood, homemaking, citizenship, and wise dealing with problems of parenthood
12, 13	Early discovery, diagnosis, treatment, and training of individuals diagnosed with handicaps; expenses to be born publicly when necessary
14	The right to be dealt with intelligently as society's charge, not society's outcast; with home, the school, the church, the court, and the institution when needed
15	To grow up in a family with adequate standard of living and the security of a stable income as the surest safeguard against social handicaps
16	Protection against labor that stunts growth, either physical or mental, that limits education, that deprives children of the right of comradeship, of play, and of joy
17	Equal opportunity for rural and city child of satisfactory schooling and health services, social, recreational, and cultural facilities
18	To supplement the home and school in the training of youth; stimulation and encouragement to the extension and development of the voluntary youth organizations
19	Minimum protections of the health and welfare of children with full-time officials (state and national) of a nationwide service of general information, statistics, and scientific research, including protection from abuse, neglect, exploitation, and hazard

As you read through Chapter 1 (and subsequent chapters) make notes of changes, emphasis, and commitment to our present-day children with regard to the preceding 19 rights. How would you score our leaders for the past 70 years? If you were in a position to put pressure on our resources (people and funds), where would you put your greatest emphasis?

3. Identify at least three early educators, briefly describe their philosophies, and note how (or what) they contributed to the current philosophy with which you identify. (See appendices at the end of this chapter.) Example: Margaret McMillan coined the word *nursery school*, recognized and worked with the "whole" child, initiated teacher training and the outdoor nursery, and was concerned about the physical health of each child. (Who encouraged music in the curriculum? Who thought children were innately "good"? Who thought there was too much pressure on children? What has been the outcome of historical thinking about children?)

4. *Begin* to formulate your own philosophy about how children should be educated. Remember that time, knowledge, interaction, experience, and other factors may change your thinking over time.

5. Inquire about the needs of children and families in your community and how these needs can be met. Take a cursory survey of your community to determine the different options parents have for child care.

6. On a card or piece of paper, list Elkind's five adult misconceptions about the way children learn, leaving a space beside each statement for marking *T* or *F*. Take a survey of at least 10 people over the age of 18 (married or single). Use this information to introduce the correct principles to others and to give yourself an understanding of the learning process in young children.

7. Observe a group of children (indoor or outdoor, formal or informal) to see if you can identify their interests, social skills, and stages of development (see Figure 1–2).

8. Ask 10 parents what their child-care needs are, if any. (Some may need occasional babysitting, and others may need 24-hour care.)

9. For parents considering or using child-care centers, ask them to prioritize their needs according to type of center, program of center, location, cost, convenience, and other considerations.

10. Place yourself in the hypothetical situation of needing care for your children, aged 6 months, 2½ years, and 5 years. List the concerns you would have and attempt to resolve them on paper.

11. Using the system suggested in exercise 1 or 6, make an entry for the historical contributors discussed early in the chapter. Explain whether their ideas appeal to you and find some additional information about each one you selected. (See also appendices at the end of this chapter.)

12. With your instructor or a classmate, plan a staff meeting or class period where you lead the group discussion on a current problem facing young children (homelessness, abuse, multiethnic families, etc.). Read at least three articles on the selected topic.

13. If you were suspicious that something unusual was bothering a young child, how would you go about investigating your suspicions? Include how you would record information and how and when you would present it to a supervisor/teacher.

14. Decide what would be most beneficial to you at this stage of your education. Write and complete it as a participator.

15. Inquire about the prevalence of and solutions for homelessness in your community. How are mistreated, abused, and misbehaving children identified and assisted?

REFERENCES

Alkers, J. 1992. Modern American homelessness. In C. Soloman & P. Jackson-Jobe (Eds.), *Helping homeless people: Unique challenge and solutions* (pp. 7–14). Alexandria, VA: American Association for Counseling and Development.

Almy, M. 1968. Introduction. In S. Isaacs (Ed.), *The nursery years.* New York: Schocken.

Baker, E. 1937. The kindergarten centennial: 1837–1937. Washington, DC: Association for Childhood Education International.

Bandura, A. 1986. *Social foundations of thought and action: A social cognitive perspective.* Upper Saddle River, NJ: Prentice Hall.

Barnard, H. (Ed.). 1890. *Kindergarten and child culture papers on Froebel's kindergarten* (rev. ed.). Hartford, CT: Office of Barnards American Journal of Education.

Bassuk, E. L. 1990. The problem of family homelessness. In E. L. Bassuk & E. M. Gallagher, The impact of homelessness on children. *Child and Youth Services,* 14(1), 19–23.

Bassuk, E. L., & Rubin, L. 1987. Homeless children: A neglected population. *American Journal of Public Health,* 78, 1232–1233.

Berger, K. S. 1991. *The developing person through childhood and adolescence* (3rd ed.). New York: Worth.

Bloom, B. 1964. *Stability and change in human characteristics.* New York: Wiley.

Blow, S. E. n.d. The history of the kindergarten in the United States. *The Outlook.*

Boxill, N. A. 1994. Making a place for Nona. *Exchange,* 95, 35–37.

Bradburn, E. 1976. *Margaret McMillan.* Nutfield, England: Denholm Press.

Braun, S. J., & Edwards, E. P. 1972. *History and theory of early childhood education.* Worthington, OH: Charles A. Jones.

Bredekamp, S. 1997. NAEYC issues revised position statement on developmentally appropriate practice in early childhood programs. National Institute for Early Childhood Professional Development. *Young Children,* Jan., 34–40.

Brimhall, D., Reaney, L., & West, J. 1999. *Participation of kindergartners through third-graders in before- and after-school care.* NCES 1999-013. Washington, DC: National Center for Education Statistics.

Bruner, J. 1962. *The process of education.* Cambridge, MA: Harvard University Press.

Casper, L. M., 1996. *Who's minding our preschoolers?* Census Bureau Current Population Reports, No. P70-53. Washington, DC: U.S. Department of Commerce.

Casper, L. M., & O'Connell, M. 1997. *Couple characteristics and fathers as child care providers.* Jan. 10. U.S. Bureau of the Census, Pop. Division, Washington, DC 20233.

Casper, L. M., Hawkins, M., & O'Connell, M. 1991. *Who's minding the kids? Child care arrangements.* Washington, DC: Population Division, Bureau of the Census, 1994, P70-36.

Chafel, J. A. 1990. Research in review: Children in poverty: Policy perspectives on a national crisis. *Young Children,* 45(5), 31–37.

Children's Defense Fund. 1988. FY 1989: An analysis of our nation's investment in children. *A children's defense budget.* Washington, DC: Author.

Children's Defense Fund. 1990. *Children 1990: A report card, briefing book, and action primer.* Washington, DC: Author.

Children's Defense Fund. 1992. *The state of America's children* (pp. 29–36, 35–40, 62–63). Washington, DC: Author.

Clifford, R. M. 1997. Welfare reform and you. From our president. *Young Children,* Jan., 2–3.

Clifford, R. M., Early, D. M., & Hills, T. W. 1999. Almost a million children in school before kindergarten: Who is responsible for early childhood services? *Young Children,* Sept., 48–51.

Cost, Quality, and Outcomes Study Team. 1995. Cost, quality, and child outcomes in child care centers: Key findings and recommendations. *Young Children,* 50(4), 40–44.

Cremin, L. A. 1957. The Progressive Movement in American education: A perspective. *Harvard Educational Review,* 27(4), 251–270.

Cremin, L. A. 1961. *The transformation of the school.* New York: Alfred A. Knopf.

Davidson, D. H. 1990. Child care as a support for families with special needs. *Young Children,* 45(3), 47–48.

Eddowes, E. A. 1992. Children and homelessness: Early childhood and elementary education. In J. H. Stronge (Ed.), *Educating homeless children and adolescents: Evaluating policy and practice* (pp. 99–114). Newbury Park, CA: Sage.

Eddowes, E. A. 1994. Schools providing safer environments for homeless children. *Childhood Education,* 48(5), 271–273.

Eddowes, E. A., & Hranitz, J. R. 1989. Educating children of the homeless. *Childhood Education,* 65, 197–200.

Elicker, J., & Fortner-Wood, C. 1995. Adult-child relationships in early childhood programs. *Research in Review. Young Children,* Nov., 69–78.

Elkind, D. 1977. Misunderstandings about how children learn. *Readings in early childhood education 78/79.* Sluice Dock, Guilford, CT: Dushkin.

Elkind, D. 1981. *The hurried child.* Reading, MA: Addison-Wesley.

Elkind, D. 1984. *All grown up and no place to go.* Reading, MA: Addison-Wesley.

Elkind, D. 1986. Formal education and early childhood education: An essential difference. *Phi Delta Kappan,* 67(9), 633–636.

Elkind, D. 1987a. The child yesterday, today, and tomorrow. *Young Children,* 42(4), 6–11.

Elkind, D. 1987b. *Miseducation: Preschoolers at risk.* New York: Knopf.

Erikson, E. H. 1950. *Children and society.* New York: Norton.

Erikson, E. H. 1963. *Childhood and society* (2nd ed.). New York: Norton.

Erikson, E. H. 1994, Sept. Seven psychological steps to a healthy personality. *Young Children.*

Fein, G. G., & Clarke-Stewart, A. 1973. *Day care in context.* New York: Wiley.

Forest, I. 1927. *Preschool education.* Upper Saddle River, NJ: Prentice Hall.

Freedman, S. G. 1990. *Small victories.* New York: Harper & Row.

FYI. (1994). Preschool-age children in poverty: Numbers increase, but most not in preschool. *Young Children,* Jan.

Galinsky, E. 1990. Raising children in the 1990s: The challenges for parents, educators, and business. *Young Children,* 45(2), 2–3, 67–69.

Gesell, A. 1939. *Biographies of child development.* New York: Paul B. Hoeber.

Ginsburg, H., & Opper, S. 1969. *Piaget's theory of intellectual development: An introduction.* Upper Saddle River, NJ: Prentice Hall.

Helm, V. M. 1992. The legal context: From access to success in education for homeless children and youth. In J. H. Stronge (Ed.). *Educating homeless children and adolescents: Evaluating policy and practice* (pp. 26–41). Newbury Park, CA: Sage.

Hewes, D. 1976. NAEYC's first half century: 1926–1976. *Young Children,* 31(6), 461–476.

Hofferth, S. L., Brayfield, A., Deich, S., & Holcomb, P. 1991. *The national child care survey.* Washington, DC: The Urban Institute.

Honstead, C. 1968. *The developmental theory of Jean Piaget.* In J. L. Frost (Ed.), *Early childhood education rediscovered* (pp. 132–145). New York: Holt, Rinehart & Winston.

Hunt, J. M. 1961. *Intelligence and experience.* New York: Roland.

Hymes, J. L., Jr. 1978. America's first nursery schools: An interview with Abigail A. Eliot. In J. L. Hymes, Jr. (Ed.). *Early childhood education living history interviews, book 1: Beginning.* Carmel, CA: Hacienda Press.

Hymes, J. L., Jr. 1991. *Early childhood education: Twenty years in review.* A look at 1971–1990. Washington, DC: National Association for the Education of Young Children.

Kagan, S. L. 1999. A5: Redefining 21st Century Early Care and Education. *Young Children,* 54(6), 2–3.

Kagan, S. L., Moore, E., & Bredekamp, S. (Eds.). 1995. *Reconsidering children's early learning and development: Toward shared beliefs and vocabulary.* Washington, DC: National Education Goals Panel.

Katz, L. G. 1983. *Talks with parents: On living with preschoolers.* Urbana, IL: ERIC Clearinghouse on Elementary and Early Childhood Education.

Kilpatrick, W. H. 1914. *The Montessori system examined.* Boston: Houghton Mifflin.

Klein, T., Bittel, C., & Molnar, J. 1993. No place to call home: Supporting the needs of homeless children in the early childhood classroom. *Young Children,* 48(6), 22–31.

Koblinsky, S. A., Taylor, M. L., & Relkin, S. F. 1990. *Teaching homeless young children: A challenge for early childhood educators.* Paper presented at the annual meeting of NAEYC, Washington, DC.

Koblinsky, S., Taylor, M., & Relkin, S. 1992. Educating homeless young children. *Day Care & Early Education,* 20(1), 24–29.

Kohlberg, L. 1968. Cognitive stages and preschool education. In J. L. Frost (Ed.), *Early childhood education rediscovered* (pp. 212–224). New York: Holt, Rinehart & Winston.

Lamb, M., Sternberg, K. J., & Ketterlinus, R. D. 1993. Child care in the United States: The modern era. In M. Lamb, K. J. Sternberg, C. P. Hwang, & A. Broberg (Eds.), *Nonparental child care: Cultural and historical perspectives.* Hillsdale, NJ: Erlbaum.

Lawson, D. E. 1939. Corrective note on the early history of the American kindergarten. *Educational Administration and Supervision,* 25, 699–703.

Lay-Dopyera, M., & Dopyera, J. 1987. *Becoming a teacher of young children.* New York: Random House/Alfred A. Knopf.

Leeper, S. H., Witherspoon, R. L., & Day, B. 1984. *Good schools for young children* (5th ed). Upper Saddle River, NJ: Merrill/Prentice Hall.

Maccoby, E. E. 1992. The role of parents in the socialization of children: An historical overview. *Developmental Psychology* 28(6), 1006–1017.

Maslow, A. 1970. *Motivation and personality* (2nd ed.). New York: Harper & Row.

May, D., & Vinovskis, M. A. 1977. A ray of millennial light: Early education and social reform in the infant school movement in Massachusetts, 1826–1840. In T. Harevan (Ed.), *Family and kin in urban communities, 1700–1930* (pp. 62–99). New York: New Viewpoints.

McCarthy, M. A., & Houston, J. P. 1980. *Fundamentals of early childhood education.* Cambridge, MA: Winthrop.

McChesney, K. Y. 1992. Homeless families: Four patterns of poverty. In M. J. Robertson & M. Greenblatt (Eds.), *Homelessness: A national perspective* (pp. 245–256). New York: Plenum.

McClinton, B. S., & Meier, B. G. 1978. *Beginnings: Psychology of early childhood.* St. Louis: Mosby.

Meddin, B. J., & Rosen, A. L. 1988. Child abuse and neglect: Prevention and reporting. In J. P. Bauch (Ed.), *Early childhood education in the schools* (pp. 290–294). Washington, DC: National Education Association.

Meisels, S. J. 1996. Performance in context: Assessing children's achievement at the outset of school. In Sameroff & M. M. Haith (Eds.), *The five to seven year shift: The age of reason and responsibility* (pp. 410–431). Chicago: University of Chicago Press.

Meisels, S. J., Atkins-Burnett, S. & Nicholson, J. 1996. *Assessment of social competence, adaptive behaviors, and approaches to learning.* Working paper #96-18, National Center for Education Statistics. Washington, DC: U.S. Department of Education, Office of Educational Research and Improvement.

Molnar, J. M., Rath, W. R., & Klein, T. P. 1990. Constantly compromised: The impact of homelessness on children. *Journal of Social Issues,* 46(4), 109–124.

Morrison, G. S. 2001. *Early childhood education today* (8th ed.). Upper Saddle River, NJ: Merrill/Prentice Hall.

National Association for the Education of Young Children. 1996. Public Policy Report. Child Care Center Licensing Standards in the United States: 1981 to 1995. *Young Children,* Sept. 36–41.

National Association for the Education of Young Children. 1997a. Who cares? State commitment to child care and early education. *Young Children,* May 66–69.

National Association for the Education of Young Children. 1997b. Highlights of the Quality 2000 Initiative: Not by chance. *Young Children,* Sept. 54–57.

National Association for the Education of Young Children. 1998a. Code of Ethical Conduct and Statement of Commitment. NAEYC #503.

National Association for the Education of Young Children. 1998b. How to plan and start a good early childhood program. NAEYC #515.

National Association for the Education of Young Children. 1999a. A time for continuity and change. *Young Children,* 54(6), 44–51.

National Association for the Education of Young Children. 1999b. A5: Redefining 21st century early care and education. From our President. Young Children, Nov., 2–3.

National Center for Education Statistics. 2000. America's kindergartners. U.S. Department of Education. Office of Educational Research and Improvement. NCES 2000-070, rev.

National Center for Education Statistics. 2000, April. U.S. Department of Education, Office of Educational Research and Improvement, NCES 2000-070 (Revised).

National Coalition for the Homeless. 1990. *Homelessness in America: A summary.* Washington, DC: Author.

National Institute of Medicine. 1988. *Homelessness, health and human needs.* Washington, DC: National Academy Press.

O'Connell, N., & Bloom, D. E. 1987, Feb. Juggling jobs & babies: America's child care challenge. *Population Trends & Public Policy,* 12, 1–12.

Osborn, D. K. 1991. *Early childhood education in historical perspective* (3rd ed.). Athens, GA: Day Press.

Rafferty, Y., & Shinn, M. 1991. The impact of homelessness on children. *American Psychologist,* 46(11), 1170–1179.

Schwartz, J. L., & D. K. Walker. 1984. The relationship between teacher ratings of kindergarten classroom skills and second-grade achievement scores: An analysis of gender differences. *Journal of School Psychology,* 22, 209–217.

Snow, C. W., Teleki, J. K., & Reguero-de-Atiles. 1996. Child care center licensing standards in the United States: 1981 to 1995. *Young Children,* Sept. 36–41.

Snyder, A. 1972. *Dauntless women in childhood education.* Washington, DC: Association for Childhood Educational International.

Spodek, B. 1988. Early childhood education's past as prologue: Roots of contemporary concerns. In J. P. Bauch (Ed.), *Early childhood education in the schools* (pp. 10–13). Washington, DC: National Education Association.

Trawick-Smith, J., & Lambert, L. 1995. The unique challenges of the family child care provider: Implications for professional development. *Young Children,* March, 25–32.

Tower, C. C., & White, D. J. 1989. *Homelessness students.* Washington, DC: National Education Association.

U.S. Census Bureau. 1995. *The cost, quality and child outcomes study.* Washington, DC: Author.

U.S. Conference of Mayors. 1990. *A status report on hunger and homelessness in America's cities: 1990. A 30-city survey.* Washington, DC: Author.

U.S. Department of Education. National Center for Education Statistics. 1996 & 1998. *America's kindergartners: Findings from the early childhood longitudinal study, kindergarten class of 1998–99,* Fall 1998, NCES 2000-070 (revised), by J. West, K. Denton, & E. Germino-Hausken. Project Officer, J. West. Washington, DC: 2000.

U.S. General Accounting Office. 1993. *Poor preschool-aged children: Numbers increase but most not in preschool.* Washington, DC: GAO/HRD-93-111BR.

U.S. General Accounting Office. 1999. *Education and care: Early childhood programs and services for low-income families.* Washington, DC: GAO/HEHS-00-11, November.

Vandell, D. L., & Corasaniti, M. A. 1988. The relations between third-graders after school care and social, academic, and emotional functioning. *Child Development* 59, 868–875.

Vinovskis, M. 1992. *School readiness and early childhood education: Some historical perspectives.* A paper prepared for the National Center for Education Statistics.

Wardle, F. 1999. In praise of developmentally appropriate practice. *Young Children,* Nov., 4–12.

Weikart, D. P. 1989. Hard choices in early childhood care and education. *Young Children,* 44(3), 25–30.

Weber, E. 1984. *Ideas influencing early childhood education.* New York: Teachers College Press.

West, J., Germino-Hausken, E., & Collins, W. 1993. *Readiness for kindergarten: Parent and teacher beliefs.* NCES 93-257. Washington, DC: National Center for Education Statistics.

West, J., Wright, D., & Germino-Hausken, E. 1995. *Child care and early education program participation of infants, toddlers, and preschoolers.* NCES 95-824. Washington, DC: National Center for Education Statistics.

White, B. L. 1985. *The first three years of life* (rev. ed.). Upper Saddle River, NJ: Prentice Hall.

Willer, B., Hofferth, S. L., Kisker, E. E., Divine-Hawkins, P., Farquhar, E., & Glantz, F. 1991. *The demand and supply of child care in 1990: Joint findings from the National Child Care Survey 1990 and a profile of child care*

settings. Washington, DC: National Association for the Education of Young Children.

Williams, C. K., & Kamii, C. 1986. How do children learn by handling objects? *Young Children,* 42(1), 23–26.

Wolfe, M. 1978. Childhood and privacy. In I. Altman & J. F. Wolhill (Eds.), *Human behavior and the environment: Children and the environment* (Vol. 3). New York: Plenum Press.

Woodill, G. 1988. *The European roots of early childhood education in North America.* In J. P. Bauch (Ed.), Early childhood education in the schools (pp. 14–21).

Zigler, E., & Gilman, E. 1993. Day care in America: What is needed? *Pediatrics,* 91(1), 175–178.

Zigler, E., & Lang, M. 1991. *Child care choices: Balancing the needs of children, families, and society.* New York: Free Press.

Zill, N., Collins, M., West, J., & Germino-Hausken, E. 1995. *Approaching kindergarten: A look at preschoolers in the United States.* NCES 95-280. Washington, DC: National Center for Education Statistics.

BIBLIOGRAPHY

Where reference is particularly appropriate for one or more educators and his or her name does not appear as the author or in the title, pertinent educator's name follows the reference in parenthesis.

Archambault, R. D. (Ed.). 1964. *John Dewey on education: Selected writings.* New York: The Modern Library.

Axtell, J. 1968. *The educational writings of John Locke.* London: Cambridge University Press.

Barnard, H. (Ed.). 1906. *Pestalozzi and Pestalozzianism.* Syracuse, NY: C. W. Bardeen.

Boyd, W. 1963. *The educational theory of Jean Jacques Rousseau.* New York: Russell and Russell.

Boyd, W. 1975. *The history of western education.* London: Adam & Charles Black. (Dewey, Owen)

Bradburn, E. 1989. *Margaret McMillan: Portrait of a pioneer.* London: Routledge.

Bremner, R. H. 1970. *Children and youth in America* (Vol. 2). Cambridge, MA: Harvard University Press. (Dewey)

Cole, L. 1962. *A history of education: Socrates to Montessori.* New York: Holt, Rinehart & Winston. (Comenius, Froebel)

Curtis, S. J. 1968. *History of education in Great Britain.* London: University Tutorial Press. (McMillan, Owen)

Dewey, J. 1909. *Ethical principles underlying education.* Chicago: University of Chicago Press.

Dewey, J. 1938. *Experience and education.* Upper Saddle River, NJ: Merrill/Prentice Hall.

Dewey, J. 1966. *Democracy and education.* New York: Free Press. (Original work published 1916)

Dewey, J., & Dewey, E. 1915. *Schools of tomorrow.* New York: E. P. Dutton.

Dobinson, C. H. (Ed.). 1970. *Comenius and contemporary education.* Hamburg: Unesco Institute for Education.

Downs, R. B. 1975. *Heinrich Pestalozzi.* Boston: Twayne.

Elkind, D. 1983. Montessori method: Abiding contributions and contemporary challenges. *Young Children,* 38(2), 3–10.

Finney, R. L. 1925. *A brief history of the American public school.* Upper Saddle River, NJ: Prentice Hall. (Froebel, Rousseau)

Fisher, D. C. 1964. *Montessori manual for teachers and parents.* Cambridge, MA: Robert Bentley.

Froebel, F. 1887. *Autobiography of Froebel.* New York: E. L. Kellog.

Froebel, F. 1893. *Mother-play and nursery songs.* Boston: Lee & Shepard.

Froebel, F. 1900. *The education of man.* New York: D. Appleton.

Froebel, F. 1902. *Pedagogics of the kindergarten.* (J. Jarvis, Trans.). New York: D. Appleton.

Froebel, F. 1976. *Mother's songs, games and stories.* New York: Arno Press.

Frost, J. L., & Kissinger, J. B. 1976. *The young child and the educative process.* New York: Holt, Rinehart & Winston. (Dewey, Pestalozzi)

Frost, S. E. 1966. *Historical and philosophical foundations of western education.* Upper Saddle River, NJ: Merrill/Prentice Hall. (Dewey, Owen)

Garforth, F. W. 1964. *John Locke's of the conduct of understanding.* New York: Teachers College Press.

Good, H. G., & Teller, J. D. 1973. *A history of American education* (3rd. ed.). Upper Saddle River, NJ: Prentice Hall. (Dewey, Locke, Rousseau)

Greenberg, P. 1990, Sept. Head Start . . . Before the beginning: A participant's view. *Young Children,* 45, 40–52.

Guimps, R. 1980. *Pestalozzi, his life and work.* New York: D. Appleton.

Handlin, O. 1971. *John Dewey's challenge to education.* Westport, CT: Greenwood Press.

Harrison, J. F. C. (Ed.). 1968. *Utopianism and education: Robert Owen and the Owenites.* New York: Teachers College Press.

Hayward, F. H. 1979. *The educational ideas of Pestalozzi and Froebel.* Westport, CT: Greenwood Press.

John Amos Comenius on education. 1967. New York: Teachers College Press.

Keatinge, M. W. 1896. *The great didactic of John Amos Comenius.* London: Adam and Charles Black.

Kessen, W. 1965. *The child.* New York: Wiley. (Pestalozzi, Rousseau)

Kraus-Boelte, M., & Kraus, J. 1892. *The kindergarten guide: An illustrated handbook designed for the self-instruction of kindergartners, mothers and nurses.* New York: Steiger. (Froebel)

Leeb-Lundberg, K. 1977. Friedrich Froebel: A friend. *Childhood Education,* 53(6).

Locke, J. 1892. *Some thoughts concerning education.* London: C. J. Clay & Sons, Cambridge University Press Warehouse.

Lord, E., & Lord, F. 1892. *Mother's songs, games, and stories.* London: William Rice. (Froebel)

Lowndes, G. A. N. 1960. *Margaret McMillan.* London: Museum Press.

Mansbridge, A. 1932. *Margaret McMillan, prophet and pioneer: Her life and work.* London: J. M. Dent.

Marenholz-Bulow, B. 1905. *Reminiscences of Fredrich Froebel.* Boston: Lee & Shepard.

Mayer, F. 1973. *A history of educational thought.* Upper Saddle River, NJ: Merrill/Prentice Hall. (Rousseau)

McMillan, M. 1919. *The nursery school.* London: J. M. Dent.

Meyer, A. E. 1940. *The development of education in the 20th century.* Upper Saddle River, NJ: Prentice-Hall. (Dewey)

Meyer, A. E. 1965. *An educational history of the western world.* New York: McGraw-Hill. (Owen)

Monroe, W. S. 1900. *Comenius and the beginnings of educational reform.* New York: Charles Scribner's Sons.

Monroe, W. S. 1969. *History of the Pestalozzian movement in the United States.* New York: Arno Press. (Also Owen)

Montessori, M. 1964. *The Montessori method.* New York: Schocken Books.

Montessori, M. 1966. *Dr. Montessori's own handbook.* Cambridge, MA: R. Bentley.

Montessori, M. 1967. *The discovery of the child.* Notre Dame, IN: Fides Publishers.

Montessori, M. 1967. *The Montessori method* (A. E. George, Trans.). Cambridge, MA: Robert Bentley.

Montessori, M., Jr. 1976. *Education for human development.* New York: Schocken Books. (Montessori)

National Association for the Education of Young Children. 1966. *Montessori in perspective.* Washington, DC: Author.

Orem, R. C. (Ed.). 1965. *A Montessori handbook*. New York: Putnam.

Patterson, S. W. 1971. *Rousseau's Emile and early children's literature*. New Jersey: The Scarecrow Press.

Pestalozzi, J. H. 1891. *Leonard and Gertrude*. Boston: D. C. Heath.

Pestalozzi, J. H. 1969. *The education of man*. New York: Greenwood Press.

Peter, R. S. 1977. *John Dewey reconsidered*. London: Routledge and Kegan Paul.

Pickering, S. F. 1941. *John Locke and children's books in eighteenth century England*. Knoxville: University of Tennessee Press.

Price, K. 1967. *Education and philosophical thought*. Boston: Allyn & Bacon. (Dewey, Rousseau)

Ransbury, M. K. 1982. Friedrich Froebel 1782–1982: A reexamination of Froebel's principles of childhood learning. *Childhood Education*, Nov./Dec. 104–106.

Rusk, R. R. 1967. *A history of infant education* (2nd ed.). London: University of London Press. (Comenius, Dewey, Montessori, Owen, Pestalozzi, Rousseau)

Rusk, R. R. 1979. *Doctrines of the great educators*. Upper Saddle River, NJ: Merrill/Prentice Hall. (Montessori)

Sadler, J. E. 1966. *J. A. Comenius and the concept of universal education*. London: George Allen and Unwin.

Senn, M. J. E. 1975. Insights on the child development movement in the United States. *Monographs of the Society for Research in Child Development*, 40(161), 3–4. (Dewey)

Skilbeck, M. 1970. *John Dewey*. London: Collier-Macmillan.

Standing, E. M. 1957. *Maria Montessori: Her life and work*. California: Academy Library Guild.

Stevinson, E. 1923. *The open-air nursery school*. London: J. M. Dent. (McMillan)

Ulrich, R. 1968. *History of educational thought*. Dallas: American Book. (Comenius)

Weber, E. 1969. *The kindergarten*. New York: Teachers College Press. (Dewey)

American Contributors

Baylor, R. M. 1965. *Elizabeth Palmer Peabody, kindergarten pioneer*. Philadelphia: University of Pennsylvania Press.

Bloom, B. 1981. *All our children learning*. New York: McGraw-Hill.

Bredekamp, S. (Ed.). 1986. *Developmentally appropriate practice in early childhood programs serving children from birth through age 8* (expanded ed.). Washington, DC: National Association for the Education of Young Children.

Brooks, G. 1957. *Three wise virgins*. New York: Dutton. (Peabody)

Cubberly, E. P. 1920. *The history of education*. Boston: Houghton Mifflin.

Gersell, A. 1945. *How a baby grows*. New York: Harper.

Guidelines for compensation of early childhood professionals. 1990. *Young Children*, 46(1).

Hewes, D. 1976. Patty Smith Hill: Pioneer for young children. *Young Children*, 31(4), 297–306.

Hewes, D. 1985. *Compensatory early childhood education: Froebelian origins and outcomes*. ERIC Document Reproduction Service No. ED 264 980.

Hewes, D. 1987. Looking backward: Fascinating facts about ECE in the 1800s. *National Association of Early Childhood Teacher Educators Bulletin*, 26, 9–19.

Hill, P. S. 1916. Kindergartens of yesterday and tomorrow. *Kindergarten-Primary Magazine*, Sept. 4–6.

Hill, P. S. 1923. *A conduct curriculum for the kindergarten and first grade*. New York: Charles Scribner's Sons.

International Kindergarten Union Committee of Nineteen. 1924. *Pioneers of the kindergarten in America*. New York: Century.

Kaestle, C. F., & Vinovskis, M. A. 1978. From apron strings to ABCs: Parents, children and schooling in nineteenth-century Mass. In J. Demos & S. S. Boocock (Eds.), *Turning points: Historical and sociological essays on the family. American Journal of Sociology*, 84.

Lawler, S. D., & Bauch, J. P. 1988. The kindergarten in historical perspective. In J. P. Bauch (Ed.), *Early childhood education in the schools*. Washington, DC: National Education Association.

Loundes, G. A. M. 1960. *Margaret McMillan*. London: Museum Press.

Manning, M. G. (Ed.), n.d. *A heart of grateful trust: Memoirs of Abigail Adams Eliot*.

Mason, M. 1958. *Kate Douglas Wiggin, the little school teacher*. Indianapolis: Bobbs-Merrill.

Media violence in children's lives. 1990. *Young Children*, 45(5).

Neugebauer, R. 1990. Child care's long and colorful past. *Child Care Information Exchange*, 69(2), 5–9.

Omwake, E. 1971. Preschool programs in historical perspective. *Interchange*, 2(2), 27–40.

Osborn, D. K. (Ed.). 1960. *Nursery school portfolio*. Washington, DC: Association for Childhood Education International.

Osborn, D. K. 1975. *Early childhood education in historical perspective.* Athens, GA: Education Associates.

Ross, E. D. 1976. *The kindergarten crusade: The establishment of preschool education in the United States.* Athens: Ohio University Press.

School readiness. 1990. *Young Children,* 46(1).

Seifert, K. L., & Hoffnung, R. J. 1991. *Child and adolescent development.* Boston: Houghton Mifflin.

Shapiro, M. 1983. *Child's garden: The kindergarten movement from Froebel to Dewey.* University Park: Pennsylvania State University Press.

Smith, N. A. 1925. *Kate Douglas Wiggin as her sister knew her.* Boston: Houghton Mifflin.

Spodek, B. 1981. *The kindergarten: A retrospective and contemporary view.* ERIC Document Reproduction Service No. ED 206 375.

Steinfels, M. O. 1973. *Who's minding the children? The history and politics of day care in America.* New York: Simon & Schuster.

Strickland, C. E. 1982. Paths not taken: Seminal models of early childhood education in Jacksonian America. In B. Spodek (Ed.), *Handbook of research in early childhood education* (pp. 321–340). New York: Free Press.

Swift, F. H. 1931. *Emma Marwedel, 1818–1893: Pioneer of the kindergarten in California.* Berkeley: University of California Press.

Tenenbaum, S. 1951. *William Heard Kilpatrick.* New York: Harper & Bros.

Tharp, L. H. 1950. *The Peabody sisters of Salem.* Boston: Little Brown.

Vandewalker, N. 1913. *The kindergarten in American education.* Upper Saddle River, NJ: Prentice Hall.

Washington, V. 1988. Trends in early childhood education. In J. P. Bauch (Ed.), *Early childhood education in the schools* (pp. 51–55). Washington, DC: National Education Association.

Weber, E. 1949. *The kindergarten.* New York: Teachers College Press.

Webster, N. 1984. The 5s and 6s go to school revisited. *Childhood Education,* 45, 325–330.

Wiggin, K. D. 1889. *The story of Patsy.* Boston: Houghton Mifflin.

Wiggin, K. D. 1916. *The Birds' Christmas carol.* Boston: Houghton Mifflin.

Wiggin, K. D. 1917. *Rebecca of Sunnybrook farm.* New York: Grosset and Dunlap.

Wiggin, K. D. 1923. *My garden of memory.* New York: Houghton Mifflin.

Wiggin, K. D., & Smith, N. A. 1896. *Kindergarten principles and practices.* Boston: Houghton Mifflin.

Zigler, E., & Anderson, K. 1979. An idea whose time had come: The intellectual and political climate. In E. Zigler & J. Valentine (Eds.), *Project Head Start: A legacy of the war on poverty* (pp. 3–19). New York: Free Press.

Educator	Significant European Contributions	Influenced by
Martin Luther (1493–1546) Saxon (German) village of Eiselben Liberal	Formal schooling to teach children how to read for socialization, religious, and moral purposes; family was important in schooling of children; encouraged libraries for children and adults; music.	Religious beliefs; importance of family
John Amos Comenius (1592–1670) Moravia (Czechoslovakia) Humanist, realist	Early education; designed the first children's textbook, *Orbis Pictus* (Visible World), which used illustrations; textbooks with illustrations; emphasis on training the senses; "discovery method"; direct experience over verbal learning; adaptation of teaching materials to abilities (known to unknown); natural sequences of learning ("unfolding"); education of all children rich and poor, male and female, bright and dull; "school of the mother's lap."	Religious beliefs; nature; importance of family
John Locke (1632–1704) Somerset, England Social realist	Importance of the environment, parents, and experience; early and enjoyable education; placed little stock in idea that intelligence was innate and present in the mind at birth; believed in individual differences in children; saw advantages in play; sensory training; blank tablet to be "written on by training and circumstances"; parents to teach by practice, praise, adaption to child's capacity and individuality, modeling, respect, and lack of force; teach about God, character, and good breeding.	Nature; environment; importance of family
Jean Jacques Rousseau (1712–1778) Geneva, Switzerland Utopianist	Remove pressure from child (however, some ideas were extreme); innate goodness of children; individual growth patterns in children; return to nature and a natural approach to educating children; encourage happiness, spontaneity, and inquisitiveness; make the school fit the child instead of the child fit the school.	Religious beliefs; nature; environment; Comenius; importance of family;
Johann Heinrich Pestalozzi (1746–1827) Zurich, Switzerland Realist, philosopher	Education is more than children relying on their own initiative; everyone is capable of learning and has the right to develop skills that would make them successful and enable them to fulfill their own potential; thus, he provided a variety of exercises that met educational, moral, and vocational needs; emphasis on sensory teaching; teacher training (best teachers taught *children* not subjects); multi-age grouping; unfolding; importance of parental teaching; individuality, respect for child.	Rousseau; importance of family
Robert Owen (1771–1858) Great Britain Environmentalist	His infant schools (forerunner of the modern-day nursery school) preceded kindergarten by about 25 years; influenced educators as to the importance of early education and the relationship between education and societal improvements; sought to reform society and provide a better world for all through education.	Political and social affairs; environment; Locke; Rousseau; Pestalozzi; importance of family

Educator	Significant European Contributions	Influenced by
Friedrich Wilhelm Froebel (1782–1852) Oberweissback, Germany Idealist	"Father of kindergartens"; areas of learning [emphasized the importance of play, and relied on observations for activities and objects); methodology ("the first educator to develop a planned, systematic program for educating young children" (Morrison, 2001, p. 58)]; curriculum ["gifts" (objects for children to handle and use in learning shape, size, color, and concepts involved in counting, measuring, contrasting, and comparing) and "occupations" (materials designed for developing various skills, primarily psychomotor, through activities such as sewing cards, drawing pictures by following dots, clay, cutting, stringing, weaving, drawing, pasting, and paper folding)]; "unfolding" of child; childhood not merely preparation for adulthood but has special value; finger plays; circle games; songs to reinforce concepts; respect for the individual; teacher training (first educator to encourage young, unmarried women to become teachers; materials and instruction for parents, especially mothers). He was a deeply religious man and his "mission was to demonstrate the unity of God's creations in both the *gifts* and *occupations*" (Braun & Edwards, 1972, p. 70).	Rousseau; Pestalozzi; Comenius; environment; religious beliefs; importance of family. [For differences between Dewey and Froebel, see Osborn (1991, p. 96).]
Margaret McMillan (1860–1931) Westchester County, New York (raised in Scotland) Socialist, environmentalist	Coined word *nursery school,* worked with the "whole" child; teacher training; early education; medical and dental care; daily health inspection; outdoor activities ("open-air nursery"); emphasized play, nurture, and work with parents (including home visits); sensorimotor learning.	Environment; Seguin; importance of the family. Opposed Montessori.
Maria Montessori (1870–1952) Italy Physician, psychiatrist, educator	Individuality of the child; importance of early years; sequential tasks of learning; awareness of learning abilities of disabled children; small-sized furniture; learning and self-correcting materials; sensory training; curriculum emphasized practical life exercises, sensorial exercises, language, mathematics, and cultural exercises; the teacher as a facilitator; joy of learning; the discovery process; teacher training.	Rousseau; Locke; Itard; Seguin; Froebel; Pestalozzi; religious beliefs; importance of the family
Jean Piaget (1896–1980) Switzerland Epistemologist	Children "construct" their own knowledge; teacher as facilitator; supporter of play; systematic stages of cognitive development; development is continuous, results from maturation and transactions between children and the physical environments; observations; popularized age/stage approach to cognitive development; provided reproducible tasks; stimulated study of infants and young children; coined theoretical terms; children actually think differently than adults; children's thought processes change as they grow.	Froebel; Rousseau; Montessori; Binet, Simon

Educator	Significant Contributions
Charles Darwin (1809-1881)	Study technique of the baby biography—written accounts by parents concerning the early growth of their children.
G. Stanley Hall (1844–1929)	Considered the father of the child psychology and child development movement in the United States, used questionnaires to assess children's knowledge of natural phenomena. First psychologist-educator to relate child study experiments to actual teaching. His scientific approach was a contributing factor in the move away from Froebelianism, which he considered superficial and sedentary. This view made him popular with some educators and very unpopular with the strict Froebelians. He conducted a seminar to report his child development research and invited a group of kindergarten teachers in the summer of 1895. His criticism of Froebel and his emphasis on the new psychology so infuriated the group that only two teachers (Anna Bryan and Patty Smith Hill) remained.
Sigmund Freud (1856–1939)	A neurologist and physician, aimed to understand and clarify the adult personality by tracing its development through early childhood and possible unresolved conflicts. There was wider acceptance of Freud's theories in the fields of child development and nursery school education than by kindergarten teachers. "Freud's theory was seen as championing permissiveness in child rearing. It was thought that if some of the child's innate characteristics conflict with ideas of proper behavior, the stress of development can be removed by removing some of the usual demands placed on children. It should be repeated that this reasoning was only inferred from Freud's work and should not be credited to him" (McClinton & Meier, 1978, p. 14). Almy states (1968, p. ix): "Psychoanalytic theories dominated child development research and permeated the child-rearing advice of many experts. Too often, the free expression of impulse rather than its eventual mastery and direction was made to seem to be the primary goal for the nursery years."
Alfred Binet (1857–1911)	Conducted intelligence testing in the early 1900s to determine the children's level of mental functioning. Wanted to develop a reliable technique for identifying children who would not benefit from schooling, and to determine the age at which most children could perform certain tasks—establishing both an IQ and a mental age.
John Dewey (1859–1952)	(See Appendix 1D).
Arnold Gesell (1880–1961)	Studied developmental changes in motor behavior, language, visual capabilities, adaptive functions, and personal and social relations of children from birth to 10 years. Was a catalyst in the child study movement—studied with G. Stanley Hall; encouraged Abigail Eliot to study in England; used moving picture photography in recording behavior of children in a "natural" setting; identified normative behavior for children as indices of likely behavior, but warned that "ages and stages" concept had been interpreted too literally; encouraged nursery schools as vital part of educational system; emphasized the importance of the early years (the preschool period) stating it "is biologically the most important period in the development of an individual for the simple but sufficient reason that it comes first in a dynamic sequence; it inevitably influences all subsequent development" (Osborn, 1991, p. 121).

Educator	Significant Contributions
John Watson (1878–1958)	Founder of behaviorism, studied emotional development. Felt that only the observable behavior of the child is important and that early reflexive behaviors are the base from which more complicated behaviors develop through learning. "For example, Watson believed that fear, rage, and love are unlearned reflexes of infants and that from these three reflexes the child's emotional system develops" (McClinton & Meier, 1978, p. 13).
Erik Erikson (1902–1994)	A neo-Freudian, noted for his psychosocial theory of development. Identified eight stages and ages through which children pass: Trust vs. Mistrust (birth to 1 year); Autonomy vs. Shame and Doubt (1–3 years); Initiative vs. Guilt (3–6 years); Industry vs. Inferiority (7–11 years); Identity vs. Role Confusion (adolescence); and Intimacy vs. Isolation (adulthood); Generativity vs. Self–absorption (adulthood); and Integrity vs. Despair (adulthood). His first three stages were well accepted as the framework for practical application in the nursery school. The theme for the 1950 White House Conference, *Personality in the Making,* represented Erikson's theory.

Name	Influence
Henry Barnard (1811–1900)	Established the first educational journal (*American Journal of Education*) in 1855. It seems quite likely that through this journal the American educational community first learned of the kindergarten (educational) movement. Referred to as the father of the American kindergarten. First saw Froebel's ideas at an exhibit in London in 1854. Published an article entitled *Froebel's System of Infant Gardens* (July 1856), the first article on the kindergarten to appear in America. Charter member of the American Froebel Union and early advocate of women kindergarten teachers. Influenced by Rousseau and drew inspiration from the liberalism of the French Revolution (Osborn, 1991).
Hon. William Torrey Harris (1835–1909)	Superintendent of schools in St. Louis; later United States commissioner of education. Called attention to the kindergartens and suggested that experiments be made by primary teachers with a view to introducing into the public schools such features of the system as might prove practical and helpful. "With the endorsement of Dr. Harris the cause acquired both dignity and momentum, and many leading educators who had previously ignored it began seriously to consider its claims" (Blow, n.d. p. 935). Strongly influenced by Elizabeth Peabody and Susan Blow. Established an experimental kindergarten program in the Des Peres School during the 1872–1873 academic year.
William Nicholas Hailman (1836–1920)	Published and practically maintained a kindergarten magazine. Translated and printed at his own expense a number of German pedagogic pamphlets and made large contributions to Froebelian literature. Taught courses in kindergarten education at Cook County Normal School in Illinois (1880s). Mrs. Hailman published a collection of songs and games, and wrote articles on kindergarten (Blow, n.d.). Husband and wife started a kindergarten in Milwaukee.
Col. Francis Parker (1837–1902)	Emphasized the value of child study and helped influence the establishment of child study associations (1874–1880) (Baker, 1937). In 1880, the first person to utilize the Froebelian philosophy as part of the curriculum of an elementary school. Taught courses in kindergarten education at the Cook County Normal School in Illinois (Osborn, 1991).
William Heard Kilpatrick (1871–1965)	Best known in kindergarten circles for his "project method" and his stopped . . . in this country." His major criticisms were that the method was based on faulty psychological theory and the sensorimotor materials used in the classroom. The project method involved motor, aesthetic, and intellectual activity and emphasized becoming involved in "real-life" experiences rather than mere preparation for life. The project method (study unit) was used extensively by kindergarten teachers for many years and can still be seen, in modified form, in some kindergartens today (Osborn, 1991, pp. 113–114).
Mrs. Quincy A. Shaw (Pauline Agassiz) (circa 1870)	Established and supported free kindergartens for children of the poor in Boston and Jamaica; cost $30,000–$50,000 annually in 1870s.

Name	Influence
Mrs. Sarah B. Cooper d.1896	In 1879 Mrs. Cooper visited the Silver Street Kindergarten in San Francisco (taught by Kate Douglas Wiggin), became a convert to the cause, and along with the members of her Bible class undertook the support of a free kindergarten. From this beginning her work grew into the Golden Gate Kindergarten Association, which through her power of inspiration and genius for administration became the largest, wealthiest, best organized, and most flourishing of all philanthropic associations for the extension of the Froebel system. First president of IKU.
Mrs. Leland Stanford (circa 1870) **Mrs. Phebe A. Hearst** (Golden Gate Kindergarten Association, 1879–1959)	Honorary president of the Golden Gate Association, gave $190,000. Supported seven kindergartens and established a free lecture course for mothers and kindergartners.

Other contributors could be cited here, but this information is given to indicate trends that were developing rather than be a complete report of individuals, theories, and research.

To be sure, many philanthropists remained anonymous, and many known names have been lost and/or forgotten. Their contributions to poor children, to new educational programs, and to families came at a very important period and their efforts will not be forgotten.

A few of the philanthropists who contributed to the care and education of young children are written about during this period by Blow (n.d., p. 936).

It is unfortunate that more information about the philanthropists of the early 1900s is not readily available for they made great contributions to the care and education of young children, to the lives of families, to the training and support of teachers, and to the promotion of child-centered programs.

Name	Contributions
Elizabeth Palmer Peabody (1804–1894)	Began teaching career at age 16. Took up kindergarten cause late in life. Championed cause of blacks and Native Americans. Met Margaret Schurz. Became interested in kindergarten movement. Opened first English-speaking American kindergarten in Boston in 1860. Published first American (Froebelian) kindergarten textbook with Mary Peabody Mann in 1863. Studied kindergartens in Europe where she met Frau Louise Froebel and Emma Marwedel, student of Froebel. Returned to United States and revised textbook. Goal was to establish kindergartens from coast to coast. Set up a number of kindergarten training institutions. Instrumental in getting School Superintendent William Harris to organize the first public school kindergarten in the United States in St. Louis, Missouri (disputed by Lawson, 1939). Promoted Froebel by authoring books, articles, letters, and essays rather than teaching the children.
Emma Jacobina Christiana Marwedel (1818–1893)	Student of Froebel and one of the most capable interpreters of his philosophy (Osborn, 1991). Recruited to the United States by Elizabeth Peabody. Conducted private Froebelian kindergartens in St. Louis, Washington, D.C., Los Angeles, and later in Berkeley, California. Teacher/trainer of Kate Douglas Wiggin and Anna M. Stovall, later principal of the Golden Gate Association Training School.
Madame Matilda Kriege and daughter, Alma (1820–1899)	Trained by Froebel. Recruited to United States by Peabody and taught in Peabody's Boston kindergarten. Alma trained well-known students: Mary J. Garland, R. J. Weston, Emilie Poulsson (first editor of The *Kindergarten Review* published by Milton Bradley Co.), Harriet Jenks Greenough (author of collection of kindergarten songs), Sara E. Wiltse (for stories and contributions to child study literature), Laliah B. Pingree (director of kindergartens in Boston); and Elizabeth Lombard (associated with Mrs. Shaw's philanthropic work) (Blow, n.d.).
Margarethe Meyer Schurz (1832–1876)	Attended Froebel's lectures in Germany. Took precise notes that were lost in mail to Froebel. Her sister and brother were also involved in Froebel's kindergartens. Married Carl Schurz (later to become an American statesman), moved to England, taught kindergartens, and then moved to Watertown, Wisconsin, where she established the first kindergarten (German speaking) in America in 1856 in her own home. Met and influenced Peabody to join the kindergarten movement.
Maria Kraus-Boelte (1836–1918)	"In 1872 Miss Haines, of New York, decided to introduce the kindergarten into her school, and invited Miss Boelte, a German lady of high culture, to conduct the experiment. Boelte had studied three years with Froebel's widow, and later had done most efficient work in England as assistant to Madame Ronge. She had also won a high reputation in Germany through a kindergarten which she established. . . . Married Prof. John Kraus and established an independent kindergarten and normal class. Educated hundreds of intelligent young women for the kindergarten work, and through her pupils made her influence widely felt. In conjunction with Professor Kraus (John, whom she married) she has written an excellent practical guide to the Froebel 'Gifts and Occupations' " (Blow, n.d. p. 933). Founded a training school in New York in 1872. Susan Blow attended the Kraus training school (Osborn, 1991).

Name	Contributions
Susan Blow (1843–1916)	Volunteered to teach in kindergarten in St. Louis without pay. Dr. Harris sent her to Kraus training center in New York. Leading proponent of Froebel in America; believed in strict adherence to his teachings. Patty Smith Hill and others were fierce opponents to Blow in the interpretation of Froebel's ideas. Served as conservative subcommittee chairperson of International Kindergarten Union's Committee of Nineteen. Patty Smith Hill, the liberal subcommittee chairperson of IKU, and Blow jointly lectured at Teacher's College, Columbia, from 1905 to 1909. Wrote five books and presented innumerable papers and lectures defining Froebelian principles and philosophy.
Kate Douglas Smith Wiggin (Mrs. Riggs) (1856–1923)	Kate met Caroline Severance, a friend of Elizabeth Peabody, who convinced Kate that kindergartening was her calling. Kate attended the kindergarten training school in Los Angeles under the direction of Emma Marwedel. After a year of study, Kate opened a private kindergarten in Santa Barbara called The Swallow's Nest. Offered a principalship of the Silver Street Kindergarten, supported by volunteer contributions, which undertook missionary work among the children of the neediest and most depraved class, later depicted in Kate's touching story of "Patsy." Before accepting, she traveled to the east coast to study with Peabody, Harris, and other Froebel promoters. She accepted the position and opened the famed Silver Street School in 1879, the first free kindergarten west of the Rockies (Osborn, 1991). She opened a training school for teachers in conjunction with the kindergarten. This school remained in operation until the great earthquake in 1906. During that period over 400 teachers received training (Osborn, 1991). Kate was joined by her sister, Miss Nora A. Smith, who became her assistant and successor when Kate married and moved to the east coast. In 1880, Kate founded the California Kindergarten Training School. She was active in the Golden Gate Association (which encouraged kindergartens in public schools) and the California Froebel Society, of which she was its first president. Until 1892 Kate and Nora trained all of the Golden Gate Association teachers. Best known for her children's writing which include: *The Story of Patsy* and *Rebecca of Sunnybrook Farm*. A prominent kindergarten educator and potent force in the movement for nearly 40 years.
Anna Bryan (1857–1901)	Graduated from Chicago Free Kindergarten Association and opened a kindergarten for the poor and a training center in Louisville, Kentucky. Patty Smith Hill was a student in Anna's first training class (Osborn, 1991). Her training was rigidly Froebelian, but her contacts with Colonel Parker and others at the Cook County Normal School were modifying influences (Snyder, 1972) and caused her to question much of that training. In her school, she deviated from Frobelian philosophy and emphasized practical life and problem-solving situations. Visitors came to observe her innovative practices. She returned to Chicago in 1893 as principal in the training department of her alma mater. Bryan, Hill, Dewey, and Hall were prime movers in the new progressive movement in the kindergarten (Osborn, 1991). Bryan and Hill attended Hall's seminar in 1895. Hall's criticism of Froebel and his emphasis on the new psychology caused all kindergarten teachers, except Bryan and Hill, to leave. Bryan and Hill worked with Hall during the summer and were convinced of the importance of the multidisciplinary approach in the study of children (Osborn, 1991). Details of Bryan's untimely death are vague.

Name	Contributions
John Dewey (1859–1952)	Dewey was not the first to promote his kind of ideas. "Professor Cremin has pointed out that J. M. Rice's articles in *The Forum* from 1892 onwards were the first shots in the campaign for nation-wide progressivism as a movement transforming all the schools. Bronson Alcott had advocated and practiced 'learning by doing' from the 1830s; Stanley Hall's child-measurement and observations were the basis of 'child-centered curricula'; and Francis W. Parker's advocacy of new methods in schools and teachers' colleges from 1875 onward infected Dewey himself. It was Parker's surmises that led to the elaboration of the Project Method for 'problem solving,' to use Dewey's phrase. As Dewey was sometimes such an obscure (and occasionally self-contradictory) writer, much of the credit for Dewey's appeal must be given to W. H. Kilpatrick at Columbia University from 1918 onward. He elucidated Dewey's dicta, relating them realistically to school and a rapidly changing social order (Boyd, 1965, p. 407; Cremin, 1961)." Significant contributions: "progressivism"; child-centered curriculum and schools; living for the present (not preparation for the future); child's interest; project method (involved motor, aesthetic, and intellectual activity and emphasized becoming involved in "real-life" experiences); action on the child's part; respect for individuality; "teachers who correlate subjects, utilize the unit approach, and encourage problem-solving activities"; learning is a socialization process; disciple of new psychology and child study movement; importance of family curriculum for both boys and girls; play (directness of social and personal relations); "sub-primary" to distinguish lab school experiment (founded in 1896 with Mrs. Dewey) from strict Froebelian kindergartens of the time; along with Hall, Dewey criticized the limitations of Froebelian practices (Spodek in Osborn, 1991); had international educational influence; published now-famous *School of To-Morrow* in 1915 with daughter, Evelyn, which gave glimpses of the Francis Parker School at Chicago, Caroline Pratt's Play School in New York, the Kindergarten at Teachers' College at Columbia University, and the public school of Gary and Indianapolis. The book went through 14 printings in 10 years—a remarkable feat (Cremin, 1957).
Harriet Johnson (1867–1934)	A nurse, former teacher, and staff worker at the Henry Street Settlement House, Johnson opened the City and County School in New York in 1919 for the Bureau of Educational experiments (later the Bank Street College of Education). Two different kinds of work with children were just beginning: research organizations studying child development and experimental schools—Bureau combined these two. Staff: doctors, psychologists, social workers, teachers, all of whom had worked directly with children. The Bureau started its own nursery school— believed by some to be the first genuine nursery school in the United States (Osborn, 1991).

Name	Contributions
Patty Smith Hill (1868–1946)	Student in Bryan's first training class in Louisville, Kentucky (Osborn, 1991). Conducted a kindergarten class at the 1893 Chicago World's Fair. Took over principalship at Louisville when Bryan returned to teach at Chicago. Attended Hall's seminar in 1895 with Bryan. Both remained while all other kindergarten teachers walked out as Hall criticized Froebel and emphasized the new psychology. Smith and Bryan worked with Hall, convinced of the importance of the multidisciplinary approach in the study of children (Osborn, 1991). While following many of the Froebelian principles, she instituted the child's free choice and a highly flexible schedule. Debated with Blow (and others) about the interpretation of Froebel's ideas. Was the liberal subcommittee chairperson of IKU (International Kindergarten Union). Joined the faculty of Teachers' College of Columbia in 1905, became head of the kindergarten department in 1910, and a full professor in 1922. Worked closely with Dewey and Kilpatrick. Helped to develop Speyer School, a neighborhood school for immigrants that served the needs of very young children, school-age children, and their parents (Osborn, 1991). Hill and Blow jointly lectured at Teachers' College from 1905–1909. Published *A Conduct Curriculum for Kindergarten and First Grade* in 1923. Her curriculum included nature study, literature, music, games, dolls and doll families, art materials, and blocks. She once said, "Observe the children and then follow their lead." She designed a set of large blocks that became known as Patty Hill Blocks. Kindergarten objectives included learning to work and play together (social adjustment), habits of purposeful work, self-reliance, and good thinking. "About 1916, Hill became interested in the nursery school movement which was beginning in England under the direction of the McMillan sisters (See Appendix 1A). Hill and Gesell were instrumental in getting Abigail Eliot to go to England to study the new movement in education" (Osborn, 1991, pp. 92–93). Hill wrote the song "Happy Birthday," which is sung daily wherever children are. Worked on Committee on Nursery Schools in the early 1920s, and was instrumental in organizing The National Association for Nursery Education (NANE), which became The National Association for the Education of Young Children (NAEYC) in 1964.
Abigail Eliot (1892–1992)	Social worker who became interested in the nursery school movement, which was beginning in England under the direction of the McMillan sisters. Influenced by Hill and Gesell to get training in England. Perhaps because of her "background in social work, coupled with the general multi-disciplinary approach taken by nursery educators, made Freud's theory of infantile sexuality more acceptable to the preschool movement" (Osborn, 1991, p. 87). Eliot is generally credited with bringing the nursery school movement to the United States (Osborn, 1991). She organized the Ruggles Street Nursery in Boston on January 2, 1922. She supervised the Eastern region of WPA nursery schools in the 1930s.

APPENDIX 1E PIONEERS OF CARE/EDUCATION BY BIRTH DATE

Elizabeth Palmer Peabody	1804–1894
Charles Darwin	1809–1882
Henry Barnard	1811–1900
Emma Jacobina Christina Marwedel	1818–1893
Matilda H. Kriege	1820–1899
Margarethe Meyer Schurz	1832–1876
William Torrey Harris	1835–1909
William Nicholas Hailman	1836–1920
Maria Kraus-Boelte	1836–1918
Col. Francis W. Parker	1837–1902
Susan Elizabeth Blow	1843–1916
G. Stanley Hall	1844–1924
Elizabeth Harrison	1849–1927
Kate Douglas Smith Wiggin	1856–1923
Anna E. Bryan	1857–1901
John Dewey	1859–1952
Harriet Johnson	1867–1934
Patty Smith Hill	1868–1946
Maria Montessori	1870–1952
William Heard Kilpatrick	1871–1965
J. B. Watson	1878–1958
Arnold Gesell	1880–1961
Lawrence K. Frank	1890–1968
James L. Hymes	1913–1994

International Kindergarten Union (1892–1913)	Established for four major purposes: (1) To disseminate knowledge of the kindergarten movement throughout the world, (2) to bring into active cooperation all kindergarten interests, (3) to promote the establishment of kindergartens, and (4) to elevate the standard of professional training for kindergartners (teachers). Differences in philosophy among its members became apparent at the 1898 meeting. "By 1903, the controversy within the IKU was so great that the membership decided to issue a statement which would clarify agreements and differences in philosophical positions. A committee was appointed to 'formulate contemporary kindergarten thought.' This group became known as the 'Committee of Nineteen' " (Osborn, 1991, p. 103). There were annual IKU meetings for 10 years. A final report was made in 1913 that indicated some commonalities, but the situation was unresolvable. There was a split among the membership, which served as a forerunner to change from traditional Frobelian to new psychology. Patty Smith Hill was the leader of the new movement (Osborn, 1991). Eventually turned into Association for Childhood Education International (ACEI). Began publishing a journal, *Childhood Education,* in 1924.
National Committee on Nursery Schools (Early 1920s) (forerunner to National Association of Nursery Education)	When the IKU no longer suited the needs of all its members, Patty Smith Hill called together a group of 25 persons interested in nursery education and the National Committee on Nursery Schools was formed. They held yearly meetings and then in 1929 decided to establish a more formal organizational structure. At this time the name was changed to the National Association for Nursery Education (NANE).
National Association for Nursery Education (1925–1964) (later the National Association for the Education of Young Children)	An outgrowth of the National Committee for Nursery Education. It was multidisciplinary in nature and included teachers (nursery school and home economics), psychologists and social workers, and medical personnel. In 1956 NANE established affiliate groups. Its publication was called *The Journal of Nursery Education.* Its name was changed to National Association for the Education of Young Children in 1964 to provide a broader scope of membership.
The Children's Bureau (1912)	"The creation of the Children's Bureau was the first recognition by the Federal government of its responsibility to promote the health and welfare of the children of the entire nation. . . . The Children's Bureau Act of 1912 gave the Bureau broad powers. It authorized research and the power to investigate child health, delinquency, dependency, and child labor (Lathrop, 1912). . . . Today the Children's Bureau is located in the Administration for Children, Youth and Families (ACYF) and is a division of the Department of Health and Human Services" (Osborn, 1991, pp. 112–113).
The Works Progress Administration (1933)	In 1933, during the Great Depression, the Federal Emergency Relief Administration set up funds for the relief of unemployed teachers. Part of the relief came as the Works Progress Administration (WPA) established nursery schools for children between the ages of 2 and 6 years. Osborn reports that "nearly 2,000 schools were in operation by 1935 and over 74,000 children were enrolled" (1991, p. 135). Hewes (1976) records the employment of 6,770 adults as teachers, clerks, and maintenance workers. Of great importance were the opportunities for children of unemployed parents in an environment that would promote their physical and mental well-being. The WPA nurseries continued until the beginning of World War II.

The Lanham Act (1940)

In 1940, the Lanham Act provided money for child care to mothers employed in defense-related industries in war-impacted communities. Nearly one third of America's women aided the war effort in defense plants or factories. Child-care programs were in 41 states, provided 2,000 daily nurseries, and were operated by the public schools. About 600,000 children attended these centers. This child-care support ended with the war in 1945 (Osborn, 1991).

One of the more familiar child-care centers during World War II was established at the Kaiser Shipyard in Portland, Oregon, under the managership of James L. Hymes, who continues to have a tremendous influence on the field of early childhood education. The Kaiser Child Care Centers provided 24-hour child care for children of working mothers, and also provided other important and useful help to these mothers (shopping, medical attention for their children, meal services, etc.).

The Economic Opportunity Act of 1964

This was passed at the beginning of the war on poverty and was the foundation for Head Start.

National Association for the Education of Young Children (1964) (formerly National Association for Nursery Education)

Began as The National Committee for Nursery Education in early 1920s; name and focus changed to National Association for Nursery Education (NANE) in 1925; name changed to National Association for the Education of Young Children (NAEYC) and membership enlarged in 1964. Its publication is called *Young Children.* Following the organizational change, membership growth was phenomenal. In 1990, NAEYC had 73,000 members. For a review of NAEYC, see Hewes (1976).

(See Chapter 3 for highlights of years 1990–2000.)

Association for Childhood Education International (1930) (formerly International Kindergarten Union)

This organization is an outgrowth of IKU (which included primary teachers). When it became an international organization, the name was changed to add "International." It is a healthy organization, has a publication called *Childhood Education,* holds annual meetings, has a prestigious membership, and includes affiliate groups across the country. Many advocates for young children are members of both ACEI and NAEYC.

National Committee for Day Care of Children (1957)

Established during a meeting of the National Conference on Social Work in Philadelphia. Concerned about the quality of day care since the lapse of the Lanham Act. The scope was broadened and the name changed to the Day Care and Child Development Council of America in 1968 (Osborn, 1991).

Head Start (1965)

In 1965 federal money was allocated for preschool education and the early programs were known as "child development centers." It was an attempt to break the poverty cycle of families and to give children educational and nurturing environments. For more information, see Chapter 3.

Chapter 2

Programs for Children

Guide for Readers

❖ *One needs to be aware that both children and parents have rights.*

❖ *Factors that influence a child's school success include educational level of the mother or father, the primary language spoken in the home, the number of parents in the home, and early care of the child.*

❖ *There are many different types of care for young children.*

❖ *Parents must be selective in the type of out-of-home care used for their infant, toddler, or preschooler.*

❖ *Some parents need care for school-age children.*

❖ *There are state and federal licensing requirements for those who care for young children.*

❖ *Many parents are unaware of the important guidelines in choosing quality care for young infants, toddlers, or preschoolers.*

❖ *Parental concerns for child care should be on quality, affordability, and availability.*

❖ *Students seeking a career in early childhood education have many resources to aid in decision-making.*

INTRODUCTION

Rights of Children/Parents

Many have asked the question, "When do children's rights supersede the rights of their parents"? Or "Where do children's rights begin and parents' rights end"? One organization that advocates on behalf of children, who cannot vote, lobby, or speak for themselves, is the Children's Defense Fund (CDF). This agency is based in Washington, D.C., and has state and local offices throughout the country. It (a) gathers data and disseminates information on key issues affecting children and monitors the development and implementation of federal policies; (b) provides information, technical assistance, and support to a network of state and local child advocates; and (c) pursues an annual legislative agenda in the U.S. Congress and litigates selected cases of major importance. CDF is a private organization supported by foundations, corporate grants, and individual donations. (More about CDF in later chapters.)

Caregivers can be strong advocates for children's rights, speaking for and on behalf of children and reporting abuse when they find it—in the home, in the center, in the community. Some caregivers, guilty of abusing children and their rights, must be removed from situations where they could inflict harm or danger. Caregivers must also be sensitive to the rights of parents and families and try to assist them in their roles by providing parent education and support.

The Families and Work Institute [330 Seventh Avenue, 14th Floor, New York, NY 10001, (212) 465-2044] has published a number of brochures of particular interest to child care. One is a practical,

---

Facts and Figures

- "According to the report *America's Kindergartners,* characteristics such as a mother's or father's education level, the primary language spoken in the home, and the number of parents heading the household can contribute to stark differences in learning abilities among children. The study also found that children's success in school—or lack thereof—is in part related to events and experiences, including early child care, that occur prior to children entering kindergarten for the first time. One finding revealed children's performance in reading, mathematics, and general knowledge increased with the level of a parent's education. Home activities such as reading to the child or interacting through play were also found to be linked to a child's future success in school." [Early Childhood Longitudinal Study, Kindergarten Class of 1998–99. A hard copy can be requested by calling toll free at 1-877-4ED-PUBS (1-877-433-7827).]

- The labor force of mothers of children younger than 6 has increased about 50 percent since 1975. (U.S. Dept. of Labor, Bureau of Labor Statistics, n.d.)

- A total of 17,714,000 have been served by Head Start since it began in 1965 (Internet). Annual enrollment in Head Start has doubled since the mid-1970s, reaching more than 750,000 children in 1995 (Internet 2000. *Webmaster@acf.dhhs.gov.*). (See information later in this chapter and Chapter 3 regarding Head Start.)

- Families headed by single fathers are the fastest growing segment, growing 34 percent in the past 5 years to more than one million, according to the Bureau of Labor Statistics (*Wall Street Journal,* May 27, 1992). . . . For these Americans, child care is not just a "woman's issue" (Duncan & Thornton, 1993, p. 53).

hands-on guide to involve fathers and other significant males in children's lives (Publication #C-93-02) (Levine et al., 1993). Publication #C-94-01 summarizes findings from the first-in-depth study of family child care and relative care since the 1980s (Galinsky et al., 1994). Still another publication is the first complete guide to the supply, cost, and quality of child care in the United States; it includes corporate initiatives to improve quality of child care and education and concludes with the authors' personal vision of an early childhood system for the 21st century (Publication #C-93-01) (Galinsky & Friedman, 1993).

Definitions

Continuing issues in early childhood education include who should bear responsibility for funding, operating, and monitoring programs, how early education should begin, what kinds of teachers to employ, what kind of curriculum to teach, and how programs should be evaluated (Seefeldt, 1990). Different factions put emphasis on different issues. Changing political and economic conditions create and reduce problems. However, until these issues have been dealt with to the satisfaction of parents, educators, legislators, and others involved with rearing of young children, they will remain in the forefront.

Early childhood programs of high quality can ensure that children are well cared for in appropriate sized groups, have loving and well-trained teachers, participate in developmentally appropriate curriculum and activities, and have their personal, health, and safety needs met. High-quality programs for employees ensure that they are well trained, fairly compensated, and active in the field of early childhood education. High-quality programs for families ensure the emotional, social, physical, mental, and spiritual growth of each member. High-quality programs for administrators include a healthy environment for all, sound financial conditions, and an atmosphere of congeniality and teamwork.

Elkind (1988) states that healthy early experiences " *in combination* with comprehensive health care, education, and job training for parents would go far towards alleviating some of the social problems of our society." The environment for young children should be warm, nurturing, and positive; a hostile or punishing psychological environment may be as harmful as physical effects, resulting in possible loss of self-esteem, increased anxiety and fear, ego impairment, helplessness and humiliation, stifled relationships, aggression and destruction, limited attention span, and hyperactivity.

Throughout the field of early childhood education are terms that are used loosely, inconsistently, and personally. Here are some definitions that apply to you as a reader of this text:

Teacher-centered: The teacher prepares and presents curriculum, imposes behavioral rules, and is in control.

Child-centered: The child has interests, abilities and needs that, when followed, lead the child to activities, time periods, and individuals with whom to be involved. The child has more responsibility for personal behavior. Katz (1993) describes it as *child-sensitivity.*

Developmentally appropriate (behavior, activities, etc.): The entire setting (materials, activities, expectations, etc.) is in line with the child's age, culture, past experiences, individuality, established within early childhood "norms," and other reasonable considerations.

Quality: This is more than the usual connotation of the word. It implies direct, focused, and successful attempts to make things "best." In describing programs for children, "quality" or "high quality" may mean "highest" quality but leave the readers to provide their own definition, which may be accurate or inaccurate.

Trained: In reference to those who lead and guide our young children, this word connotes specific instruction and experience offered by qualified individuals to dispense information and evaluate outcomes.

Accredited: This refers to programs that have followed and accomplished prescribed duties, behaviors, paths, and assessments prescribed by an organization or team that has the expertise to deliver and evaluate such conditions.

Assessment: This is a means of determining if prescribed outcomes have been achieved by means of appropriate measurement.

Other terms, when presented, will be defined throughout the text. See the glossary at back of book for other listings and definitions.

TYPICAL PROGRAMS FOR YOUNG CHILDREN

Depending on their own preferences and abilities to pay, parents have a multitude of options from which to select care for their children. Some are half-day and some are full-day programs. Most programs charge a fee; however, costs may vary with different circumstances. The most common types of programs are the following:

Half-Day or Part-Time

Preschool, nursery school, or child-care center

Prekindergarten or junior kindergarten

Neighborhood grouping

Government program (e.g., Head Start)

Special needs—disabled, gifted, and so on. Most disabled children's programs have been combined with regular programs. See Chapter 3.

Parent-child center

Laboratory school (university or college)

Vocational training

Church or community center

Parent cooperative

Public schools

Multifunded center (elderly, preschool, extended day)

Full-Day

Infant/toddler centers

Child-care center or day-care center

Laboratory school

Family day care

In-home care

On-site, industry-initiated center

Church or community

Private—personal, industry, franchise

Parent cooperative

Vocational training

Public school

Government funded (e.g., Head Start)

Special needs—disabled, gifted, and so on. Most disabled children's programs have been combined with regular programs.

Other

The sponsorship of programs varies from private to public and from independent to nationwide franchise or chain. Ownership may be a proprietorship (single person), a partnership (two or more persons), or a corporation (single or multiple entity). A franchise allows an investor to operate an outlet for its service by using name and management know-how. A chain is a number of similar establishments under one ownership, which may be a proprietorship, partnership, or corporation. Sponsorships of early childhood programs may be identified as follows:

Private nonprofit	Church groups, Community Chest
Private profit	Owner-run, franchises
Private (service to personnel)	Universities, business firms, hospitals, industries, other
Public (federal)	Head Start, parent-child centers, Title XX of Social Security Act

Figure 2–1 Primary child-care arrangements for all infants and toddlers.
Source: Hofferth, S., Brayfield, A., Deich, S., & Holcomb, P. *The National Child Care Survey 1990.* 1991. Washington, DC: The Urban Institute.

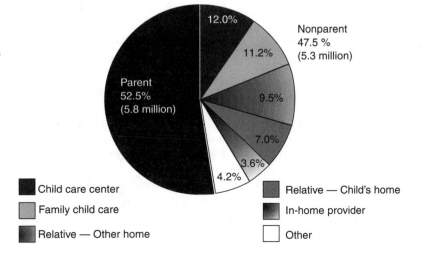

Arrangement	Percent
Center/preschool	33.0
Parent*	37.1
Relative	11.7
In-home provider	2.3
Family day care	10.1
Other	5.8

Figure 2–2 Primary child-care arrangements for all children ages 3 through 4.
Source: Hofferth, S., Brayfield, A., Deich, S., & Holcomb, P. *The National Child Care Survey 1990.* 1991. Washington, DC: The Urban Institute, p. 31.

Public (state)	State funded; may be administered through local school districts or social service agencies
Public (local)	Locally funded public school programs
Parent cooperatives and play centers	Neighborhood or community groups governed and maintained by the parents of children being served

NOTE: A given program can have multiple sources of funding and sponsorship.

Some facets of programs will be similar; others will be diverse. Although all types of programs must meet licensing requirements, possible diversities could exist between church- or industry-sponsored centers in instruction, staff training, facilities, extent of family resources, services offered, and cost. Both churches and industry provide important support to families and children. Figure 2–1 shows types of child-care arrangements for infants and toddlers. Figure 2–2 shows primary child-care arrangements for children ages 3 and 4.

Most of these program types are familiar and plentiful; however, two types of programs will receive additional discussion in this text: *extended-age programs* (such as infant/toddler care) and *employer options.*

Extended-Age Programs

Many centers meet the needs of working parents of preschool children during regular daytime hours, but other parents and children need special consideration.

Infants and Toddlers. This section briefly outlines the care necessary for infants and toddlers.

Need for Care. There is great need for appropriate care for infants. American children today are experiencing increases in the following:

Infant mortality (Children's Defense Fund, 1988)

Homicides (U.S. House Select Committee on Children, Youth and Families, 1989)

Diseases, death, and acute hospitalization from preventable diseases

One-parent families

Income and education play a strong role in determining mothers' decisions to work and their choice of child-care alternatives. Women who have more education and can earn more are more likely to work, but they are also more likely to provide the most age-appropriate care for their children. High school graduates and women with some college education are more likely to use day-care centers or nursery schools for their older preschoolers than are persons who have not completed high school. College graduates are significantly more likely to use paid in-home care for younger preschoolers. "Older preschoolers, whose mothers can afford neither to stay home nor to provide stimulating day care for their children, may be most at risk of developmental harm under existing circumstances" (Leibowitz et al., 1988).

After the birth of her baby, a woman who is employed outside the home has serious decisions to make: for example, whether to leave her job, work part-time, or continue on a full-time basis after a leave of absence. These decisions are not easily made; however, some employers are willing to give maternal or paternal leave for a period of time without jeopardizing the employee's job. Some women have no alternative but to return to work quickly and on a full-time basis.

If a woman opts to work full- or part-time, she must find care for her infant. In many instances this is informal care by relatives, friends, or others. It may be in the baby's home or at the home of the provider. At any rate, the woman may experience not only an emotional strain but also a monetary one as well.

The demand for out-of-home care for infants is a reality. The rate of employment of women with newborn children increases steadily. The women with the highest rate of increase were 30 to 44 years old; white; divorced, separated, or widowed; and had completed a year or more of college (O'Connell & Bloom, 1987).

Within each chapter of this text you will encounter "Stimulators." At the end of each chapter you will note "Participators." Both of these will give you opportunities to practice what you are reading. Read through each one carefully. Ponder its message. Then follow the directions. Doing each one will help you have a better understanding of the written material while you are having a "hands-on" experience.

Parents need to decide whether they are just looking for care that is custodial (i.e., protects the child from harm) or care that duplicates a nurturing home environment and considers the child's developmental needs. Both types of services can be found in different settings.

❖ Stimulator Ask for permission to observe a group of toddlers or preschool children. Spend 20 to 30 minutes watching their activities. Be observant (noncritical and noninterfering) as you carefully note the following:

1. Number of children and their approximate ages; also the adult-child ratio
2. The safety precautions taken
3. The health precautions taken
4. The arrangement of the physical facilities
5. The number and kinds of activities available
6. Specific toys to stimulate the four areas of development
7. The emotional response of the children to each other and the activities provided

The news media have been reporting a great need for infant and toddler care in your area. You decide you could meet this need better than anyone else by setting up your own center. You visit the only infant/toddler-care center in town. Child care looks so easy. Besides, everyone just loves those cuddly, cute babies! You go down to the local licensing agency having no appointment and no plans. After being given "the runaround," you finally identify the proper agency and are told, "Take a seat and the next available agent will see you." Twenty minutes later you are ushered into an office, where the agent begins asking you questions, giving you forms and brochures, and outlining procedures you must follow. When you leave the office, your options are these:

1. Forget it!
2. Investigate further!
3. Accept the challenge and go for it!

Explain what you would do and why. Consider many aspects of child care—not just outward appearances and short-term planning. Carefully itemize and evaluate personal elements (energy, commitment, flexibility), finances (initial investment, long-term financing, returns), value to parents and community, and other unique and overlapping ideas. Ask yourself whether the venture would be worth the time and struggle or if the idea of opening an infant/toddler-care program is a passing fancy.

❖ ❖ ❖ ❖

Program. Although there are differences between the care of infants and that of toddlers, for discussion purposes they will be combined here. No formal program is feasible for infants because their needs are immediate and intense. Infants' needs should be met on an individual basis due to their total dependence on caregivers. Inasmuch as their physical growth and development are more rapid now than during later periods, infants are vulnerable and are unable to handle discomfort or stress. They feel safest in a warm, loving environment and in the presence of warm, loving, and social adults (see National Association for the Education of Young Children, 2000).

Toddlers' needs and likes are often similar to those of infants; however, as young children gain mobility, they require different kinds of attention and activity. Toddlers also are dependent, though they strive for independence; they are egocentric and curious. They respond to children and adults in ways that are physical and somewhat clumsy. Toddlers like to do simple activities, hear stories, play with toys, and explore. They seldom play with other children, but respond when children or toys are in motion. The tantrums of toddlers are due to their inability to accomplish the things they want to do. Caregivers may plan simple creative activities involving music or art but should not expect toddlers to be attentive or involved for long periods of time.

Schedules. Depending on the length of the infants' and toddlers' day at the center, the caregiver may vary the schedule, but most infants and toddlers prefer repetition for security—and they spend most of their time eating, sleeping, or resting. They enjoy and need the undivided attention of the caregiver.

Toys. Infants use few toys, but as they develop muscles and eye-hand coordination, they become more aware of their environment and rely more heavily on their senses. They enjoy seeing patterns, colors, faces, and objects; they listen intently; they put objects, body parts, and clothing in their mouths; they rub against fabrics, themselves, and objects; and they respond to smells. Essentially their toys should stimulate their five senses and be safe and washable.

Toddlers, too, like toys that stimulate their senses. They like items that are easy to transport, such as cuddly toys, wheel toys, and containers. They are attracted to household items and enjoy

From the following list, mark *I* for the activities that are appropriate for infants; mark *T* for activities that are appropriate for toddlers; mark *N* for activities that are generally inappropriate for both infants and toddlers.

_____ Stringing beads	_____ Rolling a ball
_____ Looking at books	_____ Eating a cookie
_____ Petting an animal	_____ Finger painting
_____ Cutting with scissors	_____ Moving to music
_____ Sharing a toy	_____ Mixing paint
_____ Riding a tricycle	_____ Making cookies
_____ Catching a ball	_____ Playing instruments
_____ Doing a worksheet	_____ Stacking toys
_____ Playing peek-a-boo	_____ Slicing apples
_____ Doing finger plays	_____ Batting a mobile
_____ Playing with blocks	_____ Spreading butters
_____ Looking in mirrors	_____ Dressing oneself

playing with replicas of the real world. (See Chapter 10.)

Staff. Caregivers for children of all ages must be patient, warm, friendly, and able to respond to the individuality of each child. Contrary to the myth that anyone can take care of children, those giving infant and toddler care accept great responsibility and, therefore, need training in these areas: growth and development of infants and toddlers, milestones for normal and disabled babies, healthy environments, importance of positive interaction, and good communication skills. These individuals need some special personal attributes (e.g., commitment, permanence, enjoyment of very young children, low frustration levels, and acceptance of one-sided social and physical interaction). That infants and toddlers sleep most of the time, allowing one person to care for many at once, is a myth. Time with these youngest children can cause frayed nerves, frustration, discouragement, disappointment, and fatigue. Burn-out and staff turnover are common. Frequent breaks and assignment changes help these caregivers feel refreshed and appreciated.

Standards for the staff-to-infant ratio vary from 1:3 to 1:5 in most states. Standards for the staff-to-toddler ratio vary from 1:4 to 1:6. (The National Association for the Education of Young Children suggests groups for 2-year-olds with no more than 12 children and a ratio from 1:4 to 1:6.) Howes (1987) reports: "Both families and children appear to have more optimal development when infant and toddler child care includes one adult for a small number of children, stable care givers, and care-giver training" (p. 87). Ratios need to be low for optimum growth and development of the child and stamina of the adult.

Facilities. The physical environment (floor space, equipment, room arrangement, heating and ventilation, and sanitation) for infants and toddlers is dictated by the standards applicable to the particular center. The director and the caregiver should use their creativity and ingenuity to make the setting as aesthetically pleasing and as inviting as possible. (See Chapter 10.)

Cost. Care for infants and toddlers is expensive. Licensing agents, directors, and caregivers agree that the staff-to-child ratio must be small; therefore, the cost is substantially increased. See "Affordability" later in this chapter.

School-Age Children

Need for Care. Working parents sometimes feel relieved when their children reach school age, but simply reaching this age does not mean that children can (or should) be left unattended, especially for long periods of time. Child-care problems do not disappear with attainment of school

Facts and Figures

- "Historically, the word *latchkey* has carried negative associations: 'The house key tied around the neck is the symbol of cold meals, of a child neglected and shorn of the security of a mother's love and affection' (Zucker, 1944, p. 43). The term *latchkey* emerged during the 18th century. . . . At the turn of the century in the United States, latchkey kids were referred to as *dorks* because they had their own door keys to get inside their homes (Wolff, 1985, p. 3). . . . The meaning should no longer carry the negative stigma of yesteryear. . . . Latchkey kids are not, as a rule, eating cold meals, nor are they neglected or deprived of the security of their parents' love and affection."

- "At least 3.5 million school-age children in the United States regularly spend after-school time unsupervised by adults or older teenagers, and most discussions of this reality begin with the assumption that lack of supervision is problematic for children; and credible studies have reported poorer outcomes for children who spend after-school time with older siblings, babysitters, after-school teachers, and their own mothers, than for children who spend after school time on their own" (Bell, 1999, pp. ix, 35).

- In 1991, according to the U.S. Bureau of the Census (1994), "there were 36.7 million children between ages 5 and 14 years living in the United States. Of these, 21.2 million lived with a mother who was employed, an additional 953,000 lived with an unemployed mother currently seeking employment, and 999,000 lived with a mother enrolled in school. An estimated 912,000 children in this age range lived with a single father who was employed, and 70,000 with a single father who was unemployed and currently looking for work or was enrolled in school. In light of these statistics, in the 1990s, there are approximately 24 million school-age children who do not go home to Mom or Dad and cookies after school" (p. 6).

- According to the National Child Care Survey (Hofferth et al., 1991) 3.5 million U.S. children under age 13 were in self-care on a regular basis (based on a low estimate of about 7 percent of children from age 6 to age 13).

- Many U.S. children no longer have a parent at home to supervise their after-school activities. Maternal and paternal employment is normative.

- "The minimum wage was lower in 1995, adjusting for inflation, than it was in 1950, and the average hourly wage in 1995 was lower than it was in 1968 (Folbre & the Center for Population Economics, 1995). Half the new jobs created in the 1980s paid a wage lower than the poverty figure for a family of four (Coontz, 1992), and more than one third of all two-parent families in 1998 would be poor if both parents did not work (Coontz, 1992). Close to half of all children will spend time in a single-parent household, usually one headed by a mother, before they are 18 (Furstenberg, 1994). Among the 165 low-wage working mothers interviewed by Edin and Lein (1997), none could completely support their families on income from their full-time jobs, and three fifths of these women worked overtime at their main jobs or took a second job to make ends meet" (p. 3).

continued

Facts and Figures (continued)

- "Latchkey children are not receiving adequate training (Kraiser et al. (1990). With parental permission Kraizer and colleagues simulated phone calls from strangers and simulated package deliveries to homes of latchkey children. All children in this study supposedly had been trained by their parents regarding safety issues, yet all children followed appropriate safe procedures when answering the telephone call from a stranger. All parents in this study were surprised by their children responses, and researchers point out that latchkey children are probably at risk in spite of training" (p. 12).

- "Some studies report problems for unsupervised children, others find no differences between supervised and unsupervised children. (Bell, 1999, p. 35).

- "Girls, urban children, and children in low-income communities more often seem to experience problems associated with lack of supervision than do boys, suburban children, and children in economically secure communities . . . suggesting that the risks of unsupervised time do not diminish with age" (Bell, 1999, p. 35).

- "The proportion of employed married women with young children increased from 18% in 1960 to 30% in 1970 to 45% in 1980, and to 70% by 1995" (U.S. Bureau of Labor Statistics, 1997).

- "The three most common locations for before- and after-school programs were child-care centers (35%), public schools (28%), and religious institutions (14%), with approximately one half of the programs using shared space" (National Study of Before- and After-School Programs prepared for the U.S. Dept. of Education by RMC Research Corporation, n.d.).

---

age, they just change. The problem hours are before and after school and during vacations. Although some parents feel no need of care for their school-age children, other parents believe that continuing dependable, quality out-of-home care is vital.

It has been estimated that the number of latchkey children (those in self-care) is between 1.4 and 15 million (Zigler & Lang, 1990). For 1984 to 1985, the most recent year for which data are available, the Survey of Income and Program Participation (SIPP) found that an estimated 2.1 million school-age children were in self-care, approximately 18 percent of the total number of children with working mothers. Of 11- to 13-year-olds, 25 percent are likely to care for themselves while 5 percent of 5- to 7-year-olds are likely to do so (Cain & Hofferth, 1987).

In studies comparing children in self-care with those cared for by adults, Rodman and coworkers (1985) and Steinberg (1986) found no differences in self-esteem, adjustment, or susceptibility to negative peer pressure. Vandell and Corasniti (1988) found no differences between latchkey third-graders and those cared for by their mothers on grades, standardized test scores, conduct in school, or self-reporting of competence. But a study by Richardson et al. (1989) of nearly 5,000 eighth-graders in California found self-care to be a significant risk factor for substance use (alcohol, cigarettes, and marijuana) regardless of income, intactness of family, grades, or activity in sports. However, they also report "a large proportion of those in self-care not using these substances" (p. 564). Long and Long (1983) reported that first- to third-grade latchkey children in a sample of black parochial school children experienced problems of loneliness, fear, and stress.

The National Study of Before- and After-School Programs (prepared for the U.S. Department of Education by RMC Research Corporation in collaboration with the School-Age Child Care Project at Wellesley College and Mathematical Policy Research, Inc.) provides the following information:

- Approximately 1.7 million children in kindergarten through eighth grade were enrolled in 49,500 formal before- and/or after-school programs in 1991.
- Children enrolled in before- and/or after-school programs were overwhelmingly in prekindergarten through third grade—90 percent of the before-school enrollments and 83 percent of the after-school enrollments.
- The three most common locations for before- and after-school programs were child-care centers (35 percent), public schools (28 percent), and religious institutions (14 percent), with approximately one half of the programs using shared space.
- The study included "formal programs that offer enrichment, academic instruction, recreation, and supervised care for children between the ages of 5 and 13 before and after school, as well as on vacations and holidays."

Consider the research findings about two forms of after-school care: self-care and formal programs. Several conclusions can be drawn about the effects of after-school care. Each has implications for policies and efforts to support children's development.

1. Self-care should be used sparingly and selectively, if at all. Unsupervised time with peers is particularly problematic.

2. Formal after-school programs offer an especially good alternative to self-care for some children.

3. After-school programs can serve as valuable enrichment for children growing up poor and as a safe haven for children who live in high-crime neighborhoods.

4. If after-school programs are to support children's development, program quality must be maintained.

5. Subsidized after-school programs are necessary if programs are going to be available to children most in need of services.

6. After-school programs need to do a better job of meeting the needs of older school-age children.

7. Children's involvement in out-of-school activities provides a model of the kinds of offerings that appeal to older children.

8. Cost is a major barrier that restricts access to out-of-school activities for many families.

"Needs for age-appropriate after-school programs are likely to intensify. Fortunately, an emerging literature base can be used to inform parents and practitioners about how such programs and activities might be structured (Vandell & Su, 1999, pp. 62–71).

Information available shows that before- and after-school child care for school-age children is in short supply. It has been estimated that about 75 percent of the time mothers are working, their children are involved in classroom or school activities—leaving 25 percent of the time that they need some type of adult supervision. When both parents work, many work different shifts and alternate child care. In 1990, 62 percent of school-age children were enrolled in some kind of child care, but the demand is estimated to reach 77 percent of that population—or 30 million children—in 1995. The average fee for after-school child care was about $26 per week (Zigler & Lang, 1990).

Statistics from industry suggest that concerns of parents whose children are home alone manifest themselves on the job through the "3 o'clock syndrome" in terms of productivity slumps, increases in assembly-line accidents, and absenteeism (Pecoraro et al., 1984, cited by Bell, 1999).

As an employed parent of young school-age child(ren), rank the following options to suggest to your employer to make *you* more effective after the 3 o'clock syndrome: flextime; job sharing, voluntary part-time status; working at home; flexible spending accounts; cafeteria-style benefit plans; child-care vouchers; information and referral assistance; on-site child care; or others that would best fit your situation.
Or

❖   ❖   ❖   ❖

As an employer of women who have school-age children, and using the above options for working women, suggest some ways you could ease the 3 o'clock syndrome and still make your business profitable.

Parents may place too much responsibility or trust in their young children who are not able to accept being home alone—or in charge of other young siblings. All children can benefit from learning about in-home and out-of-home safety, emergencies, strangers, food safety, and so on. Current studies may reflect differences in self-esteem, adjustment, peer pressure, drug and alcohol use, violence, and other behaviors in latchkey children. We do know that children are joining gangs at younger and younger ages and that these gangs do have a negative effect on children, families, and communities. The main roadblocks to after-school services for poor children are lack of funding to help low-income parents pay weekly fees, lack of transportation, restrictive licensing, and lack of special outreach programs.

When parents are working longer hours than children are in school, it poses many problems for parents, children, and employers—who may or may not feel responsibility for child-care arrangements. Some employers, however, do make some attempts to ease this burden through financial assistance (child-care vouchers, subsidies, flexible benefits, etc.), sponsoring before- and after-school programs near the worksite, or contracting with outside agencies when employees are working and children are not in school.

Program.   As more and more school-age children need care while their parents are working, it is important that quality school-age care programs offer a wide range of activities and experiences that al-

low school-agers to feel industrious and that capture the interest of all program participants.

Staff should plan activities and experiences that foster positive self-concept and a sense of independence; encourage children to think, reason, question, and experiment; enhance physical development and promote a healthy view of competition; encourage sound health, safety, and nutritional practices and the wise use of leisure time; and develop an awareness of and involvement in the community at large. When programs focus on this wide range of activities and experiences, children's and youth's school-age child-care experiences are enriching and rewarding (Albrecht, 1993).

Research suggests that both children who are in poor-quality, after-school, custodial child-care centers and unsupervised latchkey children are at risk for emotional disturbance and school failure. (Long & Long, 1983; Steinberg, 1986; Vandell & Corasniti, 1988). Outcomes are more positive for children who attend high-quality, after-school child-care programs that are extensions of the child's program in elementary school. Some school districts provide before- and after-school care for their registered children, recognizing that it has advantages, such as the children's seeing continuity between school and the care program, feeling they belong, knowing the expectations and privileges provided, and being involved in activities with other individuals.

The need for care for school-age children is not new; however, its importance is becoming more recognized. The National Association for the Education of Young Children has developed materials, curricula, and protocols to accredited school-age programs following the format previously initiated for younger children (National Association for the Education of Young Children, 2000).

Because children come for varying amounts of time before and after school, activities should be appropriate for the available amount of time. Goals should be well articulated and specific to the growth and development, interests, and abilities of the age group.

Programs must be more than custodial. Teaching materials such as books, art and model projects, physical exercise, board games, and media, as well as educational materials and areas for study, must be available and stimulating for these older children. Planning can make difficult times easier. Activities, initiated by both staff and children, should be varied, plentiful, and appropriate for a mixed range of ages.

Staff. Personnel should be knowledgeable about the growth and developmental patterns of children of this wide age span. They should show interest, concern, knowledge, and the ability to meet individual and group needs. A genuine liking for children of these ages and the stamina to keep up with them are important requisites for adults who work with these children.

When schools run an extended-day program, some certified teachers become the before- and after-school staff. Some qualified people not employed by the school may direct or participate in special activities (sports, art, music). No matter what staff members are involved, it simply is not sufficient to put one teacher aide in a classroom with 30 school-age children after school, pay close to minimum wage, and expect a viable program to emerge.

Facilities. When extended-day programs are held in local schools, they use the same facilities (such as the lunchroom, the art room, the gymnasium) and often the same materials or staff. When these programs are held in connection with ongoing child-care centers, the space required for older children is often unavailable. Alternative sites to schools or centers may include church, government, YWCA, YMCA, community, recreation center, or private facilities.

School-age children should not be expected to fit into classrooms that are equipped for younger, smaller children. Provision must be made for their increased size, capacities, interests, and needs.

Cost. Costs of extended care (educational or creative materials, staff, utilities, rent, transportation, food, insurance, athletic equipment, field trips, etc.) may or may not be important to parents. Some would gladly pay for it if it were available. One national survey reported that 59 percent of all parents were willing to pay for after-school educational programs, and 52 percent were willing to pay for after-school noneducational programs. The median weekly payment made by parents for child care for children between the ages of 5 and 14 was $40.10. However, variation was found within the survey results, with payments going as low as $10 to $19 per week and as high as $70 and over per week.

In past years, federal dependent care block grants have made possible start-up and development of center-based care programs for school-age children in 48 states. Pending the cooperation of their respective states' governments, providers might see more financial resources made available through the federal Child Care and Development Block Grant Act of 1990. The text of the act recognizes school-age care as a service in its own rights. Fourteen states and most major cities have legislated and funded support to center-based program development.

Costs will vary, depending on the facility, licensing requirements, and the goals and sponsorship of the program. Most schools have the space and equipment appropriate for school-age children; however, they may need some additional items not covered through their regular budget. Unless these programs are funded through school districts, taxes, or special funds, parents should expect to pay the costs. Some organizations (government or private) will help finance the cost for low-income or qualifying children. Fees should cover curriculum materials, field trips, transportation, food, wages, rent (if applicable), insurance, sports equipment, and other items for the education and development of the children.

For additional information about equipment and space utilization, see Chapter 10.

See NAEYC publication #214 "Activities for School-Age Child Care," $6.00, or Video #841 "After School Planning" (2 videos, $79.00).

Employer Options

Employer-sponsored child care dates back to 1863 when provisions were made for children of hospital workers and "mothers who made clothing for Civil War soldiers" (Salkever & Singerman, 1990). Several large companies (Kaiser Shipyard, for example) built and maintained child-care centers during World War II (see Braun & Edwards, 1972).

Employers do have options as to how much support will be given to child-care services in the community, financial assistance (discounts, vouchers, flexible benefits), solving community child-care problems, and flexibility in employee working conditions (job sharing, parental leave, and other matters).

The number of employer-sponsored child-care centers has increased from 110 employers in 1978 to more than 4,100 in 1989 (Galinsky, 1989a). Zigler and Lang (1990) report an increase from 600 in 1982 to 3,300 in 1988. There are differences because of the way different researchers classify the amount and kind of services offered.

Employers who do provide some form of child-care support do so because they believe it will reduce absenteeism, tardiness, and turnover; increase employee productivity, morale, and health; provide a safe, educational, and healthy place for children; and boost the corporate image. In a review of studies, Dana Friedman found that, "contrary to employers" perceptions and consultants' claims, on-site child care *does not have much effect on absenteeism . . . .* The major effect of on-site

child care seems to be on recruitment and retention" of employees (Galinsky, 1989b).

> The companies that have been in on the first wave of employer-supported child care have emphasized quality. They have seen quality as a protection against liability problems. They have understood that their child care efforts are not only aimed at improving the productivity of the current workforce, they also can improve the education of the future workforce, today's children. (Galinsky & Morris, 1993)

Some employers argue against getting involved with family and community school-age child care (SACC) using arguments such as those posed by Coleman and coworkers (1991): These programs already exist; there is no need for more; school-age children are old enough to care for themselves; anyone can care for school-age children; there is no money for SACC; and that parents are more concerned with affordable than quality SACC. In many existing programs, too much emphasis has been placed on recreation rather than meeting the needs of individual children. Some do need recreation, but others need education, enrichment, study time, creative expression, and other personal attention. Some staff members of SACC programs need additional training in the skills, developmental characteristics, and needs of school-age children.

Conclusions from two studies of employers and child care conducted by the Families and Work Institute state the following:

> Employer-supported child care has evolved much faster and spread much wider than expected. Employers have become major players in the field and their involvement will be a force, perhaps a very powerful force, in shaping the future of the early-childhood landscape. The impact of this involvement remains to be seen. (Galinsky & Morris, 1993)

On-Site or Near-Site Care.   According to one survey, in 1978 there were only nine industry-sponsored child-care centers in the United States

(Perry, 1982). A decade later there were an estimated 500 to 1,000 such programs (Costello & Hunter-Sloan, 1988; Galinsky, 1987).

On-site care is provided by the employer on company property. It can be administered as a department of the company; as a wholly owned, profit-making subsidiary of the company, designed and operated by a nonprofit or for-profit agency hired by the employer; contribute start-up funds as a contribution or may contribute funds on a loan basis; or own the center and set overall policy, hiring management firm to run the daily operations. The company may or may not subsidize the child care.

Parents like on-site care for several reasons: more time spent with children (travel, center visits), proximity in case of accident, illness, or stress; reliable source of care (trained staff, permanency of center; fees may be deducted from paycheck; hours are coordinated; and other personal reasons).

Near-site care would probably be privately owned, but the company subscribes to a specific number of slots for their employees. The site is near the company for employee convenience; however, the company may or may not subsidize the care.

Many companies believe that on-site care is too expensive [costs are conservatively estimated at $250,000 for a 60-child program; companies would have to have at least 1,000 employees to make the program worthwhile (Salkever & Singerman, 1990)], requires too much space (indoor and outdoor), carries high liability, and/or only meets the needs of some employees. Therefore, many companies prefer near- or on-site care for employees children—leaving the cost and management of the center to someone who knows more about that type of business.

Financial Assistance. Instead of on-site care, many companies offer other types of assistance to their employees who need child care:

Voucher and vendor plans are a type of reimbursement program when the employer subsidizes all or part of an employee's child care (frequently determined by individual income and/or family size—sliding fee scale), but parents select the program. Options are based on employer standards and availability of licensed or registered care in the community (see Hayes et al., 1990). The assistance does not require employer investment, liability, or competition with community centers.

The family decides if this type of arrangement meets their needs. The employer may be required to reserve and guarantee payment for spaces a year in advance, and may involve some paperwork for the company (declaring the value of the voucher or allowance for federal taxation) and center (personal records of child and for management purposes). This type of assistance is more effective where adequate community services/resources exist.

Consortium-based care is when two or more employers jointly sponsor a child-care program. Costs are shared and some slots go to consortium members' employees on a subsidized or nonsubsidized basis. This option is most popular in areas where many employers are concentrated.

Purchased slots are either in child-care centers or family care. The company contracts with selected care providers for a specified number of slots, thereby reserving slots and protecting the employer and employee against a tight child-care market. Parents select from lists of availability. The employer may make payment directly to the provider and charge employees a discounted rate or the employer may not subsidize the cost of the care.

Child-care resource and referral counseling (R&R) through local or national affiliation is another form of employer assistance. Employers help parents select and locate care suited to their needs, preferences, and ability to pay; however, liability rests with the parents. The National Association of Child Care Resource and Referral Agencies (NACCRRA) is an organization committed to building a diverse, high-quality child-care system with parental choice and equal access for all families (Hayes et al., 1990).

Founded in 1972, NACCRRA's mission is to "promote the growth and development of high-quality resource and referral services, and to exercise leadership to build a diverse, high-quality child care system with parental choice and equal access for all families." In a brief 7 years NAC-CRRA built a strong record of accomplishments and a membership of over 400 community-based agencies (NACCRRA Fact Sheet, N.D.).

The value of resource and referral services to employers and employees includes current information on child-care programs, satisfaction for diverse child needs, parental options for diverse needs, visibility of public relation efforts, quality and availability of child-care centers, information for employee relocation, and a deduction for a business expense.

Resource and referral services may not meet the needs of all parents, but it is a beginning. If information is continually updated, it can be helpful to those seeking and those offering child care. See Figure 2–3 for a list of child-care resource and referral services of the Utah State Office of Child Care.

Financial assistance for employees includes the following:

The Dependent Care Assistance Plans (DCAPs), or the cafeteria benefit plan, was authorized in 1981 in the Economic Recovery Tax Act. With DCAP an employer may provide dependent-care assistance of up to $5,000 in value as a nontaxable fringe benefit to employees (and a deductible business expense to the employer). It allows employees to pay for certain expenses with untaxed or pre-tax dollars rather than with after-tax dollars, the common case; reduces the amount of taxes the employee pays and increases the amount of money received by employees after deductions; and reduces the wages that are subject to FICA taxes and workers' compensation premiums, reducing the employers' costs. (Caution: Check with a CPA or tax laws for current rules.)

Flexible time and leave policies include flextime, parental leave, and family leave.

Work-family support includes work-family seminars and counseling, assistance programs, and other services.

Other services include laundry service, take-home food, and special shopping.

Management change includes emergencies related to stress and health problems, supervisory training, work-family coordinators, and work-family handbooks.

Other options that may be available at some businesses: compressed work schedule, voluntary

Figure 2–3   Services of child-care resource and referral (Utah).
Source: Utah State Office of Child Care. N. D. *Employer's guide to child care resources.* 324 South State Street, Ste. 200, Salt Lake City, UT 84111 (810) 538-8733 or (800) 622-7390.

Parents	**Providers**
Child-care referrals	Start-up support
Consumer information	Free referral listing
Quality checklist	Consultation and training
Program information	
Financial considerations	
Employers	**Communities**
Employee seminars	Supply and demand data
Services to employees	Issues forums
Benefit information	Resource development
Workforce data	Collaborative projects
Consortium opportunities	

reduced worktime; regular part-time; job sharing; phased retirement; flexiplace telecommuting (working at home); flexible leave policies (personal, half-day, vacations, sick leave, extended maternity, contract work; paternity leave; adoption leave). These and other options may reduce or increase the need for care of small children.

Besides child care while the parent is working, there arises the problem of how to care for school-age children who are out of school (holidays, vacations, before- and after-school hours), emergency hours (overtime), and for children who are mildly ill and center policy excludes them during incubation periods or when the child is unable to function in the group (recuperation from illness, accident, or surgery, for example). This causes absenteeism from work until a satisfactory solution can be found. Absenteeism due to child care emergencies cost companies $3 billion in 1990.

There are benefits for all parties involved when employers get involved in the care of employees' children (Waxman, 1991):

Corporation: Less employee stress; an improved public image

Parents: Access to their children while at work; a more relaxed attitude while working; reduced commuting time (families travel to and from work together); the assurance of being nearby if child becomes ill or hurt, anxious or frightened; an opportunity for informal meetings with staff and observation

Staff: Get to meet parents often; can better assist child because of increased knowledge about home situation and family; feeling of parental closeness; more informal parent–staff meetings

With few exceptions, working parents' needs for sick child-care programs, summer, before- and after-school programs, holiday programs, drop-in services, and emergency hours (overtime) are still unmet.

Three international corporations are headquartered in our community, and the local hospital also has numerous employees. At one corporation, the board of directors voted against involvement with child care, listing costs, liability, and space as reasons for this action. Getting and keeping employees is no problem for them. A second corporation has a resource and referral program. They, too, have plenty of job applicants. The third corporation is in the process of getting established, enlarging its headquarters, and hiring additional personnel, but the average age of current employees is 26, indicating a possible need for child care. No decision has been made about company involvement in child care at this time. The hospital operates a child-care program across the street. Their needs have been increasing, especially for infants, and additional space has been acquired and occupied. It is difficult for them to keep enough nurses to staff the hospital.

LICENSING AND LICENSING AGENCIES

Just as there is diversity of settings for child care across the country, there is also diversity in licensing and enforcing systems for staff ratios, group size, and teacher/staff preparation. There is more consistency regarding space requirements and age appropriate curriculum.

An early but final report of licensed/regulated child care is shown in Table 2–1.

States vary in their licensing procedures from merely registering programs to actually enforcing standards. Requirements may vary depending on enrollment, part-time or full-time, exemptions, and sponsors—churches, private colleges and universities, parent cooperatives, military, or other organizations.

Preparing and enforcing standards is a costly and difficult procedure for many states; however, for the protection of children, parents, employees, employers, and others, standards must be set and followed.

Child-Staff Ratios and Group Size

Research conducted in 1977 (the National Day Care Study) indicated that staff-child ratio and group size were strongly related to program quality.

Table 2–1   Licensed/regulated child care and the total number of children cared for over a 10-year period.

	1978		1988	
	Number Licensed/ Regulated	Number Children Cared for	Number Licensed/ Regulated	Number of Children Cared for
Child-care center	18,300	1.0 million	66,400	3.7 million
Family day care	100,000	400,000	170,000	680,000

Source: 1978 data are from Ruopp, R., Travers, J., Glantz, F., & Coelen, C. 1979. *Children at the center: Final report of the national day care study.* Cambridge, MA: ABT Associates. 1978 data are from Children's Defense Fund. 1988. *State child care fact book.* Washington, DC: Author.

Guidelines for number of staff and group size for children of different ages were developed from the research study, for example:

Age	Number of Children	Number of Adults
4	Not to exceed 20	2 or more (one trained)

States differ in their ratio requirements. Only a small number of facilities fall within the range recommended by the research study. The national median is also the number recommended by the National Association for the Education of Young Children (NAEYC) for high-quality child-care programs. NAEYC recommends a maximum of three infants per staff member if the group size is limited to six, or four if the group size is limited to eight, for example. By 1995, 33 states met NAEYC's recommended ratio for infants, 28 states for toddlers. . . . Although more states had adopted group-size regulations in 1995, only 57% of those states (17 of 30) met NAEYC's recommendations.

As for staffing, it was recommended that there be two adults in a preschool classroom, at least one of which should be a certified teacher. However, teachers certified at the elementary level often lack a critical requirement for teaching young children: a comprehensive knowledge of early childhood development. In the absence of an appropriately trained preschool teacher, this person should be involved in intensive training by specialists in early childhood education.

According to the Children's Defense Fund (1990):

Parents place quality at the top of their childcare concerns; however, only 30 states met child-to-caregiver staffing requirements for the care of infants in child-care centers that meet the professionally accepted minimum safety standards. (p. 8)

Space Requirements for Centers and Family Day-Care Homes

Most states require day-care centers to have 35 square feet of indoor space and 75 square feet of outdoor space per child. For family day-care homes, most states have no space requirements. In states with space requirements, the minimums are generally similar to those for centers. Safety and health of the children and caretakers are provided for by facility requirements and inspections from appropriate agencies (fire marshal, health department, etc.).

Age-Appropriate Program Content

Nearly every state requires centers to provide a written plan for a developmental program, and 34 states have similar requirements for day-care homes. In addition, about one-half of the states require centers to express their educational philosophy in writing. This is a very good reason to formulate *your* personal philosophy—whether you are an employer or an employee.

Teacher Training

There are two types of training: preservice (prior to employment) and inservice (continuing throughout employment). Most centers prefer teachers with a background in child development and some practical experience. Many states recognize the child development associate (CDA) credential, offered through the NAEYC. (See a discussion on this credential in Chapter 3.) It is a national competency-based credential that usually involves a training program and a competency assessment. States differ widely in educational qualifications required for different positions in child care (directors, teachers, assistants, others).

The revised edition of *Accreditation Criteria and Procedures of the National Academy of Early Childhood Programs* (NAEYC 1998c) addresses criteria for high-quality early childhood programs, such as interaction among staff and children, curriculum, staff-parent interaction, staff qualifications and development, administration, staffing, physical environment, health and safety, nutrition and food service, and evaluation.

It is difficult to give a percentage (or number) on family child-care homes that are not licensed or registered. Many states fail to specify *any staff* qualifications beyond a high school education in their licensing standards. There are no requirements for experience or any form of education required in some states for *family day-care providers;* some states require preservice training, and fewer states require some inservice training. States who do not regulate day-care homes have no educational qualifications for day-care providers.

Why do we need licensing agencies? More mothers are working away from the home, existing services are insufficient, staff qualifications are low or nonexistent in child-care centers, caregivers are underpaid and untrained, many children spend their days in unlicensed or unregistered child-care environments, some young children are totally unattended, and our country has no national child-care policy. The 101st Congress (1990) passed several bills that will aid in the availability, affordability, and quality of care for young children, including the Child Care and Development Block Grant and expansion of the Title IV-A and tax credits for low-income families. For more details, see Chapter 3.

General Licensing Information

It is difficult to identify requirements for a child-care center; however, the NAEYC issued a public policy report that established guidelines for developing legislation. State requirements differ in the methods used to meet the needs of children receiving care. Centers that receive federal funds are required to follow federal guidelines. New centers must comply with all existing regulations, whereas continuing programs have a time frame within which to bring their centers into compliance.

Child-care regulations change in response to current politics, new research, and monetary restrictions. Some agencies will want full control of out-of-home care for young children, and others want little; some make recommendations, and others enforce rules. In most states, licensing is supervised by social service agencies or departments of education, public health, or child welfare. Nevertheless, every licensing agency should be aware of current research findings, meet the needs of families, and use funding wisely.

Most regulatory agencies require specific information about the following:

- Children who will be enrolled:
  Age, number (based on floor space and staff ratio), nondiscriminatory admittance policy (children with special needs, multicultural, ethnic backgrounds), health requirements
- Staff members
  Qualifications, number, responsibilities
- Programs
  Types, policies, curriculum, and discipline
- Food services and nutrition

Visit your local agency in charge of child care (Department of Health; county or state licensing agency, etc.)—whomever it may be. Ask for brochures, pamphlets, and all available information. Get the names and addresses of other agencies responsible for licensing, funding, and/or servicing all out-of-home care for infants and preschool children as well as before- and after-school care in your community or state. Study this information very carefully. If possible, plan to visit some of the different types of services. Ask informational questions, make precise notes, consider special talents you could offer, and formulate your early impression of services available for infants and preschoolers in your area.

- Environment
  Indoor and outdoor space
- Health and health records
  Immunizations, medication, emergency medical care, surveillance measures, resting/sleeping
- Records of children and personnel
- Equipment and play materials
- Transportation
  Parking, parental delivery and pickup, services provided by center
- Safety measures
- Insurance and liability
- Custody
- Financing

Licensing should ensue from careful consideration of its value and benefit to children and should positively affect both children and adults. Rigid standards and hazy guidelines are difficult to interpret and enforce. They should be written and monitored in the spirit of the regulation, that is, protecting children in out-of-home care, rather than in an effort to define and enforce power. The "letter of the law" interpretation creates a barrier among the agency, the center, and often the parents. Some agencies catch the vision of the regulation; others misinterpret it. Where there are multiple agencies to satisfy (fire marshal, public health department, federal regulations, social service agencies, and others), conflicts can arise. However, differences must be acknowledged and met.

Besides state and federal laws, there may be local requirements, such as zoning, that differ in philosophy and administration from licensing.

Some communities are fairly liberal about the types of businesses they allow in different parts of the city; some cities restrict businesses in residential areas. Checking city zoning (and other city laws) before making a market survey or selecting a particular location will save time and effort.

Most cities require specific plans before they issue a building or remodeling permit. Codes must be met that cover electrical safety, plumbing, and general building construction. Again, checking with the appropriate agency before making commitments to architects, builders, or realtors is wise.

Centers that provide transportation for children must conform to state motor vehicle regulations. Some centers find it profitable to provide transportation to and from the center, and others find it impossible because of high insurance and liability. If transportation is offered, it must conform to *all* requirements.

Licensing agencies may require proof of ability to fund the center. This assures staff and clients that the center has made the commitment and procured the assets to make it a bona fide business. Because of the great variation in requirements, individuals should refer to specific state and local agencies for information, requirements, and procedures.

The sole purpose of strong licensing laws is to protect the well-being, health, safety, and development of the children who receive the services and the staff members who render the services. Children should not be exploited or harmed, and workers must receive similar safeguards.

In their article on child-care licensing standards in the United States between 1981 and 1995, Snow, Teleki, and Reguero-de-Atiles (1996) compare requirements for three critical indicators of child-care quality: child-staff ratio, group size, and caregiver educational requirements. They found both positive and negative changes. *Positive side:* "child-staff ratios and group-size limits have improved for infants . . . and more states are now meeting recommended child-staff ratio in group size. . . more states have established licensing standards for infants separate from those for toddlers, a trend that appears to have benefitted young infants more than toddlers for both child-staff ratio and group size. . . ." (p. 40). *Negative side:* "The child-staff ratio and group-size regulations for four-year-olds eroded in many places. . . may be attributed to economic and political factors—weakening rather than strengthening standards. . . . There have been gains in the number of states requiring inservice training, but little change in terms of requiring more stringent preservice educational standards" (p. 40).

Licensing Procedure. Some child-care centers may be exempt from licensing requirements; this will be determined individually based on the purpose of the center.

> Exceptions to the licensing requirements are available usually where, for example, the child care is in the form of religious instruction, or is provided by a certified educational institution or on federal premises, or where it is provided briefly so that parents can shop or attend religious services or is provided by a public entity like a school. (U.S. Department of Health and Human Services, 1981, p. 72)

Obtaining a license can be a long and complicated procedure. Delays are not uncommon, and coordination among agencies is less than smooth; however, some agencies and directors get along amicably. Vermont, for example, formed a coalition of agencies that resulted in systematic processing. Whatever the licensing process, the center operator's most important step is to determine which agencies must be consulted, in what order, and for what purposes. Planning and organizing subsequent steps is important. It is even possible to work with different agencies simultaneously on overlapping, but not requisite, matters. However, one step missed or out of order could cause a domino effect, undoing months of work.

Initially, a licensing official will conduct an on-site inspection, followed by additional inspections by appropriate health and sanitation, fire, and safety officials, and others as deemed necessary. When the agencies have determined that the center is close to meeting *all* requirements, they may issue a provisional or temporary license. This permits a center to operate for a limited period of time if the center specifies the ways deficiencies will be corrected within an allotted time period.

A license is a certificate of compliance; it must be posted in a conspicuous place in the center. It identifies the name of the center's operator, the kind of program permitted, the number of children allowed, and the period for which the license is effective. The center can expect periodic visits by licensing or supervisory agencies to ensure continued conformity to regulations.

Owners and operators of child-care centers will be held accountable for licensure. Obtaining and learning the *current* federal, state, and local requirements must be a priority item.

In 1981, the Department of Health and Human Resources reported:

> Beyond learning and complying with these regulations, it is important that providers communicate with one another and, perhaps, with the licensing agency about the difficulties posed by unnecessary or unfeasible requirements. Licensing regulations must be clear, understandable, measurable, reasonable, and consistently interpreted. If they fall short they can be changed and the agency can be held accountable for its enforcement practices. Providers, as well as consumers, have a right to press for such changes and hold their licensors accountable.

Administrators are encouraged to apply for child nutrition reimbursement funds if their program qualifies.

Facts and Figures

- "No matter what the name or the setting, it is crucial that children be safe and that their development and learning be enhanced." (NAEYC, 1999a, p. 36)

- "Numerous recent studies suggest that, despite the fact that the majority of America's children spend at least some of their time in child care, many programs for preschool children in centers and homes fail to provide a level of care that enhances or maximizes children's early development and learning. . . . In addition, many school-age care programs do not effectively engage children in their program activities and operate in inadequate facilities" (Seppanen et al., 1993).

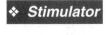  If you could be part of a delegation to discuss child-care issues with important government, business, educational, religious, and community leaders (at the White House, at the governor's mansion, at the mayor's office, with the state school board, with a large corporation—you choose the setting), what are *your* optimistic dreams? How objective and helpful could you be to improve conditions for children, families, child-care workers, and so forth?

CHOOSING A GOOD CHILD-CARE CENTER

This section is approached from the viewpoints of both parents seeking placement for their children and caregivers seeking employment. No one center will meet all the desires of parents or employees. Each consideration must be thoughtfully and completely contemplated and then some value attached to it. Determining each center's total value will help parents and prospective employees select a center.

Select and complete one or more of the following Stimulators.

From a Parent's Point of View

When parents place their child in a group setting, they should carefully consider each child, their family needs, their reasons for the placement, the potential benefits to each child, the distinctive characteristics of available child-care facilities, and the personalities of the caregivers. As parents have different needs, they seek solutions in various ways. Some place children in groups without ever having visited the center of enrollment or

doing any comparison shopping. Most parents need information and assistance to select a quality program for their children.

Some parents seek an experience that is educational as well as social and frequently enroll their children in nursery schools or preschools where their children can interact with peers and where they can attend from one to five half-days per week. This experience supplements the home experience. Parents who place high value on intellectual development (reading, math, science) sometimes enroll their children in academic programs where the satisfaction of other developmental needs (emotional, social, and physical) is not emphasized. Still other parents believe that time away from their children gives strength and freedom to both children and parents, and they look for a center that can fill these needs.

Parents like to be personally involved, because involvement increases their confidence in the program, encourages them as to the value of further schooling, improves their family relationships, and enables them to be better employees. What parents dislike is low involvement, insufficient discipline for their children, and poor community support. In a questionnaire designed by Galinsky of Bank Street College of Education and conducted by the Gallup Organization, *Fortune Magazine* (Chapman, 1987) asked working parents which child-care benefits they would like employers to introduce and which existing benefits were the most valuable. The two lists did not always correspond. Five years ago parents most wished for merit raises and management training—seemingly unrelated to child care. The next most popular choices were work-family seminars,

 Check the column that best identifies characteristics of a good-quality program for toddlers and/or preschool children and briefly state the rationale for your choice:

	Important	Desirable	Unnecessary	Rationale
Low child–teacher ratio				
Teachers educated in child development				
Experienced administrators				
Inexperienced "food handlers"				
Staff stability and training				
High standards for children's safety				
Mediocre health requirements				
Frequent movies or TV watching				
Live animals to pet				
Latest computers for children				
Frequent visitors				
Poorly equipped playground				
Current licensing				
A lounge and a break for teachers				
Staff/management/parent interaction				
Personal preference(s)				

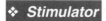 Discuss your selections with other individuals involved in child care. Do you agree on choices?

 On an initial (first) visit to a child-care center, a preschool, or an in-home care setting, note the following:

1. The general appearance of the facility
   a. Safety precautions
   b. Health precautions
   c. Physical facilities (such as lighting, heating, ventilation, traffic flow, etc.)
   d. Toys (placement, rotation, large/small muscle opportunities)
   e. Posted material (license, information for staff, information for parents, etc.)
   f. Learning "centers" or random activities

2. The appearance of individuals (adults and children):
   a. Number, ratio to children, involvement, etc.
   b. Expressions, interactions, interest
   c. Trained/inexperienced/insecure
   d. Focus of interest (children, adults, self, facilities, etc.)
   e. Philosophical basis of child rearing

Answer *T* (true) or *F* (false) to the following statements.

1. Mothers who want care for an infant or toddler can find it easily.
2. The requirements for out-of-home care for infants and toddlers are more rigid than they need to be.
3. The fee for infant and toddler care should be relatively low because the caregiver needs to do so little.
4. The space required for infant/toddler care is the same per child as that for preschoolers.
5. If care were available for school-age children, few parents would use it.
6. Without modification of staff, activities, or equipment, school-age children can simply join an ongoing preschool group when they finish school each day.
7. Staff needs for an extended school day can be met by individuals with little or no training.
8. Before- and after-school care for children requires much money and space.

Answers differ by locality and by center; what is crucial to one center may be insignificant to another. Which of the eight conditions are true in your community?

subsidized child care, ability to use salary deductions for child care, partial reimbursement of child-care expenses, and flexible working hours. Working parents who already had child-care options claimed that flextime, resource and referral services, and personal control over their work schedules were the most valuable company child-care policies. Would today's parents look for computers, language opportunities, originality, or other options like pick-up and delivery of children, sports training, and personal services?

Parents need to consider carefully the personal and professional qualities of adults who will care for their children; the program activities and equipment available; and the ability of the center to meet the varied demands of young children, their families, and the staff. The following points should be considered:

1. The program (based on sound principles)
   - Compatibility with family philosophy and goals
   - Quality
   - Convenience
2. The staff (good personal and communication skills)
   - Teacher-child ratio
   - Teacher training and experience
   - Teachers' personality and warmth
   - Rapport with children
   - Priorities for children (socialization, living skills, discipline, academics)
3. The children (happy, relaxed, involved with peers and materials)
   - Ages
   - Number per group
   - Diversity
   - Teacher-child ratio
   - Developmentally appropriate curriculum
4. The curriculum (appropriate, balanced)
   - Type and breadth
   - Pressured or relaxed
   - Child- or adult-centered
   - Good nutrition (based on federal guidelines)
   - Variety of opportunities
5. The facilities (properly maintained, accessible)
   - Location
   - Condition
   - Access

- Cleanliness (health)
- Developmentally appropriate equipment
- Safety

6. The cost (affordable)
   - Total tuition, payment schedules
   - Privileges and responsibilities

Directors can anticipate the most common questions from care-seeking parents, including the following:

1. *Curriculum.* Is the center licensed? What is the educational philosophy? (This is a major and a loaded question! Some parents will have specific ideas in mind regarding discipline, curriculum, approach, or expectations; other parents do not have the slightest idea of what they are asking, but they have been told to ask a particular question. State center goals simply and precisely.) Are the children prepared for kindergarten or first grade? What is the daily schedule? Do children play or learn? Are there outdoor facilities? Are they used often? Do children get to choose what they want to do or are activities always group oriented? Is there variation in the curriculum? Do the activities cover all areas of development (social, emotional, cognitive, and physical)?

2. *Convenience.* What are the center hours? Is transportation provided? Where is the center located? Is the traffic congested around the center during delivery and pickup times? What would be the best route to get there? What is the policy regarding ill children—is there an isolation room or must they remain at home? Are there any openings? What ages does your license cover? Does the center have a brochure that could be mailed?

3. *Caregivers/Educators.* How many teachers and children are there per group? What kind of training do teachers have? Do they have credentials (if required by state)? How long have they been with the center?

Do they like children? What are they like personally? Do they work together cooperatively and harmoniously? Is the staff updated through workshops, classes, meetings, or other ways? Do they know how young children learn and grow?

4. *Clients.* Could I contact some current patrons of the center? Do any enrolled children live near our area? What are the requirements and privileges of parents and families? When are visits permitted? Are individual needs of children and families considered? How are the health and safety of the children protected? Are there any disabled, foreign, or bilingual children?

5. *Costs.* What are the costs? When are fees due? Are there allowances for absences? If enrollment is unsatisfactory, what about refunds and withdrawals? Do other centers charge the same amount as this center?

Not all children benefit from the same kinds of programs; some perform better in a structured, one-focus group (often adult- or academic-oriented), and others perform better when the setting is relaxed and multifocused (often child-centered and oriented toward the whole child).

Parents do have a choice about the kind of center in which they enroll their children. Some parents know the kinds of questions they should ask when looking for a center. Some are unaware of different educational philosophies and do not take into account the fact that some philosophies are incompatible with the values of some children and families. One sure method to help parents choose a center is for them to visit the center when children are present—more than once, if possible. How children look and respond at a center should give parents an idea about how the children are faring. Parents should put much more weight on the way the children are treated than on the location of the center or its cost!

Figure 2–4 identifies possible problems for parents to consider in selecting a child-care center.

Figure 2–4 Signs of poor care for young children.
Source: T. Harms, Child care action campaign flyer, and personal teaching and parenting experiences.

CAUTION!! TROUBLE AHEAD!!

Parents, employees, employers: Be on guard for the following signs of poor care for young children:

If child:
- resists being left at center (after initial period).
- expresses fear of caregiver or other children.
- experiences a high number of injuries.
- has few toys, play areas, materials, activities or stimulation.
- is permitted to engage in negative or destructive play.

If parents:
- are discouraged from visiting the center.
- have no individual considerations: financing, conferences, education, participation, or information.

If caregivers (teachers, administrator, or other staff):
- are limited in number or training.
- meet child at entry and escort him/her to classroom.
- are dissatisfied, less than friendly, or turn over frequently.
- are harsh, uninterested, or unavailable.
- are intolerant of diverse needs of children (culture, disabled, etc.).
- ignore the health and safety needs of children.
- are more "self" than "child" oriented.

From an Employee's Point of View

Parents want the best teachers for their children; employees want the best working conditions. As a prospective employee, one should be as careful in looking for employment at a child-care center as parents are in placing their children there. Evaluate the personal and professional opportunities of each center. If possible, visit centers when children and teachers are in a usual setting. Then ask yourself some straightforward questions, such as the following:

1. *Those who care for children.* How do the adults express their feelings, love, and concern about and for the children? How important are the children? Are all developmental needs of the children considered? Do staff members work cooperatively for the good of the children and for the improvement of the center? How do they feel about themselves and their colleagues? How do they record and keep information about the children? What opportunities are there for in-service training? Is the ratio of children to adults adequate to run the center smoothly?

2. *Program activities and equipment.* Are activities age-appropriate? Are there sufficient materials to do the kind of job you feel is important? Are children encouraged in all areas of development? Do children have the opportunity to practice their communication skills—speaking and listening? How are problem-solving situations handled? Is there opportunity to be creative in curriculum planning and implementation? Is outdoor play considered important?

3. *Relationship among staff, family, and community.* What provisions does the center have for staff-family interaction? Are staff members free to suggest or initiate ways to support families individually or collectively? In what ways does the center expect employees to become involved with the community? Are parents valued and continually informed about their child and the center?

4. *Facility and program needs of young children, their families, and the staff.* What measures have been taken to protect the health and safety of all those involved with the center? What nutritional measures are taken to meet the needs of the children? Are minimum licensing standards met? How can families contribute to the effectiveness of the center? Could use of the facility be increased for family and social gatherings?

To this four-point list suggested by NAEYC, an additional, vital component regarding present and prospective employees needs to be added:

5. *Personal and professional opportunities at the center.* Am I dependable, trustworthy, and honest? What can I contribute to the center? Am I well trained (or could I be) to fill the job? What are my job responsibilities and privileges? What are my opportunities for advancement in the field and at the center? What are my personal benefits (wages, increases, insurance, and retirement)? How do I feel about my superiors and colleagues? Does the director value and appreciate the employees? If I had some concerns about myself, the children, the parents, my colleagues, or other center matters, could I discuss these comfortably with my supervisor? Is my philosophy compatible with that of the center? Do I really want to work in child care?

Additional Concerns of Parents, Providers, and Others

Often the main concerns of parents seeking child care, identified and addressed by NAEYC, are related to a "quadrilemma," namely availability, affordability, quality, and other aspects. Kagan (1999b) expands this list to five A's (Figure 2–5): *access* ("to high quality programs for all school-age and all children"), *affordability* ("for all parents, children, and entire workforce"), *appropriateness* ("to understood as developmental and pedagogical"), *accountability* ("creating policies that foster high-quality programs and a high-quality system"), and *advocacy* ("a vision of what early care and education must be and then adapt the policies so as to meet our vision") (p. 243). These concerns will be addressed in this section.

Accountability is always important. Child-care workers should have a goal of making the best possible experience for the children, coworkers, parents, and others. NAEYC (1997a) has a booklet (#538) that addressed accreditation, by asking seven questions about "high quality." It refers to comfort and happiness of the children, the number of adults with specialized training, appropriate expectations of children of different ages, a balanced developmental

Figure 2–5 Kagan's five A's.

program, regular planning and evaluation, interaction with parents, and alertness to health and safety of the children and themselves.

Care for infants and toddlers has been especially unavailable due to costs, untrained caregivers, infant-adult ratios, and fatigue factor. A good caregiver for infants and toddlers is loving, responsible, and satisfied with a one-way conversation. When care is available, it may be in the child's home, in family child care, or center care. A nearby child-care resource and referral agency may have a listing of licensed infant/toddler care.

NAEYC's (1998b) *Code of Ethical Conduct amd Statement of Commitment* (brochure #503) addresses professional ideals, principles, and relationships related to: (1) children, (2) families, (3) colleagues, and (4) community and society (See Figure 2–6). The Preamble, in part, reads:

> Standards of ethical behavior in early childhood education are based on commitment to core values that are deeply rooted in the history of our field. We have committed ourselves to:
> Appreciating childhood as a unique and valuable stage of the human life cycle
> Basing our work with children on knowledge of child development
> Appreciating and supporting the close ties between the child and family
> Recognizing that children are best understood in the context of family, culture, and society

---

NAEYC's Code of Ethical Conduct

Members of NAEYC identify and commit the following: (condensed from NAEYC Pamphlet: "Code of Ethical Conduct and Statement of Commitment" (1998b, #503). Used with permission.

A. **To Children:** That teachers will be: knowledgeable; well-trained; healthy; promoters of social, emotional, intellectual, and physical opportunities; respecters of each child's learning and play environment; and further that children with disabilities will be served with the appropriate and convenient support settings. Teachers will avoid practices that are "harmful, disrespectful, degrading, dangerous, exploitative, intimidating, emotionally damaging, or physically harmful to children." Teachers who suspect child abuse or neglect will report it, inform parents of the referral, and follow up on it.

B. **To Families:** That members will acknowledge the strengths and competencies of families and build relations of mutual trust and support in their nurturing of their children, respect their customs, enhance their skills as parents, and help provide them with community and professional resources. Families will have access to their child's classroom, and other resources for the protection and well-being of their children. Families will not be exploited.

C. **To Coworkers:** That members will develop and use good professional relationships. Differences will be resolved collegially and with relevant information.

D. **To Employers:** Members will provide the highest quality of service by being positive, within the guidelines of the Code/center policies, and in compliance with employment agreements.

E. **To Employees:** Members will foster mutual respect, trust, and positive solutions in the best interest of children, families, employees, and employers by utilizing one's own training/experience to improve one's performance. Employees may not be terminated without documented evidence and due cause.

F. **To Community and Society:** Members will provide high-quality education/care programs and services that are appropriate to the needs and welfare of individual children, their families, and center employees.

Figure 2–6 Code of Ethical Conduct.

Respecting the dignity, worth, and uniqueness of each individual (child, family members, and colleague)

Helping children and adults achieve their full potential in the context of relationships that are based on trust, respect, and positive regard. (NAEYC, 1996a, p. 57)

In June 1998, a conference was sponsored by the McCormick Tribune Foundation to review trends in accreditation policies and the impact of quality services to children and families. From that meeting, the following recommendations (in the form of accreditation policies) were established: (1) support for a strong regulatory system, but not regulation replacement; (2) increase of public awareness about regulation and accreditation in support of young children's healthy development and learning during critical early years and during out-of-school time; (3) identification of accrediting bodies to ensure integrity, validity, and reliability of accreditation decisions; (4) financial incentives to cover ongoing costs of maintaining high-quality services; (5) provide resources to meet diverse needs of child-care administrators, workers, and advisory boards in meeting accreditation criteria; (6) support of a highly qualified, stable early childhood and school-age care professional workforce; and (7) to promote an overall plan for improving the system of childhood care and education and outcomes for children and families to use achievement of accreditation as one of many benchmarks to help track progress.

Follow-up on this study has not been located; however, it is interesting to note the sponsor and the recommendations of this civic-minded group.

Quality, Availability, Compensation, and Affordability Related to Early Childhood Programs

Consider some selected topics from *Young Children* publications. One study (NAEYC, 1995d) found that while child care varies widely within and between states and sectors, most child care is

mediocre in quality—sufficiently poor to interfere with children's emotional and intellectual development. Market forces constrain the cost of child care and at the same time depress the quality of child care provided to children. (See also the May 1995 issue of *Young Children* for highlights of this study and reflections of key leaders in the field as to its implications for NAEYC's efforts to improve quality, compensation, and affordability in early childhood programs.)

Consider the following from NAEYC (1995e):

Quality. All children have the right to attend good programs that promote their development and learning. High quality care and education programs have been documented to promote children's development and learning, whereas poor-quality programs may place children's development, even their health and safety, at risk. . . .

Compensation. All early childhood programs should provide staff equitable salaries and benefits commensurate with their qualifications and job responsibilities. . . .

Affordability. High-quality early childhood programs should be available to all families who want or need their service at a price that each family can afford. (pp. 39–41)

In Schulman and coworkers (1999) some interesting findings are discussed:

In most cases, state spending is insufficient to provide prekindergarten to all children who need it.

Spending and eligibility restrictions limit the number of children served.

Good prekindergarten programs provide children with experiences that help them develop to their full potential.

Effective state initiatives consider the various factors associated with program quality, including facilities, teacher qualifications and compensation, staff-child ratios, class size, health and social services, parent involvement, etc.

Prekindergarten programs with comprehensive services better prepare children for school entry and later success.

Also a variety of approaches to prekindergarten initiatives has emerged as each state makes choices regarding school settings, model programs, high-quality experience for children, comprehensive approach to children's nutritional, health care, social services, full-day programs to meet needs of working parents, etc.

It would be time well spent to study this publication and to make recommendations to educational leaders in each state. (This article is adapted from *Seeds of Success: State Prekindergarten Initiatives*, 1998–99. For a complete report, contact Children's Defense Fund, Publication Department at 25 E Street, NW, Washington, DC 20001, or phone 202–662–3509.)

Whitehead and Ginsberg (1999) provide the following advice: "Excellent early childhood programs are characterized by caring and responsive interactions between adults and children, developmentally appropriate programming, partnerships with families, qualified staff, low staff-child ratios and small group sizes, provision of a safe and healthy environment, and nutritious food" (p. 4).

Three components to be considered in creating a familylike program in large child-care centers are: (a) the physical environment, (b) the caregiving climate, and (c) family involvement.

In a landmark study of 400 licensed centers in four states, the relationship between costs, quality, and child outcomes was documented. This study tracks children from their preschool experience through second grade. The findings of this study link high-quality child care to children's higher achievement of cognitive skills (e.g., math and language) and social skills (such as peer interactions and prosocial behaviors) that help them be prepared for kindergarten and to succeed in school. Children who attended high-

quality programs as 3- and 4-year-olds benefitted from their child-care experiences in kindergarten and, in many cases, through the second grade. "Children whose family backgrounds put them at risk for school failure gained the most from positive child care experiences and were more negatively affected by poor program practices and environments" (NAEYC, 1999b, p. 46).

In a Public Policy Report Adams and Poersch (1997) ask: "Who cares? State commitment to child care and early education." They continue:

The states' 1994 commitment . . . reveals several patterns: (a) a wide variance nationally and between neighboring states;

(b) inadequate service to the many children and families who need help;

(c) many states with large proportions of poor children did not commit to these services;

(d) action clearly depended more on state "will" than state "wallet";

(e) in general, states placed child care and early education low in priority; and

(f) more than half of the states spent *at least 30 times* as much on highways as on child care and early education assistance for families. (pp. 66–69)

Information and recommendations posed by Adams and Poersch (1997) included: (1) Financial commitment to child care and early education must be increased by all sectors, and (2) child care and early education funds must be used for good-quality, comprehensive services that help prevent dependency now and in the future.

In a delegation of 30 child-care teachers, family child-care providers, their friends, and supporters met with White House advisors at the White House on December 1, 1995, for the purpose of carrying a strong message to the president about what it is like to provide high-quality child care on poverty-level wages and to describe what budget cuts proposed under welfare reform would mean to children, families, and caregivers across the country (NAEYC, 1996e). The White House staff was extremely respectful, attentive, and sympathetic. "Forty-two percent of all presidential appointees are women, and all have been asked to go home and organize events to gather information and testimony from 'ordinary women' in the communities."

Focusing always on a positive outcome, try the following steps:

1. Work toward developing trust between all participants. Always focus on the positive outcome.

2. Build rapport by paying attention, remaining unemotional, reflecting words, watching for good behavior and commenting on it. Help each other look for and use positive behavior—anger and violence breed more anger and violence. Refer to Chapter 8 (Health) and Chapter 9 (Safety, Abuse, and Violence) for more information.

3. "In a collaborative conversation the meeting moves quickly; conversations are effective ways to build parent-school relationships and acknowledge the abilities that all partners in the process possess" (Koch & McDonough, 1999, p. 14).

The Group

The Accreditation Procedures of NAEYC (NAEYC, 1998c) and the National Research Council (1991) recommend the following ranges for group size:

6 to 8 infants

6 to 12 one-year-olds or 2-year-olds

14 to 20 three-year-olds

16 to 20 four- and 5-year-olds

Note: These groups are listed by specific age; however, some centers prefer combining ages (called "family grouping") not to exceed a one-year span. Individuality within the larger age span allows children to learn from and teach each other. It makes an interesting experience for children and staff.

Group Ratio

4	infants or 1-year-olds for each caregiver
4 to 6	2-year-olds for each caregiver
5 to 10	3-year-olds for each caregiver
7 to 10	4- or 5-year-olds for each caregiver

Howes and coworkers (1992) found that the addition of even one child to a group made a meaningful difference in quality. Others have found the quality of the caregiver-child relationship to be related to group size, caregiver-child ratios, and caregiver training.

Caregivers with specific training in child care and child development provide more sensitive and responsible care than do those without such training. However, overall educational level of caregivers appeared to be less important (Scarr et al., 1994). (See Stimulator on page 84.)

The Teaching Staff

There are several aspects to consider when selecting teaching staff.

Qualifications/Training. Teaching staff members will promote quality care for young children and their families when they (1) understand and apply the principles of child development, (2) provide stability in the classroom—generally related to lack of compensation, appreciation, and advancement (see Chapter 8), (3) individualize for every child whether or not he has special needs, (4) respect parents, (5) select materials and activities that respect children's needs, abilities, and interests, (6) provide a safe, orderly, and stimulating physical environment, (7) appreciate and allow for diversity, and (8) keep abreast of literature in the field (Koralek et al., 1993).

Staff turnover is a common measure of quality of care. High turnover means dren have fewer opportunities to affectionate relationships with et al., 1994).

Attachment of provides a bas

❖ Stimulator

In your preschool group, you have a child who is frequently disruptive, withdrawn, has anger outbursts, and tries to physically harm teachers and other children. Try to avoid: (1) extensive dialogue about the problem, (2) blaming others for the problem, (3) designating only certain individuals to deal with the outbursts, (4) identifying the child as impaired or unreasonable, or (5) demeaning the child's reactions. Identify the procedures you will follow, stating reasons for your actions. What specific results do you want to achieve? How can you strengthen relationships between children and adults and help children become more responsible for appropriate behavior? Be optimistic! Look for effective ways to build teacher-child, teacher-teacher, teacher-parent, and child-child relationships. Find solutions for getting response other than through using force—even though some cultures have individual ways of disciplining children.

❖ ❖ ❖ ❖

and social relationships. Caregivers need to be sensitive and responsible to young children, especially infants.

Number and Ratio. For the safety and protection of the children, there should always be two teachers (over 18 years of age in most states) in a group, regardless of the group size. An emergency, a child needing immediate attention, an unexpected occurrence, curriculum being used other than intended, unpredictable weather or room conditions, and so on call for two adults—at least one with experience and training; the other could be an aide, trainee, or assistant.

Personal Characteristics. To be most effective, adults working with children should be kind, patient, flexible ... daptable, loving, tolerant, teachable, and ot... amed modifiers, and be consistent, ... lert, fair, and open-minded ... ld know how to react in fa... mstances. The chil-...

... for Early Child-... scribed its vi-... ntified major ... 01 as (a) at-... d educa-... nd bu-... ation ... rais-... is-...

and ACE, National Board for Professional Teaching Standards), plans for "ongoing training," new use of Childhood Career Development Block Grant (CCDBG), establishing an early childhood career development system, adoption of new early childhood certificates, a certificate for master teachers (National Board for Professional Teaching Standards), new training and more consistent requirements for CDA, state funding for career development and loan forgiveness (amendment to federal Higher Education Act), and other benefits. It will be interesting to see what progress they have made—or what additional needs they have found.

USA Child Care (formerly Child Care Association of America) began on July 11, 1993, in Alexandria, Virginia, when a group of child-care advocates met to talk about the formation of a national organization to provide leadership for child-care providers, children, and families. They wanted a voice in debates about child care and welfare reform, Chapter One reauthorization, Head Start reauthorization, Child Care and Development Block Grants, and Title IVA At-Risk Child Care reauthorization. Feeling that their participation in these important matters would help shape future programs and improve the quality of child care for children and families, they formed their mission statement.

And a final observation from Kagan (1994):

> Finally, professionals in the field of early care and education have begun to take stock of their own situation: fragmentation of services; competition with

colleagues for scarce resources, including space, staff, and children; discontinuity and isolation from mainstream services, often including schools; less than optimally effective training and advocacy; and inequitably and unjust compensation and benefits . . . the field has recognized both the opportunity and the responsibility such attention brings with it . . . the field of early care and education has begun to coalesce, to set priorities, and to voice its concerns. (p. 187)

Quality

In child-care centers quality is measured by observation and interview—*regulatable variables*—(such as ratios of teachers to children, group sizes, and teacher training), and in *process-oriented* dimensions (such as adult-child interactions and developmentally appropriate activities). Of the regulatable variables, teachers' highest wage proved to be the best indicator of quality (Scarr et al., 1994, p. 137).

Numerous studies point to group size, staff-child ratios, and personal characteristics and tenure of caregivers (including training and compensation) as determinants of the quality of a child-care program. Although parents place quality high on their list of child-care concerns, only 60 percent of the states maintain staffing requirements for the care of infants that meet the professionally accepted minimum safety standards (Children's Defense Fund, 1990).

The highlights of major findings and recommendations of the National Child Care Staffing Study Revisited (1993) include some of the same concerns as in the initial 1988 study: education of teaching staff, staff wages and benefits, and staff turnover (Whitebook et al., 1993).

The 1999 NAEYC Annual Report is a review of the association's mission, as articulated in its three primary goals (some important changes have occurred over the last 5 years):

Goal 1. "Facilitate improvements in the professional practice and working conditions in the field of early childhood education through (a) NAEYC annual conference, (b) leading edge satellite video-conference, (c) National Institute for Early Childhood Professional Development, (d) literacy forums (NAEYC and IRA), (e) publications, (f) professional preparation review, and (g) Young Children International."

Goal 2. "Advocating for high-quality early childhood programs:" (a) federal advocacy, (b) affiliate issues, (c) accreditation, and (d) other projects and activities [such as (1) Week of the Young Child and (2) collaborative projects with American Psychological Association (APA), National Partnership for Excellence and Accountability in Teaching (NPEAT), working on health issues and projects with American Academy of Pediatrics, and other agencies].

Goal 3. "Building and maintaining a strong, diverse, and inclusive organization" through membership, website, revised organizational structure, and other means (*Young Children*, November 1999, pp. 44–51, used with permission).

The NAEYC governing board adopted a position on the quality, compensation, and affordability in early childhood programs to include access to high-quality early childhood programs for all children with trained teachers, developmentally appropriate curriculum, group size and adult-child ratios based on ages and needs of children served, salaries and benefits commensurate with the skills and qualifications of staff, and high-quality programs to families wanting or needing their services at prices they could afford (NAEYC, 2000).

The cry is loud and clear: Determinants of a quality program depend on two major factors: (1) the group—size, ages, child-adult ratio, individual needs—and (2) the teaching staff—qualifications, training, stability, number, compensation, and personal characteristics. See Figure 2–7 for a description of the characteristics of high-quality and poor-quality child-care programs.

❖ **Stimulator**

Which of the following items are characteristics of good-quality programs [as defined by *Cost, Quality, and Child Outcomes Study Team (1995)*]?:

_____ Small child-adult ratio   _____ Large child-adult ratio

_____ Low educated teachers   _____ College-educated teachers

_____ General administrators   _____ Experienced ECE administrators

_____ Low staff turnover   _____ Frequent staff turnover

_____ Public licensing (local, state and/or NAEYC standards)

_____ No licensing and voluntary standards (own ideas)

_____ High standards for children's safety, health, and learning

❖ ❖ ❖ ❖   _____ Low/no standards for children's safety, health, and learning

High Quality	*Poor Quality*
Low teacher-child ratio	High teacher-child ratio
Low teacher-staff turnover	High teacher-staff turnover
Ample space	Cramped space
Sufficient developmentally appropriate toys/ materials of high quality	Inappropriate number, developmental level, or quality of toys/materials
Happy, congenial staff	Negative or uncaring staff (stern faces, harsh voices)
Interaction with children without taking over	Little/no interaction with children or adults
Flexibility	Strict rules, threats
Confident, well trained	Insecure staff/children
Enjoyment of children, others	Unsure of relationships
Optimistic about self, future	Dread of setting, activities, future
Stimulating environment, activities, routine, people	Dull, unchanging environment, activities, routines, people
Parent/staff interaction	Limited parent/staff contact
Nutritious snacks/meals	Unappetizing snacks/meals
Children act confidently	Children react fearfully
Healthy, vibrant adults/children	Unhealthy, lethargic adults/children

Figure 2–7 Characteristics of high-quality and poor-quality child-care programs.

Quality, Compensation, and Affordability

Six things directors can do to improve staff compensation and quality (NAEYC 1996d):

1. Use your annual operating budget as a working tool. Most decisions have budgetary implications.

2. Recognize that budget is policy; be actively involved in the development of the annual budget.

3. Get support from a financial analyst or business administrator when necessary.

4. Polish your leadership and negotiating skills to effectively guide the budget development process.

❖ Stimulator

What is a career in early childhood education like?

1. Do you provide planned educational experiences for groups of young children and/or services to their families? Y _____ N _____

2. Do you help children develop their imagination, curiosity, and concepts about the world? Y _____ N _____

3. Do you help children develop their language skills? Y _____ N _____

4. Do you assist children to learn about their world through play activities and literature? Y _____ N _____

5. Do you learn new things about yourself? Y _____ N _____

6. Do you acquire new ways and information to promote skills in safety, health, and relationships? Y _____ N _____

7. Do you further your knowledge about the importance of play in children's lives? Y _____ N _____

8. Do you know how to handle children who are ill, frustrated, antisocial, handicapped, etc.? Y _____ N _____

9. Could you converse with others about the Head Start program? Y _____ N _____

10. Have you decided upon your future career? Y _____ N _____

11. Would you consider volunteering at a child-care center or Head Start group? Y _____ N _____

12. Do you know the varied areas of education that are involved in working with young children? Y _____ N _____

13. Do you know a person or an educational institution that could help you decide if a career in early childhood education is for you? Y _____ N _____

5. Don't forget strong human resource skills in working with staff.

6. Make sure your program offers a career lattice.

Findings from a 1999 study on quality, compensation, and affordability (CQO) provide powerful evidence of the importance of good quality in licensed child care for children's school success (NAEYC, 1999b, p. 46). This newest report tracks children from their preschool experience through second grade.

Structural features of child-care settings (such as group size, child-staff ratio, caregivers' qualifications, stability and continuity of caregivers, structure and content of daily activities, and organization of space) may influence the quality of child care. In addition, child development professionals view two other structural aspects of child care as important components of quality: parental involvement and the recognition of active appreciation of children's cultures. Head Start has also played a pioneering role in making multicultural sensitivity an integral part of its program. Developmental research underscores the importance of providing a child-care environment that builds and sustains the self-esteem of children from minority cultures. Some studies show links between minority children's academic competence and their identification with their own culture, which suggests that cultural affirmation may be an important component in the quality of child care (National Research Council, 1991).

Availability

Three factors impact the availability of child care in the future: household incomes, public subsidies, and employer support. For details, see Casper and coworkers (1994).

Care for infants and toddlers has been especially unavailable due to costs, untrained caregivers, infant-adult ratios, and fatigue. A good caregiver for infants and toddlers is loving, responsible, and satisfied with a one-way conversation. When care is available, it may be in the child's home, in family child care, or center care. A nearby child-care resource and referral agency may have a listing of licensed infant/toddler care and a longer list of requests for care. Although recommendations of other parents, friends, and coworkers are often helpful, one should always visit a potential caregiver and make a personal judgment about a caregiver or program before enrolling a child of any age (Dittman, 1993).

The question of demand for and supply of child care in the United States must take into consideration the location, economy, supply, and demand of workers, and other local, state, and national conditions. In general, the number of preschool children declined until about 1980 and since then has steadily increased. Labor force participation by mothers of preschool children has steadily increased over the same period.

With confidence that preschool population would start declining in the 1990s, demographers predicted a decline in the need for child care. In fact, there has been a soaring demand for child-care services as the number of children under age 5 with working mothers has steadily increased. In 1990 over 4.2 million babies were born in the United States—the highest in any year since the peak of the baby boom in 1961.

In 1990, the National Research Council of the National Academy of Sciences published a comprehensive report on child care (Hayes et al., 1990). Its findings identified the most urgent needs for organized programs: care for infants and toddlers; before- and after-school programs for the nation's estimated 2.1 million latch-key children; child care and preschool programs for children with disabilities; and comprehensive child development programs for economically disadvantaged children. The panel reached seven general conclusions (Can you see any differences in the need for quality child care today?):

1. Child-care services in the United States are inadequate on meeting the needs of children, parents, and society as a whole.

2. Many children are now cared for in settings that neglect their health and/or developmental stages.

3. Families from varying income levels need child care.

4. Finding quality child care can be difficult, stressful, and time-consuming for families of low incomes at a disadvantage.

5. Because of varying needs of children and families, no single policy or program fills everyone's needs.

6. Individuals, families, voluntary organizations, employers, communities, and all levels of government should share the responsibility for meeting the needs of the nation's child care.

7. The role and responsibilities of families should be supported through child-care policies (Carnegie Corporation of New York, 1990).

Parent Information.   Parents must know the location of and have access to their children at all times. A consumer education program must be established, providing parents and the public with information regarding licensing and regulatory requirements and complaint procedures. Many states maintain a list of substantiated parental complaints and make it available on request.

Since the early 1990s the enrollment of preschool children in centers by working mothers surpassed, for the first time, the number cared for by parents (at work), relatives, nannies, and family day-care providers (Neugebauer, 1994). During the 1960s, centers were the least popular choice of child care by working parents. In the early 1960s, only one out of every 20 preschool children of working mothers was enrolled in a

---

Facts and Figures

- In 1999 approximately 6.6 million children who had not yet entered kindergarten regularly attend centers, and an additional 3 million such children regularly attend family child-care programs where they are cared for by a nonrelative in the provider's home (estimates are based on data from West et al., 1995).
- School-age care is said to be the fastest growing segment of the child-care arena, with estimates of approximately 2 million school-age children attending some 50,000 programs and nearly 5 million school-age children left unsupervised during a typical week (National Institute of Out-of-School Time, 1997).
- "No matter what the name or the setting, it is crucial that children be safe and that their development and learning be enhanced" (NAEYC position statement, 1999a).
- "Numerous recent studies suggest that, despite the fact that the majority of America's children spend at least some of their time in child care, many programs for preschool children in centers and homes fail to provide a level of care that enhances or maximizes children's early development and learning (various references). . . . In addition, many school-age care programs do not effectively engage children in their program activities and operate in inadequate facilities" (Seppanen et al., 1993).

---

child-care center; today, nearly one in three attends a center (Neugebauer, 1994).

NAEYCs varied role as a change agent is the focus of its 1998 annual report, including all three of its goals: (1) improving professional practice ("by promoting standards of excellence among and providing information and resources to early childhood professionals"), (2) improving public understanding and support ("among parents, general public, policymakers and the media"), and (3) "building and maintaining a strong, inclusive organization" (p. 43).

Affordability

Some of the main reasons child care is so expensive include the following:

The number of adults per children (especially for infants and toddlers, but preschoolers as well).

Costs vary by type of center, ages served, geographical location, and services offered.

High rate of adult turnover (half of all teachers in the program leave for another job within 1 year) (NAEYC, 1992a).

High turnover rate have serious effects on program quality and ultimately affect children.

Low salaries; many employees terminate.

Low respectability from the public.

Burn-out of employees.

Of the 13 findings by the Cost, Quality, and Child Outcomes Study Team (1995), the following applies to "costs":

Finding 6: Center child care, even mediocre-quality care, is costly to provide, averaging $95

Facts and Figures

- Quality child care is labor intensive and expensive. Estimates are that good quality full-day programs cost a minimum of $4,000 per child per year.

- A two-tiered child care system is developing—quality programs for those who can afford them, and inappropriate and even unsafe programs for those who cannot afford quality ones (Kahn & Kamerman, 1987). Child care is the fourth largest family expense after housing, food, and taxes (National Association for the Education of Young Children, 1992a).

- Child-care teaching staff in 1992, as in 1988, continue to earn less than half as much as comparably educated women and less than one-third as much as comparably educated men in the civilian labor force. . . . Even the highest paid teachers in 1992, 70 percent of whose counterparts in 1988 had completed some college or a bachelor's degree, earned barely half as much as a male who has completed high school and only two thirds as much as women who have completed high school but have no college background (National Center for the Early Childhood Work Force, 1993).

- Rather than the weekly (monthly) cost of child care consider the proportion of family income that is spent on care. In the Hoffereth and coworkers (1991) survey, some families spent 10 percent overall on child care (comparable to expenditure for food) while low-income families spent 20 to 26 percent (comparable to housing costs).

---

per week per child expended (cash cost) or $2.11 per child per hour for mediocre care.

Finding 7: Good-quality services cost more than mediocre quality, but not a lot more.

Finding 8: Center enrollment affects costs.

Finding 9: Cash payment from government and philanthropies are sources of center revenue that demonstrate a social commitment to sharing the expenses of child care. On average, these cash payments represent 28 percent of center revenue.

Government Programs. Although not technically a child-care program, Head Start provides daytime care (part- or full-day) for many 4-year-olds whose parents may or may not be in the workforce.

As reported in the Public Policy Report (1991): The Head Start program was reauthorized at its highest level ever, providing full funding to serve all eligible 3- through 5-year-olds by 1994. (For additional information see the discussion about Head Start in Chapter 3.)

States have considerable flexibility as to how funds should be spent, within the broad constraints of improving child-care affordability, quality, and availability. There are two large categories for funding: (1) activities for improved quality and availability of before- and after-school care and early childhood development services and (2) activities for improved affordability and other activities.

Of the funds 75 percent must be used to make child care more affordable or for activities to improve quality and availability.

Public School Programs. Public schools are also involved in early childhood education programs for these reasons:

1. They are good educationally.

2. They can improve the cognitive and social development of the young child.

3. They are cost-effective, particularly for disadvantaged children, and lead to substantial long-term savings for society.

4. They meet the needs created by dramatic changes in family life.

Those in need of child-care subsidies should check with programs of their choice (local offices of child care and human services, employers, churches, and/or other community groups) to discuss payment flexibility and personal needs.

Parents should consult with local tax preparers to decide if they qualify for the Earned Income Credit (EIC) or Credit for Child and Dependent Care, which forms to use, how to file, and how the credits can benefit them. Information can also be obtained by calling the IRS toll-free number, 1-800-TAX-1040, or by contacting a Volunteer Income Tax Assistance (VITA) center, which provides free tax help, in their own community.

Funds assist different income-level families in different ways. Head Start funds, for example, serve low-income families primarily through providing part/full-day services for 3- and 4-year-olds. It cannot be looked on as a child-care program for working parents. Two other programs enacted in the past, Child Care and Development Block Grant (CCDBG) and the Family Support Act (FSA), also target resources for lower-income families. Under these programs, parents may obtain vouchers that they can use to purchase child care from a wide range of providers. Middle- and upper-income families have received a tax credit through the Dependent Care Tax Credit (DCTC) program.

The Worthy Wage Campaign, launched in November 1991 by a group of child-care advocates from around the country in response to the crisis of low wages in child care, is built on the belief that fair and decent employment for child-care workers must be the cornerstone of affordable, high-quality services for children and families. Its ultimate goal is to promote the vision of a revamped and fully funded national child-care system, one that recognizes the essential link between the needs of all three child care constituencies: parents, children, and caregivers.

Compensation

The NAEYC (1993) position statement regarding compensation for early childhood professionals recommends the following guidelines: equal pay for equal qualifications, experience and job responsibilities regardless of the setting of their job; no differentiation on the basis of the ages of children served; encouragement and remuneration for professional preparation; adequate benefits packages; and career ladders providing additional salary based on performance and participation in professional opportunities.

Family child-care providers play a critical role in our society. Because they care for so many of our nation's children, their impact on our future is immeasurable. In spite of the unique stresses of their professional lives and the complex collection of competencies that are required to do their job well, their contributions are not always recognized or rewarded. Training and support programs are needed that reflect respect for and sensitivity to the unique role of these professionals.

Family care providers differ from other care programs in that they: (1) must, at one time, meet the needs of children representing an extremely broad developmental range, (2) work and live in the same space (a major challenge), (3) often care for their own children within their programs, (3) must administer and manage their own programs, and (5) are among the loneliest and least appreciated of all professions working with children (Trawick-Smith & Lambert, 1995).

To not provide for quality early childhood programs would be a grave and expensive mistake.

 **Stimulator**   Now that you have studied this chapter, and hopefully had actual experiences observing or participating with young children, answer the following questions and determine if the experience was of "high" (Yes) or "low" (No) quality:

Yes	No	
_____	_____	In general, the children were happy, comfortable, and involved in various activities.
_____	_____	The toys and activities matched the skill, interests, and needs of the children.
_____	_____	The teacher-child ratio was adequate.
_____	_____	There was healthy interaction between the children and teacher(s).
_____	_____	There were sufficient toys, materials, and activities to interest all the children.
_____	_____	There were opportunities for children to use or increase knowledge and skills.
_____	_____	There were opportunities for children to enhance their development of cognitive, social, emotional, and physical skills.
_____	_____	Teachers demonstrated prior planning.
_____	_____	When parents (or other adults) were in the classroom, they were treated with interest, courtesy, and respect without detracting from the teacher's attention to the children.
_____	_____	The teacher was aware of health, safety, and individuality in planning the activities.
_____	_____	You can identify the educational approach of the teacher (facility).

If you were the teacher tomorrow (or next week), what kinds of changes would you make or what things would you be more likely to encourage or discourage?

Do you learn more as an observer or a participator?

 **Stimulator**   How can you hold public and organizational officials accountable for making children's well-being and learning a national commitment—in actions as well as words?

1. Speak out on behalf of children as often as the opportunity presents itself.

2. Do something to improve the life of one child beyond your family or classroom.

3. Join organizations that commit to the welfare and education of young children and their families.

4. Recruit, convince, and support others to join this cause (Adapted from NAEYC, 1995a).

Many people from various disciplines concur that to care, nurture, and educate the young should be our highest priority because young children represent the future of our society.

The state of the economy is most critical. Since over 80 percent of the income of all centers is derived from parent fees, a healthy economy with rising household incomes, will have a positive impact on centers (Neugebauer, 1994).

CHAPTER SUMMARY

1. There are organizations, literature, advocates, and volunteers that can help parents find good child care for their infant/preschool children.
2. The labor force of mothers of children younger than 6 has increased about 50 percent since 1975. Parents are concerned about the quality of out-of-home care.
3. Early childhood programs of high quality can ensure that children are well cared for in appropriate settings, by well-trained teachers, with age-appropriate activities, and in healthy and safe ways.
4. There are many different kinds of child care: full-day, half-day, part-time, before and after school, in one's own home, in private homes, in group settings, by educational or religious groups, at one's employment, by relatives, and through special arrangements. One type of care does not meet the needs of all children and families.
5. One can learn much about young children and their care through observing their activities.
6. Many parents and caregivers are unsure about the characteristics and needs of young children.
7. School-age children who are unattended before and after school may be at risk. Parents of these children, sometimes called latch-key children, may also feel anxiety about this situation. In some communities there are programs available for these children; in other communities there is nothing.

8. On-site care or near-site care is desirable, convenient, and sometimes available; however, it may be limited, costly, and demanding.
9. Licensing of child care is enforced in most states. Such things as child-staff ratio, group size, space requirements, curriculum, teacher preparation, and safety and health measures are closely monitored.
10. Parents seeking quality care for their child(ren) should investigate before enrolling, keep in close contact while child is enrolled, inquire about concerns, and be teachable.
11. Some important factors that influence placement of young children include: availability (what options do they have), access (to their children, information, etc.), accountability (flow of information to and from parents/school), affordability (costs to families, and income to caregivers), and attitude (parents, children, and caregivers).
12. The National Association for the Education of Young Children (NAEYC) has an ethical code of conduct to children, to families, to coworkers, to employers, to employees, and to the community and society. It would be well for students, parents, and caregivers to familiarize themselves with it. A copy is shown in Figure 2–6.
13. The NAEYC also recommends the number and ages of children per group.
14. The teaching staff members should be well-trained, healthy, enjoy young children, and be professional in their work.
15. Quality in human relationships is vital.
16. The National Research Council of the National Academy of Sciences published a comprehensive report on child care (Hayes et al., 1990).
17. The NAEYC issued a position statement regarding compensation for early childhood professionals. It is summarized on page 91.

PARTICIPATORS

1. Survey the kinds of centers available for young children in your community. Include program, location, cost, center hours, number and ages of children enrolled, staff and their training, and other services available to parents and children.

2. Contemplate opening a new center. Make a checklist of the agencies you need to contact (in order of priority) and the items you need to handle. You may wish to use the following headings:

   WHO   WHEN   PURPOSE   RESULTS   FOLLOW-UP

3. Write to your state department of education, child welfare, or social services for a copy of the current regulations for a child-care center.

4. Check with city zoning and building departments about the requirements for a child-care center in your city.

5. Call or visit the department of motor vehicles and ask about requirements for transporting young children.

6. Visit some local preschools or child-care centers and inquire about their experience in getting a license. What information could they offer that would help a prospective care provider avoid common pitfalls or delays?

7. Describe a day as a provider of infant/toddler care. Compare your ideas with those of someone who is currently giving this type of care.

8. Describe a typical before- and after-school program. Compare your ideas with those of someone who is currently giving this type of care.

9. Make a list of community resources that could be helpful for school-age children and their parents.

10. Determine the balance between *need for* and *availability of* child care in your area.

11. If possible, ask a group of parents which factors influenced them to place their children in the particular centers they chose. (Seek information but do not make the parents defensive.)

12. Design a short child-care questionnaire and administer it to a number of parents of young children. Include questions about programs, staff, facilities, and cost. Determine parents' priorities when they seek a child-care center.

13. Interview a number of students interested in child care. Ask them to identify why they would like to be employed in child care.

14. What training has been provided at the center to help staff members interact favorably with children with physical, mental, social, or intellectual disabilities? If you have a special-needs child in your center, design an activity that would help you better understand the child and would increase the child's sense of self-worth.

15. Talk to caregivers at a local center and ask them how they deal with the following:

    a. Violence (aggression) in the center, if present

    b. Teacher turnover. How many caregivers have been employed in this center for over 6 months? 1 year? longer? What has been the main reason for termination?

    c. Diversity. How many children in the group (or center) come from ethnic backgrounds other than white?

    How do teachers integrate customs from minority groups (food, dress, celebrations, etc.) into healthy attitudes for children and adults?

REFERENCES

Adams, G., & Poersch, N. O. 1997. Who cares? State commitment to child care and early education. Public Policy Report. *Young Children,* May, 66–69.

Albrecht, K. 1993, Jan. Joining the quality circle: Developmentally appropriate practice in school-age care. *Exchange,* 89, 19–22.

Ball, J., & Pence, A. R. 1999. Beyond developmentally appropriate practice: Developing community and culturally appropriate practice. *Young Children,* Mar., 46–50.

Bell, D. 1999. *The after-school lives of children.* Mahway, NJ: Lawrence Erlbaum Assoc.

Braun, S. J., & Edwards, E. P. 1972. *History and theory of early childhood education.* Worthington, OH: Jones.

Cain, V., & Hofferth, S. L. 1987. *Parental choice of self-care for school-age children*. Paper presented at the annual meeting of the Population Association of America, Chicago.

Carnegie Corporation of New York. 1990. Annual Report. A decent start: Promoting healthy child development in the first three years of life. New York: Author.

Casper, L. M., Hawkins, M., & O'Connell, M. 1994. *Who's minding the kids? Child care arrangements*. 1991, Fall. pp. 70–36. Washington, DC: Population Division, Bureau of the Census.

Chapman, F. S. 1987. Executive guilt: Who's taking care of the children? *Fortune*, Feb. 16, 30–37.

Children's Defense Fund. 1988, 1994, 1995, 1996, 1997, 1998, 1999. State of America's Children Yearbook. Washington, DC: Author.

Children's Defense Fund. 1990. Children 1990: *A report card, briefing book, and action primer*. Washington, DC: Author.

Coleman, M., Robinson, B. E., & Rowland, B. H. 1991. School-age child care: A review of five common arguments. *Day Care & Early Education*, 18(4), 13–17.

Coontz, S. 1992. *The way we never were: American families and the nostalgia trap*. New York: Basic Books.

Costello, A., & Hunter-Sloan, K. 1988. Dependent child care. In J. S. Rosenbloom (Ed.), *The handbook of employee benefits* (2nd ed.) (pp. 269–297). Homewood, IL: Dow Jones-Irwin.

Cost, Quality, and Child Outcomes Study Team. 1995. *Cost, quality, and child outcomes in child care centers, executive summary*. Denver: Economics Department, University of Colorado at Denver.

Dittmann, L. L. 1993. Finding the best care for your infant or toddler. *Zero to Three*. Washington, DC: National Association for the Education of Young Children. Arlington, VA: The National Center for Clinical Infant Programs.

Duncan, S., & Thornton, D. 1993. Marketing your center's services to employers. *Exchange*, 89, Jan., 53–56.

Early Childhood Longitudinal Study, Kindergarten Class of 1998–99. 2000. *America's kindergartners*. Washington, DC: U.S. Department of Education, Office of Educational Research and Improvement. NCES-2000-070 (Revised).

Edin, K., & Lein, L. 1997. *Making ends meet: How single mothers survive welfare and low-wage work*. New York: Russell Sage.

Elkind, D. 1988. Educating the very young: A call for clear thinking. In J. P. Bauch (Ed.), *Early childhood education in the schools* (pp. 65–70). Washington, DC: National Education Association.

Galinsky, E. 1987. "MacNeil/Lehrer News Hour," June 16.

Galinsky, E. 1989a. Is there really a crisis in child care? If so, does anybody out there care? *Young Children*, 44(5), 2.

Galinsky, E. 1989b. Update on employer-supported child care. *Young Children*, 2, Sept., 75–77.

Galinsky, E., & Friedman, D. E. 1993. *Education before school: Investing in quality care*. New York: Families and Work Institute.

Galinsky, E., & Morris, A. 1993. Employers and child care. *Pediatrics*, 91(1), 209–217.

Galinsky, E., Howes, C., Kontos, S., & Shinn, M. 1994. Publication #C-94-01. Families and Work Institute.

Hayes, C. D., Palmer, J. L., & Zaslow, M. J. (Eds.). 1990. *Who cares for America's children? Child care policy for the 1990s*. Washington, DC: National Academy Press.

Hoffereth, S. L., Bray, A., Deich, S., & Holcomb, P. 1991. *The national child care survey*. Washington, DC: Urban Institute.

Howes, C. 1987. Quality indicators in infant and toddler child care. In D. Phillips (Ed.), *Quality in child care: What does research tell us?* (Vol. 1) (pp. 81–88). Washington, DC: National Association for the Education of Young Children.

Howes, C., Phillips, D. A., & Whitebook, M. 1992. Thresholds of quality: Implications for the social development of children in center-based child care. *Child Development*, 63, 449–469.

Kagan, S. L. 1994. Early care and education: Beyond the fishbowl. *Phi Delta Kappan*, Nov., 184–187.

Kagan, S. L. 1999a. From our president. Going beyond "Z." *Young Children*, Mar., 2.

Kagan, S. L. 1999b. Redefining 21st century early care and education. *Young Children*, Nov., 2–3.

Kahn, A., & Kameran, S. 1987. *Child care: Facing hard choices*. Dover, MA: Auburn House.

Katz, L. G. 1993. Child-sensitive curriculum and teaching. *Young Children*, 48(6), 2.

Koch, P. K., & McDonough, M. 1999. Improving parent-teacher conferences through collaborative conversations. *Young Children*, March, 11–15.

Koralek, D. G., Colker, L. J., & Dodge, D. T. 1993. *The what, why, and how of high-quality early childhood education: A guide for on-site supervision*. Washington, DC: National Association for the Education of Young Children.

Kraiser, S., Witte, S., Fryer, Jr., G. E., & Miyoshi, T. 1990. Children in self-care: A new perspective. *Child Welfare League of America*. .

Leibowitz, A., Waite, L. J., & Witsberger, C. 1988. *Child care for preschoolers: Differences by child's age*. Washington, DC: National Institute of Child Health and Human Development.

Levine, J. A., Murphy, D. T., & Wilson, S. 1993. *Getting mean involved: Strategies for early childhood programs*. New York: Families and Work Institute.

Long, T. J., & Long, L. 1983. *The handbook for latchkey children and their parents.* New York: Arbor House.

National Association for the Education of Young Children. 1992a. Goal 1: Problem or Promise. *Young Children,* 47(2), 38–40.

National Association for the Education of Young Children. 1992b. *Where your child care dollars go.* NAEYC #545. Washington, DC: Author.

National Association for the Education of Young Children. 1993. *Compensation guidelines for early childhood professions: A position statement of NAEYC #546.* Washington, DC: Author.

National Association for the Education of Young Children. 1994. *Using NAEYC's code of ethics: A tool for real life. Young Children,* Nov., 62.

National Association for the Education of Young Children. 1995a. Be a children's champion. NAEYC #592. Washington, DC: Author.

National Association for the Education of Young Children. 1995b. Cost, quality, and child outcomes in child care centers: Key findings and recommendations. Special research report. *Young Children,* 40–41.

National Association for the Education of Young Children. 1995c, Jan. From our readers. Worthy wages for child care workers. *Young Children,* 3–4, 82.

National Association for the Education of Young Children. 1995d. Quality, compensation, and affordability. Landmark study released on economics of early care and education. *Young Children,* March, p. 48.

National Association for the Education of Young Children. 1995e. Revised position statement on quality, compensation, and affordability. *Young Children,* Nov., 39–41.

National Association for the Education of Young Children. 1995f. Quality, compensation, and affordability. Jan. p. 79; May, p. 42. See also 1994: Jan., p. 65; Mar., p. 79; May, p. 65; July, p. 49; Sept., p. 49; Nov., p. 44.

National Association for the Education of Young Children. 1996a. Code of ethical conduct: Guidelines for responsible behavior in early childhood education. *Young Children,* March, pp. 57–60 (NAEYC #503).

National Association for the Education of Young Children. 1996b. *Guidelines for preparation of early childhood professionals.* Washington, DC: Author.

National Association for the Education of Young Children. 1996c. Annual report. A time for continuity and change. *Young Children,* Nov., 44–51.

National Association for the Education of Young Children. 1996d. Quality, compensation, and affordability. Six things directors can do to improve staff compensation and quality. *Young Children,* Sept., unnumbered.

National Association for the Education of Young Children. 1996e. Quality, compensation, and affordability. At the table: Child care teachers and providers speak out at the White House. *Young Children,* March.

National Association for the Education of Young Children. 1996f. Using NAEYC's code of ethics. Why don't you teach babies? *Young Children,* July, pp. 48–49.

National Association for the Education of Young Children. 1996g. Using NAEYC's code of ethics. When a staff member violates ethical principles, what should a parent do? *Young children,* Nov., 66–67.

National Association for the Education of Young Children. 1996h. What are the benefits of high quality early childhood programs? NAEYC #540. Washington, DC: Author.

National Association for the Education of Young Children. 1997b. Careers in early childhood education. NAEYC #505. Washington, DC: Author.

National Association for the Education of Young Children. 1998a. NAEYC position statement on licensing and public regulation of early childhood programs. NAEYC #536. Washington, DC: Author.

National Association for the Education of Young Children. 1998b. Code of Ethical Conduct and Statement of Commitment. NAEYC #503. Washington, DC: Author.

National Association for the Education of Young Children. 1998c. *Accreditation criteria and procedures.* Washington, DC: Author.

National Association for the Education of Young Children. 1998d. Annual Report. *Young Children,* pp. 43–54.

National Association for the Education of Young Children. 1998e. Choosing a good early childhood program: Questions & answers. NAEYC #525.

National Association for the Education of Young Children. 1998f. Early childhood program accreditation. NAEYC #538.

National Association for the Education of Young Children. 1999a. Position statement on developing and implementing effective public policies to promote early childhood and school-age care program accreditation. *Young Children,* July (adopted April 1999), 36–40.

National Association for the Education of Young Children. 1999b. Quality, compensation, and affordability. New longitudinal evidence supports investments in quality and compensation. *Young Children,* Sept., 46.

National Association for the Education of Young Children. 1999c. Using NAEYC's code of ethics: What would you do? *Young Children,* Nov., 56–57.

National Association for the Education of Young Children. 1999d. Annual report. *Young Children,* 44–51.

National Association for the Education of Young Children. 2000. *Guidelines for developing legislation creating or expanding programs for young children.* Washington, DC: Author.

National Association for the Education of Young Children (Revised). Developmentally appropriate practice. NAEYC #234. Washington, DC: Author.

National Center for the Early Childhood Work Force. 1993. *The National Child Care Staffing Study revisited: Four years in the life of center-based child care.* Washington, DC: National Center for Early Childhood Work Force (formerly the Child Care Employee Project).

National Institute of Out-of-School Time. 1997. School-age care. Fact sheet prepared for the White House Conference on Child Care. October. Washington, DC.

National Research Council. 1991. *Caring for America's children.* Washington, DC: National Academy Press.

Neugebauer, R. 1994. Impressive growth projected for centers into the 21st century. *Exchange,* 95, Jan., 80–87.

O'Connell, N., & Bloom, D. E. 1987. *Juggling jobs and babies: America's child care challenge.* Washington, DC: Population Trends and Public Policy.

Perry, K. 1982. Survey and analysis of employer-sponsored day care in the United States. In M. Vanzaro-Lawrence, D. LeBlanc, & C. Hennon (Eds.), *Industry-related day care: Trends and Options. Young Children,* 37(2), 4–10.

Public policy report. 1991. 101st Congress: The children's congress: Historic legislation enacted in child care Head Start, and children's television. *Young Children,* 46(2), 78–80.

Richardson, J. L., Dwyer, K., McGuigan, K., Hansen, W. B., Dent, C., Johnson, C. A., Sussman, S. Y., Brannon, B., & Flay, B. 1989. Substance use among eighth-grade students who take care of themselves after school. *Pediatrics,* 84, 556–566.

Rodman, H., Partto, D. J., & Nelson, R. S. 1985. Child care arrangements and children's functioning: A comparison of self-care and adult-care children. *Developmental Psychology,* 21, 413–418.

Salkever, M., & Singerman, J. 1990. The origins and significance of employer-supported child care in America. In C. Seefeldt (Ed.), *Continuing issues in early childhood education* (pp. 43–54). Upper Saddle River, NJ: Merrill/Prentice Hall.

Scarr, S., Eisenberg, M., & Deater-Deckard, K. 1994. Measurement of quality in child care centers. *Early Childhood Research Quarterly,* 9, June, 131–151.

Schulman, K., Blank, B., & Ewen, D. 1999. State prekindergarten initiatives: A varied picture of states' decisions affecting availability, quality, and access. *Young Children,* Nov., 38–41.

Seefeldt, C. (Ed.). 1990. *Continuing issues in early childhood education.* Upper Saddle River, NJ: Merrill/Prentice Hall.

Seppanen, J., Love, D., & Bernstein, L. 1993. *National study of before and after school programs.* Washington, DC: U.S. Department of Education.

Starting points. 1994. Public policy report: Executive summary of the report of the Carnegie Corporation of New York task force on meeting the needs of young children. *Young Children,* 49(5), 58–61.

Steinberg, L. 1986. Latchkey children and susceptibility to peer pressure: An ecological analysis. *Developmental Psychology,* 22, 433–439.

Trawick-Smith, J., & Lambert, L. 1995. The unique challenges of the family child care provider: Implications for professional development. 1995. *Young Children,* March, 25–32.

U.S. Department of Health and Human Services. 1981. *Legal handbook for day care centers.* Washington, DC: Office of Human Development Services, Administration on Children, Youth and Families. Office of Developmental Services.

U.S. House Select Committee on Children, Youth, and Families. 1989. *Children and families: Key trends in the 1980s.* Washington, DC: U.S. Government Printing Office.

Vandell, D. L., & Corasniti, M. A. 1988. The relation between third graders' after-school care and social, academic, and emotional functioning. *Child Development,* 59, 869–875.

Vandell, D. L., & Su, H. 1999. Child care and school-age children. *Young Children,* Nov., 62–71.

Waxman, P. L. 1991. Children in the world of adults—Onsite child care. *Young Children,* 46(5), 16–21.

West, J., Wright, D., & Hausken, E. 1995. *Child care and early education program participation of infants, toddlers, and preschoolers.* Washington, DC: U.S. Department of Education. NCES 95-824.

Whitebook, M., Phillips, D., & Howes, C. 1993. *National Child Care Staffing Study revised: Four years in the life of center-based child care.* Oakland, CA: Child Care Employee Project.

Whitehead, L. C., & Ginsberg, S. I. 1999. Creating a family-like atmosphere in child care settings: All the more difficult in large child care centers. *Young Children,* Mar., 4–10.

Zigler, E., & Lang, N. E. 1990. *Child care choices: Balancing the needs of children, families, and society.* New York: Free Press.

Zucker, H. L. 1944. Working parents and latchkey children. *Annuals of the American Academy of Political and Social Science,* 235, 43–50.

Chapter 3

Programs for Diverse Populations

Guide for Readers

❖ *A revised position statement on developmentally appropriate practices (DAP) issued by the National Association for the Education of Young Children in 1997 identified major issues as: (1) what is taught (curriculum and assessment), (2) by whom it is taught (role of the teacher), (3) how culture is retained (role of culture in development), (4) personal interest in each child (individual attention), and (5) interaction within and outside the family circle (relationships with others). Each of these areas will be discussed in this chapter.*

❖ *Meeting the needs of children and families from dissimilar backgrounds requires active awareness and constant pursuit.*

❖ *Our diversity requires that we consider the goals and values of all people. It is often easier for young children to learn and respect others than it is for those who feel prejudice and malice.*

❖ *Learning to respect people of other races is an important foundation upon which children can build. Adults (teachers, family members, etc.) can help children accept and appreciate others.*

❖ *Multicultural education can provide a social foundation from which all can benefit.*

❖ *The more comfortable an adult is with various cultures, the more their children will embrace people who are different from themselves.*

❖ *People of all ages, cultures, and walks of life have disabilities. These disabilities, whether mild or severe, can be used to strengthen or weaken one's outlook.*

❖ *Studies show that children (and adults) develop biases about people who are different.*

❖ *Head Start programs introduce children and their families to people of varying backgrounds, beliefs, and attitudes. National, state, local, federal, and private organizations help those people to accept themselves and those around them.*

❖ *There is a great need for people who can work with special needs infants, school age, and older children. Frequently these children are mainstreamed into private and public programs in which both sets of children learn much from each other.*

❖ *Special needs children may have one or more of the following impairments: visual, hearing, hearing/visual, language, orthopedic, mental, behavioral, cognitive, emotional, motor, or any combination. The IDEA (Individuals with Disability Education Act) provides many services to help children and adults deal with their disabilities.*

❖ *There are various programs for gifted/talented children.*

❖ *Diverse family structures are found in every community.*

DEVELOPMENTALLY APPROPRIATE PRACTICES

In 1997, the National Association for the Education of Young Children (NAEYC) issued a revised position statement on developmentally appropriate practices (DAP) in early childhood programs (Bredekamp, 1997). The revised statement expands and clarifies the definition of the term "developmentally appropriate practices." Some of the major issues of practice are identified as: (1) curriculum and assessment, (2) role of the teacher, (3) role of culture in development, (4) attention to the individual child, and (5) relationships with families. The revised edition of DAP includes input from special educators, cultural context folks, those who confuse DAP with anti-bias curriculum, core curriculum disciples of E.D. Hirsch (1990), and a new group of critics—deconstructionists—who believe established knowledge or raising and teaching children should be rejected because it imposes on everyone dominant ideology about educating children (Bredekamp & Copple, 1997). There also continues to be discussion within the field as to whether or not DAP guidelines and strategies are sufficient to meet the needs of all children with disabilities (Carta et al., 1993).

Developmentally appropriate practices result from the process of professionals making decision about the well-being and education of children based on at least three important kinds of information or knowledge: What is known about:

1. Children development and learning
2. The strengths, interests, and needs of the individual children in the group
3. The social and cultural contexts in which children live

The revision states:

> The position statement on developmentally appropriate practice is a political document about what NAEYC and its members believe constitutes quality care and education for young children as a constant process of professional decisionmaking guided by a knowledge base but also constructed through daily interactions with children, families, and colleagues. Our goal is to establish standards that demand both informed judgment and negotiations of diverse perspectives to move our practice and our profession forward in the future. (Bredekamp, 1997, p. 40)

DIVERSITY

Diversity, as used in this text, refers to programs that are designed to meet the needs of children and families from dissimilar backgrounds: specifically, educational, economic, cultural, and personal settings.

Consider the following about diversity. It is a quality, state, fact, or instance of being diverse; different, dissimilar, varied, and/or diversified. It is multiformity, not necessarily "good" or "bad." Children within a family are of different heights, builds, talents, and predispositions. Does this mean that one is better than another? Families accommodate to the "differences" in their members. Society should be able to make similar adaptations. Diversity, in a positive sense, can bring understanding, tolerance, comradeship, learning, love, equality, and other positive attributes. We, in early childhood education, can help this happen.

Many children from low-income families and those from some minority groups (primarily African Americans, Hispanics, Native Americans, and some Asians) have a higher drop-out rate, grade retention, and special education placements than do other children. If this situation is permitted to continue, more students will lack skills necessary for economic and civic survival in our country, which increases our social instability. Action must be taken to design educational solutions to prevent or reduce the number of school failures (Bowman, 1994).

There are two models of school practice that have dominated American educational theory during this century, both with different goals and conceptions of the teaching and learning process, and both have been used in educating children "at risk" — poor and minority.

1. The "cultural transmission" (uniformity) approach with traditional school policies and practices emphasizing standardized and lockstep curricula (Kohlberg & Mayer, 1972).
   a. Common knowledge that must be learned by all (learning objectives)
   b. Instructional strategies of teaching

2. Identified with progressive education (diversity—or developmentally appropriate practices), which stresses the individual and personal nature of education and proposes diversity in goals and methods (Dewey, 1938; Gardner, 1985; Piaget, 1962).
   a. Learning should be personal and responsive to individuals.
   b. Instructional methods should have maximum diversity.
   c. Delaying academic socialization in the belief that children will acquire academic knowledge and skills through their own interests and abilities. However, at-risk students have not learned the same things as quickly as their more economically advantaged peers.

In line with these two strategies, a third one has evolved. Bowman (1994) writes:

Some educators have suggested that the rules of development for poor and minority children are different from those that pertain to middle-class and white children. Believing so, some teachers have focused exclusively on basic skills, creating school programs that build neither on children's prior knowledge and competence nor on their interests and strengths. Other teachers, responding to the notion that some children are unable to learn from methods that engage other children (Jensen, 1972), have concentrated on rote learning, thereby providing fewer opportunities for children to learn to understand and to think. Neither of these strategies has proved successful. In fact, ignoring developmental considerations has often caused children to disengage from school learning. (p.220)

Bowman offers a more culturally embedded way of thinking about educating children from diverse groups:

Rules of development are the same for all children, but social contexts shape children's development into different configurations. When children's families, communities, and schools all provide opportunities to learn similar skills and knowledge, we can be confident that the slow and informal introduction of academics will not jeopardize children's achievement. However, children who come from groups that are outside the main-stream and whose families do not rear them with the motivations, beliefs, opportunities to learn, and reinforcement of school learning that are common to the mainstream will find school more difficult. If teachers ignore the powerful role of social context in preparing children for school and rely primarily on either individually determined learning or alien, standardized curricula, many children will not have the experiences they need to succeed in school. (pp. 220–221)

Schooling is both individual *and* cultural. Schools should strive for a better understanding of the balance between a child's potential for personal growth and the socializing practices of the child's home environment.

Children should be encouraged in cultural competence (Knapp et al., 1990), which includes satisfying social relationships with family and friends, language acquisition, perceptional organization, and categorical thinking, imagining, and creating, which are learned in a similar fashion by all children and occur in predictable sequences across various cultural and racial groups, but allow for individual differences in development (Bowman, 1994).

If schools are to maintain the critical balance between educational excellence and cultural diversity, educators' knowledge of child development must be embedded in a broader social context. . . . To educate culturally and linguistically diverse students, teachers must be sensitive to the similarities and differences between themselves and their students and their families. (Bowman, 1994, p. 224)

General Diversity

Gouch (1993) writes the following about diversity: Many of the faces now appearing at our classroom doors bespeak racial and cultural origins that are neither white nor European. And this "browning of America" is pushing school people to apprehend two facts: (1) Ignoring cultural differences can inhibit students' learning and (2) failing to teach children to respect people who are different from themselves does not augur well for the nation's future.

Writing in the spring 1990, American educator, historian Diane Ravitch cut to the heart of the matter. "What we should be teaching our children is that race hatred is wrong, racial chauvinism is wrong, and racism is wrong. People are people. Cut us and we bleed. If we love a child, we cry. . . . It is the job of public education to teach everyone, whatever their ancestry, that we are all Americans and we all reside in the same world. . . ." For, as Ravitch points out, "we are a multicultural people, but also a single nation knitted together by a common set of political and moral values" (p. 3). And herein lies our strength.

CULTURE

In all settings (including child care) teachers can avoid classrooms that are culturally assaultive by teaching true concepts and beliefs of other cultures (see Clark et al., 1992). My frustration is that teachers (near and far) teach erroneous principles about Native Americans—outmoded dress, customs, habitat, and violence—even when a Native American child is in their classroom! ("We always do a pilgrim-Indian Thanksgiving!") In other areas frustration may be for other cultures, races, traditions, or differences. (See Billman, 1992; Brady, 1992; Dimidjian, 1989; Greenberg, 1992a; Little Soldier, 1992; Shaffer, 1993.)

Teachers can talk with children about the different cultures represented in their classroom or community, use authentic visuals, invite visitors, remove stereotypes, value differences, feel what it is like to be in the minority, and provide other "here and now" experiences that the children can participate in and learn from. Ponder this quote from Clark, and coworkers (1992):

> Research by ethnobiologists such as Conrad Lorenz and John Bowlby suggests that the early years are an especially sensitive period for imprinting language, visual, and other sensory stimuli, and for developing the capability for lifelong attachments. We ought to imprint our children with a variety of people. Their teachers and peers, as well as pictures on the walls, books on the shelves, and babies in the play areas, should all reflect cultural diversity. If your center has enrollment of primarily one ethnic or racial group, you should work double hard to bring this diversity in.
>
> We should work *with* rather than *against* the child's egocentrism in our curriculum, keeping a base curriculum of salient similarities and universal needs as the underlying theme of our more visible surface curriculum. Children want to learn about things that are immediately applicable to their lives. They like to talk about family and friends, food and pets, what they saw on the way to school, and the plans for their birthday party. They like to sing about silly and funny things and show their competence with language by repeating new words and sounds. This is the most important curriculum, developmentally, for preschool. We have decided to be certain that when we present this curriculum and talk about grandmothers and how they tell bedtime stories, we bring in grandmothers of other ethnic backgrounds to tell stories. (pp. 8–9)

By 2 years of age, children not only notice, they also ask questions about differences and similarities among people (Derman-Sparks et al., 1980).

How we answer children's questions and respond to their ideas is crucial to their level of comfort when learning about diversity (Derman-Sparks & ABC Task Force, 1989).

Between 2½ and 3½ years of age, children also become aware of and begin to absorb socially prevailing negative stereotypes, feelings, and ideas about people, including themselves (Derman-Sparks & ABC Task Force, 1989).

Facts and Figures

- Due to our mobile society, demographic changes are necessary because of (a) cultural diversity (It is estimated that about one third of all Americans will be African-Hispanic, or Asian-American by 2020), (b) a changing workforce (mothers of infants and toddlers are the fastest growing segment), and (c) "a changing family and community structure in which mutual support within and among families is often lacking" (Decker & Decker, 1997).
- Early childhood educators have been researching bilinguistic and cultural diversity for many years (Derman-Sparks, 1992/94; Derman-Sparks & ABC Task Force, 1989; Spodek & Brown, 1993; and others).
- "In just five years, Hispanics will be the largest U.S. minority. By 2050, nearly one-quarter of our population will be Hispanic" (U.S. Department of Education, May 2000).
- "The operating cost of U.S. child-care centers has remained about the same since the 1970s, but public funds have supported a smaller and smaller proportion of this cost, leaving parents to pay more and more" (Whitebook, Howes, & Phillips, 1990, cited in Zigler & Finn-Stephenson, 1995).
- "The proportion of employed married women with young children increased from 18% in 1960 to 30% in 1970 to 45% in 1980, and to 70% by 1995" U.S. Bureau of Labor Statistics, 1997.
- "Almost 4.5 million children with various disabilities received special education services during the 1992–3 school year" (U. S. Dept. of Education).
- "Between 1979 and 1989 the number of children in the United States from culturally and linguistically diverse backgrounds increased considerably" (NCES, 1993), and according to a report released by the Center for the Study of Social Policy (1992), that diversity is even more pronounced among children younger than age 6. Contrary to popular belief, many of these children are neither foreign born nor immigrants but were born in the United States (Waggoner, 1994).
- Approximately 9.9 million of the estimated 45 million school children, more than one in five, live in households in which languages other than English are spoken (Waggoner, 1994).
- "For optimal development and learning of all children, educators must **accept** the legitimacy of children's home language, **respect** (hold in high regard) and **value** (esteem, appreciate) the home culture, and **promote** and **encourage** the active involvement and support of all families, including extended and non-traditional family units" [Responding to Linguistic and Cultural Diversity— Recommendations for Effective Early Childhood Education: An NAEYC Position Statement (1996). Brochure #550].
- Head Start reports that the largest number of linguistically and culturally diverse children served through Head Start are Spanish speakers, with other language groups representing smaller but growing percentages (Head Start Bureau 1995).

continued

Facts and Figures (continued)

- In a review of more than 100 studies, Scott and Scau (1985) found that: "Pupils who are exposed to sex-equitable materials are more likely than others to: (1) have gender balanced knowledge of people in society, (2) develop more flexible attitudes and more accurate sex-role knowledge, and (3) imitate role behaviors contained in the material."

- Smith and Zeedyk (1997) found that, while preschool girls said they preferred feminine-typed toys and neutral-typed toys, they actually played more with neutral-typed toys. Preschool boys said they preferred both masculine-typed and neutral-typed toys, but spent more time playing with the masculine-typed toys.

- Contrast the above study (Smith & Zeedyk, 1997) with earlier research studies that found that in the preschool years, girls prefer swinging, stringing beads, playing at houskeeping, painting, drawing, doing artwork, playing with dolls, and engaging in table activities while boys prefer to play with toy guns, toy trucks, carpentry, blocks, and riding toys and to engage in rough-and-tumble play (Clark et al., 1969; Maccoby & Jacklin, 1974; Sprafkin et al., 1983).

- "Teachers must take biased or racist remarks very seriously and validate the feelings of the child who is on the receiving end. . . . It becomes clear that some children suffer long-term effects from what might be considered the 'rough and tumble' of everyday life in preschool. . . . Early childhood educators must take a positive stance on issues of inclusion" (Elswood, 1999, pp. 63–64).

- "When racist remarks have been made, the children hurt need to hear that others want to play with them *not* in spite of their color, but because they are who they are. Children value everything they are, including their color" (Elswood, 1999, p. 64).

"Throughout the early childhood period, children continue to construct and elaborate on their ideas about their own and other's identities and their feelings about human differences. . . . Some researchers believe that after age 9, racial attitudes tend to stay constant unless the child experiences a life-changing event" (Aboud, 1988).

The research literature also points to the great damage racism, sexism, and classism have on *all* children's development.

"Racism attacks young children's growing sense of group, as well as individual identity. Thus, the children are even less able to resist racism's harm" (Derman-Sparks, 1993/94, p. 68).

White, English-speaking children also experience psychological damage. Limited research suggests some disturbing problems:

First, racism teaches white children moral double standards for treating people of racial/ethnic groups other than their own.

Second, children may be constructing identity on a false sense of superiority based on skin color. White children's self-esteem will be rather vulnerable if/when they come to realize that skin color does not determine a person's value.

Third, racism results in white children developing fears about people different from themselves. They do not gain the life skills they need for effectively interacting with the increasing range of human diversity in society and the world. (Derman-Sparks, 1993/94, p. 68)

Teachers working with culturally different children (and adults) should actively seek information that will help them understand that cul-

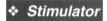 **Stimulator**   Several children are playing together. One child doesn't get the role she wanted and decides to disrupt the entire activity by calling the other children unacceptable names. The teacher's choices could be:

1. "If you can't play nicely, you'll have to sit in your locker."

2. "Maria, you may not tell the other children they can't play because they are black (white or any other reason). It hurts them when you say that. I will help the children tell you that it is wrong to say those things, and I will help you tell the children why you are upset with them."

3. "I will call your mother to come and take you home if you say those words again."

4. "Can you tell me what made you angry so I can help you tell the children how those things/words made you feel?"

5. "Are you angry because the other children wouldn't let you play? Tell me how you felt when they said those things to you. Can you think of a better way to be included in the group play?"

6. Make up three or four of your own alternatives for future use.

ture (differences in hair textures, diet, ways of communicating, learning styles, and so forth).

Race is an intimate part of an individual's self-esteem, and racial issues must be recognized and addressed by those who have powerful influence on children's lives—teachers. Boutte and coworkers (1993) conclude: "Unless educators provide encouragement and a nurturing environment in which all children and older students can learn and excel, negative misconceptions about their academic, communication, and social abilities will be perpetuated. In a diverse society, we as educators must learn to recognize subtle, negative, racial attitudes. Prejudice is no joke—it is ignorance" (p. 23)!

All educators need to openly state and defend their convictions about diversity and equality, regardless of their expectations for immediate results. If multicultural education is designed to prepare individuals for social and political realities, then professionals must be prepared to confront the reality of continued discrimination in the economic, education, and political life of America (Children's Defense Fund, 1992).

Fennimore (1994) encourages others to think through possible prejudiced answers and responses *before* the situation actually arises. The article concludes:

Students need opportunities to practice making assertive responses to prejudiced comments in risk-free classroom environments. . . . Students must be given the opportunity to evaluate situational problems or questions about prejudice and stereotyping in class. . . . Remember that we can make an important contribution to positive acceptance of diversity by asserting our own beliefs and personal commitment to human equality in our everyday actions. In a world so endangered by hatred and inequality, all of us share the responsibility of standing against prejudice. (p. 204)

Derman-Sparks (1993/94) suggests that the most useful way to overcome our own prejudice is to join with others (staff or staff and parents) in support groups that meet regularly over a long period of time. By collaborating, sharing resources, and providing encouragement, we can work on our self-awareness issues, build and improve our practices, strengthen our courage and determination, and maintain the joy and excitement of education.

As the population of the United States increases, it becomes more diverse. Howard (1993) writes:

It is time for a redefinition of white America. As our percentage of the population declines, our commitment to the future must change. It is neither appropriate nor desirable to be in a position of dominance. . . .

It will take time to learn to fully embrace our emerging multicultural partnerships. . . . We now have an exciting opportunity to join with Americans of all cultures in creating a nation that actually tries to move to the tune of its own ideals. These are my people, and this could be our vision. (p. 41)

TEACHER'S ROLE

Teachers can build an enriching, positive curriculum—free from fear, apprehensions, anxiety, and low self-esteem—when they include multicultural curriculum and experiences that reflect their own community and classroom diversity. (For further information, see Neugebauer, 1992.)

Multicultural education seeks to recognize a host of other individual differences, including race, ethnicity, religion, gender, socioeconomic class, age, ability, and family life-style. Sometimes the words used confuse rather than clarify (*antibias, bias-free, diversity, bicultural, cross-culture education,* etc.). One well-known approach to multicultural education is the antibias approach pioneered by Derman-Sparks and the ABC Task Force (1989). It involves children in planning and decision-making processes, stressing that children must develop skills for effectively functioning in their own society and those across the globe (Derman-Sparks, 1993/94). Through this approach children learn not only to be more aware of injustices but also to act to correct such situations as a means of achieving a more equitable society (Derman-Sparks & ABC Task Force, 1989; York, 1991). Teachers play a very important role in establishing and supporting antibias in their classrooms and among their students.

The Harvard Family Research Project indicates that child-care resource-and-referral agencies (CCR&Rs) often offer (a) multidisciplinary training for parents and providers that focus on health, (b) ways to work with parents, (c) information about child development, (d) the logistics of either providing or arranging for child care, (e) links between business, education, university, and state and federal offices, and (f) a model of integrated referral services across agency boundaries (Kreider & Hurd, 1999, p. 76).

Discussions in this chapter are designed to address the following topics: (a) educational programs [for preschool children (such as Head Start) and ongoing programs for infants and children with special needs], (b) economics (to combat poverty, homelessness, to aid single parents and latch-key children); (c) culture (to address ethnicity, religion, customs), and (d) personal (family and family situations, such as gender and aging).

Regardless of the sponsor of the learning, all settings should be for the specific children involved. NAEYC calls it a "responsive learning environment" (RLE) and gives suggestions for working with children, with families, for professional preparation, and for programs and practice [NAEYC brochure #550 (#551 in Spanish)]. The pamphlet suggests that the best way to help linguistic and culturally diverse children and families is to acknowledge and respond, in the educational setting, to the importance of the child's home language and culture.

 ❖ **Stimulator**

For the teacher who has only English-speaking children in the classroom: Bring in some familiar objects (e.g., food, colors, family members, toys, etc.) and teach the children the names of the objects in a language they are most likely to encounter in their environment. As they learn the new name, add other objects and the new language or use a new object and teach its name in still another language. Base the experience on the readiness of your children.

For the teacher who has several ethnic children in the same classroom: Bring in some familiar objects (e.g., food, colors, family members, toys, etc.) and teach the children the name of the object in one language at a time until they have learned it. Add additional languages for the same object as the children show readiness to learn. Provide meaningful experiences where the children are encouraged to use the new words.

❖ ❖ ❖ ❖

Facts and Figures

- Research in integrated preschool classrooms has consistently demonstrated that children with disabilities are rarely chosen as playmates by their typically developing peers (Devoney et al., 1974; Guralnick & Groom, 1987; Snyder et al., 1977).

- "Recent research suggests that children as young as 4 years of age are aware of physical and behavioral differences in their peers" (Diamond, 1994, p. 51).

- In 1990, more than 75 percent of programs that identified themselves as regular nursery schools included at least one child with a disability in their classrooms (Wolery et al., 1993b).

- For children with disabilities, peers' negative attitudes may be just as effective as physical, architectural barriers in limiting their opportunities to participate fully in schools and communities (Stoneman, 1993).

- If the cues to which children attend are associated only with less competent behavior, it would not be surprising that preschool children generalize these characteristics and increasingly come to see their peers with disabilities as less competent and less valued as friends and playmates.

- Children's explanations of disability include references to age and immaturity (e.g., "He's a baby") or accident and trauma (e.g., "She broke her leg"). . . . Interestingly, several children who used immaturity as an explanation also offered the possibility that the child would acquire the specific skills that were delayed with age, as typical infants do as they grow (e.g., "He'll be able to walk when he gets older"). . . . It is clear that children are responding to observable physical cues, including adaptive equipment and classroom location, in their efforts to understand their peers.

- There are at least 8.6 million families with children in which one or both parents have a disability or work limitation, comprising about 12 percent of all American families (LaPlante et al., 1996).

- Program staff should: challenge their own attitudes and assumptions about disabled mothers; programs can include women with disabilities on the board of directors or advisory committees; programs should get accurate information on physical access and program accommodations; and programs should become familiar with disability laws and learn about disability resources (LaPlante et al., 1996).

- "Between 1979 and 1989 the number of children in the United States from culturally and linguistically diverse backgrounds increased considerably (NCES, 1993), and according to a report released by the Center for the Study of Social Policy (1992), that diversity is even more pronounced among children younger than age 6. Contrary to popular belief, many of these children are neither foreign born nor immigrants but were born in the United States" (Waggoner, 1993).

- Head Start reports that the largest number of linguistically and culturally diverse children served through Head Start are Spanish speakers, with

continued

Facts and Figures (continued)

other language groups representing smaller but growing percentages (Head Start Bureau, 1995).

- In 1993, 9.9 million children younger than age 5 needed care while their mothers worked (Bureau of the Census 1995). About 1.6 million of these children lived in families that had monthly incomes of less than $1,500. Another 22.3 million children ages 5 to 14 had mothers who worked, and many of these children required care outside school hours.

- More than one half of all infants younger than one year receive some form of nonmaternal care, with most enrolled in programs for 30 hours or more each week (Hofferth et al., 1991).

- Early childhood models should be concerned with programs designed for all children that foster positive attitudes and behaviors concerning diversity (Spodek & Brown, 1993).

- Studies in the 1950s showed how children developed biases and how these attitudes affected their intergroup behaviors. Curricula were designed to counteract biases.

- Derman-Sparks and the ABC Task Force (1989) designed the *Anti-Bias Curriculum* to teach children to actively confront biases and to respect diversity, while realizing that some parents may disagree with this curriculum.

- Over time, early childhood programs have been designed to meet various societal goals, such as: (a) an extension of the home; (b) for custodial care while parents work or prepare skills; (c) a stable environment; and (d) providing compensatory education. Intervention programs for children with special needs began major expansion after the passage of P.L. 94-142 and P.L. 99-45

- The Children's Defense Fund (1998) recommends that all investments in child care and early education ensure that children from low-income families have access to comprehensive services, including health, nutrition, social services, and education, and that parents have access to education and support services. Integrated networks of support may help to buffer the stresses associated with poverty and increase the capacity for family empowerment (Barclay with Breheny, 1994, p. 74).

The summary encourages early childhood professionals and families to work together to achieve high-quality care and education for *all* children.

EDUCATIONAL AND ECONOMIC PROGRAMS

The final report of a recent study by the National Center for Children in Poverty (NCCP) is a collaboration with Mathematica Policy Research, Inc., under the auspices of the Department of Health and Human Services, published in a full report as *Enhancing the Well-Being of Young Children and Families in the Context of Welfare Reform: Lessons from Early Childhood, TANF (Temporary Assistance to Needy Families), and Family Support Programs*. It is an attempt to answer questions regarding: (1) new welfare policies and practices, (2) kinds of partnerships among support providers and families with low incomes and young children, and (3) emerging opportunities and challenges between early childhood programs and welfare agencies in an effort to improve outcomes for adults/parents and young children (Knitzer & Cauthen, 2000).

As to the usefulness of developmentally appropriate practices (DAP) with children who have disabilities; there continues to be a discussion within the field as to whether or not DAP guidelines and strategies are sufficient to meet the needs of all children with disabilities (Carta et al., 1993).

The reader is encouraged to review the information in Chapter 2 about Head Start. It has been a highly successful program throughout the nation. Numerous programs for young children with physical and learning disabilities are also discussed in Chapter 2.

Head Start and Other Programs for Children

About children who attend a high-quality Head Start (Source: Schweinhart et al., 1993; *http://www. nhsa.org/research/bites.htm*, and others).

One-third more graduated from high school

Spend 1.3 years less in some form of special education placement

Are less likely to be retained a grade

Are three times as likely to be home owners by age 27

(Young women) are one-third less likely to have out-of-wedlock births

Are five times less likely to be arrested repeatedly by age 27. ("It has been estimated that the annual cost to victims of crime was $92.6 billion in 1985. Even if an expanded Head Start could cut this by 1/20th, it will have paid for itself.)

During the 1997–1998 operating period:

1. Of the Head Start enrollment 13 percent consisted of children with disabilities.

2. Of the Head Start teachers 88 percent had degrees in early childhood education or had obtained the Child Development Associate

---

Facts and Figures

- Reported in Public Policy Report in the September 1995, issue of *Young Children*, p. 63: In 1993, 9.9 million children younger than age 5 needed care while their mothers worked (Bureau of the Census, 1995). About 1.6 million of these children live in families that had monthly incomes of less than $1,500.

- Another 22.3 million children ages 5 to 14 had mothers who worked, and many of these children required care outside school hours. More than half of all infants younger than one year receive some form of nonmaternal care, with most enrolled in programs of 30 hours or more each week (Hofferth et al., 1991).

- "A study was conducted using four criteria to assess the outcomes of alternative programs for children. Head Start came out extremely well in two of the criteria. One criteria states that it is important for these programs to possess 'incentives' that encourage people to eventually decrease their participation in the program . . . and the second criteria was an assessment of the program value as an 'investment.'. . . It was concluded that Head Start's benefits greatly outweigh the money put into it, as seen in the large positive outcome and improved used of preventive care" (Curie, 1997).

(CDA) credential or a state certificate to teach in a preschool classroom.

3. As many as 668 programs operated a home-based program.

4. A total of 4,840 home visitors provided home-based services to 42,743 children.

5. Of the staff 29 percent were parents of current or former Head Start children.

6. Over 808,147 parents volunteered in their local Head Start program.

7. Of Head Start families 55 percent have income of less than $9,000 per year and 72.7 percent had yearly incomes of less than $12,000. (http//www.2.acf.dhhs.gov/programs/hsb/about 99_hsfs.htm)

Head Start fiscal and year data 1965–1998 (in 5 year increments)

	Year	Enrollment	Appropriation
Summer only	1965	561,000	$ 96,400,000
	1970	477,400	325,700,000
	1975	349,000	403,900,000
	1980	376,300	735,000,000
	1985	452,080	1,075,059,000
	1990	540,930	1,052,000,000
	1995	750,606	3,534,128,000
	1998	822,316	4,347,433,000

Ages	
Number of 5-year-olds and older	6%
Number of 4-year-olds	59%
Number of 3-year-olds	31%
Number under 3 years of age	4%

Racial/Ethnic Composition	
Native American	3.4%
Hispanic	26.4%
Black	35.8%
White	31.5%
Asian	2.9%

This program has served a total of 17,714,000 children since it began in 1965 (Source: webmaster@acf.dhhs.gov).

Some condensed, but important, historical milestones of Head Start include:

1964   The Economic Opportunity Act was passed—the beginning of the War on Poverty.

1965   Federal money allotted for preschool education and early programs were known as "child development centers."

1967   The Follow Through Program was initiated to extend Head Start into primary grades.

1972   Head Start was a contributing force in mainstreaming children with disabilities.

1981   Head Start was extended to provide effective delivery of comprehensive services to economically disadvantaged children and their families.

1991   Changes in authorization allowed funds to be used for operating resources and referral and school-age child care.

1993   Head Start received the largest funding increase in its history—raising its total funding to $2.77 billion in fiscal year.

1994   The needs of families and children living in poverty were more complicated and urgent than ever before: more violence and substance abuse, interrelated problems of homelessness, lack of education, unemployment, single-parent families, etc. Recommendations were to: (1) ensure that every Head Start program strive for excellence in serving children and families, (2) expand number of children served and scope of services, (3) encourage Head Start to forge partnerships with communities and community services. Funding increased to $3.3 billion.

1995   Funding totaled $3.53 billion, an increase of $210 million.

1997   Expanded health coverage for as many as 5 million uninsured children. Funding for the America Reads! Program; and a

❖ Stimulator

Suppose you were given a chance to further your education, expenses paid, if you would go to some remote (or even different language) community to work with young children. How would you respond? How much information about the situation would you need to make a decision (cultural values, purposes of experience, parental/community involvement, etc.)? Briefly outline your decision making, your questions, and your expected outcomes for yourself, the children you would teach, their families, and the community. Who learns the most? What are the goals for the "teacher" and the "learner"?

$500 per child tax credit. The Child Care Quality Improvement Incentive Program establishes a $240 million competitive grant program to assist states in improving the quality of child care.

1999   From the president's budget: $4.66 billion for Head Start and $1.8 billion for CCDBG; appropriations of $350 million for Early Head Start. Head Start funds allocated for staff training, higher education, and higher compensation. (Washington Update, *Young Children*, Oct 9, 1998, p. 55)

"The NICHD Study of Early Child Care focused on determining the unique contribution of child care to the development of children. . . . on children's first 3 years of life. Higher quality was related to: higher cognitive performance of children in child care, better language comprehension in children, and higher level of school readiness. Lower quality predicted: more problem behaviors, poorer cognitive and language ability, and lower school readiness scores" (Internet February 28, 2000).

CHILDREN WITH SPECIAL NEEDS

Introduction to Working with Children with Special Needs

"It is critical that the teacher consider the *uniqueness* of the child and gain specific information about each individual child" (Stewart, 1999).

Establishing the philosophical base for educating young children with special needs is very important. Not only is it important to carefully consider the children who have special needs but

also the children who are without disabilities in the same classrooms and how they will try to explain and understand the disabilities of their peers and the importance of well-trained adults who work with both types of children. Recognizing my own limitations in special education, the importance of it in the field of early childhood education, and the vast references by professionals in the field, much of the information in this section has been drawn from the literature and some from hands-on experience.

One summer I was teaching a classroom/lab experience for early childhood education majors. The Special Education Department needed space to train some of its majors. Even though the current thinking was "not to integrate," we thought the experience would be beneficial for both sets of students and both sets of preschool children. We had separate preparation and teaching rooms, but one group at a time would be on the playground. (We thought our children were too active and loud; the teachers from Special Education thought their group needed protection—and not competition!) It was hot and the children would stand at the window, watch the other group, and beg to be outside. So we decided to use the playground simultaneously, but in doing so, children in both groups became less verbal, less active, and more concerned: "Will something happen to me so I can't run and climb?" "How come he can run and play and I can't?" "If I do something bad (or good) will I be unable (able) to play like she can?" All teachers found it difficult to reassure all the children. So, after much thought and study, both sets of teachers agreed that we could all be on the playground, interact with each other, and all have a terrific first-hand experience! By the end of the term, nonhandicapped children were learning to use crutches, practicing being blind, being more patient, helpful, and kind. The handicapped children had learned new ways of navigating, new skills, more reassurance, patience, and so forth. We all learned valuable information, skills, and experiences. We, teachers and children, found we needed each other!

Mainstreaming preschool programs have been gaining impetus for over a quarter of a century. Those who care for and educate young children need an excellent foundation in child development and the typical developmental patterns at various ages, as well as understanding that no two children are alike. Temporary problems in any area of development may occur or temporary phases of complaining about physical problems or behaving in unusual ways are not unusual for some children (Culpepper, 1992). In an effort to help adults understand the abnormal behavior of young children, Culpepper has written a two-part article: Part I examines physical development, including hearing, vision, motor, and language impairments (1992). Part II focuses on problems in cognitive and emotional development (1993). You, the reader, would be wise to spend time with these articles, and other related ones, to increase your knowledge and understanding of young children who have developmental deviations.

"The earlier that a handicap is discovered and intervention is begun, the more the child will benefit. Early childhood professions are responsible for knowing typical patterns of child growth and development and for closely observing children in their group to detect any atypical growth or behavior that appears lasting and that creates problems," writes Culpepper (1993, p. 39). Know age characteristics and habits of young children, seek help when necessary, find appropriate referral agencies, and meet with families. Culpepper (1992) also issues this caution:

> Many of the indicators of exceptionalities which have been listed may be seen in preschoolers and may be age-appropriate or temporary. Adults must not become alarmed when observing a symptom a single time and must not prematurely assume that impairments are present. Be sure to watch children over a period of several weeks to determine the number of exceptional characteristics observed and their frequency. As a teacher or director, you have a unique opportunity to view children for large periods of time, and some of them may be depending on you to help them obtain needed assistance; the sooner, the better. The key is to be cautious in objectively detecting genuine disabilities, and to act only on repeated and prolonged signals. . . .
>
> *Note*: Your local or state department of education will assist teachers and parents in locating services and programs available for exceptional children. You can obtain a listing of early intervention programs in your state, as well as parent support and advocacy groups, by calling 1-800-999-5599, the National Information Center for Children and Youth with Disabilities. Request the source sheet for your state. (p. 43)

Special Needs for Infants and Toddlers

The Association for Childhood Education International (ACEI) has issued a position statement regarding the needs of infants, toddlers, and their families (Sexton et al., 1993). Included in the statement is the belief that all young children and their families have a fundamental right to quality care, education, and special intervention. The NAEYC offers a publication "Setting up for Infant/Toddler Care," #228. Your local or state Department of Education will assist teachers and parents in locating early intervention services and programs. A current book, *Adapting Early Childhood Curricula for Children in Inclusive Settings* by Cook, Tessier, and Klein (2000) is highly recommended for teachers and parents of young children who have poor or delayed learning skills. The appendices of this book are thorough and useful.

Early notable and highly respected pioneers in special education are Jean-Marc Itard, Maria Montessori, and Jean Piaget. Their contributions paved the way for the development of circular adaptations to accommodate young children with special needs in a variety of settings.

Educators of all children should focus on: (1) all children mature at varying rates, (2) early childhood education tends to focus on the *process* more than the product, (3) materials usually found in ECE centers are conducive to the development of all young children, (4) accepting and even appreciating individual differences, (5) noting that young children respond to each other without making judgment and comparisons, and (6) that ALL children should be in the *least restrictive environment*.

Students entering education as a career must realize that in any case, including special education, the *child* must be viewed as an individual first—and then in the context of her family and extended environment. Training, experience, and future expansion will be constantly evolving as new theories and research become available. What happens during one period may be abandoned in another period or it may be the foundation for greater advancement. One needs to look carefully at the past and present researchers, what they have learned, and in what direction to advance.

Special Needs for Preschool-Age Children

There are many different kinds and degrees of developmental impairments and ways teachers can assist young children.

Visual Impairments.   Among other things, the teacher should familiarize the child with a visual impairment with the center; describe the room layout; describe particular objects (which the child handles); introduce other children and adults (explaining to them how to assist the child); describe the sequence of activities; help the child find her place for personal items (locker, cubby); tour the playground with the child; and other things that have relative importance to the particular classroom and surroundings.

Many of the children enrolled in mainstreamed programs will have some functional vision. Visual impairments do affect other areas of development. . . .

Delay in the use of the hands results in delay of concept development. Language differences may become more noticeable after the age of 3 years, approximately. Many children with severe visual impairments experience difficulty with personal and possessive pronouns. In general, both cognitive and language development are hindered by lack of stimulation. (Cook et al., 2000, p. 191)

Hearing Impairments.   Among other things, for children with hearing impairments the teacher should demonstrate (act out) rules of the center, post pictures indicating areas of play and expectations, help other children to communicate with the hearing impaired child (use simple language, look at child, have child look at speaker), use items that have both visual and tactile stimulation, and look for nonverbal roles the child can fill while playing with other children (Huyett, 1994). Children with hearing impairments may exhibit inappropriate behavior due to lack of understanding or resulting socialization problems (Cook et al., 2000, p. 189).

Hearing and Visual Impairments.   "Children having problems with hearing and/or vision are likely to have problems cognitively and socially" (Culpepper, 1992, p. 42). Among other things, the teacher should speak slowly and carefully (avoiding loudness and exaggeration, and making the child feel uncomfortable); listen attentively; get the child's attention before speaking (noting if the child misunderstands the message, turns head to listen, doesn't respond to own name, shows signs of ears hurting, etc.); watch child's facial and physical actions (squinting, frowning, blinking, lack of response).

Language Impairments. Untrained adults may not be able to discriminate between a temporary language habit and a permanent disorder. Among other things, adults can watch for mispronunciation, sentence structure, length of message, work meanings (different from earlier patterns—short, choppy sentences, confused meanings, etc.), refusal to speak, stuttering, the child's understanding of the message, emotion in child's speech, and so on.

Children who have moderate and mild retardation will often be able to learn to talk and understand speech and language in the expected sequences, although at a slower pace. It is especially important to provide these children with a **language-nurturing environment** matching their linguistic age, rather than their chronological age. (Cook et al., 2000, p. 304)

Motor Development. Recalling the characteristic patterns of normal development (and the great variation in gross and fine-motor abilities of infants through preschool age), the adult must observe over a greater period of time before determining motor delays. Walking, climbing, running, throwing, eye-hand coordination, pincer-prehension, concentration, strength, dependency, and other characteristics may or may not be signals of delayed or permanent motor abilities. Nevertheless, the teacher should watch for progress, regression, frustration, and withdrawal from activities involving motor development. If teachers note children not participating in motor activities, or moving in unnatural ways for their age (*and* depending on the severity of the inappropriate behavior), they should do further observations, ask others to observe, or speak with the parents without creating undue alarm. There is even greater variation in the small motor activities of young children. (It seems that all parents want their children to learn cutting skills before beginning public school—and sometimes it just doesn't happen! Some of our 2-year-olds have better stringing ability than our 4-year-olds!)

> The extent to which children become proficient in these (motor) skills is dependent on muscle development as well as opportunity for muscle use. However, it must be remembered that even in the most optimal situations, large and uneven growth spurts do occur. To provide the stimulation needed, safe environments free from obstacles and full of encouragement are needed (Cook et al., 2000, p. 255).

Orthopedic Impairments. Caregivers should make sure the room is properly arranged, with ample space, for children who must maneuver wheelchairs, walkers, and/or crutches. Unless at-

tention is given to ways children with different impairments can interact with nonimpaired children, the impaired children may become more isolated and their impairments more emphasized. With orthopedically impaired children, teachers can encourage play and activities that will include them, plenty of space, safe use of materials, roles and props in various kinds of play (housekeeping, dramatic), and times when their impairments are advantageous (crutch to reach things that roll under cupboards, their own chair at low tables, etc.).

Mental Impairments. Children with mental impairments may need more teacher assistance than children with other impairments. The environment may become so stimulating that these children are unable to control themselves. Teachers working closely with these children can limit the number of choices (activities), introduce new items gradually, allow for learning and practice time, demonstrate over and over, invite peers to model and instruct, describe sequences and allow plenty of time for child to react, and offer encouragement to try things and praise on progress (Huyett, 1994).

Guralnick and Groom (1987) compared the behaviors of preschool children with mild mental retardation in integrated and in segregated play groups. They found that children with disabilities in the integrated groups participated in as much social interaction and displayed higher levels of plan than did children in segregated groups.... Increases that have been observed in the social behaviors of children with disabilities in integrated settings can be attributed to the higher frequency with which normally developing peers suggest ideas for playing together. The positive regard in which children with disabilities hold nondisabled classmates may also be important in fostering and maintaining children's higher levels of play. (Guralnick, 1990; Diamond et al., 1994, p. 69)

Behavioral Impairments. Children with behavioral impairments have difficulty participating in large open areas, where rules are unenforced and numerous or where there are abrupt changes. Rather, they need adult praise and support for appropriate interactions with materials, activities, and other children (Huyett, 1994).

> Young children with disabilities often learn new and more adaptive behavior through imitating their nondisabled peers. The modeling effect is a strong argument for integrating children with and without disabilities in early education programs. (Cook et al., 2000, p. 209)

Cognitive Disabilities. Certain physical disabilities, particularly when severe or untreated, seem to delay cognitive development. Other factors such as heredity, birth defects, and brain injuries may also impair thought processes (Culpepper, 1993). Children with atypical cognitive development also have a greater chance of success the earlier the disability is diagnosed and treated and make rapid strides in cognitive development during the preschool years—using their senses during the learning process (Culpepper, 1993). Adults who work with preschoolers may suspect a cognitive disabling condition if any of these behaviors are seen: "disorganized thinking; poor memory and recall; seeming to withdraw from reality; extremely short attention span; poor verbal skills; failure to learn developmental tasks (e.g., eating, dressing self); poor motor coordination; delayed speech and language development; frequent fascination with unimportant details" (Culpepper, 1993, p. 40).

> Three basic processes related to information processing are important to the development of cognition: attention, perception, and memory. . . . Attention is the focusing of the individual's perceptual processes upon a specific aspect of the environment. . . . Perception is the "process of becoming aware of and interpreting objects and events that stimulate the sense organs" (Silverman, 1975, p. 366). . . . Memory is the process by which information that is received through attention and perception is stored in the central nervous system. (Cook et al., 2000, pp. 342–343)

Emotional Disabilities. Most common emotional problems of young children are a result of

emotional or physical abuse, emotional deprivation, or other experiences that affect cognitive, social, and perhaps physical development (Culpepper, 1993). The age and severity of the deprivation are expressed in different ways and in different intensities, but most of them are derivatives of distance from people, disinterest in surroundings, inappropriate or no emotional response, repetition of words with no response, no verbal communication, refusal of physical closeness, distress with changes, aggressiveness and hostility, shyness, temper tantrums, and a highly negative self-concept (Culpepper, 1993). Adults working with these children must show love, patience, and a desire to build a trusting relationship.

Conclusions

1. "In many ways play is probably the single most important concept in early childhood special education. It is important both as a teaching context and as an end in itself. Play is an important skill. Typical young children can often learn play skills with little guidance from adults. Many children with special needs, however, must be assisted in learning these skills. Thus the teaching of play as a social skill is considered an important part of the early education curriculum" (Cook et al., 2000, p. 175).

2. Play can help children with special needs acquire the same important skills and concepts as their typical peers who are at the same *level* of development, but not necessarily the same age (Huyett, 1994, p. 43).

3. Teachers may need to help a special-needs child find appropriate ways to enter play and to interact with other children. Children with special needs often do not respond when their peers approach them during play (Huyett, 1994).

4. Play is an important part of the life of all children, including those children who have special needs. Techniques for enhancing the learning center environment to facilitate the play of children with specific

disabilities apply only to a certain type of disability. This leads to the conclusions that children are more alike than different and that all children are special (Huyett, 1994, p. 44).

5. Recent efforts to develop a comprehensive system of intervention for infants and toddlers with special needs entails constructive attention to ensuring access to services for all children, developing and enforcing quality control assurance standards, training personnel and administrators to meet the needs of an extremely diverse population in developmentally appropriate ways, and requiring public policies that provide resources to achieve the collaboration necessary to improve child care and education, which benefit all infants and toddlers and their families, as well as society in general (Sexton et al., 1993).

6. Parents of typical children perceive their children's enrollment in mainstream programs as beneficial in developing greater responsiveness to the needs of others and increased acceptance of human diversity (Peck et al., 1992). In a study by Green and Stoneman (1989) they found that (1) although parents expressed concerns about whether or not teachers and classroom staff would be able to fully address the educational needs of all children, the parents were generally supportive of the concept of integration, and (2) parents with previous experiences with integrated programs held significantly more positive attitudes toward this educational approach than did parents who had not experienced an integrated program.

7. Because preschool children focus on concrete, observable features when characterizing themselves and others, it is likely that the presence of a disability in another person will be a particularly salient cue for children of this age.

8. In the only study in which preschool children's knowledge of disability has been investigated, Conant and Budoff (1983) found that while 3- to 5-year-old children were able to understand that it is possible for someone to have visual, auditory, or orthopedic impairment, these same children had considerable difficulty understanding mental retardation (Diamond, 1993a).

9. With regard to number and types of activities for classrooms adapting to children with disabilities, the following findings are relevant:

   a. Mainstreamed programs reported using a wider range of activities than did nonmainstreamed programs.

   b. Mainstreamed programs rated activities and areas as more easily adapted to accommodate children with disabilities than did nonmainstreamed programs.

   c. Respondents from both mainstreamed and nonmainstreamed programs tended to rate activities as *easy to moderately easy* to adapt (Wolery et al., 1992, 1993b).

10. The major issues in programs that did not survive (programs that became resegregated into regular and special education early childhood classrooms) reflected struggles between professionals (Giangreco et al., 1993; Peck et al., 1993; Rose & Smith, 1993).

Referrals

With the 1997 amendments to IDEA (Individuals with Disability Education Act) many early childhood and special education personnel have a new task: that of helping to identify and refer children who may qualify for special education. Some disabilities, such as Down syndrome or spina bifida, are easier to identify than others. Those with less obvious disabilities (such are a learning or behavioral problem) are more difficult to identify. The main reasons referrals are made, typically, are because a child is struggling with preacademic tasks in her current learning environment, and it is suspected that the child may be significantly delayed in one or more areas of development, such as motor or communication skills.

Cook and coworkers (1992) have prepared an article to provide a rationale for identifying eligible children, to caution against unnecessary referrals, and to instruct how to make appropriate referrals. Because the exact steps may differ in localities, individuals making referrals should contact their local school district and proceed as directed. One of the potentially harmful effects of referring or testing young children is the categorical labeling, which may be misleading, believed permanently, and detrimental to the child receiving an appropriate education. To avoid the potential negative labeling, some states and programs use a noncategorical approach to identify children (Harbin et al., 1991). This approach encourages programs to develop intervention plans based on the child's individual needs, rather than on potentially detrimental and inaccurate labels (Cook et al., 1992).

Referral Process.   A referral is made to the local school system. A representative of the school collects all information and submits it to a screening committee. If a comprehensive evaluation is warranted, the school system must obtain the parents' permission and inform them of their rights (in writing) in the evaluation process (Cook et al., 1992).

Early intervention has a significant, positive effect on the developmental progress of young children with disabilities (Cole, Dale, & Mills, 1991). Young children with identified disabilities and children at risk for developmental delays who are enrolled in early intervention programs make greater gains in their developmental skills than do children with disabilities who receive no intervention services (Bailey & Wolery, 1992). With the passage of Public Law 99–457 . . . increasing numbers of young children with identified disabilities have begun to receive early intervention services. The 1987–1988 report to Congress on implementation of the Education for the Handicapped Act showed that 29,699 infants and toddlers (birth to three years) and 335,846 preschool children (three to five years) received early intervention services nationwide, a 26% increase from the previous year. (Diamond et al., 1994, p. 68)

The Teacher's Role

Fair and appropriate education as defined by PL 42–242 requires a "comprehensive educational assessment of every handicapped child, an annually updated, written IEP (Individualized Education Program), and education in the least restrictive environment compatible with the child's handicap. . . . Thus, the IEP is viewed as the focus or the guide for planning an educational program for an individual child with special needs" (Pavia, 1992, p. 38). Figure 3–1 shows what Pavia lists as the roles of the different types of teachers.

Facts and Figures

In a study of four preschool groups, Wolery et al. (1993b) found that more early childhood programs of various types are enrolling children with diagnosed disabilities than they did 5 years ago.

- Programs reported enrolling children with certain disabilities more than they do children with other disabilities . . . 57.5% with speech/language impairments, 30.6% with developmental delays, 24.1% with behavior disorders, and 20.8% with physical handicaps. Less than 15% of the programs enrolled children with mild mental retardation, moderate to severe mental retardation, visual impairments, hearing impairments, and autism. (Wolery et al., 1993b, p. 79)

Regular Teacher's Role in Special Education

Special educator's views	*Regular educator's views*
1. Briefly assess what the child needs that special educators cannot provide	1. Enable the child to relate to peers
2. Keep mental assessments of child's improvements	2. Implement parts of the IEP that are workable in the classroom
3. Do not go out of the way to do things they are not trained to do	3. Help the child to feel part of the classroom
4. Acquire knowledge about the child and her capabilities	4. Establish a standard of normal developmental expectations
5. Plan ahead for special help if an activity requires it	

Special Educator's Role in the Regular Classroom

Special educator's views	*Regular educator's views*
1. Help child in transition to regular classroom	1. Support regular teacher
2. Go in and adapt the environment	2. Suggest how to adapt the environment
3. Gather anecdotal comments from the regular teacher	3. Physically step in when extra person is needed
4. Help with specific skills and/or conflicts	4. Teach regular teacher what to do ("They are the experts")
5. Establish a dialogue with the regular teacher	5. Keep teacher informed
6. Stay in contact by scheduling regular times to meet	6. Act as a resource for expanding the regular teacher's understanding of special needs

---

Figure 3–1 Roles of different types of teachers.

For example, the regular teacher in special education is seen from two views: (1) that of the *special educator* as assessing each child's needs, making mental assessments of the child's improvements, doing only what one is trained to do, acquiring new knowledge, and planning ahead for help with special activities; and (2) that of the *regular educator* as helping the child to relate to peers, implementing workable IEP parts into the classroom, helping the child feel part of the classroom, and establishing normal developmental expectations for the child.

The special educator's role in the regular classroom is seen from two views: (1) that of the *special educator* as helping the child make a transition to the regular classroom, adapting the environment, getting anecdotal comments from the regular teacher, helping the child with special skills and/or problems, and arranging regular meetings with the teacher; and (2) the *regular educator* as supporting the child's teacher, making suggestions on environmental adaptation, physically stepping in when needed, providing instruction to teachers when needed, keeping teachers informed, and acting as a resource for expanding the regular teacher's understanding of special-needs children (Pavia, 1992).

When early childhood education teachers and special education teachers work together, the young disabled child will reap the benefits of such a cooperative approach (Pavia, 1992).

Summary

The early childhood community has an excellent opportunity to benefit from both past experiences and the research literature on mainstreaming and teacher change. This work suggests that teachers' feelings and attitudes about mainstreaming must be addressed in dynamic relation to their needs for information and skills as they change over time. Teachers, directors, and teacher educators need help in understanding that teachers' development and the development of the children they teach are inextricably linked. (Volk & Stahlman, 1994, p. 17)

MAINSTREAMING (INCLUSIONS)

Mainstreaming was the original name of programs where handicapped and nonhandicapped children were merged in the same classroom. The more recent term, which is softer and more gentle, is "inclusions"— all individuals are included! The two most frequently cited benefits of mainstreaming/inclusion were that (1) exposure to one another results in children with and without disabilities learning to accept differences, and (2) it provides more normalized experiences and opportunities for socialization for children with disabilities (Wolery et al., 1993b).

Barriers to inclusion, in order of their occurrence, were: "untrained staff and lack of consultation; inadequate staff-child ratios; objections of parents, teachers, and administrators; lack of funds, space, equipment, and transportation, and architectural or structural restrictions" (Wolery et al., 1993b, p. 81).

Inclusion, a practice of enrolling children with special needs in programs designed for typically developing children, has been studied for 20 years. It is thought to (1) help children learn about diversity among individuals, (2) help children develop positive attitudes toward people with disabilities, (3) provide competent role models for children with special needs, (4) provide opportunities for typically developing children to learn altruistic skills, (5) provide children with special needs with real-life experiences similar to those of their peers, (6) provide supportive learning environments for children with special needs, and (7) allow communities to use their early education resources effectively by limiting the need for specialized programs (Bricker, 1978; Peck & Cooke, 1983).

Justification exists for inclusion in early childhood programs: Model programs have been effective, family members are generally supportive, and guidance exists on how to mainstream. The major task before the fields of early childhood education and early childhood special education is to ensure that the staff, when mainstreaming occurs, receive the support needed to provide appropriate, high-quality early education experiences for all children (Wolery et al., 1993b).

Although inclusion is popular with some parents, educators, and students, others feel differently. An editor's note in *Phi Delta Kappan* (1994) states: "Full inclusion, in which the regular education teacher must learn a monumental number of additional skills in order to deal with both special and regular education students, may be state-of-the art education for the Nineties—the 1890s, that is—according to Messrs. Smelter, Rasch, and Yudewitz." Smelter and coworkers (1994) state:

> Inclusionists generally use three main arguments to substantiate their case: 1) that all children learn best in the regular education classroom (which is tantamount to saying that all children learn best in large groups as opposed to smaller groups), 2) that the goal of social equity that is met by keeping children mixed with their peers is of greater importance than how much children learn, or 3) that pull-out programs are a violation of the civil rights of children with special needs because they segregate them from their peers. (pp. 36–37)

They reject all three arguments as intellectually indefensible and a mismash of ultraconservative thinking and not very taxing from an intellectual standpoint.

The inclusive education movement also received support from provisions in the 1990 ADA (PL 101–336) and further IDEA amendments. The Individuals with Disabilities Education Act Amendments of 1991 (PL 102–119) required that, when appropriate, early intervention for children with special needs should be provided in "natural environments," meaning homes and community programs serving typical children (Deiner, 1993;

Sexton et al., 1993). In 1992 another provision of ADA became effective, making it illegal to prohibit children with special needs from attending any home or center-based child-care or nursery school facility that accommodates the public (Surr, 1992).

These legal mandates make it clear that including children with special needs must be a part of our plans to serve all children. The implementation methods are, however, still a source of debate among professionals in the fields of early childhood and early childhood special education (Bredekamp, 1993; Carta et al., 1991, 1993; Johnson & Johnson, 1992, 1993; McLean & Odom, 1993). Until a body of research develops in this fledgling field, teachers will have to rely on a common-sense approach (Walley, 1994/95).

Conclusion

Implementing programs for all children requires teachers to evaluate both their attitudes toward diversity and the instructional strategies they choose to employ in the classroom. At the heart of a program for all children is the flexibility to adapt lessons to more closely fit children's individual needs. The program's goals and implementation strategies should be continuously evaluated and adjusted to reflect changes in the classroom's composition. The framework of practical strategies presented in this article is intended to serve as both a guide for implementation and a tool for monitoring progress. (Walley, 1994, 1995, p. 118)

GIFTED/TALENTED CHILDREN

In considering the needs of children, one must consider the gifted as well as disabled or disadvantaged children. Foster (1993) notes the following about young gifted children.

1. They are rarely served by special preschools for the gifted because there is a shortage of these kinds of programs in the United States. . . . Preschool teachers need to take responsibility for meeting the needs of this group, as well as the needs of other special needs children in their classroom.

2. They enjoy many of the same activities that nongifted children enjoy but to a greater degree and in more depth and detail (p. 28).

3. They are very verbal. Activities that introduce advanced vocabulary would be an excellent source of enrichment for gifted preschoolers.

Barclay and Benelli (1994) recommend the work of Piaget (1952) and Vygotsky (1978), along with contemporary theorists such as Glazier (1988) and Resnick and Klopfer (1989), who emphasize the dynamic interactions between the individual and the physical and social environments. Children construct their own knowledge through repeated interactions with people and materials. For all young children, including those who may be intellectually gifted, the following aspects of learning are accepted as true (Barclay & Breheny, 1994).

The quality of social interactions has an impact on children's intellectual and affective capabilities. New information must be examined in light of what children already know in order for them to develop more complex concepts and solve novel problems. Central to motivation for learning is the child's interest and "need to know." Children's ability to assess what is needed to solve problems is a developmental process.

Using mediating strategies that will evoke higher-order thinking requires teachers to use considerable skill. They must set the stage, recognize the responses that occur and follow through with the necessary support. More basic than these important skills is an underlying philosophy of attending to the development of the whole child through an integrated curriculum of intellectual integrity and use of interactive teaching methods. . . . Both preservice and inservice education programs will be needed to address the content and methods that will result in appropriate educational experiences. (Barclay & Benelli, 1994, p. 135)

Teachers of gifted children, like teachers of disabled children, often come under fire because they are not doing as well as they could with the children in their classrooms. Classroom teachers of both kinds of students feel suddenly caught in a no-win situation. *National Excellence: A Case for Developing America's Talent* (1993) criticizes general education's inability to challenge the specifically talented and illuminates the goal of providing optimum education for all students. The booklet states that gifted American students achieve below the level of their foreign counterparts on international tests.

Conclusions

Child care specialists, childhood development workers and educators need to remember that although gifted preschoolers may think like 8-year-olds, they are still preschoolers. The key to enriching gifted preschoolers lies in knowing their interests and offering activities and materials to expand these interests.

Gifted preschool children can test the patience of both parents and teachers. Interesting and challenging activities at home and in preschool will help channel their energy and intellectual curiosity in positive ways. It is the job of parents and teachers to see to it that these children receive appropriate educational experiences so that boredom and underachievement don't occur. (Foster, 1993, p. 30)

GENDER

We can and should teach young children to respect and value both sexes. Being thoughtful to one's sex should be as important as being thoughtful to the opposite sex. Courtesy goes a long way in creating friendships; it should be practiced more in our present-day society.

Years of research, reams of notes, hours of observation, and careful evaluation have pinpointed some gender differences in children in kindergarten through the sixth grade in Michigan and southern California multicultural (Spanish-speaking) schools.

Thorne (1993), like other researchers, agrees that segregation by gender exists and begins early. Children who occasionally play with the other gender are often teased by their peers, a form of criticism. Some findings include the following:

Boys, when they approach girls, are more often "invading" or bothering the girls' domain, rather than desiring friendly play. Girls, on the other hand, work hard to follow the boys' rules and expectations when they cross over to the male domain. Girls are likely to initiate games of "chase

---

Facts and Figures

Education researchers have focused increasing attention on the identification of young gifted children from all population groups (Barbour, 1992; Frasier, 1991; Shaklee, 1992). Children from disadvantaged and culturally diverse environments are of particular concern because of their underrepresentation in the few existing programs for young gifted children (Frasier, 1991; Karnes & Johnson, 1991). Although appropriate programming has been addressed, it has not received the necessary attention that would lead to an understanding of the best practices (Barclay & Benelli, 1994).

Karnes and coworkers (1982) share this view: Potentially gifted children from low socioeconomic-level homes may not have had their talents nourished and as a result may not appear to be as gifted as their gifted peers from more advantaged homes (Barclay & Benelli, 1994).

Based on classroom examples, we question the need for *teaching* children how to think. Experiences that elicit and support higher-order thinking may be more appropriate (Barclay & Benelli, 1994).

the boys" and to talk about these games later on. Most girls want the chasing game to cease if it gets too physical.

In Thorne's study, many children indicated being friends with the opposite gender in their family, church, or neighborhood but kept these friendships quiet at school for fear of teasing.

Girls play in smaller groups and have more best friends than do boys. Boys dominate playground space for ball games; girls use smaller spaces (closer to the buildings) for jumping rope, hopscotch, and handball.

Some competition between genders is created by adults who set up practice sessions, drills, games, or contests with girls and boys on opposing sides. Lining up is so often done according to gender that children frequently do it without being told.

Children's absorption of gender stereotypes limits their development. As young as 3 and 4, children begin to self-limit their choices of learning experiences because of the gender norms they are already absorbing. One of the negative consequences of this process is a pattern of uneven cognitive development, or "practice deficits," related to the types of activities boys and girls choose (Serbin, 1988, p. 5).

FAMILIES

Separation/Divorce

In 1990 it was reported that close to one third of the children in the United States can expect that before their eighteenth birthdays, their parents will be divorced (Strangeland et al., 1989).

Teachers may become aware of a pending separation or divorce through abrupt change in a child's classroom behavior. Separation and divorce have powerful effects on children: anger, sadness, anxiety, abandonment, loneliness, being out of control, or being overburdened with the prospect of possibly increased responsibilities can result (Frieman, 1993).

Being supportive and letting the troubled child know that the teacher is understanding and willing to listen can be a valuable tool in helping the child. Emotional needs can be met through the use of developmentally appropriate means that facilitate the child's growth: empathetic listening, expressive art materials, unit blocks, music and movement, relevant books, uninterrupted play, friends, and other means.

Diverse Family Structures

The following reminder appeared in an issue of *Young Children* and is related to the Wickens (1993) article:

> Editor's Note: Early childhood educators are expected to create an environment of tolerance and justice for all people, including those unlike us in some way (religion, color, sexual orientation, family format, ability, socio-economic status), and to promote tolerance and justice even for people with whom we disagree and whose behavior we disapprove. This is the way of democracy, and democracy is the ideal of our country.
>
> There are 8 to 10 million children in 3 million gay and lesbian families in this country.

Knowing that the curriculum for young children is about the family, Wickens (1993) interviewed families with young children and wrote an article about lesbian parents. Teaching about diverse family structures may not be comfortable for some caregivers, but it is important even if these conditions do not currently exist in their classrooms. As part of the interview, Wickens found that some teachers began examining their curriculum, modifying stories and songs to present parents of both sexes in protective and nurturing roles, and creating a climate in which a child could talk about family structure, regardless of how conventional or unconventional it was. Other teachers thought about the risks involved of teaching about different family structures. One principal reported: "We have a very diverse population here, with all kinds of interesting differences from each other. We have physically disabled children, from shelters, parents who have lots of money and send kids to private schools, wide ethnic mix. It's a very diverse population added to the diversity we already have. Our teachers and our parents work very hard to preserve that diversity" (Wickins, 1993, p. 28).

AGING

We live in a society where the population of those over 65 is rapidly approaching 20 percent.

We believe our children should hold a heightened sensitivity to the needs and concerns of all people, yet as child-care workers and teachers we seem to do considerably little in the way of combating the ageistic prejudices that exist toward the elderly (Kupetz, 1994).

Children even as young as 3 have begun to form perceptions about the elderly (Burke, 1981; Jantz et al., 1977), and unfortunately these views coincide with those of the adults in our society.

Young and old alike view aging in a negative sense and believe a variety of myths and misconceptions related to the elderly such as being senile, miserable, set in their ways, crabby and mean, socially isolated and lonely, unhealthy, and unable to carry out their normal activities (Kupetz, 1994).

In valuing all individuals, we need to help young children value the "golden years": They are inevitable, memorable, and a part of the life cycle. We can highlight and enhance the intergenerational relationship through involving senior citizens in the classroom as volunteers for individuals or groups, for sharing real-life experiences, for specific curriculum areas (art, music, literature), and for interaction.

> When young children digest behaviors, images, and perceptions, they will begin to form attitudes that have a powerful influence on their present and future behavior. It is only as young and old alike are able to understand and develop healthy attitudes toward their own aging process and cultivate the positive attitudes that allow them to develop intergenerational relations that they will be able to realize their own full potential. (Kupetz, 1994, p. 37)

Reviews of children's literature reveal ageist language (Treybig, 1974), ageist and negative attitudes toward elderly (Burke, 1981; Click & Powell, 1976), attitudes that are difficult to change (Bennett, 1976; Burke, 1981), negativism toward the elderly (McGuire, 1993), few older characters, minor/boring roles, and uncomplimentary descriptions (Dodson & Hause, 1981; McGuire, 1993); however, a few authors do portray aging in a sensitive manner and others beautifully incorporate aspects of their own family memories and history.

In selecting children's books about elderly people, adults should do the following:

1. Look for themes that portray the elderly with accurate descriptions—focusing on vitality, fully developed, positive, and accurate descriptions—avoiding derogatory descriptors, nonproductive, stereotyped roles of ethnic or racial groups, inappropriate visuals, or other negative characteristics.

2. Discourage those with language that demean, patronize, or stereotype the elderly (American Association of Retired Persons, 1984).

3. Select those with minimal exposure to death, dying, illness, or disability.

4. Select those with intergenerational plots (see McGuire, 1990).

OTHER ASPECTS

The National Commission on Children was charged with developing a national agenda for public and private sectors to improve the opportunities for every young person to become a healthy, secure, educated, economically self-sufficient, and productive adult. Recommendations addressed nine broad areas: (1) ensuring income security, (2) improving health, (3) increasing educational achievement, (4) preparing adolescents for adulthood, (5) strengthening and supporting families, (6) protecting vulnerable children and their families, (7) making policies and programs work, (8) creating a moral climate for children, and (9) costs and financing. The commission estimates that the federal share of the costs would be approximately $52 to $56 billion in new federal funding in the first year (Hayes, 1991).

Providers must, at minimum, be registered with the state. States must impose health and safety requirements applicable to all providers receiving funds under the act. Standards must address prevention and control of infectious disease, including immunizations, building safety requirements, and health and safety training for providers. States are free to impose more stringent requirements. States must do a one-time review of their licensing requirements unless it has been done during the previous 3 years.

According to the "Public Policy Report" (1993), plans under consideration in many states include a review of funds and child-care policies, rather than solely relying on block grant funds; using broad-based advisory committees in developing a state plan; providing for resource and referral; setting up special committees to review present training opportunities and to develop new ones; reviewing reimbursement rates to encourage more providers to serve low-income children; expanding eligibility for child-care assistance; adding licensors; and considering contracts and grants in an effort to service certain target populations.

The following are considered key elements for an effective early childhood development system (Blank, 1991):

1. State and local advisory groups
2. Interagency coordination
3. Child-care resource and referral
4. Uniform licensing
5. A career development system
6. Quality incentives for programs and providers
7. Incentives to ensure adequate supply of all types of services, including programs for infants and toddlers, school-age children, and children with special needs

8. Incentives such as special grants or higher rates to promote comprehensive services and to allow opportunities and technical assistance for all types of health and family support services for low-income families
9. Incentives to provide full-day programs
10. Reimbursement rates that promote a stable supply of quality child care (e.g., payments for normal absences of sick children and holidays for providers)
11. A mixture of payment mechanisms (certificates, contracts, and grants)
12. Sliding fee scales
13. Coordinated eligibility criteria
14. Two-tiered eligibility scales that include one-income cut-off for entry into subsidized programs and another, higher, income cut-off for families to leave the system
15. Coordinated intake that provides either a single place or process through which families can find out about and apply to all programs for which they are eligible
16. Uniform reporting requirements

There are several ramifications associated with federal standards: According to Olmstead (1989):

> First, in states with minimal regulation systems, parents have difficulty obtaining information about the availability or quality of specific settings. Second, considering the high staff turnover rates, a parent cannot assume that the staff present in a center is the staff that was presented at the time of the latest licensing inspection nor that a given family daycare home will still be in operation even 6 months in the future. Finally, with the lack of education qualifications required of child-care staff in both centers and homes, there are few assurances for parents regarding the quality of care in most settings. (p. 386)

EMPLOYER SUPPORT

For many years, educators, parents, employers, and others have explored the relationship of child care and the workplace. Needs of specialized children were seldom specifically addressed. Issues have changed and there is need for dialogue about the needs of the workplace and the home. Accreditation projects of the NAEYC and, more recently, the Americans with Disabilities Act are emphasizing the unique needs of families with special-needs children.

Flexible Spending Accounts.

This option does not require a major commitment on the part of an employer, and it does offer many families a significant savings on dependent care expenses, especially for families with special-needs children. Employers making flexible spending accounts available to their employees must follow the regulations in Internal Revenue Code 125. Reimbursement from the dependent care account is made when the employee presents a receipt for eligible expenses. Neither the employee nor the employer must pay federal taxes on the amount withheld for dependent care, an advantage for both parties (Martin, 1992).

Resource and Referral Services.

Some employers provide child-care resource and referral services to employees as a service without becoming financially involved. Some communities have an additional listing of centers and family day-care homes that serve the special-needs children (Martin, 1992).

Child-Care Centers.

Few employers provide on-site or nearby child-care centers for young children of their employees. Employers who offer child care must follow national and local guidelines for quality, adult-child ratios, teacher preparation, meeting the individual needs of all children, and a method of communicating with parents. Estimates in 1992 suggest that approximately 1,000 employers provided this option; most employers have not addressed the needs of disabled children, but when they do, they must adhere to modifications in physical environment, programs, teacher preparation, communication with parents, and other specific requirements.

Notable change of perspective is the realization that services for special-needs children must take into account the child in context. Services must be family based (IFSP—Individual Family Service Plan) and must be adapted to the needs of the individual child and the individual family. The child with special needs can be enrolled in a variety of settings and served by professionals or paraprofessionals with diverse backgrounds (Cook et al., 2000).

The 5th edition of Cook and coworkers (2000) lists four focal points to help the giver of care to special-needs children including: (1) the nature of young children and how they learn; (2) understanding the young child within the context of the family; (3) development through understanding of each of these complex domains: social-emotional, motor, communication, and cognitive skills; (4) and a synthesized view of the whole child. . . . the whole child is much greater than the sum of his or her parts.

Guralnick (1990) a decade ago wrote: "Perhaps the single most significant achievement in the

---

 **Stimulator**   As an employed parent of young school-age child(ren), rank the following options to suggest to your employer to make *you* more effective after the "3 o'clock syndrome": flextime; job sharing, voluntary part-time status; working at home; flexible spending accounts; cafeteria-style benefit plans; child-care vouchers; information and referral assistance; on-site child care; or others that would best fit your situation. . . . Statistics from industry suggest that concerns of parents whose children are home alone manifest themselves on the job through the 3 o'clock syndrome in terms of productivity slumps, increases in assembly-line accidents, and absenteeism (Pecoraro et al., 1984 cited by Bell, 1999).
Or

❖ ❖ ❖ ❖   As an employer of women who have school-age children, and using the above options for working women, suggest some ways you could ease the 3 o'clock syndrome and still make your business profitable.

Facts and Figures

- "No group has been as overlooked and as inadequately presented in children's books, young readers' books, adult books, and the popular press than individuals with disabilities . . . they were often depicted with extreme characteristics (i.e., as people of evil or godliness . . .) difference or deviance—not a balance of strengths and weaknesses—was often the main personality or behavioral trait held up for the reader. Now in this time of heightened awareness and sensitivity to differences and to portraying people with mental and physical disabilities in more positive roles, it is distressing that the depiction of people with disabilities remains generally negative in the mass media although the situation is improving. . . " (Blaska & Lynch, 1998, p. 36).

- "All children must be routinely represented in the children's fiction and nonfiction we select for our classrooms. We need to incorporate books that include people with disabilities into every program, just as we include books with people representing racial and cultural diversity. . . . Their use should not be limited to classes in which children with disabilities are mainstreamed" (Blaska, 1996).

- A list of story books regarding children and disabilities was compiled by Blaska and Lynch (1998). An editor's note encourages adults to look at all books "before using them to ensure that the language, art, and message meet your standards of excellence. Not all books are equal. We want to use books which make children feel that they are equal."

- Some resources that may be helpful to the reader:

  Council for Exceptional Children
  1110 North Glebe Rd, Ste. 300
  Arlington, VA 22201
  http:www.cec.sped.org

  Division for Early Childhood
  http:www.dec-sped.org

  Young Exceptional Children
  Division for Early Childhood of the Council for Exceptional Children
  1444 Wazee Street, Suite 230
  Denver, CO 80202
  Phone: 303-620-4576

---

field of early childhood education in the decade of the 1980s was the repeated demonstration that mainstreamed programs can be implemented effectively" . . . and should be designed to maximize its effectiveness (p. 3).

In one of my many groups over the years, I had a handsome Japanese preschooler named Roman. He was smaller than most of the other children; his language was limited; his behavior was isolated. The word "Jap" was frequently heard when the children referred to Roman. I also had a male "trainee" who had spent two years in Japan. We watched Roman and tried to get him to associate with the other children—and to get them to accept him. I had a special interest in Japan so when the trainee asked if he could plan a unit on Japan, I was impressed. He brought in kimonos and clogs, oriental toys, books, bowls and chopsticks, and

Stimulator

What would you do if

1. A child brought the book *Little Black Sambo* to class and demanded that it was "my favorite book and I want you to read it to all the children."

2. A parent of a child in your group asked that her child "not play with the special-needs children"?

3. A child in your group suddenly and vigorously became afraid of a special-needs child?

4. There were no special-needs children in your group, but shortly several children of differing disabilities were going to be placed in your group? How would you prepare yourself, the enrolled children, the environment, and the "new" children?

5. A parent brought a birthday surprise to school (without first checking with you) that was degrading to other ethnic children (costumes, toys, food, etc.)? [Derman-Sparks et al. (1989) provide some interesting and positive approaches that will help teachers and children develop positive attitudes and behavior toward reducing bias in your classroom.]

6. Children never ask questions about race, disability, or gender. How would you set up situations in class, in books, in activities, and so forth that teach positive concepts?

talked to the children in Japanese. The winner was when we prepared Japanese food! Roman was so interested and enthusiastic that the children noticed a great difference in him. They kept asking Roman the names of the food, how to use the chop sticks, how to put on the items of clothing, and on and on. From that day on, Roman was sought after as a playmate, children learned words in both languages—and it turned from a negative bias to wonderful comradeships. The children became more friendly with others who were "different" from themselves when we repeated the experience using different cultures. It was almost as if the children were saying, "Thank you for helping me understand about others."

INDIVIDUALS WITH DISABILITIES

The Americans with Disabilities Act is a federal civil rights law that went into effect in 1992. The act states that people with disabilities are entitled to equal rights in employment, state and local public services, and public accommodations such as preschools, child-care centers, and family child-care homes. Children with disabilities can share learning opportunities with their peers in

early childhood settings, foster caring attitudes, and learn about interdependence and tolerance of human differences (Turnbull & Cilley, 1999).

There are specific provisions in the law that implement these principles: zero rejection (educating all and excluding none), nondiscriminatory evaluation (to determine disability), appropriate education, least restrictive environment, procedural due process mediation or impartial hearing officers or judges, and parental and student participation. It does not incorporate the 1998 regulations.

Caregivers must develop a plan of action to provide for children with disabilities. They may need to modify structures for easier physical accessibility, begin a recruitment/enrollment plan, change routines, incorporate services for sensory-deprived (sight, hearing) individuals, hire specialists, and begin a staff training program.

Research on children's development of ideas and feelings about disabilities indicates that by ages 2 and 3, they notice, are curious about, and sometimes fear people with a disability and their equipment (Froschl et al., 1984). Derman-Sparks (1993/94) writes:

Individuals with Disabilities

Children's fears appear to come from developmental misconceptions that they might "catch" the disability, as well as from adults' indirect and direct communication of discomfort. Moreover, the impact of stereotypes and biases about people with disabilities affects primary age children's treatment of any child who does not fit the physical "norms" of attractiveness, weight, and height. . . . Research also suggests that young children who learn about people with disabilities through a variety of concrete activities are much more likely to see the whole person, rather than just focusing on the person's disability. (pp. 68–69)

The Individuals with Disabilities Education Act (IDEA) was amended in 1997. Three important questions are now being asked about (1) its governing principles, (2) specific provision of implementation, and (3) the significance of the provisions added by Congress in the 1997 amendment.

Conclusions

Implementing programs for all children requires teachers to evaluate both their attitudes toward diversity and the instructional strategies they choose to employ in the classroom. At the heart of a program for all children is the flexibility to adapt lessons to more closely fit children's individual needs. The program's goals and implementation strategies should be continuously evaluated and adjusted to reflect changes in the classroom's composition. This article is intended to serve as both a guide for implementation and a tool for monitoring progress (Walley, 1994/95, p. 118).

Russell-Fox (1997) has some very good suggestions on working with children who have *health* needs, *hearing* needs, *learning* needs, *visual impairments*, *communication* needs, and *physical* needs. It would be well for anyone working with young children, inexperienced children, or special-needs children to review his article.

In programming and placement of special-needs children, parents and teachers should consider the individual characteristics of the child,

the parental support and commitment needed and expected, and the other program considerations to which the child is being admitted (De-Haas-Warner, 1994).

Several solutions for dealing with children with difficult behaviors include:

1. Separating the problem from the individuals involved; generate multiple solutions; evaluate the solutions; and decide which solutions to try (Galinsky, 1988).

2. Define the *goals* for the child; identify *individual characteristics* of the child; consider the *needs* of the people involved; evaluate the *feelings* of those involved (Heath, 1994).

3. In addition to the above considerations, other issues include criteria for the safety of the disabled child; the health of others; the modifications of policies, practices, and procedures to accommodate the child; extra "auxiliary aids and services" required for those affected in hearing, vision, or speech; and architectural/physical barriers to provide *ready accessibility* to the disabled child (Cohen, 1995).

As mandated by U.S. Public Law 101–476, special education services are to be offered in the least restrictive environment (LRE). This LRE policy states that "removal of children with disabilities from the regular educational environment occurs only when the nature or severity of the disability is such that education in regular classes with the use of supplementary aids and services cannot be achieved satisfactorily" (1990, Sec. 612). Research has reflected the benefits of placing preschoolers with developmental delays with typically developing peers in least restrictive environments. . . . Early childhood specialists continue to support this important effort.

There are several discrete goals to ensure that *all* children with disabilities have available to them: (a) "a free appropriate public education that emphasizes special education and related services resigned to meet their unique needs and prepare them for employment and independent living"; (b) "to protect the rights of children with disabilities and parents of such children;" (c) "government funded educational services for early intervention for education of all disabled children;" (d) "to assist States in the implementation of a statewide, comprehensive, coordinated, multidisciplinary, interagency system of early intervention services for infants and toddlers with disabilities and their families"; (e) "tools to improve educational results for children with disabilities and their families"; and (f) "to assess and ensure effectiveness of, efforts to educate children with disabilities" (Turnbull & Cilley, 1999).

Young children, over the course of the preschool years, are "gradually figuring out that they are *like* other people in many ways and *different* in others. Children's learning experiences in these early years can help them to form a strong, positive self-concept and grow up to respect and interact comfortably with people different from themselves" (Derman-Sparks et al., 1989).

Consider the following two situations I have experienced.

Recently my husband and I had dinner with our two young Samoan granddaughters, Lea (just turned 4) and Bre (1½). Out of nowhere came a casual statement from Lea: "You are white and I am brown." We were somewhat surprised at the informal statement. I said, "That's right, and aren't we beautiful!" She matched her skin to each of the three of us. She continued, "Mama is brown, and Daddy is white." I said, "That's right, and aren't they beautiful!" It was a pleasant exchange that ended as casually and abruptly as it had started!

The year was 1966—before much integration had taken place. We had moved from Utah to Tallahassee, Florida. It was a totally different experience for our family. Our son, David, was in high school and Brad was in third grade. One day Brad came home and was telling us about his first day of school. He described his teacher, the activities, and some of the children. One comment was: "I made a new friend. His name is Danny—and I think he is a negro, but I'm not sure." He was right, and he and Danny became great friends. I had a similar experience. As a Head Start consultant, I visited many "black" centers. On one occasion, the children were fascinated with my appearance, which was different than theirs. We all had black hair, but my skin was white. Individually or in small groups, the children would gather around me, talk to each other, and take turns feeling my skin and hair. It helped me know what they were thinking about a "different" kind of person.

"Research tells us that between ages 2 and 5, children become aware of gender, race, ethnicity, and disabilities. They also become sensitive to both the positive and negative biases attached to these

 **Stimulator** Which choice would help to prevent prejudice in young children:

   1. a. Stories that promote fear, prejudice, and inaccurate concepts against others (race, sex, age, etc.). Think of some good examples.
      b. Stories that teach true concepts and acceptance of others. Think hard!

   2. a. Only invite guests of the same race as most of the children.
      b. Invite guests from various races.

   3. a. Favor children with similar characteristics (sex, race, ability).
      b. Treat all children fairly.

   4. a. Ignore actions that are discriminatory.
      b. If children never ask questions about race, disability, gender, and so forth, set up situations in class, in books, in activities, in play situations, talk with parents, and bring in "aids" (wheelchair, crutches, braces, language, dress, food preferences) that will "educate" your children against prejudice.

four key aspects of identity, by their family and by society in general. Young children develop "pre-prejudice": misconceptions, discomfort, fear, and rejection of differences that may develop into real prejudice if parents and teachers do not intervene" (Derman-Sparks et al., 1989, p. 1).

CHAPTER SUMMARY

1. Programs, practices, expectations, and relationships should be within the developmental ability of each child.
2. Diversity may come in many forms.
3. Culture is one form of diversity and will be different for individuals within or outside of any particular culture.
4. Educators must accept, respect, value, promote, and encourage involvement and support of all families.
5. Biased and racist remarks are not to be tolerated.
6. Teachers can build an enriching, positive curriculum; they must include multicultural curriculum and experiences that reflect their own community and classroom diversity.
7. If the cues to which children attend are associated only with less competent behavior, preschool children likely will generalize these characteristics and increasingly come to see those with disabilities as less competent and valued.
8. Head Start is a program that values diversity. It has grown rapidly in the number of children served through government appropriations.
9. Children with and without special needs can learn from each other in the classroom.
10. Infants and toddlers with and without disabilities can benefit from being together.
11. Some impairments of children include vision, hearing, vision and hearing, language, motor, orthopedic, mental, behavioral, cognitive, emotional, and combinations.
12. Referrals for special-needs children are covered through the 1997 Amendments to IDEA (Individuals with Disabilities Education Act).
13. The teacher in special education and regular classrooms plays an important role.
14. Inclusion (originally called "mainstreaming") refers to the "no exclusion" policy whereby everyone can receive care and an education.
15. Gifted/talented children also need a proper education.
16. Children of both genders should receive respect and an education.
17. Different types of families have different needs.
18. All people should show respect for all other individuals. Aged people are sometimes lonely and neglected.
19. Many variables help young and old to live a self-sufficient and productive life.
20. Employers sometimes recognize and meet the needs of families.
21. Individuals with disabilities need to be respected and accommodated.
22. Some highlights of the National Association for the Education of Young Children (NAEYC), beginning in 1926, are impressive, valued, and visonary.

PARTICIPATORS

1. Identify an age group (within a one-year span), observe a child of that age over a period of time (minutes, hours, days), and see if you can match that age to expected "norms."
2. Specifically, what does "developmentally appropriate practice" mean to you?
3. How do you define "diversity"? Give some examples.
4. List some of the characteristics of the "culture" to which you belong.
5. Describe the teacher's role in dealing with (a) preschool children, (b) multiculture, (d) prejudice, (e) parents, and (f) community expectations.

6. Visit a Head Start center. Note the role of the teacher, the activities provided, parental expectations, responses of the children, cultural makeup of the group, and anything of particular interest to you. Being positive about your experience, describe it to someone.

7. Make a list of the reasons why you would like to work with preschool children, children with special needs, and/or both.

8. Elaborate on your own thoughts about inclusion for young children.

9. Try to observe or interact with a gifted/talented child. How would you act differently to this child than to a handicapped child?

10. Ponder your own thoughts about gender of children you teach, diverse family situations from which children come, interacting with elderly people or disabled individuals, and other things that might cause you to reconsider teaching as a profession.

REFERENCES

Aboud, F. 1988. *Children and prejudice.* London: Basil Blackwell.

Albrecht, K. 1993, Jan. Joining the quality circle. Developmentally appropriate practice in school-age care. *Exchange*, 89, 19–22.

Ball, J., & Pence, A. R. 1999. Beyond DAP practice: Developing community and culturally appropriate practice. *Young Children*, March, 46–50.

Barclay, K., with C. Benelli, 1994, Spring. Are labels determining practice? Programming for preschool gifted children. *Childhood Education*, 70(3), 133–136.

Barclay, K. H., & Breheny, C. 1994. Letting the children take over more of their own learning: Collaborative research in the kindergarten class. *Young Children*, Sept., 33–39.

Berkeley Planning Associates, 1996. *Meeting the needs of women with disabilities: Summary of round one Delphi responses.* Oakland, CA: Author.

Blaska, J. K. 1996. *Using children's literature to learn about disabilities and illness.* Moorhead, MN: Practical Press.

Blaska, J. K., & Lynch, E. C. 1998. Is everyone included? Using children's literature to facilitate the understanding of disabilities. *Young Children*, 53(2), 36–38.

Boutte, LaPoint, & Davis. 1993, Nov. Racial issues in education: Real or imagined? *Young Children*, 49(1), 19–23.

Bowman, B. T., & Beyer, E. R. 1994. Thoughts on technology and early childhood education. In J. L. Wright, & D. D. Shade (Eds.), *Young Children: Active learners in a technological age.* Washington, DC: NAEYC.

Bowman, B. T., & Scott, F. M. 1996. Understanding development in a cultural context: The challenge for teachers. In L. Mallory & R. S. New (Eds.), *Diversity and developmentally appropriate practice.* New York: Teachers College Press.

Bredekamp, S. 1997. *NAEYC issues revised position statement on DAP in Early Childhood Programs.* National Institute for Early Childhood Professional Development. *Young Children*, Jan., 34–40.

Bredekamp, S., & Copple, C. (Eds.) 1997. *Developmentally appropriate practice in early childhood programs*, (Rev. Ed.). Washington, DC: NAEYC.

Bredekamp, S., & Rosegrant, T. (Eds.). 1992. *Reaching potentials: Appropriate curriculum and assessment for young children* (Vol. 1, #225). Washington, DC: NAEYC.

Bricker, D. 1978. Early intervention: The criteria of success. *Allied Health and Behavior Sciences Journal*, 1, 567–582.

Bromer, J. 1999, Nov. Cultural variations in child care: values and actions. *Young Children*, 72–78.

Burke, J. L. 1991. Young children's attitudes and perceptions of older adults. *International Journal of Aging and Human Development*, 14, 205–22.

Caldwell, B. M. 1993. *From research to practice: Informing Head Start today and in the future.* Minutes of a conversation hour at the Annual National Head Start Research Conference, Washington, DC.

Carnegie Corporation. 1974. Racism and sexism and children's books. *Carnegie Quarterly* 22, 1–8.

Carta, J. J., Atwater, J. B., Schwartz, J. S., & McConnell, S. R. 1993. A reaction to Johnson & McChesney Johnson. *Topics in Early Childhood Special Education* 13, 243–254.

Chandler, P. *A place for me: Including children with special needs in early care and education settings.* NAEYC #237. Washington, DC: NAEYC.

Chang, H. N. L. 1993. *Affirming children's roots: Cultural and linguistic diversity in early care and education.* San Francisco: California Tomorrow.

Child Health Insurance and Lower Deficit (CHILD) Act. 1997. *Young Children*, June, 44.

Children's Defense Fund. 1998. *The state of America's children: Yearbook 1988.* Washington, DC: Author.

Clark, et al. 1992. Teaching teachers to avoid culturally assaultive classrooms. *Young Children*, 47(5), 4–9.

Clark, A. H., Wyon, S. M., & Richards, M. P. M. 1969. Free play in nursery school children. *Journal of Child Psychology and Psychiatry*, 10, 205–216.

Cohen, A. J. 1995. From our readers. *Young Children*, Jan., 5. San Francisco, CA: Managing Attorney, Child Care Law Center.

Cook, R. E., Tessier, A., & Klein, M. D. 2000. *Adapting early childhood curricula for children in inclusive settings* (5th ed.) Upper Saddle River, NJ: Prentice Hall/Merrill.

Coontz, S. 1992. *The way we never were: American families and the nostalgia trap*. New York: Basic Books.

Council for Exceptional Children (CEC). http:www. cec.sped.org.

Crowley, A. L. W. 1999. Training family child care providers to work with children who have special needs. *Young Children*, July, 58–61.

Culpepper, S. 1992, Winter. Early childhood special education: How to recognize handicaps in preschoolers. Part I: Hearing, vision, motor, and language impairments. *Day Care and Early Education*, 20(2), 41–43.

Culpepper, S. 1993, Spring. Early childhood special education: How to recognize handicaps in preschoolers. Part II: Cognitive and emotional exceptionalities. *Day Care and Early Education*, 20(39), 30–40.

Cummings, J. 1986. Empowering minority students: A framework for intervention. *Harvard Educational Review*, 56(1), 18–33.

Decker, C. A., & Decker, J. R. 1997. *Planning and administering early childhood programs*. Upper Saddle River, NJ: Prentice Hall/Merrill.

DeHaas-Warner, S. 1994. The role of child care professions in placement and programming decisions for preschoolers with special needs in community-based settings. *Young Children*, July, 76–78.

Delpit, L. D. 1996. *Other people's children: Cultural conflict in the classroom*. New York: New Press.

Derman-Sparks, L. 1992. Reaching potentials through antibias, multicultural curriculum. In S. Bredekamp & T. Rosegrant (Eds.), *Reaching potentials: Appropriate curriculum and assessment for young children* (Vol. 1, pp. 114–127). Washington, DC: NAEYC.

Derman-Sparks, L. 1993/94, Winter. Empowering children to create a caring culture in a world of differences. *Childhood Education*, 70(2), 66–71.

Derman-Sparks, L., & A. B. C. Task Force. 1989. *Antibias curriculum: Tools for empowering young children*. NAEYC #242. Washington, DC: NAEYC.

Derman-Sparks, L., Guitierrez, M., & Phillips, C. B. 1989. *Teaching young children to resist bias: What parents can do*. NAEYC #564. Washington, DC: NAEYC.

Diamond, K. E. 1993a, April. Preschool children's concepts of disability in their peers. *Early Education and Development*, 4(2), 123–129.

Diamond, K. E. 1993b. Factors in preschool children's social problem-solving strategies for peers with and without disabilities. *Early Childhood Research Quarterly*, 9(2), 195–205.

Diamond, K. E. 1994, Jan. Integrating young children with disabilities in preschool: Problems and promise. Research in review. *Young Children*, 49(2), 68–74.

Dodson, A. E., & Hause, J. B. 1981. *Ageism in literature. An analysis kit for teachers and librarians*, Acton, MP: Teaching and Learning About Aging Project. (Available from Center for Understanding Aging.)

Dryfoos, J. G. 1990. *Adolescents at risk: Prevalence and prevention*. New York: Oxford Press.

Edin, K. & Lein, L. 1997. *Making ends meet: How single mothers survive welfare and low-wage work*. New York: Russell Sage.

Elam, S. M., Rose, L. C., & Gallup, A. M. 1992. The 24th annual Gallup/Phi Delta Kappa poll of the public's attitudes toward the public schools. *Phi Delta Kappan*, 74, 42–53.

Elswood, R. 1999. Really including diversity in early childhood classrooms. *Young Children*, July, 62–66.

Fallon, B. J. (Ed.). 1973. *40 Innovative programs in early childhood education*. Belmont, CA: Fearon.

Fennimore, B. S. 1994, Summer. Addressing prejudiced statements: A four-step method that works! *Childhood Education*, 70(4), 202–204.

Fiene, R. 1993. *National early childhood program accreditation* (annual report). Harrisburg, PA: Bureau of Child Day Care.

Folbre, N., & the Center for Popular Economics. 1995. *The new field guide to the U. S. economy*. New York: The New Press.

Foster, S. M. 1993. Meeting the needs of gifted and talented preschoolers. *Children Today*, 22(3), 28–30.

Frieman, B. B. 1993, Sept. Separation and divorce: Children want their teachers to know—meeting the emotional needs of preschool and primary school children. *Young Children*, 48(6), 58–63.

From Our Readers. 1995. It is important that child care providers understand the legal framework that governs the rights of individuals with disabilities. *Young Children*, Jan., 3–5.

Fuchs, V. R. 1988. *Women's quest for economic equality*. Cambridge, MA: Harvard University Press.

Fulgham, R. 1989. *All I really need to know I learned in kindergarten*. New York: Villard Books.

Furstenberg, F. F. 1994. History and current status of divorce in the United States. *The Future of Children*. 4(1), 29–43.

Galinsky, E. 1988. Parents and teacher-caregivers: Sources of tension, sources of support. *Young Children*, 43(3), 4–12.

Gardner, H. 1985. *Frames of mind*. New York: Basic Books.

Giangreco, M., Dennis, R., Coninger, C., Edelman, S., & Schattman, R. 1993. "I've counted Jon": Transformational experiences of teachers educating students with disabilities. *Exceptional Children*, 59, 359–372.

Glazier, R. 1988. Cognitive and environmental perspectives on assessing achievement. In *Assessment in the service of learning. Proceedings of the 1987 ETS invitational conference* (pp. 37–43). Princeton, NJ: Educational Testing Service.

Gordon, L. 1994. *Pitted but not entitled: Single mothers and the history of welfare*. Cambridge, MA: Harvard University Press.

Gouch, P. B. (Ed.) 1993, Sept. Dealing with diversity. *Phi Delta Kappan*, 75(1), 3.

Green, A., & Stoneman, Z. 1989. Attitudes of mothers and fathers of handicapped children towards preschool mainstreaming. *Journal of Early Intervention*, 13, 293–304.

Guillean, T. (Ed.). 1991. *A world of difference: A prejudice reduction activity guide*. Los Angeles: Anti-Defamation League of B'nai B'rith.

Guralnick, M. 1990. Social competence and early intervention. *Journal of Early Intervention*, 14, 3–14.

Haktua, K., & Garcia, E. 1989. Bilingualism and education. *American Psychologist*, 44(2), 374–370.

Hayes, C. D. 1991, Sept. Highlights on the recommendations of the National Commission on Children. *Young Children*, 46(6), 30–33.

Heath, H. E. 1994. Dealing with difficult behaviors—Teachers plan with parents. *Young Children*, July, 20–24.

Hofferth, S. L., Brayfield, A., Deich, S., & Holcomb, P. 1991. *The national child care survey*. Washington, DC: The Urban Institute.

Howard, G. R. 1993, Sept. Whites in multicultural education: Rethinking our role. *Phi Delta Kappan*, 75(1), 36–41.

Hurd, T. L., Lerner, R. M., & Barton, C. E. 1999. Integrated services: Expanding partnerships to meet the needs of today's children and families. *Young Children*, March, 74–80.

Huyett, B. 1994. Involving the special needs child in learning centers. Early Childhood Special Education. *Day Care & Early Education*, 21(4), 43–44.

James, J. Y., & Kormanski, L. M. 1999. Positive intergenerational picture books for young children. *Young Children*, May, 32–38.

Jantz, R. K., Seefeldt, C., Galper, A., & Serlock, K. 1977. Children's attitude toward the elderly. *Social Education*, 41, 485–523.

Kaiser, B., & Raminsky, J. *Meeting the challenge: Effective strategies for challenging behaviours in early childhood environments*. NAEYC #300. Washington, DC: NAEYC.

Knapp, M. S., Turnbull, B. J., & Shields, P. M. 1990, Sept. New Directions for educating the children of poverty. *Educational Leadership*, 4–8.

Knitzer, J., & Cauthen, N. K. 2000. Innovative strategies support children and families coping with welfare changes. *Young Children*, Jan., 49–51.

Kohlberg, L., & Mayer, R. 1972. Development as the aim of education. *Harvard Educational Review*, 42, 449–469.

Kraiser, S., Witte, G., Fryer, G. E. Jr., & Miyoshi, T. 1990. Children in self-care: A new perspective. *Child Welfare League of American*, 69(6), 571–581.

Kreider, H., & Hurd, T. L. 1999. *Child care resource and referral agencies: Training child care providers to support families*. Cambridge, MA: Harvard Family Research Project.

Kupetz, B. 1993. Bridging the gap between the young and the old. *Children Today* 22(2), 10–13.

Kupetz, B. N. 1994. Ageism: A prejudice touching both young and old. *Day Care & Early Education*, 21(3), 34–37.

LaPlante, M. P., Carlson, D., Kaye, H. S., & Bradsher, J. E. 1996. *Families with disabilities in the United States*. Disability Report, No. 8. Washington, DC: U. S. Department of Education, National Institute on Disability and Rehabilitation Research.

Little Soldier, L. 1992. Working with Native American children. *Young Children*, 47(6), 15–21.

Lukins, R. 1995. *A critical handbook of children's literature* (5th ed.). New York: HarperCollins.

Maccoby, E. E., & Jacklin, C. N. 1974. *The psychology of sex differences*. Stanford, CA: Stanford University Press.

Marshall, N. L., Roseson, W. W., & Keefe, N. 1999. Gender equity in early childhood education. *Young Children* July, 9–13.

Martin, K. A. 1992, Fall. Employer support. Early education for the handicapped. *Day Care & Early Education*, 20(1), 45–57.

Mayer, R. S. 1971. A comparative analysis of preschool curriculum. In R. H. Anderson & H. G. Share (Eds.), *As the twig is bent*. New York: Houghton Mifflin.

McCracken, J. B. *Valuing diversity: The primary years*. NAEYC #238. Washington, DC: NAEYC.

McGuire, S. 1993. Promoting positive attitudes toward aging: Literature for young children. *Childhood Education*, 69(4), 204–207.

McLean, M. E., & Odom, S. L. 1993. Practices for young children with and without disabilities: A comparison of DEC and NAEYC identified practices. *Topics in Early Childhood Special Education*, 13(3), 274–292.

McGuire, S. L. 1993, Summer. Promoting positive attitudes toward aging: Literature for young children. *Childhood Education*, 69(4), 204–207.

Meisels, S. J. 1992. *The work sampling system: An overview*. Ann Arbor, MI: Author.

Meisels, S. J. 1993. Remaking classroom assessment with the work sampling system. *Young Children*, July, 48(5), 34–40.

Meyerhoff, M. 1994. Of baseball and babies: Are you consciously discouraging father involvement in infant care? *Young Children*, May, 17–19.

National Academy of Sciences. 1990. *Who cares for our children?* Washington, DC: Author.

National Association for the Education of Young Children, 1988. NAEYC position statement on standardized testing of young children 3 through 8 years of age. *Young Children*, March, 43(3), 42–47.

National Association for the Education of Young Children. 1991. *Accreditation criteria and procedures: A position statement of the National Academy of Early Childhood Programs* (rev. ed.). Washington, DC: Author.

National Association for the Education of Young Children. 1992. Goal 1: Problem or promise? *Young Children*, 47(2), 38–40.

National Association for the Education of Young Children. 1993. *Understanding the ADA: The Americans with Disabilities Act*. NAEYC #514. Washington, DC: Author.

National Association for the Education of Young Children. 1996. *Responding to linguistic and cultural diversity: Recommendations for effective early childhood education*. NAEYC550. Washington, DC: Author.

National Association for the Education of Young Children. 1998. Code of Ethic: A tool for real life. *Young Children*, Nov., 62. NAEYC #503. Washington, DC: Author.

National Association for the Education of Young Children & National Association of Early Childhood Specialists in State Departments of Education. 1991. Guidelines for appropriate curriculum content and assessment in programs serving children ages 3 through 8. *Young Children*, 46(3), 21–30.

National Center for Educational Statistics (NCES). 1993. *Language characteristics and schooling in the United States, a changing picture: 1979 and 1989*. NCES 93-699. Washington, DC: U. S. Department of Education, Office of Educational Research and Improvement.

National Center for Fair and Open Testing. 1991. *Standardized tests and our children: A guide to testing reform*. Cambridge, MA: Author.

National Child Care Information Center. 1995. Including children with disabilities in child care. *Child Care Bulletin* (5).

National Commission on Testing and Public Policy. 1990. *From gatekeeper to gateway: Transforming testing in America*. Chestnut Hill, MA: Author.

Neugebauer, B. (Ed.). 1992. *Alike and different: Exploring our humanity with young children* (rev. ed.). NAEYC #240. Washington, DC: NAEYC.

New, R. S. 1999. Here we call it "drop off and pickup:" Transition of child care, American style. *Young Children*, March, 16–17.

Norton, D. 1995. *Through the eyes of a child* (4th ed.). Upper Saddle River, NJ: Prentice Hall.

Olmstead, P. O. 1989. *How nations serve young children*. Ypsilanti, MI: High/Scope Press.

Pallas, A. M., Natriello, G., & McDill, E. L. 1989. The changing nature of the disadvantaged population: Current dimensions and future trends. *Educational Researcher*, 18, 16–22.

Partnership for Family Involvement in Education. 1999. Community Update. No. 72, Nov./December, p. 3. Washington, DC; U. S. Department of Education.

Pavia, L. 1992, Spring. Early education for the handicapped. Introducing the early childhood teacher to IEP. *Day Care & Early Education*, 19(3), 38–40.

Peck, C. A., Odom, S. L., & Bricker, D. D. (Eds.). 1993. *Integrating young children with disabilities into community programs*. Baltimore: Brookes.

Phillips, D. A., & Cabrera, N. J. (Eds). 1996. *Beyond the blueprint: Directions for research on Head Start's families*. Washington, DC: National Academy Press.

Piaget, J. 1952. *The origins of intelligence in children*. New York: International Universities Press.

Piaget, J. 1962. *Play, dreams, and imitation in childhood*. New York: Norton.

Public Policy Report. 1994a. "Raising a child takes love. Understanding. Patience. And money." *Young Children*. January, 52.

Public Policy Report. 1994b. "A primer on welfare reform, young children, and early childhood services." *Young Children*, May, 67–68.

Public Policy Report. 1995. Facts and Figures. *Young Children*, Sept., 63.

Resnick, L. B., & Klopfer, L. E. 1989. Toward the thinking curriculum: An overview. In L. B. Resnick & L. E. Kloper (Eds.), *Toward the thinking curriculum: Current cognitive research* (pp. 1–8). Alexandria, VA: ASCD.

Responding to linguistic and cultural diversity: Recommendations for effective early childhood education. 1996. #550 (#551 in Spanish). Washington, DC: NAEYC.

Rose, D., & Smith, B. 1993. Public policy report. Preschool mainstreaming: Attitude barriers and strategies for addressing them. *Young Children*, 48(4), 59–62.

Rose, D., & Smith, B. J. 1994c. Providing public education services to preschoolers with disabilities in community-based programs: Who's responsible for what? *Young Children*, September, 64–68.

Rudman, M. K. 1995. *Children's literature: An issues approach.* (3rd ed). New York: Longman.

Russell-Fox, J. 1997. Together is better: Specific tips on how to include children with various types of disabilities. *Young Children*, May, 81–83.

Sandall, S., & Ostrosky, M. (Eds). 1988. *Practical ideas for addressing challenging behaviors.* NAEYC #380. Washington, DC: NAEYC.

Saracho, O. M., & Spodek, B. 1983. *Understanding the multicultural experience in childhood education.* Washington, DC: NAEYC.

Schultz, T., & Lombardi, J. 1989. Right from the start: A report on the NASBE task force on early childhood education. *Young Children*, 44(2), Jan., 6–10.

Schweinhart, L. J. 1993. Observing young children in action: The key to early childhood assessment. *Young Children*, 48(5), July, 29–33.

Schweinhart, L. J., McNair, S., Barnes, H., & Larner, 1993. Observing young children in action to assess their development: The High/Scope child observation record (COR) study. *Educational and Psychological Measurement*, 53, Summer, 445–455.

Schweinhart, L. J., & Weikart, D. P. 1988. Early childhood development programs: A public investment opportunity. In J. P. Bauch (Ed.), *Early childhood education in the schools* (pp. 36–43). Washington, DC: National Education Association.

Schweinhart, L. J., & Weikart, D. P. 1993. Summer, *Changed lives, significant benefits: The High/Scope Perry preschool project to date.* Ypsilanti, MI: High/Scope Educational Research Foundation.

Scott, K., & Schau, C. 1985. Sex equity and sex bias in instructional materials. In S. Klein (Ed.), *Handbook for achieving sex equity through education*. Baltimore, MD: Johns Hopkins University Press.

Seefeldt, C. 1990. Assessing young children. In C. Seefeldt (Ed.), *Continuing issues in early childhood education* (pp. 311–330). Upper Saddle River, NJ: Prentice Hall/Merrill.

Seefeldt, C., & Warman, B. with Jantz, R., & Galper, A. 1990. *Young and old together.* Washington, DC: NAEYC.

Seligson, M. 1991. Models of school-age child care: A review of current research on implications for women and their children. *Woman's Studies Int. Forum*, 14(6), 577–584.

Serbin, L. 1988. Play activities and the development of visual-spatial skills. *Equal Play*, 1(4), 5.

Sexton, D., Snyder, P., Sharpton, W. R., & Stricklin, S. 1993. Infants and toddlers with special needs and their families. *Childhood Education*, 69(5), 278–86.

Shaffer, D. D. 1993, Summer. Making Native American lessons meaningful. *Childhood Education*, 69(4), 201–203.

Smelter, R. W., Rasch, B. W., & Yudewitz, G. J. 1994, Sept. Thinking of inclusion for all special needs students? Better think again. *Phi Delta Kappan*, 35–38.

Smith, M., & Zeedyk, M. S. 1997. *What's a mother to do? Differences in children's verbal and play preferences for sex-typed toys.* Poster presented at the biennial meeting of the Society for Research in Child Development, Washington, DC.

Snyder, L., Apolloni, T., & Cooke, T. P. 1977. Integrated settings at the early childhood level: The role of the nonretarded peers. *Exceptional Children*, 43, 262–266.

Spodek, B., & Brown, P. C. 1993. Curriculum alternatives in early childhood education: A historical analysis. In B. Spodek (Ed.), *Handbook of research on the education of young children* (pp. 99–104). New York: Macmillan.

Sprafkin, C., Servin, L. A., Denier, C., & Connor, J. M. 1983. Sex-differentiated play: Cognitive consequences and early interventions. In M. B. Liss, (Ed.), *Social and Cognitive skills.* New York: Academic.

Squires, S. 1990. Day care: Hard to find, hard to afford. *Washington Post Health Supplement*, 6, March, 12–15.

Stewart, S. L. L. 1999. Good questions to ask: When a child with a developmental delay joins your class. *Young Children*, Sept., 25–27.

Stoneman, Z. 1993. Attitudes toward young children with disabilities: Cognition, affect and behavioral intent. In C. Peck, S. Odom, & D. Bricker, (Eds.), *Integrating young children with disabilities in community programs: From research to* implementation. Baltimore: Brookes.

Strangeland, C. S., Pellegreno, C. C., & Lundholm, J. 1989. Children of divorced parents; A perceptual comparison. *Elementary School Guidance & Counseling,* 23(2), 167–174.

Strong, M. F. 1999. Serving mothers with disabilities in early childhood education programs. *Young Children,* May, 10–17.

Sturn, C. 1997. Creating parent-teacher dialogue: Intercultural communication in child care. *Young Children,* 52(5), 34–38.

Surr, J. 1992. Early childhood programs and the Americans with Disabilities Act (ADA). *Young Children,* 47(5), 18–21.

Thorne, B. 1993. *Gender play: Girls and boys in school.* New Brunswick, NJ: Rutgers University Press.

Turnbull, R., & Cilley, M. 1999. *Explications and Implications of the 1997 amendments to IDEA.* Upper Saddle River, NJ: Prentice Hall.

U. S. Department of Education. 2000, May. Community Update. Issues #77. Addressing the future of Hispanic Education. (A full copy of the speech is available at: http://www.ed.gov/Speeches/03-2000/00315.html.)

U. S. Department of Health and Human Services. 1995. *Passages to inclusion: Creating systems of care for all children.* Monograph for State, Territorial, and Tribal Care Administrators. Washington, DC: Author.

U. S. Department of Labor, Bureau of Labor Statistics. 1991. *Working women: a chartbook.* Washington, DC: U. S. Government Printing Office.

Vandell, D. L., & Corasniti, M. A. 1988. The relation between third graders' after-school care and social, academic, and emotional functioning. *Child Development,* 59, 869–875.

Volk, D., & Stahlman, J. I. 1994, Spring. 'I think everybody is afraid of the unknown'; Early childhood teachers prepare for mainstreaming. *Day Care and Early Education,* 21(3), 13–17.

Vygotsky, L. S. 1978. *Mind in society: The development of higher psychological functions.* Cambridge, MA: Harvard University Press.

Waggoner, D. 1994. Language minority school age population now totals 9.90 million. *NABE News* 18(1):1, 24–26.

Waggoner, V., & Andrews, J. D. (Eds). *Children of 2010.* Washington, DC: NAEYC.

Walley, C. 1994/95. Winter. Special trends in education. *Childhood Education,* 71(2), 118.

Wanerman, T. 1999. The open-door policy: Enhancing community in a part-time preschool program. *Young Children,* March, 16–17.

Washington, V., & Andrews, J. D. (Eds.). *Children of 2010.* NAEYC #390. Washington, DC: NAEYC.

Wellesley College Center for Research on Women. 1995. *How schools shortchange girls–the AAUW Report.* New York: Marlowe.

What would you do? 1999. Using NAEYC's Code of Ethics to negotiate professional problems. *Young Children,* Sept., 44–45.

Whitebook, M., Howes, C., & Phillips, D. 1990. The child care crisis: Implications for the growth and development of the nation's children. Cited in E. Zigler & M. Finn-Stephenson, 1995. *Journal of Social Issues,* 5(3), 215–231.

Wickens, E. 1993, Mar. Penny's question: I will have a child in my class with two moms—What do you know about this? *Young Children,* 48(3), 25–28.

Wolery, M., Schroeder, C., Martin, C. G., Venn, M. L., Holcombe, A., Brookfield, J., Huffman, K., & Fleming, L. A. 1992. *Classroom activities and areas: Regularity of adaptability by general early educators.* Manuscript submitted for publication.

Wolery, M., & Wilbers, J. S. (Eds.). *Including children with special needs in early childhood programs.* NAEYC #145. Washington, DC: NAEYC.

Yawkey, T. D. 1987. Project P. I. A. G. E. T.: A holistic approach to early childhood education. In J. Roopnairene & J. Johnson, (Eds.), *Approaches to early childhood education* (pp. 197–212). New York: Merrill/Macillan.

York, S. 1991. *Roots & wings: Affirming culture in early childhood programs.* St. Paul, MN: Redleaf Press.

Zigler, E. 1993. From research to practice: Informing Head Start today and in the future. Minutes of a conversation hour at the Annual National Head Start Research Conference, Washington, DC. Nov. 4–7.

Zucker, H. L. 1994. Working parents and latchkey children. *Annuals of the American Academy of Political and Social Science,* 235, 43–50.

Chapter 4

Philosophy of the Center

Guide for Readers

❖ Curriculum has been described as child-centered, developmentally appropriate, and child-sensitive.

❖ Philosophical views about children's care and education encompass:
   a. The way young children learn
   b. The needs of parents
   c. The personal qualities of the teacher
   d. Evaluation of programs
   e. Center-community relationships

❖ Curriculum, the number and variety of activities provided for the children, includes values, attitudes, preferences, and restrictions.

❖ In defining the philosophical basis for a program, carefully consider:
   a. Who will be involved in its planning and implementation
   b. Its accuracy and understandability
   c. The relationships between individuals (children, parents, and staff) to ensure cohesiveness and success

❖ Organizations, individuals, licensing agents, and centers encourage quality programs for children as well as a good relationship between the center and the community.

❖ Programs can be evaluated by organizational, state, national, local, or personal standards.

❖ The needs and progress of children should be assessed carefully, accurately, and with appropriate measures.

CURRICULUM

In order to distinguish among practices that more fully involved children compared with teacher-controlled programs, a new descriptive term came into use early in this century—*child centered*. More recently another term was coined: *developmentally appropriate practices*. Sometimes the two terms are used interchangeably, which may be confusing. *Child-centered* means that the child initiates an activity, has more control over the amount of time and type of activity, accepts suggestions but makes personal decisions, and achieves personal feedback. Katz (1993) proposed a new term, *child-sensitive,* for two reasons: first, to some the term *child-centered* means "anything goes: or a child-indulgent approach to curriculum and teaching"; and second, a *child-sensitive* program is one that capitalizes on children's inborn impulse and curiosity.

In another source, Katz (1994) writes about *expressive environments,* or how best to respond to children's resistance to limits and rules, or being sensitive to children versus being intimidated by them, stating "the main idea of these distinctions is to let children know that we understand their feelings about the limits or rules and that we respect their right to those feelings, but this does not mean that we give in to them" (p. 2). But we can keep the number of limits and rules down to a bare minimum, based on rules of effective group functioning and respect for individual rights "to serve and act on behalf of needs, rights, and well-being of all young children" (p. 2).

Values

Curriculum is the number and variety of activities provided for the children. With it comes attitudes, preferences, and restrictions. In telephone interviews with 1,326 adults ages 18 and older, conducted from May 20 to June 8, 1994, by the Gallup Organization for Phi Delta Kappa (a national professional association of public school educations), about half the nation's adults said personal values and ethical behavior should be taught in the public schools. Only 4 in 10 said these matters should

be left to parents or the churches of the community. Twelve percent said that ethics and values should be taught in schools, in homes, and in churches of the community.

What were the values the people wanted taught in schools? Nine adults in 10 believe students should be taught respect for others, industry or hard work, persistence or the ability to follow through, fairness in dealing with others, compassion, civility and politeness, and self-esteem. Only 3 in 4 adults expect the schools to teach the value of thriftiness to their students.

As to the effectiveness of teaching ethics and values and thereby reduce violence in the schools, 6 out of 10 thought it would be very effective; 27 percent said it would be somewhat effective, and 12 percent said it would have little or no effect.

Brainstorming with a group of young children about ways to value their feelings and the feelings of others may elicit the following suggestions:

1. Instead of taking something from someone, offer something in return. ("I'll let you use the rake if I can use the shovel.")

2. Set a time limit. ("You ride around the circle twice and then let Hillary ride around twice.").

3. Help children empathize with others ("It made you mad, Ned, when Alicia pushed you off the trike you were riding. And it made Alicia mad when you wouldn't let her have a turn with her favorite trike. What do you think we could do so that both of you would be happy?")

4. Sharing means that both (several) children can play with a toy. ("Pietra had the doll first. Let her play with it for a few minutes and then she will let you have a turn.")

5. Ownership means more than "self-possession." ["The animal belongs to Xeena and she wants to tell us about it; then she'll let you (handle, feed, pet, or whatever). Listen to her carefully so her pet won't be frightened, hurt," etc.]

6. "It makes both of you happy when you play friendly together."

7. Ask children for suggestions as to how they could include other children in their play (those who have physical, social, emotional, or intellectual impairments; those who are new in the setting; those who speak a different language, etc.).

EDUCATIONAL PHILOSOPHY

Parents, teachers, nonteaching staff, community, and support groups must accurately envision the goals of the school. The center director or another knowledgeable person should take time to explain—or show through an open house or social event—what the school stands for and how it contributes to the care and education of the children and families it serves.

A complete philosophy of child care and education contains specific thoughts about children, parents, employees, and curriculum. It should be based on research and experience. It provides methods by which major goals and short- and long-term objectives can be reached. It takes into consideration the environment and the materials and equipment needed to promote the goals and provides checkpoints to measure progress. The philosophy defines what will take place at the center.

The educational philosophy of a care center should be established in a thoughtful, systematic manner. Anyone responsible for a center's educational philosophy needs to consider these three very important points:

1. What are the needs, characteristics, and learning patterns of young children?

2. What are parents' needs to raise responsible, happy children?

3. What are the desired personal qualities of teachers, and how should teachers be trained?

These questions help to formulate an educational philosophy, which must then be clearly and understandably written to facilitate implementing, enforcing, and evaluating it.

Administrators feel a great responsibility to be effective, to develop a program philosophy with valid goals and objectives, and to evaluate the effects of the program and curriculum on the children. These three components will be addressed in this chapter.

Program Descriptions

Deciding on terms and goals can be a major problem for center administrators. Some theorists emphasize one area of development over another (affective, cognitive, psychomotor, moral); some espouse a holistic or eclectic approach. Theories go into and out of fashion periodically.

Some basic issues must be addressed in each school's philosophy. Of major importance is that the philosophy builds and enhances the self-image of children, parents, and center employees. Another important issue is that of content versus process, sometimes interpreted as school orientation versus human orientation. Those who believe in *content orientation* state that the goal of education is to help children succeed in school as it exists. Their focus is on preparation for the next step in schooling, and achievement is evaluated by relating children's progress to norms or grade level. The goal of education for those who believe in *human orientation* is the upward movement of children, as independent learners, to higher levels of intellectual competence. Learning and problem-solving skills are more important than content mastery. Autonomy and assertiveness are valued, and the years in school are considered an integral part of life itself. Schooling is not viewed primarily as preparation for later school or for life. Achievement does not depend on reaching a norm or the next grade level, but on the ability to cope with the here-and-now.

Each teacher must resolve this issue: whether to help children live happily and healthily now (process) or to prepare them academically for the next step in schooling (content). Some adults want emphasis on cognitive or intellectual

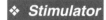 **Stimulator**

A certain community has a number of different types of child-care programs:

1. A Head Start group housed in a city-owned facility has 15 children, a teacher, an untrained support teacher, and a volunteer parent. The children are free to socialize, explore, and play.

2. Another group is similar to that in type 1; however, each teacher has an individual group of five children. One group is doing an art project, another is discussing a letter of the alphabet, and the other is preparing a snack.

3. A parent co-op, held in a local church, has 20 children, 4 adults, and different activities going on throughout a large, undivided room. No attempt to involve children in activities or to station adults at strategic points is apparent.

4. A private, for-profit center has 12 children, one teacher, and a part-time support teacher. The children, seated on small chairs with their arms folded, repeat numbers as if they were a choral group. The teacher encourages group response, but discourages the children's interaction.

5. A large, franchised chain enrolls 150 children, some full-time, some part-time. Eight full-time and 14 part-time staff handle the infant through the after-school programs. Teacher schedules cover a wide range of hours and age groups.

Place yourself in each of these centers. What assumptions can you make about the following:

1. Theories on which the philosophy is based

2. How children learn

3. Parent involvement and influence

4. How teachers should teach

5. What effect environment has on children and learning

development; others desire affective or social development; still others seek a combination of both aspects of development.

Teacher Involvement

The amount and quality of teacher involvement are other important considerations in developing a program philosophy; there is more direct teacher involvement in some models and more indirect teacher involvement in other models.

Early childhood programs have been categorized by the degree of teacher-child interaction:

1. Preacademic (high teacher direction)

2. Discovery (teacher provides stimulating environment)

3. Cognitive discovery (broad curriculum framework; no set daily structure)

Based on the objectives of the program—whether they are determined by the teacher or children—and on the structure, Bissell (1973) identified program types as follows:

1. Permissive-enrichment (determined by children's needs)

2. Structured-cognitive (concepts taught by teacher during structured periods and practiced, reinforced, and expanded during directed play periods)

3. Structured-informational (teacher-prescribed learning activities; more structured than type 2)

4. Structured- (or prepared-) environment (self-correcting and self-instructing materials; children have freedom to choose among materials)

Weikart (1972) looked at teacher involvement differently and grouped curriculum models according to how teachers and children interact with each other and activities:

1. Child-centered (the teacher guides, the child initiates)
2. Programmed (a teacher initiates and implements; the child responds)
3. Open-framework (teacher initiates ideas and responds to child's actions)
4. Custodial (more protective than educative)

Stevens and King (1976) reported teacher involvement in four different ways:

1. Stimulus-response (direct teaching, assessing, diagnosing, prescribing, structuring the environment, modeling and reinforcing selectively)
2. Cognitive interactionist (observing and assessing interests and skills; structuring the environment according to child's interest and skills, questioning, expanding, and redirecting)
3. Psychosexual-interactionist (observing, helping child recognize and resolve problems, supporting mastery and autonomy, and structuring the environment)
4. Maturationist (observing and structuring the environment)

Four preschool curriculum models by Mayer (1971) are based on the amount of interaction between teacher and child, child and child, and child and materials. The *child-development model* and the *sensory-cognitive model* feature low teacher-child interaction, high child-material interaction, and moderate child-child interaction. In the *verbal-cognitive model*, interactions are high for teacher-child, child-material, and child-child. The final model, *verbal-didactic*, uses high teacher-child interaction and low child-material and child-child interactions.

More research on the relationship of teacher effectiveness and program success is needed. Some believed that the success of a program is more dependent on teacher variables than on the philosophy and goals of the program. Based on research on the relationship of children's progress and teaching style, others found that, rather than a polarity between formal and informal classrooms, a definite continuum of teaching styles exists and concluded the teacher's role is the most important variable in the effectiveness of the program.

Each theory can be analyzed from many different viewpoints: the nature of the learning process; the nature, scope, and sequence of content; the expected outcomes; the children's role; the purpose of the program; examples of models; supporters; and facilities. Therefore, each person must carefully examine goals and means of accomplishing them with emphasis on the particular children receiving care and/or education.

Philosophical Beliefs

Administrators define beliefs about children, parents, and employees as a basis for establishing the educational philosophy of the center. If the policy of a center is already established, employees should apply to centers that are compatible with their own personal and professional beliefs. Accepting employment in a center whose philosophy conflicts with personal goals and values will lead to friction, dissatisfaction, and turmoil.

There *are* different philosophies indicating that some individuals (children and adults) function better under one type than they do under another; that children who have had rich language experiences, explored their community, and had social opportunities would be happier in a more open, thinking type of program than would those with more limited experiences. There is no right or best philosophy under which all individuals reach their potential. Nonetheless, the program philosophy must reflect the values, beliefs, and the needs of the director, the program planners, and the families who will participate in the program. Programs without specific goals, objectives, aims, and guidelines would appear to be no more than baby-sitting services.

Administrators, teachers, and parents are certain to have prejudices and desires related to employment or placement of children in centers. New research and better methods can help adults more clearly see and better meet the individual needs of children and adults.

Following are some examples of how children respond in different types of environments. They are presented here as examples of different educational philosophies and for pondering by readers.

Comparison of Teaching Philosophies.   An interesting longitudinal study was reported in *Young Children* entitled "Today's Research Practices: Highlights from *Early Childhood Research Quarterly*" (1997, pp. 62–63). It is a 30-year follow-up study by Schweinhart and Weikart (1997). It reports on 68 children living in poverty who were randomly assigned to preschool programs following one of three early childhood curriculum models: (1) High/Scope, (2) direct instruction, and (3) traditional nursery school. The nursery school model represented the child-centered approach; the direct instruction emphasized teacher-directed academic instruction; and the High/Scope model used constructivist theory to engage children as active learners. All three models were well implemented and of high quality. The former participants in the three curriculum models did not differ at age 23. Note the following conclusions:

> The High/Scope group surpassed the direct instruction group in highest year of schooling planned. . . . Graduates of the 3 curriculum groups did not differ significantly in their employment rates or earnings. . . . At age 15, the High/Scope participants had reported committing significantly fewer acts of misconduct than the direct-instruction graduates. However, the direct instruction graduates had significantly more felony arrests at age 23, significantly more arrests for property crimes than the High/Scope group, and was the only group that had participants cited for assault with dangerous weapons (19%). (p. 63)

Schweinhart and Weikart (1997) hypothesized that "the High/Scope and nursery school curricula would lead to greater adult success and personal responsibility because of their influence on positive dispositions of planning, decision making, and social reasoning." The authors suggest that these long-term group differences (a) "may be related to the exclusive focus of the direct-instruction model on academic skills rather than on planning or social objectives, and (b) that their findings support the preventive value of early childhood education based on child-initiated activities rather than on scripted, teacher-directed instruction" (p. 63).

Developmentally Appropriate Practice (DAP). Wein's work (1996) shows how a teacher's use of developmentally appropriate organization may either undermine or support his or her use of that practice. Use of time as a rigid "production schedule" (specifying when activities had to begin and end) often clouds the way teachers and children acknowledge and reflect upon learning experiences. When time is scarce:

1. Teachers rush children and content; quality is lost.

2. Insisting that all events "begin and end on time" frustrates children who are "slow-beginners" and "reluctant-enders."

3. Preestablishing what each child must accomplish and in what time span may cause "no action at all."

4. Presetting time and accomplishment goals destroy initiative.

5. Some children (disabled, shy, undeveloped, etc.) may never feel satisfaction, growth, or "closure."

Wardle (1999) gives strong support to the DAP philosophy, stating: "I sincerely believe that as an educator, parent, and member of society, I have a responsibility to implement what I believe to be best for all of our children" (p. 4) [based on her own childhood, a Ph.D. in early childhood education (ECE), diverse experiences in the early childhood field, including Head Start, and raising her four children].

She continues:

Since the publication of the revised edition of DAP in EC Programs (Bredekamp & Copple) in 1997, each of us has had the opportunity to reflect on the relationship of this philosophy to our own teaching beliefs and practices and to examine criticism by detractors of this approach. While the new volume carefully includes input from special educators and cultural context folks, we still hear their concerns (references). Added to these critics are those who have confused developmentally appropriate practice with antibias curriculum, and the Core curriculum disciples of E. D. Hirsch (1990). A fairly new group of critics are the deconstructionists (Lubeck 1996; O'Brian 1996) who believe established knowledge of raising and teaching children should be rejected because it imposes on everyone dominant ideology about educating children. (p. 11)

These are Wardle's 12 beliefs in praise of DAP: [Each belief is accompanied by justifications, sound reasoning, and documented support. The reader is encouraged to obtain, read, and study the complete article by Wardle (1999).]

1. It is theoretically valid.
2. It encourages academic rigor.
3. It benefits all children.
4. It provides an excellent philosophy for our field.
5. It is "a radical, cutting-edge approach."
6. It should be creatively and sensibly implemented.
7. It is best for our children.
8. It reflects Wardle's educational values.
9. It prepares minority groups for success.
10. It encourages cooperative and collective learning.
11. It encourages cooperation between home and program.
12. Its practice encourages meaningful learning.

She concludes:

I believe the developmentally appropriate early childhood philosophy is the best framework for continuing to meet the diverse needs of all the young people we serve. I believe it provides protection from the continual assaults on our children—programs that are too academic, pushing down curricula, forcing children into custodial child care so parents can work, in inappropriate TV and computer programs, and politically motivated outcome-based programs. . . . DAP is a set of guidelines designed to further our practice and discussion; it is *not* a set of rigid rules carved in stone. We need to commit ourselves to a greater implementation of the philosophy and develop nuances and variability within it. (p. 11)

Other Theories, Practices, and Support. Individuals have "favorite" theories; some have lasting support, others fade quickly. Some practices are aimed at specific ages, socioeconomical groups, or income levels.

CHILDREN

One who believes that children are born evil or that they are empty vessels to be filled will act differently from one who believes that children are born good and need experiences and opportunities as they show interest and readiness. Hunt (1974), discussing the importance of the relationship between the child's environment and his sensorimotor capacities (the "problem of the match"), explained that adults who are guiding the development of young children must "find and arrange the circumstances that will provide a development-fostering match for the ready-made achievements of the individual children in their charge."

Children respond differently to different types of instruction. Bennett (1977) found that the structure of teaching style had these effects:

1. Disadvantaged children taught in programs with teacher-prescribed objectives and direct teaching show greater achievement than children taught by an informal teaching style.

2. Anxious and insecure children do better in a structured environment.

3. In general, the least effective programs were those at extreme ends of the continuum—the very structured and the very informal.

It is imperative that the director, staff, and parents understand and support the program philosophy of their center. In planning for the education and care of young children, it is helpful, if not essential, to ask the following questions:

- What roles do heredity and environment play in the lives of young children? Is one more important than the other?

- Are there critical periods of development that should be of particular concern to parents and teachers?

- How can children's individual differences be recognized and met?

- How can children be motivated to strive toward their potentials?

- What are parents' aspirations for their children? Are they realistic?

- What goals and objectives should be set for a child-care center?

- How is the effectiveness of the center's philosophy, goals, objectives, and experiences evaluated?

- What roles do teachers, directors, parents, and other community members play in caring for and educating young children?

Answering these questions is an important step toward clarifying and formulating a written philosophy.

For a discussion on children with disabilities (special needs), cultural and other diversities, see Chapter 3.

Child-Centered Programs

A child-centered curriculum should include a broad mix of peers, ample provision for activities and options for student involvement, items and ideas that are workable, communication and the sharing of ideas, activities grouped under labels and definitions according to kinds of activities (not subject matter), and a teacher who is more of a support and encourager than a director. Conversation should include dialogue among the children and between children and adults, with encouragement to reflect, solve problems, make observations and assumptions, and use probing questions rather than ones seeking specific answers. There should be integration between subjects. Play provides fascinating and vital opportunities for the children because it "blends language, thought, affect, and imagination. . . . It leads development and stimulates children to extend their self-directed, rule-governed behavior" (Fromberg, 1990, p. 238). From the components listed above, "it seems reasonable to hypothesize greater long-term gains in learning and development from these programs than from those with the conventional academic emphasis" (Lay-Dopyera & Dopyera, 1990, p. 220).

The purpose of the National Association for the Education of Young Children's (NAEYC's) (1991b) guidelines for appropriate curriculum content and assessment is to guide teachers and supervisors to: (1) make informed decisions about appropriate curriculum content (how, what, and when) and assessment, (2) evaluate existing curriculum and assessment practices, and (3) advocate for more appropriate approaches. The conditions of *how* children learn include *when* their physical and psychological needs are met, through repeated experiences and interactions with people and materials, through socialization, through awareness (exploration, inquiry, and utilization), through play, through interests, and by individual variation. *What* they should learn includes values of the culture and community, important information, personal autonomy, and the ability to think, reason, and make decisions. *When* they learn is when their physical and psychological needs are met.

If you know how children learn, what they should learn, and when they learn you can plan appropriate curriculum to meet their needs. You can plan both short- and long-range goals for all domains of development. Your plans should include things that are relevant and meaningful to children; goals that are realistic and attainable for children; and activities geared to individual and group needs and interests (i.e., activities should incorporate cultural and linguistic diversity, build on prior knowledge, integrate concepts, and become more complex over time). The plan should specify ways to teach intellectual integrity and teach efficiently and effectively while actively involving the children. It should emphasize thinking, reasoning, decision making, and problem solving rather than looking for quick or "right" answers; value social interaction; encourage competence and enjoyment; and teach with flexibility so that information and activities can be adapted to individual children or groups (adapted from National Association for the Education of Young Children, 1991a).

PARENTS

In a survey of program directors by Austin and Morrow (1985/1986), the fourth most pressing concern of the respondents was establishing ef-

fective parent-center communications. Parents (and teachers) should consider two important factors in deciding whether a child is ready for a group experience: (1) the child's emotional readiness to separate from the primary in-home caregiver and (2) the parent's readiness to share the care and education of the child. If the child is not ready for a center experience, other arrangements should be made—even temporarily—for in-home or small-group care or for the parent to linger at the center until both parent and child feel more secure. Parents need to understand fully the center's educational philosophy, what is expected of them, and what they can expect in return. They may also need help identifying good centers (see Chapter 3).

Parents can make a valuable contribution to the center. A brief form, such as the form in Figure 4–1, could provide important data. Other items on the form could include contacts for equipment or supplies; ways parents could serve the center (committees, advisory board, newsletter, substitute, field trips); donation and repair of toys; assistance with bookkeeping; and legal advice. The parents should complete the form and bring it to the

```
Name of parent _____Date _____
Name of child enrolled _____Group_____
Occupations of parents _____
Interests, hobbies, collections that would be of
   interest to young children _____
Musical talents _____
Family pets _____
Special things to share (religious, cultural, other) _____
_____
_____
Willingness to help in classroom, on excursions,
   in special activities (specify) _____
Family members and things they could share _____
_____
Other information _____
_____
_____
```

Figure 4–1 Parent questionnaire.

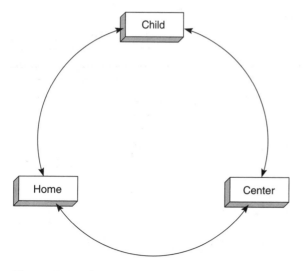

Figure 4–2   Three-way communication.

orientation meeting, giving the director and teachers an early opportunity to review the information.

Though children are the connecting link between the home and the center, they cannot carry the full load of communication and adjustment. Ways to facilitate the kind of three-way communication shown in Figure 4–2 must be established.

A handbook, a parent education program, and written and verbal communications between home and center are vehicles by which information can be transmitted. All these components should be introduced at the orientation meeting.

For information in selecting child care, see Chapter 2.

Orientation Meeting

The main goal of this meeting is to introduce children and parents to the facilities, staff, policies, and procedures of the center. The meeting could be conducted in several ways:

1. New parents and children go to the children's classrooms. A second teacher interacts with the children (in sight of the parents for the children's security), while the lead teacher informally instructs the parents. Afterward, the children and parents take a short tour of the building and playground.

2. Only parents come to the meeting. The director or teacher gives them an overview of the center's goals and the parents' roles. At a different but scheduled time, newly enrolled children and their parents come to the center for a short visit when other children are present. The teacher and parents set up a schedule for the new children's adjustment to full attendance.

3. Only parents attend the meeting. Before the children visit the school, the head teacher visits them in their homes. Then, by appointment, the children visit an ongoing session individually. As in item 2, the teacher and parents arrange a schedule for full attendance.

Parents and teachers should make a plan of action to help hesitant children feel comfortable and secure as they begin attendance at the center and to help the child build trust in people and the environment.

Handbook

A handbook, presented to the parents at an orientation meeting, could include (but not be limited to) the following:

- Personnel at the center and ways to contact them
- Brief goal statement
- Health and safety policies
- Procedure to follow when bringing and picking up children
- Car pools
- Daily program outline
- Snacks and meals served
- Policies on toys from home
- Absence
- Dress code for children
- Celebration of holidays and birthdays

- Visitors
- Calendar of events
- Family services
- Request for parental input

See Appendix A for a sample handbook.

Parent Education

The education of parents should be a high priority at the center. Although some parents may want to leave the education of their children to those with more training and experience, they—the parents—are the most important teachers their children will ever have; they do not have the option not to teach their children. Most parents want information and experience to help them in their complex roles. Those who are unwilling to participate in parent education should seek a center in which involvement is unavailable or voluntary.

Simple instructions for flying, cooking, and investing are easily found. Driving instruction is required in most states before a license is granted. But where does one go for help in parenting? Our most important responsibility is expected to simply *happen.* Private and public classes, workshops, and counseling frequently have low attendance or commitment because some parents feel it is a sign of weakness or guilt to attend.

Parents should know what the opportunities and expectations at a center are before they enroll their children. When they realize that their participation can help them get (1) more value for their money, (2) personal help, (3) information and input into current issues related to children and families, (4) an opportunity to discuss situations with parents in similar circumstances, and (5) confidence in themselves as parents, they are more willing to become involved.

Successful education of parents includes carefully assessing the parents' needs and interests and then matching those needs and interests to the center's resources. The value gained from participating will be unique for each family. Strong, friendly relationships between home and center will increase the benefits for all involved.

The center and home should share their values and priorities with each other, thereby helping the children to learn value systems that can be used in the home, center, and elsewhere. Because children spend varying amounts of time away from home, parents need help in establishing and continuing value systems in their children and families.

The center may require parental participation as a condition of enrollment of their child; however, this can be done in numerous ways:

Group parent meetings (monthly, quarterly, etc.): Research shows that the lecture method is an ineffective way of learning. Telling is not always teaching; listening is not always learning. For an example of a parent meeting, see Appendix A.

Reading program: For convenience, the center may compile a list of basic books for parents to check out from the center, obtain at the local library, or purchase at a bookstore. Topics may be predetermined or selected by the parents. Parents who read to their children show the value of books and encourage children to read.

Commercial media: The center could have a media room in which materials such as tapes and recorders, records, videos, films, CDs, and filmstrips can be used or checked out for home use. Or the center could rent such media on a different topic each month, posting viewing times in advance. (To reduce center costs, some of these materials can be checked out of the local library or borrowed from a local or regional childcare/early childhood organization.) Probe questions, informal discussions, or formal groups could be provided for evaluation and implementation of materials. As with other parent education options, the parents are a valuable source of feedback to the center.

Home visits: Home visits are a conditional part of enrollment in some programs (Head Start, private centers, etc.); however, some public and private centers may make them on request. A home visit is a way to further build parent-center-child relationships and to meet the children and parents in their own environments. Because some parents may feel their privacy is being invaded or that they are being evaluated and compared, they may not permit a visit until they have developed a fairly strong relationship with staff members. Center staff should show sensitivity when requesting and making visits to the individual homes.

Home visits can be child-centered or can function as a means of bringing information to parents. When the focus of the visit is the parents, it should be arranged at their convenience and not exceed one hour. The child may or may not be present. Child-centered visits put a greater emphasis on seeing the child in his familiar setting—a good way to plan for the child's needs at the center.

School Participation. In some groups (e.g., parent cooperative, Head Start) parents are expected to spend a specified time each month assisting at the center. In other types of centers, depending on legal implications, parents may accompany field trips, demonstrate skills or talents in the classroom, make visual aids, assist with office work, prepare for meetings and socials, take occasional responsibility for a curriculum area, help acquire equipment, or serve as members of a committee or board. Figure 4–1 is very helpful in planning program topics and inviting parent participation.

Individual Needs. Whenever parents have individual needs or problems, a member of the center staff may design a method to gather pertinent information and share it with the parents. Families coping with serious situations such as illness or separation may require greater assistance than the center can provide. In these cases, the director can refer families to community resources that best meet their needs.

Written Communications. Regardless of the ages of their children, parents appreciate know-ing what happens each day at school. Many teachers post a daily lesson plan for parents to read. Informed parents support teachers and programs, reinforce concepts, correct misconceptions, and let the children know that adults are willing to listen to them and to discuss topics. Some centers send home weekly or monthly fliers or newsletters, a service appreciated by parents and other family members. Knowing the topics presented to the children and the times they will be discussed increases parent awareness in the home.

Written communications should include simple suggestions for ways parents can reinforce center learning. Figure 4–3 shows a sample flier.

Staff members or parents can work on newsletters. Items to consider are as follows:

- Parent education/child rearing
- Curriculum topics
- Special activities at school during the month (field trips, holidays, special guests)
- Community events (concerts, voting, drives)
- Uses of the local library (story hour, audio-visual materials)
- Recommended TV programs for children and parents
- Short educational messages
- Recipes for art activities
- Children's favorite songs or finger plays
- Parent column (consumer information)
- Appreciation (thank you to parents, children, or staff for participation, ideas, materials, etc.)
- Needs of the center for parental support (field trips, policy)
- Parents' requests

There is no question that providing a parent education component adds time and work to center personnel; however, the rewards to the children, parents, and center employees far exceed the efforts.

Dear Parents:

This week at school we will be discussing the five senses, as follows:

Monday—TASTE—We will have a tasting table. We will talk about taste buds and the four main tastes (sweet, sour, bitter, salty).

Tuesday—SIGHT—We will talk about eyes seeing pleasant things and keeping us from danger. We will review eye care and use of glasses.

Wednesday—HEARING—Children's voices will be individually taped, following which the tape will be played back and the children will guess who is speaking. We will listen to a tape of sounds of the home, animals, and vehicles. Using a replica of an ear, we will talk about the care of ears. We have a hearing-impaired child in our group, so we will discuss ways to communicate with her.

Thursday—SMELLING—We will have small vials of nonharmful substances with various odors. We will also present various foods, compare their odors, and cook some to show how smells can change. We will discuss the relationship between taste and smell; we will show the proper way to blow a nose.

Friday—TOUCHING—We will have a texture matching game, and our art activity will include a collage of various textured materials. The children will feel objects that are inside fabric bags and try to guess what they are. After the "feeling" opportunities, gloves will be put on and the same "feeling" experiences will be repeated to increase the children's awareness of touch.

We are using the above concepts as an introduction to later teaching about the senses. We hope you will use the opportunities at home to help your children apply these concepts in their daily lives.

Figure 4–3 Sample flyer.

Other Contacts. Other contacts can aid in parent education:

- Informal chats while children are in school or at other times
- Displays of children's art or stories they have dictated
- Informal discussions on current topics

TEACHERS

Many texts outline the personal qualities desired in teachers of young children and define what constitutes adequate teacher training; therefore, only two general examples will be given.

In most states, the minimum age required for directors and main care-givers or instructors is eighteen or twenty-one years, and the maximum age permitted is sixty-five or seventy years. Assistant care-givers or instructors, who are never alone with children, must be a minimum of sixteen or eighteen years of age.

Minimum educational and experience requirements are given in most state licensing manuals. In most states, directors and main care-givers or instructors must have a high school certificate; a few states require two years of education beyond high school, with courses in child development and nutrition. . . . Finally, most states require that a plan for staff training and development be submitted to the licensing agency. (Decker & Decker, 1984, pp. 181–182)

As a prerequisite before hiring a potential employee, the center must conduct a federal fingerprint check, a pedophile and abuse check, and a criminal record check. Singling out undesirable or harmful individuals can save the center, the children, and the candidate time, money, and embarrassment.

It is important, however, to note that many authors and studies emphasize that the most important factor in young children's learning is the teacher. In establishing the teacher-child ratio, prevailing standards regarding age and number of children must be followed. Licensing agencies specify adult-child ratios based on ages of children, floor space, and other considerations. Adult-child ratios are very important if both child and adult needs are to be met. Stevens and King (1976) report an interesting ratio-related incident: From our own experience, teachers in a half-day program for four-year-olds reported much more difficulty in simply managing children and perhaps less time teaching or interacting when the ratio increased on a trial basis from 1:7 to 1:10 (p. 291).

PROGRAM EVALUATION

Assessment

Too frequently, evaluation is based on a single category such as quality or affordability rather than being based on a multifaceted one. Quality should not oppose affordability; rather, optimum affordable quality should be the goal. Parents, especially lower-income ones, who need the services of a child-care center want the best opportunities and care for their children but are limited by what they can afford. Often the center that parents can afford has insufficient slots available (as specified by that center's license) to fill parents' needs. (See discussion in Chapter 2 on ratios, affordability, and other related information. See Chapter 8 for employee information.)

Schweinhart (1993) says that "assessment emerges as an endeavor that will literally define the success of the early childhood field" (p. 29).

For years there has been a demand to show the learning of school children. When emphasis was placed on the education and care of young children, there was also a means of measuring their learning. Unfortunately, the measuring of older children and younger children were similar. Now, realizing the harm that can be done to the younger children, early childhood educators are developing new practices, such as performance-based assessment, that are consistent with the early childhood profession's process goals (Schweinhart, 1993).

Parents want assurance about the experiences the children are being exposed to outside the home—and parents should be reminded not to demand more than is healthy from their children. Early childhood educators need the proper tools to assess children's development, if their time is well spent and if their experiences are laying the foundation for their future success. Teachers need to know how to plan for children in general and for individual children. Administrators and funding agents need good assessment tools as they promote programs and evaluate how well monies are spent. A Gallup/Phi Delta Kappa poll found that 74 percent of the American public believe that preschool programs will help children from low-income families do better in school in their teenage years (Elam et al., 1992).

Tools to Assess Young Children.   As with all educational assessment, tools must measure what they intend to measure. For young children, this would include the following:

1. Measuring what is developmentally appropriate for the age and individuality of the child
2. Reliability ("scored in the same way by various scorers and internally consistent across items")
3. Validity ("correlating as expected with concurrent measures of children's development and background characteristics and future measures of school success")
4. Being user-friendly ("easy for teachers or other scorers to use and meaningful in their day-to-day experiences with young children") (Schweinhart, 1993, p. 38)

Developmental Appropriateness.   "National associations of educational researchers, psychologists, and measurement specialists have published general *Standards for Educational and Psychological Testing* (1985), but these do not deal with the criterion of developmental appropriateness" says Schweinhart (1993, p. 30). Examples of inappropriate testing methods for young children include one right answer; focuses on curriculum such as numbers, letters, shapes, or colors; and ignoring personal characteristics such as initiative, creative (art, music, movement) representation, and social relations. In other words, testing is for teacher ease in scoring and judgment "because tests are designed to be teacher-proof and achieve their high reliability by minimizing the role of teacher judgment in the assessment process," inappropriate to various cultures and day-to-day experience (National Center for Fair and Open Testing, 1991).

Several efforts are under way to develop appropriate assessment tools for young children. Work on multiple intelligences by Howard Gardner at Harvard University has led to an effort to develop better assessment techniques. Samuel Meisels and his colleagues at the University of Michigan developed and field tested The Work Sampling System TM for preschool through third grade in schools around the country. The Project Construct National Center, directed by Sharon Ford Schattgen at the University of Missouri–Columbia, has developed for the state of Missouri a matrix of developmentally appropriate activities for children from 3 to 7 years old (Schweinhart et al., 1993).

With funding from the national Head Start Office, the High/Scope Educational Research Foundation completed development of the High/Scope Child Observation Record for Ages 2½ to 6 (COR) for use in all developmentally appropriate early childhood programs, regardless of whether or not the High/Scope curriculum is used. A two-year study found the COR to be feasible, valid, and reliable when used by 64 Head Start teaching teams in southeastern Michigan (Schweinhart et al., 1993).

Reliability and Validity. Schweinhart (1993) suggests:

> Use anecdotal notes to complete developmental scales of established reliability and validity. Such an approach permits children to engage in activities anytime and anywhere that teachers can see them. . . . It embraces a broad definition of child development that includes not only logic and language but also initiative, creative representation, social relations, and music and movement. (pp. 31–32).

Informal ways of data collection include observing and recording children's behavior in typical classroom situations, such as using records (narrative, running, anecdotal), logs, journals, checklists, rating scales, brief notes, volunteers, tapes or videos, samples of children's work, or other means. With many children to observe, teachers need methods that they can use easily and are appropriate for the child being observed. Appropriate assessment makes it possible for the teacher to share with others who take responsibility for the child's educational progress: parents, administrators, other adults, and children within the classroom.

User-Friendly. The COR evaluation system is used by a trained teacher to assess each child's behavior and activities by observing and taking notes two or three times a year in six categories of development: initiative, creative representation, social relations, music and movement, language and literary, and logic and mathematics. [One caution: In addition to observing and recording, "teachers must reflect on *what* they have seen and written in relation to program goals and objectives for each child" cautions Hills (1993, p. 26).] The COR has also been used by trained outside observers for research on programs themselves. The COR respects both the methods of the assessment field and the process and outcome goals of the early childhood field (Schweinhart et al., 1993).

Purposes of Assessment

Standardized tests, previously used as assessment tools, are inadequate reflections of what children learn though instruction (National Commission on Testing and Public Policy, 1990). Children are often unable to express what they are "taught" or what is tested (Bergan & Feld, 1993). Since the 1980s, testing of 4-, 5-, and 6-year-olds has been excessive and inappropriate. Under a variety of different names, leftover IQ tests have been used to track children into ineffective programs or to deny them school entry. Prereading tests held over from the 1930s have encouraged the teaching of decontextualized skills. Shepard

(1994) says, "in classrooms, we need new forms of assessment so that teachers can support children's physical, social, and cognitive development. And at the level of public policy, we need new forms of assessment so that programs will be judged on the basis of worthwhile educational goals" (p. 212).

The Westinghouse Learning Corporation/ Ohio University 1969 study used standardized IQ measure to assess the learning of children in Head Start programs and was a widely quoted study at the time it was conducted. Later these measures were determined to be inappropriate because of their lack to consider cultural diversity, the sweeping social and demographic changes occurring in the country, and the rapid advances of scientific knowledge about children's learning (Bergan & Feld, 1991).

Assessment should not be used to determine how well children fit into categories—especially categories that are inappropriate for the stage of development and age of the individual child. Assessment can be successfully used in educational planning and communicating with parents, identifying children with special needs, and program evaluation and accountability. It should require teachers to discover what children know and can do and where they are in their development and learning as a basis for deciding how they can be assisted in their future growth and learning. Identifying the needs of young children, especially from birth to age 8, may reduce or eliminate problems in their growth, behavior, or later achievements.

NAEYC (1999) formulated guidelines that endorse the integration of curriculum, instruction, and assessment based on what we know about the development, individual differences, and cultural diversity of young children and work to the children's benefit.

The proposed national early childhood assessment system conforms to NAEYC's guidelines for standardized testing and appropriate assessment. The system draws on multiple sources of information, collected over time, from the individuals who know the child best, parents and teachers. Most important, the assessment system uses a national sampling procedure to ensure that the results cannot be used to label, track, or harm individual children in any way, but rather the aggregated results are intended to be used to benefit all young children. (National Association for the Education of Young Children, 1992, p. 39)

The innovative approaches to assessment should enable teachers and parents to assess children's development in ways that will increase their understanding of how each child learns; plan learning opportunities; make educational decisions; help parents create supportive learning environments; and document the extent to which early childhood programs are fulfilling their educational mission by promoting learning suited to each individual (National Association for the Education of Young Children & National Association of Early Childhood Specialists in State Departments of Education, 1991).

A developmental assessment by Bergan and Feld (1993) covered six areas: language, early math, nature and science, perception, early reading, and social development (which included fine and gross motor development). The focus of teaching is on larger structures, not on isolated skills and facts. The revised version of their assessment, MAPS (Measurement and Planning System), "comprises three observational assessment instruments designed to assess cognitive and socioemotional development during the preschool years, cognitive and socioemotional development in kindergarten, and physical development in children in preschool and kindergarten programs" (Bergan & Feld, 1993, p. 43). Observations may be done by teachers, classroom staff, volunteers, or parents at different times, in different places, with different people, and using different materials. And further:

Systematic observation with MAPS identifies what each child already knows and is able to do and can help teachers integrate this information with curriculum objectives to plan developmentally appropriate learning environments. . . . It also encourages children to participate in self-evaluation and addresses what children can do independently and what they can do with assistance. . . . Teachers use an array of tools and a variety of processes . . . to obtain an accurate picture of children's accomplishments and learning needs, which are communicated on a regular basis to parents to help them provide supportive home learning environments. (p. 45)

Bergan and Feld (1993) conclude: "Our belief is that the tension between measurement and teaching will persist until we adopt an approach that unites assessment, teaching, and curriculum and, at the same time, is capable of documenting that educators teach abilities, not isolated sets of behaviors" (p. 43).

Meisels (1993) stated: "Tests have the power to change teachers' and children's perceptions of themselves and their view of the entire educational process. Teachers and researchers have studied this phenomenon extensively (See Bredekamp & Rosegrant, 1992), but our daily experience provides the most convincing evidence about how powerful tests have become" (p. 34). Meisels encourages teachers to use *checklists, portfolios of children's work,* and *a summary report,* consisting of a brief summary of the child's classroom performance and is based on teacher observations and on records that teachers keep as part of the work sampling system, completed for each child three times a year. Meisels concludes:

With this method of assessment, parents become participants in the assessment process. They can be guided to see that whole-group standardized tests and report-card rankings are pale substitutes for the richness of parents' examining their own child's work and watching its progress over time. Parents can be supported in learning how to interpret their children's work. Although most parents know that comparing children with their brothers and sisters is not helpful, for parents to give up comparing their children to schoolmates using percentile scores or rankings on conventional texts will take some time. Parents need to be taught a new way of looking and seeing. This type of assessment gives parents permission to use their own natural gift of valuing what children do and to recognize the importance of their own perceptions. (p. 40)

As reported by Schweinhart and Weikart (1993) on the importance of assessment:

Fundamental to any effort to improve Head Start quality is widespread *formative assessment* of current Head Start program-implementation and outcomes for young children. This assessment must focus not only on the performance of teaching staff in implementing high-quality, active learning programs but also on the outcomes regarding young children's development. The assessment tools used should embody a vision of what such programs are about and what they can accomplish. For the assessment or teaching staff, two such tools are the Early Childhood Environment Rating Scale (Harms & Clifford, 1980) and the High/Scope Program Implementation Profile (High/Scope Educational Research Foundation, 1992; Epstein, 1992). Much support is given by researchers, educators, and others for the national Head Start program and similar programs—to not only serve all 3- and 4-year-olds living in poverty but also provide each of them with a high-quality, active learning preschool program, as identified in Head Start proposals.

Guidelines for Appropriate Assessment

According to the National Association for the Education of Young Children (1991b), "in early childhood programs, assessment serves several different purposes: (1) to plan instruction for individuals and groups and for communicating with parents, (2) to identify children who may be in need of specialized services or intervention, and (3) to evaluate how well the program is meeting its goals" (p. 32).

In order for young children to be served effectively, there needs to be collaboration among schools, child-care agencies, and families. Services need to be expanded and improved, and there needs to be better communication with parents and other agencies caring about and for young children. Finances need to be a blend of federal, state, local, and parental sources. Clearly, children who participate in high-quality early childhood programs come to school with improved health, self-concept, and social skills, and better attitudes toward learning.

A simple evaluation of learning and effectiveness may be to see how children in a given program stack up against Fulgham's (1989) list in *All I Really Need to Know I Learned in Kindergarten.* Can they share, be friendly and supportive, be responsible, observe health habits and take care of themselves, and enjoy a balanced life? Do they have a sense of wonder about their world? Do they function effectively, productively, and happily in society? And do they remember the first word they learned in the Dick-and-Jane books— "the biggest word of all—LOOK?"

Leavitt and Eheart (1991) state the purpose of assessment in early childhood programs is "to help caregivers and parents better understand, appreciate, and respond to the growth, development, and unique characteristics of each child in their care" (p. 4). An accurate and thorough assessment requires information from many sources: parents, teachers, children, and others. "The comprehensive profile of the child emphasizes her capabilities and points out her possibilities" (p. 6).

High-quality programs are good investments. Schweinhart and Weikart (1988) identified aspects of a high-quality program as one that (1) takes into account the total development of the child—social, intellectual, physical, and emotional; (2) pays close attention to the number and qualifications of staff members; and (3) has staff/parent relationships "built on mutual respect and a pooling of knowledge about individual children and child development principles" (p. 41).

Researchers have proposed a radical shift from objectives-based or standards-based evaluations to a focus on issues, which will improve teachers', parents', and caregivers' understanding of how children relate to, and benefit from, experiences that contribute to resolving major social problems.

Testing.   In 1988 NAEYC took a position on standardized testing in early childhood programs that

> restricts the use of tests to situations in which testing provides information that will clearly contribute to improved outcomes for children ... standardized tests

are only one of multiple sources of assessment information that should be used when decisions are made about what is best for young children. . . . Rather than to use tests of doubtful validity, it is better not to test, because false labels that come from tests may cause educators or parents to alter inappropriately their treatment of children. . . . The burden of proof for the validity and reliability of tests is on the test developers and the advocates for their use. The burden of proof for the utility of tests is on administrators or teachers of early child programs who make decisions about the use of tests in individual classrooms. (p. 47) (See also Seefeldt, 1990, pp. 327–328; National Center for Fair and Open Testing, 1991; National Commission on Testing and Public Policy, 1990.)

Accreditation and Self-Evaluation of Programs

For five years, the National Early Childhood Program Accreditation (NECPA) pursued visionary development, evaluation, testing, and piloting. In March 1993 it announced its new accreditation program. It is a

> self-evaluation instrument based upon criteria in the following content/component areas: administration and general operations; professional development and work environment; indoor environment; outdoor environment; developmental programs; parent and community involvement; formal school linkages; and health and safety. Development of the criteria was aided by input from practitioners, academia, and most importantly, parents. (White, 1994, p. 59)

It consists of demographic information, comprehensive self-evaluation on topics listed above, an on-site visit to verify information, scoring of program's profile, and completed package presented to NECPA's National Accreditation Commission for evaluation and feedback.

The indicator (AAIS—Automated Accreditation Indicator System) approach was developed by Dr. Richard Fiene, a professor of psychology and education at Pennsylvania State University at Harrisburg. It is a compilation of key predictor items or indicators that have been identified as

Name of center _____ Date _____

Address _____

Person contacted _____

Experience of director _____

_____

Major responsibilities of director:

    Teacher training _____ Bookkeeping _____ Buying _____

    Teaching _____ Working w/parents _____ Other _____

Number of staff _____

Training of teachers _____

_____

Wage/salary scale of teachers _____

_____

Best method of advertising _____

_____

Goals _____

_____

_____

Philosophy _____

_____

Do they have a board of directors?   Yes _____ No _____

    If so, what kind? Governing _____ Advisory _____

                           Elected _____ Appointed _____

Handbook for parents? _____ Handbook for employees? _____

Number and ages of children _____

_____

Hours in session _____ Full _____ Part _____

Fees _____ Due _____

Allowances for additional children? _____   Is the center eligible for federal

Allowances for absences? _____   nutrition funds? _____

Estimated costs in percentages:

    Wages _____ Equipment and toys _____ Supplies _____

    Insurance _____ Maintenance _____ Other _____

Parent education or opportunities _____

_____

Greatest administrative problems and creative solutions _____

_____

Other comments or information _____

_____

_____

Figure 4–4 Interview form.

predicting the overall quality of a program and/or positive development outcomes for children. It has been used across the United States and in Canada.

White (1994) states: "In a study done last summer, Fiene measured the NECPA programs against the NAEYC accreditation program. 'If we can assume that NAEYC accreditation measures quality,' he explains, 'then, on the basis of our findings, we can assume that NECPA is also measuring quality.'. . . Fiene observes that there was a 'very, very high correlation' between the scores centers obtained on both accreditation programs" (p. 17).

"NECPA's association with Dr. Fiene and the use of his 20 years of research on the indicator methodology has created an accreditation program which is cost effective and efficient," states Katherine Depuydt, President of the NECPA Commission. She continues:

> The NECPA is simply another step in the evolution of accreditation systems. In the 1970s, we were introduced to instrument-based program monitoring; during the 1980s, the indicator systems were born; and in the 1990s, we are fortunate to be able to provide an automated accreditation indicator system which takes full advantage of nationally recognized quality standards and state-of-the-art technology. (White, 1994, p. 17)

The NECPA Commission has an advantage in being able to access the nation's private early childhood community, which up until now was not availing itself in great numbers of the very positive benefits of self-study and accreditation.

Benefits of NECPA. In less than a year since August 1994, there were over 125 programs in self-study or accredited. NECPA publishes an annual report that identifies several significant trends, such as the overall compliance rated with the indicators has changed significantly in a very positive direction, staff are more qualified, training opportunities have increased, there is more parental involvement, salaries have increased slightly, and programs appear to have additional resources. Because of these results, the NECPA weighting system has been adjusted accord-

ingly—this is a unique feature of the accreditation system, in that it is sensitive to changes in the national database. Because NECPA collects voluntary data on program demographics from centers in accreditation, the annual report includes a section reflecting those demographics. Center owners, directors, and administrators will find the information helpful in operationally benchmarking their programs with national data.

The NECPA Commission believes that any accreditation system is constantly evolving and should build on improvements and suggestions made by those involved with its use (program owners, directors, staff, parents, and educators).

Besides the benefits listed, Fiene (1993) reported another result, based on evaluative and research studies conducted in the summer of 1993, that clearly shows that group size and staff-child ratios appear to have a significant effect on the scoring system. A recommendation was made to the National Accreditation Commission and board of directors to reconsider these significant indicators in the weighting and scoring systems of NECPA. It is the hope of the National Commission and board that the NECPA accreditation system will continue to improve all early care and education programs across the country regardless of affiliation.

In addition, NAEYC (1991a) outlined some conditions that would upgrade child care, specifically the following:

1. *Staff qualifications and development:* specified training in early childhood education/child development and appropriate personal characteristics for the teaching position held and for working with young children, promotes smooth and unregimented transitions, allows for flexibility, encourages self-help especially in routines

2. *Curriculum:* encourages active involvement and self-selection in learning process, has a written statement of philosophy and goals for the children, provides balanced daily activities, and makes appropriate modifications and/or referrals for children with special needs

CENTER-COMMUNITY RELATIONSHIP

Every attempt should be made to integrate the center into the community. This can be done with either the center or the community taking the lead. The procedure and extent of community involvement may vary depending on the sponsorship of the center (government, private, university, community, etc.).

Center-Initiated Interaction

Center personnel can apprise themselves of community goals, needs, and resources related to child care and other local matters and offer to share their time and talents when feasible. The following are ways the center can become involved in the community:

Periodically, during start-up time or reorganization, the center could provide some timely articles and photographs to the local media, giving pertinent information about the center. From time to time, the center could sponsor public or low-cost lectures, workshops, or panels on topics of child rearing, health, or legislative bills.

The center could hold an annual open house. This would be exciting for the children, families, and personnel and would be a good opportunity for community residents to become better acquainted with the center. Programs that put undue stress on the children should be avoided.

Opportunities to set up information booths at local bazaars, fairs, or educational meetings should be considered. This and the previous suggestions are ways that center personnel can get acquainted with community people—professionals in medicine, law, education, and social agencies; lay people; artists; teenagers who want to do volunteer work; or citizens of all ages.

All center personnel should take an initiative to promote goodwill in the community. When centers remain aloof from community activities, needs, or interests, the community may develop an attitude of indifference or in some instances obstruct efforts to improve standards or encourage legislation affecting young children.

Personnel represent the center. Their social, personal, and professional behaviors reflect directly on the center. Activities, conversations, and happenings at the center that are of a private nature should be kept strictly confidential.

The National Association for the Education of Young Children sponsors an annual Week of the Young Child. Usually celebrated in March or April, it receives national media coverage; many governors, mayors, churches, educational organizations, and other interested individuals and groups endorse this effort. Centers across the country find this week a good time to hold open houses and workshops, make displays, and provide special activities for young children.

Advertising

Advertising can be done by newspaper, radio, television, brochures, fliers, coupons, posters, letters to families who have preschool children, and many other creative methods. The best way to advertise the center depends on its enrollment size, cost, location, hours, space, personnel, philosophy, length of school year, parental involvement, geographical location of the community, and so on. Good advertising includes the right amount of pertinent information and reaches those who need the services.

Neugebauer (1983) reported a study in Detroit in which 89.2 percent of a random sample of parents with children enrolled in day-care centers selected centers through recommendations from friends, relatives, and coworkers. Word of mouth is one of the best methods of advertising. Satisfied children and parents will bring in other satisfied children and parents.

Community-Initiated Interaction

Residents can actively seek information or visit centers. They can share knowledge or possessions and offer their services—many senior citizens feel new zest by being around children.

Local newspapers can volunteer to publish press releases as news (not advertising) items.

The chamber of commerce, civic groups, public agencies, clubs, and individuals may provide information or services or spotlight a center.

Different organizations might request use of center facilities, personnel, or expertise. If provision is made in the policies to cover such requests, compliance or refusal is easily handled.

CHAPTER SUMMARY

1. Establishing the educational philosophy of a center requires much thought, study, and consideration.
2. The children should be the main focus of any center, regardless of its philosophy, funding, or management.
3. In management, psychology, and education, popular views of human development and learning change from time to time, are categorized differently, and are evaluated by different standards.
4. Children attend centers for a variety of reasons.
5. Upon enrollment, parents should submit information that will help center personnel meet each child's physical, social, emotional, and intellectual needs.
6. Ethics and values are important in teaching young children.
7. The amount and quality of teacher involvement are important considerations in developing a program philosophy.
8. Studies indicate that some children function better under one type of philosophy than they do under another.
9. Studies with disadvantaged children show interesting results.
10. Parents' involvement in their child's education is very important.
11. Personal qualities of a teacher influence a child's learning.
12. Parents should be aware of the program goals, teacher attitudes and training, overall philosophy, and accreditation of any preschool program before enrolling their child(ren).
13. Parent education and involvement can be achieved in a variety of ways and can improve quality of life of the family (perhaps the center has a handbook for parents, a bulletin board, center activities, written communications, on-site visits, phone calls, etc.). See Appendix B.
14. Center personnel should treat inquiries with courtesy and professionalism. They can anticipate common questions about costs, convenience, caregivers/educators, clients, curriculum of their program, as well as other general or specific matters. The involvement of teachers varies in different learning models.
15. Administrators need to affirm their beliefs about the ways children grow, develop, and learn; about the role of parents; and about the personal qualifications and training of teachers.
16. Testing should be restricted to situations in which it provides information that will clearly contribute to improved outcomes for children.
17. A number of reliable measures are available to accredit and self-evaluate the effectiveness of programs for young children.
18. An important part of the success of the center is center-community relationships.

PARTICIPATORS

Select and complete the activities that will increase your skills, knowledge, and training.

For Those Currently Involved in a Center

1. If they do not currently exist, write the educational philosophy and goals for the center. Include information related to children, parents, and staff. If educational philosophy and goals have been written for your center, review them and make appropriate suggestions to your administrator.
2. Prioritize the goals in item 1 in order of importance. For each goal, include such information as time required, funds needed, staff available, and space allotted.

3. If one does not currently exist, prepare a handbook for center employees. If one exists, make updates and enhance the appearance of it.

4. Review your center-community relationships and design new ways to strengthen them.

5. Make a list of the circumstances in which you used referral agencies in the community. List the satisfactory and unsatisfactory results. How could relations be improved?

6. From your past advertising, rank methods from the most effective to the least effective in terms of recruiting patrons. Keep a file for future needs.

7. If you had the opportunity to rename the center, would you do it? If so, list five to seven possible names and discuss the appropriateness of each with the staff. If the present name is preferred, discuss why it is the best selection.

8. Form a panel to identify major issues related to early childhood education in your area.

9. Make an evaluation list to help parents to determine whether a care center provides a good setting for their children.

10. Propose to the administrator or staff that the center investigate being accredited or conduct a self-evaluation.

For Students or Prospective Center Directors/Owners

1. Begin to write an educational philosophy with which you could work comfortably. Include information related to children, parents, and staff.

2. Outline a manual for center employees.

3. Write a tentative policy statement and goals for a child-care center (item 1 asks for a philosophy; this item asks for policy statements and procedural methods).

4. Prioritize the goals of item 3 in order of importance. For each goal include the time required, funds needed, staff available, and space allotted.

5. From the philosophy statement of a child-care center, determine which theoretical philosophy it follows: environmental (Thorndike, Watson, and Skinner), maturational (Freud and Gesell), interactional (Piaget), eclectic, social learning (Sears, Bandura, and Walters), or others. Also determine to what extent it is content- (norm or grade) and human- (problem solving, coping) oriented. (See Chapter 1.)

6. Visit several centers in the community and compile the information requested on the form in Figure 4–4. Keep the information confidential!

Child Information and Parent Education

See Appendix C for further discussion.

1. Use of forms and records

   a. Prepare an application form for (1) a part-time group and (2) a full-time group. Note the differences and similarities.

   b. Design a form for acquiring personal information on children. Support your need or use for each item. Eliminate superficial items.

   c. Prepare and evaluate a health record for a child. Justify the entries.

   d. Write and discuss procedures for handling emergency or illness. Prepare and post an emergency list. (See Chapter 9.)

   e. List advantages and disadvantages of requiring a physical examination before a child enters your center. What should the center know about the child's physical condition?

   f. What information is valuable to collect and retain on children who attend a child-care center? How would this information be used? How would it be interpreted by staff members or parents?

2. Parent education and information

   a. Prepare a handbook for parents or make changes in the one suggested in Appendix A.

   b. Select topics for six monthly parent meetings. Describe ways you plan to involve parents in each meeting. Prepare the agenda and conduct a parent meeting.

   c. How valuable do you think feedback on parent education materials would be for (1) parents and (2) staff?

d. If you were the director of a full-day child-care center, would you provide parent education? If not, why not? If so, what options would you implement? Why?

e. Prepare a newsletter for parents. How often should one be prepared? How could you involve parents in it?

f. Make a list of local or state social and health agencies and the services they offer. What is the center's referral procedure for children and parents?

g. Assuming a moderate amount of funds and a room 9 ft × 12 ft, design a parent-resource room. Suggest ways to motivate parents to use it.

h. You are invited to speak to parents in your community about out-of-home care and education of children under the age of 6. Outline your discussion.

i. Carefully make some assumptions about a fictitious child who is aggressive, shy, antisocial, or physically above or below norms. With a colleague or supervisor, practice ways you could conduct a conference with the child's parents. After several minutes, switch roles with your partner and repeat the conference. Did you gain new insights by role-playing both positions?

j. Make a list of desired philosophy components for a center and trace their roots from information in Chapter 1 (individual differences, hands-on, etc.).

REFERENCES

Austin, A. M. B., & Morrow, S. 1985/1986. Common concerns of child care administrators as modified by education, experience, and ownership of facility. *Educational Research Quarterly*, 10(2).

Bennett, N. 1977. *Teaching styles and pupil progress.* Cambridge, MA: Harvard University Press.

Bergan, J. R., & Feld, J. K. 1991, June. *Measuring the abilities of Head Start children: Past accomplishments and future challenges.* Paper presented at the national working conference, "New Directions in Child and Family Research: Shaping Head Start in the Nineties," sponsored by the Administration for Children, Youth, and Families; The National Council of Jewish Women; and the Society for Research in Child Development, Arlington, VA.

Bergan, J. R., & Feld, J. K. 1993, July. Developmental assessment: New directions. *Young Children*, 48(5), 41–47.

Bissell, J. S. 1973. The cognitive effects of preschool programs for disadvantaged children. In J. L. Frost (Ed.), *Revisiting early childhood education* (pp. 223–240). New York: Holt, Rinehart & Winston.

Bredekamp, S. 1997. NAEYC issues revised position statement on early childhood programs for early childhood professional development. *Young Children*, Jan., 34–40.

Bredekamp, S. & Copple, C. 1997. *Developmentally appropriate practices in early childhood programs.* Washington DC: NAEYC.

Bredekamp, S., & Rosegrant, T. (Eds.). 1992. *Reaching potentials: Appropriate curriculum and assessment for young children* (Vol. 1) (#225). Washington, DC: NAEYC.

Bye, E. A. 1995. Why many child care providers are rated so low. Special Research Report, *Young Children*, May, 41–45.

Decker, C. A., & Decker, J. R. 1984. *Planning and administering early childhood programs* (3rd ed.). Upper Saddle River, NJ: Merrill/Prentice Hall.

Elam, S. M., Rose, L. C., & Gallup, A. M. 1992, Sept. The 24th annual Gallup/Phi Delta Kappa poll of the public's attitudes toward the public schools. *Phi Delta Kappan*, 74, 41–53.

Epstein, A. S. 1992. *Evaluation of the High/Scope training of trainers project* (final report). Ypsilanti, MI: High/Scope Educational Research Foundation.

Fantuzzo, J., Childs, S., Stevenson, H., Collahan, K., Ginsburg, M., Gay, K., Debnam, D., & Watson, C. 1996. The Head Start teaching center: An evaluation of an experiential, collaborative training model for Head Start teachers and parent volunteers. *Early Childhood Research Quarterly*, 11(1).

Fromberg, D. 1990. Play issues in early childhood education. In C. Seefeldt (Ed.), *Continuing issues in early childhood education* (pp. 223–241). Upper Saddle River, NJ: Merrill/Prentice Hall.

Fulgham, R. 1989. *All I really need to know I learned in kindergarten.* New York: Villard Books.

Harms, T., & Clifford, R. M. 1980. *The early childhood environment rating scale.* New York: Teachers College Press.

High/Scope Educational Research Foundation. 1992. *High/Scope child observation record.* Ypsilanti, MI: Author.

Hills, T. W. 1993. Assessment in context—Teachers and children at work. *Young Children,* 48(5), 20–28.

Hunt, J. M. 1974. *Reflections on a decade of early education.* Urbana, IL: ERIC Clearinghouse.

Katz, L. G. 1993. Child-sensitive curriculum and teaching. *Young Children,* 48(6), 2.

Katz, L. G. 1994. Perspectives on the quality of early childhood programs. *Phi Delta Kappan,* Nov., 200–205.

Lay-Dopyera, M., & Dopyera, J. E. 1990. The child-centered curriculum. In C. Seefeldt (Ed.), *Continuing issues in early childhood education* (pp. 207–222). Upper Saddle River, NJ: Merrill/Prentice Hall.

Leavitt, R. L., & Eheart, B. K. 1991. Assessment in early childhood programs. *Young Children,* 46(5), 4–9.

Mayer, R. S. 1971. A comparative analysis of preschool curriculum. In R. H. Anderson & H. G. Share (Eds.), *As the twig is bent.* New York: Houghton Mifflin.

Meisels, S. J. 1993. Remaking classroom assessment with the work sampling system. *Young Children,* 48(5), 34–40.

National Association for the Education of Young Children. 1991a. *Accreditation criteria & procedures: A position statement of the National Academy of Early Childhood Programs* (rev. ed). Washington, DC: Author.

National Association for the Education of Young Children. 1991b. Guidelines for appropriate curriculum content and assessment in programs serving children ages 3 through 8. *Young Children,* (46)3, 21–38.

National Association for the Education of Young Children. 1992. Goal 1: Problem or promise? *Young Children,* 47(2), 38–40.

National Association for the Education of Young Children & National Association of Early Childhood Specialists in State Departments of Education. 1991. Guidelines for appropriate curriculum content and assessment in programs serving children ages 3 through 8. *Young Children,* 46(3), 21–39.

National Center for Fair and Open Testing. 1991. *Standardized tests and our children: A guide to testing reform.* Cambridge, MA: Author.

National Commission on Testing and Public Policy. 1990. *From gatekeeper to gateway: Transforming testing in America.* Chestnut Hill, MA: Author.

Neugebauer, R. 1983. How to stimulate word of mouth. *Child Care Information Exchange,* 44(2), 5–10.

Schweinhart, L. J. 1993. Observing young children in action: The key to early childhood assessment. *Young Children,* 48(5), 29–33.

Schweinhart, L. J., McNair, S., Barnes, H., & Larner, M. 1993, Summer. Observing young children in action to assess their development: The High/Scope child observation record (COR) study. *Educational and Psychological Measurement,* 53, 445–455.

Schweinhart, L. J., & Weikart, D. P. 1988. Early childhood development programs: A public investment opportunity. In J. P. Bauch (Ed.), *Early childhood education in the schools* (pp. 36–43). Washington, DC: National Education Association.

Schweinhart, L. J., & Weikart, D. P. 1993, Summer. *Changed lives, significant benefits: The High/Scope Perry preschool project to date.* Ypsilanti, MI: High/Scope Educational Research Foundation.

Schweinhart, L. J., & Weikart, D. P. 1997. The High/Scope Preschool curriculum comparison study through age 23. *Early Childhood Research Quarterly,* 12(2).

Seefeldt, C. 1990. Assessing young children. In C. Seefeldt (Ed.), *Continuing issues in early childhood education* (pp. 311–330). Upper Saddle River, NJ: Merrill/Prentice Hall.

Shepard, L. A. 1994. The challenges of assessing young children appropriately. *Phi Delta Kappan,* Nov, 206–212.

Stevens, J. H. Jr., & King, E. W. 1976. *Administering early childhood education programs.* Boston: Little, Brown.

Wardle, F. 1999. In praise of developmentally appropriate practice. *Young Children,* Nov., 4–12.

Weikart, D. P. 1972. Relationship of curriculum teaching and learning in preschool education. In J. C. Stanley (Ed.), *Preschool programs for the disadvantaged: Five experimental approaches to early childhood education.* Baltimore: Johns Hopkins Press.

Wein, CA. 1996. Time, work, and developmentally appropriate practice. *Early Children Research Quarterly* (ECRQ), 11(3): 377–403.

White, L. 1994. The national early childhood program accreditation: A parent driven accreditation. *Early Childhood News,* July/Aug., 16–19.

Chapter 5

Organizational Structure

Guide for Readers

- ❖ *The success of a center depends on the personal characteristics and professional background of the administrator.*
- ❖ *The attitude of each employee plays an important role.*
- ❖ *For a center to be effective, policies and procedures must be established for children, parents, and employees.*
- ❖ *A center may or may not have a board of directors.*

 **Stimulator**

As a leading candidate for the director of a *new*, prestigious child-care center, you are asked to prioritize some of your procedures regarding:

1. Processing of applications for:
   a. Teaching staff
   b. Office staff
   c. Support staff
   d. Children

2. Equipping the center:
   a. Office
   b. Classrooms
   c. Support areas (kitchen, outdoors, etc.)
   d. Financial limitations

3. Formulating policies and procedures for:
   a. Employees (expectations, benefits, advancement/termination, vacations, staff meetings, etc.)
   b. Enrollment of children (ages, fees, health/safety, withdrawal, attendance, etc.)
   c. Parent participation (fees, arrival/departure times, visiting, etc.)

4. Unforeseen possibilities/events:
   a. Severe weather conditions
   b. Contagious diseases
   c. Family emergencies—yours and clients' (illness, job changing, financial, etc.)
   d. Unexpected low enrollment or greater demand for higher enrollment
   e. Lack of funds or energy; no community support

5. Personal preferences toward:
   a. A teaching philosophy—is it really the best approach for *these* children?
   b. Experiences for children, families, staff, others
   c. Self-dedication

Where do you start? Are you prepared to attack all of these procedures—either singly or collectively? *Where do you start?*

CENTER LEADERSHIP

For a center to function properly, the personal and educational characteristics of the administrator are very important. One who does not know how to get along with others or does not have the educational background and experience will be less likely to succeed. The following characteristics of an *ideal* early childhood administrator include (but are not limited to) the following:

1. *Education/experience:* Current broad awareness of disciplines related to early childhood education:
   a. *Child development:* Growth and developmental patterns, family relationships, observation, research
   b. *Education:* Curriculum development and instructional theory, research, certification, classroom participation, relationships, assessment
   c. *Finance:* Budgeting and resources
   d. *Management:* Of people and organizations, discipline
   e. *Psychology/philosophy:* Theories, trends, research

2. *Socioculture:* Relationships, diversity, research

3. *Personal characteristics:* Attitude, health, goals, values

See Figure 5–1 for a description of the duties of a child-care center's administrator or director.

General

Secures licensing; meets state, local, and city requirements
Sets goals for center and personnel policies for staff
Reports to board of directors (if applicable)
Supervises curriculum
Helps to implement and maintain goals and objectives
Provides leadership
Keeps records: inventories, repairs, food, personal records of children and staff
Orders supplies, etc.
Prepares budget and oversees expenditures (payroll, equipment, supplies, insurance, etc.)
Collects fees and tuition
Keeps report of expenditures current
Has legal responsibility for safety
Implements values that will further development and provide a healthy environment for each person at
    the center

With/for Staff

Is friendly; interacts with staff on both formal and informal occasions; is caring
Values each person and considers his or her ideas; implements ideas when feasible; does not compro-
    mise on important issues
Prepares job descriptions
Recruits, hires, and oversees staff
Assists in implementing curriculum and school goals
Observes staff and provides frequent feedback
Listens to staff and seeks solutions to problems/suggestions
Provides current staff handbook
Keeps personnel records current and confidential
Encourages staff to join and participate in local, regional, and national organizations, issues, and legislation
Provides "personal space," library and curriculum materials, opportunities for preparation and interaction
    with others

With/for Children

Is friendly; interacts with children on both formal and informal occasions; is caring
Values each child as an individual
Enrolls children and keeps a waiting list
Plans for their health and safety needs
Keeps current records about health of children enrolled

Figure 5–1 Duties of an administrator/director.

For different types of program settings (toddler, Head Start, on-site, private, government, etc.), see Chapter 2. Different types of programs and ownership require different management approaches. This chapter covers management of centers in general; the reader is encouraged to adapt the information to particular settings. See also Chapter 3.

DIRECTOR'S ROLE AT THE CENTER

In this chapter, the role of the director is considered in relationship to the center as a whole and the overall management of it. Chapter 6 will consider the allocation of resources and the management of time. Chapter 7 deals more directly with interactions with people.

With/for Parents

Is friendly; interacts with parents on both formal and informal occasions; is caring
Values parents, their roles and concerns for their children
Informs parents and others about the center; involves them when possible
Prepares a parent handbook and keeps it current
Conducts orientation meetings
Plans and implements parent education activities
Involves parents in school activities when possible
Confers with parents regarding their child's progress
Consults with parents and recommends community agencies for special help when necessary

About Facility

Responsible for building, physical plant, equipment
Plans, allocates, and uses space effectively
Provides custodial care and equipment maintenance
Plans for present and future space needs

For Self

Is friendly, self-confident, and knowledgeable
Values self and all others at the center
Evaluates self and professional responsibilities
Plans and participates in professional growth
Has membership in professional organizations and provides appropriate feedback/support

With/for Community

Is friendly; interacts with community on both formal and informal occasions; is caring
Knows needs of community and participates in activities
Promotes and advertises school
Maintains effective public relations
Knows of and uses referral to community agencies
Is active in professional and legislative activities; encourages staff to join and participate

---

Figure 5–1 *continued*
Source: Some ideas adapted from Click and Click (1990).

Responsibilities and Behaviors of the Director

In his 1989 book *The 7 Habits of Highly Effective People*, Covey describes the characteristics of people who work effectively. In essence, they (1) act responsibly and in a positive manner, (2) have the end goal in mind, (3) prioritize (put first things first) and learn to say *yes* and *no*, (4) think positively—win-win, (5) seek information (to understand) and then to be understood, (6) open their minds and hearts to new options (synergize), and (7) "sharpen the saw" by involving all four dimensions of nature—physical, spiritual, mental, and social/emotional—rather than relying on one or two. Novices would be hard pressed to attempt all seven of these characteristics at one time, but one must begin somewhere. Change takes time, patience, practice, and commitment. Reviewing and practicing Covey's habits can help one to become more effective in the job and more satisfied with oneself. (To practice these habits in an early childhood environment, see participator number 2 under "For either Current or Prospective Center Director/Owners" at the end of this chapter.)

As a follow up, Covey and coworkers (1994) have elaborated on habit 3, "First Things First." (See Chapter 6 for application in early childhood settings.)

In Organization. Seldom does a new administrator step into a job in which all decisions have been made and all problems have been solved— and even if that did happen, there will be adjustments of some magnitude.

The director must carefully study the new surrounding, its people, its physical attributes, its material resources, its goals, its philosophy, and its potential. Either by oneself or with the assistance of others (board, owner, employees, professionals, organizations, etc.), the director will consider the circumstances regarding good educational, financial, and other pertinent criteria. Are procedures mandatory or could alternatives be considered or implemented? How much flexibility is there in adopting, implementing, and evaluating a plan of operation?

In Supervision. The director will be in a supervisory role to all employees, even if job roles are further subdivided. In this capacity, the director will provide program leadership in the development of personnel, curriculum, programs, and contact with individuals outside the center (parents, colleagues, vendors, etc.). Within the center, current literature suggests that supervision is composed of three functions:

1. Improving the quality of instruction ("most important because the only purpose of any program is to help the children and their parents . . . requires specific training or re-

training . . . because of new knowledge, methodological techniques, and even attitudes") (Decker & Decker, 1992)

2. Mutual growth of supervisor and teacher ("both must be committed to a relationship that fosters growth, learning, and exchange of ideas") (Caruso & Fawcett, 1986)

3. Evaluation (supervisor as a role model; observing and conferencing, "collegial rather than hierarchial") (Decker & Decker, 1992)

In Promoting a Healthy Atmosphere. Stress, or burnout ["a syndrome of emotional exhaustion and cynicism that can occur in individuals who spend much of their time working closely with other people" (Pines & Maslach, 1980)], is becoming more and more job related. It comes from several conditions:

> (1) the unexpected is common because of the age of the children and the fact that the curriculum designs in many programs are not highly structured; (2) undesirable working conditions often plague teachers such as unpaid overtime, inability to take scheduled breaks due to staff shortage, and the lack of fringe benefits including medical coverage; (3) early childhood positions are not considered high status jobs by some persons who see play activities as less than real teaching; (4) early childhood teachers are so indoctrinated in the importance of the early years of the child's life that they often feel let down when they do not achieve their lofty goals regardless of the underlying cause (e.g., the teacher, the child, the parents' lack of follow-through, the teaching-learning situation such as lack of equipment or space, or problems in scheduling); and (5) teachers are unable to maintain a detached concern (i.e., they see themselves as surrogate parents). (Needle et al., 1980)

Considering these causes of burnout, it is easy to see that caregivers of young children are most susceptible. Stress may occur as a result of off-the-job conditions as well. Research from the National Day-Care Study found that 30 percent of the caregivers were the sole support of their families and 69 percent provided more than half of their family's income (Ruopp et al., 1970). On the other hand, the

Stimulator   From the following two-column list, identify the behavior (A *or* B) that encourages a good relationship between administrators and staff:

A	B
Interest and respect	Ignoring and discourteous
Friendly treatment	Bias toward races, religions, cultures
Rigidity in practices	Encouragement to be innovative, original
Physical or negative discipline	New ways to handle problems unoffensively
Comfortable, relaxed atmosphere	Strained, offensive atmosphere
Encouragement to discuss problems	Expected to follow "rules" unquestioningly
Blind obedience	Affection, interest, respect, responsive
Cooperative problem solving	Fearful of making mistakes
No time for unnecessary talk	Encouragement to talk about feelings and ideas
Talking behind one's back	Open, constructive discussions

National Child Care Staffing Study found high job satisfaction (Whitebook et al., 1989).

Jorde-Bloom (1988) defined 10 dimensions of organizational climate that, when positive within a program, can help individuals avoid stress. They are: (1) collegiality (i.e., supportive, cohesive staff); (2) professional growth (i.e., emphasis placed on growth); (3) supervisor support (i.e., facilitative leadership); (4) clarity (i.e., clear policies and job descriptions); (5) reward system (i.e., fairness in pay and fringe benefits); (6) decision making (i.e., staff involved in decisions); (7) goal consensus (i.e., staff agreement on goals/objectives); (8) task orientation (i.e., emphasis placed on good planning and efficiency in job performance); (9) physical setting (i.e., spatial arrangement helps staff); and (10) innovativeness (i.e., organization finds creative ways to solve problems). Jorde-Bloom (1988) developed an *early childhood work environment survey* that measures the organizational climate.

Stress may be stimulating unless it is prolonged or gets out of control. Ways stress can be eliminated, or greatly reduced, in a child-care setting include: (1) knowing the developmental stages and expectations of the young children served, (2) planning with flexibility but completeness, (3) keeping records of children's progress in all areas of development, (4) being empathetic but not overly involved emotionally, (5) maintaining good health,

and (6) having someone with whom you can confide (Decker & Decker, 1992, p. 136).

Management Style

There are different styles of management; some directors use a consistent style and others change their styles when confronted with a different situation. In general, management methods can be classed as the following:

Authoritarian: Person in charge makes and implements the decisions, the policies, and the rewards/punishments based on what seems "right" to him/her. There are no choices, no suggestions, no personal decisions. Some employees function well under this type of leadership; others feel smothered.

Laissez-faire: Person in charge is passive, leaves decisions and policy making to others, may give suggestions but does not participate or provide leadership. There are no rules, no boundaries. Experienced employees function better than new ones in this atmosphere.

Democratic: Person in charge involves others in decisions and policy-making processes. It is people- rather than task-oriented. It can be difficult, time consuming, and fluctuating.

According to a classic study by White and Lippitt (1953), there was more productivity, higher quality of work, less discontentment, greater cohesiveness and satisfaction, less absenteeism, and more independent behavior in this group than the other two.

Management is a process whereby, under the direction of a leader, goals of a group can be attained with the least amount of time, energy, and money expended. As noted, there are different management approaches with different outcomes. As is true in many fields (not just child development, finance, business, etc.), theories are accepted, rejected, modified, and misinterpreted. They may be used singly (to strengthen a point) or they may be combined with other fields, such as those in a child development center (child development, finance, social studies, psychology, law, health, and many others). For a more detailed discussion about management, see Chapters 6 and 7.

Beginning and Ongoing Responsibilities

Licensing. Licensing is a major responsibility for the director/manager. Sometimes the owner will be involved, but generally the follow-through for licensing will fall to the director. Before a center can operate, licensure is required by different agencies: city/community, state, federal, and sometimes those of the sponsoring agency. These policies must be carefully followed to assure safety regarding physical facilities (building, playground, vehicles, etc.) and that of the individuals (staff, children, patrons). Space requirements, adult/child ratios, ages of children, transporting children, staff qualifications, and other items covered by licensing are discussed in other parts of this text.

Accreditation. Another of the director's responsibilities will be to see that the center is run in a highly efficient manner. The National Academy of Early Childhood Programs, a division of the National Association for the Education of

Young Children (NAEYC), has set standards for high-quality programs in its pamphlet *Guide to Accreditation* (NAEYC, 1991), which has since been revised as *Guide to Accreditation, Self-Study Validation and Accreditation* (1999). It is designed to improve the quality of care and education provided for young children in group programs in the United States.

The Academy accomplishes this purpose by developing training resources, by providing public information about the importance of high quality early childhood programs, and by accrediting those programs that voluntarily demonstrate substantial compliance with the Academy's Criteria for High Quality Early Childhood Programs. The accreditation process involves three steps:

Step 1—Program personnel conduct a self-study to determine how well the program meets the Academy's Criteria, make needed improvement and report the compliance with the Criteria on the Program Description.

Step 2—Validators make an on-site visit to verify the accuracy of the Program Description.

Step 3—A three-person Commission considers the validated Program Description and makes the accreditation decision. (p. 3)

Accreditation with NAEYC or any other organization (such as National Early Childhood Programs Accreditation—NECPA, discussed in Chapter 4), is entirely voluntary; however, centers that accept and fulfill the requirements can be accredited by the academy (or other programs)—a distinction valued by administrators of early childhood schools and child-care centers because of outside validation of high quality of their programs. Examples of NAEYC accreditation are found in applicable chapters throughout this text.

Some program directors hesitate to seek accreditation for fear their center will not meet the requirements. Before making such a decision, each one should inquire about the qualifications and responsibilities associated with accreditation. Accreditation is actually a self-study process, which frequently shows that such programs can qualify easier than they had thought. All programs have strong and weak areas—they need to be identified and strengthened. One needs to consider the quality of all areas of the program—enrollment procedures, program planning, health and safety needs of children and families, philosophy regarding young children, support and encouragement to staff—and many other facts. Self-study brings out the best in programs and can also change the weakness to strengths.

The accreditation system of the National Academy of Early Childhood Programs is designed to meet two major goals:

1. To help early childhood program personnel become involved in a process that will facilitate real and lasting improvements in the quality of the program serving young children, and

2. To evaluate the quality of the program for the purpose of accrediting those programs that substantially comply with the criteria for high-quality programs.

The governing board of NAEYC voted to explore the feasibility of a "center endorsement project" in 1980 in response to serious concerns about the (a) quality of early childhood programs, (b) the lack of uniform standards across the nation, and (c) the lack of a consensual definition of quality.

"Perhaps the greatest frustration of the last decade" write Bredekamp and Glowacki (1996) "has been that the early childhood profession has evolved a much clearer concept of what quality is in early childhood programs and even what it costs (Willer, 1990) but still cannot begin to figure out how to pay for the full cost of quality." They continue: ". . . we need to do some careful thinking about how our system needs to change internally to be more responsive to programs and parents and better able to sustain continued expansion. . . . These events include policy and regulatory changes, public awareness and demand, and financing. The crisis in quality is now well established in the research; among the solutions is accreditation" (p. 44).

Child Development Associate Credential

Another procedure whereby the administrator can increase the quality of service given and also aid teachers in becoming more satisfied and proficient in their job performance is the Child Development Associate (CDA) credential. A more detailed discussion is found in Chapter 6. Basically, it is established by the Child Development Associate Consortium and is administered by the CDA National Credential Program, headquartered in Washington, DC. It consists of six core competency areas:

1. Set up a safe and healthy learning environment for young children

2. Advance their physical and intellectual competence

3. Build their positive self-concept and individual strength

Facts and Figures

As of January 1996, the National Academy of Early Childhood Programs has enrolled in the accreditation process:

13,258 programs from 54 states, U.S. territories, and commonwealths, and 13 foreign countries; this includes 8,731 in self-study and 4,527 accredited. (Bredekamp & Glowacki, 1996, p. 44)

4. Organize and sustain the positive functioning of children and adults in a group learning environment

5. Bring about optimum coordination of home and center child-rearing practices and expectations

6. Carry out supplementary responsibilities related to the children's program (Sciarra & Dorsey, 1990)

The CDA credential is granted after a candidate has been assessed about the following procedures established by the CDA National Credentialing Program in Washington, DC: teaching behavior with a group of children in a classroom and review of candidate's portfolio demonstrating preparation to be a child caregiver. A parent representative may be asked to provide a summary of evaluations gathered from all parents of children with whom the candidate works. Some colleges provide credit-based CDA courses. Although there are fees associated with participating in this credentialing process, there are also scholarships available and some agencies pay all or part of the fees (Sciarra & Dorsey, 1990).

Few states mandate certification of prekindergarten teachers, however, many states do mandate licensing of child-care programs. CDA credentials are encouraged; Montessori certification is available to graduates of accredited Montessori training programs.

Update on the CDA is reported by Decker and Decker (1997):

Teacher Qualifications in Head Start and Child Care Programs. The Head Start Act mandates that, by 1994, every Head Start classroom will have a teacher with a Child Development Associate (CDA) credential or other appropriate qualification, such as an associate degree in early childhood education/child development. The CDA Consortium grew out of efforts by Head Start to recognize competent performance of staff. (The CDA Award system is described later in this section). (p. 68)

Because of the meager requirements for Head Start and child care teachers, these teachers have far less formal training than teachers in public school programs. The National Child Care Staffing Study (Whitebook, & Associates, 1993) found that only 12% of center staff had bachelor's or graduate degrees in a field related to early childhood education and that 38% had no education related to early childhood education at all. Other staff members were in-between. Although child care is still seen by many as an unskilled occupation, states are beginning to strengthen regulations. Different guidelines are used for minimal staff qualifications and for training. These guidelines include *Federal Model Child Care Standards* (U.S. Department of Health and Human Services, 1985), *Accreditation Criteria and Procedures for the National Academy of Early Childhood Programs* (NAEYC, 1984), and the *Family Day Care Accreditation Profile* (National Association for Family Day Care, 1988).

The CDA credential is used by teachers in a variety of child-care settings, including Head Start. The CDA program has had an interesting history. Launched in 1972, the consortium's goals were to establish competencies needed for working in early childhood education, to develop methodologies for assessing such competencies, and to issue appropriate credentials. On March 25, 1975, the board of directors formally adopted the Credential Award System and authorized the awarding of the CDA credential to anyone who could demonstrate competence by completing the requirements of the consortium. Because of federal funding cutbacks, the consortium disbanded in 1979, and credentialing was shuffled around. In 1985, the NAEYC took responsibility for credentialing, establishing a separate, not-for-profit corporation—the Council for Early Childhood Professional Recognition.

Policies and Procedures

A center functions more smoothly when it has written policies regarding operation, employees, children, and parents. These policies should show consistency of philosophy, goals, and implementation. In some cases there will be a board of directors, a governing board that establishes policies. Mutual agreement and feasibility are

Stimulator Using the following four familiar areas of your teaching space (indoor and outdoor), suggest ways to plan for "all children" (handicapped/nonhandicapped, immature/mature, younger/older, social/nonsocial, active/quiet, etc.):

Area	Props Provided	Outcomes Expected
Housekeeping		
Creative arts		
Outside (large muscle, group)		
Language (stories, etc.)		

Children within your group include: six children on appropriate developmental schedule (whatever that is!), two children with disabilities (you select what kind), and two "ethnic" children. How do you plan so the day will be rewarding to each child? [Some directions for thought: weather, group or individual play, large/small muscles, active/quiet, health/safety, age appropriate, activities that could be expanded/reduced, routines (relaxed/rushed).]

important considerations; however, available resources are also a factor.

For policies to be effective, they must (1) be clearly defined as rigid (due to laws, liability, and so on) or flexible so as to inform staff and patrons about those policies that can be changed by decision of the administrator (or owner) and those policies that are outside the control of the administrator (owner), and (2) make a clear distinction between statements that are *policies* and that are *procedures to implement a policy.* In this text, *policy* and *procedure* are used as shown in Figure 5–2.

For convenience and clarity, each center should have an operations manual that includes the center's philosophy, policies, procedures, bylaws, job descriptions, salary schedules, and other important information about the center (e.g., possible sponsorship, funding, and history). Each employee and board member should have access to the operations manual and the parents' handbook (see Appendix A). (Note: Privately owned nonincorporated schools are not required to have bylaws; however, bylaws are required by the Internal Revenue Service if the center is a corporation seeking tax-exempt status. Bylaws strengthen written policies and explain how the business will be conducted.)

Job descriptions and responsibilities must be carefully outlined and impartially distributed. In-

dividuals at the center must be valued and respected for their personal contributions, regardless of assignment, age, sex, culture, or pay.

Need for Policies and Procedures. Policies and procedures should be written for the following important reasons:

1. To clarify direction and provide checkpoints
2. To provide consistency and ensure fair treatment
3. To protect the rights of the center, board members, employees, children, and parents
4. To help orient board members and employees
5. To assist with proposals, funding, and licensing
6. To provide evidence in legal matters
7. To support financial records for auditors
8. To use in advertising

All individuals involved with the center should be covered in the policies and procedures. Employees who know to whom they are directly responsible generally feel more at ease and perform their tasks better (see Figure 5–3). The center must plan for its growth and development, promote personal development in individuals, be

Figure 5–2 Distinctions between policy and procedure. *Note:* For clarity, indicate which policies are mandated by federal or state laws (unchangeable).

Policy	**Procedure**
What is to be done	*How* it is to be done
By whom: Board, owner, other	*By whom:* The director (and/or staff)
Areas of coverage: Center, board, personnel, children's programs, parent involvement (see Figure 5–4)	*Areas of coverage:* Same as policy
Degree: General, flexible but implementable, mandated	*Degree:* Detailed for clear and uniform implementation, but some allowance for freedom/ creativity; short rationale; input from staff when possible

Figure 5–3 Organizational chart.

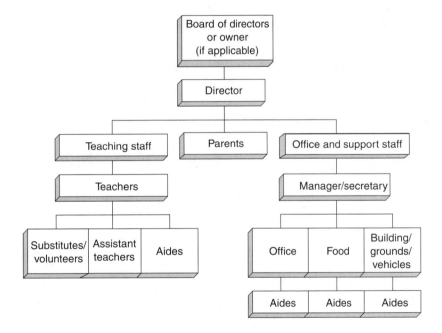

a basic support system to the family, and give employees the opportunity to share their talents while gaining knowledge and experience. The children should gain self-confidence and self-control in a healthy, harmonious, happy, and safe environment. Families can gain strength and support from the center through awareness of their roles and appropriate expectations for parents and their children. The center can offer support to the community through educating the public about children and group care, teaching about different cultural and ethnic groups, providing quality child care and employment, and developing mutual understanding and respect.

Centers that carefully define and enforce policies run more smoothly. For example, consider a policy about tuition. When the policy is clear, less income will be lost due to absenteeism of children, turnover, and delinquent payments. The fee policy should meet the center's needs and include the following:

1. A deposit when parents commit to enroll their child. This can be applied toward the first tuition payment or retained until the child is withdrawn from the center and all monetary commitments have been met. The amount of the deposit varies among centers from a full month's tuition to a percentage of that amount to retain a place for the child.

2. Notice of a specified number of weeks before the child is withdrawn from the center

(The deposit helps cover costs if advance notice is not given.)

3. Information about refunds or allowances regarding frequent, periodic, or extended absence of a child

4. Response time limit within which replacement children must be enrolled without losing their place on the waiting list

5. Definition of what the fee covers (tuition, insurance, meals, etc.)

6. Payment particulars—when, how, and where

Policy Characteristics and Categories. Some characteristics are common to all policy statements. Policies must conform to laws and regulations, be all-inclusive and complete, reflect philosophy and goals, be noncontradictory, be consistent

---

 **Stimulator**

The Family Care Center is opening soon. The director and teachers hold a planning meeting. As the meeting unfolds, it is evident that organizational policies and procedures are vague, hard to implement or evaluate, slanted in favor of management, and ineffective. The policies need to be proposed, discussed, and established so employees understand and support them. Critical issues are as follows:

1. Authority lines—What is the chain of command? How many levels does it have? How much power is there at each level? How are grievances handled? Are there other issues?

2. Job descriptions—What are the responsibilities of each employee? How are changes initiated, negotiated, or assigned? How are coordinated and overlapping jobs handled?

3. Center responsibility—What does the center expect from each employee? What are the privileges given each employee? How are expectations and rights conveyed to the employee? What steps are taken to ensure the rights of both the center and the employee?

4. Policy implementation—Which policies are mandated by others (laws, liability, funding agency, etc.)? How can policies be reviewed, clarified, modified, deleted, or added? How are infractions resolved?

Assume the role of chairman of the policy-making group. Outline the procedure and priority for dealing with each issue. Note that this Stimulator could be a common malady of various centers.

Note: The reader may wish to refer to Chapter 2 to review the different types of centers, as policies and procedures are reviewed there. Different sponsorship (nursery schools, parent cooperatives, public schools, and Head Start) requires a different approach to policies and procedures.

in their interpretation and follow-through (with allowance for infrequent or unusual circumstances), be specific, and provide relative constancy but allow for revision, if warranted. Each of these facets needs careful consideration. Most early childhood and child-care programs use the general policy and procedure categories summarized in Figure 5–4.

Developing Policy That Supports Organizational Structure.   Consistency between center policy and organizational structure facilitates the center's operation. Such detriments as "responsibility without authority, lack of support, low participation in decisions, competition or lack of it, may make us silent, resentful, poor team players, and less than ideal members of an organization"

states Michael T. Matteson (Short Takes, 1983, p. 26). Definite authority lines must be established; an incomplete organization can create stress. Peter Drucker explains, "The only things that evolve by themselves in an organization are disorder, friction and malperformance" (Short Takes, 1983, p. 26).

The key to developing an organizational structure is to focus on *goals* and *activities* rather than on the people in the organization. This requires reviewing the program and objectives, designing short and clear job descriptions, allowing freedom to act, and assigning positions to maximize knowledge and skills.

The ways center employees feel and react toward others and toward their jobs affect the center's success. Conflict can be a healthy sign if it is

Figure 5–4 Procedural responsibilities by category.

Category	Responsibility
Administrative	Board of directors, director, operations
Staff/personnel	Recruiting, hiring, assigning, tenure, terminating, salary and benefits, leaves, evaluation, training and career development, promotion, progress (Decisions are generally made by the director, subject to board approval.)
Business	Funding, budgeting, purchasing, accounting
Children	Selection, admission, attendance, number, age span, teacher-child ratio, programs, records, welfare, admission of handicapped or ethnic children, hours, days, year-round or school-year (The board must approve the director's recommendations.)
Parents	Needs, staff involvement, confidentiality, education, participation, suggestions or complaints, procedure for admission and withdrawal of children, fee payment, involvement with staff
Records	Confidential or open to staff; types for children and staff, responsibility for location
Public relations	Advisory committees, volunteers, use of facilities, agency and association interaction, communication, support to and from community, publicity

viewed and handled constructively. Administrators sometimes confuse their personal or professional goals with the goals of the center, causing them to feel they have failed if problems arise, if goals are not readily achieved, if they or others feel discouraged, or if ideas are challenged. A realistic attitude toward such problems can actually improve the center *and* move the administrator toward his or her personal goals.

As administrators organize "WHAT should be done, by WHOM, with WHAT RESOURCES, to achieve WHICH OBJECTIVES, by WHAT TIME (Streets, 1982), they should consider end goals and methods of reaching them rather than looking at and solving small, and sometimes insignificant, problems. Procedural steps include identifying and grouping goals and objectives, selecting qualified people, setting the time frame and work site, outlining the plan, and correlating the tasks. Subdividing tasks and specifying sequences then seem less complicated and more achievable.

Two important guidelines should be considered in determining policies: (1) They should provide parameters to reach predetermined goals, being concrete enough to coordinate ideas, reflect ethics, and support a plan of action. (2) They should provide for evaluation or modification and be based on reliable, relevant research evidence, educational theory, or data related to a particular population or center.

It would be elaborate, and perhaps of little value, to list the organizational structure for different types of centers, as regulations bylaw, personal preference, type of ownership, ages served, and so on make each situation unique.

Because organizations change name, location, and sponsorship, it would be of little value to list them in this publication. Check with your local library or specific organizations.

To check the climate at the center, Neugebauer (1990) has prepared an organizational health checklist of 40 items covering such areas as planning and evaluating, motivation and control, group functioning, staff development, decision making

and problem solving, financial management, and environmental interaction. This author issues two cautions in using checklists: (1) the items should be looked at as goals to strive for, not minimum standards, and (2) administrators may not be too objective in the evaluation. However, it is worthwhile for an administrator to look over the checklist as an indicator of the climate of the center.

Governance Structure

Board of Directors.   The Child Welfare League of America (established in 1920), a principal organization in establishing standards for child-care agencies, publishes the *Guide for Board Organization and Administrative Structure.* It notes that most states require *not-for-profit* programs to have a board of directors or a governing board comprising the people that program serves. Under its bylaws, the board usually (1) formulates major policies for achieving overall goals of the program, (2) adopts all proposed policies planned by the director, (3) supports the annual budget, (4) approves the hiring of all personnel, (5) develops criteria for evaluating the program, and (6) participates in community relations (Decker & Decker, 1988, pp. 169–170). Figure 5–5 summarizes the kinds of things usually covered by bylaws.

When a board does exist, several important questions need to be asked, such as the following:

1. What is the function of the board?
2. How are members selected?
3. How long is a term of office?
4. What provisions exist for reelection, reappointment, or removal from office?
5. What are their individual duties and responsibilities?
6. When does the board meet?

Board Duties and Responsibilities.   The major responsibilities of the board are to define the scope and services of the center, determine policies and procedures, hire personnel who support the

Article I.   Name, address, and telephone number of center

Article II.   Purpose of center

Article III.   Board of Directors
    3.1   The board of directors shall consist of _____ (list whether it is a set number or a minimum and maximum number) of members.
    3.2   Board members will be selected based on the following criteria:
        _____.
    3.3   Board members will be elected for a _____ year term of office.
    3.4   Functions (powers, responsibilities) of the board are as follows (give particulars such as amending policy, preparation of financial statement, etc.): _____
    3.5   Vacancies (reelection, reappointment, or removal of board members) shall be handled _____ (state the conditions).
    3.6   State all conditions as they apply to your particular center.

Article IV.   Officers
    4.1   The following officers shall be elected for a term of office as noted (or chairperson, etc.):
        President   ___ years   Secretary   ___ years
        Vice-president   ___ years   Treasurer   ___ years
    4.2   The officer shall have the following responsibilities (itemize each one separately and completely):
        President (or chairperson):   Secretary:
        Vice-president: Treasurer:
    4.3   The replacement of officers, at expiration of term or for other conditions, shall be as follows (give specifics):

Article V.   Committees
    5.1   The following committees will be formed (give specifics):
    5.2   Board members will be selected to serve on the committees by the following procedure (give specifics such as to replace outgoing members, by their expertise, as needed, etc.):

Article VI.   Amendments
        Addition, deletion, or change in bylaws shall be done in the following manner (specify conditions such as at annual meeting, by majority or unanimous vote, etc.):

Article VII.   Meetings
    7.1   Meetings will be held _____ (specify).
    7.2   Emergency meetings can be called or canceled by (specify):
    7.3   Items for discussion must be submitted to the secretary by _____ (specify).
    7.4   A quorum will require _____ members to conduct center business.

Article VIII.   Other matters
    8.1   Employee grievances not resolved by the director can be referred to the board in the following instances and manner (specify):
    8.2   Grievances of the director will be resolved by (specify):
    8.3   Make clear and precise methods to handle urgent or unusual items of business.

Figure 5–5   Suggestions for bylaws for a child-care/education center.

center's philosophy, provide necessary training, and oversee the total operation of the center. In carrying out these functions, the board develops and implements the annual budget, provides facilities and equipment, evaluates the ongoing program and personnel, solves major problems, and recognizes the relationship between the center and the community.

Boards function in different ways; some make most decisions, and others make few or no decisions but rely heavily on the discretion of the director. Board members should be interested and responsible; they should be given adequate direction and the freedom to pursue it. They should neither make all decisions nor merely approve recommendations. Board members may be compensated with pay or privileges; however, many serve because of interest and civic pride, satisfaction being their only reward.

Each member of the board should have a clear and precise job description. As new members come onto the board, they are given a committee assignment, preferably within their area of expertise. Sometimes they will serve on the same committee as the member they are replacing, but committees may be reorganized as individuals with different expertise are added to the board. One member (or one committee) may be responsible for policies, another for budget, and still another for public relations. Thus, each board member is a contributing member and an authority in handling the assigned area. Figure 5–6 gives a checklist for board members to use in evaluating their performance on a board of directors. Figure 5–7 lists some of the committees common to most boards.

For clarity and protection, a center may wish to add additional information to the bylaws regarding parliamentary authority, amendments, nondiscrimination, handling of funds (deposits, check-writing, investments, etc.), and/or dissolution of the organization. These items may or may not be of value; therefore, careful consideration should be taken to ensure adequate bylaw coverage for each particular center.

Selection of Board Members. Some states specify how many members boards are required to have. The number should be large enough to handle the duties, but not so large as to be unwieldy or unproductive. Small centers may have five or fewer board members, each being a chairperson of a committee, with all other members assisting;

Figure 5–6 Checklist for board members.

1. How well were you oriented for your duties and responsibilities?
2. How easy or difficult will it be for the board to accomplish individual and group assignments? Is there commitment? Do some members dominate or withdraw from discussions?
3. How often does the board review the goals of the center to see if they are on target?
4. Is there sufficient dialogue to inform and convince members of issues and options? Who (individuals or committees) makes final decisions?
5. What input does the board receive on policy and financial matters?
6. Recall your qualifications to serve on the board and ways you can make a positive difference in the operation of the center. Recall the qualifications of other members and how you can work together effectively as a team.
7. What constructive suggestions could you bring to the attention of the board?

Executive: This is a very powerful committee. During emergencies, it can act in place of the total board. It assigns members to committees, considers needed changes and possible action, and gives information to appropriate committees.

Personnel: This committee takes responsibility for the personnel at the center—mainly the director—by preparing job descriptions, advertising for personnel, interviewing, hiring, and firing when necessary. It helps locate and screen candidates for vacancies and may make recommendations for additional or specific personnel or action. The committee, the director, or the total board may make final hiring decisions, depending on the bylaws.

Finance: This committee prepares the budget and oversees expenditures, so it must be familiar with the general operation of the center. It arranges for an annual financial audit and may be responsible for salary schedules and major purchases.

Building (or Building and Grounds): If the center is looking for land, a building to purchase or lease, or an architect, this committee would investigate and advise on the appropriate action. The committee also purchases, repairs, and maintains the center's equipment and facilities, both indoors and outdoors.

Program: This committee is responsible for programs for the children, the parents, and the staff. The program for the children includes all procedures involving the children. Parent programs include parent education, participation, social services, and other matters. The staff program includes in-service training, promotion, evaluation, and general staff needs.

Nominating: Whether board members are elected or appointed, this committee prepares a slate of candidates and assumes the responsibility of orienting new board members.

Figure 5–7   Committees common to most boards.

large centers may have a chairperson and members of each committee, with no members serving on more than one committee.

Members may be appointed or elected, and membership is contingent on fulfilling the assignment as well as willingness to serve. Professionals, parents, and members of the community should be diversely represented, with consideration given to future board members based on their backgrounds, personalities, occupations, sexes, ethnic groups, ages, and points of view. The board may wish to specify that a certain percentage of the board consist of parents of currently enrolled children or people in specific occupations. Centers have different ways of orienting new board members. Some prepare a packet of materials and hold an orientation meeting similar to those for new employees (see Chapter 6). Some invite new members to the final meeting of the board before they take office; some assign a "buddy" on the board;

some have new members meet individually or collectively with the director; still others invite new members to visit informally with staff and parents. A combination of any of these options is helpful to new board members. Being well versed in their positions gives new members a better understanding of the center and their responsibilities as governing agents.

If board members are elected rather than appointed, clear information about the needs of the center and responsibilities of the board members should be disseminated among those voting. Only the best people should be recruited. People who have insufficient time, skills, or knowledge to function effectively on the board can volunteer in their fields of expertise at appropriate times, but should not attempt to serve on the board.

Term of Office and Duties of Members.   The terms of office, tenure, and the duties of the board members, whether elected or appointed, and methods of removing or replacing members will be carefully described in the bylaws of the center.

An experienced board will have valuable suggestions about the length of service, replacement for unexpired terms, deficiencies in the board, training new members, and other matters that apply specifically to a center.

Someone is responsible for planning and making an agenda for each meeting—whether it be a governing board or an advisory committee. All important topics should be listed with time to respond to each. Rushing through a meeting or agenda may expedite the present but make serious problems for the future. All members of the meeting should feel that the time has been productive and will make a difference to the people they serve.

Boards constructed for new organizations may be entirely appointed; ensuing boards are usually elected following a process stated in the bylaws and required by law. As future members are appointed or elected, careful consideration should be given to the personality and experience of the candidate, along with the current composition of the board so that meetings and governance of the center will proceed productively. People from the fields of health, education, finance, and law are often desirable candidates for board members because of the expertise they bring to the center. However, candidates who may not understand or support the goals and philosophy of the center should not be approached for service even though they may bring a new dimension to the board.

Prospective board members should be informed about liability insurance. Sciarra and Dorsey (1990) report: "Large agencies usually provide liability coverage for board members, but smaller organizations may be unable to afford this coverage. Prospective board members should be informed that they must provide their own liability coverage if that is the case. Director liability is controlled by state law and additional information on this topic can be obtained from your insurance agent or attorney" (p. 47).

The board should have continuity. A good procedure is for members to serve staggered terms, with new members being oriented by continuing members. Terms of office vary. One year barely gives members a chance to understand and respond in a helpful way; however, some individuals are willing to serve only a 1-year term. A 3-year term, with members going off and coming onto the board yearly, gives time for members to gain understanding of what the center is and does; however, some people may be reluctant to serve for this length of time.

Tenure, requirements for membership, number of members, and duties must (1) be specified in the bylaws, (2) be supportive of program philosophy, and (3) be in accordance with state laws.

Reelection, Reappointment, and Removal.   The bylaws of the center should include clear statements about reelection, reappointment, and methods of removal if members fail to perform as expected. When reelection and reappointment are permitted, the number of consecutive terms should be precisely stated, as should the method for filling vacancies created by unexpired terms. Removal may be requested by the individual, center, parents, or board. Each case should be considered individually, with options, recommendations, and support from the entire board for actions taken. See Figure 5–8 for a list of questions to use when considering a candidate for a child-care center board.

Board Meetings.   In the early stages of orientation or reformation, board meetings may be held more frequently, for longer time periods, or in subgroups. Regardless of the frequency or duration of meetings, they should always be conducted in an organized way with recorded minutes that are read at the next meeting for corrections or approval.

Boards can be assets or liabilities to the center. When they devote most of their time to unimportant matters, recruit unqualified members, and delegate authority to members who lack the knowledge to make appropriate decisions, they

1. Do you understand your responsibilities as a board member?
2. Is the board well organized to accomplish its responsibilities?
3. Is there an ongoing board development process? (recruit)
4. Are board members committed to the mission of organization?
5. Does the board closely monitor the performance of the organization?
6. Do board members make well-informed budgetary decisions?
7. Does the board exercise effective oversight of the organization's financial management?
8. Is there a healthy tension in relationships between board and staff members?
9. Does the board have an effective system for evaluating the performance of the executive director?

Figure 5–8 Board member questions.
Source: Nine questions for the dedicated board member, 1990.

exhibit their shortcomings. Boards are most effective when they are informed, when they respond quickly to problems, when they have good public relations with the community, when they support the director and staff, and when they provide appropriate legal, financial, and moral support for the operation of the center. Board members can be helpful in informal ways as well—finding equipment to be donated, involving community members as resources, promoting the center, and obtaining financial support.

When there is no number of board members stipulated, it is best to keep the number small and limit the expectations from these members. Some owners/directors, recognizing their limitation in certain areas, may seek board members who have specific expertise. The important issue is to see that there are enough board members to cover the needs of the center, whether it is large or small, recognizing that fewer numbers have more individual power than a larger number. Board members, generally unpaid, must be willing to fulfill the assigned responsibility and not feel overwhelmed or burdened by it.

Centers Without Boards of Directors

Having a board is not always necessary or feasible. Small centers, private profit-making corporations, employer- or union-subsidized day care, public school systems that operate child-care programs, and university programs usually do not use a board. Some centers have no need for a board, and others may be governed as part of an existing organization (such as those listed previously) and must comply with overall policies and procedures, thus making a central board inoperative.

When boards of directors are not needed for legal or structural reasons (check state statutes), centers may elect to have an advisory board. When there is no board, the tasks usually assigned to the board belong to the director or proprietor.

CHAPTER SUMMARY

1. Policies and procedures are necessary, contain certain characteristics, and can be categorized.
2. The organizational structure of the center reflects consistency in philosophy, goals, and purposes but may change as these components are evaluated. The structure defines lines of authority, assigns duties and responsibilities, and shows regard and

respect for all individuals involved regardless of ages, responsibilities, or pay rates.

3. The director, whose personal characteristics and training are very important in the leadership of the center, is responsible for setting and enforcing the policies of the center. The director also performs (or assigns) all administrative tasks when there is no board of directors.

4. When there is a board of directors for the center, the director works with it to ensure a safe and healthy environment for children, families, and employees.

5. There are two kinds of boards: governing and advisory.

6. Governance over a board of directors includes setting meetings, conforming to bylaws, supporting committees, replacing members whose terms expire (or request replacement), and other matters as they arise.

7. Where there is no board of directors, administrative tasks are performed by the director, proprietor, or assignee.

PARTICIPATORS

For All Students

Write your own personal philosophy about young children including (among other things):

1. Your attitude toward child care—working with infants/preschoolers

2. Your enjoyment of young children

3. Your ability to work with adults (colleagues, parents, others)

4. Your personal attributes that you can share with children and adults

5. Your future goals toward child care and/or teaching young children

6. Your flexibility in working with children from diverse backgrounds (cultures, ability/disabilities, socioeconomics, others)

7. Your perception of how young children learn—appropriate curriculum, "balanced curriculum," age-appropriate behavior, introduction of new ideas, meeting individual needs, etc.

8. Perception of others regarding early childhood education—and how it affects you

9. Add items of personal current or future interest, expertise, and/or concern regarding your future with young children

For Those Currently Involved in a Center

1. Review the educational philosophy for the center and determine ways to implement it into policy and procedural steps. What are the pitfalls? How can they be made more palatable (or changed)?

2. Prioritize the items in number 1 in order of importance and include resources required to implement them.

3. If the center has a board of directors and it does not currently have an operations manual, prepare one to distribute to board members. If an operations manual has been written for the center, review it and make appropriate suggestions to the administrator.

4. If the center has a board of directors, consult them about ways to improve meetings, strengthen interpersonal relationships, and increase revenue. If your center does not have a board of directors, contemplate the value of forming at least an advisory board.

5. You are the new director of an ongoing center. There is currently no board of directors. The owner asks you to prepare an item for the monthly staff meeting regarding your recommendation about adding a board of directors. Begin your preparation by listing advantages and disadvantages. Prepare a convincing, thoughtful, and unbiased recommendation. Following a group discussion, be prepared to make a recommendation.

6. Review current center-community relationships and design new ways the board (where applicable) can strengthen them.

7. Visit different kinds of centers. Ask to see governing flowcharts. Compare private-ownership, school-district, industry-based, and community-sponsored programs (with and without boards of directors).

8. Analyze your own needs. Identify a bothersome organizational problem you would like to reduce or eliminate. Design and implement a procedure, allowing enough time for a true test. Evaluate your progress. Do you need to try a different strategy, is the present strategy worth continuing, or has it reduced or eliminated the problem?

For Students or Prospective Center Directors/Owners

1. Prepare an operations manual to distribute to future board members.

2. Write a tentative policy statement and goals for a child-care center.

3. Prioritize the policies from number 2 in order of importance. Specify implementation methods, the needed funds, the required staff, and the allotted space.

4. Visit different kinds of centers. Ask to see governing flowcharts. Compare private-ownership, school-district, industry-based, and community-sponsored programs (with and without board members).

5. From a copy of the bylaws (or an interview with a director) of a child-care center that has a board of directors, determine the following: (a) number of members, (b) selection procedure, (c) term of office, (d) duties, (e) committees and their responsibilities, (f) meeting frequency, and (g) other items of interest.

6. If possible, interview a board member of a child-care center. Ask about specific duties, initial involvement with the center, general

feeling between the board and the center, and expertise. Keep the interview constructive and short.

7. You have been hired as the director of a new child development center. It is optional whether or not there will be a board of directors. One of your assignments is to prepare an item for the first staff meeting regarding your recommendation about a board of directors. Begin your preparation by listing advantages and disadvantages. Prepare a convincing, thoughtful recommendation.

8. Formulate some guidelines for the center and decide if they are policies or procedures (see Figure 5–2).

For Either Current or Prospective Center Directors/Owners

1. Using the stress reducers suggested by Jorde-Bloom or Decker and Decker in this chapter, prioritize the ones that would be most effective in reducing *your* stress *or* make and prioritize your own personal list of stress reducers. Make a conscious effort to keep your stress under control by doing something about it before it gets out of hand.

2. Refer to the discussion of Covey's *7 Habits* (Chapters 7 and 8). Practice each habit in an early childhood setting:

   a. Act responsibly and positively. For at least a 2-hour period, jot down on a small note pad occasions where you or a teacher have listened carefully to another adult or child and responded with a positive comment or gesture.

   b. Before you begin an activity, have clearly in mind what results you can expect from the children—their abilities, their creativeness, their frustrations.

   c. As you formulate a lesson plan, make a prioritized list of the steps to accomplish the purpose of the plan. (Ask how can this topic or these activities benefit the children, what steps are necessary, and what ones are insignificant or even confusing?)

d. Select a specific relationship (adults, children, or child-adult) where you would like to develop a win-win agreement. Propose a situation (either verbal or participant), involve the individuals, and be prepared to mediate, if necessary, so that the situation can be resolved in a win-win situation for both (children taking turns, adults reaching consensus, etc.).

e. Watch for a situation where you and another person (adult or child) tend to confront each other. Pause, think of what the person is saying, then try to understand what the words and tone are really saying. Respond with understanding rather than judgment.

f. Next to the names of a few people who irritate you list a few reasons why this occurs with each person. In another column write some things *you* could do to reduce this irritation—look for new possibilities, new alternatives, new commitments.

g. Following the "7 habits philosophy," make a list of things you can (and will) do to "sharpen your own saw":

Physically	*Spiritually*
Mentally	*Socially-emotionally*

3. Consider writing management goals for (a) a new center, (b) an ongoing center, (c) one with public or federal money, or (d) one as a part of a larger organization (university, chain, on-site). How are they similar? How are they different?

REFERENCES

Bredekamp, S., & Glowacki, S. 1996. NAEYC accreditation: The first decade of NAEYC accreditation: Growth and impact of the field. *Young Children*, March, 38–44.

Caruso, J. J., & Fawcett, M. T. 1986. *Supervision in early childhood education: A developmental approach.* New York: Teachers College Press.

Click, P. M., & Click, D. W. 1990. *Administration of schools for young children* (3rd ed.). Albany, NY: Delmar.

Covey, S. R. 1989. *The 7 habits of highly effective people.* New York: Simon and Schuster.

Covey, S. R., Merrill, A. R., & Merrill, R. B. 1994. *First things first.* New York: Simon & Schuster.

Decker, C. A., & Decker, J. R. 1988. *Planning and administering early childhood programs* (3rd ed.). Upper Saddle River, NJ: Merrill/Prentice Hall.

Decker, C. A., & Decker, J. R. 1992. *Planning and administering early childhood programs* (5th ed.). Upper Saddle River, NJ: Merrill/Prentice Hall.

Decker, C.A., & Decker, J.R. 1997. *Planning and administering early childhood programs* (6th ed.). Upper Saddle River, NJ: Prentice Hall/Merrill.

Jorde-Bloom, P. 1988. *A great place to work: Improving conditions for staff in young children's programs.* Washington, DC: NAEYC.

National Association for the Education of Young Children. 1991. *Accreditation criteria & procedures: Position statement of the National Academy of Early Childhood Programs* (revised). Washington, DC: Author.

National Association for the Education of Young Children. 1999. *Guide to Accreditation, Self-study, Validation, and Accreditation.* Washington, DC.

Needle, R. H., et al. 1980. Teacher stress: Sources and consequences. *Journal of School Health*, 50, 96–99.

Neugebauer, R. 1990. Organizational health checklist. *Exchange*, April, 38–41.

Nine questions for the dedicated board member: Exchange evaluation instrument. 1990, June. *Exchange*.

Pines, A., & Maslach, C. 1980, Spring. Combating staff burn-out in a day care center: A case study, *Child Care Quarterly*, 9, 6.

Ruopp, R., Travers, J., Glantz, F., & Coelen, C. 1970. *Children at the center* (Vol. 1 of *Final report of the national day-care study*) (p. 224). Cambridge, MA: ABT Associates.

Sciarra, D. J., & Dorsey, A. G. 1990. *Developing and administering a child care center* (2nd ed.). Albany, NY: Delmar.

Short takes. 1983. *Child Care Information Exchange*, Sept./Oct., 26.

Streets, D. T. 1982. *Administering day care and preschool programs.* Boston: Allyn & Bacon.

White, R., & Lippitt, R. 1953. Leadership behavior and member reaction in three "social climates." In

C. Cartwright & A. Zander (Eds.), *Group dynamics* (pp. 585–611). New York: Row, Peterson.

Whitebook, M., Howes, C., & Phillips, D. 1989. *Who cares? Child care teachers and the quality of care in America: Executive summary national child-care staffing study.* Oakland, CA: Child Care Employee Project.

Whitebook, M., Phillips, D., & Howes, C. 1993. *National Child Care, Staffing Study revised: Four years in the life of center-based child care.* Oakland, CA: Child Care Employee Project.

Chapter 6

Management of Personnel

Guide for Readers

❖ All teachers and staff must be emotionally stable, physically healthy, professionally trained, and must work harmoniously to provide the best environment and experiences for all who participate at the center.

❖ One important source for preparing early childhood professionals, The National Association for the Education of Young Children (NAEYC).

❖ The Child Development Associate (CDA) program lists qualifications for teachers and/or directors.

❖ There are essential characteristics for early childhood education programs.

❖ Research studies emphasize the importance of teacher education, relationships, sensitivity, involvement, interaction, and compensation.

❖ Accreditation of early childhood programs is available.

❖ There is an increasing, not decreasing, demand for quality care of young children outside their home.

❖ Good maintenance of child care personnel can be provided through organizational goals, motivation, communication, supervision, evaluation, and compensation.

INTRODUCTION

This chapter begins with reference to the goals from the Accreditation Criteria (National Association for the Education of Young Children, 1991a):

Administration (Goal E): Goal/Rationale: to efficiently and effectively provide for the needs and growth of children through good-quality care, for parents through good communication skills, for the staff members through good working conditions, for the community through support, and for the center through financial stability and overall concern for what happens at the center.

Staffing (Goal F): Goal/Rationale: sufficient, trustworthy, and trained staff capable of promoting the development of the whole child (physically, socially, emotionally, cognitively, and spiritually), allowing for individualized care, small group, and teacher/child interaction, and opportunities for cooperation and understanding among children.

ADMINISTRATION

To ensure that a program runs efficiently and effectively, the director should keep written policies, procedures, records, and relationships current. Reviewing any and all of these areas frequently and conscientiously will facilitate a smooth operation at the center. Staff meetings may be devoted to any of these topics. The director should meet periodically with employees, parents, and board members (if applicable), and arrange to meet with potential clients, employees, and community members as needed.

At least annually, the director and staff should have an assessment of written policies and procedures of: the program, employees, children, the board (if applicable), financing, insurance, emerging procedures, community resources, staff meetings and other pertinent happenings (adapted from Administrative Report of NAEYC, 1999c, pp. 51–54).

STAFFING

Group Size and Composition

Each teacher will be given primary responsibility for specific children within a designated space. In this way, a teacher can have personal contact with, develop attachment to, plan meaningful learning experiences for, and provide for the individual and group needs of each child. The ratio of staff to children will be in compliance with licensing regulations taking into account the ages of the children, whether or not there are special-needs children, the amount of space, the type of program activity, time of day and season, and other factors.

Additional staff, substitute staff, and volunteers brought into the group must meet the appropriate staff qualifications with the exception of parents (or guardians) who come to make special presentations or for specific purposes.

The NAEYC Guidelines for Preparation of Early Childhood Professionals, adopted in 1994(a), identifies the field of early childhood education, which is unified by a common core of "knowledge that deepens and expands with specializations" at advancing levels of preparation. At each of these levels, "the professional is expected to reflect on his or her practices that result in improved programming for children and also contribute to continuing professional development. In addition, at each of these levels, the professional is expected to advocate for policies designed to improve conditions for children, families, and the profession."

1. At the associate level: The graduate demonstrates knowledge of theory and practices necessary to plan and implement curriculum for individual children and groups.

2. At the baccalaureat level: The graduate demonstrates the ability to apply and analyze the core knowledge and to systematically develop curriculum and develop and conduct assessments of individual children and groups.

3. At the master's level: The graduate demonstrates greater capacity to analyze and refine the core knowledge and evaluate and apply research to improve practices.

4. At the doctoral level: The graduate conducts research and studies practices to expand the knowledge base and influence

systems change. At each of these levels, the professional is expected to reflect on his or her practices to result in improved programming for children and also contribute to continuing professional development. In addition, at each of these levels, the profession is expected to advocate for policies designed to improve conditions for children, families, and the profession.

It is noted that this document "does not promote any single route to the acquisition of an early childhood certificate, license, or degree but rather calls for all teachers of young children from birth through age 8 to be adequately prepared to demonstrate the knowledge, performance, and disposition specific to their teaching specialization, regardless of their employment setting or their position" (pp. 3–4).

Qualifications and Roles of Personnel

Good health: physical, psychological, emotional, social, personal, and moral

Personal qualities necessary to work with young children

Qualifications for a specific role

Teaching staff (frequently called primary program or classroom personnel) includes supervisors, teachers, associate teachers, assistant teachers, substitute teachers, trained aides or volunteers, curriculum specialists, and others.

Support personnel (support or facilitate caregiving and instructional program): dietitians, cooks, medical staff, psychologists, caseworkers, maintenance and grounds staff, dual-capacity people, general office workers, transportation drivers, general volunteers, and others. These people may or may not be on-site continually.

Auxiliary staff may include repair people, board members, accountant, sanitation services, and others.

Director. This title is frequently given to the person legally responsible for the total program and services. This role includes but is not limited to:

- Director-teacher wherever needed
- Resembles principle in public school
- Business manager
- Go-between the center and board (when applicable)
- Initiator/enforcer of program philosophy and goals
- Center policymaker, interpreter, enforcer, recruiter, employer
- Supervisor and trainer of teaching staff
- Supervisor of building, program, and employees
- Record keeper for center, children, and employees
- Preparer of budget
- Overseer of income and expenses

The qualifications of a director vary depending on the program's organizational pattern, ownership of center, and funding. (See Figure 5–1). The director needs to be able to do the following:

- Meet state and federal licensing requirements (including department of education certification)
- Exhibit physical and mental stamina
- Be warm and sensitive to children and adults
- Have personal sense of security and honesty
- Pass antiabuse and anticriminal checks

Teaching Staff. Several principles must be kept in mind when working with the teaching staff. They need to (1) understand and support the program's philosophy, (2) consider the development and needs of children they teach, (3) take a holistic approach to children and families, (4) have clear plans about what they are teaching, and (5) have ways of evaluating what has been presented.

Despite the well-established link between staff training and the quality of child-care services, more than two thirds of the states fail to require preservice training for child-care center teachers (Morgan et al., 1993).

Early Childhood Teacher Assistant

Role. Helps implement program activities under direct supervision

Qualifications. Previous training/experience are optional

Early Childhood Associate Teacher

Role. Helps implement program activities independently and may be responsible for a group of children

Qualifications. Minimal early childhood preparation (may hold a CDA credential or an associate degree in early childhood education/child development)

Early Childhood Teacher

Role. Responsible for a group of children

Qualifications. A professional with an undergraduate degree in early childhood education/child development; experience helpful

Support Personnel. The responsibilities vary because of the diverse needs of the center. However, each person must be well trained, experienced, healthy, and add a dimension of their expertise so the center will function healthily, profitably, and professionally. Some federal or state requirements may be imposed for specific jobs.

PROFESSIONALISM

There is sufficient evidence from the frequent turnover and low wages that our national community is not valuing employees who work with young children. It has been suggested that "the time is ripe for advocates to press for greater collaboration among agencies serving young children to meet their full range of needs" by urging increased funding to Head Start, expanded child-care assistance to needy families, welfare reform to guarantee AFDC (Aid to Families with Dependent Children) families access to good-quality child care, and strong state/community partnerships regarding child care (Children's Defense Fund, 1992).

The National Association for the Education of Young Children (NAEYC) has worked more than 60 years to promote high-quality early childhood programs for all young children and their families, with two major efforts to support this goal:

1. Facilitating the professional development of individuals working for and with young children from birth through age 8

2. Improving public understanding and support for high-quality early childhood programs (NAEYC, 1994b)

The article outlines a framework with four components:

1. Current diversity of early childhood programs and preparation of service providers with (a) roots from social welfare and education, traditional part-day preschool/ nursery programs, and little consideration of parental needs for full day programs; (b) need for before- and after-school programs; (c) need for care and education of interdisciplinary, family-based services for infants and toddlers or developmental delays in the least restrictive environment; (d) diversity of settings; and (e) preparation of providers, which varies between states and within states.

2. A lattice description of professional knowledge, performances, and dispositions connected with the early childhood profession's diverse roles, levels, and settings: (a) hands-on training of teachers; (b) need for teacher certification; (c) programs to meet needs of children and families; and (d) adequate compensation for teachers. "In 1990 half of all teachers in child care centers nationally earned less than $11,000 annually, while the annual earnings of family child care providers before expenses averaged less than $10,000 per year" (Willer et al., 1991,

p. 71); (e) need to distinguish the early childhood *field* ("anyone engaged in the provision of early childhood services") from the early childhood *profession* ("those who have acquired some professional knowledge and are on a professional path . . . such as the CDA credential and/or transformed into credit toward another professional credential or degree") (Willer et al., 1991, p. 71).

3. Key elements regarding professional development that include experiences and training in (a) child development, (b) individualizing teaching practices and curriculum, (c) safety and health for children and environments, (d) developmentally appropriate curriculum for all aspects of development, (e) guidance and group management, (f) relationships with children and families, (g) diversity of children, families, cultures, society, and (h) management—with a commitment to professionalism.

4. Guidelines for compensation that link increases in professional development and improved performance to increased compensation NAEYC, 1994b. Early childhood professionals with comparable qualifications, experience, and job responsibilities should (a) receive comparable compensation regardless of the setting of their job, (b) receive compensation equivalent to that of other professions with comparable preparation, experience, and job responsibilities, (c) not experience a differential in compensation because of the age of children served, (d) be encouraged to seek additional preparation and should be rewarded accordingly, (e) receive an adequate benefits package, and (f) have a career ladder with increased compensation based on performance and participation in professional development opportunities (p. 77).

Spodek and coworkers (1988) identified at least three meanings for the term *professional*, stating that as long as the focus is on any one of the definitions, individuals will embrace one of the terms and reject the others.

1. To distinguish someone who receives payment for doing something without describing their skill, for example, "professional singer"

2. To denote a high level of skill and competence, as in "a professional performance"

3. To refer to the learned professions (medicine or law) or the semiprofessions (teaching and social work) that are characterized by specialized knowledge not available to others and less direct contact with the client

The March 1992 issue of *Young Children* included pros and cons of professionalizing the early childhood field. The May 1993 issue of *Young Children* contains information about the advantages of professionalization, minimizing the potential negative effect, and resulting in higher-quality early childhood programs. One article (Willer & Bredekamp, 1993) proposes a need for a new paradigm that builds "upon the key dimensions of each definition, that is, that early childhood professionals be well-prepared, knowledgeable individuals who demonstrate high-quality performance resulting in better outcomes for children" (p. 63). They note that the early childhood profession was among the first groups in the nation to recognize the value of a competency-based assessment system, and continue: "The challenge now is to identify comparable assessments of core knowledge for all of the roles and settings for which assessment is needed. At the same time, such a conceptual framework must identify steps to professional development and bridges from one role or setting to another" (p. 63). They conclude:

A new paradigm will only result if we ensure that professional preparation

is meaningful, relevant, and accessible to all early childhood practitioners in all roles and settings;

contributes to an increased understanding and respect for all families and children and fosters communication and trust between parents and teachers/caregivers, rather than increasing the separation between professional and client;

is linked to opportunities for higher compensation and status for individuals with greater skills and knowledge; and enhances individuals' knowledge and competence for providing high-quality, developmentally appropriate programs for all young children. (p. 66)

As of 1991, the most comprehensive national study to collect baseline data on state policies affecting career development in early care and education was *Making a Career of It: The State of the States Report on Career Development in Early Care and Education* (Morgan et al., 1994). The study documented policies that affect the training of practitioners, both those who prepare in advance, before employment, and those who receive specialized training after beginning their work with young children. The study's timing provides baseline data prior to the implementation of the Child Care and Development Block Grant.

As noted in the study, three major policy areas that influence practitioner training and career development in the United States [based on data from all states' child-care licensing agencies, departments of education, and lead agencies for the Child Care and Development Block Grant (CCDBG) higher education institutions, and key informants (also District of Columbia and New York City)] are as follows:

1. Regulation (licensing and teacher certification)
2. Training opportunities (all options, including noncredit and credit training)
3. Financing of training (federal, state, and local public funds for training and private sector funding)

The summary, highlights, and major findings of the study stated: "millions of practitioners are not required to have any early childhood training. Training that develops the full range of essential early care and education knowledge and skills is not consistently available, accessible, or linked coherently. Financial support to pursue training is frequently insufficient" (Morgan et al., 1994, p. 82).

The vision from the study suggests

regulatory, training delivery and funding policies are inextricably tied, so altering only one of them will not produce viable, long-term solutions. From our study, we developed and refined a new vision for career development for the field, which consists of five elements:

1. *Systemic planning.* Understanding how the parts of the whole—regulation, training delivery, and financing—need to fit together.
2. *Effective quality controls for the profession* . . . should reflect the field's knowledge base, ensure skills, be appropriate for specific roles, and be effectively implemented.
3. *Progressive, role-related, appropriate, and articulated training* . . . need not be a dead-end career. . . . Training should be appropriate to specific roles and child populations and should be offered at different levels of knowledge and skills. . . . Credits from individual courses and certificate and degree programs should count toward, or articulate with, one another.
4. *Recognition and reward systems* . . . rewarded with increased responsibility, compensation, and status.
5. *Expanded and coordinated financing.* . . . Funding should be available not only to those pursuing their training prior to employment but also to those who need help paying for ongoing career development while employed.

Making a Career of It makes many policy recommendations among the following: planning, regulations—progression of roles; training—make it count, improve access to credit-bearing training, articulate programs, offer leadership training; and funding—increase reimbursement rates to government subsidy, restructure pay schedules (publish recommended salary scales by role), allocate 5 percent of direct service funds to training. And a note that "most of the action to improve the quality of training will have to occur at the state level, with strong federal leadership and support . . . needed changes, multiyear efforts" (Morgan et al., 1994, p. 83).

Additional findings about training as reported in the Morgan et al. (1993) study include ineffectiveness because it is repetitive, does not address the full spectrum of needs of the early childhood field, inequities between both noncredit and credit training, and few linkages among and between noncredit and credit training programs. These facts paint a bleak picture. In addition, training is inaccessible to many practitioners, advanced career training is not addressed, there is little articulation between and within noncredit training and higher education, and only limited and sporadic funding is available for training.

Code of Ethics

The NAEYC (1994a) has published a code of ethics for early childhood education personnel. (See Also Chapter 4.) The commitment details ethical responsibilities to four groups: children, families, colleagues (employers and employees), and community and society. For each group there are ideals and principles. For example, Section I (ethical responsibilities to children) includes the following:

Ideal (I-1.5) To create and maintain safe and healthy settings that foster children's social, emotional, intellectual, and physical development and that respect their dignity and their contributions

Principle (P-1.1) Above all, we shall not harm children. We shall not participate in practices that are disrespectful, degrading, dangerous, exploitative, intimidating, psychologically damaging, or physically harmful to children. *This principle has precedence over all others in the code.*

It is important that NAEYC has provided "A Code of Ethical Conduct and Statement of Commitment" as a tool in working with young children; and it is helpful to recall the priorities, issues, and support for the "ideas and practices we all aspire to but don't always articulate clearly" (NAEYC, 1994b, p. 56).

The code is a tool to better understand our role in the lives of children and families. It helps us to be ethical and professionally responsible through three steps:

The first step . . . is to decide what makes a troubling situation a dilemma. Are the best interests of various people in conflict, a lack of staff agreement or from the practice of school clashing with the needs of a child or family?

The second step is to sort out the issues that must be addressed by different people—the teacher, the parent, the director.

The third step is to refer to the Code of Ethics for help in thinking about priorities and responsibilities in determining a plan of action. (p. 57)

Not only should employees sign a code of ethics similar to the cited NAEYC code, but employees should also sign a code of confidentiality specific to the center. Child-care workers are privy to a plethora of family and child information and must realize that disclosure of such information to certain parties would be grounds for dismissal.

CDA Information

For those who are new to the CDA program, the initials stand for the Child Development Associate program. (See Also Chapter 4.) It represents a national effort to credential qualified caregivers who work with children from birth to age 5. The Council for Early Childhood Professional Recognition operates the CDA credentialing program as a major national effort to improve the quality of child care. Focusing on the skills of child-care providers, the program is designed to provide performance-based training, assessment, and credentialing of child-care staff, home visitors, and family child-care providers.

To the question, What is a CDA?, the Council pamphlet (CDA professional preparation program, 1989) states:

A CDA is an individual who has successfully completed a CDA assessment and who has been awarded the CDA Credential. S/he is able to meet the specific needs of children and works with parents and other adults, to nurture children's physical, social, emotional, and intellectual growth in a child development framework.

The CDA has demonstrated competence in the CDA competency goals through her/his work in a center-based, home visitor or family day care program. In addition, a person who has demonstrated bilingual competence is a CDA with a bilingual specialization. (p. 3)

The CDA is listed as a qualification for teachers and/or directors in the licensing regulations in 46 states and the District of Columbia. Thirty-seven states include the CDA as an "equivalent qualification" for director positions; 21 states plus the District of Columbia include the CDA as an "equivalent qualification" for teaching positions. Learning is divided into three phases: fieldwork (participation in a child-care program on a daily basis, readings, and exercises), course work (series of group seminars), and final evaluation (organize and practice a cohesive set of practical skills while working with young children, guided by a field advisor). The Council sponsors a CDA Scholarship Act, for which interested candidates (at least 18 years of age and holding a high school diploma or GED) may apply by contacting the agency in their state or call the Council for assistance at (800) 424-4310, ext. 211.

Six competency goals demonstrated by CDAs are as follows:

Goal 1: To establish and maintain a safe, healthy learning environment

Goal 2: To advance physical and intellectual competence

Goal 3: To support social and emotional development and provide positive guidance

Goal 4: To establish positive and productive relationships with families

Goal 5: To ensure a well-run, purposeful program responsive to participant needs

Goal 6: To maintain a commitment to professionalism

Findings from the 1994 survey (Latest CDA survey results are in!, 1994) revealed

many consistencies among this population, with few changes from previously surveyed CDAs. The data indicate that (1) CDAs are fairly well-educated, having taken some college courses before obtaining the CDA Credential . . .; (2) salary increases do come with obtaining the CDA. . . . However, the actual amount of the increase has been consistently low (less than $500 a year); (3) more CDAs than ever before are now able to obtain early care and education CDA training at a postsecondary education institution and in the community. As a result, there has been an increase in CDAs seeking that training. Also, more child care workers outside Head Start are seeking the nationally recognized CDA; (4) few CDAs leave the child care field. On average, from 1983 to 1994, 95% of CDAs remained in child care after obtaining the nationally recognized CDA.

Certification

The Association of Teacher Educators and the National Association for the Education of Young Children issued a joint position statement regarding early childhood teacher certification (NAEYC, 1991c). (See Also Chapter 4.) These guidelines were developed to inform decision makers about certification standards for teachers in programs serving children from birth through 8 years of age to ensure that all young children and their families have access to qualified early childhood teachers by guiding teacher educators and policymakers to "(1) make informed decisions about early childhood educator teacher certification, (2) evaluate existing teacher certification standards, and (3) advocate for more appropriate early childhood teacher certification standards" (p. 16).

Several hundred early childhood and teacher education professionals participated in developing these guidelines. An initial draft was reviewed at an open hearing by participants at the NAEYC Annual Conference, and a revised draft was then sent to a selected national sample of over 900 early childhood teacher educators, state department certification specialists, and the NAEYC Teacher Education Guidelines Panel. Two separate mailings requesting feedback were sent to selected Association of Teacher Educators (ATE) members. Feedback was also sought from 27 related professional organizations. It was adopted by the executive boards of the ATE and the National Association for the Education of Young Children in July/August 1991.

NAEYC (1991c) announced the National Institute for Early Childhood Professional Development in September 1991.

One of the goals of the Institute is to influence the quality and content of early childhood teacher preparation programs and to advocate for policies that promote an articulated career development system for the field. . . . Our goal is to achieve specialized early childhood certification in every state, which in turn will influence the content and delivery of preparation programs throughout the nation. (p. 16)

The significance of specialized knowledge in early childhood education is also confirmed by research findings that early childhood teachers with a strong background in early childhood development and education interact with children in ways that are more growth promoting (Ruopp et al., 1979; Weikart, 1989). (See also Chapter 5 for supporting information.)

Essential Characteristics of Early Childhood Educators

Teachers of early childhood education must do the following:

1. Be educated in the liberal arts and in a variety of disciplines to be able to use interactive teaching strategies that will advance children's developing understandings

2. Be well informed about developmental theorics and their implications for practice

3. Understand the significance of play and ways to facilitate enriching play in their classrooms

4. Understand families as the primary source of children's learning, respect diversity in family structure and values, and develop skills in interacting with parents to enhance education success of their children

5. Acquire ability to work cooperatively with other adults

6. Reflect on their own present professional development and seek further knowledge and experience

The joint statement further recommends that state departments of education (certifying agencies)

ensure free-standing certification distinctive from existing certifications for elementary and secondary education, . . . set age- and content-congruent standards across the 50 states for reciprocity reasons and education by appropriately prepared teachers, . . . meet the standards of early childhood preparation programs set forth in this document, . . . recognize that teacher preparation programs are inseparable regarding the care *and* education of children, . . . initiate articulation agreements between two-year and four-year institutions within a state in order to provide a continuum of teacher preparation opportunities, promote professional development, and facilitate professional growth, . . . and create ways to coordinate the efforts of those who teach children in public and private school settings. (Latest CDA survey results are in!, 1994, p. 19)

Certification standards for teachers of children from birth through age 8 will require demonstration of professional knowledge, abilities, and application regarding (1) child growth, development, and learning; (2) family and community relations; (3) curriculum development and implementation appropriate for specific age and ability levels; (4) health, safety, and nutrition; and (5) field experiences and professionalism. All of these requirements will be carefully defined in the certification.

Training and certification requirements vary from state to state; however, some states are providing more stringent standards for child care, preschool, kindergarten, and primary personnel. More states are requiring mandatory training

Name	Type of Training	Certification
Certificate	High schools and vocational programs	Child-care aide
Associate degree	Community colleges	Child-care aide, primary child-care provider, assistant teacher
Baccalaureate	Four-year college programs (ages and grades vary from state to state—prekindergarten and kindergarten may require extra hours)	Teacher certification
Master's degree	Varies by state	Program directors, assistant directors, career in teaching
CDA National Credentialing Program (a)	CDA Professional Preparation Program: meet age (18) and education (high school or GED) requirements; have professional advisor, field work, course work, and final evaluation	Caregivers in center-based, family day care, and home visitor programs
CDA National Credentialing Program (b)	CDA Direct Assessment Method: meet age (18) and education (high school or GED) requirements; have work experience, formal training in ECE, be observed, Professional Resource File; written assessment and interview	Caregivers in center-based, family day care, and home visitor programs.

Figure 6–1   Types of programs.
Note: For additional information about CDA, see the information in this chapter and Chapter 4.

before certifying a person as a child-care worker (Morrison, 1991). Figure 6–1 shows the types of certificate programs available.

Teacher's Interaction with Young Children: Results of Several Research Studies

1. Teacher Training.   The NAEYC has developmentally appropriate practice guidelines regarding teachers' classroom interactions (Bredekamp, 1987; Bredekamp & Copple, 1997) as do the ac-

creditation guidelines by National Academy of Early Childhood Programs (Bredekamp, 1985).

Teacher training programs place a heavy emphasis on effective teacher interactions with children (e.g., Hendrick, 1996; Spodek & Saracho, 1994). Changes in licensing regulations regarding training of child-care providers probably can improve the quality of teacher-child interactions (Kontos & Wilcox-Herzog, 1997, p. 11).

Research consistently shows that training is an important predictor of involved, sensitive teacher-child interactions. It is therefore very important to have trained teachers in classrooms and child-care homes.

Differences in training are frequently found to relate to variations in how teachers interact with children:

1. A study based on two large data sets revealed that teachers with more education are more responsive and sensitive in their interactions with children than those with less education (Howes, 1997).

2. Changes in licensing regulations regarding teaching of child-care provider improved the quality of teacher-child interactions in Florida classrooms (Howes et al., 1995).

3. Teachers with CDA training were more sensitive but not more involved than teachers without CDA training.

4. Teachers with better training tend to interact with children more responsively and sensitively.

5. In a study of family child-care providers, those with more family child-care training tended to be more sensitive and less detached than did providers with less training (Kontos et al., 1994).

6. Research contradicts the notion that a good teacher is "born to the job" and that sensitive, responsive interactions are inhibited by advanced training (Howes, 1997). In spite of this evidence, most states still do not require child care to have specialized training (Hayes et al., 1990). Consequently, the responsibility for seeking and completing training falls to individual teachers. To attract teachers, the training needs to be affordable and accessible, as well as available at both entry and advanced levels. Although the responsibility for seeking advanced training will probably always lie to some degree with individuals, it is also important for early childhood educators to advocate for more stringent state regulations on training for child care staff (Kontos et al., 1994).

Research has shown that classrooms with a teacher-directed, didactic focus typically have teachers who exhibit less warmth, sensitivity, and verbal stimulation (Kontos & Dunn, 1993; Stipek et al., 1995). Although it is not clear whether curriculum shapes teachers' behavior or if teachers choose a curriculum that fits their style, it is reasonable to assume that when teachers work to enhance the developmental appropriateness of their program, they are probably also enhancing their interactions with children. (Kontos & Wilcox-Herzog, 1997, p. 10).

Part of teacher training should be to impart knowledge to the learners, but also to teach them how to think, learn, and also how to evaluate, adapt, and disseminate what they learn—learning is a lifelong process requiring critical thinking, reflection, application, and self-direction. The idea of memorizing meaningless facts for the satisfaction of a teacher is archaic, wasteful, and intolerable. As teachers in early childhood education, we need to prepare ourselves to be active, lifetime problem solvers for the benefit of ourselves, young children everywhere, and the future for all.

Volunteers in the early childhood classroom are a largely untapped resource. "In our aging society, well-educated, accomplished baby boomers, retiring early and eager for volunteer work that leaves them free to travel or hold part-time jobs, have many skills and talents to offer young children. . . . It seems a match made in heaven—the wisdom of age paired with the wisdom of young. I predict your child care center will benefit immensely from bringing the outsiders in, welcoming talented, caring volunteers into your playroom" (Horsfall, 1999, pp. 35–36).

Adult Education Principles.   Knowles (1980) advocates four basic principles regarding the characteristics of adult learners: (a) the self-concept of an adult is one of an independent, self-directed human being; (b) adults have an extensive bank of experiences; (c) adults' readiness to learn is closely related to the developmental tasks of their social roles; and (d) the adult's perspective on

 **❖ Stimulator**

Make a list of suggestions about how and where you can recruit volunteers. How can you make the experience meaningful to them? How can you retain them? How do you decide what quality, characteristics, and talents would benefit your group of young children?

In some communities there may be an agency where volunteers can be identified. Before you seek volunteers, carefully prepare information that identifies the job to be done, the requirements of volunteers, and value/benefits to the person, the hours, the type of work, and so forth so there will be no misunderstandings. If there are choices of how the person can serve, make them known at the beginning. Look for community volunteers that meet your specific needs. Make an appointment for them to see the center, meet some of the teachers, children, and parents. Be sure to give your volunteer back-up support and guidelines regarding activities, discipline, choices, interaction with children/adults, activity schedule, and the like. Make the experience a healthy, rewarding one for all concerned!

❖ Stimulator

When beginning an experience in a new classroom or with new children, as quickly as possible, learn the name, age, and a brief physical description of each child—have an interaction with each child, where possible. Note how you became acquainted with each child. Make a self-commitment to further these relationships or build new relations with each child.

learning is one of immediate application of knowledge rather than on future application.

Implications for Teachers in Helping Young Children Learn (Wadlington 1995)

1. Help them to identify "what" it is they want to do and "how" they can do it.

2. Assist them in clarifying their desires through means they understand (discussion, role playing, creative problem solving, participation, etc.).

3. Assist them in tasks and roles, acquiring materials, and basing their actions on their developmental abilities and safe actions.

4. Meet the needs of the children (abilities, objectives, etc.).

5. Assist them in analyzing problems, suggesting solutions, practicing safe solutions, and evaluating various outcomes.

2. Teacher/Child Relationships. Sensitive caregivers are important to parents (Kontos et al., 1994). Research is beginning to help us to sort out how and why teacher-child interactions are important. As that relationship grows, it fosters other aspects of children's development (Kontos and Wilcox-Herzog, 1997).

The importance of relationships between adults and children's development has been documented (Elicker & Fortner-Wood, 1995). One study in university preschool classrooms found that children were playing with teachers very close by (but not necessarily interacting) just over half of the observation time (Kontos & Wilcox-Herzog, 1996). A companion study revealed that when teachers were near a child (within 3 feet), they interacted with that child only about 18 percent of the time (Wilcox-Herzog & Kontos, 1996). In public school pre-K classrooms, children were observed in proximity to teachers 29 percent of the time (Farran et al., 1991). The above data are consistent with those from the national Life in Preschool study conducted in Head Start, child-care, and preschool classrooms in which nearly one-third (31 percent) of the children received no individual attention during the lengthy observation and, incredibly, in 12 percent of the classrooms, one half or more of the children received no individual attention (Layzer et al., 1993).

Teachers are not necessarily inattentive; they were shown to be actively involved with children about 71 percent of the time. From the child's per-

Stimulator Using Wadlington's (1995) list for helping young children learn, prepare an activity that would help adults to build relationships with children. Consider:

Strategy 1: Getting acquainted with the children—help them to know and trust each other.
What self preparation will you do? How can you learn the names, ages, physical description, etc. of each child involved? Make your information positive! How will you record information so that it will be useful?

Strategy 2: Identify your individual feelings regarding each child involved.
What are your interests? What props do you need? How will you handle interruptions?

Strategy 3: Initiating the activity:
How will you approach each child?

Strategy 4: Keep daily or weekly information regarding individual children (developmental changes, particular activities, own attitudinal changes, etc.).
How will you document your notes so they will be useful now and later?

Strategy 5: Identify different stages in young child; watch for changes as they mature in different areas of development.
Can you identify changes in development?

Strategy 6: Understand your own temperament and that of individual children.
How does each child relate to you? Are you comfortable with different behaviors?

Strategy 7: Write your personal philosophy about early childhood education; enhance your own interaction with others (children and adults). Eventually you may wish to investigate two sides to an issue. Share your findings with others.
Are there some philosophical issues related to early childhood education that you do not understand or that make you uncomfortable? If so, what can you do?

Also consider issues such as how you will interest and involve the children; by whom and how will observations be recorded (time, number of children, etc.); how can you determine the developmental abilities of the children to make sure the experience will be worthwhile; how much do you know about the interests, developmental skills, and cooperation of the participants; why are you interested in these particular individual children; what do you hope to learn from this experience; how to you propose to use the information obtained?

Alternate Stimulator Select *one* of Wadlington's (1995) strategies and do an indepth study of it.

---

spective, the data are likely to show that each child interacts with teachers relatively infrequently, but when it is conducted from the teacher's perspective, the data frequently show that teachers are very involved with children (Erwin et al.,1993; Layzer et al., 1993).

Children outnumber teachers in early childhood classrooms; therefore teachers distribute their attention across children in varying ways. Teachers interact more frequently with children who seek adult contact, whose behavior requires frequent intervention, who spend more time in activities that require adult assistance, and who are personally more appealing to the individual teacher. Studies documenting the low frequency of children's interactions with teachers in early childhood classrooms suggest that the influence of teacher-child interactions on children must be exerted through quality rather than quantity (Kontos & Wilcox-Herzog, 1996, pp. 4–5).

Researchers, parents, and expert teachers all agree about the importance of teacher-child

❖ **Stimulator** With a child in your classroom, or in another appropriate setting, consider these activities for both male and female children. Select a child who especially needs some individual attention and ideas about the male role. The activities listed can be with one's own children, with one child, with a group of children (as in child care, school, church, public meeting, etc.).

1. If you have males in your family (husband, father, brother, grandfather, uncle, friend, etc.) ask one to join the children in an activity of his specialty such as woodworking, sports, pets, occupation, dancing, food preparation, etc. The activity need not be exclusively "male." Provide appropriate "props" so the children can safely practice the activity often.

2. Invite male and female parents to visit or participate when convenient.

3. Show interest in things children bring each day—pictures from home, special gifts, souvenirs, or books. Have a special place to keep the items from being lost or destroyed during the day.

4. Go on field trips where males work, play, and so forth.

5. Pay special attention when fathers bring or pick up their children.

6. Encourage parents to have special routines at home where the child can interact with males—bedtime, physical activity, or sharing time.

7. Include activities often that involve male models (books, puzzles, building, games, etc.).

8. Initiate various activities that meet the needs of individual children in your classroom and involve male models.

9. Remember that many of your children need to see good female models, too! And some children need to learn techniques of getting along with peers and adults!

10. Suggest ways males (dads, friends, etc.) could interact with preschoolers.

11. Review your own attitudes about contributions men make to the development of young children.

12. Review your own relationship with a male model during your early years. How has this influenced your attitude toward men and young children?

13. Suggest ways you could encourage more male contacts in one's home or a child-care center.

interactions in early childhood classrooms, yet researchers have only recently begun to more formally document exactly how these interactions take place and how variations in these interactions are related to behaviors and other outcomes in children (Kontos & Wilcox-Herzog, 1997).

Men in the Lives of Young Children (Involving men in the lives of children, 1999.   National Association for the Education of Young Children.) Many young children have little involvement with a male model. Teachers of young children (especially infants and preschoolers) are dominantly female. Where can a child from a single-parent family (usually mothers) learn about the male role? In my university experience, there have been excellent male professors and outstanding male students. Children (both girls and boys) flock around these men whenever they come into the laboratories. Many children have little or no exposure to men in their lives—at home or at school. Where do they get their role models? Television, videos, movies, computer games, and books are limited and questionable sources because they frequently depict men as being harsh and violent.

3. Teacher's Role.

In general, the teacher's role focuses on interactions with children and includes (among other things) socializing each individual, providing appropriate ways for them to act and react, encouraging their play activities, monitoring their behavior for safety, creating a stimulating environment, giving them a "thirst for knowledge," and meeting the needs of individual children and families. What an important undertaking!

Early in the discussion of the teacher's role, attention should be focused on an important fact: *Too few teachers are aware of how rarely each child in their classroom receives individual attention—and some even less than others;* perhaps this is partially due to individual characteristics and the nature of the relationship between the adult and each child. Thus, it is important that teachers/caregivers consciously try to distribute their attention among all the children in their classroom/home. The NAEYC accreditation guidelines (Bredekamp, 1985) place a high priority on individual interactions between teachers and children throughout the day.

In one study of teachers and children involved in dramatic play, researchers not surprisingly found that teachers frequently shift roles depending on children's play behavior (Enz & Christie, 1994).

When children were roughhousing and~~ ~~ing over toys, teachers tended to use mor~ directive roles rather than socializing, co~ ones. There was also some evidence that tea~ tended to prefer one role over another and~ their preferred role more frequently (Enz~ Christie, 1994).

Conversations between teachers and childre~ can be measured in two ways: <u>how often</u> and <u>what type.</u> There is typical teacher-child talk all the time, but individual conversations between child and teacher are infrequent:

1. In one university-laboratory setting of teachers talking to children, the children are very likely to be recipients of stimulating questions or bits of information rather than directives (Wilcox-Herzog & Kontos, 1996).

2. Teachers generally did not express feelings or attitudes with the children or talk to them about social relations (McCartney, 1984).

3. During 2-hour classroom observations in midwestern child-care centers that were judged mediocre in quality, the most frequently observed interactions between teachers and children were positive guidance (e.g., praise, nurturance, and redirection) and limit setting. Least frequent interactions involved divergent questions and elaboration of children's play activities. Data suggests: (a) the caregivers' interactions with children tend to center around guidance, not on facilitation of children's free-play activities and (b) that teachers' talk to individual children is relatively infrequent and that the quality of that talk is likely to be related to the quality of the program (Kontos & Dunn, 1993).

Bloom (1997) states: "Achieving a~ ~ quality of work life is both a goal ~ it is something we work ~ means by which w~ mate makes i~ the ne~

Goal consensus—staff support of philosophy, goals, and objectives

Task orientation—good planning, efficiency, and cooperation

Physical setting—conducive to carrying out one's responsibilities

Innovativeness—center adaptation to change; ways to solve problems.

4. Teacher Sensitivity. This refers, generally, to how warm and attentive teachers are with the children in their classrooms and how quick they are to comfort children in times of need as opposed to teachers who are detached, generally unresponsive, harsh, critical, and quick to punish.

A large study of child-care centers (Cost, Quality, & Child Outcomes Study Team 1995) found that on a scale of 1 (never true) to 4 (often true), trained observers typically rated teachers 3 on sensitivity and 2 on harshness/detachment. Another study reported similar results for child-care center teachers' sensitivity and slightly lower results for harshness and detachment. Results also were similar with a sample of family child-care providers (Kontos et al., 1994). Overall, these data indicate that teachers are typically somewhat sensitive and not very harsh or detached.

"Researchers demonstrate a pattern of positive relationships between children's sensitive, [involv]ed interactions with teachers and chil[dren's] enhanced development. The impact of [the]se of interactions are likely to be seen in [children's] cognitive, socioemotional, and lan[guage develo]pment" (Kontos & Wilcox-Herzog, [1997; see] discussions on teacher/child re[lationship, teac]her's role involvement, and [involvemen]t, and influences on teacher-[____ in] this chapter.)

[Do teac]hers moderate their behavior [toward such ch]aracteristics as gender, per[sonality, or soc]ioeconomics? Research [has be]en observed to:

[____ 1975; Kontos &

Give more affection to girls (Botkin & Twardosz, 1988; Kontos & Wilcox-Herzog, 1997)

Respond more negatively to boys (Wittmer & Honig, 1988)

Respond more favorably to girls (Galejs & Hegland, 1982)

Researchers do not believe that teachers necessarily make these distinctions intentionally; rather the differentiation is more likely the result of deeply ingrained patterns or behavior typical of our culture. We know less about how other child characteristics, such as personal style, ethnicity, or socioeconomic status, relate to ways in which teachers interact with children. Several studies indicate that teachers do moderate their behavior as a function of these child characteristics (Galejs & Hegland, 1982; Ogilvy et al., 1992; Quay & Jarret, 1986). (Kontos & Wilcox-Herzog, 1997, p. 401).

5. Teacher Involvement. Teacher involvement refers to the intensity and responsibility of teachers' interactions with children (Howes & Stewart, 1987) and can vary from nonexistent or ignoring to physical means, such as verbalizing, interactive play, or comforting a child. "Research provides inconsistent information on how typical each level of involvement is in early childhood programs (Kontos & Wilcox-Herzog, 1997, p. 401). One study reported very low levels of teacher involvement in center-based care, reporting that when teachers were within proximity of a particular child, they ignored that child 61 percent of the time if he was an infant and 79 percent of the time if he was a preschooler. Infants in this study received responsible involvement only 27 percent of the time, but preschoolers received responsive involvement just 10 percent of the time (Whitebook et al., 1989a).

Another study, in contrast, reported that infants in center-based care were ignored by teachers 27 percent of the time, whereas preschoolers were ignored 28 percent of the time. Responsive involvement occurred 43 percent of the time for infants and 31 percent for preschoolers—an encouraging change (Cost, Quality, & Child Outcomes Study Team, 1995).

Family child-care providers were observed ignoring children 20 per cent of the time when they were in proximity and being responsive 54 percent of the time (Kontos et al., 1994). Thus "family child care providers appear to be more involved with the children in their care than center-based teachers. These results may reflect the smaller groups of children and the more intimate homelike setting" (Kontos & Wilcox-Herzog, 1997, p. 6).

Researchers have provided some evidence that children's cognitive development is related to teacher-child interactions. For example, in the family care study Kontos and coworkers (1994) found that children who engaged in more frequent and higher quality play with objects experienced more frequent responsive interactions with their family child-care providers. In a study in British child-care centers Melhuish and colleagues (1990a, 1990b) demonstrated that children who received less verbal communication and less responsiveness from their teachers displayed poorer language development. And further, in the National Child Care Staffing Study, children who experienced more responsive teacher involvement exhibited higher levels of language development (Whitebook et al., 1989a).

Preschool children (but not infants or young toddlers) in center-based care were more competent in their peer interactions when they had more frequent responsive involvement with their teachers (Whitebook et al., 1989a). File and Kontos (1993) also reported that teachers' interactions with children were related to children's competence with peers. Results from the Bermuda day-care study (Phillips et al., 1987) indicated that children who experienced more verbal interactions with their teachers were more intelligent, task-oriented, considerate, and sociable. Interestingly, the amount of positive teacher interactions and teacher *un*involvement were both positively related to children's competence with peers.

Children's emotions in early childhood programs are related to their interactions with teachers. Hestenes, Kontos, and Bryan (1993) found a relationship between amount of teachers' responsive involvement and children's affect in child care centers: Children who experienced more frequent responsive involvement from teachers displayed more intense positive affect (taking into account the child's temperament).

Love, Ryer, and Faddis (1992) found evidence that when teachers are attentive and encouraging to children, children exhibit less stress. The low frequency of children's interactions with teachers in early childhood classrooms suggest that the influence of teacher-child interactions on children must be exerted through quality rather than quantity and, further, that teachers may need to be quite conscious of how they distribute their attention among children so that the same children are not ignored every day.

Ratio and Group Size. States regulate adult-child ratio and group size because they realize that having too few teachers will have a negative effect upon sensitive, responsive relationships with each child.

1. Results of a Florida study revealed that teachers were more sensitive and responsive in their interactions with children when there were fewer children per adult (Howes et al., 1995).

2. The Cost, Quality, & Child Outcomes Study (1995) (using data from the Florida study) demonstrated that in classrooms that did not meet professional adult-child ratio, teacher-child interactions were less responsive and sensitive than in classrooms that adhered to professional recommendations (Howes, 1997).

3. Ratios and group sizes in child-care centers directly and indirectly influence the types of interactions between teachers and children (Howes, 1997).

4. Regulations on adult-child ratios in classrooms and family child-care homes vary from

Stimulator   When teaching in a setting where the organizational climate is well defined, how do one's efforts further support the success of the experience for oneself, other staff, parents, and children. Be creative!

1. Describe the characteristics you think are important in a person working with young children. How would you prioritize these characteristics?

2. If you were a supervisor (lead teacher) how would you observe and guide a new employee?

3. Outline a 6-month "meeting schedule" for:
   a. Individual center employees
   b. All center employees
   c. Only lead/head teachers
   d. Only support (trainees, volunteers, etc.) staff
   e. Nonteaching staff
   f. Others (parents, etc.)

4. How would you handle differences between:
   a. Individuals of the same rank (lead teachers, aides, etc.)
   b. Hierarchial ranks (longevity, title, etc.)
   c. Teaching and nonteaching staff

state to state. NAEYC has recommended Voluntary national standards and ratios [see following table]. Teachers and caregivers should voluntarily adhere to the recommended ratios, but they also should advocate for state regulations on adult-child ratios that are consistent with the recommended ratios (Kontos & Wilcox-Herzog, 1997, p. 10).

NAEYC Recommended Adult-Child Ratios

Age of Children	Adult : Child
0 – 1 year	1:3
1 – 2 years	1:5
2 – 3 years	1:6
3 – 5 years	1:8
5 – 6 years	1:10

6. Influences on Teacher-Child Interactions.

Few teachers are aware of how rarely each child receives individual attention and why some children receive even less than others. These variations in attention reflect, in part, individual characteristics and the nature of the relationship that has developed between the adult and each child. Thus, it is important that teachers/caregivers consciously try to distribute their attention among all the children in their classroom/home. The NAEYC accredita-

tion guidelines (Bredekamp, 1985) place a high priority on individual interactions between teachers and children throughout the day. Conscious reflection on individual attention is more likely to occur in classes with recommended ratios and with trained teachers.

Examining the types of activities children engage in and highlighting typical/atypical gender roles through the curriculum may help teachers reflect on their own classroom behaviors. There is some evidence that there is a relationship between children's cognitive development and teacher-child interactions. In a family child-care study children who engaged in more frequent and higher quality play with objects experienced more frequent responsive interactions with their family child-care providers (Kontos et al., 1994). In the Bermuda day-care study children who experienced more verbal interactions with their teachers were more intelligent and task oriented (Phillips et al., 1987).

A relationship between teacher-child interaction and children's language development has been shown. In British child-care centers, Melhuish and his colleagues (1990a, 1990b) demonstrated that children who received less verbal communication and less responsiveness from their teachers displayed poorer language development. In the National Child Care Staffing Study, children who experienced more responsive teacher involvement exhibited higher levels of language development (Whitebook et al., 1989a). (See also discussions on teacher/child relationships, teacher's role, teacher sensitivity, and teacher involvement in this chapter.)

7. Compensation for Early Childhood Professionals.

Economic and social conditions have been changing the family patterns regarding employment, composition, educational opportunities, and other individual situations and families. However, families alone cannot be expected to bear the additional costs. The demand for early childhood services has grown dramatically in recent years due to the change in family employment patterns, family composition, educational opportunities, and many situations that fit individual families.

The National Association for the Education of Young Children believes that the lack of resources facing many early childhood programs and the concomitant inadequate compensation of early childhood personnel is rooted in this nation's chronic indifference toward young children. More young children—one out of every five children—are in poverty than are members of any other age group, even though they are the most vulnerable. As a nation, we historically have placed less value on any type of work done for or with young children. Pediatricians earn less than other types of physicians. Kindergarten and elementary school teachers earn less than secondary school teachers (Bureau of Labor Statistics, unpublished analyses).

These were NAEYC's revised recommendations in 1993 (Brochure #546):

> Early childhood professionals with comparable qualifications, experience, and job responsibilities should receive comparable compensation regardless of the setting of their job. This means that a teacher working in a community child-care center, a family child-care provider, and an elementary school teacher who each hold comparable professional qualifications

should also receive comparable compensation for their work.

> Compensation for early childhood professionals should be equivalent to that of other professionals with comparable preparation requirements, experience, and job responsibilities.

> Compensation should not be differentiated on the basis of the ages of children served.

> Early childhood professionals should be encouraged to seek additional professional preparation and should be rewarded accordingly.

> The provision of an adequate benefits package is a crucial component of compensation for early childhood staff.

> Career ladders should be established, providing additional increments in salary based on performance and participation in professional development.

Accreditation

Accreditation in self-evaluation is based on standards set by the accrediting agencies, such as professional groups. The staff and parents objectively and subjectively make judgments in the evaluation process. According to Decker and Decker (1992),

> Accreditation is defined as a process of self-regulation; thus, regulations governing programs (e.g., certification of staff, licensing, registration) differ from accreditation in several ways. Regulations are mandatory minimum standards requiring 100 percent compliance, are determined or set by government or funding agencies, and often are imposed at the local and state levels, although some regulations have federal scope (e.g., IRS regulations, Civil Rights Acts, P.L. 94-142). Conversely, accreditation standards are voluntary high-quality standards, and operated at the national level. Failure to meet regulation standards means legal sanctions, but failure to become accredited signifies failure to gain professional status. Early childhood programs accredited by a particular association or agency are not necessarily superior to other programs, although they are often superior because staff members have voluntarily pursued a degree of excellence. (p. 92)

Facts and Figures

The *National Child Care Staffing Study* (Whitebook et al., 1989a) found that child-care center teaching staff earned annual wages less than one-half of those paid to comparably educated women in other professions and less than one-third of those of comparably educated men.

"Given the importance of the early childhood years in shaping later development and learning and the increasing number of families relying on early childhood programs, it is crucial that such programs employ personnel with the knowledge and ability needed to provide good care and education for our nation's youngest citizens" (p. 30).

"Because low- and moderate-income parents are unable to afford the full cost of a quality program, the price has been depressed. What parents, even in upper-income families, typically pay is far below actual cost, especially when adequate compensation is figured into the equation. Since personnel costs are the largest component of the program budget (60 percent or more), they are the most affected when program resources are inadequate" (p. 30).

The process of self-regulation (accreditation) involves three major steps:

1. Application, fee payment, and a completed and submitted self-study (The National Academy of Early Childhood uses a 3-point rating scale [criterion fully met, criterion partially met, criterion not met] for its program description.)

2. On-site validation by highly qualified professionals with association training to interpret the accreditation standards and procedures

3. Decision-making process by accrediting agency after which the decision, along with strengths and weakness of the program, are written and sent to the applying program

For accrediting programs, there is a term of accreditation; in order to stay accredited, program officials must reapply and successfully complete the entire process before the term expires and submit annual reports. The accrediting organization has the right to revoke accreditation for violations. For deferred programs, there are appeal procedures and also association assistance plans for helping them to meet standards and become accredited.

Several accreditation agencies are involved in early childhood programs.

1. In 1982, NAEYC began developing an accreditation system for programs serving a minimum of 10 children within the age group of birth through 5 years, in part- or full-day group programs and 5- through 8-year-olds in before- and after-school programs. No home-based day-care programs were included at this time. A new organization—the National Academy of Early Childhood Programs—was initiated. The academy has completed two follow-up studies: (a) 1 year following accreditation of its programs, and found "high standards were not only maintained but were being improved upon" (Mulrooney, 1990, p. 60); and (b) 3 years after original accreditation, the study suggested that "because of changes in programs, a complete self-study/evaluation leading to reaccreditation every three years is appropriate" (Mulrooney, 1990, p. 60).

2. The National Association for Family Day-Care developed an accreditation program in

1988 in an effort to give family day-care programs an opportunity to gain professional recognition. Providers rate their programs using the Assessment Profile for Family Day-Care to measure 186 criteria, which fall into seven categories: indoor safety, health, nutrition, interaction, indoor play environment, outdoor play environment, and professional responsibility. Parents participate through questionnaires and observation instruments. A validator observation is also used. Contact the following for more information: National Association for Family Day Care, 725 Fifteenth St., N.W., Suite 505, Washington, DC 20005 (202) 347-3356.

3. The Child Welfare League of America provides accreditation to child welfare agencies such as Child Day-Care-Center Based, Child Day-Care-Family Based, and Child Protective Services through its Council on Accreditation of Services for Families and Children. The agency may begin the accreditation process if no major questions are raised.

4. The National Council for the Accreditation of Teacher Education (NCATE) for teacher preparation institutions uses the standards prepared by NAEYC for accredited early childhood programs (i.e., a 4- or 5-year teacher preparation curriculum for those who want to be teachers of children from birth through age 8). In 1985, NAEYC completed its guidelines for early childhood education programs in associate degree granting institutions.

From a 1993 NCATE study, the most frequently cited reasons for supporting accreditation are that it did the following:

1. Provided another way for centers that already know or thought they had a good program to show quality (36.7 percent)

2. Confirmed or validated that the centers had a good program (33 percent)

3. Served as a vehicle to improve or update programs to enable them to provide the highest quality (32 percent)

4. Promoted awareness of what constitutes high-quality early childhood programs and what motivates staff (32 percent)

5. Promoted prestige and recognition at the local and national levels (27 percent)

Directors overwhelmingly (95 percent) reported that program reaccreditation would be sought when the 3-year accreditation term expired, for the following reasons:

1. There was the perception that accreditation was beneficial and that directors wished to keep on track (49 percent).

2. Accreditation was a seal of quality and the accredited program is a model for others (39 percent).

3. Accreditation reflected professionalism (24 percent).

4. Accreditation positively affected staff and parent morale, serving as a source of pride (24 percent) (Herr et al., 1993).

An excerpt from the National Child Care Staffing Study further supports accreditation:

It appears that the process of becoming accredited enhances center quality; for example, the recently accredited centers had the lowest four-year turnover rate (33%) and paid higher wages to teachers and assistants than all other centers in the sample. (Whitebook et al., 1993, p. 35)

DEMOGRAPHIC CHARACTERISTICS OF CENTERS

1. For-profit centers provided significantly poorer-quality care than nonprofit centers.

2. For-profit centers were more likely to have closed than were nonprofit centers.

3. Number of children served did not change significantly.

Child-Care Teaching Staff

The changes were as follows:

- Average size of the teaching staff had increased from 14.3 to 16.2.

- There were more assistant teachers, who were younger and less well-trained.

- There was minimal evidence of opportunities for career advancement so teachers were leaving centers, but directors were quite stable.

Compensation

The teaching staff continue to earn less than half as much as comparably educated women and less than one third as much as comparably educated men in the civilian labor force.

Benefits

Health benefits for employees were neither improved nor reduced.

Teaching Staff Turnover

Staff turnover averaged 41 percent, as reported by directors, in the original staffing study. A second, recent study of typical center-based care has replicated this 40 percent turnover rate (Scarr et al., 1993). Even studies that include part-day Head Start and school-based programs among their sample consistently report annual turnover rates around 25 percent (see Kisker et al., 1991). A striking comparison is offered by public school teachers who left their jobs at a rate of 5.6 percent in 1987–1988 (National Center for Education Statistics, 1992).

Conclusion

The Staffing Study Revisited suggests that the overall quality of centers remains worrisome as indicated by the low wages, lack of health coverage and high turnover among child care teaching staff. As a nation we like to believe that children are our most precious resource; our current child care delivery system reveals a very different reality. America depends on child care teachers. Our future depends on valuing them. (National Center for the Early Childhood Work Force, 1993, p. 13)

THE INDIVIDUAL

The way individuals view themselves is important. Belief in and satisfaction with oneself are important attributes that contribute to personal and center success. Happy, contented people are more pleasant to work with than discontented or negative people. Cheerfulness is contagious, as is negativism. Building relationships with people who are self-critical is difficult. Each individual's total attributes, both personal and professional, must be included in self-evaluation. Self-evaluation is necessary because individuals' inner feelings affect their feelings about their jobs and other people. The attributes of a good caregiver include, but are not limited to, nurturance, empathy, knowledge, experience, flexibility, curiosity, enthusiasm, and dependability. Unhappy or insecure people do not exhibit these feelings as often or as openly as happy ones.

Personal Security

People who enjoy a job and remain in it usually know what they want out of life. They know their direction and have taken time and effort to identify their strengths and to capitalize on them. They have learned how to plan, organize, implement, and evaluate personal and professional goals.

In general, people who know what they want out of life know their limitations; they exhibit some or all of the following characteristics:

- Can say no without feeling guilt or jeopardizing personal relationships

- Work for results, not rewards

- Stand back occasionally and survey their day-to-day work

- Communicate in clear and honest ways

- Know how to overcome loss and rejection—consider failure a stepping stone, not a stumbling block

- Give credit where credit is due and do not try to build themselves up at the expense of others
- Feel secure in their relationships with others and consider risk-taking a growth step
- Relieve tension in constructive ways
- Maintain high levels of energy and enthusiasm
- Value total health and work to maintain it
- Have the courage to be themselves

Because child-care workers have a lasting influence on the children they care for, they should have positive personal characteristics and qualities (e.g., commitment, security, enthusiasm, and health). Individuals with these attributes make excellent teachers, although they are sometimes called into leadership positions because of their self-confidence and ability to work successfully with others.

JOB SATISFACTION

In an attempt to investigate job stability and job satisfaction among family day-care providers, Bollin (1993) found that the more stable the providers are, the more likely they report high levels of job satisfaction, are willing to work longer hours, and to have held child-related jobs previously. Short-term providers indicate that problems with parents and job stress influenced their decisions to give up their FDC (family day care) business. Insufficient income was another primary reason for discontinuing the service.

Job satisfaction is positively correlated with perception of social support, especially in the area of client support, but is negatively correlated for staff and other parents by the presence of the provider's own children. In most studies of FDC, providers express high levels of satisfaction with their actual work with children but low levels of satisfaction linked to perception of support for their work, particularly from their parent clientele and their own family members (Bollin, 1993). In another report (Whitebook et al., 1989c), child-care staff were dissatisfied with their salaries and benefits programs but were highly satisfied with their day-to-day work contributing to the growth and development of children, positive relationships with coworkers, and job autonomy (Jorde-Bloom, 1988; Powell & Stremmel, 1989; Whitebook et al., 1982).

Staff turnover in child development centers is epidemic, reaching as high as 41 percent (Whitebook et al., 1989b).

Studies have shown that high rates of turnover are related to poor-quality child care, having detrimental effects on children in child-care facilities (Clarke-Stewart, 1987; Galinsky, 1990a; Whitebook et al., 1982). Variables associated with high staff turnover are low wages, poor working conditions, and minimal benefits (Havercamp & Everts, 1992, p. 28).

A job satisfaction study conducted in Reno, Nevada, found that a fun-filled, challenging, and caring environment is essential to building a cooperative and empowering spirit among staff and their center director and also reduces staff turnover (Havercamp & Everts, 1992). Major ideas to motivate child and family staff members are having personal values and challenges, feeling appreciated, and empowerment, or having the ability to influence their work situation.

❖ Stimulator You have been employed as a head teacher at the Green Hills Child-Care Center for 2 years. Due to popularity and community need, the center is expanding. You are promoted to supervisor. Two of the teachers under your supervision have been at the center longer than you. Both are good teachers, but they have different attitudes about themselves. Helena is jovial, outgoing, cooperative, and confident. Chelita is quiet, insecure, and keeps to herself. In your new role, how do your personal attributes help you build effective relationships with Helena and Chelita (and the other teachers), and how do you propose to provide a growth-promoting environment for them?

Ingredients from survey	Ways to implement ingredients into early childhood setting
1. Interesting and challenging work	Work with different adults, ages of children, new curriculum; be creative!
2. *Management that makes employees feel they are important as individuals	Management that is honest and prompt with evaluations
3. Never being bored at work	Looking for ways to involve children, staff, and self
4. *Management that provides feedback on performance	Management that observes and evaluates each employee
5. A job where rewards are strongly related to performance	Employees who know procedures, are conscientious, work hard; get feedback/encouragement
6. *Having a management that is good at setting goals	Management aware of problems, solutions, and input
7. A job that provides status	Frequent opportunities and recognition. Sharing ideas
8. A job with opportunities for advancement	Specific steps, encouragement, and reward
9. Having been consistently successful in your job	Personal satisfaction in and center approval of efforts
10. *Getting along with your boss	Be teachable, responsible, and cooperative
11. *Having a management that avoids "crisis management"	Recognize and solve problems before they get out of hand; offer constructive criticism
12. *Having a management that assigns reasonable work loads	Help establish workable schedules, assignments; work for results

Figure 6–2 Twelve ingredients of a satisfying job.
Source: Ingredients from the survey are from *Working Woman*, 1986, p. 48.
*Note that half of these items deal directly with management! Managers can encourage motivation in employees by clear, frequent, and honest communication. Discipline is sometimes necessary, and when it is used, it should be direct, accurate, and finished.

According to a magazine survey, 12 ingredients of a satisfying job in order of importance were as shown in Figure 6–2.

Burnout

Another condition that prevents a person from performing well is *burnout*. Burnout is exhibited in a number of ways, including negativism, dissatisfaction, boredom, unpreparedness, tardiness, forgetfulness, tiredness, depression, and frequent illness. It can be caused by events at work or elsewhere. Individuals who work in high-energy, highly emotional jobs are bound to feel stress and/or burnout. Working with young children is highly rewarding but also highly fatiguing. (The National Institute of Occupational Safety and Health has indicated that teachers and teacher aides rank in the top 20 most stressful occupations.) Burnout occurring at the center may be caused by poor personal relations, insufficient resources to perform required tasks, ambiguous communications, or inappropriate working conditions. Insecurity about teaching methods and materials, lack of recognition as a professional, time pressures, unrealistic view of one's role, classroom management problems, administrative incompetence/insensitivity, or personal ability to use and develop talents, can also result in burnout. Regardless of its causes, individuals who recognize the signs can do something about them. Some possible solutions include the following:

- THINK POSITIVELY!
- Change in assignment/hours
- Better communication skills
- More classroom resources
- More support of talents/abilities
- Change in center/occupation
- More knowledge about children
- Better personal health habits
- Change what can be changed
- Deal with current problems
- More classroom training
- Discussion with director
- Time off
- Less regimentation
- Physical outlets (sports)
- Be better prepared daily
- Take periodic breaks
- Join a support group

Several recent studies have been conducted in relationship to child-care workers. The first study assessed the extent to which personality (neuroticism, extraversion), background characteristics (education/training, work experience), and perceptions of the work setting (work role conflict, work role ambiguity, organizational commitment, job satisfaction) were associated with three facets of burnout (emotion exhaustion, depersonalization, personal accomplishment). Manlove (1993) found that

> the results indicate that neuroticism, work role conflict, and work role ambiguity were positively associated with higher levels of burnout as measured by all three facets. Higher levels of organizational commitment were significantly associated with less emotional exhaustion and greater personal accomplishment. Those reporting better supervisor and

co-worker relations as well as more autonomy at work reported significantly lower levels of depersonalization. Those with more education/training and work experience reported significantly higher levels of personal accomplishment. (p. 449)

The second study examined emotional exhaustion in relation to job satisfaction, communication within the center, and background variables among child-care directors, teachers, and assistant teachers (Stremmel et al., 1993). The findings in this study suggest that "satisfactions with working conditions and the work itself predicted lower emotional exhaustion among directors, teachers, and teaching assistants, but satisfactions with professional development and monetary rewards did not" (p. 229).

In still another study, Powell and Stremmel (1989) found that "staff communication influences satisfaction with working conditions and the work itself, and that these satisfactions buffer against emotional exhaustion; . . . that feelings of emotional exhaustion may be reduced by adopting organizational practices that enhance job satisfaction" (opportunities for teachers and assistant teachers to discuss children's needs and share information useful in dealing with daily classroom concerns, in particular: assistant teachers, who typically have limited training and often rely on center-based sources of information and center directors, who typically are perceived as helpful staff development resources).

THE PROFESSIONAL

Keeping Current

Individuals involved in child care and early childhood education (ECE) need to keep abreast of research and information in the field by attending workshops, lectures, conventions, organizational meetings, and other means. They should read current books, articles, pamphlets, and other materials to find ways they can apply these findings and ideas to their own center. They can also listen to tapes, watch videos, and discuss current topics with colleagues and parents.

Awareness of new research and information helps individuals enhance and strengthen personal styles of thinking and acting, rather than providing norms, groups, or points of view to which individuals must conform.

Other ways to support the field and keep current are joining national and local organizations, reading their publications and being an active member, supporting and lobbying for principles and ideals of early childhood education, and running for an office in a professional organization.

Be aware of community, state, and national goals and accomplishments. Also be a part of the team that makes good things happen for young children, families, and teachers of young children by knowing what is being proposed, who is supporting it, the impact it will have in your immediate situation (self, center, community) and expanding area (state, national, international).

For a list of professional organizations and/or publications to which one can turn for information, materials, and support, see the end of this chapter.

Working with Others

Director/Coordinator. The terms director and coordinator are used interchangeably. In a national survey, Austin and Morrow (1985–1986) questioned 200 child-care directors in Head Start, day-care, preschool, and university-based programs about their most pressing administrative concerns. Almost everyone targeted the following four areas: (1) evaluating one's own effectiveness as an administrator (see Chapters 2 and 7 and this chapter), (2) developing a philosophy for the center and establishing curriculum goals and objectives consonant with this philosophy (see Chapter 4, (3) evaluating the effects of the center and the curriculum on the children (see Chapters 2 and 4), and (4) establishing effective parent-center communications (see Chapters 2 and 4).

A director/coordinator has varied and serious responsibilities—great influence on the philosophy of the center, the maintenance or support given to employees and clientele (both children and parents), the structure and policies of the organization, the record keeping, the budget, and the use of space and the facility. Directors must be understanding and accepting of themselves and others, as well as have the skills, knowledge, talent, and ability to maintain a high profile in such a multifaceted job.

The director will have contact with most people who come to the center, including employees. The following traits are important:

- Make a good impression through personal appearance, good physical and mental health, enthusiasm, humor, flexibility, and empathy
- Feel comfortable with both adults and children
- Recognize individual and group needs
- Be self-confident
- Have integrity
- Use organizational skills effectively
- Be a source of help to employees
- Know the field of early childhood education well enough to be a resource to the staff in the performance of effective classroom practices, curriculum development, discipline, assessment, and fulfillment of individual needs
- Facilitate group cohesiveness
- Be willing to observe, participate, and/or advise

A successful director also provides social support for his subordinates, clarifies overall goals, maintains a friendly but professional role differentiation, and provides general supervision. The director may have varied duties; however, the job description can be divided into two simple categories: working with people and performing jobs. Because the director's responsibilities are so important to the employee's success and the success of the program, several duties will be discussed in depth.

❖ Stimulator   From the following list of duties of a director, indicate which items are personnel matters (PM) and which are task-oriented (TO):

_____ Determining the number of employees	_____ Writing job descriptions for employees
_____ Evaluating goals and progress with employees	_____ Interviewing, hiring, reprimanding, and terminating employees
_____ Planning preservice and in-service training	_____ Conducting workshops
_____ Building effective relationships with employees	_____ Conducting staff meetings
_____ Supervising employees in various jobs	_____ Building a strong center/home bond
_____ Planning for and meeting the needs of each child and each family	_____ Acting as a liaison between center and board of directors (where applicable)
_____ Being aware of community events and key people; working together cooperatively and professionally	_____ Knowing and supporting local and federal licensing agencies
_____ Knowing and using appropriate referral agencies for the benefit of the children and families	_____ Formulating, implementing, evaluating, and enforcing the center's educational philosophy and policies
_____ Assisting teachers in the classroom	_____ Keeping current in the field
_____ Discovering and handling problems quickly and tactfully	_____ Handling correspondence
_____ Keeping records	_____ Scheduling the use and maintenance of the center
_____ Budgeting expenses efficiently	_____ Raising funds

As the score is tallied, note that fewer of the items are strictly personnel (people) matters, and at least half can be considered both personnel (people) and task (thing) matters. Does this mean that accomplishing tasks is more important than building relationships with personnel? Be prepared to discuss your opinion.

The director is an advocate for children and families, as well as a strong supporter of staff personnel. Neugebauer (1991) has compiled a list of qualities employees like in an employer. It is adapted in Figure 6–3. See how well you match up, then return to each question and ask yourself just how you do (or could) accomplish each item with each employee, child, and parent.

PERSONNEL POLICIES AND PROCEDURES

It is strongly recommended that the center prepare basic information related to employment to ensure consistency in policies and protect the center from disgruntled employees and possible lawsuits. Some find it worthwhile to give handbooks to new employees. Preparing such handbooks in

Do you:	Always	Sometimes	Never
believe in people from the beginning?			
recognize and build on their strengths?			
give feedback?			
view their welfare as a high priority?			
contribute to team spirit?			
inspire commitment?			
set high standards?			
remove obstacles to their success?			
encourage them to take risks?			
make working fun?			
cultivate professional pride?			
help them see results?			

Figure 6–3   Qualities employees like in employers: A self-assessment.

loose-leaf form allows information to be updated without reprinting entire manuals or justifying outdated material with new rules.

Criminal Record Checks

Information about criminal record checks can be found from Child Care Action Campaign, Information Guide 5, 330 Seventh Avenue, 17th Floor, New York, NY 10001. See also Chapter 5.

In addition to the personal and professional references, the director must make a criminal and abuse check on each individual before considering the applicant as a serious contender for the job. One cannot be too cautious when hiring individuals who will work closely with and strongly influence young children. Children and staff can be safeguarded by screening out people who do not belong in the field. Public Law 92–544 grants authority to the Federal Bureau of Investigation to ex-

change background information on potential child-care providers with their employers. This law applies only in those states requiring background checks—today, at least 20 states have established background check programs, according to the FBI, and use checks to verify the employment and criminal histories of potential providers to work in child-care programs or to become licensed. Thirty-six states check records at the state level.

Criminal record checks do infringe on the rights of those who have records. In the child-care field, however, the rights of adults with criminal records must be subordinate to the rights of children—who trust and depend on the caregiver. Efforts to prevent child abuse should include the following:

- Mandate that parents can visit programs at any time
- Parent involvement in checking that licensing requirements are met

- Required, ongoing training of staff
- Credentialing of family day care
- Strict regulation of field trips
- Requirements that children can be taken from the program only by adults with parents' authorization
- Clear, effective complaint procedures

(*Source:* Information from Child Care Action Campaign. n.d., "Do Criminal Record Checks Protect Children?" Information Guide 5.)

Statement of Personnel Policies

A statement of personnel policies is a written document covering employer-employee relations. It spells out the conditions of employment. Given to new employees, this kind of document will convey information about the job in a concise manner. It can ask employees to sign a statement that they have read it and should be short and to the point, clear, and organized into logical sections.

A personnel handbook will include job description, advancement opportunities, termination of employment, and grievances.

Job Descriptions

Job descriptions can be assets if they are accurate and complete, but they can be deficits if they are misleading or vague. For efficiency, each job at the center should have a detailed description that outlines the specific job and shows how related jobs fit with it. The description should eliminate any misunderstandings about the task, the person who performs it, or the way it is supervised. The job description should be altered whenever situations change; revisions should be pointed out and changes justified. In some industries, job descriptions are called *job models* because they supplement or operationalize the job description.

The best kind of job description is for a specific opening and should be accompanied by a brief description of the school's educational philosophy and goals. For examples, see Appendix F.

Recruiting, Hiring, and Retaining Good Child-Care Employees

Across the country, there is a real shortage of workers in child care because of low salaries, noncompetitive benefits, lack of status and career ladders, and poor working conditions. There is a 41 percent annual turnover in child care. The projected demand for preschool teachers and child-care workers is expected to increase between 40 and 56 percent in the next decade (Sheerer & Jorde-Bloom, 1990; Willer & Johnson, 1989). It is vital to recruit and retain competent workers. Start by looking for workers in logical places—local community colleges, 4-year institutions, businesses, and others who train early childhood personnel. A close relationship with potential sources of employees is important.

The typical director should give frequent, even weekly, attention to recruitment; however, many of them believe that recruiting quality staff is the single most perplexing and complex problem now facing preschools. About the only protection a director has is to have a backlog of applications of qualified people who can be called for further interviews.

In making a final selection, the director must consider all information available—the application (including education and experience), personal appearance, personal references, criminal and abuse checks, and the responses to interview questions. The immediate supervisor of the job being filled may sit in on part of the interview and may have valuable information to add. Remember that most applicants are somewhat nervous in meeting new people and in being interviewed—some may perform naturally and some may not. If the applicant is being seriously considered, ask that he or she spend some compensated time in one of the classrooms.

Soon after the deadline closes for applications, send a letter of acceptance to the successful applicant and letters of nonplacement to all others. See Figure 6–4 for an example of an acceptance letter.

Personnel can be retained for longer periods of time when employers provide good working

---

SandyHill Child-Care Center

This agreement is made the _____ day of _____ , 20 _____ , between SandyHill Child-Care Center and
_____ (employee).

It is mutually understood that you will be employed in the position of _____ for a
period of _____ (specify time—usually 1 year), beginning _____ , 20 _____ .

Specific duties include: _____ ; as outlined in the center's policies or by
the board of directors.

Terms of your contract include (probationary period; vacation and sick days; benefits; notification and conditions for termination and other conditions):

It is agreed that you will be paid the sum of _____ , to be paid at the rate of _____ per calendar month, beginning _____ , 20 _____ .

_____   _____
Signature of Employee   Signature of Director

Dated _____   Dated _____

Approved: _____
_____ Board Member (if applicable)

Figure 6–4 Sample acceptance letter.

conditions (compensation, hours), show respect for and appreciation of personnel, provide benefits (insurance, retirement, etc.), compensate personnel for extra efforts (home visits, in-service meetings, parent conferences, etc.), encourage and support membership and participation in professional organizations (fees, conferences), encourage additional schooling and training (scholarships, part tuition, CDA work, low-interest loans for books/tuition), offer opportunities for advancement, encourage leadership, provide an opportunity for talent sharing, involve employees in decision making and problem solving, and offer incentives for extra and/or quality performance (vacation days, classroom materials, etc.). See also "Job Satisfaction."

When seeking a new employee, consider these questions:

- What personal and professional qualifications are required?
- What is the best way to advertise the job—local newspaper, posters, employment office?
- How much lead time is there before the job must be filled?
- For what period of time will applications be accepted?
- When will interviews be conducted?
- Are salary and hours negotiable or fixed?

The serious applicant will want to know about the benefits provided (sick leave, retirement, vacations, and special holidays), the school calendar, and job security (possible layoffs, probation, termination, opportunities for advancement, etc.). He or she may ask about pay periods, savings plans, and taxes. Whether a center hires many or few employees, it should prepare an application form that meets the center's specific needs. Commercial forms or verbal means of gathering information are insufficient.

The Equal Opportunity Act of 1972 prohibits employers from discriminating against any individual on the grounds of race, creed, color, sex, national origin, or age. Employers must hire on merit and competence and must base job qualifications on bona fide occupational requirements. Recruiting and hiring practices must follow affirmative action guidelines in an effort to change discriminatory practices against minorities and women (Equal Opportunity Commission, 1980). The Equal Opportunity Act and the Affirmative Action Guidelines of the Equal Opportunity Commission specify what questions may be asked in an interview. It is legal—and important—to determine whether the applicant has any record of child abuse or criminal offenses.

Employers must also adhere to the conditions set forth in the Americans with Disability Act of 1990.

For information regarding employment discrimination and affirmative action issues and questions, contact Public Information Unit, Equal Employment Opportunity Commission (EEOC) 2401 E Street, NW, Washington DC 20507 (800) USA-EEOC or (202) 634–6922.

The applicant may bring a personal vita as well as a completed application. The vita, or an application, which gives supplemental information, may be sufficient for some centers.

Before an interview, the director should consider having the immediate supervisor of the job position be part of the interview process. A checklist (based on the job description) may help directors and supervisors make objective and fair evaluations of candidates.

The interview room should reflect a friendly atmosphere. The applicant will feel more at ease seated next to the interviewer than behind a barrier such as a desk. The director may skim the vita or application and then talk informally with the applicant, asking for clarification and additional information or getting a spontaneous response related to curriculum, discipline, or other teaching matters. The director may ask pointed questions: Why are you applying to this center? How do you feel about young children? How comfortable are you around parents? What are your plans for professional development? The interview should be a two-way discussion, with the applicant being given an opportunity to ask about the center. If the applicant is a serious contender for the job (he or she is interested in the job and the

interviewer or director is interested back), take the applicant on a tour of the center, give him or her the opportunity to observe and visit with other employees, have another staff person interview him or her, and later have the applicant demonstrate teaching and classroom management skills.

A poll conducted by *Career Digest* revealed 10 reasons candidates are rejected at the interview level: (1) poor personal appearance, (2) lack of interest and enthusiasm, (3) failure to look at the interviewer when conversing, (4) late to the interview, (5) asks no questions about the job, (6) is too overbearing, (7) know-it-all attitude, (8) inability to express self clearly, (9) poor voice, diction, grammar, and (10) lack of planning for career; lack of purpose or goals (Brigham Young University, 1986).

Naturally, the employer will look for the best match between personal qualities and the job to be filled. The ideal applicant is mature and stable, has realistic goals, is well trained, is willing to learn and share, is congenial, and enjoys working with adults and children. A prospective employee should also be interested in the congruence between his or her ability and the job and in the job's potential for personal and professional growth.

Interview techniques can be verbal or written. Questions should be open-ended. (Example: "What kinds of music activities would you provide for 2-year-olds?" rather than "Would you use music with 2-year-olds?") Neither discussions nor questions should lead the candidate's responses. The director should ask, "Tell me more," or rephrase the candidate's answer rather than add a personal interpretation. Nonverbal communication (facial expressions, body language) can indicate understanding or misunderstanding, agreement or disagreement, likes or dislikes. Nonverbal cues are often subconscious and may convey more than words do; thus, misunderstandings and misinterpretations may result. When both parties have gained sufficient information, the interview is terminated in a friendly way by telling the applicant when and how notification will be given about the decision.

Even an employee who has the qualifications that fit the job should be hired on a temporary or probationary basis. The length of the probation and the conditions for continuation or termination are set by the employer and must be clear to the employee. Such a probation also gives the employee time to determine whether he or she wants to remain at the center. At the end of the specified period, the employee and director should meet and discuss the experience. Either party can terminate the employment; or, by consensus, it can continue.

Many centers use a written contract that includes the employee's name, duties (or a job description), salary and pay periods, and special conditions, such as vacations, holidays, leaves of absence, the school calendar, evaluation period for pay raises, and so on. Verbal agreements make it difficult for either party to review the specific conditions. Although verbal agreements may seem less binding and the parties may feel less committed, they are difficult to use in legal issues!

Directors should check the personal and professional references carefully for accuracy and completeness. Gaps in employment or frequent job changes may indicate personal or professional problems, but they may be explained by logical events or activities.

Hiring Older Adults.

Based on the 1980 census, Collins (1987) reported that persons older than age 55 accounted for 13 percent of all child-care workers. More recently there is optimism that more people of this age group will join this field to relieve the chronic shortage of younger workers.

Some older adults are looking for meaningful, productive, and valued work in financial or personal relationships. Those who come without work experience or child-care training will need time to adapt to and learn new procedures. Training will be an important and necessary part of their service in child care. Newman and coworkers, (1992) state:

> Older adults can make a significant contribution to child care, to children, to other staff members, and to parents. Children benefit through contact with

older adults who can share the wisdom obtained from a life-time of learning and experience, who can model successful aging, and who can form nurturing intergenerational relations . . . older adults can benefit physically, economically, emotionally, and cognitively from productive, meaningful work . . . can increase older adults' self-esteem, energy level, competence, and overall sense of community participation.

In hiring older men and women, the center will need to give attention to preparation of current staff to work with adults who may be older and less experienced in the field, to prepare older staff members in ways that are more appropriate to their experience and abilities—being understanding but not condescending, to children, non-teaching staff, and parents.

In summary, Newman and coworkers (1992) state:

> The successful inclusion of productively employed older adults in child care will depend on the degree to which employers are sensitive to the needs of their older and younger workers and are willing to use resources such as these guidelines to support the creation of positive and supportive environs for all their workers.

Recruiting Males.

Less than 1 in 20 workers in child-care centers is a male. For a variety of reasons, the profession has been unsuccessful in recruiting significant numbers of men: social attitudes, low pay, director attitudes (some believe that women have a natural ability to nurture children and that men fail to have this instinct). Some directors won't consider hiring a male without an early childhood degree but hire females without a degree; won't consider allowing males to change diapers or toilet train toddlers; feel that male teachers would be more likely to molest children than females; would play too roughly and injure children. Some directors are suspicious and give direct assertions or indirect innuendoes that child-care work means that a man is unable to land a job worthy of a man. Isolation—few opportunities to talk with other males—is another deterrent (Neugebauer, 1994c).

The National Day Care Study (Ruopp et al., 1979), found that in 1977 just over 6 percent of all center classroom staff were men. The National Child Care Staffing Study (Whitebook et al., 1989b), reported that in 1988 men comprised only 3 percent of the teaching staff in their survey, which reinforces and perpetuates the myth that only women have the ability to nurture.

Recruiting Patrons. Without a viable program, good teachers, and appropriate goals, the center will not sell itself (Wassom, 1994). In a survey of nearly 300 parents, the results indicated that competence and training of the staff was the first reason parents choose a particular child-care center. Another study indicated the director and staff were the primary deciding factor for parents.

Child-care companies are competing for customers like never before. They entice parents with a variety of "benefits."

"In 1993, mid-size early childhood organizations expected to expand their capacity 11%, while large organizations projected 16% expansion" (Status report #8 on early childhood education, 1993).

Center owners, directors, and companies find a variety of methods to showcase their center—an advertisement in the Yellow Pages, a good brochure, an occasional newspaper ad, fliers at places where parents frequent, word of mouth, center open-houses, and unique eye-catchers will attract parents.

Price will be a major factor in recruiting children to your program. It should be competitive and fair. Tell parents what your child-care services will do for the child and the family. Highlight some of the center's best features: well-trained and experienced teachers, a developmentally appropriate program, highest quality care, safety and health measures, and happy children!

❖ Stimulator

Code each of the following examples:

    A. Supervisor (superior) should set the goal.

    B. Subordinate should set the goal.

    C. Supervisor and subordinate should set the goal together.

    D. The goal needs modification.

Example 1: There are no preschool/child-care centers in your town. A new paper mill, expected to employ 200 people, is being built.
Goal: Build a center immediately that can care for 50 children

Example 2: In 3 months there will be openings for aides, teachers, and supervisors in your child-care center. Several present employees could prepare themselves for these openings by receiving educational training that is available in the community; the center can provide limited funds.
Goal: Determine who should take advantage of this opportunity

Example 3: A high-school student visits your center; he hopes to set up a preschool/child-care center on graduation in the spring. His only experience has been in a 1-day-per-week class, and he "just loves children!"
Goal: To open his own center

Example 4: One lead teacher in the preschool excludes music entirely from the curriculum. Because the center stresses the importance of music, something must be done in this classroom.
Goal: To incorporate more music with this classroom's activities

❖ ❖ ❖ ❖   Give ideas and rationale for solutions selected for each example. (Answers depend on the reader's ability to identify the issues and defend the reasoning.)

Job Orientation.   A new employee deserves an orientation to the workplace and job. The employee's first exposure to the center should be friendly, informative, and productive. If possible, he or she should be given a packet or handbook for employees containing important center documents (philosophy, policies), general information, and personal information (such as procedure for absenteeism, place for personal items, etc.). The director should review for each new employee the objectives of the center, special center jargon, chain of command, employee benefits, payroll deductions, layout of the facility, and other matters. The new employee should be given opportunities to ask questions as they arise or at the end of the orientation session.

Well-planned orientation programs are invaluable. They can reduce or eliminate misconceptions, inform workers, help them feel more at ease, review employees' responsibilities and their importance to the center, introduce a precise view of the center's overall goals, and acquaint them with other employees.

Preservice training may be necessary to help new employees understand the specifics of the center. This may be a part of, or separate from, classroom participation. Additional training will depend on the employees' status and progress. The director or trainer should be available as a continual resource to employees. Observations and evaluations are valuable for both trainers and trainees.

Ongoing training takes the form of classes, workshops, conferences, demonstrations, observations, and other methods with frequent opportunities for the teaching staff to share their experiences. Qualified teachers can help less experienced employees gain confidence and experience.

The contract should be a statement of all the conditions of employment.

Grievance Procedures.   Close contact with each employee, periodic scheduled or spontaneous evaluations, and immediate feedback can prevent grievances. Catching problems early can mean easier and quicker solutions to problems.

An alert director or supervisor can recognize signs of dissatisfaction and should immediately set out to identify and reduce or eliminate its causes. Some signs of dissatisfaction are absenteeism/tardiness, lack of interest in details, poor classroom appearance, defensiveness, changes in productivity, lack of follow-through, or changes in an employee's usual pattern or attitudes.

The prospective employee should be informed about the process of presenting grievances and getting a fair hearing. He should also recognize the differences between information gathering, problem solving, or suggestion making, and disagreements, rebellion, or defiance.

One cannot always foresee and avoid problems. Grievances are certain to appear sometime. If employees know how to present their problems, the problems can be addressed and solved. When no grievance procedure exists, or when an employee is afraid of being fired or punished, problems tend to be inflated. Both employees and employers have a responsibility to see that grievances reach a logical conclusion.

Centers should have a policy regarding grievances. Figure 6–5 shows some of the questions to consider when writing a grievance policy. Before formal grievances are presented, try to resolve the problem through discussion. Even when policies are inflexible (safety, health, ownership, or funding), a discussion could clear the air.

The first step in resolving the situation is for the person initiating the grievance (employee or supervisor) to discuss the matter directly with the other person involved. Most problems can be resolved this way; but if no solution can be reached, involve the next direct supervisor.

Terminating.   There must be just cause and due process in the termination of an employee. If conditions related to employment are clearly defined and all employees have a copy of these conditions or know what they are, they know when they are in violation. Periodic evaluation with each employee will eliminate problems before they become too severe; however, some one-time events—such as endangering the health and safety of the children—may warrant immediate

Figure 6–5 Questions that need to be addressed by a grievance procedure.

1. Who can submit a grievance (full-time employees only)?
2. Can it be verbal or must it be written?
3. To whom should it be presented? Where? When?
4. How is it reviewed?
5. How is a decision on the grievance reported to the employee (verbal, written)?
6. Is there a time limit between problems and reporting them; between submitting a grievance and receiving a reply?
7. If there is a hearing, who can attend (employee, supervisor, board member, witnesses/supporters)?
8. Is the employee to submit possible remedies or just the problem?
9. Is there a method of appeal for either employee or supervisor?

dismissal. Each situation must be assessed according to its seriousness.

Problems should be handled as they arise, not left to become worse. Discipline involves both written and verbal action. The written documentation is progressive and may eventually lead to termination; it protects the director if formal grievance actions are initiated by the employee. The employee should be informed of the infraction, given a warning, and told the consequences of repeating it. The director should consider the evidence carefully, determine appropriate consequences, and be prepared to follow through if the infraction recurs or the consequences need to be administered.

If the center has a board of directors, the director informs them of the problem and the intended actions. The board may interview the employee, depending on the seriousness of the offense. For protection and future use, information on employees who are fired, indicating the reason(s) for the action, is recorded. This form should be signed by both parties, and each should have a copy of it.

The Exit Interview   An exit interview is suggested (Olsen, 1993). The information gained from it can be used in a number of positive ways at the center: (1) information may be unknown to the di-

rector, (2) reasons may be common (but unrecognized by director), (3) reason may deter unfair employment practices (e.g., sexual harassment), (4) compensation may be unfair, (5) center practices may be inequitable (personality clashes with supervisors or others, unfair, competition unbearable, evaluations unfair, training and working conditions too strict, etc.) (Drost et al., 1987), or (6) management disagreement over management practices (Woods & Macaulay, 1987).

Research suggests that telephone interviews or mailed questionnaires, conducted 3 to 6 weeks after termination of employment, are more effective than personal interviews conducted as the employee leaves an organization (Tenoschok, 1988). For telephone exit interviews to be successful, interviewers should be credible, trustworthy, and trained in interview techniques. Short, specific questions and answers done in comfortable settings, lasting no longer than 45 to 60 minutes, are optimum (Olsen, 1993).

Exit interviews will not solve all problems of staff turnover in each child-care program. Sherwood (1983) noted, "An exit interview program will not, of course, be the answer to employees problems, but . . . maintain morale, mini . . . efforts, and . . . tions" (. . .

Figure 6–6 Conducting successful exit interviews. *Source:* Adapted from Olsen (1993, p. 73).

- Put person at ease; explain confidentiality, how record will be kept, and how the information will be used for future hiring, training, etc.
- For consistency, use checklist or interview form to make sure all items are covered, but allow the employee to elaborate
- Use mainly open-ended questions so as not to lead answers
- Understand that the terminated employee may be reticent
- Be consistent in holding exit interview—voluntary and involuntary resignations
- Have someone other than the director or the employee's supervisor conduct the interview
- Encourage questions that allow for interchange
- Conduct the interview on a day other than the employee's last work day
- Employee benefits, severance pay, and other matters should be conducted separate from the exit interview

several management tools that can help an administrator be more effective and responsive to teachers and staff. For the benefit of the children who are served, lowering employee turnover in child-care programs must be accomplished (Olsen, 1993, p. 73). Figure 6–6 shows some successful exit interviewing techniques.

Substitutes. To plan on hiring a full staff is important; however even with every job filled, occasions arise ＿ ＿h substitutes are needed—either in ｆ＇ ＿n or in supporting jobs. Most c＿ ＿f the applications of potent＿ ＿these applications, c ＿ ＿ly hired or come in ＿ is short-staffed. ＿hod of provid-＿permanently ＿ a list of ＿come on ＿eferral ＿Ad-＿or

the part of the substitute and the center. Recently, other methods of filling staff positions for short or long terms have been initiated: leasing a teacher may be less expensive and more convenient than keeping applications from which to draw; some senior citizens find fulfillment and pleasure in working at a center periodically; some service organizations provide assistance on request. Using a referral service or leasing a teacher may ensure getting an experienced person, whereas using volunteers may not.

No matter the source of substitutes, have each applicant come into the center to get acquainted with the children, the routines, the parents, the program, the facilities, and other aspects that would make for good continuity.

A substitute/volunteer must feel wanted, needed, and valued! To assist in "belongingness" have a written handbook that outlines basic policies, guidelines, responsibilities, and expectations on the part of the center as well as the substitute.

If possible, invite each prospective substitute/volunteer to interact with a small group of children or participate in a variety of activities with the children *prior* to the time they are needed. After the per-＿n has worked in the center, the director should sit

---

Facts and Figures

While the average rate of growth between 1982 and 1995 for all occupations is projected to increase by 25 percent, employment in preschool education and child care (not including private household care) is expected to increase by 41 percent (NAEYC, 1985; Taeuber & Valdisera, 1986).

Despite the well-established link between staff training and the quality of child-care services, more than two thirds of the states fail to require preservice training for teachers in licensed or regulated child-care centers. Few states require preservice training for assistant teachers or family child-care providers (Morgan et al., 1993).

From research on relations between teacher characteristics and teacher behaviors we know that sensitive and involved teachers have more formal education and are likely to have taken courses in child development (Howes et al., 1993) . . . if we are to promote secure teacher-child relationships, we need to retain well-educated teachers who are fluent in child development (Howes & Hamilton, 1993, p. 30).

---

down and evaluate the experience with the person. How did the substitute/volunteer feel? What questions does he have? Does she want to be on your substitute roster—and would the director and other teachers want her to return? How did the children respond to him? Does she have any limitations to helping again—transportation, home responsibilities, physical or mental impairments that make it difficult to move quickly or to get up and down with the children?

Training

It is logical to think that a person who has some specific training from pre-entry vocational programs will perform better than one who has had no training at all. However, many directors find little or no choice as to whether prospective employees come with any training or experience. When they do find college-trained early childhood teachers, they can't afford to pay them enough to entice them to join the center staff. There is a serious shortage of trained entry-level people. In many cases, individual child-care facilities are forced to develop on-the-job training procedures for untrained staff (Shirah et al., 1993).

A main reason for the high employee turnover rate is inadequate and immediate on-the-job training or preservice training of unskilled employees. They don't know what to expect or what to do. Vocational training increased the retention of graduates–82 to 87 percent were still employed after 6 months and 68 percent continued in their position after 1 year. Providers consistently show employment preference for hiring program graduates over other applicants (Shirah et al., 1993).

Teacher-training programs need to include training in staff development and other management skills, expand the number of caregivers enrolled in the CDA and other credentialing processes, increase use of on-site staff development programs, and produce graduates with knowledge of child development principles.

In an article in *Phi Delta Kappan*, Phillips (1994) discusses the challenge of training and credentialing early childhood educators, stating, "Nowhere is the opportunity for collaboration clearer than in the training and credentialing of two groups of educators: teacher/caregivers for early care and education and teachers for elementary schools" (p. 214). The article focuses on center-based group programs for young children who have yet to enter the public schools, and refers to the National Child Care Staffing Study, which surveyed 1,309 classroom personnel at 227 child-care centers in four major cities (Whitebook et al., 1993, 1989b). They report the following preservice experience:

Bachelor's or graduate degree in related field	12%
At least one high school course in ECE	24%
Vocational training related to ECE	7%
Some college education related to ECE	19%
No education related to the field at all	38%

NAEYC has been especially important in defining standards of quality for programs for young children as well as standards for teacher preparation (National Association for the Education of Young Children, 1991a).

NAEYC (1994a) published a conceptual framework for the professional development of early childhood educators that included what early childhood professionals must know and be able to do. Among the items listed were to demonstrate and apply in practice an understanding of child development, to plan and implement a developmentally appropriate curriculum, and to establish and maintain productive relationships with families.

Representing a professional ideal, actual information reveals that some of these areas are inadequate or missing. State regulations govern the licensing of child-care centers and the certification of teachers and introduce a remarkable degree of inconsistency from state to state. Moreover, licensing for child care and teacher certification places different emphases on experience and training. While child-care licensing accepts experience in place of formal training and favors early access to employment over preservice training, the route to formal teacher certification usually prefers academic preparation to on-the-job training and values college degrees at the expense of work experience (McCarthy, 1988).

There are various approaches to training, education, and credentialing used in early childhood education. Some of the most common are: (1) multiple entry paths, (2) training based on principles of child development, (3) cooperative

and differentiated leadership in the classroom, (4) a meaningful role for parents, and (5) response to cultural pluralism (Phillips, 1994).

In many states and training institutions, credentialing of elementary education and the early childhood community have been unable to mutually agree on process or content. Jointly they need cooperation, not competition, and certification and licensing should be done under one area of leadership. They should develop new and creative patterns of program staffing—multiple teachers with a variety of credentials and certification. And third, they should collectively resolve funding and finance issues (*A quest for coherence*, 1990). Career ladders that link increased salaries and benefits to increased educational preparation and years of experience afford incentives for people to stay in the field and pursue advanced training, through grants and scholarships, and to promote diversity among personnel by making advanced training opportunities available for mature individuals of poor and minority backgrounds.

There is an increasing, not decreasing, demand for the care of young children outside the home, which means that the highest quality of services is needed for them. Separate traditions for the preparation of professionals for schools and for child care have created two distinct realms that are "fraught with problems, yet rich with resources. Collaboration between the two realms is a signal that the field is coming of age" (Phillips, 1994, p. 217).

Bredekamp (1995) asks, What do early childhood professionals need to know and be able to do?, and then offers some profound but workable solutions (content revisions to the guidelines), such as the following:

Changing the name from "teacher education" guidelines to "professional preparation" guidelines

Greater depth of preparation (environments, families/other adults, supervision)

More preparation in working with children with disabilities and special learning and developmental needs

Cultural and linguistic diversity

Individualization of instruction

Use of technology with children

Specificity on health, safety, and violence

A more family-oriented approach

A better base for working with children

Newer perspectives on professionalism

Demonstrating "an understanding of basic principles of administration, organization, and operation of early child programs, including supervision of staff and volunteers and program evaluation" (p. 69)

Advocates for improved quality for early childhood programs across the full age span of birth through age 8 can use the revised guidelines for several purposes:

1. Specialized, more consistent early childhood licensure standards in every state

2. Improved professionalism: national accreditation of teacher education programs, performance-based licensure (of teachers) required to practice

3. Certification of accomplished teachers through the National Board for Professional Teaching Standards (NBPTS) (Wise & Liebbrand, 1993)

To make recommended revisions, different sectors will have to work together—government and public agencies, trainers (including educational institutions), practitioners, communities, professional organizations, foundations, and child-care advocates (Morgan et al., 1993).

Training of teachers of young children has also been supported by business.

Family-To-Family Project. The Family-To-Family Project is administered by Dayton Hudson Foundation, Mervyn's, and Target Stores. It recruited more than $10 million over an 8-year period. In 1991, the average site received a grant of $216,000 for a 3-year period. The target population is family child-care providers and parents of children in care.

The project developed a four-part approach to support family child-care and improve quality: (1) training, (2) accreditation, (3) association building, and (4) consumer education. In 1991 the Family-To-Family Project was evaluated by the Families and Work Institute, and judged an enormous success.

Goals

1. Offer a training course of at least 15 hours to 8,000 providers in 32 communities

2. Help 1,200 providers become accredited by recognized organizations

3. Start or support a provider association in each community. These strong associations facilitate the improvement and support of quality care.

4. Educate consumers (parents) on the importance of training and accreditation for family child-care providers

5. Institutionalize the training, so that communities will continue to offer it after the Family-To-Family funds run out

ORIENTATION

When orienting new employees, a checklist is very useful to make sure that the candidate has been oriented to the policies for which he or she will be responsible. This gives the candidate an opportunity to ask questions, clarify issues, and become more familiar with employment expectations. The interviewer could have the candidate initial the items as they are discussed. The interview (and checklist, if used) should include: (1) an explanation of the orientation process; (2) a hiring conference when job description is discussed, a contract is signed, the candidate receives a center policy handbook, timetable for introductory phase is provided, there is a discussion about the probationary period, and a date is set for the first day of work; (3) routine procedures and policies are discussed (daily schedule, completion of payroll paperwork, health certificate, child abuse and criminal check form, call-in procedures, and pay dates); (4) professional responsibilities are discussed while reviewing the handbook (dress, code of conduct, discipline policies, supplies for work); (5) orientation to school (tour of facilities, issued keys and supplies, introduced to staff members, children and parents, emergency procedures, etc.); and (6) probationary conference (further discussion of handbook, results of initial observation skills shared, clarification of in-service expectation, and opportunity to ask and answer questions) (Hildebrand, 1993).

PERSONNEL MAINTENANCE

Goals

All center personnel should formulate personal and professional goals relating to their jobs at the center. These goals may be long- or short-range and should do the following:

1. Be stated specifically and simply
2. Be prioritized
3. Be challenging
4. Provide checkpoints and time lines to measure progress and completion
5. Be attainable

When employees know what personal and professional goals they want to achieve and make those goals known to their supervisors and fellow workers, they can help each other move toward achievement. For example, one worker may tell another about a workshop or publication related to that employee's goal. Another employee may share new knowledge or experiences in an effort to inform others or to clarify personal ideas. If an employee wanted to lose weight, other employees could suggest low-calorie foods, encourage exercise, and notice weight reduction.

Decision Making

Decision making can be easy or difficult. Some choices are serious; others are not. Some are fre-

quent and automatic; others require professional assistance. If people have had little experience in making choices (they were always told what to do and when to do it) or have generally made inappropriate choices, their ability to make good choices is diminished. A decision is not a goal in itself. People need a process of collecting information to form judgments to be used in making decisions. Click and Click (1990) suggest that a typical decision-making process involves four steps: (1) clarify or identify the problem, (2) develop a list of alternatives, (3) put alternatives in a priority order, and (4) choose an alternative to implement. Results and objectives need to be compared. If they match, continue; if they do not match, choose another alternative. Through this decision-making process, the ability to predict outcomes and, thereby, to make better decisions increases.

When outcomes involve other people, they should be included in the decision-making process as much as possible. Alternatives should be determined and stated clearly without attempts to influence the decision. Alternatives, however, should be offered only when there is a choice. When a certain procedure *must* be followed, the facts should be stated in the expected direction, but not in a demanding or negative way. Logical explanations encourage employees to move in the necessary direction. Example: "You'll need to get your report in on time in order to complete the budget for the annual meeting," not "Can you get your report in on time?" "No." "Well, you don't have that option."

When a legitimate choice is offered, the response should be accepted unquestioningly.

Motivation

Whereas an individual can be motivated through self-reward, motivating another person is more difficult. This is because being motivated is an individual's decision. The effectiveness of motivation is based on its quality and force; a motivator can be stimulating to one person and valueless to another. A motivator can be universal or unique to the individual and the situation.

Expectations can influence results, as shown by a scientific experiment with 60 preschool children enrolled in a summer Head Start program. Some teachers were told that the children in their classrooms were relatively slow learners, and other teachers were told their children had excellent intellectual ability and learning capacity. Which group learned more quickly? The second one, of course. "A teacher's expectations for her pupil's intellectual competence can come to serve as an educational self-fulfilling prophecy!" (Rosenthal & Jacobson, 1968).

Discuss this incident and its implications.

The way an employee is treated greatly influences personal performance. If the employee is treated as directionless, irresponsible, insecure, unreliable, immature, and lazy, he or she is likely to perform in this manner—needing specific directions, close supervision, constant encouragement, and incentives. On the other hand, if the employee is treated as self-directed, creative, and self-controlled, he or she is likely to respond as a productive, important member of the team. In general, the better employees are treated, the better they perform their jobs. They are more devoted, more congenial with peers and superiors, more satisfied with their jobs, and have less absenteeism, turnover, and conflict.

To encourage motivation, approach employees with a positive, supportive attitude; remember that individual willingness determines the ability to be motivated. Look for approaches with which employees feel individually comfortable. Be friendly—letting employees share personal goals and identify time lines, procedures, and guidelines helps them determine the feasibility of options. (Perhaps several minigoals will be more worthwhile than one major goal.) Certain employees who have a rapport with the others may be willing to assist in motivation strategies by being sounding boards, being supportive, and suggesting self-rewards without becoming watchdogs, whip-crackers, or enablers of employees who waste time, lose track of goals, or become discouraged.

Communication

Communication is often associated only with spoken language, but nonverbal elements such as tone of voice and gestures are important in communication, too. Conflicting verbal and nonverbal messages can cause confusion, misinterpretation, and misunderstanding. Was the speaker really asking a question, or was he seeking approval or support? If a choice was offered, was it really valid? Are there multiple meanings of what was said? How should joking, sarcasm, and ridicule be interpreted? How can one be sure that the message sent was the one received? How can a compliment or reprimand be given to a person so she will understand its true intent and message?

Individuals rely on communication to express themselves and to send and receive messages. Keeping channels of communication open should be a goal of each employee in the center. Misinterpretation of words, meanings, or gestures can lead to mishandled tasks, damaged relationships, or destroyed goals.

Body language is a powerful means of communication. The way heads are held, the distance between those interacting, presence or lack of physical contact, facial expressions, postures, and movements are strong nonverbal messages. Some nonverbal ways to keep communication lines open are the following:

1. Smile
2. Show interest by leaning into rather than away from the conversation, by posture, and by relaxing and giving the other person a chance to talk
3. Use facial expressions and head movements to show interest or a need for more information

4. Shake hands, give a pat on the back, or gently squeeze a hand when appropriate

5. Sit face-to-face to show cooperation rather than competition

6. Avoid facial expressions that convey negative ideas such as dislike, boredom, doubt (frowning, yawning, or wrinkled brow)

7. Maintain eye contact

8. Arrange seating so that both participants are on the same (eye) level (or both stand)

9. Consider the physical setting of the conversation (informal, uncluttered, unhurried)

10. Make actions and words support each other

11. Be honest and give frequent feedback (in both verbal or nonverbal communication)

Delegation

Delegating appropriate tasks has advantages. More work is accomplished, even though delegation may take more time at first. Employees gain new skills, self-respect, and knowledge and become more motivated as they expand their overall job understanding. The director is freed from routine tasks and can attend to more critical tasks. She may gain credibility among the staff members.

Administrators usually have two problems with delegation: (1) they delegate the wrong tasks and (2) the tasks they delegate are done improperly or late. In some cases, administrators assign tasks to the available employee rather than to the employee whose skills match the task, thus wasting valuable resources. Administrators may also fail to prioritize what needs to be done—urgent items go unattended, and minor items are completed quickly. Some administrators delegate only when they feel pressure, and then become frustrated because someone else fails to meet the deadline or omits important details. Although leaders have the authority and responsibility to delegate, they often choose not to for personal, economic, or personnel reasons. They sometimes forget that employees complete tasks on the basis of their understanding rather than the delegator's meaning.

Causes of ineffective delegation can be divided into three categories:

1. *Communication problems:* Disagreement on the specifics of the task delegated, insufficient guidelines or standards, improper training of delegatee, and unclear organizational objectives—all of these could be resolved by a short discussion, written instructions, or checkpoints.

2. *Emotional problems:* The administrator may feel personally insecure and be unwilling to work cooperatively toward a common goal.

3. *Job performance:* When employee has no clear job description or follow-up procedures, he procrastinates, is unsure of his responsibility, or fails to see consequences of not doing the job—clarification of these points would help the subordinate understand and complete the task.

These steps lead to effective delegation:

1. Explain what is to be done
2. Tell why the job is important
3. State desired results
4. *Provide the authority necessary to do the job*
5. Set completion date and time
6. Ask for feedback on the assignment
7. Provide ways to determine progress
8. Review the completed task with delegatee

Both the person who delegates the job and the one who is to perform it must work with—not against—each other. The delegator makes the reporting process clear: Is the delegatee to (1) investigate and report back, (2) investigate and suggest action, (3) advise on planned action, or (4) take action and then report back? Figure 6–7 provides an outline for delegating a task.

Periodically, one delegated task overlaps with another. To have tasks flow smoothly, both parties need to know the purpose, status, and progress of each task. Shared tasks bring satisfac-

Center's Name, Address, Telephone Number

Person assigned _____ Date _____

Task (explain briefly) _____

_____

_____

Importance and purpose of task _____

_____

Authority delegated (check one):
_____ Investigate and report back
_____ Investigate and suggest action
_____ Investigate and advise on planned action
_____ Investigate and take action without reporting back

Timeliness (outline steps and time required) _____

_____

Deadline for completion (write specific date) _____

Assignment reviewed and clarified: ___ Yes ___ No

Is this an independent task, or are others depending on information/action (give information) _____

_____

_____   _____
Delegatee   Delegator

Action taken _____

_____

Task completed (date) _____

Reported to delegator (by phone, in writing, in meeting) _____

_____

Further action, if any _____

_____

Figure 6–7   Delegated task form.

tion to individuals involved, expedite matters, build relationships, and introduce new methods of handling situations at the center.

Staff Meetings

Meetings with the staff should be held as often as is productive. Before scheduling a meeting, decide exactly what is to be accomplished (solve problems, receive reports, plan strategies, give directions to or train staff, clarify issues, share honors or information). What would the consequences be if no meeting were held? All meetings should be thoughtfully, not haphazardly, scheduled. Changes in regular meeting times require ample notice. If possible, circulate a written agenda (with prioritized items) a day or two before the meeting so staff can focus on issues. Schedule the most important items when most staff members are present. Avoid repeating items for those who arrive late, and don't use time for announcements that can be made by memo.

The timing of meetings should be considered carefully. Some days are better than others; some hours of the day are better than others. Ask for time preferences from those who will be involved.

Indicate on the agenda the sequence of topics and the approximate amount of time allotted for each. Items that need more than the scheduled time can be left for future meetings or continued;

other items can be postponed. Flexibility and consideration are important when conducting a meeting. An item scheduled to take 10 minutes may be very important to some employees and require much more discussion, deliberation, or information before a suitable conclusion can be reached. Stalemated issues should be rescheduled for another time so that the meeting can move forward. Moods, needs, and interests of those present set the tempo of the meeting. If the meeting moves more rapidly than expected, end it early.

When possible without lengthening the meeting, a short but pertinent *highlight* adds interest and participation. Assigned staff members can share important research findings, stimulating articles, new curriculum ideas or activities—a good way to keep employees abreast of important events.

If possible, follow up on the meeting with brief notes on the topics and decisions. Circulate copies to employees. This creates a future reference, informs those who were absent, and provides clarification.

Further meeting considerations include the following: Will substitutes be needed to handle classrooms, or can duties be rearranged with staff members who are not involved in the meeting? Is it necessary for all staff to be involved in each meeting? Will the meeting promote good feelings and relationships? Can different individuals introduce or discuss various topics so that everyone participates? How will people who monopolize the meeting be handled? How can the quiet person be encouraged to participate?

Both issues for discussion and issues requiring decisions come up at meetings. A clear distinction between them should be made for the staff before the meeting begins. On decision issues, agree, as a group, that they will be resolved. Will it be by majority (most) or consensus (all)? Both systems have advantages and disadvantages that should be considered carefully. Outspoken staff members may sway others, and less verbal or less opinionated members may feel ignored. Some members may take an indifferent attitude just to move the meeting along. Consensus requires each person to be involved, but may encourage feelings of coercion. Consider the ground rules for participation. Will individuals be allowed to take all the time they want in discussions, or will they be limited in number of comments and time? Of course, some items will require much serious discussion and even become emotional issues; others will be decided quickly. Figure 6–8 provides a sample staff meeting agenda.

Beginning and ending meetings on time encourages prompt attendance. When a serious or urgent matter cannot be resolved in the allotted amount of time, consensus from the group about continuing the meeting or recessing until a specific time in the near future helps members feel their input is valued.

Figure 6–8 Staff meeting agenda.

Date of meeting _____

From _____ To _____

Who should attend: _____

Please bring: _____

Highlight by: _____

	Agenda Item (by priority)	Time Allocated	Action Taken
1.			
2.			
3.			
4.			

Supervision

Supervision is very important in the successful operation of a child-care center. It may be performed by the director, the coordinator, or a person designated as supervisor. Supervision should be a support system for the employees, not a spy ring for the supervisor. Employees will feel supported if supervisors help them solve problems, use creativity and spontaneity, and feel they are an important part of the center staff. They will feel lack of support if they are controlled, treated as inferior, or evaluated harshly.

The method of supervision will depend largely on the philosophy of the center and the director. If the philosophy is that the employees must be told what to do and closely supervised, then the supervisor will be authoritarian. If the philosophy is that employees will be self-directed, cooperative, creative, and motivated, the supervisor will be supportive, friendly, and trusting.

Cahoon (1983) outlined four important steps in supervision:

1. The supervisor teaches correct principles.
2. The teacher directs herself by selecting and being guided by goals consistent with correct principles.
3. The supervisor prepares herself to be a source of help to the teacher, who in turn actually calls on the supervisor for help.
4. The teacher periodically gives an accounting to the supervisor of his progress toward his goals.

However jargon may differ, basic supervisory responsibilities remain the same: know the jobs to be done, their priority and timing, who is to do them, and the acceptable performance quality, then give full support to the person being supervised.

As a supervisor works with individual teachers, she must remember that each one is at a different stage. Katz (1972) defined the sequential steps as: survival (approximately the first year and a half of the experience); consolidation (approximately the end of the first year to the beginning of the third year—with overlapping steps); renewal (beginning after two and a half years of experience and extends beyond five years); and maturity (begins after three and a half years for most teachers and continues throughout their careers).

There are many different ways to supervise and interact. The supervisor must develop a leadership and interpersonal style that matches the objectives to be achieved and the people involved. However, the supervisor can do the most good in observing and interacting with others by taking a positive approach. Look for, write down, and give feedback on the good things employees do. Don't ignore undesirable behavior—but emphasize the positive.

People react differently to each other. For example, some people like closeness and share their feelings, ideas, and peculiarities. Some feel offended when others do not level with them, reveal emotions, or become serious. Supervisors should react to ideas, rather than people, as they observe and give feedback.

In an article about the emerging profile of supervisors, Caruso (1991) outlined supervisory positions and responsibilities as executive director, program director, educational coordinator, head teacher, and other early childhood supervisors with their multiple roles. Characteristically, supervisors are generally young, predominantly white, and virtually all female. They have diverse educational backgrounds—from only a high school diploma to university doctorates. One study showed that fewer than 10 percent of supervisors had degrees in early childhood education; only 50 percent had had prior experience in early childhood education before becoming supervisors. The National Child Care Staffing Study reveals that the average length of tenure for directors in a program is 5½ years, teachers remain in their programs for 2½ years, and assistant teachers remain only 18 months. Therefore, directors and other supervisors learn much of their supervisory craft through trial and error.

Some supervisors do have formal study in preparation for their role, but there is a critical need for professional preparation. Caruso (1991) suggests that

> as early childhood educators often find themselves in leadership positions at a fairly young age, perhaps training in supervision and staff development should be offered . . . as part of associate and bachelor's degree programs . . . perhaps linking early childhood education with field-based training for supervisors in settings where students are placed might serve the dual purpose of preparing both more effective teachers/caregivers and more effective supervisors. (p. 24)

State departments of education, licensing agencies, and professional organizations could do more to encourage directors to establish networks at local levels.

Several conclusions emerge from the need for supervisors in the field of early childhood education: Supervisors are a diverse group of people in diverse programs, the field needs more research reflecting comprehensive descriptions of supervisors, supervisory practices affect program quality, and directors and supervisors plan to stay in the fields of early childhood education and human services (Caruso, 1991).

Supervisors may have multiple roles in addition to administrative and teaching roles (fund-raising, curriculum development, staff development, program planning, recruiting, communicating with parents, coordinating, keeping records, hiring, working with social service staff, purchasing materials, and cleaning). Supervisors have the potential to influence the quality of a program significantly, especially with respect to their responsibilities in the areas of staff and curriculum development. Their education, training, and experience are among a number of factors that have a bearing on their effectiveness (Caruso, 1991).

The range of educational preparation of individuals in supervisory positions suggests that many come with limited knowledge of group care for young children; they learn much of their skills through trial and error, experiencing great anxiety and, often, pain in the process. Some su-

pervisors, however, *do* come from positions within early childhood programs. NAEYC (1985) estimates that more than 40 percent of all child-care workers in educational and service positions need to be replaced each year just to maintain the existing supply of child-care providers.

Training in supervision is certainly desirable. The most critical need for coursework is in staff development and supervision. Formal study of supervision principles and practices, experience working with children, and administration practice can ease many burdens of supervision.

According to Morgan's (1989) view of child-care regulations, only a few states stipulate that directors have coursework in administration, and 17 states require ongoing training for directors.

Staff Evaluation at Centers

Too often, *evaluation, review, annual accounting,* and similar terms connote criticism, onesidedness, and judgment. Personal measurement can be threatening even for employees who have major roles in establishing and fulfilling their personal goals. In this discussion, the term *performance appraisal* will be used and is intended to be positive rather than negative. It indicates two-way negotiation, in that both the supervisor and the supervisee have input into goals, both understand the target behavior or goals, both are working toward accomplishment, and both are aware of current research. Both know when they are on track.

Performance appraisals are evaluations about the quality, quantity, and timeliness of work performed by individual employees. These appraisals serve primarily two functions. First, they provide information needed to manage employee productivity; second, they provide information needed for proper salary administration. Evaluations about the effectiveness of employees' work are necessary if supervisors are to capably guide and support employees' contributions to the organization. Moreover, employees must know what is expected of them and how well they are performing in relation to those expectations if

❖ Stimulator   At his annual performance appraisal, Lester expressed personal concern about his interaction with the children—namely, his being authoritarian and negative, and expecting more than is possible for the children to do. He determined that his first efforts would be directed toward learning what is developmentally appropriate for the age span and interests of the children in his group. He felt that through greater knowledge about children, he would become more positive with the children and also less authoritarian (high expectation, high motivation). He talked about his ideas and approach with his supervisor. He outlined his procedure, initiated his plan, conferred periodically with his supervisor, and began to feel a greater cohesiveness with the children and more satisfaction in his job. Contrast the situation just described (including Lester's satisfaction and progress) with a scenario in which the supervisor sets the same goals for him.

❖　❖　❖　❖

they are to perform effectively, develop personally, and feel pride in accomplishment (Brigham Young University, 1986).

Directors, coordinators, or supervisors should give frequent and immediate feedback and should not save it for the scheduled review. Employees should know where they stand at all times and not be surprised in a scheduled review.

A review should be conducted with each employee at specific intervals, with additional reviews scheduled at the request of the supervisor or subordinate. They should be handled with diplomacy, professional etiquette, and privacy.

Some supervisors rank employee performance on a scale of poor, fair, good, excellent; others find more value in using a scale of frequently, occasionally, never. One state provides a self-evaluation form that covers two broad areas: general work habits and attitudes and skills (with children, parents, class, coworkers, and professional development). Examples of behaviors are observed and there is a summary of the discussion and evaluation conference in which strengths and leadership are identified, further goals or improvements are identified, action is agreed on, and both employee and supervisor sign and date the form (Carter, 1992).

Several steps can make the appraisal more successful. Before the interview, the supervisor and the employee each fill out an identical form about the employee's performance, recording only first-hand knowledge. This facilitates the appraisal. The supervisor should notify the person well in advance of the time and place of the meeting. During the actual review, the information should be discussed in a friendly, sincere, and helpful way. See Figure 6–9 for an example of a performance appraisal form.

Many employees view an evaluation as having three steps: praise, reprimand, and praise. When this is the procedure, most employees regard the praises as mere "coatings" for the reprimands, but place more stock in the reprimands. Evaluation tends to be viewed by these employees as a time for them to be told their mistakes, rather than a time for them to work with their supervisors to assess the positive and negative aspects of their performances for future improvement. Gaps in the appraisal can be narrowed by having either the employee or the supervisor reiterate at the end of the session the important points. It cannot be overemphasized that this meeting involves *both participants* in listening, discussing, and planning. The tone of the meeting is not judgmental, accusatory, or authoritarian. Rather, evaluation should be viewed constructively as growth-promoting and reflective, as well as being an opportunity for further planning.

When disciplinary action is necessary, the supervisor should conduct a thorough preliminary investigation of the infraction and its circumstances. He should then meet with the employee for an informal, friendly talk that includes an oral warning or reprimand, followed up with a written warning indicating penalties if the problem recurs (layoff, demotion, transfer, discharge).

```
(LOGO)          Center's Name, Address, and Telephone Number

Employee _____ Date _____
Job title _____
Job description (listed here or attached) _____
Goals for present year (prioritized) _____
_____
_____

Progress on above goals (results achieved) _____
_____

Things that have gone well _____
_____
_____

Further work on above goals (additions, changes) _____
_____
_____

Performance goals for next period (prioritized) _____
_____
_____

Working document for following period _____
_____

Game plan _____
_____

Resources needed _____
_____

Method of evaluation _____
_____
_____
_____


_____        _____
           Employee                               Supervisor
Comments of supervisor (may be on past or future goals, present performance,
recommendations, etc.) _____
_____
_____
_____
```

Figure 6–9   Performance appraisal form.

Feedback

The value of feedback is helping us become more aware of what we do and how we do it—thus increasing our ability to modify and change behavior.

Teachers need affirmation and constructive criticism. It is sometimes difficult to recognize effective behaviors and evaluate how effective they are. With proper feedback, teachers can improve their performance in the classroom.

Feedback should be specific, timely, consistent, direct, creditable, based on observed behavior, and constructive. It may be provided through verbal comments, checklists, written summaries, observation protocols, videotape reviews, or other ways convenient to a specific facility. Teachers usually get (or expect) feedback in the areas of environmental arrangement, classroom performance, teaching style, and personal aspects.

Things to Remember When Providing Feedback. George Lehner (1978), professor of psychology at the University of California, recommends the supervisor focus on the following:

- Specific behaviors rather than personal traits
- The "what" rather than "why"
- Observations rather than inference
- Defining behaviors on a continuum "more to less" rather than "either/or"
- Sharing ideas and information rather than giving advice
- Addressing behavior in the "here and now" rather than in the abstract
- The amount the person can comfortably receive rather than the amount of data collected
- The value it holds to the recipient and not the emotional release it may provide the supervisor

Some evaluations are planned and some are spontaneous. Some are for specific reasons (horizontal or vertical movement on the career ladder, raises, etc.) and some are for general feedback, encouragement, and relationship building. (See Perreault, 1989; Sciarra & Dorsey, 1990.)

When you are dealing with a procrastinator, a number of specific steps reduce frustration for those involved:

- Make sure expectations or assignments are specific. Ask for clarification if you feel there are any doubts or questions.

- Help the individual break the assignment into manageable segments.
- Observe how the person works so that suggestions are effective and compatible with behaviors. Decide if any out-of-the-ordinary solution may be applicable.
- Model if appropriate. Talk about what the task or assignment should look like.
- Avoid power struggles or threats. (See Hobbs, 1987; Ideas for Directors, 1989.)

Offer some sincere, timely compliments on things that have gone especially well for the person. Buffington (1989) reports that "individuals who compliment each other tend to disagree less, cooperate more, and generally think that similarities exist between them. Individuals who use compliments also tend to utilize positive voice inflections more frequently" (pp. 65–66).

Each member of the center staff should have the opportunity to make self-evaluations. Peer evaluations and evaluations with others (director, board members, etc.) may be helpful and positive if conducted in a proper manner—looking for the good and respecting feelings of others.

In conclusion, the administrator of a child-care facility has varied responsibilities, the most prominent of which are personal development and interaction with teaching and supporting staff. In addition, the director will plan for and have contact with children, parents, the board of directors (when applicable), and community residents as discussed in various chapters of this text.

Compensation

The importance of the work performed by child-care personnel is not reflected by the amount of

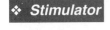 

A training manager once explained supervision this way. The five most important words: "I am proud of you." The four most important words: "What is your opinion?" The three most important words: "Will you please?" The two most important words: "Thank you." The one most important word: "You" (Leon, 1971).
Express your reaction when the above words are said to you.

Facts and Figures

Real earnings by child-care teachers have actually declined by nearly one quarter since the mid-1970s (Kisker et al., 1991; Whitebook et al., 1989b).

The National Child Care Staffing Study (Whitebook et al., 1989b) found that 70 percent of the teaching staff included in their sample worked without a written contract, and 40 percent had no written job description (Jorde-Bloom, 1989).

While there are some promising federal and state initiatives to enhance child-care staff compensation (Boyer et al., 1990; Child Care Employee Project, 1992; Whitebook et al., 1990), and increased attention is being focused on the issue through the Worth Wage Campaign and the Full Cost of Quality Campaign, we need not wait for the results of these national efforts to improve the plight of the early childhood workers in our programs. There are important steps that can immediately be taken to improve policies and practices regarding employee compensation (Jorde-Bloom, 1993a,b).

the compensation offered, the status granted, or opportunities offered for advancement in the field. The first national organization dedicated exclusively to improving the status and working conditions of early childhood staff was the Child Care Employee Project in the 1980s.

As discussed in Chapter 2, compensation is a very important factor in quality of centers and longevity of employees. As a nation, we historically have placed less value on any type of work done for or with young children. Pediatricians earn less than other types of physicians; kindergarten and elementary school teachers earn less than secondary school teachers (U.S. Bureau of Labor Statistics, 1989).

The *National Child Care Staffing Study* (Whitebook et al., 1989b) found that child-care center teaching staff earned annual wages less than one half of those paid to comparably educated women in other professions and less than one third of those in comparably educated men.

"Given the importance of the early childhood years in shaping later development and learning and the increasing number of families relying on early childhood programs, it is crucial that such programs employ personnel with the knowledge and ability needed to provide good care and education for our nation's youngest citizens."

The *Position Statement on Guidelines for Compensation of Early Childhood Professionals* by NAEYC states that families alone cannot be expected to bear the additional costs for quality child care and that these costs should be distributed more equitably among all sectors of society. The statement also says that early childhood professionals with *comparable qualifications, experience, and job responsibilities* should receive comparable compensation regardless of the setting of their job (community child-care center, family child-care provider, elementary school teacher) or ages of children served. Early childhood professionals should be encouraged to seek additional professional preparation (with appropriate reward); they should be provided with an adequate benefits package; and there should be a career ladder established that provides additional increments in salary based on performance and participation in professional development opportunities (National Association for the Education of Young Children, 1994a).

From an informal survey, 30 percent of directors, teachers, and parents agreed that child-care workers were somewhat underpaid—but 60 percent agreed that they are significantly underpaid. (*Parents,* etc., 1992). In this same article four strategies for raising teacher wages were clearly the most popular: lobbying federal legislators to increase child-care subsidies; national media campaign to highlight the value of early childhood education; working with employers to increase their support of child-care costs; and lobbying state officials to raise reimbursement rates.

In addition, "the most disconcerting finding of the survey was the degree of pessimism respondents displayed about the prospects for making progress on the wage issue. Nearly two thirds of all respondents predicted that the wages of teachers in early childhood centers will increase at a rate slower than the rate for all US employees over the next five years. Teachers were especially pessimistic" (Parents, teachers, and directors have their say on raising teachers' wages, 1992).

Jorde-Bloom (1993a) makes a distinction between internal and external equity within a center, school, or agency.

> Internal equity refers to the relationships of different jobs within a center, school or agency. It has two aspects: the relative similarities and differences in work content of jobs and the relative value or contribution of the work to the center's goals. . . . External equity refers to the relationships among employees in the external labor market. External equity is established by determining the going rate for similar work in relevant labor markets. . . . People evaluate their jobs by comparing what they give to it (their inputs—time, energy, commitment) with what they get from it (their outcomes—pay, recognition, security, friendship). . . . most people work best when they know the philosophy underlying their compensation and their potential for promotion. . . . A philosophy statement should . . . include a statement about beliefs regarding the confidentiality of compensation information . . . and a statement that acknowledges that teachers make a financial sacrifice to work in child care. (pp. 66–67)

In the second part or her article, Jorde-Bloom (1993b) continues:

> Good compensation systems are based on differentiated staffing patterns. . . . Movement in the system may be horizontal (between different jobs with similar pay) or vertical (between different jobs requiring greater responsibility and paying more). Vertical movement is based on increasing levels of education, experience, and performance in carrying out assigned roles. (p. 66)

Jorde-Bloom (1993a) also suggests five steps for program administrators in determining wages: (1) do a job analysis of each position, (2) write a job description for each position, (3) evaluate jobs to determine comparable worth, (4) set salaries and determine benefits, and (5) determine how individuals advance within the center. This process works best when a committee of varying degrees of seniority in the organization is appointed for establishing, reviewing, maintaining, and monitoring the compensation system.

When program budgets do not provide adequate compensation, children suffer the consequences. Low salaries, few benefits, and difficult working conditions result in higher rates of staff turnover; research demonstrates that children enrolled in programs with high staff turnover are especially vulnerable to impairment in the critical areas of social-emotional and language development (Whitebook et al., 1989b).

In reviewing salary schedules, Neugebauer (1994b) found a strong bias toward paying for knowledge and skills. In some centers, two teachers performing the same job with the same level of performance may be paid at significantly different levels. In yet another study, Neugebauer (1994a) provides guidelines for fine tuning the salary schedule for child-care workers. For example, he writes,

> the average Lead Teacher salary is 150% of the average Teacher Aide salary, based on a review of over 200 salary schedules; Executive Director 320%, Center Director 230%, Educational Coordinator 190%, Assistant Director 180%, Center Director 230%, Lead Teacher 150%, Administrative Asst. 150%, Custodian 130%, Assistant Teacher 120%, Substitute Teacher 120%, Cook 120%, Bus Driver 110%. (p. 55)

Four factors were used to measure the monetary value of employees: responsibility, training, experience, and performance.

Using the average pay for high school graduates as the base (100 percent), the following are the average increases provided for education:

MA degree in ECE-related field	135%
MA degree in unrelated field	130%
BA degree in ECE-related field	130%
BA degree in unrelated field	125%
AA degree in ECE-related field	125%
AA degree in unrelated field	115%
High school diploma or equivalent	100%

Two additional findings of Neugebauer (1994b) are worth attention: (1) "Research findings now make it clear that teachers with college degrees or college level ECE training will typically do a better job" and (2) "experience tends to be a poor predictor of teacher performance. . . . Teachers with more years on the job are not necessarily better performers than less experienced teachers. Therefore, centers are probably exercising good judgment in not investing heavily in longevity" (p. 7). In other words, pay for performance is better than pay for longevity.

In making or refining a salary schedule, consider simplicity, security (long-range view—options and opportunities), clarity, flexibility (to add, upgrade or downgrade positions), liability (affordability), and relevancy (rewarding most important factors) (Neugebauer, 1994c).

And from the Worthy Wage Campaign (1993):

> The situation is indeed a crisis. Every year, nearly half of all child care workers leave their jobs, and researchers have shown that a constant change in caregivers can have very negative effects on children's development. A major reason for the turnover is low pay: over 70% of this predominantly female work force earns an income below the poverty level. And when adjusted for inflation, the average child care wage actually decreased more than 20% in the past decade. (p. 43)

The Worthy Wage Campaign's overall goal is to secure fair and decent employment for child-care workers, as the cornerstone of quality services for children and families. To build a unified voice at the national level, the campaign is targeting its efforts in three areas: outreach and empowerment training for child-care workers (to encourage them to play a critical role in solving the staffing crisis); public education for child-care consumers; and the development of public policy initiatives, including salary enhancement and health benefit legislation, mechanisms to reward caregivers' training and experience with better compensation, and industrywide standards for a safe and fair work environment. The Child Care Employee Project, a nonprofit resource and advocacy organization founded in 1977, serves as the campaign's national coordinator.

Turnover

As an example of high turnover, the results of an informal employer-needs analysis of 20 child-care facilities in Mobile County, Alabama, revealed that the turnover rate of recently hired, lower paid employees ranged from 70 percent to in excess of 100 percent; most terminations and resignations came within 5 weeks of employment; and one job may turn over several times during a year (McNair, 1985). It is believed that the reasons for the employee turnover rate include no preservice training or inadequate immediate, on-the-job training of unskilled employees (Shirah et al., 1993). In a more recent study,

the results seem to warrant several modest observations. First, the vocational approach has increased retention of graduates. We find that 82 to 87% are still employed after six months and that 68% continue in their position after one year. Second, providers consistently show employment preference for hiring program graduates over other applicants. Finally, we note a trend toward career motivation (further training).

In addition to refining teacher-training programs to include training in staff development and other management skills, expanding the numbers of caregivers enrolled in the CDA and other credentialing processes, expanding the numbers of programs involved in NAEYC's accreditation process, increas-

---

Facts and Figures

. . . child-care workers have the highest turnover rate of all occupations. During the past decade, staff turnover in child-care centers nearly tripled, from 15 percent in 1977 to 41 percent in 1988, and another 60 percent of all child-care workers in private household settings left the field. This is more than double the average replacement rate of 19.4 percent for all occupations (National Association for the Education of Young Children, 1985; Galinsky, 1990b; Whitebook et al., 1991).

    The three main causes of this turnover rate are usually identified as low pay, lack of benefits, and stressful working conditions (National Association for the Education of Young Children, 1985; Children's Defense Fund, 1990; Kagan, 1990; Whitebook et al., 1991). A fourth major cause of turnover may be a lack of training in critical safety job skill competencies and knowledge of child development. For most of this century, NAEYC has supported the idea that a major factor in the quality and effectiveness of programs for young children is the specialized education of child-care staff; in recent years a great deal of research has emphasized this point (Shirah et al., 1993, p. 27).

---

ing use of on-site staff development programs, the child care industry needs viable vocational programs that will produce graduates with knowledge of child development principles. (Shirah et al., 1993, p. 30)

A recent study calls attention to the potentially serious effects of staff turnover on children's subjective experiences of a program (Howes & Hamilton, 1993). The extent to which program sponsors provide contexts that are hospitable and supportive of staff members should be given serious attention in assessing program quality. Evaluations should consider how staff members would feel "answering questions about respect, program philosophy, organization, etc." (Katz, 1994, p. 202).

Nationally, child-care center teachers have a 42 percent annual turnover rate. Therefore, there is concern for three types of teacher change: (1) when a child loses his primary teacher in the center, (2) when the child leaves the center, and (3) when the relationship between the teacher and the child changes (Hayes et al., 1990).

Changing a primary teacher influenced withdrawing behaviors in younger children. Older children who changed primary teachers to a less positive teacher-child relationship were most aggressive. "When children had secure teacher-child relationships, particularly if these relationships changed in a positive direction, children were more positive with peers" (Howes & Hamilton, 1993, p. 29), indicating that children use their child-care teachers for emotional support, and that teacher-child relationships are not unimportant or interchangeable.

"If we are to retain teachers who can promote secure teacher-child relationships as well as teachers who will stay in the field we must improve both compensation and training" (Howes & Hamilton, 1993, p. 30).

The tenure rate or length of time individuals are in a given position or in a given field is not good. The Bureau of Labor Statistics data on tenure for 1987 show 2.7 years for the job category "Child Care Worker, Except Private Household" versus 6.6 years for the average of all jobs (Decker & Decker, 1992; Whitebook et al., 1989b).

Although teachers in the National Child Care Staffing Study expressed very high levels of satisfaction with their work, the most important predictor of staff turnover was wages (Whitebook et al., 1989b). Other causes of termination were lack of benefits (e.g., health, retirement), lack of career ladder, and a low social status.

Compiling information from various sources, the following conclusions can be drawn:

1. Children who changed primary teachers as young toddlers regardless of the qualitative nature of their relationship with their teachers were more aggressive than children who did not change their primary teacher.

2. Changes in primary teachers are difficult for young children, even for those fortunate enough to have a new primary teacher who fosters emotional security.

3. When older children changed primary teachers and changed to a less positive teacher-child relationship they were most aggressive.

4. A more secure child is better prepared to adjust to the loss of a primary teacher and to develop a positive relationship with the new teacher than is an insecure child.

5. Many children may have little opportunity to develop a stable primary teacher relationship because of accordion staffing, pooling classes, or using different teachers for outdoor or special activities.

CHAPTER SUMMARY

1. Administration and staffing goals have been identified in the Accreditation Criteria by the National Association for the Education of Young Children.

2. Current written policies, procedures, records, and healthy relationships among center personnel are critical to the success of the experience for children and adults.

3. Staffing a child-care program requires qualified personnel in all positions.

4. High-quality early childhood programs support two goals: professional development of staff and improving public understanding and support.

5. Professionalism is highly valued in early childhood settings—keeping current is an important part of professionalism.

6. Professionals in early childhood programs believe in and support a code of ethics, which outlines responsibilities to children, families, colleagues, and community.

7. CDA training, available to child-care workers, is a valued accomplishment. Certification helps ensure the quality of teachers and programs and enhances center quality.

8. Specific characteristics of teachers (such as training, teacher-child relationships, sensitivity, involvement, dependability, teachableness, etc.) enhance the program for children and families.

9. Participation in some or all **Stimulators** gives an opportunity to solidify one's thinking about child care and to learn in a meaningful way.

10. There should be written personnel policies and procedures regarding job descriptions; recruiting, hiring, and (voluntary and involuntary) terminations; job orientation; substitutes; and other matters pertinent to each center. Well-defined goals, involvement of individuals, and congeniality are important for personnel maintenance.

11. Preservice, in-service, and ongoing training benefits the children, the success of the program, and longevity of teachers.

12. Supervisors teach correct principles, help supervisees set appropriate goals, and prepare themselves to be resources.

13. Personnel at all levels need and want constructive feedback. To be effective, performance needs to be carefully planned and appraised by both employee and supervisor in a constructive and growth-promoting way.

14. The high turnover of workers in child care affects the quality of the program, the stability of the children, and the morale of the staff.

PARTICIPATORS

Select and complete those activities that would increase your present knowledge, skills, value to a center, or professional training.

Self

1. Write a personal assessment. Include strengths/weaknesses, successes/failures, skills, talents, preferences, and so on. Consider your multiple roles (home, work, church, community, leisure), the people who depend on you, the people you depend on, the purposes and outcomes of these relationships, and your own satisfaction.

2. Write your personal and professional short- and long-range goals.

3. Evaluate your progress toward one of your goals. Can you proceed or do you first need to make some modifications? Is your goal attainable, considering present resources (e.g., time, money)? Is the goal valuable enough to pursue?

4. Given no restrictions on money, time, skills, or other means, outline your 5-year goals. How realistic are these goals?

5. Prepare a list of constructive ways to reduce stress and burnout; prioritize them.

6. On a scale of 1 (strong) to 5 (weak), rate yourself on the following traits:
   a. Team member
   b. Participator
   c. Friendliness
   d. Rigidity
   e. Energy
   f. Communication skills
   g. Constructiveness
   h. Creativity
   i. Preference to work with people
   j. Preference to work with machines, data, and programs

7. Evaluate your personal health in terms of nutrition; exercise; rest; use of alcohol, drugs, and tobacco; and so on.

8. Give an example of turning a negative teaching experience into a growth-promoting one.

9. Write or update your personal resume using information in the chapter as a guideline.

10. Write a job description for a director.

11. Evaluate your effectiveness as an administrator of a child-care center. What components are important?

12. List five of your greatest motivators. List five of your "un-motivators."

13. Using time sheets from Chapter 7, note the order in which you completed several tasks. (Note the steps followed: liked or disliked, familiar or unfamiliar, easy or difficult, quick or time-consuming, scheduled or unscheduled, self-initiated or requested, crisis or routine, interesting or uninteresting, rewarding or nonrewarding.)

14. Make a list of things you tend to procrastinate doing most often. Star the items you are currently putting off. Decide why you procrastinate or what you do instead of the task. If you are a procrastinator, how do you feel about it? What are the causes of your procrastination? Outline some steps and deadlines to reduce or eliminate procrastination.

15. Using the time management information in Chapter 7, plan daily, weekly, and monthly schedules so you are more productive—but still enjoy daily life!

Working with Staff

1. Prepare and evaluate an application form.

2. Prepare an interview form.

3. Write a letter of acceptance to a new employee. Write a letter telling a potential employee that he did not get the job.

4. Role-play an interview. After 3 minutes, switch roles and have the interviewee become the interviewer.

5. Prepare a written contract for a new employee. Indicate whether employment is permanent or probationary. Specify details.

6. Prepare a termination form for an employee.

7. Prepare an orientation packet for a new employee.

8. Prepare a questionnaire related to in-service training.

9. Write job descriptions for the following: preschool teacher, teacher's aide, custodian, secretary.

10. Help a peer or subordinate write goals; include short- and long-range, personal, and professional goals.

11. List three group decisions that need to be made. Agree whether the decisions will be made by majority vote or consensus. Hold a discussion about one of the problems, make a decision, and implement it.

12. Propose a goal and ask four to six people to make, through consensus, a plan of action to achieve it.

13. List at least three ways to get others to do what you want them to do. How does it make those people feel?

14. Discuss barriers you have encountered in talking with another person (such as contradictory body language, insufficient information, misunderstanding, prejudice, etc.). For what possible reasons do such barriers present themselves? What can you do to reduce or remove these barriers? Name the person you like to talk with most and state the reasons you enjoy the conversation.

15. For a period of 2 days, carry a piece of paper and a pencil for the purpose of noting your own and others' nonverbal behavior. Record whether you were the sender or receiver of the message. What did the message convey to you? What do you suppose it meant to the other person? Were your messages positive (smile, wink, nod) or negative (frown, shrug, glare)?

16. Evaluate the delegation form in Figure 6–7. Suggest modifications. Use the form at least

three times as you delegate tasks to others. Revise it to better fit your needs.

17. Write three letters of professional recommendation; write two letters of personal recommendation.

REFERENCES

Austin, A. M., & Morrow, S. 1985–1986. Concerns of child care administrators as modified by education, experience, and ownership of facility. *Educational Research Quarterly*, 10(2).

Bellm, D., & Whitebook, M. 1987a. Improving your center's substitute policies and procedures. *Child Care Information Exchange*, Jan., 16–18.

Bellm, D., & Whitebook, M. 1987b. A good sub is hard to find: Establishing a substitute referral system. *Day Care and Early Education*, Summer, 16–20.

Bloom, P J. 1997. *A Great place to work: Improving conditions for staff in young children's programs* (Rev.). Washington, DC: NAEYC.

Bollin, G. G. 1993. An investigation of job stability and job satisfaction among family day care providers. *Early Childhood Research Quarterly*, 8, 207–220.

Botkin, D., & Twardosz, S. 1988. Early childhood teacher's affectionate behavior: Differential expression to female children, male children, and groups of children. *Early Childhood Research Quarterly*, 3, 167–177.

Boyer, M., Gerst, C., & Eastwood, S. 1990. *Between a rock and a hard place: Raising rates to raise wages.* Minneapolis: Child Care Workers Alliance.

Bredekamp, S. (Ed.) 1985. *Guide to accreditation by the National Academy of Early Childhood Programs.* Washington, DC: NAEYC.

Bredekamp, S. (Ed.) 1987. *Developmentally appropriate practice in early childhood programs serving children from birth through age 8* (Ex. Ed.). Washington, DC: NAEYC.

Bredekamp, S. 1995. What do early childhood professionals need to know and be able to do. National Institute for Early Childhood Professional Development. *Young Children*, 50(2), 67–69.

Bredekamp, S., & Copple, C. (Eds.) 1997. *Developmentally appropriate practice in early childhood programs.* (Rev. ed.). Washington, DC: NAEYC.

Brigham Young University. 1986. *Personnel update*, 10(1).

Buffington, P. W. 1989. Compliments. *Sky,* Jan., 65–66.

Cahoon, O. W. 1983. *Successful supervision: Principles and practices for early childhood education.* Provo, UT: Author.

Carter, M. 1992. May. Evaluating staff performance. *Exchange,* 85, 5–8.

Caruso, J. J. 1991. Supervisors in early childhood programs: An emerging profile. *Young Children,* 47(6), 20–26.

CDA Professional Preparation Program. 1989. *Essentials for child development associates,* draft copy. Washington, DC: Council for Early Childhood Professional Recognition.

Cherry, L. 1975. The preschool teacher-child dyad: Sex differences in verbal interaction. *Child Development,* 532–535.

Child Care Employee Project. 1992. On the horizon: New policy initiatives to enhance child care staff compensation. *Young Children,* 47(5), 39–42.

Children's Defense Fund. 1990. *S.O.S. America: A children's defense budget.* Washington, DC: Author.

Children's Defense Fund. 1992. Child care and early childhood development. *The state of America's children* (pp. 29–36). Washington, DC: Author.

Clarke-Stewart, K. 1987. In search of consistencies in child care research. In D. A. Phillips (Ed.), *Quality in child care: What does research tell us?* (pp. 105–119). Washington, DC: NAEYC.

Click, P. M., & Click, D. W. 1990. *Administration of schools for young children* (3rd ed.). Albany, NY: Delmar.

Collins, G. 1987. Wanted: Child care workers, age 55 and up. *The New York Times,* Dec. 15, 1, 8.

Cost, Quality, & Child Outcomes Study Team. 1995. *Cost, quality, and child outcomes in child care centers.* Denver: Economics Department, University of Colorado.

Decker, C. A., & Decker, J. R. 1992. *Planning and administering early childhood programs.* Upper Saddle River, NJ: Merrill/Prentice Hall.

Drost, D., O'Brien, F., & Marsh, S. 1987. Exit interviews: Master the possibilities. *Personnel Administrator,* Feb., 104–110.

Elicker, J., & Fortner-Wood, C. 1995. Research in review. Adult-child relationships in early childhood settings. *Young Children,* 51(1), 68–78.

Enz, B., & Christie, J. 1994. Teacher play interaction styles and their impact on children's play and emer-

gent literacy. Paper presented at the annual meeting of the American Educational Research Association, April, New Orleans.

Equal Opportunity Commission. 1980. *Affirmative action: A guidebook for employers* (Vols. 1 & 2). Washington, DC: Author.

Erwin, E., Carpenter, E., & Kontos, S. 1993. What preschool teachers do when children play. Paper presented at the annual meeting of the American Educational Research Association, April, Atlanta.

Farran, D., Silveri, B., & Culp, A. 1991. Public school preschools and the disadvantaged. In L. Rescorla, M. Hyson, & K. Hirsh-Pasek (Eds.). *Academic instruction in early childhood: Challenge or pressure?* No. 53, (pp. 64–74). San Francisco: Jossey-Bass.

File, N., & Kontos, S. 1993. The relationship of program quality to children's play in integrated early intervention settings. *Topics in Early Childhood Special Education* 13(1), 1–18.

Galejs, I., & Hegland, S. 1982. Teacher-child interactions and children's locus of control tendencies. *American Educational Research Journal,* 19(2), 293–302.

Galinsky, E. 1990a. The costs of not providing quality early childhood programs. *Annual Editions: Early Childhood Education,* 91/92, 233–240.

Galinsky, E. 1990b. *Reaching the full cost of quality in early childhood programs.* Washington, DC: NAEYC.

Havercamp, M., & Everts, J. 1992. Creating cooperation and empowerment in a child care center. *Day Care and Early Education,* 19(4), 28–31.

Hayes, C. D., Palmer, F. L., & Zaslow, M. 1990. *Who cares for America's children: Child care policy for the 1990s.* Washington, DC: National Academy Press.

Hendrick, J. 1996. *The whole child.* Upper Saddle River, NJ: Prentice Hall.

Herr, J., Johnson, R. D., & Zimmerman, K. 1993. Benefits of accreditation: A study of directors' perceptions. *Young Children,* 48(4), 32–35.

Hestenes, L., Kontos, S., & Bryan, Y. 1993. Children's emotional expression in child care centers varying in quality. *Early Childhood Research Quarterly,* 8, 295–307.

Hildebrand, V. 1993. *Management of child development centers.* Upper Saddle River, NJ: Merrill/Prentice Hall.

Hobbs, C. R. 1987. Thirteen ways to procrastinate efficiently and gain control of your time. *Working Woman,* Oct., 96–97.

Horsfall, J. 1999. Welcoming volunteers to your child care center. *Young Children,* Nov., 35–36.

Howes, C., & Hamilton, C. E. 1993. The changing experience of child care: Changes in teachers and in teacher-child relationships and children's social competence with peers. *Early Childhood Research Quarterly,* 8, 15–32.

Howes, C., Phillips, D. A., & Whitebook, M. 1997. Teacher characteristics and effective teaching in child care: Findings from the National Child Care Staffing Study. *Child Care Quarterly.*

Howes, C., Smith, E., & Galinsky, E. 1995. *Florida quality improvement study: Interim report.* New York: Families & Work Institute.

Howes, C., & Stewart, P. 1987. Child's play with adults, toys, and peers: An examination of family and child-care influences. *Developmental Psychology* 23(3), 423–430.

Ideas for directors. 1989, April. *Exchange,* 66, 21.

Involving men in the lives of children. 1999. National Association for the Education of Young Children. NAEYC #593. Washington, DC: NAEYC.

Jorde-Bloom, P. 1988. Factors influencing overall job satisfaction and organizational commitment in early childhood work environments. *Journal of Research in Childhood Education,* 3, 107–122.

Jorde-Bloom, P. 1989. Professional orientation: Individual and organizational perspectives. *Child and Youth Care Quarterly,* 18(4), 227–240.

Jorde-Bloom, P. 1993a. 'But I'm worth more than that!' Addressing employee concerns about compensation. Full cost of quality report. Part 1. *Young Children,* 48(3), 65–68.

Jorde-Bloom, P. 1993b. "But I'm worth more than that!": Implementing a comprehensive compensation system. Full cost of quality report. Part 2. *Young Children,* 48(4), 67–72.

Kagan, S. 1990. *Excellence in early childhood education: Defining characteristics and next-decade strategies.* Washington, DC: Outreach Staff of Information Services, Office of Educational Research and Improvement.

Katz, L. G. 1972. Developmental stages of preschool teachers. *Elementary School Journal,* Oct., 50–54.

Katz, L. G. 1994. Perspectives on the quality of early childhood programs. *Phi Delta Kappan,* Nov., 200–205.

Kisker, E., Hofferth, S. L., Phillips, D., & Farquhar, E. 1991. *A profile of child care settings: Early education and care in 1990.* Washington, DC: U.S. Department of Education, Office of the Under Secretary.

Knowles, M. 1980. *The modern practice of adult education.* New York: Cambridge University Press.

Kontos, S., & Dunn, L. 1993. Caregiver practices and beliefs in child care varying in developmental appropriateness and quality. In S. Reifel (Ed.), *Advances in Early Education and Day Care,* Vol. 5 (pp. 53–74). Greenwich, CT: JAI Press.

Kontos, S., Howes, C., Shinn, B., & Galinsky, E. 1994. *Quality in family child care and relative care.* New York: Teachers College Press.

Kontos, S., & Wilcox-Herzog, A. 1996. Influences on children's competence in early childhood classrooms. Unpublished manuscript.

Kontos, S., & Wilcox-Herzog, A. 1997. Teachers' interaction with children: Why are they so important? *Young Children,* Jan., 4–12.

Latest CDA survey results are in! 1994. *Competence, News for the CDA Community,* 11(3).

Layzer, J., Goodson, B., & Moss, M. 1993. *Observational study of early childhood programs, Final report, Vol. 1: Life in preschool.* Washington, DC: U.S. Dept. of Education.

Lehner, G. 1978. Aids for giving and receiving feedback. *Exchange,* June.

Leon, R. O. 1971. *Manage more by doing less.* New York: McGraw-Hill.

Love, J., Ryer, P., & Faddis, B. 1992. *Caring environments—Program quality in California's publicly funded child development programs: Report on the legislatively mandated 1990–91 staff/child ratio study.* Portsmouth, NH: RMC Research Corporation.

Manlove, E. E. 1993. Multiple correlates of burnout in child care workers. *Early Childhood Research Quarterly,* 8, 499–518.

McCarthy, J. 1988. *State of certification of early childhood teachers: An analysis of the 50 states and the District of Columbia, an NAEYC policy perspective.* Washington, DC: National Association for the Education of Young Children.

McCartney, K. 1984. Effect on day care environment on children's language development. *Developmental Psychology,* 20(2), 244–260.

McNair, R. H. 1985. *Survey of twenty child care facilities in Mobile, Alabama.* Unpublished manuscript.

Melhuish, E., Lloyd, E., Martin, S., & Mooney, A. 1990a. Type of child care at 18 months—II. Relations with cognitive and language development. *Journal of Child Psychology and Psychiatry, 31*(6), 861–870.

Melhuish, E., Mooney, A., Martin, S., & Lloyd, E. 1990b. Type of child care at 18 months—I. Differences in interactional experience. *Journal of Child Psychology and Psychiatry, 31*(6), 849–859.

Morgan, G. 1989. *The national state of child care regulations, 1989.* Watertown, MA: Work/Family Directions.

Morgan, G., Azer, S. L., Costley, J. B. Elliot, K., Genser, A., Goodman, I. F., & McGimsey, B. 1994. Future pursuits: Building early care and education careers. National Institute for Early Childhood Professional Development. *Young Children, 49*(3), 80–83.

Morgan, G., Azer, S. L., Costley, J. B., Genser, A., Goodman, I. F., Lombardi, J., & McGimsey, B. 1993. *Making a career of it: The state of the states report on career development in early care and education.* Boston: Center for Career Development in Early Care and Education, Wheelock College.

Morrison, G. S. 1991. *Early childhood education today* (5th ed.). Upper Saddle River, NJ: Merrill/Prentice Hall.

Mulrooney, M. 1990. Reaccreditation: A snapshot of growth and change in high quality early childhood programs. *Young Children, 45*(2), 58–61.

National Association for the Education of Young Children. 1985. *In whose hands? A demographic fact sheet on child care providers.* Washington, DC: Author.

National Association for the Education of Young Children. 1991a. *Accreditation criteria and procedures of the National Academy of Early Childhood Programs.* Washington, DC: Author.

National Association for the Education of Young Children. 1991b. Announcement of National Institute for Early Childhood Professional Development. *Young Children, 46*(6), 16.

National Association for the Education of Young Children. 1991c. Early childhood teacher certification: A position statement of the Association of Teacher Educators and the National Association for the Education of Young Children. Adopted July/August 1991. *Young Children, 47*(1), 16–21.

National Association for the Education of Young Children. 1994a. NAEYC position statement: A conceptual framework for early childhood professional development. NAEYC #503. *Young Children, 49*(3), 68–77.

National Association for the Education of Young Children. 1994b. Using NAEYC's code of ethics: A tool for real life. *Young Children, 49*(5), 56–77.

National Center for the Early Childhood Work Force. 1993. *The National Child Care Staffing Study revisited: Four years in the life of center-based child care.* Washington, DC: Author.

National Center for Education Statistics. 1992, Nov. *Issue brief: Teacher attrition and migration (IB-2-92).* Washington, D.C.: U.S. Department of Education.

Neugebauer, R. 1991, Jan./Feb. Twelve reasons people love to work for you. *Exchange, 77,* 5–8.

Neugebauer, R. 1994a, May. Guidelines for fine tuning your salary schedule. *Exchange, 97,* 55–64.

Neugebauer, R. 1994b, Mar. Is your salary schedule up to speed? *Exchange, 96,* 6–17.

Neugebauer, R. 1994c, May. Recruiting and retaining men in your center. *Exchange, 97,* 5–11.

Newman, S. M., Vander Ven, K., Ward, C. R., & Generations Together. 1992. *Guidelines for the Productive employment of older adults in child care.* NAEYC #763. Washington, DC: National Association for the Education of Young Children.

Ogilvy, C., Boath, E., Cheyne, W., Jahoda, G., & Schaffer, R. 1992. Staff-child interactions styles in multiethnic nursery schools. *British Journal of Developmental Psychology, 10,* 85–97.

Olsen, G. 1993, July. The exit interview: A tool for program improvement. *Exchange, 92,* 71–75.

Parents, teachers, and directors have their say on raising teachers' wages. 1992, May. *Exchange, 85,* 13–18.

Perreault, J. 1989, April. Developing the employee handbook: Grievance procedure. *Exchange, 66,* 41–44.

Phillips, C. B. 1994. The challenge of training and credentialing early childhood educators. *Phi Delta Kappan,* Nov., 214–217.

Phillips, D., McCartney, K., & Scarr, S. 1987. Child-care quality and children's social development. *Developmental Psychology, 23*(4), 537–543.

Powell, D. R., & Stremmel, A. J. 1989. The relation of early childhood training and experience to the professional development of child care workers. *Early Childhood Research Quarterly, 4,* 339–355.

Quay, L., & Jarrett, O. 1986. Teachers' interactions with middle- and lower-SES boys and girls. *Journal of Educational Psychology, 78*(6), 495–498.

A quest for coherence in the training of early care and education teachers. 1990. New York: Rockefeller Brothers Fund.

Rosenthal, R., & Jacobson, L. 1968. *Pygmalion in the classroom.* New York: Holt, Rinehart & Winston.

Ruopp, R., Travers, J., Coelen, C., & Glantz, F. 1979. *Children at the center: Final report of the National Day Care Study* (Vol. 1). Cambridge, MA: ABT Associates.

Scarr, S., Phillips, D., McCartney, K., Abbott-Shim, M. 1993. Quality of child care as an agent of family and child care policy in the United States. *Pediatrics,* 91(1), 182–188.

Sciarra, D. J., & Dorsey, A. G. 1990. *Developing and administering a child care center* (2nd ed.). Albany, NY: Delmar.

Sheerer, M., & Jorde-Bloom, P. 1990, April. The ongoing challenge: Attracting and retaining quality staff. *Exchange,* 72, 11–16.

Sherwood, A. 1983. Exit interviews: Don't just say goodbye. *Personnel Journal,* Sept., 744–750.

Shirah, S., Hewitt, T. W., & McNair, R. H. 1993. Preservice training fosters retention: The case for vocational training. *Young Children,* 48(4), 27–31.

Spodek, B., & Saracho, O. 1994. *Right from the start: Teaching children ages three to eight.* Boston: Allyn & Bacon.

Spodek, B., Saracho, O., & Peters, D. 1988. Professionalism, semiprofessionalism, and craftsmanship. In B. Spodek, O. Saracho, & D. Peters (Eds.), *Professionalism and the early childhood practitioner.* New York: Teachers College Press.

Status report #8 on early childhood education. 1993, May. *Exchange.*

Stipek, D., Feiler, R., Daniels, D., & Milburn, S. 1992. Effects of different instructional approaches on young children's achievement & motivation. *Child Development,* 66, 209–223.

Stremmel, A. J., Benson, M. J., & Powell, D. R. 1993. Communication, satisfaction, and emotional exhaustion among child care center staff: Directors, teachers, and assistant teachers. *Early Childhood Research Quarterly,* 8, 221–233.

Taeuber, C. M., & Valdisera, V. 1986. *Women in the American economy* (Series P-12) (No. 146). Washington, DC: U.S. Department of Commerce, Bureau of the Census.

Tenoschok, M. 1988. When teachers resign, ask why—And then learn from what they tell you. *American School Board Journal,* Sept., 26–27.

U.S. Bureau of Labor Statistics. 1989. *Current population survey.* Unpublished analyses. Washington, DC: Author.

Wadlington, E. 1995. Basing early childhood teacher education on adult education principles. *Young Children,* May, 76–79.

Wassom, J. 1994, May. The center will sell itself . . . and other child care marketing myths. *Exchange,* 97, 17–21.

Weikart, D. 1989. *Quality preschool programs: A long-term social investment.* Occasional paper No. 5, Ford Foundation Project of Social Welfare and the American Future. New York: Ford Foundation.

Whitebook, M., Howes, C., Darrah, R., & Friedman, J. 1982. Caring for caregivers: Staff burnout in child care. In L. Katz (Ed.), *Current topics in early childhood education* (Vol. 4) (pp. 212–235). Norwood, NJ: Ablex.

Whitebook, M., Howes, C., & Phillips, D. 1989a. *The National Child Care Staffing Study: Who cares? Child care teachers and the quality of care in America.* Final report. Oakland, CA: Child Care Employee Project.

Whitebook, M., Howes, C., & Phillips, D. A. 1989(b). *Who cares? Child care teachers and the quality of care in America. Final Report of the National Child Care Staffing Study.* Oakland, CA: Child Care Employee Project.

Whitebook, M., Howes, C., Phillips, D., & Pemberton, C. 1989c. Who cares? Child care teachers and the quality of care in America. *Young Children,* 41–45.

Whitebook, M., Howes, C., Phillips, D., & Pemberton, C. 1991. Who cares? Child care teachers and the quality of care in America. In K. M. Paclorek & J. H. Munro (Eds.), *Annual editions, early childhood education,* 91/92 (pp. 20–24). Guilford, CT: Dushkin.

Whitebook, M., Pemberton, C., Lombardi, J., & Galinsky, E. 1990. *From the floor: Raising child care salaries.* Oakland, CA: Child Care Employee Project.

Whitebook, M., Phillips, D., & Howes, C. 1993. *The National Child Care Staffing Study Revisited.* Oakland, CA: Child Care Employee Project.

Wilcox-Herzog, A., & Kontos, S. 1996. The nature of teacher talk in early childhood classrooms and its relationship to children's competence with objects and peers. Manuscript under review (1997), Department of Child Development and Family Studies, Purdue University, West Lafayette, IN.

Willer, B., & Bredekamp, S. 1993. A "new" paradigm of early childhood professional development. *Young Children,* 48(4), 63–66.

Willer, B., Hofferth, S. L., Kisker, E. E., Divine-Hawkins, P., Farquhar, E., & Glantz, F. G. 1991. *The demand and supply of child care in 1990: Joint findings from The National Child Care Survey 1990 and A Profile of Child Care Settings.* Washington, DC: National Association for the Education of Young Children.

Willer, B., & Johnson, L. C. 1989. *The crisis is real: Demographics on the problems of recruiting and retaining early childhood staff.* Washington, DC: National Association for the Education of Young Children.

Wise, A., & Liebbrand, J. 1993. Accreditation and the creation of a profession of teaching. *Phi Delta Kappan* 75(2), 133–136.

Wittmer, D., & Honig, A. 1988. Teacher re-creation of negative interactions with toddlers. *Early Child Development and Care*, 33, 77–88.

Woods, R., & Macaulay, J. 1987. Exit interviews: How to turn a file filler into a management tool. *The Cornell HRA Quarterly*, Nov., 39–46.

Worthy wage campaign. 1993. An emerging voice for the child care work force. *Day Care & Early Education*, 20(4), 43.

Chapter 7

Management of Programs, Resources, and Time

Guide for Readers

❖ *Managerial functions for programs, resources, and time include planning, organizing, implementing, and evaluating.*

❖ *Directors/managers must deal with individual goal setting, decision making, motivation, communication, and time management.*

❖ *Different theories, applied to early childhood education settings, can support program goals.*

❖ *On or off the job, time-use habits need contemplation and sometimes adjustment.*

❖ *When directors/managers prioritize needs, the program functions more smoothly.*

INTRODUCTION

Management skills must be acquired. Good managers may make their jobs appear easy, as if the ability to do it comes naturally. But just like the ease and confidence of U.S. Olympic team competitors, the things-just-fall-into-place impression made by a good manager comes only through the investment of time and energy. Even then, challenges and setbacks happen. This text is designed to help experienced and inexperienced child-care providers administer early childhood programs to make the programs economically feasible and to create centers that are exemplary places for both children and adults.

Administrators know that personal and organizational success depends on how well they meet the needs of their clients and employees. This means that the needs of each child and her immediate family members are carefully considered. The center should be a place where children feel safe and loved; parents should believe their children are in good hands. To employees, organizational success means they are valued for themselves and for their contributions.

In the broad sense, to *manage* is to coordinate the efforts of two or more people toward attaining a goal. *Manage* can be viewed from two extremes— to barely get along (under a plan) or to function successfully. Managing gets the job done, sometimes through prescribed or procedural means and sometimes through innovative means.

Cooperation among authority figures and subordinates brings about the most successful early childhood programs. Coercion does not foster healthy attitudes and optimal development. Leaders are more than authority figures. They must be good goal setters, decision makers, motivators, communicators, and time users. They must be interested in people as well as programs. Frightened children, anxious parents, or insecure employees at the child-care center may need warmth and understanding. The administrator knows that processes and interactions are more important than the job title.

MANAGERIAL FUNCTIONS OF THE PROGRAM

Managerial functions include *planning* (what is to be done), *organizing* (the way it is to be done and by whom), *implementing* (carrying out the plan), and *evaluating* (assessing the plan's appropriateness). Diagrammatically it looks like Figure 7–1.

Target goals must first be defined; then, methods to achieve them are identified and coordinated; next, the plan is tried. If it is effective, the process continues. If it is ineffective, one or more steps may be faulty. A careful review of the steps will reveal weaknesses or omissions. Once the problem has been identified, the necessary adjustments can be made. The plan is then tested and retested until a successful solution is found.

The director must take responsibility for identifying problems, determining priorities, defining tasks, delegating responsibilities, establishing guidelines and time lines, and weighing results, as well as successfully coordinating the talents, skills, and motives of the employees. The center can run smoothly only when people feel appreciated for doing their jobs. The perceptive director knows how to prioritize tasks and to select the people who can do them best.

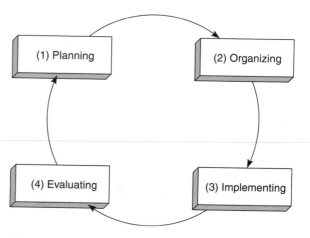

Figure 7–1   Managerial functions.

Planning. Planning is the foundation on which the other managerial functions are built. Thorough and thoughtful planning simplifies later functions. Successful planning requires predetermination of goals, objectives, priorities, and methods based on available resources (time, people, funds, and space), a procedure known as *pre-assessing.* Clearly state objectives. To formulate objectives, consider past, present, and future conditions to identify goals and determine progress. Well-defined objectives contribute to positive results. The route from the objectives to the results is the method used. Creative and responsible choices of methods—part of good planning—distinguish successful management.

One needs to be meaningfully involved in decision making to achieve trust and commitment to organizational goals. When one is committed, endeavors can yield positive benefits with respect to improved employee morale, job satisfaction, and commitment to the organization. In some settings, decisions are made at a higher level than the individual center—such as federal, state, company, or other. This makes it very difficult for employees to make "adoptable" suggestions.

Involvement of others, frequently called *participatory management*, means they have a right to be involved in making choices that affect their lives, and that involvement gives them a greater stake in those decisions than those who are uninvolved. Individuals who hold different positions (or responsibilities) in the organization likewise view decision-making processes differently. Levels of participation from others could include: (a) *unilateral* (where director makes the decisions and announces them to the staff), (b) *consultive* (where director makes a tentative decision and solicits reactions from the staff—after which the director makes the decision), (c) *collaborative* (where director and staff define and analyze problems; generate and evaluate alternatives), and (d) *delegated* (where decision is made by a subgroup of staff with or without input of others; or decision is made by individual staff members unilaterally (Bloom, 1988, p. 57).

In a study conducted of the current and desired decision-making influence of 2,709 early childhood workers in 315 centers, Bloom (1995, p. 55) found: 70 percent of directors who agreed with the statement: "The director values everyone's input in major decisions," only one-half of the teachers in these centers concurred; two-thirds of the directors believed that "people are encouraged to be self-sufficient in making decisions," whereas only one-half of the teachers agreed with that statement. One-third of the teachers thought that "people provide input, but decisions have already been made"; only 19 percent of the directors concurred with that statement. Overall, fully 78 percent of the teachers involved in the study indicated that they have less influence in centerwide decisions than they would like to have. These results support previous research on teachers' perceptions of the decision-making practices at their centers (Neubauer, 1975; Whitebook et al., 1982, 1989).

Types of decisions in the early childhood setting differ by ownership, goals, expectations, and other collective or individual means. They could include supervision and personal development of human resources (staff, teachers, etc.), instructional practices (grouping, scheduling, etc.), financial policies, facilities management, evaluation practices (children, staff, center, curriculum, etc.), and other general and specific matters.

In shared decision making, interpersonal trust is essential. It begins with one-on-one connections and involves getting to know staff (and oneself) without pressuring individuals to participate. Incentives, when offered, should be attractive enough to interest qualified people. Divergent points of view should be encouraged, and should value the orientations by cultural traditions, experience, and deeply held beliefs. "The problem with uniformity is that it can produce an uncritical acceptance of an idea. This can result in 'groupthink' " (Kostelnik 1984, p. 59). The facilitator of ideas should remain neutral, but could "assign someone as 'devil's advocate' to underscore the importance or considering all sides of an issue" (Bloom, 1995). "The only way leaders can truly communicate that they value differing perspectives on issues is to employ empathetic listening skills. In Covey's words, effective leaders 'seek first to understand, then to be understood' " (1991, p. 58).

Keep in mind that an open trusting environment is cultivated when directors avoid "one right answer"—in any of a number of good, constructive ways. "Keeping options open and exploring new, creative ways to define and solve problems communicates to staff that different perceptions of the issue are both valued and valuable in generating ideas for collective action" (Bloom, 1995, p. 60). Problem solvers are encouraged to use a variety of skills—effective questioning strategies, eliciting and receiving feedback, conflict resolution, brain storming, and peer coaching . . . so that the group can function cohesively and effectively (Saphier et al., 1989).

Bloom (1988, p. 60) concluded the following about participatory management:

1. It depends on issues, the people, and the external constraints of the program.

2. It is the means to an end—not an end in itself. It is to "improve program practices for children and families and the quality of work life for staff. . . . Greater collegiality may be a positive outcome of shared decisionmaking, but it should not be the driving force of our efforts."

3. The end goal is shared decision making, a balance of meeting both organizational needs and individual needs. If it is to be successful, it requires frequent cooperation and

teamwork—"illustrating that the whole is truly greater than the sum of its parts."

To plan time well, one must know what activities need to fit into what time line. To get started on a plan, use Figure 7–2 (pie chart) to divide your typical day into a 24-hour period. Realize that no two days are the same.

If helpful, use Figures 7–3 (daily plan), 7–4 (weekly time planner), and 7–5 (monthly time planner) or a system that would help you identify how your time is spent during different time periods.

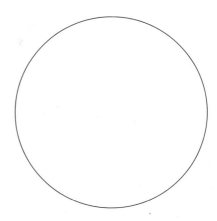

How you use your day in:

1. Sleeping
2. Working
3. Traveling
4. Eating
5. Personal hygiene
6. Leisure
7. Other

Figure 7–2   Pie chart.

From your own experience, or using your best educational imagination, respond to how decision making may differ in the following settings:

1. Public or private school (share playground, various ages, etc.)

2. Small private child care (narrow age span, high income group, etc.)

3. Government facility

4. Before- and after-school program in a public school

5. Variation in interest, socioeconomic level, wide age span, etc.)

Things To Get Done						Time Schedule
Task	Importance	Sequence	Time Allotted	Completed	Tim	
					6:00	
					30	
					7:00	
					30	
					8:00	
					30	
					9:00	
					30	
					10:00	
					30	
					11:00	
					30	
					12:00	
					30	
					1:00	
					30	
					2:00	
					30	
					3:00	
					30	
					4:00	
					30	
					5:00	
					30	
					6:00	
					30	
					7:00	
					30	
					8:00	
					30	
					9:00	
					30	
					10:00	
					30	
					11:00	
					30	

Preparation:
1. Material needed
2. Persons to contact in advance
3. Special notes
4. Future follow-up

Figure 7-3 Daily Plan for those who prefer to plan this way.

	SUNDAY	MONDAY	TUESDAY	WEDNESDAY	THURSDAY	FRIDAY	SATURDAY
6:00							
7:00							
8:00							
9:00							
10:00							
11:00							
12:00							
1:00							
2:00							
3:00							
4:00							
5:00							
6:00							
7:00							
8:00							
9:00							
10:00							
11:00							
12:00							

Week _____

_____ 20 _____

Figure 7–4 Weekly time planner for those who prefer to plan by the day and time.

Month & Year _____

SUNDAY	MONDAY	TUESDAY	WEDNESDAY	THURSDAY	FRIDAY	SATURDAY

Figure 7–5 Monthly time planner.

ORGANIZING

The aspects of organizing considered here are individual goal setting, decision making, motivation, communication, and time management.

Individual Goal Setting

Because a goal is a desired achievement and is action-oriented, it must be specific; the more clearly the goal is defined, the more visible progress becomes. The goal should challenge staff members to expand their present skills and knowledge; staff commitment is necessary to attain the goal (Blanchard & Johnson, 1982).

Who originates goals? How easily can they be reached? Studies show that when people select and have control over their own goals, set high expectations, discuss these goals, and value the outcome, they are more likely to reach those goals. Other research studies on goal setting (by individuals, by supervisors and individuals, and by groups) confirm that when challenged to "do their best," most people perform as if they had no goals (Sashkin, 1982). Monetary incentives, time limits, and knowledge of results do not affect performance level independently of individuals' goals and intentions. However, managers' expectations and treatment of subordinates will largely determine their performance and career progress, inasmuch as subordinates usually do what they believe they are expected to do.

Directors of child-care centers can enhance the self-esteem of their employees by acknowledging their individuality and by demonstrating trust in them through letting subordinates set quality goals (those that are important, challenging, productive), determine methods (ways that express uniqueness but are comfortable for them), and set time standards (reasonable time increments and encouragement to meet deadlines), and means of measurement (checkpoints, methods of determining quality, completeness, and value). Employees under these conditions will be more effective in monitoring their own work.

Goal statements should be explicit and should contain four specific elements:

- _Who_ is responsible for achieving the goal(s)?
- _What_ is the desired outcome?
- _How_ is it to be accomplished?
- _When_ is the outcome to be measured?

Personal objectives can be designed in the format of the pyramid shown in Figure 7–6. More complex and important goals carry more weight, take longer to reach, and should receive more careful consideration.

Decision Making

Decisions are necessary in all phases of personal and professional development. Every situation has alternatives. Choosing among alternatives is influenced by environmental and behavioral factors, values, perceptions, and personalities. Decision making can be a creative process having unique results whenever the following steps are taken:

1. Recognize the real problem rather than its symptoms (the heart of the issue)
2. Determine priorities (importance for present and future)
3. Gather and evaluate information (accuracy)
4. Develop options that provide solutions (immediate steps)
5. Act on the chosen method (which idea to follow first)
6. Appraise the procedure and results (constructively evaluated and conveyed to others)

One form of management, _participative management,_ involves employees in making relevant decisions. Increased employee commitment, job satisfaction, knowledge, energy, and creativity result. Employees become resources in problem solving, cognitively and emotionally committed to making each decision work. The degree of employee participation and its success depend on whether participation is forced or voluntary, formal or informal, and direct or indirect (Gibson et al., 1982; Tuney & Cohen, 1980). Studies of em-

Figure 7–6 Pyramid of personal objectives.

Daily

Weekly

Monthly

Quarterly

Annually

Lifetime

ployee participation in decision making show the following:

1. Employee commitment increases job satisfaction.
2. Motivation techniques are not effective among generally unmotivated employees.
3. Participation does not always lead to better performance, and may even be inappropriate.

Cooper (1991) identifies keys to participative management: Listen carefully with attentive posture. Choose your words carefully, ask smart questions (open, focused, groundwork, empowering others), reduce mistakes, and overcome objections. Clarify your perceptions and say what you really mean. Give sincere compliments and control anger and criticism.

The success of decision making depends on the available time, the employees' desire to par-

ticipate (commitment), the reward system, and the nature of the task (Gibson et al., 1982).

In a study of early childhood programs, 18 percent of the teaching staff were included in major decision making; over half of them said they were dissatisfied with the arrangement (Whitebook, 1981). Peters and Waterman (1982) allude to a study of group decision making related to "listening to one's clients," "fostering leaders and innovators throughout the organization," "thinking of the rank and file as the root source of quality and productivity gain," and "becoming decentralized by pushing autonomy down to nonadministrators."

When staff members of early childhood programs work together, they can create new proposals, novel ideas, and innovative strategies (Decker & Decker, 1992). One's thoughts might add to previous thoughts or create entirely new solutions. It's the dialogue that is stimulating, and it's the

❖ Stimulator

Suppose you are in a life-threatening situation: A gunman threatens to kill you unless you surrender certain information. Your first impulse may be that there is no choice. But Arnold (1978) states: "With a gun pressed against your head, your seven choices are: (1) defiance, (2) surrender, (3) counterattack, (4) lying, (5) reasoning, (6) pleading ignorance, and (7) stalling" (p. 5).

Ask yourself: Which approach should I take, and why is it better than another? If I think longer, would there be other options? Are there really options to all situations?

Studies strongly suggest that without objectives, individuals lose their purpose and drive (Douglas & Douglas, 1980). In many cases, hard-working executives who have looked forward to retirement die soon after retiring because of inadequate goals. Maltz (1970) offers the following:

> When we have no personal goal which we are interested in and means something to us, we have to go around in circles, feel lost, and find life itself aimless and purposeless. . . . People who say that life is not worthwhile are really saying that they themselves have no personal goals that are worthwhile. . . . Always have something ahead to look forward to.

comradeship that makes it work. Formal means of presenting and solving problems help staff members to become more aware of the center as a whole and of the need to work together for solutions.

There are situations that cannot be solved by merely meeting, discussing, presenting solutions, voting, and moving on. In these cases, employees need to know that some situations are open to discussion and (hopefully) amicable solutions; others are beyond the director's control (restraints placed by chain franchise, rules governing a larger organization—of which the center is a minor part, licensing bodies, management, money, time, and others).

Motivation

Employees need both motivation and stimulation to perform their jobs efficiently. Motivation comes from some inner drive, impulse, intention, and so on that causes a person to do something or act in a certain way; it's a personal incentive or goal. Stimulation is an external drive, act, or the condition of being stimulated by the hope of reward, prospect of recognition, and so on. In other words, something is done to the organism in hopes of causing internal motivation.

The quality and force of motivation determine the success of goals and decisions. Some employers try to stimulate their employees with incentives. If employees do not particularly value incentives, they will be unaffected by them. For example, consider the "Stimulators" in this text—if one sees value or use, one will read them carefully and try to discover some personal value in completing them. If not, one may skip over them, perform the task sloppily, or not at all. People do not change unless they are ready to change, and different incentives stimulate people differently.

A number of motivational theories, which have differing foci and support, have been proposed. The following brief review of five of them, in random order, reveals their uniqueness and possible application to child-care centers.

Theory X and Theory Y (Douglas McGregor). Theory X says that most people prefer to be directed, don't want to assume responsibility, hold security as their highest priority, view work as a necessary evil, and expect to be told how to do their jobs. Theory X managers view their employees as unreliable, irresponsible and immature, motivated only by money, fringe benefits, and threat of punishment.

Theory Y states that most people can be self-directed, creative, and self-controlled; for them, work can be as natural as play. Theory Y managers believe that people have the *potential* to be mature and self-motivated, directing their own efforts toward accomplishing goals and viewing superiors as supportive and facilitating (McGregor, 1960).

Carefully read each of the following examples, then make and justify your decisions.

1. The week has been extremely hectic for you. A good friend whom you seldom see, calls to invite you to dinner and a movie. You have a pile of work to complete by morning.

2. You have just settled into a new house or apartment. You are near friends, like the area, and enjoy your job. You are offered a job in a distant city, but you know no one there and have little information about the company. The pay is slightly higher than your present salary, but there is no commitment about salary increase or job permanency.

3. You are invited to join an exclusive club that offers many of your favorite activities and the opportunity to meet influential people; however, the fee is beyond your budget.

4. Your boss calls you into his office and asks for your help on a complicated report he should have completed earlier. He must present it to the board of directors today. You know he has been using his time unproductively, he is often cool toward you, and, furthermore, you are in the middle of the annual budget.

5. There will soon be an opening in your center that would advance you in salary and position. You have not been punctual in getting to your classroom or staff meetings. Your reports are last-minute and sloppy; your lesson plans are barely complete. However, you are helpful and friendly to colleagues, parents, and children. Will you apply?

These two theories seem to oppose each other, but in fact they are complementary. Some individuals perform better under one set of conditions than they do under the other. For example, some teachers prefer a teacher-centered classroom (closer to Theory X). Montessori, a pioneer in early childhood education, developed sequential steps in her self-help activities for deprived children. To compensate for the children's lack of experience and skills, the tasks were broken down into small and precise steps (Theory X). Experienced children prefer a setting that permits and encourages them (and their teachers) to interact with people and materials and to modify programs to meet their individual needs and interests (closer to Theory Y).

Immaturity-Maturity (Chris Argyris). Maturity brings changes in personality development. Individuals begin as passive, dependent infants; their behavior is limited by shallow interests, short time perspectives, dependency, and egocentrism—characteristics of immaturity. Characteristics of maturity include action, independence, autonomy, a broad repertoire of behavior patterns, and deep and strong interests over a long perspective. Argyris (1976) contends that characteristics of immaturity-maturity can be evident when an individual takes a new job. He may be given minimal control over his job—and, thus, encouraged to follow rigid performance rules, seek frequent permission, and behave in other immature ways. Argyris (1976) has challenged management to provide work opportunities in which the individual has a chance to grow and mature personally and as a member of a group. He contends that when properly motivated, a person can be self-directed and creative in his work.

For example, this theory of immaturity-maturity can be applied in a child-care center. Employees who are treated as incompetent, dependent, stagnant, and unimportant will act as though they are, whereas those who are treated as competent, creative, flexible, and important will exhibit these characteristics. Surely, children who are placed with people whose jobs match their talents, interests, abilities, and goals are happier, more eager to learn, and more willing to extend themselves. The center is more likely to prosper, and its employees are more cooperative and satisfied.

Motivation-Hygiene   Theory   (Frederick Herzberg).   Herzberg (1968) identified two categories of needs that are independent of each other and affect behavior differently: *hygiene*, or maintenance, factors (job satisfaction), and *motivators.* Hygiene factors are generally outside the employees' control (such as policies and administration, supervision, working conditions, interpersonal relations, money, status, and security) and do not motivate superior performances or affect individuals' willingness to work. An example of a hygiene factor is job enrichment (defined by Herzberg as deliberate upgrading of what is expected from employees and making their work more challenging). It gives employees an opportunity to demonstrate their ability to gain promo-

tions and feel personal satisfaction (Herzberg, 1968). Motivators are factors within the employees' control—achievement, professional growth, recognition for accomplishment, challenging work, increased responsibility, and growth and development. An example of a motivator would be a workshop for center employees conducted by an employee on a subject for which he has just finished a course of study.

For example, employees at a child-care center (as in other fields) may feel that control of their jobs is out of reach. However, if they focus on the aspects of their jobs that are within their control, they can become motivated and feel satisfaction with their assignments, progress, work relationships, and working conditions. The process is circular: Job satisfaction brings motivation, and vice versa.

Hierarchical   Needs   (Abraham   Maslow). Abraham Maslow's hierarchical needs are briefly described and shown in Figure 7–7.

Figure 7–7   Maslow's hierarchy of human needs.
Source: Adapted from Maslow, A. B. 1954. *Motivation and personality.* New York: Harper & Row.

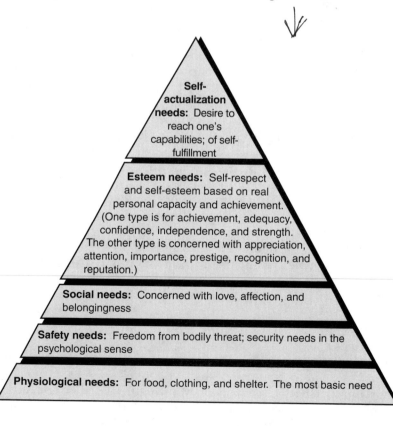

Self-actualization needs: Desire to reach one's capabilities; of self-fulfillment

Esteem needs: Self-respect and self-esteem based on real personal capacity and achievement. (One type is for achievement, adequacy, confidence, independence, and strength. The other type is concerned with appreciation, attention, importance, prestige, recognition, and reputation.)

Social needs: Concerned with love, affection, and belongingness

Safety needs: Freedom from bodily threat; security needs in the psychological sense

Physiological needs: For food, clothing, and shelter. The most basic need

Maslow, a research psychologist whose ideas had a major impact on management education and practices, envisioned a ladder or pyramid. (Some psychologists envision a number of overlapping circles, each representing one of Maslow's steps, which would then portray each need as interacting and overlapping with all the other needs.)

Maslow proposed that once the basic needs were satisfied (physiological needs), the person would become concerned about the next higher level, the need for safety and security. On meeting the needs of each level, the needs in the next higher level would come into prominence.

In addition to the five basic categories of needs identified above, Maslow suggested two further basic desires: (1) the desire to know: to be aware of reality, to get the facts, and to satisfy curiosity; and (2) the desire to understand: to systematize and look for relations and meanings. Taken as a whole, Maslow's concepts of basic needs and desires form a comprehensive look at the diversity of human motives in the work environments.

"Abraham Maslow, one of the fathers of modern psychology, developed a 'needs hierarchy' in which he identified 'self-actualization' as the highest human experience. But in his last years, he revised his earlier theory and acknowledged that this peak experience was not 'self-actualization' but 'self-transcendence,' or living for a purpose higher than self" (Covey et al., 1994, p. 49).

For example, adapted to early childhood education, Maslow's theory may appear that adults who must worry about their personal physiological needs (housing, food, shelter, perhaps job security) will be less able to meet the needs of children under their care. Adults who fear for their own safety may spend more time and effort on their own insecurities than those of the children. The progress from one need to the next will differ in degree of importance and at different times in the life of a child or an adult. Through efforts of all, the child development center can become a haven for young and old, where they will be able to fulfill their needs, interact favorably, and grow peacefully. A high-quality center will be the result.

Habits and Priorities. Covey (1989) identifies the following seven habits of effective people: *Anticipating problems*

1. They are proactive, positive, and in control of their language, actions, and life.
2. They begin with the end in mind; they are responsible.
3. They put first things first; they organize and execute around priorities.
4. They think positively—the win/win paradigm.
5. They seek understanding first—then to be understood.
6. They synergize by simply opening their minds and hearts and expressions to new opportunities and options.
7. They "sharpen the saw" through renewing the four dimensions of nature—physical, spiritual, mental, and social/emotional.

Example in the early childhood setting: Adults think and act in positive ways, the "I can do." They show in their organizing and planning what they want to accomplish. They seek to understand what needs to be done, and formulate ways to gain support of others to accomplish the tasks. They engage all parts of their natural being in the performance of the tasks.

First Things First. In his later writing with Merrill and Merrill (Covey et al., 1994), Covey builds on habit number three—first things first—stating the following:

> The key to motivation is motive. It's the "why." It's what gives us the energy to stay strong in hard moments. It gives us the strength to say "no" because we connect with a deeper "Yes!" burning inside. . . . (p. 142)
>
> Without principles, goals will never have the power to produce quality-of-life results. You can *want* to do the right thing, and you can even want to do it for the right reasons. But if you don't apply the right principles, you can still hit a wall. A principle-based goal is all three: *the right thing, for the right reason, in the right way.* (p. 146)

As an example in an early childhood setting, one may state:

My goal is (the what): To use music more effectively with the children

(The why): So that the children will gain a better appreciation for the role of music in their daily lives, so that music can help them in their personal development, and so that I will enjoy the experience more with the children

(The how): By writing and implementing specific ways and means to accomplish the following goal, such as using a variety of specific ways to make it a fun experience for all, using specific appropriate props, using it specifically and spontaneously throughout the day, by teaching specific accurate concepts

According to Covey and coworkers (1994),

The power of principle-based goal setting is the power of principles—the confidence that the goals we set will create quality-of-life results, that our ladders are leaning against the right walls. It's the power of integrity— the ability to set and achieve meaningful goals regularly, the ability to change with confidence when the "best" becomes the "good." It's the power of the four human endowments working together to create the passion, vision, awareness, creativity, and character strength that nurture growth. (p. 152)

The principle-based goal-setting process is most effective when it includes: 1) setting "context" goals, 2) keeping a "perhaps" (or a generic "to do") list, and 3) setting weekly goals (which are often not urgent but are important). (p. 146)

Covey and coworkers (1994) support making a list of priorities and then placing them in a quadrant of (1) things that are urgent and important, (2) things that are not urgent but are important, (3) things that are not important but are urgent, and (4) things that are neither urgent nor important.

We have just reviewed five theories that can be applied to early childhood education—and life.

Urgent and important	Not urgent but important
Not important but urgent	Neither urgent nor important

There are others that are also helpful. The director (board or governing power) must decide what principles are most helpful in the present situation and how to use them most effectively.

Money.   In this discussion money has not been stressed as a motivator, but in some cases it can be used to stimulate employees' performance. Money can be used as an incentive if a person needs or wants it, if it is a large amount, and if receiving it has meaning (Donnelly et al., 1981). On this subject, Sciarra and Dorsey (1990) state:

Certainly, low salaries and poor working conditions can lead to dissatisfaction, but the promise of more money, or the threat of less, will probably not have far-reaching nor long-lasting effects on individual or group performance levels. In addition, if a leader is using dollars to control and motivate performance, it becomes increasingly more difficult to find the necessary supply to meet the demand. . . . Two of the strategies that seem particularly applicable to the child care setting are use of encouragement and provision of job enrichment. . . .

Use of rewards or reinforcements may motivate the staff, but they tend to increase dependency on the one who controls the source of rewards and also heighten competition, thus defeating the overreaching goal of developing a sense of a cooperative community. Encouragement, on the other hand, tends to build self-confidence and a sense of intrinsic job satisfaction. . . . Job enrichment is a management strategy which enhances job satisfaction by presenting more challenges and increasing responsibility which, in turn, produces a sense of personal achievement and on-the-job satisfaction . . . there is evidence to suggest that, more often than not, the person who is challenged and who "stretches" to assume more responsibility will feel a sense of pride and achievement. (p. 7)

Stimulator How the quadrants shown on page 264 are filled out and how they are addressed depends on the individual, the motivation, and personal and other resources. For example, make a random list of at least 20 things that need to be done, or are "bugging" you—they may be personal items (grooming, exercise, diet), housekeeping items (taking care of your home, car, etc.), work-related items (more schooling, reading new information, better job), inter- personal items (family, friends), or items just specific to you. After listing the items that occur to you first, try to place them in the four quadrants. Do some quadrants contain many items and some contain none? Review the items to see that you have placed them in the right quadrants. Is this item really important—or not important? Is it really urgent—or not urgent at all? Most of us should be working at quadrant two (not urgent but important) level—far too many of us are spinning our wheels on quadrant four (neither urgent nor important). Use this exercise to prioritize what is important and what is urgent! How do you plan to change the way you identify and attack your "to do" list?

Because of the short duration that child-care workers spend at a center (or in the field), the rapid turnover, and lack of recognition, there is good reason to believe that money is a major factor. (See "Quality" in Chapter 2).

Communication

Authority figures should strive to understand and to be understood by others. Articulate lead- ers convey information quickly and accurately, promote teamwork, show individual respect, and help their employees. Good communication skills give leaders a sense of control, a balance of au- thority and obligation, attention from subordi- nates, and recognition from superiors.

Feedback is important in communication. Em- ployees who receive feedback are more confident and friendly, whereas lack of feedback inspires low confidence and hostility. Most employees ap- preciate positive feedback for jobs well done, ini- tiative in solving problems, or cooperation with other employees. Feedback about their overstep- ping their authority or being possessive of mate- rials and ideas is appreciated, too.

Effective communication can be obstructed by many barriers. Messages may be sent or received from different points of reference, or a person may hear only what she wants to hear. The sender or re- ceiver may incorporate personal judgments, based on past experience with that person, into a conver- sation. Different groups use words differently or use jargon that is unfamiliar to others. A threatened person may withhold or distort information. Any of a number of factors can prevent clarity in send- ing and receiving messages.

What about nonverbal messages? In general, research (Gibson et al., 1982) indicates that

> facial expressions and eye contact and movements provide information about the type of emotion, while such physical cues as distance, posture, and gestures indicate the intensity of the emotion. These conclusions are important to managers. They indi- cate that a communicator often sends a great deal more information than is contained in the message. To increase the effectiveness of our communication, we must be aware of the verbal as well as nonverbal content of our messages. (p. 410)

Incongruent verbal and nonverbal messages can create problems. For example, if a supervisor compliments an employee while frowning and avoiding eye contact, the verbal message is not re- ceived accurately. If a child hears the teacher say, "It's time to go outside," as the teacher turns to cleanup or other tasks, the child may feel confused. Generally, an individual adheres more to the non- verbal message in the presence of a contradiction between spoken words and body language.

Techniques that reduce the chance of being misunderstood include the following:

1. Have eye contact when the person is present

2. Use clear words and statements; avoid jar- gon and ambiguity

3. Have a two-way conversation (discussion)

4. Pause occasionally; ask for and give clari- fication

5. Use open-ended questions when questioning; care about answers

6. Use a pleasant, nonthreatening tone of voice, but be candid

7. Use written messages when appropriate

8. Seek information before making judgments

9. Give immediate and frequent feedback

10. Listen for meaning

11. Try to see things from different sides

12. Practice what you will say (preferably before a mirror) before having important or emotional conversations

13. Pay attention to your body language

14. If a disagreement exists, try to agree on what the *problem* is; use facts and figures; make goals or agreements on which feedback is requested

15. Summarize the conversation

16. Follow up on the conversation

At times the purpose of a conversation will be to praise or reprimand. These procedures need not be long or painful if you follow steps outlined by Blanchard and Johnson (1982). *Praising* works well when people know *up front* that you are going to let them know how they are doing. They need the feedback immediately—specifically what they did right. Pause as you let them "feel" how good you feel. Encourage them to do more of the same; shake hands or touch people in a way that makes it clear that you support their success.

The *reprimand* is similar to the praising. Again, let the people know from the beginning that you'll keep them informed of how they are doing. No holds barred! When reprimands are necessary, give them immediately, being specific about the transgression. Pause for the feeling that accompanies uncomfortable silence to let them know how you feel. Then shake hands or touch people in a way that makes it clear that you support them, but not their performance in this particular situation. Then "realize that when the reprimand is over, it's over" (p. 59).

❖ **Stimulator**   Patrick arrived at the center early Monday morning to plan in solitude for a busy week. He considered three plans that included quick and easy tasks, major projects, and preparation that would ease his work the following week:

Plan A: Starting promptly on the budget and working diligently until it is finished, then preparing the advertising campaign for fall enrollment.

Plan B: Writing that short thank-you note to a visitor for bringing a beehive to the center, making the agenda for Thursday's staff meeting, reminding the cook to serve lunch family-style, balancing his own checkbook to make sure his last check was covered, ordering a plane ticket for next month, and then working on the budget and advertising.

Plan C: Starting on the budget, but slipping in a few quick jobs so he feels he is making progress; jotting frequent notes that are related to upcoming advertising.

The most valuable thing Patrick could have done was to *plan to plan*. He soon found his valuable quiet time gone, and no progress made.

Consider the options. Now that Patrick has outlined what needs to be done, he must prioritize the tasks according to his method of doing them.

Plan A: If he does not do the budget and advertising campaign first, will his budget be smaller or the enrollment lower?

Plan B: If he does small, bothersome jobs first, will that help or hinder him when it comes to bigger tasks?

Plan C: Does he work better if he breaks bigger tasks into smaller ones, completes them, and then rewards himself with diversions? Give your reactions to the various plans and your method of approach.

Examples of praise and reprimand may be helpful here. The Midland Child Care Center is having difficulty because employees are arriving late for their assignments, and promptness is important to the smooth operation of the center. Examples of praise to those who are prompt might include: "Your efforts to be here on time have helped parents get to their other commitments, other employees to be relieved on time, and children to feel secure here. Thanks for your efforts to help the center function smoothly." To reprimand those who are continually tardy, the director might tactfully include such remarks as: "When you are late, there is a domino effect on the center. Parents get frustrated, employees who have finished their assignments are delayed, and children feel a sense of insecurity. Everyone is counting on you to be here and ready to start when your assignment begins."

Time Management

The main objectives in this section are to define the use of personal time, to structure it more effectively, and to identify the value of time as a step to success. Adages such as haste makes waste and a stitch in time saves nine pertain to time as well as to energy. Without planning, an administrator is like the cowboy who jumped on his horse and rode off in all directions—he got nowhere at an undefinable rate of speed!

Time Planning. An essential part of time planning is recognizing that much of our time is spent on conditions (regulations, funds), people (staff, parents, others), situations (understaffed, weather), and other things that are beyond our control. Some individuals refuse to plan their time because they feel planning breeds rigidity and unfriendliness. (Some overplan their time and it *does* breed rigidity and unfriendliness!) However, lack of time planning can result in an aimless use of time. The advantages of administrative time planning are as follows:

1. Support for and interactions with individual employees, parents, and children

2. Task delegation

3. Professional development (of administrator)

4. Better overall planning (e.g., financial, facilities, community)

5. Less burnout

6. Job satisfaction

See Figures 7–8 through 7–12.

The person who is unaccustomed to planning time may argue that he or she is performing at his maximum and doesn't want to "save" or plan time better. Scheduling would create unnecessary pressures. Others may feel they don't have control over their lives; but they should not confuse busyness with productivity. The two are not necessarily related.

Research on various time concepts has produced some common myths—such as, most active people get the most done; decisions made at high levels are better than those made at lower levels; tasks are completed faster and better when done by oneself; the open-door policy improves teamwork; problem identification is the easy part of problem-solving; and no one has enough time to complete plans or projects. For example, some busy people spend all their time being busy—they should work for important results, regardless of the amount of time required; decisions may be made by administrators who have the power, but they may lack necessary information to make and enforce those decisions. Employees in the trenches can supply important facts and examples that could help administrators make even better decisions. (For example, some legislatures pass bills but fail to provide funds or methods for their enforcement.)

People have different mental energy levels. Morning people rise and get going quickly; evening people do their best thinking and working during late evening and early morning hours. Dorothy Tennov, a behavioral consultant and professor of psychology at the University of Bridgeport, has suggested that different energy levels are "peak, good, average, relaxed, and low." When one is at "peak" level, things can be learned, ideas

Planning Period:		Date:
Employee:		

DAYS	PROJECTS		CALLS		OTHER
Monday					
Tuesday					
Wednesday					
Thursday					
Friday					

Figure 7–8 Daily objectives for those who prefer to plan this way.

Planning Period:		Date:	

FUNCTIONS	3 MONTHS	6 MONTHS	9 MONTHS
Forecast			
Objectives			
Strategies			
Budgets			
Policies			
Miscellaneous			

Figure 7–9   Short-term goals for those who prefer to plan this way.

Planning Period:	Date:

FUNCTIONS	ONE YEAR	TWO YEARS	THREE YEARS
Forecast			
Objectives			
Strategies			
Budgets			
Policies			
Miscellaneous			

Figure 7–10   Long-term goals for those who prefer to plan this way.

Date	✓	Name	Phone	Incoming	Outgoing	Result

Figure 7–11   Phone log.

Week of _____, 20____

TELEPHONE (In & Out Calls)					VISITORS (Unscheduled)					OTHER (Specify; Meetings, Etc.)				
Person(s)	Purpose	Time		Total	Person(s)	Purpose	Time		Total		Purpose	Time		Total
		Start	End				Start	End				Start	End	

Figure 7–12 Interruptions—note which activities you initiate and which ones are initiated by others.

can be generated, and individuals can be creative. "Good" brings above-average performance, and most things can be done at this level. People spend most of their time at the "average" level, at which they carry out, but don't learn, complex activities. People at the fourth level, "relaxed," can perform easy tasks. When one is at the "low" level, one does not want to think or make decisions. Some people work best when they are slightly hungry; others just after eating or following physical exercise. Knowing peoples' levels can help administrators plan schedules to take advantage of their employees' peak working times.

There are many methods of planning and expending one's time—ranging from no planning (the "Johnny-on-the-spot" people) to not getting started until every detail is firmly ordered and written (the marble statue people). Surely, one should have some plan of attack and a method that works for them—or they never get anything done and it doesn't matter anyway.

Time Saving or Time Wasting.   Each individual must set priorities and organize time to fit responsibilities, interests, and body clock. A useful technique for one director is to leave things in sight until they are completed, to prevent the "out of sight—out of mind" syndrome; other directors set a timer to check progress; still others use lists, or make plans while doing routine tasks. Some managers advocate spending short periods of time (5 to 30 minutes at a time) on a particular task, then evaluating whether to terminate the task or continue it for another period; others find such short periods of time worthless. Some people reward themselves for their diligence by following productive periods with things they really enjoy, such as an evening out, extra time with the family, or other favorite pastimes. Use Figure 7–13 as a guide for timesaving tips.

Wasting one's own time may be excusable, but wasting others' time is unpardonable. Careful examination of time use by subordinates may reveal that their biggest loss comes from lengthy, unimportant chatter with their supervisors.

Every center employee is responsible for the use—or misuse—of time. See Figure 7–14 for some potential time wasters.

Figure 7–13   Timesaving tips.

- Record key events and work around them (prioritize)
- Use a time log to show where and how time is consumed; however, a log may become unrealistic or unchallenging whenever goals are set too high to be attained, are vague, or general entries are made, or random, unpredictable events occur
- Make written plans or notes
- Coordinate related tasks
- Reserve time every day for reading, thinking, and reflecting
- Consider main objectives and time allowances
- Use transition periods productively
- Build around personal attributes
- Delegate when possible
- Prepare the schedule for the following day before leaving work or prepare the day's agenda first thing each morning
- *Include frequent opportunities to stop and smell the roses.* Make all areas of your life as enjoyable as possible

- Poor organization
- Inaccuracy, incompletion, or improper handling
- Excessive detail
- Procrastination
- Interruption
- Failure to delegate or delegating improperly
- Mediocre or unprepared personnel
- Trivialities
- Personal affairs unrelated to job
- Time logs (see Figure 7-13)

Figure 7–14   Potential time wasters.

Setting Personal Limits: Procrastination.

Unless individuals take precautions to protect themselves from the quantity of tasks, from personal availability, from the complexity of tasks, and from completing all tasks personally, they are open to any and all interruptions. Four time-management techniques that have proven helpful are shown in Figure 7–15.

Procrastination results from unpleasant, difficult, or unclear tasks. Some people do unpleasant things first to get them out of the way; others delay, hoping to avoid them altogether. Such delaying of unpleasant tasks can actually cause more frustration than doing them to begin with. Difficult or unclear tasks may be avoided because of desire for perfection, fear of failure, insecurity, fear of rejection by others, or lack of motivation.

Although undesirable tasks can be made more palatable by breaking them into smaller segments and allotting short time periods to focus on one part at a time, to really correct the problem, procrastinators should admit their procrastination, desire to change, and then work diligently toward completing the task.

Necessary to discourage procrastination are the following:

- Confidence in one's ability
- Desire to do the job quickly and efficiently
- Self-reward; satisfaction with work
- Initiative; good work habits
- Tools to complete the job (e.g., knowledge, time, materials, space, assistance when needed)

Applying a Time Plan.

Clear, precise plans for using time are tested in their application. Will they really work? Will they save time and frustration? Ideas that could win a prize for simplicity, thoroughness, and realism sometimes fail when put to the test.

A procedure's value depends on the strength of its application and enforcement. For example, a teacher is injured on the way to the center. The employee handbook says an employee must request time off at least 48 hours in advance and provide a suitable replacement. Obviously, the regular procedure cannot be used in this situation. An alternative is to refer to a list of substitute teachers who are available and well trained and can be at the center within minutes. Calling begins. One after another, the names are checked off as the substitutes are ill, have prior commitments, or are out of town. Time is flying and, still, no one can come. The children will be arriving soon, and there will not be enough teachers! Another alternative is having a regular teacher come in a little earlier—or stay a little later—until the problem

Opinions differ as to the world's greatest or most useful invention. Some say the wheel, others say current technology, some say the plastic bag, others say TV or CDs, and yet others say sports equipment. There are even those who believe it is the Internet! There are many great timesavers; but lack of knowledge increases time and money spent on them and causes great frustration.

Decide what timesavers you value!

Figure 7–15 Helpful time-management techniques.

Insulation	Limit the amount and type of tasks to accept, then stay within the limits. Plans should be flexible enough to include or exclude activities, if necessary, but should not exceed allotted amounts of time or energy.
Isolation	Remove yourself from ready accessibility to others. It provides times and means of contact, but also ensures a degree of privacy from drop-ins and trivialities.
Simplification	Provide for work to be completed as easily and quickly as possible. Involve few steps and individuals to complete the tasks. Applies to routine or unique tasks.
Delegation	Can increase or decrease a director's work load and time allotment. In general, a leader should handle enjoyed activities, those concerned with policy, and discretionary matters. Routine correspondence and meetings, as well as recurring problems, should be delegated. For detailed information about delegation, see Chapter 6.

can be resolved. Perhaps a nearby child-care center also has a list of available substitutes. The point is clear: Good planning is important, but may not eliminate all problems—implementing procedures may be far more difficult than it seems. (See Figure 7–15.)

Evaluating Time Use. Evaluation of different aspects of the center plays a very important role in the success of the center. When evaluation is ig-nored or slighted, the children, staff, parents, and center suffer. In evaluating time use, you may need to make changes in habits, procedures, or schedules, if more time, not less, is being consumed. Give the changes a fair trial by evaluating them objectively and without bias.

A time log can be of great assistance in evaluating time use. Take the example of unexpected visitors. Although the time spent with them may be perceived as the problem, the real time stealer

❖ **Stimulator**

You have identified your biggest time waster at the center to be unexpected visitors. You want to do something about it. You begin by brainstorming: Keep your door closed so you are not visible; post a note for visitors to see the secretary for information/appointments; list a time when visitors are welcome; do not answer the door; be rude; see visitors but let them know you are busy; receive visitors cordially; stand at the door and talk to them; or recognize that many interruptions can result in increased enrollment. In fact, if a caller asks about enrolling a child in your center, your response is, "Come to the center and see if our program meets your needs!" You are undoubtedly going to get many of your clients this way, and you want to treat them with courtesy. If it is impossible for you to talk with these visitors at the moment, you might ask another employee to show them around while you rearrange your activities; ask the employee to take over your task so you can talk with the visitor; or decide that you will always be available to possible clients.

❖ ❖ ❖ ❖

Week of _____, 20____

Activity	Person(s)	Time taken	Purpose	Outcome
Telephone (in & out)				
Visitor				
Procrastination				
Poor planning				
Doing more than one task				
Failure to complete task before beginning another				
Work space cluttered				
Socializing				
Paperwork (mail, reports, etc.)				
Ineffective delegation				
Meetings—scheduled & unscheduled				
Lack of motivation (self-discipline)				
Crises				
Daydreaming				

Activity	Person(s)	Time taken	Purpose	Outcome
Materials unavailable				
Waiting				
Distractions				
Reading unscheduled materials				
Work left from previous day				
Routines				
Poor communication, repeating				
Personal disorganization				
Failure to say no				
Fatigue				

Figure 7–16 Time wasters' log for those who want to know where their time is spent.

could be socializing with the teachers. An administrator might try to blame outsiders for her feeling guilty about not reading current materials and spending more productive time with the staff. A time log would reveal the actual time waste (see Figure 7–16).

The director may also want to consider seriously a variety of ways to handle emergencies such as being understaffed. How do other centers deal with such situations? What suggestions could the staff members make? Is someone assigned to another task who is (or could be) trained and reassigned temporarily? Could other names be added to the list? Are there trained parents who could come in occasionally? How would you handle the absence of two or more scheduled employees?

Albert Einstein is credited with this profound statement: The significant problems we face cannot be solved by the same level of thinking that created them.

IMPLEMENTING

The third component of management is implementation. The *what* (planning), the *how* and *by whom* (organization) have been decided; implementation puts them into operation. On paper or in planners' heads the plans may seem superb. The real test is whether they are realistic and appropriate enough to work.

In implementing management principles, ask questions such as these:

- What changes are necessary?
- Is this the appropriate time?
- How many changes will be made concurrently?
- Will they deplete, strain, or enhance resources of staff, funds, time, and energy?
- How much input will be required for desired output?
- Are the goals short- or long-term?
- Have guideposts been established to determine the progress and effectiveness of the changes?

Figure 7–17 shows a plan for successful time management.

Lewin (1951) described a technique to determine discrepancies between goals and progress. He listed the forces that support the goal and forces that retard or prevent progress (or, "for" forces with "against" forces). When driving forces are more powerful than restraining forces, the driving forces dominate. However, if restraining forces are stronger, change is difficult to achieve. If the driving and restraining forces are about equal, it is possible to make a change by pushing the driving forces and converting or immobilizing some or all of the restraining forces. Sometimes driving forces are preferred, and sometimes restraining forces are preferred. Some things are right to do and some things are wrong to do!

Regardless of one's personal method of organization (i.e., no notes or system—in-head planning only; scribbled notes or key words; notes and checklists; detailed calendars and appointment books; someone else to make, keep, and remind about schedules), once the plan of attack has been divided up—one needs to put it in operation. It can embrace all the strengths and (hopefully) eliminate all the weaknesses of the above methods. Covey and coworkers (1994) state: "More than an evolution, we need a revolution. We need to move beyond time management to life leadership . . . based on paradigms that will create quality-of-life results . . . based on the 'importance' paradigm. Knowing and doing what's important rather than simply responding to what's urgent is foundational to putting first things first" (p. 32).

Time, energy, and resources are important and will be used in personal ways. Different methods may be used for types of decisions within a category (personal, social, professional, spiritual, recreational, educational, etc.). But it still remains: *How do we decide what should come first?* Do we have a hierarchy for each category and then prioritize between categories? Do we do pleasurable things first—or last? Do we tackle the biggest jobs first— or last? Do we do the most costly things first—or last? Do we do group tasks first—or last? Is the decision a personal matter or are others involved?

Figure 7–17 Successful time management.

1. *In general*
   Prioritize items
   Set time limits on every task
   Do things right the first time
   Learn to act rather than react
   Conquer procrastination
   Finish what you start
   Set aside quiet time for important things
   Develop a personal philosophy of time's value in your life
   Make and take personal time for dreaming, relaxing, and living!

2. *In preparation*
   Write objectives clearly and simply
   Focus on them and not on activities
   Analyze everything in terms of your objectives
   Eliminate unnecessary actions
   Keep a time log

3. *In planning*
   a. Daily:
      Make the first hour of each workday productive if you are a morning person (or the last hour if you are an evening person)
      Make a daily to-do list of objectives, priorities, and time estimates
      Set and achieve at least one major objective each day
   b. Weekly:
      Make a written plan for each week
      Eliminate at least one time waster each week

4. *In evaluating*
   Determine the workability of time management by testing your ideas
   Have back-ups for the original plan
   Be flexible and receptive to alternatives

In implementing plans, one may prepare a checklist or a preliminary outline asking and answering the what, where, when, why, who, and how questions. Change is not easy for people or groups unless they can see that the change will enhance themselves or the group. Influencing agents are those that can facilitate change.

EVALUATING PROGRAMS

The fourth, and final, managerial function is evaluation, sometimes referred to as *control*. It involves critical analyses of the functions, feedback, and follow-up of the program to determine progress and the accomplishment of goals. If goals have been al-tered, parallel adjustments may be needed. To support, correct, or improve situations, evaluation requires the development of performance standards, a measurable means of assessing resources, procedures for making adjustments, a review process, and a method of feedback. (For employee evaluation, see Chapter 6.)

To a certain extent, evaluation is subjective. In dealing with services rather than goods (as in the operation of a child-care center), accountability is often difficult to measure. Thus, it is important that evaluation information be relevant, accurate, and complete. Evaluators must understand the purposes of the evaluation, the criteria used, pitfalls to avoid, the evaluation methods suitable to

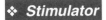 **Stimulator** The director of a preschool wants to use more fresh fruit and vegetables for snacks. A schedule is made and posted, only to provoke numerous complaints from the staff. The director calls the staff together, and they decide to apply Lewin's force-field theory to this problem. The force-field looks like this: (See Chapter 6 for discussion.)

Driving Forces	Restraining Forces
Inexpensive	Time-consuming
Children enjoy the food	Late delivery
Children learn about crops	Unhappy teachers
Children eat new foods	Wasted food
	Frequent late snack
	More dishes
	Slow cleanup
	Food too ripe or green on scheduled day

The restraining forces outnumber the driving forces and appear to be stronger. The director feels the driving forces are important and wants to maintain them, if possible, by exploring with the staff the possibilities of changing each restraining force into a driving one. The discussion shows the revised field as this:

Driving Forces	Restraining Forces
Inexpensive (in season)	
Children enjoy new food	Delivery often late
Children learn about crops	
Children involved in food preparation and cleanup	
Snack on time—teachers more flexible	More dishes
Teachers more careful in amount of food prepared or plan to use leftovers	Food too ripe or green on scheduled day

Several internal changes were made easily, but the problems of delivery and food selection still exist. The nutritionist says she will work with the produce market to see what can be done; the teachers suggest more flexibility in using the fresh produce. They are excited about having the children help with the preparation and cleanup—they wonder why they didn't think of that sooner! And the entire staff got involved in a project using good organizational skills.

specific purposes, and the significance of the evaluation to the people and the organization. Besides being judgmental and developmental, the evaluation can be motivational and provide improved understanding to the evaluator and the program being evaluated.

One of the most important components of evaluation is feedback. Prompt feedback is more important for changing behavior and procedures than intense feedback. Feedback needs to be both vertical (between management, between supervisors and subordinates) and horizontal (between individuals of the same rank). (See "Feedback" in Chapter 6.)

Evaluation is retrospective, permitting examination at a distance of projects that failed as well as of goals that were achieved, stepping stones for present and future goals. Evaluations can fail due to the omission of one or more of the following: important changes, clear goals, appropriate measures, lasting effects, and anticipated outcomes. To prevent failure, evaluations should be necessary,

 **Stimulator**

You are the director of a large child development center. Place the following situations in one of the four quadrants identified by Covey and his associates and justify your placement: (See Chapter 6 for discussion.)

1. The board of directors has called an emergency meeting.
2. Edgar fell from the slide and just wants to sleep.
3. The eggs in the incubator have just hatched.
4. Stephen brought his five puppies—unannounced!
5. The cook can't come today because of a funeral.
6. It's the annual picnic—but it's raining heavily.
7. Two teachers are ill, and licensing committee is coming.
8. The fire alarm goes off.
9. The visual aids for your presentation to the governor's Committee on Children have been lost at the printers.
10. Several influential people are coming to visit the center for possible enrollment of their children. You are short of staff and must substitute in the classroom today.
11. Six parents report ill children—possibly chicken pox.
12. Every time you work on the budget (due tonight) you are interrupted by phone, visitors, and mini-emergencies.
13. The owner is bringing potential buyers for the center; you are a candidate for the new directorship; the wind has blown down a big tree in the yard; the power is out!
14. Three children, two of them seriously, are experiencing allergic reactions from something they ate at lunch.

Quadrant 1: Urgent and important	Rationale for placement:
Quadrant 2: Not urgent but important	Rationale for placement:
Quadrant 3: Urgent but not important	Rationale for placement:
Quadrant 4: Not urgent and not important.	Rationale for placement:

purposeful, pertinent but not too precise, and include a variety of evaluation techniques—short answers to open-ended questions and responses to specific questions, interviews, and direct observations.

In conclusion, don't take yourself too seriously when you've been unrealistic, idealistic, or naive in regard to planning, organizing, implementing, or evaluating the program. Employ the "oops" principle! Simply say, "Oops!—The planning was insufficient. The goal was inappropriate and unattainable. There were not enough checkpoints. We took an indirect approach." Although this principle should, for obvious reasons, not be used too often, it can be effective in easing the tension of evaluation and in getting plans back on track.

Evaluation			
Internal	By owner, director, board, teaching and/or support staff Of one's own job; or of supporting/ overlapping jobs Overall center evaluation Of quality, of costs	**External**	By parents, children, licensing agents (health, safety, program, quality), community, educators, professional organizations

Figure 7–18   Evaulation.

See Figure 7–18 for internal and external evaluation of one's performance.

CHAPTER SUMMARY

1. *Manager, administrator, leader,* and *director* are terms used to describe authority figures in groups or organizations. Sometimes the terms are used synonymously, sometimes discriminately. *Director* is more commonly used in this text.
2. The functions of management are planning, organizing, implementing, and evaluating.
3. Goal setting and decision making must be done with precision, clarity, and realism.
4. Individuals are stimulated in different ways, but motivation must come from within the individual.
5. Directors must realize the importance of knowing theories and applying them in child-care programs.
6. Some theories of motivation are Theory X, Theory Y, immaturity-maturity, needs, hygiene, and habits.
7. For communication to be effective, it should provide frequent and prompt feedback, be open, and flow vertically and horizontally. Body and verbal language should not conflict.
8. Careful planning of personal time helps ensure that important tasks are completed. Time logs may or may not be helpful.
9. Different individuals have different mental energy levels. What may be a good use of time for one person may be a misuse for another person.
10. Delegation can be growth-promoting for administrators and subordinates; however, it is not necessarily a time saver.
11. To reduce or eliminate procrastination, admit it is a problem and develop techniques to change the behavior.
12. Administrators need to be perceptive in evaluating their own time use and that of each employee.
13. The implementation of goals and programs can determine their success or failure.
14. A useful tool in determining priorities is Covey's "urgent" and "important" quadrant.
15. Using Lewin's theory of forces can help in decision making.
16. Program evaluation should be conducted periodically, include feedback from a variety of sources, and be constructive.
17. The "oops" principle can be applied in correcting problems when used infrequently and discriminately.

PARTICIPATORS

Because readers will be in different stages of their careers in program management, they are encouraged to read through all participators and practice those that will be of the most current value to them in understanding procedures of management, resources, and time.

1. Managerial theories
   a. Reread the various theories outlined in the chapter and then decide which one(s) fit(s) your style of management. Why do you prefer one over another? Write and implement procedures from one of the theories.
   b. Briefly sketch some reminders about planning, organizing, implementing, and evaluating child-care programs.
   c. Write five goals. Check each one for precision, clarity, and realism.
   d. Give an appropriate use of the "oops" principle.

2. General techniques of time management
   a. For personal improvement, use items that will help you use time more effectively, such as checklists, rearrange your desk and work space, set time limits with visitors, use the phone effectively, employ a secretary when possible, prepare a time log, plan the next day's agenda before leaving the center, make agendas for meetings and conferences, record thoughts, use specialists or consultants, brainstorm with others.
   b. For efficiency, use visual scheduling and planning systems (charts, graphs, etc.), visualize ideas, use a chalkboard, use color coding, use templates and models.
   c. In reading, read for speed and comprehension, delegate reading, use abstracts or clippings.
   d. For correspondence, use a tickler file, write shorter letters, use more form letters or paragraphs, reply on original letter or memo, handle correspondence only once, use postcards if appropriate, have mail screened, dictate into a tape recorder or machine or give a secretary the main points to compose the answer, and so on. (A tickler file contains a folder or pocket for each day of the month. Correspondence and appointments are filed by date for future attention.)

3. Prepared forms (see forms in this chapter, use commercial forms, or make your own)
   a. Use the monthly time planner to record appointments and other time uses for 1 month. Or get a commercial time planner.
   b. Use the weekly time planner to record hourly and daily activities for 1 month. Make special notations of times of days and days of the week that you perform most efficiently.
   c. Using information from the weekly time planner, average the amount of time you spend on sleeping, working, traveling, eating, personal hygiene, leisure, and other activities. Convert the weekly averages to daily percentages and record them in the circle how you use your day.
   d. Keep a daily time log for 1 month, being careful to record information in each column.
   e. Each day before leaving the workplace, fill in your daily plan for the following day; or fill it in *first* thing each morning.
   f. Practice prioritizing tasks on the daily plan.
   g. Fill in the time waster sheet weekly for 1 month to determine what activities waste your time. Add extra categories, if necessary. At the end of the month write down ways to reduce the amount of time you waste on each activity.
   h. Fill in the interruptions sheet weekly for 1 month. Determine ways you can reduce the amount of time you spend on interruptions.
   i. Evaluate the monthly exercise. Was it helpful or detrimental to your performance?
   j. Do you usually manage your time with written forms? If the provided forms do not meet your needs, how could you modify them?

4. Progress
   a. Identify three ways you can become a better administrator by applying principles of time management from this chapter.
   b. Write down and discuss with a colleague, supervisor, or friend how you plan to make better use of your time. At the end of 1 month, report your progress.
   c. Record one to three problems you are still encountering in time management. How can you handle them?
   d. Set a goal and make a plan to initiate an element of time use that you have not em-

ployed in the past (e.g., time saving, prioritizing, delegating, time log).

e. Select an item from Section 1 or 2 to work on. Be specific in your attack and evaluation.

f. Help someone record and evaluate her use of time. Are you more objective with her time use or with your own?

g. From your time waster sheet and your daily, weekly, and monthly planning sheets (and from past experience), list your five worst procrastinators. What do you intend to do about them?

h. Throughout your month of recording time-use data, pay close attention to your ability to implement your plans. Was it easier or more difficult to plan than to carry out your plans?

REFERENCES

Argyris, C. 1976, Winter. Leadership, learning, and changing the status quo. *Organizational Dynamics*, 29–43.

Arnold, J. D. 1978. *Make up your mind.* John D. Arnold ExecuTrak Systems. New York: American Management Association.

Blanchard, K., & Johnson, S. 1982. *The one minute manager.* New York: William Morrow.

Bloom, P. J. 1988. Closing the gap: An analysis of teacher and administrator perceptions of organizational climate in the early childhood setting. *Teacher and Teacher Education: An International Journal of Research and Studies* 4(2): 111–120.

Bloom, P. J. 1995. Shared decisionmaking: the centerpiece of participatory management. National Institute for Early Childhood Professional Development. *Young Children*, May, 55–60.

Bridges, E. M. 1967. A model for shared decisionmaking in the school principalship. *Educational Administration Quarterly* 3, 49–61.

Cooper, R. K. 1991. *The performance edge: New strategies to maximize your work effectiveness and competitive advantage.* Boston: Houghton Mifflin.

Covey, S. R. 1989. *The 7 habits of highly effective people.* New York: Simon & Schuster.

Covey, S. 1991. *Principle-centered leadership.* New York: Fireside.

Covey, S. R., Merrill, A. R., & Merrill, R. R. 1994. *First things first.* New York: Simon & Schuster.

Decker, C. A., & Decker, J. R. 1992. *Planning and administering early childhood programs.* Upper Saddle River, NJ: Merrill/Prentice Hall.

Donnelly, J. H., Jr., Gibson, J. L., & Ivancevich, J. M. 1981. *Fundamentals of management.* Plano, TX: Business Publications.

Douglas, M., & Douglas, D. 1980. *Manage your time, manage your work, manage yourself.* New York: American Management Systems.

Gibson, J. L., Ivancevich, J. M., & Donnelly, J. H., Jr. 1982. *Organizations: Behavior, structure, processes.* Plano, TX: Business Publications.

Herzberg, F. 1968. One more time: How do you motivate employees? *Harvard Business Review,* Jan./Feb., 53–62.

Kostelnik, M. J. 1984. Read consensus or groupthink? *Child Care Information Exchange* 38(Aug.), 25–30.

Lewin, K. 1951. *Field theory in social science.* New York: McGraw-Hill.

Maltz, M. 1970. *Psycho-cybernetics and self-fulfillment.* New York: Grosset & Dunlap.

McGregor, D. 1960. *Human side of enterprise.* New York: McGraw-Hill.

Neugebauer, R. 1975. Organizational analysis of day care. Unpublished manuscript, Lesley College, ERIC, ED 157–161.

Peters, T. J., & Waterman, R. H., Jr. 1982. *In search of excellence: Lessons from America's best run companies.* New York: Harper & Row.

Saphier, J., Bigda-Peyton, T., & Pierson, G. 1989. *How to make decisions that stay made.* Alexandria, VA: Association for Supervision and Curriculum Development.

Sashkin, M. 1982. *A manager's guide to participative management.* New York: American Management Association.

Sciarra, D. J., & Dorsey, A. G. 1990. *Developing and administering a child care center* (2nd ed.). Albany, NY: Delmar.

Tuney, J. R., & Cohen, S. L. 1980. Participative management: What is the right level? *Management Review.* Oct., 66–69.

Whitebook, M. 1981. Profiles in day-care: An interview with Millie Almy. *Day Care and Early Education* 8, 29–30.

Whitebook, M., Howes, C., Darrah, R., & Friedman, J. 1982. Caring for the caregivers: Staff burnout in child care. In L. Katz (Ed.), *Current topics in early childhood education. Vol. 4* (pp. 212–235). Norwood, NJ: Ablex.

Whitebook, M., Howes, C., & Phillips, D. 1989. *Who cares? Child care teachers and the quality of care in America.* Oakland, CA: Child Care Employee Project.

Chapter 8

Health

Guide for Readers

Health for all who participate at the center (personnel, management, parents, and especially children) must be of utmost concern at all times.

- ❖ *Personnel should be in top physical and mental condition.*
- ❖ *Management should provide safe policies and procedures to ensure the health and safety of all participants at the center.*
- ❖ *Parents should receive written information regarding inclusion/exclusion of ill children, as well as children with special needs or chronic health conditions.*
- ❖ *Children should have a physical examination, immunizations, and other precautions to ensure their well-being and that of others.*
- ❖ *The Children's Health Insurance Program (CHIP) is designed to provide free or low-cost health insurance for uninsured families with low or moderate incomes.*
- ❖ *Food and eating experiences help children learn valuable information and skills.*
- ❖ *Environmental hazards can be reduced or avoided when given proper attention.*
- ❖ *Government programs, including licensing and immunizations, should promote wellness in children and caregivers.*
- ❖ *For additional information regarding health/learning, see Chapter 3.*

Ethical responsibilities to children:

Above all, we shall not harm children. We shall not participate in practices that are disrespectful, degrading, dangerous, exploitative, intimidating, psychologically damaging, or physically harmful to children. THIS PRINCIPLE HAS PRECEDENCE OVER ALL OTHERS IN THIS CODE! (From NAEYC's *Code of Ethical Conduct, P-1.1)*

Facts and Figures

At the time of this writing, there are many health bills under serious consideration in state, local, and federal meetings (health plans, nutrition programs, parental work programs, insurance, and others) that will affect low-income families. Only time will tell the impact the changes will have.

Closely related to safety, and certainly an integral part of the goals of the center, is the health of the children, families, and staff. When individuals are not at their optimal health, their mental attitude and physical conditions prevent them from performing their best.

- By 1994–1995, 75 percent of all two-year-olds were fully immunized, up from 55 percent in 1992.

- In 1994, only 80.2 percent of babies were born to mothers who had received early (first-trimester) prenatal care, the infant mortality rate was 8.0 deaths per 1,000 live births, and 7.3 percent of newborns were born at low birth weight (less than 5 pounds, 8 ounces).

- "In the year 2000, it is anticipated that 75% of women with children under five years of age will be employed—at least part time, at least for a number of their children's early years—and in need of child care" (Hernandez, 1995, p. 145).

- Children who attend child care programs are at increased risk for infectious diseases, most commonly upper respiratory, and diarrheal and skin diseases (Dershewitz, 1993; Holmes et al., 1996). Infectious diseases are carried home with the children, so that 15 to 25 percent of family members also become infected. Care providers too are at increased risk for disease (Pickering, 1996).

- "Every child deserves to start life with healthy bodies and minds. *All* children need access to comprehensive health and mental health services that provide preventive care when they are well and treatment when they are ill. But today, 11.3 million children—more than 90 percent of them in working families— have no health insurance." (Children's Defense Fund, 2000).

- A recent survey of licensed child-care centers found that staff in almost half (43 percent) of the centers were unaware of the association between sudden infant death syndrome (SIDS) and an infant's sleep position. Since 1992 the American Academy of Pediatrics has recommended that *healthy infants born at term be placed down for sleep on their backs or sides.* This recommendation is based, in part, on an international panel's finding of a 50 percent reduction in the rate of SIDS in countries advocating the Back to Sleep position. (FYI. *Young Children,* Sept. 1997, p. 81; Gershon & Moon, 1997).

Facts and Figures (continued)

- "Today across America 11 million preschoolers and school-age children do not have health insurance, although 92 percent of them have at least one parent who works and 66 percent have a parent who works full-time" (Bureau of Census, 1997). These children—most of whom are likely to be in child care or after-school programs every day while their parents work—suffer needlessly from preventable health problems (O'Connor, 1999).

- In 1977 Congress passed a new Children's Health Insurance Program (CHIP) designed to provide free or low-cost health insurance to children in uninsured families with low or moderate incomes. CHIP is the most significant funding increase for children's health coverage since Medicaid began in 1965 (O'Connor, 1999, p. 63). (See discussion later in this chapter.)

- Health and safety standards for the child-care force are not considered as often as the ones for young children, but they are very important. A study to assess the health status, health behavior, and health concerns of early childhood practitioners, using a random design," included 446 participants (child-care center teachers, family child-care providers, and center directors in Wisconsin). Following are some of the findings of Gratz and Claffey, (1996).

  More than 85 percent of each group rated their general health as good to excellent.

  Teachers were more prone to illness in their first years of employment.

  Tripping over toys and equipment was cited as one cause of staff injuries on the job.

  Most of the workers were not "drinkers" or "smokers."

  Researchers examined health concerns stemming from work-related stress and benefits of occupational hazards involving the physical demands of the job.

  The majority of the sample did not have health insurance, dental insurance, or life insurance as employment benefits.

  Most indicated that their jobs were stressful, with center director reporting the most stress.

- The authors of this study suggest that training in such areas as the use of appropriate furniture, footwear, and body mechanics is important to the well-being of teachers and directors. Providing sick leave policy and health benefits are other ways to promote physical and mental health and safety for those who nurture, teach, and care for children.

- Actions adults can take to ensure a healthy environment:

  Know that the safety, health, and welfare for children and themselves is priority 1.

  Encourage reasonable cleanliness with the children. Soap, water, disposable towels, and first-aid materials are available and used frequently. Children are encouraged to wash after using the toilets, before eating, and after using messy materials.

  Keep play and work areas clean and orderly.

> ### Facts and Figures (continued)
>
> Personal records include results of physical exams, immunizations, allergies, illnesses, emergency contact information, special health conditions, employment information, skills, talents, etc.
>
> New staff members serve a probationary period of employment during which their physical and psychological competence for working with children is evaluated.
>
> At least one on-site staff member is certified in emergency pediatric first-aid treatment, CPR for infants and children, and emergency management of choking. Current certificates are kept on file.
>
> Be familiar with emergency procedures (such as primary and secondary evacuation routes—and practice evacuation procedures monthly with children—operation of fire extinguishers and procedures for severe storm warnings (when necessary).
>
> Know the procedure for reporting suspected incidents of child abuse and/or neglect.
>
> Know the importance of confidentiality pertaining to children, parents, staff, and other center matters.

HEALTH FACTORS FOR PERSONNEL

Center personnel, whether they work directly with the children or in supplementary roles, should be in excellent physical and mental condition. Poor health and lack of stamina interfere with performance. Many centers require new employees to have a physical examination (including a tuberculosis check and other tests). This is especially important for employees who will work closely with children or food.

Providing medical insurance for employees is costly; however, this benefit frequently offsets its cost. Employees tend to seek medical care earlier when they have such medical coverage.

Caregivers may experience aches and pains accompanying frequent hand washing, sitting on child-sized chairs, bending to be at child level, or lifting equipment. These bodily changes are real and need attention. Aronson (1987b) acknowledges these problems and offers these simple practices to follow: maintaining good posture, standing comfortably, wearing proper shoes, and lifting correctly.

As required for most licenses, employees are to receive preemployment physical examinations, tuberculosis tests, and evaluation of any infection.

To have confidence in themselves, personnel must feel good about what they are doing, the people with whom they work, and the children for whom they care. To do these things, personnel must be well informed about their duties and be well trained with constant refreshers in curriculum, relationships, and responsibilities. Discussions and practice help keep one's mind alive; conversely, never reviewing procedures makes one apprehensive and unsure. For example, first-aid and emergency procedures should be refreshed often through discussion, reading, and practice.

The employees need health care for themselves and their families. (See Chapter 6.) But the way employees care for themselves (nutrition, exercise, health checks, personal habits, lifting procedures, cleanliness, caution, etc.) can help keep their stamina high and their resistance low.

The center employees, and especially the director, need to take frequent walks around the playground and through the facility to detect and remove environmental hazards that can affect both adults and children. Consider this list of possible environmental hazards:

Indoors: Cleaning materials, tobacco smoke, lead, asbestos, toxic art or play materials, communicable diseases, injuries

Outdoors: Lead, toxic waste including chemicals and pesticides, animals, unsafe play equipment, injuries, improper fencing, unfavorable weather conditions

Both indoors and outdoors: Chemicals, unsafe building materials, unauthorized people, clutter, inattention, improper fitting clothing (especially shoes), incomplete or outdated first-aid training, mistreated children

RESPONSIBILITIES OF THE DIRECTOR AND/OR OWNER

Establishing safe policies include hiring qualified and caring staff members; purchasing nontoxic art and play materials; screening for radon, asbestos, lead content of painted toys and equipment, soil, and water; maintaining appropriate air, ventilation, and heating in classrooms (implementing no smoking policy, venting of fuel by-products); monitoring use of pesticides, herbicides, and other chemicals; reassessing the center for potential hazards frequently; and reducing risk of harm and/or accident.

Most environmental hazards in care centers can be prevented or managed through common sense, knowing what building materials have been used in the center's construction, constant vigilance, and following the health standards for licensing of the center.

In addition to establishing safe policies, the director recognizes that children get sick, injured, or into difficulties because of their heightened sensitivities: oral (ingestion), skin (absorption), and lower body density (inhalation). (See the examples discussed in the section, "Health Factors for Children.") Hands and objects are frequently mouthed, irritants are absorbed through their thin skins, and through inhalation "due to age-specific factors such as a higher respiratory rate, greater levels of physical activity causing even faster and deeper breathing, a breathing zone closer to the ground where heavier pollutants are more concentrated, increased mouth breathing, which impairs the natural filtering process, and a greater potential for long-term exposure" (Gratz & Boulton, 1993, p. 30).

It is assumed that all staff members will obtain training in first-aid, CPR, and emergency procedures—even if they aren't required—and review them frequently as they upgrade newer and more appropriate ways of interacting with peers, children, and families.

Employees must familiarize themselves with signs of abuse and reporting methods. Because of specific statutes, no further information will be given here about child abuse; however, laws do require reporting of suspicious circumstances at home or at the center. See Chapter 9 for a discussion on child abuse.

HEALTH FACTORS FOR PARENTS

On inquiry or enrollment of their children in the center, parents should be specifically informed (verbally and/or in writing) about the health policies of the center (including enrollment physical examinations, daily routine health check, and handling of ill children). If the center is willing to administer doctor-prescribed medication, this should be clearly stated, a current form must be signed by a responsible parent/guardian with specific instructions from the child's doctor as to amount and timing of dosages. Nutrition, rest, dental hygiene, health education, transportation (if applicable), and other matters that affect the health and safety of the children and staff at the center must be clear to parents and employees.

When parents enroll their child(ren) at a child-care center, they want to assume that the child(ren) will be safe, loved, and protected from harm, accident, and illness. Common sense says that when people are gathered together (especially young children), there is exposure to common, contagious, and serious illnesses—and sometimes accidents occur.

When a child is to be absent from the center for a period of time, regardless of the reason, parents should notify the center of the reason and the expected return of the child. In this way, the staff and other children will anticipate the child's return rather than wonder about the cause of the absence—which can be upsetting to some of the other children.

Inclusion/Exclusion Policy

Parents should be specifically informed about ill and/or absent children—especially who makes the final decision about whether a child can come to the center or remain at the center if there is evidence of illness. Some centers may have established illness policies, but they may be willing to consider variables on an individual basis. Options must be *clearly understood by both parties* to avoid frustration and anger during unusual times: Both center employees and parents face a dilemma.

Even when there are written policies, parents need to recognize that some of the policies are beyond the jurisdiction of the director—such as local and/or state regulations, type and severity of illness, administration of medication, number of staff at the center, skills of staff, isolation space, or specific needs of the child. From the time the parent inquires about enrollment of a child, parents must be aware of special conditions when the parent (or their designated alternate) would have to be available on short notice. The center policy on conditions for inclusion/exclusion for illness and/or injury must be clearly understood and consistent for all parents. (Note: Utah's Department of Health Services, "Guide for First Aid and Emergency Care for Young Children," states: *"Communicable Diseases: DO NOT* provide treatment for children with apparent communicable diseases. Isolate children with signs and symptoms (cold symptoms, rash, nausea, vomiting, diarrhea, yellow eyes and skin, fatigue and malaise). Notify par-

ents and exclude children from center and urge parents to seek medical care.") See Appendix C, for children's records.

Aronson (n.d.), a pediatrician and frequent medical writer of NAEYC articles, gives some basic suggestions regarding ill children and center care.

1. Child-care programs need ready access to knowledgeable medical professionals to determine contagiousness. And at best, some of these decisions are judgment calls.

2. Exclusion is rarely appropriate to prevent the spread of infection in child care; however, it is required when there is infectious diarrhea and vomiting, untreated conjunctivitis, impetigo, ringworm, head lice, and scabies. Within a day or two of treatment, the child may return.

3. Various infection-spreading particles can be carried in the nose, mouth, stool, and urine particles without a child showing symptoms of illness. Some children shed infectious material before showing signs of illness; some children shed infectious material after symptoms are gone.

4. Studies that compared child-care centers with stringent policies for excluding ill children with centers that are less stringent about exclusion show no difference in the amount of illness.

5. The decision about permitting a child with a respiratory illness to remain in child care should depend on the needs of the child and the availability of the parent to provide the needed care.

6. See pages 304–305 regarding HIV/AIDS.

Children Who Become Ill at the Center

Parents will ask: What criteria will be used to determine if the child is well enough to attend the center or sick enough to be returned home? How quickly must a parent respond if called to pick up an ill child? Checking with the local American

Red Cross, the local health department, pediatricians, other centers, and NAEYC publications may help the center to arrive at solutions that are important, fair, and consistent.

The center should advise the parents of incubation periods for certain illnesses and their policy about contagious diseases. All parents must make alternate care arrangements, though tenuous or inadequate, for illness or emergencies for their own peace of mind. (See Appendix A for more information.)

The needs of all children (well or ill), staff, and parents need to be considered—but the final decision must lie with the center.

The following are considerations for making a decision about whether a child should stay or be sent home.

Needs of the Ill Child. How much care is required (minimal, continual)? Will it require extra personnel? If so, how is cost absorbed? Does the child feel safe at the center? Does the child need medical attention or medication? How would the child who becomes ill at the center perceive isolation (punishment, frightening, rejection, etc.)?

Needs of the Center. Are there licensing or liability requirements for the care of sick children? (If all else fails, the local public health authority by law has the final word.) Is the illness contagious? What are the center's policies about administering medication?

Based on an informal survey, if the exclusion from the care center for a child with a runny nose, cough, crankiness, earache, sore throat, rash, diarrhea, or pink eye were up to (1) the child-care staff, (2) mothers, or (3) pediatricians, the child would most readily be excluded by the child-care staff and lastly by pediatricians.

Needs of the Parents. How easily can the parent find substitute care? Will immediate pick-up of the child cause employment problems for the parent? If no care can be found, would the child have to be left alone or with young siblings? What are the consequences, what are the alternatives?

If your child isn't ill but another one is, how would you feel about the ill child remaining at the center?

Readmission of a Child Who Has Been Ill

There are some basic assumptions about returning children. Generally, agreement among the center, the program, and the child will determine when the child is ready to return to group care. Exceptional cases may involve a health professional in the decision. At our university preschool, during the time we were fortunate to have a registered nurse on our staff, she made any difficult decisions about a child's health. In that way, problems were prevented between parents and teachers, director and staff, director and parents, and parents and children. (See Appendix A.)

Children with Special Needs

Families with children needing special attention because of disabilities can seek some relief and education when they enroll their child in a center with children their own ages who aren't disabled. In these centers where teachers are knowledgeable about growth and development of young children and have the child's interest at heart, activities can be provided whereby the child can feel individual success, participate with same-age peers, and give family members some relief from the child's constant care.

Some children with special needs are easier to include in groups of young children than others. The Americans with Disabilities Act, discussed in Chapter 3, provides for the inclusion of children with different needs. Aronson (1991) states: "The key to accepting children with chronic illnesses or disabilities is planning for their enrollment and reevaluating their needs on a periodic basis. Some children require intensive services that are beyond the resources of the usual program. Many have only mild manifestations of their impairment and require only intermittent or minor adjustments of the program's curriculum" (p. 171).

For a more detailed discussion, see "Diversity" in Chapter 3.

HEALTH FACTORS FOR CHILDREN

Every center caring for young children should have carefully and specifically written health goals for the children and adults. These goals should be reviewed frequently and changed as new information or procedures are available.

Child-care centers should practice preventive health care by requiring immunizations and routine checkups, treating chronic diseases, implementing special diets, helping to cope with allergies and intolerances, detecting possible problems and making necessary referrals, teaching dental hygiene, observing and documenting growth and development, teaching good nutrition and food habits, and observing the guidelines of food safety (e.g., avoid serving items that often cause choking such as nuts, popcorn, or hot dog chunks and avoiding serving honey to children under 1) (Kendrick et al., 1988).

Infectious diseases can be transmitted through intestinal and urinary tract excretions; through respiratory tract secretions from eyes, nose, mouth, and lungs; and through direct contact with infected people and surfaces. It is inevitable that children will catch infectious diseases, but they can be controlled and sometimes prevented. "In child-care settings, there are three ways to stop the spread of infectious diseases: (1) vaccinations for vaccine-preventable diseases, (2) medical care and education, and (3) proper sanitation practices, including (a) compulsive handwashing, (b) careful diapering, (c) frequent disinfecting, and (d) adequate ventilation" (Moukaddem, 1990, p. 28).

Margaret McMillan, a crusader for children's rights and a pioneer in the early organization of nursery schools in England, recognized the needs of the starving and diseased children near London. Her constant cry for children to be taken off the streets, to be fed and nurtured in a loving environment, and to be freed from disease made her both popular and unpopular. She succeeded in establishing nursery schools in certain areas, in establishing clinics for the care of young children, and in providing a food program for many children. One of her great disappointments was that diseases in slum children were not preventable; the children were temporarily cured, only to return reinfected. McMillan found that even children with severe cases of rickets and other dietary deficiencies improved in the nursery schools while living and playing outdoors and eating properly. The children attending open-air nursery schools suffered only mild cases of common diseases or experienced none at all.

McMillan insisted on cleanliness, not just to prevent disease, but because she felt that the self-esteem of the children would increase and that teachers could see conditions that required treatment (such as rickets, deformities, diseases, infections) when children were undressed and washed. McMillan often expressed the conviction that children must *feel* clean because they breathe through their skins and cannot learn if they are uncomfortable. Her own statement was, "We must try to educate every child as if he were our own, and just as we would educate our own" (Bradburn, 1976, p. 91). She felt it was a waste of money to try to educate a hungry, let alone a starving, child. Her open-air nursery schools were places of beauty, with lovely flower and herb gardens, winding paths, trees, provisions for pets, only necessary equipment, and interesting places to explore. Children who needed baths were bathed; children who were undernourished were fed; children who had little or no care were loved. The combination of these attributes brought color back into faces and strength back into bodies.

In our own country, there is evidence that good health care can improve the lives of young children. The Head Start Program, for example, has fostered many of McMillan's goals. Children need dental, medical, and emotional care. They need a good diet for their bodies to grow strong and straight. They need opportunities to learn under the best conditions. See Figure 8–1 for a description of how to teach handwashing steps to children.

Each state or jurisdiction has licensing requirements for each and every area of concern. In the

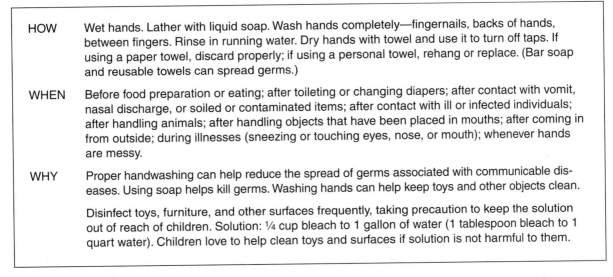

HOW	Wet hands. Lather with liquid soap. Wash hands completely—fingernails, backs of hands, between fingers. Rinse in running water. Dry hands with towel and use it to turn off taps. If using a paper towel, discard properly; if using a personal towel, rehang or replace. (Bar soap and reusable towels can spread germs.)
WHEN	Before food preparation or eating; after toileting or changing diapers; after contact with vomit, nasal discharge, or soiled or contaminated items; after contact with ill or infected individuals; after handling animals; after handling objects that have been placed in mouths; after coming in from outside; during illnesses (sneezing or touching eyes, nose, or mouth); whenever hands are messy.
WHY	Proper handwashing can help reduce the spread of germs associated with communicable diseases. Using soap helps kill germs. Washing hands can help keep toys and other objects clean.
	Disinfect toys, furniture, and other surfaces frequently, taking precaution to keep the solution out of reach of children. Solution: ¼ cup bleach to 1 gallon of water (1 tablespoon bleach to 1 quart water). Children love to help clean toys and surfaces if solution is not harmful to them.

Figure 8–1 Handwashing steps.

Utah State Department of Human Services, Office of Licensing for *Family Child Care Rules* (different than *center* care) dated January 1993, the following information is reported regarding selected areas for example only: physical examinations, immunizations, medications, first-aid and injuries, nutrition and food services:

Physical Examinations

a. Initially, no child shall be admitted for care who has not had a physical examination within the past 6 months for children under age two, within the past year for preschool age children, and within the past two years for school age children. A copy of the examination shall be available in the facility.

b. If a child shows signs of illness or communicable disease, the caregiver may request of the parent that a physical examination be carried out at any time.

Immunization

a. No child shall be admitted for care that has not had appropriate age immunizations required by state law or meet conditional enrollment requirements required by law.

b. If immunization is against the parents' religion or not advisable for medical reasons, an exception to immunization requirements may be made if it is requested in writing.

c. A current record of the child's immunizations shall be on file, updated as soon as possible or within 30 days. (A recommended Schedule of Immunization is included in packet.)

See Appendix D for contagious diseases and immunizations.

Medication

a. Caregivers shall not give drugs, either nonprescription or prescription, unless currently prescribed and approved in writing by a physician and parent. (A form is available for current information.)

b. Caregivers shall report to the parent of each child on the same day of discovery of any adverse reaction to medication.

c. Written standing orders for commonly used medications may be used to avoid the need for a health care provider's instruction or parents' written permission for every instance for every child. Parents should always be notified in every instance when medication is used from a standing order.

d. All medications, refrigerated or unrefrigerated, shall have child-protective caps, shall be stored in their original container, shall be kept in an orderly fashion, shall be stored away from food at the proper temperature, and shall be inaccessible to children. Medications shall not be used beyond the date of expiration.

First Aid and Injuries

a. The caregiver shall post and understand the "Guide for First Aid and Emergency Care for Children" in Appendix C–8. A first aid kit shall be maintained in the home. Recommended items for a first aid kit are listed in the "Guide for First Aid and Emergency Care of Children" in Appendix C–8.

b. If a child shows signs of illness after arrival, the caregiver shall contact the parent immediately.

c. When a child requires immediate medical attention, caregivers shall notify parent and obtain medical services as agreed upon by parents. (Checklist is provided.)

d. Children's injuries, i.e., falls, bumps on the head, scratches and bruises, etc., shall be reported to parents on the same day they happen and shall be documented.

Nutrition and Food Services

1. Nutrition:

   a. Meals and snacks served shall meet the nutritional requirements of the USDA Child Care Food Program. (USDA Food Chart provided.)

   b. Children shall receive meals and/or snacks according to the hours in care. (Chart provided.)

   c. Sufficient food shall be available for second servings.

   d. Only Grade A fluid milk shall be used for drinking. Powdered milk shall be used for cooking only.

   e. Children and infants shall be served special diets, formulas, or food supplements in accordance with the written instructions from a parent. Food brought from home shall be labeled and, if perishable, refrigerated.

   f. All children shall be served at the appropriate mealtime hour. With no more than three hours between the serving of meals or snacks.

2. Food Preparation:

   a. Food shall be stored under safe and sanitary conditions.

   b. Utensils, equipment, and preparation areas shall be kept clean, sanitary, and in good repair.

3. Infant Feeding:

   a. Infants who can not sit upright and hold their own bottle shall be held with heads elevated while drinking.

   b. Infant food and formula shall be labeled, refrigerated, and fed to the infant in a sanitary manner.

In all the years of my teaching preschoolers, the experience I find most memorable (and the most educational) was as a once-a-week co-teacher of toddlers for 15 years. Each child came into the group at 18 months of age and "graduated" at age 3. In the beginning each child was so dependent, frightened, emotional, and nonverbal! We made it a point to treat each child with love and respect. We saw lots of changes in the children—they became verbal, confident, independent, caring, and mature! They learned how to share toys, to enjoy story/group time, to be proud of their efforts, to enjoy other children and activities, and to serve themselves at snack time! We showed them how to hold their glass in one hand and pour their own juice from a pitcher and how to enjoy music and rhythm, story time, creative art, and other activities. It was sad to see them turn 3, but now we look at them as mature, productive, and happy individuals. What a wonderful learning experience for me!

Snacks fill several needs of young children. Besides replenishing their energy and building their health, it serves as a social time, a learning time, and a resting time: "Snack time is an intimate comforting break in which children gain physical and emotional nourishment. The environment balances their need to be cared for with the need to be independent and self-sufficient" (Murray, 2000, p. 43).

Carefully consider the following quotes:

Physical needs are met by providing nutritious food to the hungry child. Emotional needs are considered as we create a comforting and inviting atmosphere. I think of snack time as respite from the busy day's

Stimulator

Some children have strong and/or negative feelings related to food. It can mean feelings of safety, love, and well-being, or it can mean another experience of powerlessness, restriction, and conflict. Snack time is often overlooked as a positive, growing part of the child's day. It may even mean a temporary break for teachers! Planning for snack foods, table behavior, conversation, and enjoyment should be important for both teachers and children. It can be a relaxing, rejuvenating part of the day—or it can be one of frustration, limitations, and conflict. Take these two examples: Which one mimics your snack time?

1. Children are *forced* to disrupt their play—"*I said snack is* **NOW!**" They *dislike* the foods served.—"*I hate fruit—it makes me throw up!*" They resent adult imposition into their lives—"*We don't want to eat now! We want to dig in the sand.*" The children have assigned seats—mainly for the sake of the teacher! Food is dished out and children are told to finish all of it before leaving the table. Snack time is abrupt, boisterous, tearful, and frustrating!

2. The children have had previous warning about the approaching snack time. In fact, several of the children helped prepare the applesauce they will eat today. They have been reassured they can return to their prior play—but they seldom do. The children dish out their own food—and ask for seconds occasionally. They sit in unassigned places, enjoy their friends and the food—and then return to their former play or new play at their discretion.

Sometimes children use food as a weapon against adults—and sometimes teachers use food as a control of children. "Due to the strong connection that occurs between food and feelings of safety, love, and well-being, the events surrounding the activity of eating should be taken seriously by caretakers" (Lowsley, 1993, p. 31). "Snack time offers unlimited potential for learning about and meeting children's social-emotional needs, yet it may be one of the most overlooked times of the day when planning instruction in a preschool classroom" (Murray, 2000, p. 43).

Does example 1 or example 2 best represent your snack time? How could you better meet the nutritional and social needs of the children in your classroom? Are your children more or less compatible after ingesting food?

Are your children (even toddlers) encouraged, for example, to serve themselves (pour, dish, spread, combine, limit, etc.), to select wanted foods, or to eat or not eat? Review your procedures.

❖ ❖ ❖ ❖

activity. With a nurturing emotional climate established, snack time also becomes a time for learning many important preschool concepts, thus facilitating the integration of emotional and cognitive learning. (Maslow, 1972, p. 43)

Challenge to teachers: The satisfying sensory experience of taking nourishment into our bodies, being cared for at the most basic level, undoubtedly holds great possibilities for creating important early experiences in the development of self. Parents report that although their preschool child doesn't readily retell significant events from the day when asked the classic question, "What did you do today at school?" she *will* often recall what she ate for snack! (Murray, 2000, p. 52)

Designing a snack-time routine that provides utmost potential for developing a healthy sense of self is of paramount importance for preschool teachers. I challenge teachers to view snack time with fresh insight and embrace the occasion to nourish the body, mind, and spirit of each child. (Murray, 2000, p. 52)

The child's social-emotional needs serve as the foundation for all other learning experiences, cognitive goals being secondary during snack time. What comes from the child spontaneously should never be ignored or redirected into a theme-based conversation or skill lesson. Integration of cognitive goals at snack time will come naturally and incidentally to the observant, sensitive, and flexible preschool teacher. (Murray, 2000, p. 51)

For a More Productive Snack Time

1. As an observer (not a participator) closely watch and record the behavior of the children before, during, and after snack time over a period of several days.

2. After observing the group behavior, select one of two children to further track.

3. What ideas do you have about teacher behavior before, during, and after snack time?

4. What information did you gather about general and specific likes and dislikes of the children.

5. What food items encourage/discourage children's verbal expression or dependence/independence?

6. Which children are active/inactive participators at snack time and which children could be encouraged to be more/less involved with food experiences?

7. How can you encourage/discourage snack behavior?

8. How does the equipment (tables, chairs, benches, dishes, etc.) influence the behavior of the children?

9. Is food used more by children or teachers as a weapon for behavior?

10. Have you inquired of children or teachers about their food preferences? How could you enlarge their good experiences?

For More Insight Into the Snack Period

Observe a snack period. Note what *incidental* developmental teaching is occurring:

1. What social skills are being taught?

2. What physical skills are being taught?

3. What intellectual skills are being taught?

4. What emotional skills are being taught?

5. Was there evidence of ethnic teaching?

6. Did teachers or children introduce related or unrelated topics?

7. What was the role of the teacher?

8. Was the activity more "child" or "adult" oriented?

9. What ideas did you (as a teacher) gain for use in a future snack period?

10. What are the advantages and disadvantages of a snack period for young children?

Recent Developments Regarding Health Factors for Children

The Children's Health Insurance Program (CHIP) was passed by Congress in 1997. It is designed to provide free or low-cost health insurance to children in uninsured families with low or moderate incomes. It provides a significant funding increase for children's health (O'Connor, 1999).

It also provides:

$4 billion a year in federal matching funds to states.

State determined benefits and terms; most states will insure children through age 18, covering checkups, well-baby and well-child visits, prescriptions, immunization shots, and more.

Coverage for children from uninsured families whose incomes are too high to allow them to qualify under the 1997 Medicaid eligibility limits but too low to enable their purchase of private family coverage. In the majority of states the maximum allowable income for a family of four is about $32,900 a year.

Many states have developed policies that make the program completely cost-free for families with incomes between $16,450 and $24,675 annually for a family of four (CDF, 1998).

Outreach to families—but these families must be identified.

Additional steps early childhood professionals can take, after familiarizing themselves with the fund and eligibility requirements: (a) spread the word to families; (b) help families with the application process; (c) reach out to your professional networks; (d) join Children's Defense Fund's (CDF's) on-line outreach campaign; (e) track family experiences; and (f) monitor program policies.

The Children's Defense Fund can be a valuable source of assistance and information:

Website: *www.childrensdefense.org*

Phone: 800-CDF-1200 and press "2" for information

CDF's Child Health Implementation Project Coordinator: Jeannette O'Connor at 202-662-3653

Mental health is an important aspect of total health. It must be addressed in the curriculum, policies, and daily activities, thus reducing problems of poor coping and unmanaged stress in children.

"Early childhood education policy makers recommend helping child care centers link with one another and with health care systems . . . as consultants to child care programs. . . . They are often uninformed about how to make the link and what services are available. This article gives suggestions on whom to contact for such services" (Dooling & Ulione, 2000, p. 23).

The role of the child-care health consultants in a group setting include preventing illness and injury, providing positive health outcomes for children and adults (including parents) through information, guidance, and technical training, acting in child advocacy roles on local, state, and national levels, and providing knowledge of national, state, and local licensing procedures. The qualifications of health consultant should include knowledge of pediatric health care and child development, public health principles, local community resources (as a link to other agencies), local and state child-care licensing regulations, injury prevention screening such as playground equipment and environmental safety, and the ability to meet learning needs at a variety of educational levels (Dooling & Ulione, 2000, p. 24).

Common injuries of children include falls, usually from playground equipment. Most injuries can be avoided. Playground standards are published in *Caring for our Children—National Health and Safety Performance Standards: Guidelines for Out-of-Home Care Programs* (APHA & APA, 1992).

ENSURE A HEALTHY ENVIRONMENT FOR CHILDREN, PARENTS, STAFF, AND CENTER

Children

Emergency telephone numbers (police, fire, rescue, poison control, hospital, etc.) are posted near all phones.

Suspected incidents of child abuse and/or neglect by parents, staff, or other persons are reported to appropriate local agencies.

The staff is alert to health changes in each child.

Health records include current and vital information: results of recent health exam, immunizations, *emergency information, allergies, limitations,* pick-up persons, health history, etc.

When, and if, medication is administered, careful, written records are kept.

Children are encouraged to wash their hands after using the toilets, before eating, after handling pets, and after using messy materials.

Children are rehearsed frequently on emergency procedures (where to go, what to do).

Escape routes and behaviors are familiar, but not frightening.

If children are transported, vehicles are equipped with age-appropriate restraint devices and appropriate safety precautions (licensed driver, fire extinguisher, explanation of trip, etc.).

Infants' equipment is washed and disinfected frequently. Toys that are mouthed are washed daily.

Individual bedding is washed once a week and used by only one child between washings.

Individual cribs, cots, and mats are washed if soiled.

Toys are free from sharp edges, mouthable parts, and kept out of the way when not in use.

Parents

Parents are informed about center procedures and policies for (but not limited to): attendance of sick children, arrival and departure times, payment of fees, health (limitations, administration of medication, allergies, and other specific/general information), field trips (dates, time span, purpose, precautions, etc.), and other special activities.

Their questions are courteously answered.

Their requests are considered and sometimes implemented.

Staff

Know that the safety, health, and welfare for children and adults is priority 1.

Know the procedure for reporting suspected incidents of child abuse and/or neglect.

Personal records include results of physical exams, immunizations, allergies, illnesses, emergency contact information, special health conditions, employment information, training completed, skills, talents, etc.

Encourage reasonable cleanliness with the children. Soap, water, disposable towels, and first-aid materials are available and used frequently.

Keep play and work areas clean and orderly.

Be familiar with emergency procedures (such as primary and secondary evacuation routes—and practice evacuation procedures monthly with children—operation of fire extinguishers and procedures for severe storm warnings (when necessary).

Know the importance of confidentiality pertaining to children, parents, staff, and other matters.

New staff members serve a probationary period of employment during which their physical and psychological competence for working with children is evaluated.

At least one on-site staff member is certified in emergency pediatric first-aid treatment, CPR for infants and children, and emergency management of choking. Current certificates are kept on file.

Center

Meals should be served in an atmosphere encouraging healthy eating habits and where children can experience healthy nutrition, friendly conversation, proper use of utensils, good manners, child-sized tables and chairs, etc.

Licensing and accreditation certifications are current and posted in a conspicious place.

A plan exists for dealing with medical emergencies that includes a source of emergency care, written parental consent forms, and transportation agreements.

There is certification that nontoxic building materials—lead paint or asbestos—are not used in the facility.

When appropriate, screens are placed on all windows that open. Upstairs windows must have locking devices.

Toileting and diapering areas are sanitary.

The classrooms are carefully monitored: children sometimes use things in unexpected ways!

Nutritious foods are served in attractive ways so that children have a pleasant and important experience.

Smoke detectors and fire extinguishers are conveniently located and updated.

First-aid supplies are adequate and readily available. Staff know emergency procedures.

The center is cleaned daily—bathroom fixtures are disinfected. Hot water does not exceed 110°F (43°C) at outlets used by children.

Potential hazards (stairs, open windows, small spaces, obstructed areas, etc.) are carefully monitored.

ENVIRONMENTAL HAZARDS FOR YOUNG CHILDREN

Gratz and Boulton (1993), making a commitment to serve the health and safety needs of children, discuss environmental hazards and direct attention to pesticides, environmental tobacco smoke, lead, toxic art materials, asbestos, and other substances.

At the 1993 International Conference on Child Day Care Health in Atlanta sponsored by the Centers for Disease Control, the three most important areas of concern were identified as communicable disease, injuries, and environmental hazards. The ongoing research specifically on children's exposure is very limited.

Particular attention is directed to special susceptibilities of young children to environmental hazards through three pathways of exposure because of physiological and biological differences between children and adults: *ingestion* (through the alimentary tract—oral exploration of young children), *inhalation* (via the respiratory tract—young children inhale two to three times as much pollutant per unit of body weight, have increased respiratory rate, faster and deeper breathing, are closer to the ground where heavier pollutants are more concentrated), and *skin absorption* (thinner skin of children) via (1) oxygen consumption and metabolism; (2) body composition (infants have a greater percentage of water and a lesser percentage of solids in lean body tissue, which enhances absorption of toxic materials in the body; (3) developing body systems/organs (comparatively rapid growth of infants and chemical accumulation); and (4) behavioral differences (oral exploration in children, children spend more time indoors and on the floor) (Gratz & Boulton, 1993).

Pesticides/Poisons

All pesticides, cleaning materials, empty containers, and possible contaminants *must* be locked in storage spaces where children have *no* access.

There are many types of poisons. According to Intermountain Regional Poison Control Center (n.d.), "It is important to remember that any nonfood item could potentially be a poison. Some of the more common products that result in poisonings include medications, household cleaners, petroleum products, plants, tobacco smoke, drugs, and personal care products. As the seasons change and our activities move in and out of doors, certain poisons become increased hazards" (p. 2). Figure 8–2 lists poisonous plants and Figure 8–3 lists some nonpoisonous plants.

Each center should frequently review, and post in conspicuous places, the appropriate action to follow when children ingest, inhale, get in the eyes or on the skin any foreign or suspect materials. Landscapers and other outdoor caretakers should be constantly reminded about poisonous plants, cleaning materials, and discarded containers.

Autumn crocus	Azalea
Baneberry	Belladonna
Black cherry	Black locust
Buckeye	Caladium
Caper spurge	Castor bean
Cherry	Chinaberry
Daffodil	Daphne
Delphinium	Dieffenbachia (dumbcane)
Duranta	False hellebore
Foxglove	Golden chain
Hyacinth	Hydrangea
Jequirity bean	Jessamine
Jimson weed	Lantana
Larkspur	Laurel
Lily-of-the-valley	Lupine
Mistletoe	Monkshood
Moonseed	Mountain laurel
Mushrooms	Nightshade
Oleander	Philodendron
Poison hemlock	Pokeweed
Privet	Rhododendron
Rhubarb leaves	Rosary pea
Rubber vine	Sandbox tree
Tansy	Thorn apple
Tobacco	Tung oil tree
Water hemlock	White snakeroot
Yellow jessamine	Yellow oleander
Yew	

Figure 8–2   Poisonous plants (partial listing).

African violet	Prayer plant
Aluminum plant	Rubber plant
Begonia	Sensitive plant
Boston fern	Snake plant
Coleus	Spider plant
Dracaena	Swedish ivy
Hen-and-chickens	Wandering Jew
Jade plant	Wax plant
Peperomia	Weeping fig

Figure 8–3   Nonpoisonous plants (partial listing).

If you have any questions about the safety of any plants, contact an authority in your area!

Contact your State Department of Health and Family Services. Ask for Poison control. Get a phone number and procedures for reporting any environmental hazards especially regarding young children ingesting toxic materials. KEEP ALL HARMFUL MATERIALS SECURELY LOCKED UP!

Organizations with Lists of
Child-Care Health Consultants:

American Academy of Pediatrics (AAP)
141 Northwest Point Boulevard
P. O. Box 927
Elk Grove, IL 60009-0927
e-mail: *childcare@aap.org*
Phone 708-228-5005
Online: *www.aap.org*

National Association of Child Care Resource & Referral Agencies (NACCRRA)
1319 F Street, NW, Suite 810
Washington, DC 20004-1106
Phone: 202-393-5501
Online: *www.naccrra.net*

Tobacco Smoke

Smoking in the Child-Care Center.   In answer to the question, Should smoking be permitted inside a child-care center? Aronson (1993), among others, says *no* for the following reasons:

1. It increases the risk of respiratory illness for children and lowers their resistance to respiratory infections.

2. It causes loss of elasticity of body tissues, yellows the skin and teeth, causes bad breath, and is a "powerful poison."

3. It contaminates space used by smokers and nonsmokers.

Lead/Asbestos

Many factors need to be considered for the safety of children: toxic waste, unhealthy air, noise pollution, caustic materials, and lead in building materials and toys. "Lead in Children's Environ- ments" (1990) reports that even small amounts of lead can cause problems with learning and behavior that persist into adulthood. "The persistent toxicity of lead was seen to result in significant and serious impairment of academic success,

---

Facts and Figures

- The real tragedy of secondhand smoke is the effect it has on young children and unborn babies. In a current review of literature, maternal smoking is reported to be responsible for the deaths of 115,000 fetuses per year, and the deaths of 6,000 babies per year (*Journal of Family Practice,* 1995, May).

- Mothers who smoke contribute to low-birth-weight babies, infants who need intensive care after birth, babies who have illness in their first year of life. Their babies are more likely to have lower IQs and behavioral difficulties such as attention deficit disorder.

- Up to 75 percent of children are exposed daily to secondhand smoke either in the home or in other environments.

- Exposure to secondhand smoke is the third leading cause of preventable deaths in the United States (behind smoking and alcohol use), killing 53,000 adults per year—36,000 deaths from heart disease and 3,000 from lung cancer (Cox, 1995).

The 1993 report of the Environmental Protection Agency regarding passive smoking reached these major conclusions regarding children: Environmental tobacco smoke (ETS) exposure increases the risk of lower respiratory tract infections such as bronchitis and pneumonia (EPA estimates that between 150,000 and 300,000 of these cases annually in infants and young children up to 18 months of age are attributable to exposure to ETS. Of these, between 7,500 and 15,000 will result in hospitalization); increases the prevalence of fluid in the middle ear, a sign of chronic middle-ear disease; irritates the upper respiratory tract and is associated with a small but significant reduction in lung function; and increases the frequency of episodes and severity of symptoms in asthmatic children (the report estimates that 200,000 to 1,000,000 asthmatic children have their condition worsened by exposure to environmental tobacco smoke).

The 1994 report of the EPA, very similar to ones made previously by the National Academy of Sciences and the U.S. Surgeon General, concluded that secondhand smoke causes lung cancer in adult nonsmokers and impairs the respiratory health of children; is a risk factor for the development of asthma in children and worsens the condition of up to 1,000,000 asthmatic children, and causes respiratory effects in children and is widely shared and virtually undisputed. Even the tobacco industry does not contest these effects in its media and public relations campaign.

The Clinton administration supported legislation (H.R. 3434, S. 1680, s. 262) that would protect nonsmokers, including children, from secondhand smoke in most public places—but not take away smokers free choice to smoke, nor regulate smoking in the home.

including sevenfold increase in failure to graduate from high school, impairment of reading skills, and deficits in vocabulary." Contact your local EPA office or the NAEYC Information Service for ordering "Drinking Water at Nursery Schools and Day-Care Centers." (See also Kendrick et al., 1988).

According to the NAEYC (1994), lead poisoning is the most common environmental pediatric health problem in the United States. Fifteen percent of all U.S. children may have blood lead levels high enough to cause cognitive deficits and other adverse effects, including certain types of behavioral disorders and hearing impairments. These effects are persistent across cultures, racial and ethnic groups, and social and economic classes (American Academy of Pediatrics, 1994).

The Centers for Disease Control and Prevention (CDC) revised the standard establishing the level at which children are considered at risk for lead poisoning and recommended new guidelines for screening in 1991. The American Academy of Pediatrics has joined the CDC in recommending screening at age 6 months, with regular visits to follow, for those identified at high risk for lead poisoning.

Center Action. Check paint on toys, play equipment, painted room surfaces, and so on for possible toxins. Removing paint and repainting with nonlead paint may help. In some cases, items must be removed or destroyed.

Asbestos could be considered along with the hazards of lead because both are found in the child's living environment and both were not considered harmful for many years.

Resources on lead-related issues:

National Lead Information Center Hotline:
1-800-LEAD-FYI
(Available 24 hours a day, 7 days a week, in English and Spanish.)
Provides a brochure entitled *Lead Poisoning and Your Children* and a list of state/local contacts for information.

National Lead Information Clearinghouse:
1-800-424-LEAD
Trained specialists answer specific questions on lead-related issues in English or Spanish, including information on lead-related federal laws and regulations, qualified testing laboratories, and technical assistance.

For a discussion on toxic art materials, see Chapter 9. For a discussion on allergies, see "Nutrition, Learning, and Behavior" in this chapter.

Ways to Prevent Bites

Human

1. Have an adequate supply of toys and materials; give close supervision to children who are teething or who display aggressive behavior.
2. Encourage children to use verbal rather than physical means of getting something. "Instead of biting (name of child), tell him with your voice what you want"—for children who are verbal—and to children who are nonverbal, say "He thought he wasn't going to get a turn with the (toy) so he bit you."
3. Provide a substitute: "I can't let you bite (name) but if your teeth really need to bite something, you can bite (the rubber toy, a cracker, etc.).
4. Provide comfort to the attackee.
5. Maintain an adequate teacher-child ratio for the age group.
6. Teach staff members to anticipate problems and how to step in before biting occurs

Insect

1. Wear dark-colored clothing (different from flowers, etc.).
2. Keep skin covered when possible.
3. Avoid sweet-smelling perfume.

4. Stay away from areas that insects inhabit.

5. Discard food items and soft drink cans.

6. Keep garbage cans covered.

7. If necessary, have an exterminator remove nests.

8. Avoid stagnant water.

9. Check enclosures for insects before you enter (car, storage shed, etc.).

Animal

1. Enclose playground areas, if possible.

2. Teach children how to carefully handle pets and to avoid unfamiliar animals.

3. Never approach an animal that is growling or eating.

4. Never tease an animal.

5. Avoid surprising an animal.

Treatment.   If a person is known to suffer a severe systemic reaction to stings, he or she should be taken to a doctor or emergency room immediately for epinephrine treatment. The stringer should be removed carefully and not squeezed with fingers or tweezers. Ice should be applied to prevent more absorption of venom and to reduce swelling, itching, and pain. Wash the wound with soap and water to lessen the chances of infection or apply a poultice of vinegar and salt to lessen the discomfort. For one who suffers from severe allergic or systemic reactions, desensitization or immunotherapy may be needed (Sagall, 1992).

If the skin is broken from an animal or human bite, the wound should be washed with soap and water. Depending on the severity of the bite, a doctor's care may be advisable.

Medication

Deciding whether the program can accept responsibility for giving medication to children should be part of establishing the program's general health policies and procedures (Aronson, 1991). Will caregivers administer medication on all requests (medication for colds and minor ailments) or just under emergency conditions? Who will be responsible to see that the medication is administered at the proper time and in the proper amounts? If it is administered at the center, parents must sign a waiver giving permission and instructions before any member of the center staff can give the medication.

Medication kept at the center must be kept in the kitchen refrigerator stored in a separate, closed (preferably locked) container.

Caregivers are not expected to diagnose what is wrong with a child, but they are expected to accurately observe and describe the chronology of the appearance of the symptoms; therefore, they should be able to identify symptoms of illness for infectious diseases—colds, diarrhea, chicken pox, measles, and whooping cough (fever, runny nose, runny eyes, coughing, fatigue, lethargy, irritability, other)—and chronic illnesses—allergies, asthma, bronchitis, and others. (Symptoms may resemble those of infectious diseases.) For a discussion of injuries, see Chapter 9.

DIRECTORS' RESPONSIBILITIES

Under Our Direct Control

Establish and enforce no smoking policies for the center

Purchase nontoxic art materials

Screen for radon

Check the lead content of painted materials

Purchase nontoxic cleaning agents and properly store them

Building maintenance and ventilation: Clean and change filters of air conditions, humidifiers, dehumidifiers, and furnaces; control for dampness, dust, sand, etc.; open windows daily, even in winter, to allow fresh air into the center

Continuously reassess the center for potential hazards

Not Under Our Direct Control, But Important

Building construction: Materials used and their current condition (e.g., asbestos, formaldehyde-releasing insulation, etc.); location and condition of any surfaces covered with lead-based paint; ventilation and heating systems, particularly the venting of fuel by-products

The location of power lines around the center

The use of pesticides and herbicides (these may be mandated for use and cannot be controlled by the center)

The lead content of soil and water

According to Gratz and Boulton (1993), for more information, call or write to the following:

Environmental Protection Agency Public Information Center
PM 2116
401 M Street SW
Washington, DC 20460
(800) 424–9065

Toxic Substances Control Act Hotline
(202) 554–1404
(Call to order *Environmental Hazards in Your School: A Resource Handbook* and *The ABCs in Schools*)

Indoor Air Division (ANR–445)
Office of Air and Radiation
USEPA
Washington, DC 20460

Asbestos Ombudsman
(800) 368–5888

Safe Drinking Water Hotline
(800) 426–4791 (call to order *Lead in School Drinking Water*)

Radon Hotline
(800) 767–7236 (call to order *Radon in Schools*)

Alliance to End Child Lead Poisoning
600 Pennsylvania Ave. SE
Suite 100
Washington, DC 20010

National Coalition Against the Misuse of Pesticides
701 E Street, SE, Suite 200
Washington, DC 20003
(202) 543–5450

Environmental Defense Fund
1525 18th Street, NW
Washington, DC 20003

CHILDREN WITH HEALTH CONDITIONS

Children with HIV/AIDS

More and more people, young and old, are being diagnosed with HIV/AIDS, a fact that concerns nations, communities, health service workers, and families. Child-care providers are mandated to respond to parents and children who have HIV/AIDS or are afraid of getting it. Legal attempts to exclude children with HIV/AIDS from group care and educational settings have largely been unsuccessful.

Public and private schools, day-care centers, and Head Start programs who do not currently enroll children with HIV/AIDS should anticipate serving them. A recommendation by the American Academy of Pediatrics Task Force on Pediatric AIDS (1992) states that children with HIV/AIDS who are well enough to participate should be accepted into existing programs. Additionally, legislation mandates that children with HIV/AIDS cannot be excluded from participation in programs in which normal children typically participate (U.S. Congress, 1990). According to the American Academy of Pediatrics Task Force on Pediatric AIDS (1992), most recommendations state that the majority of children with HIV infection should be allowed to attend schools and day-care centers. (See also Chapter 3.)

Facts and Figures

"Infants and toddlers who are HIV positive or have AIDS also present challenges to child care providers. Though obviously an infant will not be the source of such information, the caregiver could learn from comments by neighbors, relatives, or well-meaning informants" (Black, 1999, p. 39).

Early childhood educators and caregivers are faced with issues of childhood innocence, fairness, and anger toward the suspected source of the infant's or toddler's infection and with concerns about how to maintain personal and classroom safety. Is it really safe to change diapers or to clean up an infant's vomit? What about biting? What about sick infants, toddlers, and young children who become orphaned as a result of AIDS-related parental death (Bowlby, 1980; Mahler, 1961; Norris-Shortle et al., 1993).

Some conclusions regarding HIV/AIDS and young children:

1. AIDS is a disease that can affect anyone— and a growing number of families are affected by HIV/AIDS (Green, 1995).

2. Early childhood educators report confusion and difficulty in addressing the needs of young children and families who are affected by HIV/AIDS (Green, 1995).

3. Infection control guidelines remain constant regardless of the source of disease (Massachusetts Department of Public Health, 1993; National Pediatric HIV Resource Center, 1992).

4. Children who live in families affected by HIV/AIDS experience changes in nurturing, caretakers, and living arrangements as well as grief and bereavement due to the death of loved ones (Black, 1995; Jessee et al., 1993; Schonfeld, 1993; Skeen & Hodson, 1987).

5. "HIV is **not** spread by saliva. To transmit HIV via biting, there must be an exchange of infected blood with uninfected blood (an infected child, mixing the infected blood directly with uninfected blood. . . . To date, no such event has been reported" (Black, 1999, p. 45).

6. "HIV is hard to get! There are *only five ways* to get HIV: (1) from infected blood, (2) from un-

protected sex with an infected person, (3) from intravenous drug needles used by an infected person, (4) from a pregnant women infected with HIV (transmitted to her fetus during pregnancy), and (5) from breast milk of an infected mother (transmitted to her nursing baby)" (Black, 1999, p. 45).

7. "Each state has laws to protect the rights of individuals about disclosure of HIV/AIDS status. Teachers do not have a right to know if a child in their class has HIV/AIDS. According to law, individuals have a right to privacy" (Black, 1999).

Legislation mandates that children with HIV/AIDS cannot be excluded from participation in programs in which normal children typically participate (U.S. Congress, 1990).

Savage and coworkers (1993) published a pamphlet to provide accurate answers to parents and child-care providers regarding: transmission, privacy, precautions, exclusions, refusal, per acceptance, parental inquiries, and schooling.

Children with Chronic Illness

According to an estimate, 7.5 million children under the age of 18 in the United States have chronic illnesses. One million children in the United States are afflicted with severe chronic illnesses and another 10 million children have less significant chronic disorders (Goldberg, 1990). Thirty-one percent of children under the age of 18 nationwide are affected by chronic conditions (Newacheck & Taylor, 1992).

One of the problems teaching and caring for children with chronic health conditions is that the children are frequently absent. And when they do attend, they are often excluded from the play of daily attending children because of ongoing play, close relationships, and stamina.

Chronic illnesses may include, but not be limited to, asthma, allergies, diabetes, epilepsy, hypoglycemia, seizures, sickle cell anemia, or other medical conditions that require continued treatment. For symptoms of hypoglycemia, and signs of seizure in young children, see Frieman and Settel (1994).

Different ailments are caused by different reactions [e.g., asthmatic attacks—pollens, mold spores, animal dander, chemicals, aspirin and food additives, respiratory tract infections, exercise, cigarette smoke, aerosol sprays, strong odors (National Jewish Center, 1992), and common and uncommon items]. Attacks can range from short and mild to extended and severe. Different ailments require different solutions, but it is very important that the teacher/caregiver knows the symptoms, the reactions, and how to properly care for the child.

The chronically ill child should not be defined by his or her disease—nor should the child be excluded from the classroom. The teacher can expect the same standards of acceptable behavior from the chronically ill child as from any other child. However, the teacher should strive to have the classroom environment appropriate for chronically ill children—dietary restrictions, animals, strong odors, cleaning materials, ventilation, amount of physical exertion, and other activities should be monitored.

Of special importance, and a golden teaching opportunity, is for the teacher to provide information and experiences, which would help all children understand about chronically ill children, thus teaching tolerance and compassion, and helping children to be less frightened (about a seizure, for example), more capable in an emer-gency, and more accepting of "differences." Medical personnel, parents, school advisors, and community people could all participate in the experience. The teacher should avoid overwhelming the children with too much information, too much frustration (some children may wonder when they will become chronically ill), and too many types of illness at one time. If there are chronically ill children in the classroom, involve them in the teaching as they have special needs and not as oddities.

Every teacher should have committed to memory and written down the following: (1) an emergency medical plan for each chronically ill child for whom she is responsible, (2) a plan for all children in general, and (3) a plan for unexpected emergencies (fire, earthquake, etc.). In this way, the adult and children can respond in helpful, constructive, and less frightening ways.

Sources of Additional Information

"Healthy Kids: The Key to Basics" is an information and consulting service dedicated to promoting health and educational equity for children in early childhood programs who have asthma and other chronic health conditions. To receive a copy of the brochure, *Educational Planning for Students with Chronic Health Conditions*, send a self-addressed, stamped business envelope to Ellie Goldberg, M.Ed., Educational Rights Specialist, 79 Elmore Street, Newton, MA 02139.

Asthma
   Lung Line Information Service
   National Jewish Center for Immunology &
      Respiratory Medicine
   1400 Jackson Street
   Denver, CO 80206
   1-800-222-5864

Diabetes
   Juvenile Diabetes Foundation International
   432 Park Avenue South
   New York, NY 10016
   1-800-533-2873

Epilepsy
Epilepsy Foundation of America
4351 Garden City Drive
Landover, MD 20785
1-800-332-1000

Sickle Cell Disease
Sickle Cell Disease Branch
National Heart, Blood, & Lung Institute
National Institutes of Health
9000 Rockville Pike
Bethesda, MD 20892
1-301-496-6931

NUTRITION, LEARNING, AND BEHAVIOR

Combining food and nutrition with early childhood principles and practices makes an interesting curriculum. It emphasizes that malnutrition is one of our nation's major health problems. If optimal potential is to be reached by young children, they need nutritionally sound diets and good nutritional habits that they can practice throughout their lifetimes.

Food and nutrition is not an end in itself. It can easily and joyfully be combined with all areas of development and all curriculum areas (see "Health Through Curriculum" later in this chapter). Even with our safe, adequate, and nutritious food supply, malnutrition is one of our nation's major health problems.

Good nutrition is a matter of awareness, education, and application. When adults and children know what foods are available, how edibles aid or harm the body, and why good nutrition is vital to individual survival, they can develop good eating habits. Also of vital importance are the awareness, adaptation, and promotion of ethnic and cultural foods and food preferences. These considerations can be introduced through lesson planning, arranging with those who plan and serve snacks and lunch, and by inviting guests to present information (and samples) appropriate for young children.

The staff should be aware of any allergies or food preferences children have. Some children know which foods cause their allergies and avoid them; some do not. Nutritionists know which foods are the most common causes of rashes or allergic reactions in young children (eggs, citrus foods, wheat, cow's milk); some centers avoid serving these whenever possible. Center records should include food items that produce a negative reaction in individual children. (See Appendix C.)

Allergic reactions are the result of an abnormal or increased response of the body's immune system to certain substances, such as pollens, smoke, perfumes, fumes or air pollutants, dyes, insect stings, certain foods (shellfish, eggs, nuts, etc.), furred and feathered pets, molds, dust, odorous substances (paints, mothballs, tar, gasoline, kerosene, cleaning fluids), and other substances (Aronson, 1991).

Some children suffer from asthma rather than allergies. Asthma causes more hospital admissions and more missed days of school than any other chronic illness (American Academy of Pediatrics, 1987). Children may show signs of asthma after increased physical activity, when lying down, after being near a cat, at the onset of a cold, or during special occasions. Four signs of asthma trouble are wheezing, retractions (chest skin drawn in), longer exhalation than inhalation, and rapid breathing. Parents know when an attack is about to occur and can give medication, contact their physician, or take their children for emergency treatment. Caregivers need information from parents to know the appropriate response to asthmatic children.

In addition, staff members should be on the alert for signs of poisoning: overstimulation, drowsiness, shallow breathing, unconsciousness, nausea, convulsions, stomach cramps, heavy perspiration, burns on hands and mouth, dizziness, changes in skin color, unusual stains on skin or clothes, sudden changes in a child's behavior, or open bottles of chemicals or medicines out of place. Each employee should be well trained in procedures to take if they suspect that a child has ingested poisonous materials.

A list of nine specific goals for child-care centers to include in building a nutrition education

 Discussions about food intake should address allergies. Consider these situations:

1. Chocolate, strawberries, milk, and wheat are common allergens. Adults may give these foods to young children without considering that the children could be allergic to them or that their young bodies cannot absorb them easily.

2. Besides food products, children can be allergic to teaching materials (ingredients in creative materials, paint, dust, stuffed objects, detergent, vegetation, and other unidentified sources).

3. Having a problem with either of the above examples is bad enough, but consider the child who fits into both categories. Evan breaks out with a rash when he eats or drinks food that is high in ascorbic acid (vitamin C), eats wheat products, drinks milk that is not goat's milk, eats peanut butter, or even *tastes* chocolate. In addition, the same rash appears when he gets near dust (as on occasions when there were stuffed birds on the science table), tries to decorate the center's Christmas tree, wears a newly washed cover-up that was not thoroughly rinsed, finger paints with soap flakes, and dresses up in wool clothing. What can a director do? A teacher? A parent?

program, compatible with overall goals of early childhood education, are as follows:

1. Helping meet the total nutritional needs of the infant and child

2. Providing food with consideration for the cultural patterns, food practices, and social needs of the child and family

3. Encouraging the development of healthful food habits

4. Providing meals in a safe, clean, and pleasant environment

5. Providing a continuing nutrition education program for the children, parents, and staff of the center

6. Helping children learn to enjoy a wide variety of foods

7. Building the understanding that good food is necessary for strong bodies and minds

8. Developing feelings of self-assurance by encouraging children to make many choices and take appropriate responsibilities

9. Caution children about ingesting anything harmful (drugs, tobacco, some plants that are found to give a "high")

These goals are comprehensive, yet allow flexibility to meet the needs of the individual children and staff.

Nutritional imbalance (deficiency or excess of protein, calories, vitamins, minerals, or other dietary constituents) can affect behavior, learning, and health in different ways. For example, it has been shown that iron-deficiency anemia not only reduces children's resistance to disease; it also lessens their stamina, endurance, vitality, and ability to pay attention and to learn.

In the 1970s, many people believed that hyperactivity and learning disabilities in school-age children were associated with additives and salicylates (a common ingredient in aspirin) (Feingold, 1975). Caregivers and parents who reduced the intake of additives to children reported a reduction in hyperactivity of up to two thirds in these children. Because of the hyperactivity/additive concern, the scientific community, National Institutes of Health, the Food and Drug Administration, and the National Education Association have studied the issue of diet. Recommendations have been published (see Lipton & Mayo, 1983), and those which are relevant to the caregiver and parents are included in the following statements:

1. There is no evidence to recommend a ban on foods containing artificial food colorings in federally supported food programs such as those served by caregivers.

2. Because the diet has no apparent harmful effects and because the nonspecific effects of this dietary treatment are frequently benefi-

cial to families, there is no reason to discourage families that wish to use the diet as long as other therapy is continued and the child's nutritional status is monitored (Endres & Rockwell, 1994).

A 1991 study discusses the effects of sugar on aggressive and inattentive behavior in children with attention-deficit disorder with hyperactivity and normal children, concluding that hyperactivity and sucrose and aspartame use show that sucrose does not adversely affect behavior of children (Wender & Solanto, 1991).

Children who are introduced early to good foods and good eating habits may avoid some ailments and diseases, learn to plan balanced diets, and recognize that diet and exercise help promote a higher quality of life. Figure 8–4 provides a general outline of good nutrition.

❖ **Stimulator**

Using the following list of food products, plan a five-day menu for breakfast, lunch, and afternoon snack for a group of 25 children, ages 3 to 5.

A number could be attached to each entry so that items could be ordered by code number instead of name in a computer program. Codes should allow extra numbers for new items, or new items could replace unused items.

Fresh Vegetables	*Cookies/Crackers*	*Dairy Products*	*Fresh Fruits*
avocado	animal	butter	apples
bean sprouts	butter	cheese	bananas
broccoli	Fig Newtons	cheese spread	berries
cabbage	grahams	cottage cheese	cantaloupe
carrots	oatmeal	cream	grapes
cauliflower	oyster	cream cheese	lemons
celery	pretzels	curd	melons
lettuce	Ritz	eggs	nectarines
peas	saltines	ice cream	oranges
peppers	sugar	milk—canned	pineapples
potatoes	Town House	milk—dry	plums
tomatoes	Triscuit	milk—fresh	raisins
turnips	vanilla wafers	sherbet	strawberries
	wheat thins	yogurt	watermelon
	Wheatsworth		
Juices	windmill		*Miscellaneous*
apple		*Baking Needs*	catsup
grape		baking powder	Chinese noodles
lemonade	*Grains*	flour	gelatin
orange	biscuits	salt	honey
pear/grape	bread—white	shortening	mayonnaise
pine/grapefruit	bread—wheat	soda	nuts
tomato	bread sticks	sugar—brown	popcorn
V8 cocktail	cones, ice cream	sugar—powdered	pudding
other	croutons	sugar—white	soup—chicken
	mix—cake	vanilla	noodle
	mix—muffins	yeast	soup—tomato
Processed Fruits	mix—pancakes		soup—vegetable
applesauce		*Meat*	
fruit cocktail		Lean	
peaches		avoid additives	
pears			
pineapple			
prunes			

Figure 8–4   Eating right pyramid.
Source: U.S. Department of Agriculture.

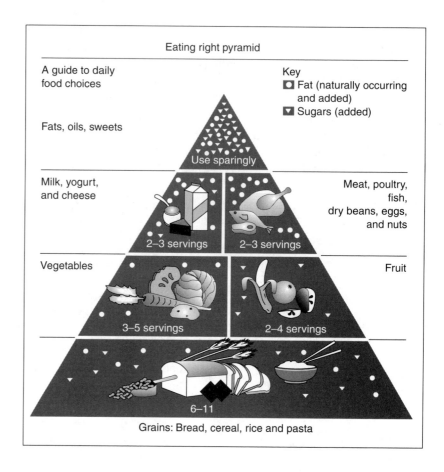

An excellent way to acquaint children with good foods and establish good eating habits is to involve them in food preparation. In some centers and under some circumstances this becomes difficult but not impossible. Teachers must be well prepared and convinced that the experience will be a meaningful one for the children. (Remember the cleanliness and safety factors mentioned in Chapters 5–9.) Foods children can prepare in the center (with supervision) include butter, sandwiches, breads, fresh and cooked fruit, fresh and cooked vegetables, soups, pasta combinations of foods (casseroles, spaghetti), and some ethnic or holiday food.

Governmental Programs

Governmental agencies are actively involved in promoting information and programs to improve the nutrition of young children. A set of national child-care health standards is being developed that will address the issues of environmental quality, prevention and control of infectious diseases, prevention and control of injuries, general health, nutrition, prevention and management of child abuse, staff health, children with special needs, health concerns related to social environment and child development, and organization and administration of the health component of programs.

The Child Care Food Program (CCFP) is a federally sponsored program that helps provide nutritious meals to children enrolled in child-care centers or family child-care programs throughout the country. It introduces young children (and consequently their families) to many different types of foods and helps teach them good eating habits. It is funded by the U.S. Department of

Agriculture and (in most states) is administered by the U.S. Department of Education as an adjunct to the School Lunch Program. The program is limited to public and private nonprofit organizations providing licensed or approved nonresidential child-care services.

Problems related to diet are heart disease, cerebrovascular diseases, stroke, cancer, hypertension, diabetes, cirrhosis of the liver, obesity, and dental decay. Although many dietary problems and their symptoms are not observed directly in young children, evidence indicates that most of these conditions begin to develop in childhood and are sustained by poor lifelong eating habits. Teachers and parents of young children can help prevent such problems.

At the present time, there are conflicting debates about federal and state monies being used for food programs for young children and families. The reader is encouraged to talk with local and federal officials about the status of subsidies for food programs.

Government Recommendations on Nutrition

The government publishes recommended dietary allowances, as well as suggested height and weight charts for males and females in different age groups. The U.S. Department of Agriculture (USDA) and the U.S. Department of Health and Human Services (DHHS) encourage Americans to eat healthily—even to change certain eating habits. Nutrition objectives for the country published in *Healthy People 2000* (U.S. Department of Health and Human Services, 1990) suggest the following dietary guidelines: "eat a variety of foods; maintain desirable weight; choose a diet low in fat, saturated fat, and cholesterol; choose a diet with plenty of vegetables, fruits, and grain products; use sodium in moderation; if you drink alcoholic beverages, do so in moderation" (p. 43).

A layperson's interpretation may be: Eat less refined sugar and less foods high in sugar content; eat less salt and foods high in salt; substitute poultry, fish, and other protein sources, such as grains and legumes for red meat; eat fewer foods high in fat; eliminate food additives (artificial colors, flavors, preservatives, etc.); and eat more fruit, vegetables, and whole grains.

Dietary changes are more likely to be lasting if they are made gradually and if their purposes are understood. Contrary to first impressions, the recommended dietary changes need not be expensive.

In addition, attention is called to exercise and measures to reduce coronary heart disease, rise in cancer, growth retardation, and other factors.

To build strong bodies, and maintain good health, six nutrients are necessary (see Figure 8–5).

Feeding Young Children

Some centers operate on a half-day schedule and others service children and families for full days. In either case, children will require snacks and/or meals.

Most centers have help in planning menus from a qualified nutritionist, from state or local personnel, or publications, but they must still pay careful attention to the types, amounts, and frequency of foods served to young children. There are some government-financed programs for centers that qualify.

Some nutritional snacks for young children include the following, which can be served alone or in combination with other foods listed (as a precaution, see information about preventing choking):

Fruit	Juices: unsweetened, mixed, or individual
	Sliced and/or peeled fruit (depending on availability) and dried
Dairy products	Milk, cottage cheese, cheese, low-fat yogurt, eggs
Grains	Whole-grain crackers, graham, whole-grain muffins, enriched bread, unsweetened cereals, unsalted crackers
Vegetables	Raw preferably

The shaded text on page 313 shows the characteristics of children who are well-nourished or undernourished:

Type	Contained in	Value to Body
Fat	Dairy fats (whole milk, butter, cream, cheese, etc.) Eggs Oils (corn, soybean, peanut, cottonseed, coconut, etc.) Meat and poultry	Provides energy Helps absorb certain vitamins Component of certain body tissues Insulates and pads some body organs Essential fatty acids
Protein	Meats Dairy products (eggs, milk, cheese) Fish Grains, legumes, seeds, and nuts	Growth of body, tissues, and life-long maintenance Restoration Builds resistance to disease
Minerals. Many different ones influence growth and bodily functions etc.	Dairy products Meat, organ meat, seafood Whole grains, seeds, legumes, nuts Dark green leafy vegetables Fruits Table salt	Varies Bone and teeth development Aids in blood clotting Carrier of oxygen and carbon dioxide Growth and rate of metabolism Other functions
Carbohydrates	Bread, cereals, and pasta Fruits Vegetables Dairy products Legumes	Source of readily available energy Body regulators Contribute to structure of certain cells
Vitamins Fat-soluble: A, D, E, K Water-soluble: C, B-complex (thiamine, riboflavin, folic acid, niacin, B6, B12)	Organ meats, dairy products, green leafy vegetables, orange fruits and vegetables, whole grains, vegetable oils, fish Citrus fruits, green leafy vegetables, nuts, vegetables, dairy products, organ meats, fish, yeast, fruit	Promote growth of bones and teeth Protect nervous system Keep skin healthy Build resistance to disease Regulate biological reactions for normal metabolism Produce energy and synthesize tissues, enzymes, hormones, and other vital compounds Aid healing wounds and broken bones
Water	Beverages Fruits Vegetables	Prevents dehydration Aids bodily functions (digestion, elimination, cooling the body, etc.)

Figure 8–5   Food nutrients.

Characteristics of Children	
Well-nourished	*Undernourished*
Alert, attentive, enter into and enjoy physical activity, less likely to become ill, recover from illness more quickly	May be quiet, withdrawn, or hyperactive and disruptive; more susceptible to infections and illness

When one Head Start program evaluated the nutrition the children were receiving, it made some startling discoveries: food provided was very high in sugar, salt, fat, and refined grains; celebrations had become unintentional endorsements of consumption abuse; there were poor eating behaviors; nutrition was unrelated to the daily classroom curriculum; parental involvement modified the center's nutritional policy; and fat and cholesterol were abundant (Wardle & Winegarner, 1992). After the study, the following steps were taken: radical revision of menus to modify recipes to reduce salt, simple sugars, saturated fats, and refined grains; parties were permitted only as an integral part of the ongoing curriculum; staff were required to interact with children during meals in a family-style service arrangement; soda vending machines were placed in areas removed from the children; parent training on good nutrition appeared in monthly newsletters; refusal of food that was incompatible with nutrition philosophy; each child visited a local store accompanied by a teacher to become familiar with food varieties; small refrigerators, available in each classroom, were stocked with fruits, vegetable sticks, cheese slices, and other wholesome foods for self-service for hungry children; teachers initiated a weekly healthy food activity in their classrooms; and cultural foods were included and expanded. As a result, (1) the children have become more willing to try new foods, (2) parents are more receptive to the center's food policy and the role of good nutrition, and (3) there has been a reduction in the stress level, especially associated with holidays. "Food has become a vital element throughout our entire curriculum—not just a reward for good behavior or the catalyst for having a good time" (Wardle & Winegarner, 1992, p. 7).

Other Precautions

Physical Examinations.   The main purposes of requiring a physical examination before children enter a center program are to discover their present physical condition, to determine whether their stage of development is within reasonable limits for their age, and to see if immunizations are current. Rather than being an unnecessary expense for low- or middle-income families, an annual physical can provide early detection of problems that could cause greater expense, not to mention children's discomfort, later.

Results of yearly physical exams should be reported to the center so that the children's health can be monitored.

Emergency Information.   There should be emergency information readily available at the center that includes the addresses and phone numbers where parents (or guardians) can be reached, and the names, phone numbers, and addresses of others who could pick up sick children or authorize their treatment in emergency cases. (See Appendix C.)

> Emergency consent signed in advance by a parent can only give consent to transport a child to a medical facility. Because the nature of the injury and required treatment cannot be known in advance, parents cannot give the informed consent which is required for medical treatment in advance. Doctors can provide life-saving treatment under Good Samaritan laws, but are limited to life-saving treatment without parental consent. Parents must understand their responsibility to be able to be contacted by phone at all times. Witnessed telephone consents are acceptable. (Aronson, 1987b, p. 37)

Centers should have established procedures for handling ill or injured children when parents are unavailable or cannot come immediately.

Daily Check-in.   Daily health procedures, including a routine check-in, should be formulated and implemented at each center. This gives the teacher (or director) regular contact with each child and the chance to note any changes in the child's body or behavior. It also provides the

 **Stimulator** As the new director of the Ideal Preschool, carefully review the advantages and disadvantages of requiring each enrolling child to have a physical examination. How do you interpret a report from a doctor or clinic? How could this information be helpful in planning for each child's needs? If center experience with a child reveals information contrary to that presented in her exam report (for example, it was reported that the child is well developed and shows no sign of deviation for a child of her sex and age, yet she has problems attending to tasks; her motor skills are uncoordinated; and she is easily upset), how should this discrepancy be handled? Should someone be notified (the doctor, the parents, or a referral agency)?

center with an opportunity to remain in contact with the parents and notify them of any unusual health situations (contagious diseases, community information, referral agencies, or other items). Few centers can afford a nurse or doctor on the premises. The director or another qualified person can perform a daily check of each child to identify bodily changes that may indicate the onset of illness, but not to diagnose or treat the child.

If a school transports children, a person riding with the children (other than the bus driver) could make a cursory check of the children as they board the bus.

Immunizations. In addition to monitoring children's immunizations, the center can alert parents to children's possible exposures to disease. Certain times of year bring increases of contagious childhood diseases. More thorough check-ins of children or awareness of the children at these times can prevent such diseases from spreading throughout the center. Parents who object to having their children immunized should consult their physician or the local health department. (See Appendix D for information about contagious diseases.)

Records. The center should have a list of agencies to which parents and children can be referred when health conditions are beyond the expertise of center personnel. (See Figure 8–6.) Record keepers at the center must conform to the rigorous minimum requirements set by licensing agencies. Information should be promptly and accurately posted to the proper record. Individual health records should be kept for each child and all personnel.

General Well-Being. The physiological condition of the body also contributes to health or sickness. Nutrition, digestion, elimination, respiration, and circulation must work harmoniously. When the body lacks nutrients, it will be undernourished. When, what, and how much food is eaten establish eating habits. Some children become dehydrated because they drink only small amounts of liquids. Food and moisture consumption, exercise, and their interaction are related to digestion and elimination. Exercise, fresh air, and rest influence respiration and circulation. In planning food intake and curriculum activities for children, the teacher must consider the needs and development of children's total bodies.

Mental health is especially important during the early years. Children need to experience success, feel good about themselves and their abilities, and feel valued, respected, and loved by others. As outlined by Erikson (1950), young children must feel trust rather than mistrust, autonomy rather than shame and doubt, and initiative rather than guilt. When they experience positive (rather than negative) feelings, they have a basis for developing a healthy personality. Each child should have guidance and experiences that will help develop a strong self-image (Taylor, 1995).

Burnout/Rest. Some children stay in centers for such long daily periods that both they and their teachers become fatigued. Adults like to take a break or have a change of responsibility. Children often sit when they are tired and run when they are restless. Frequently, teachers want children to rest because the teachers are tired, the next activity is not ready, or the teachers have nothing planned. An organized rest period may help the teacher, but it is often less than restful for the children.

Some licensing requirements call for formal resting or napping, depending on the ages of the

Figure 8–6   Suggested referrals.

> *List 1: Professionals and Their Organizations*
>   Pediatricians, nurses, dentists, general practitioners, government health officers; public school systems; health services; nutritionists, dietitians, social workers, hospital administrators, psychiatrists, psychologists, ophthalmologists; public school systems' speech and hearing specialists, learning disabilities specialists; medical technologists.
>
> *List 2: Community Sources (private individuals or groups, government or public, neighborhood, or other)*
>   Practitioners of medicine, nursing, dentistry, optometry, psychology, and so forth; health departments; school health programs; comprehensive child health centers; clinics; Title XIX Medicaid; special voluntary agencies and public agencies; dental service corporations; prepaid medical groups; insurance and prepayment plans; state crippled children's programs; community mental health centers; armed forces medical services.
>
> *List 3: Agencies*
>   Various community organizations, such as United Way, civic clubs, women's clubs, and parent-teacher organizations; religious groups of various denominations; family service associations; Lions Clubs; associations for the blind or for the prevention of blindness; associations for retarded children, crippled children, and for children with cerebral palsy and other special diseases; tuberculosis associations; mental health associations; visiting nurse associations; the Red Cross association.

children and the amounts of time they spend in the center. Center operators must carefully review their goals and activities so they match the needs of the children, who frequently require different amounts of rest. Some can regain their energy by sitting at quiet activities; others need sound sleep to refresh themselves.

At centers where naps are required, the nap room should have individual cots, be dimly lit, have a serene atmosphere, and have several adults present. Cots should be washable and spaced so the room can be easily evacuated in case of emergency. For adult information, see Chapter 6.

HEALTH THROUGH CURRICULUM

Health and curriculum go hand in hand. Each activity, each area of the classroom, each period during the day, and each person contribute to the health and welfare of another. And health is more than just physical health—it involves one's emotions, socialization, cognitive and perceptional

growth—the total person and his or her total surroundings. Consider the types of activities offered, indoors and outdoors, the personal interactions, the materials and toys used, the choices one makes, the environmental influences, and the beauties of nature around us. Health is a relative thing—we can do much to promote it!

PROMOTING WELLNESS IN THE CHILD

Unfortunately not all young children receive adequate health care. Most low-income children receive the poorest prenatal and child health services or only go to hospital emergency rooms and only when acute illness or serious injury strikes (*Starting Points*, 1994). The report continues: "Malnutrition during the first two years of life has much more devastating consequences than at any other time, inhibiting normal growth and development. Children growing up in poverty suffer from higher rates of malnutrition and anemia than other children" (p. 65).

Infections preventable by immunizations include tuberculosis, diphtheria, pertussis, tetanus, poliomyelitis, measles, mumps, rubella, and hemophilus influenza type b (Hib) infection (Aronson, 1991).

Teachers at the center can encourage children in hygienic procedures by their own attitudes, the kinds of activities provided, the procedures related to health, and the types of lavatory facilities (urinals, basins, drinking fountains, etc.). Children who feel comfortable with these procedures are more likely to see positive results from cleanliness and other means of staying well.

CHAPTER SUMMARY

1. Health, safety, nutrition, and immunizations are closely related because the quality of one affects the quality of the others. A healthy child is more likely to accept and eat nutritious food, find success in peers and opportunities, build a good self-image, enjoy a variety of activities, incur fewer accidents, recover more quickly from accidents or illnesses, be more alert and active, and have more stamina.

2. The health of adults who care for young children is as important as the health of the young children in their care—healthy and happy children influence healthy and happy adults—and vice versa.

3. There are many specific ways adults can ensure a healthy environment by maintaining their own health and being aware of health and environmental factors for children and families.

4. Director/owners can prevent environmental hazards.

5. To maintain the health of all those at the center, parents must follow center guidelines.

6. The Children's Health Insurance Program (CHIP) was passed by Congress in 1997 to provide free or low-cost health insurance to children in uninsured families with low or moderate incomes.

7. Health factors for children include physical examinations, immunizations, medication, first aid and injuries, and nutrition.

8. Well-planned snacks have many benefits for children.

9. Recent developments regarding health factors for children included in CHIP provides a significant funding increase for children's health.

10. Ways to ensure a healthy environment for children, parents, staff, and center are outlined.

11. Environmental hazards such as pesticides/poisons, tobacco smoke, lead/asbestos, and others can be detrimental to the growth and well-being of children and adults.

12. The director has full responsibility to provide a healthy environment. There are state and federal laws that guide caregivers in providing a safe and healthy environment. The reduction of environmental hazards, the attention to cleanliness and immunizations, and the overall atmosphere at the center will set the stage for healthy living.

13. Children who have chronic health conditions or learning disorders can find satisfaction in being a part of the group, even though some of their activities may be curtailed.

14. Nutrition, learning, and behavior influence the outcomes of many lives. Some government programs help improve the lives of young children and low-income families.

15. Health principles and eating habits can be taught through the daily curriculum. Promoting wellness in the child should be of great concern to child-care workers.

PARTICIPATORS

1. Prepare a checklist to assess a center's safety and health factors quickly.

2. If the center already has procedures for emergencies (fire, evacuation, earthquake, flood), review them with the staff. If no such procedures exist, compose emergency procedures and review them with the staff.

3. Make a list of health forms for each child and each employee (see Appendixes C and E). Ascertain that all forms are current and properly filed.

4. Plan snacks for a group of preschoolers for a 2-week period. Avoid sugar, salt, fat, and empty calories.

5. Obtain a list (state or federal) of daily food requirements for young children. Note recommended food sources of vitamins, minerals, and other nutrients. Plan a week's lunch menu.

6. Outline a full day's activities that would help a child develop a stronger self-image.

7. Plan and implement a month-long program to develop a child's strength and stamina.

8. From the local health department, or other resources, develop a list of the advantages and disadvantages of immunizations for children.

9. Identify a teaching area (such as outdoor play) then describe a miniplan for this area incorporating either a health or nutrition concept (activity) that would appropriately involve young children (name the age span). Using this same miniplan (concept) expand it to include other teaching areas (free play indoors, table toys, music, etc.).

10. Suggest a health or nutrition miniplan (concept) that could more easily be taught in a specific teaching area. Why is it more appropriate to one teaching area than another? Could it be revised to fit other teaching areas? (Could nutrition be taught during a large-muscle activity as easily as during snack? Could health be taught in a creative setting as easily as in an outdoor activity?) Are health and nutrition all encompassing?

11. Plan a simple food experience with the children using a written recipe as a guide. Before actually using the recipe, make it into a picture chart that will assist the nonreading children to more easily and independently make the product.

12. Using a health or nutrition concept, write a miniplan that would enhance the self-image and confidence of the child. Think of an activity that would *not* enhance the self-image and confidence of the child. Could you make it into a good experience for the child?

13. Observe at a child-care setting, home, or even public place. Record how many times a child touches his or her nose or mouth during a set period of time. Make some assumptions about how disease/germs can be spread.

REFERENCES

American Academy of Pediatrics. 1992. Guidelines for human immunodeficiency virus (HIV)-infected children and their foster families. *Pediatrics,* 89(4), 681–683.

American Academy of Pediatrics. 1994. *Pediatrics,* 93(2).

American Academy of Pediatrics. June, 1997. *Model Child Care Health Policies* (3rd ed.). Elk Grove Village, IL: Author. This edition of this publication is a must for all who care for young children. It can be purchased from American Academy of Pediatrics, Division of Publications, 141 Northwest Point Blvd., P.O. Box 927, Elk Grove Village, IL 60009-0927 (phones: 800-433-9016 or 847-228-5005) or National Association for the Education of Young Children, 1509 16th St., N.W., Washington, DC 20036-1426 [phones 800-424-2460, 202-232-8777, or 202-328-1846 (fax)].

APHA & AAP (American Public Health Association & American Academy of Pediatrics). 1992. *Caring for our children—National health and safety performance standards: Guidelines for out-of-home child care programs.* Washington, DC: Authors.

Aronson, S. 1987b. Coping with the physical requirements of caregiving. *Child Care Information Exchange,* 39–40.

Aronson, S. 1991. *Health and safety in child care.* New York: Harper-Collins.

Aronson, S. 1993. Smoke is poison and more on clean sand. *Exchange,* 92, July, 61–63.

Black, S. 1995. Increasing early childhood educators' and parents' understanding of AIDS through an early childhood AIDS program. Ph.D. diss., Nova University, Florida.

Black, S. M. 1999. HIV/AIDS in early childhood centers: The ethical dilemma of confidentiality versus disclosure. *Young Children,* March, 39–44.

Bowlby, J. 1980. *Attachment and loss: Loss, sadness, and depression.* New York: Basic.

Bradburn, E. 1976. *Margaret McMillan: Framework and expansions of nursery education.* Birkenhead, Great Britain: Wilmer.

Bureau of the Census. 1997. *Current population survey.* Washington, DC: Author.

Child Care Bureau & Maternal and Child Health Bureau. 1995. *Healthy child care America: A blueprint for action*. Washington, DC: Department of Health and Human Services.

Children's Defense Fund (CDF). 1998. *CHIP checkup: A healthy start for children*. Washington, DC: Author.

Children's Defense Fund. 2000. *http://www.childrens defense.org/healthystart.html* (May 17).

Cosgrove, M. S. 1991. Cooking in the classroom: The doorway to nutrition. *Young Children, 46(3),*

Cox, J. L. 1995. Secondhand smoke: The smoking gun. *House Calls: A Newsletter Published by IHC Hospitals in Utah County.* Spring, 3.

Dahl, K. 1998. Why cooking in the curriculum? *Young Children* 53(1), 81–83.

Dershewitz, R. 1993. *Ambulatory pediatric care*. Philadelphia: Lippincott.

Dooling, M. V., & Ulione, M. S. 2000. Health consultation in child care: A partnership that works. *Young Children*, March, 34–26.

Endres, J. B., & Rockwell, R. E. 1994. *Food, nutrition, and the young child* (4th ed.). Upper Saddle River, NJ: Merrill/Prentice Hall.

Erikson, E. 1950. *A healthy personality for young child.* Washington, DC: Superintendent of Documents, U.S. Government Printing Office.

Feingold, B.F. 1975. *Why your child is hyperactive.* New York: Random House.

Frieman, B.B., & Settel, J. 1994. What the classroom teacher needs to know about children with chronic medical problems. *Childhood Education,* 70(4), 196–201.

FYI. 1999. Child and dependent care credit. *Young Children,* 54(2), 65.

Gershon, N. B., & Moon, R. Y. 1997. American Academy of Pediatrics. Infant sleep position in licensed child care centers, *Pediatrics,* 100(1) 75–77. Send reprint requests to Dr. R. Y. Moon, Department of General Pediatrics, Children's National Medical Center, 111 Michigan Ave., NW, Washington, DC 20010.

Goldberg, B. 1990. Children, sports, and chronic disease. *The Physician and Sportsmedicine,* 18(10), 44–50, 53–54, 56.

Gratz, R., & Boulton, P. 1993. Taking care of kids: A director's concerns about environmental hazards. *Day Care and Early Education,* 21(2), 29–31.

Gratz, R. R., & Claffey, A. 1996. Adult health in child care: Health status, behaviors, and concerns of teachers, directors, and family child care providers. *ECRQ,* 11(2) 243–267.

Green, K. M. 1995. HIV/AIDS and early childhood programs: Myth and reality. Presentation at the Annual Conference of the National Association for the Education of Young Children, Washington, DC, November 28–December 2.

Hayes, C. D., Palmer, J. L., & Maslow, M. J. (Eds). 1990. *Who cares for America's Children? Child-care policy for the 1990s.* Washington, DC: National Academy Press.

Howell, N. M. 1999. Cooking up a learning community with corn, beans, and rice. *Young Children,* 54(5), 36–38.

Hernandez, D. J. 1995. Changing demographics: Past and future demands for early childhood programs. *The Future of Children,* 5(3), 145–160.

Holmes, S. J., Morrow, A. L., & Pickering, L. K. 1996. Child care practices: Effects of social change on the epidemiology of infectious diseases and antibiotic resistance. *Epidemiology Review,* 18(1), 10–28.

Intermountain Regional Poison Control Center. n.d. *Poison awareness.* Salt Lake City: Utah Department of Health, Family Health Services.

Jessee, P. O., Potett-Johnson, D., & Nagy, M. C. 1993. Fears of AIDS among day care administrators and teachers. *Early Childhood Development and Care,* 89, 19–39.

Kendrick, A. S., Kaufman, R., & Messenger, K. P. (Eds). 1988. *Healthy children: A manual for programs.* Washington, DC: National Association for the Education of Young Children.

Kontos, S., & Wilcox-Herzog. A. 1997. Research in review. Teachers' interactions with children: Why are they so important? *Young Children* 52(2), 4–12.

Lipton, M. A. & Mayo, J. P. 1983. Diet and hyperkinesis—an update. *Journal of American Dietetic Association I,* 83, 132–134.

Lowsley, J. M. 1993. Beyond food. *Montessori Life,* Fall, 31–33.

Mahler, M. 1961. On sadness and grief in infancy and childhood. *Psychoanalytic Study,* 16, 332–351.

Maslow, A. 1972. *The farther reaches of human nature.* New York: Viking.

Massachusetts Department of Public Health, 1993. Massachusetts Department of Education, Massachusetts Board of Education. *AIDS/HIV infection policies for early childhood and school settings.* Boston: Author.

Moukaddem, V. 1990. Preventing infectious diseases in your child care setting. *Young Children,* 45(2), 28.

Murray, C. G. 2000. Learning about children's social and emotional needs at snack time—nourishing the body, mind, and spirit of each child. *Young Children,* March, 43–52.

NAEYC. 1991a. Health and safety tips. Emergency planning for early childhood programs. *Young Children,* 46(4), 64.

NAEYC. 1991b. Health and safety tips. Toward safer, exciting playground environments. *Young Children,* 46(6), 26.

NAEYC. 1994. FYI: Lead!—No. 1 environmental pediatric health problem. *Young Children,* 49(4), 9.

NAEYC. 1995a. *Keeping healthy: Parents, teachers, and children.* Washington, DC: Author (Brochure).

NAEYC. 1995b. *Code of Ethical Conduct and Statement of Commitment* (Stephanie Feeney and Kenneth Kipnis). Brochure #503 (#504 for Spanish). Washington, DC: Author.

NAEYC. 1997a. FYI. Healthy children—Healthy partnerships. *Young Children,* 52(4), 74.

NAEYC. 1997b. *Position statement on licensing and regulation of early childhood programs* (Brochure). Washington, DC: Author.

National Jewish Center for Immunology and Respiratory Medicine. 1992. *Understanding asthma.* Denver, CO: Author.

National Pediatric HIV Resource Center. 1992. *Getting a head start on HIV: A resource manual for enhancing services to HIV-affected children in Head Start.* Newark, NJ: Author.

Newacheck, P. S. & Taylor, W. R. 1992. Childhood illness: Prevalence, severity, and impact. *American Journal of Public Health,* 82(3), 364–371.

O'Conner, J. 1999. Public policy report. New children's health insurance program: Early childhood professional outreach efforts can make a difference. *Young Children,* 63–65.

Poison Control Center. For the nearest center, dial 1-800-456-7707.

Pickering, L. 1996. Infections in the day care center setting—Not just for children. *Infectious Disease Watch in Pediatrics,* 6(1), 1–5.

Sagall, R. J. 1992. Day care doctor: Summertime and insect stings. *Day Care and Early Education,* 19(4), 48.

Savage, S., Mayfield, P., & Cook, M. 1993. Fall questions about serving children with HIV/AIDS. *Day Care and Early Education,* 19(4), 48.

Schonfeld, D. J. 1993. Talking with children about death. *Journal of Pediatric Health Care,* 7, 269–274.

Skeen, P., & Hodson, D. 1987. AIDS: What adults should know about AIDS (and shouldn't discuss with very young children). *Young Children,* 42(4), 65–71.

Starting points: Meeting the needs of our youngest children. 1994. New York: Carnegie Corporation of New York.

Taylor, B. J. 1995. *A child goes forth* (8th ed.). Upper Saddle River, NJ: Merrill/Prentice Hall.

U. S. Congress. 1990. *Americans with Disabilities Act of 1990.* Public Law 101–336.

U. S. Department of Health and Human Services. 1990. *Healthy people 2000: Health promotion and disease prevention objectives.* Public Health Service. Washington, DC: U.S. Government Printing Office.

Wardle, F., & Winegarner, N. 1992. Nutrition and Head Start. *Children Today,* 21(1) 5–7.

Wender, E. H., & Solanto, M. V. 1991. Effects of sugar on aggressive and inattentive behavior in children with attention-deficit disorder with hyperactivity and normal children. *Pediatrics,* 88, 960.

Whitehead, L. C., & Ginsberg, S. I. 1999. Creating a family-like atmosphere in child care settings: All the more difficult in large child care centers. *Young Children,* 54(2), 4–10.

Resources

Selected resources for early childhood professionals—organizations that publish technical standards that can apply to child-care facilities—[as listed in *Model Child Care Health Policies* (3rd ed). Elk Grove Village, IL: American Academy of Pediatrics, 1997]. See following for ordering information:

American Public Health Association
1015 15th Street, NW
Washington, DC 20005
(202) 789-5600

National Association for the Education of Young
    Children
1509 16th Street, NW
Washington, DC 20036-1426
(800) 424-2460

National Association for Family Child Care
206 Sixth Avenue, Suite 900
Des Moines, IA 50309-4018
(515) 282-8192

Poison Control Center-dial 1-800-456-7707.

Superintendent of Documents
U.S. Government Printing Office
Washington, DC 20402

The Children's Foundation
725 Fifteenth Street, NW
Suite 505
Washington, DC 20005-2109
(202) 347-3300

U. S. Consumer Product Safety Commission
Washington, DC 20005-2109
(800) 638-2772

Chapter 9

Safety in Child Care

Guide for Readers

- ❖ *Safety measures in the physical environment, with parental involvement, in different settings, in routines, in the curriculum, in cases of emergency, in indoor and outdoor play—in all aspects of the center—must be carefully considered for everyone who participates at the center.*

- ❖ *Center goals must anticipate and plan for situations that require first-aid treatment, procedures for natural disasters, minor accidents, temporary interruptions, and illness of children and staff. Teachers, staff, children, and parents should know what to do in case of any emergency.*

- ❖ *The types of play children enter into can increase or decrease safety factors.*

- ❖ *Before hiring a person who will work closely with children, it is mandatory that there be a criminal and abuse check to assure that the person has no criminal or suspected tendencies that would be harmful to the children or other individuals at the center.*

- ❖ *All personnel must be aware of and know how to deal with various situations in which children's safety may be jeopardized: abuse, violence, aggressive behavior, teasing/bullying, anger, injuries, and other causes.*

This chapter addresses safety as it relates to children, care providers, and families. These are vital issues and should not be taken lightly. Of primary importance for the safety of children is the people who care for them; personal, criminal, and behavioral checks should be serious concerns. When people feel safe, their entire outlook on life improves. When children and adults are well, happy, and secure, children are content, parents are satisfied, and caregiving employees perform efficiently.

Centers take a serious responsibility in caring for children. The safety and health of the children must be of prime importance. Rather than "trying to be careful" or "watching the children the best we can," center personnel must be totally committed to see that *all* equipment, and *all* materials are safe for the children's use and that *all* individuals are carefully screened so they will not harm the children in any way. Because children do not foresee problems that can result from their play, adults must anticipate children's responses to the environment.

CENTER GOALS

Before a new center begins operation, and periodically during operation, personnel must consider the safety goals of each facet of the program, reviewing and updating as necessary. A basic outline of safety goals should include the following:

1. Opportunities for children to practice safety (field trips, food experiences, care of pets, cooperation, etc.)
2. Specific and spontaneous classroom teaching that encourages good safety habits
3. Administration of medicine to children only under strict supervision (all medicine locked out of reach of children)
4. Purchase, maintenance, and replacement of equipment
5. Inspection and upkeep of the physical environment (all toxic and harmful substances kept out of reach in locked cabinets)
6. Compliance with licensing procedure (including emergency and personal phone numbers posted with easy access)
7. Orientation of employees and parents to safety rules and emergency procedures
8. Learning materials for parents regarding safety of children and families
9. Periodic in-service training for all employees regarding first aid, emergency procedures, accident and injury reporting, and personal responsibility
10. Understanding liability and purchasing of insurance
11. Special attention to safety of learning-disabled or special-needs children

❖ **Stimulator**   Miriam has had a lifelong dream of having her own child-care center. For years she had been studying, reading, visiting, saving, and preparing for the time when her dream would become a reality. The time is *now*. She has leased a modest facility, hired a skeleton crew, budgeted her funds wisely, and has received her license. Her greatest fear is that a child will be injured while playing outdoors. Nevertheless, she has divided the playground into areas for four types of activities:

- Riding and playing with wheeled toys
- Digging and planting
- Running and free play
- Dramatizing and quiet play

   With these activities, she must provide space for storage, guidelines for playing, and opportunities for the children to be creative and to explore freely. What suggestions (or cautions) would help Miriam to reduce her fear, yet allow and encourage outdoor learning and play?

12. Thoroughly checking the background of each employee to ensure there is no evidence of abuse or violation against children (sexually, physically, etc.)

13. Where there is question or litigation about the legal custody of a child, confirming and following court procedures

14. Safety being taught in each curriculum area (art, music, social studies, etc.), in routines (clean-up, change of activities, lavatory use, etc.), in various locations (indoors, outdoors, on field trips, etc.), and by all individuals (adults and children). Children learn best about safety from caregivers who model, practice, and counsel safety.

15. Preparing for all kinds of disasters—common/uncommon, expected/unexpected, minor/serious

OVERALL PLAN

Every setting where children congregate must have a plan for the safety and protection of both the children and adults who spend time there—one's home is also included. The focus should be on prevention rather than treatment.

One needs to develop and follow a procedure with attention focused on individuals and groups, acquisition and maintenance of furnishings and equipment, well and ill children, peaceful times and crises, needs and relationships, families and caregivers, first-aid and emergency treatment, floor space and activities, preparing and eating food, cleanliness and hazard-free environment, transporting and housing children, and developmentally appropriate programs and materials.

Centers should make emergency plans for all types of disaster—whether or not they are common to the area. Earthquakes, floods, tornadoes, bombings, hostage situations, toxic waste spills, and other types of disasters are known to happen at unexpected times and places. Rather than take an alarmist point of view, take a precautionary-prepared view to save lives, to reassure people,

and to act with confidence. Each center should discuss, write, and practice evacuation routes, classroom procedures, emergency treatment, meeting locations, and accountability of people. If a disaster occurs, what are some spin-offs one must consider—types of injuries (broken bones, head injury, burns, bleeding), loss of energy supply (fumes, fire, explosions), collapsed structures, and so on?

Making a Plan

Safety begins before the children arrive. It includes the philosophy of the center, the planning of the curriculum, the interaction among individuals, the use of materials, the hiring of teaching and non-teaching staff, the allocation of funds, and the arrangement of the environment. Safety encompasses the purposes for which the center exists.

Every center should have a *written evacuation emergency plan* for different kinds of disasters. In preparing or updating the plan, it is wise to invite a safety specialist (fire marshal, fire fighter, insurer, etc.) to walk through the building and play yard with you. This person can offer recommendations about extinguishers, fire exits, alarms, hazards, escape routes, and maintenance. The written plan should specify where children in each room are to gather, who will take attendance and personal records, who will check children's names against the rolls, who is to assist insecure children, who is to make necessary calls and/or check facilities for children, and how and when children are to return to their previous activities for all possible or probable situations.

Another important point of the plan is to inform parents (verbally, in writing, in diagrams, and in frequency) where and how to pick up their children in case of an emergency. Traffic patterns, distraught children, worried parents, emergency personnel, and other unforseen conditions could turn an emergency into a nightmare. Anticipating events can lessen problems—but if an emergency does occur, expect children, parents, employees, and emergency workers and yourself to be under great stress.

The evacuation plan should be practiced often enough for children to know the procedure, but not so often that it becomes a game. It is serious, and should help children to be reassured if an emergency ever arises. It should be practiced at different times of the day (playtime, resting time, group or individual time, indoor or outdoor time, etc.), during different types of weather, and with different adults so children will not be confused or frightened if a particular pattern is not followed. Some centers will have to be concerned about removing infants and/or children who are unable to help themselves. If the center maintains the proper ratio of adults to children, evacuation should be no problem.

For insurance and other purposes, keep records in a safe, fireproof container and make sure there is an accurate list of all center property (with a copy at another location).

False alarms should be treated as seriously as real emergencies and *all* people should follow the

 **❖ Stimulator**

A teacher is stationed near areas of possible danger—the climbing apparatus, toys with mouth-sized pieces, activities that may need attention as children play, and children who have unpredictable temperaments. Added precaution has been taken by placing a mat underneath the gym, monitoring activities, and providing a variety of play materials. In some areas, teachers act as overseers only, letting the children initiate their own play; in other areas children might leave because of the absence of a nearby adult. The children move freely among the activities until their interest dwindles; then they help with cleanup. By removing debris and storing toys for future use, the children make their playroom safer. No parts get lost, no objects are left lying around for children to place in their mouths or slip on, and children develop good work and safety habits. Teachers do not lecture the children about cleanliness or threaten to withhold toys or activities, and the children do not resist helping.

After the opening period, the children move to a group or gathering activity. To begin with, the teacher plays a record, asking the children to listen and follow the directions. (When guidelines are set before the activity, the children know what to expect and how to act.) Should they move around or be stationary? If they do move, what pattern should they follow? What is expected of them at the end of the record. Careful teacher planning can prevent misbehavior and accidents.

The children sing songs and listen to a story. By now they are getting restless and hungry. The teacher reminds them to walk to the rest room, use the toilet if necessary, wash their hands, and find a place at the snack tables. In reiterating the expected behavior, the teacher, again, models safety. Running or hurrying can cause injuries, unmet personal needs may cause toilet accidents, and dirty hands spread germs and disease.

At the snack table, the children have individual, small plastic knives, containers of peanut butter, and quartered slices of bread. The teacher and children engage in an informal discussion about the properties and uses of knives. Some children are reluctant to use knives (possibly from past experiences), but they have opportunities to satisfy their curiosity about knives under optimal conditions. In this way, the children become aware of both the danger and value of knives. After the snack, children wipe their hands and mouths with their napkins, place their dishes on the snack cart, and prepare for outdoor play.

As the children hurry to the playground, several safety factors should be considered. First, is the playground adequately supervised? Second, are toys readily available or do sheds need to be opened and toys removed? Do the toys and activities meet the needs of the involved children? Are toys of the appropriate size, number, and construction for the children to benefit from their use? Third, are there activities that allow children to participate in play according to their individual needs and desires—active or quiet, solitary or cooperative, gross muscle or fine muscle, intellectual or social, sustained or short-lived. Do children have opportunities for child-child relationships without unnecessary interference from adults? Even though the play yard is checked and rechecked, what are some possible hazards there?

emergency plan. Children need to know that whenever an alarm goes off, they are to follow emergency procedures for practice and for safety. (See Health and Safety Tips, 1991a, 1991b; Levin, 1991.)

The various considerations for safety of the children and staff will be introduced later in this chapter, including the following: transportation (to and from center, off center trips), unsafe art materials, noise pollution, choking because of unsafe toys/objects, and relationships with peers and others—including violent play and toys. Other equally important factors (toxic waste, caustic building materials, unhealthy air, personal cleanliness, ill children, and so on) were introduced in Chapter 8 and apply equally to safety.

The director, owner, or supervisor must carefully follow the state, local, and federal guidelines to assure reasonable safety and protection for the children in their care. (Refer to Chapter 2 for general information.) The safety of the children in all areas of development and in all activities must be protected.

Safety policies (goals) should be as specific as possible. Obviously, many safety items will be consistent for all centers, but implementation can vary widely. Most accidents can be prevented if center personnel are familiar with policies, prevention, reasons, and procedures. Note the many safety precautions in the following description of a typical day at a child-care center.

THE PHYSICAL ENVIRONMENT

Teachers and directors can make safer play areas for children through good planning and careful supervision. From the first footsteps onto the center property to the last footsteps off it, owners and operators are liable for hazardous conditions. Precautions— the best solutions—can be taken to remove or reduce obstacles that may cause injury or harm to individuals on the premises. Immediate repairs, removal of foreign objects, and safety guidelines protect children and adults.

Codes outlining safety factors required for the operation of a center vary from area to area; therefore, it is mandatory that the operator check carefully with licensing agents to conform to standards and avoid penalties. Common guidelines deal with transportation of children (loading and unloading zones, adequate parking), premise requirements (drained, free of insects and rodents), play yard enclosure and openings, placement of climbing equipment (over soft surfaces such as grass, sand, or artificial material), and use of the playground (a separate play area for younger children when there are distinct age differences among the children). Every building must meet fire and safety requirements.

Unsafe climbers, slides, and other playground equipment should be modified or eliminated. Hazardous activities require closer adult supervision than do activities with a lower injury rate. Architectural features, such as doors and indoor floor surfaces, require special attention. Children must always travel in seat restraints in cars or vans and must follow school-bus safety rules in larger vehicles. Training and resources to change hazardous conditions should be available to all staff.

It is mandatory that all staff members be especially conscious of when children are most accident-prone: when they are hungry, when they are fatigued, when they are inexperienced with the equipment, and when the equipment is new and challenging. *All* staff members are responsible for the safety of *all* children—not just those that are the closest or at the most interesting activities. Staff should note the possible hazards of climbing equipment (whether used indoors or out), of tools (woodworking, cooking), of overstimulated children, and of crowded facilities. Young children *can* be taught how to properly use toys and equipment to further their knowledge and development. (See Figure 9–1.)

Many injuries occur from children falling to the ground. Aronson (1990) notes:

> The key role played by surfacing under play equipment is underscored by several other studies of injury in early childhood settings. These studies show that whenever children can climb above the ground, falls to the surfaces under equipment are the leading cause of injury. To date, no ideal, low-cost playground surfacing material is available. Each material has drawbacks and advantages. (p. 54)

Name of Child _____ Birth date _____
Parent/guardian _____
Address _____ Phone number _____
Usual source of health care _____
Date of injury _____Time _____ Age ____ Sex ____
Type of injury (circle):   Bite   Broken bone   Bruise   Burn   Choking   Cut
Eye injury   Foreign body   Head injury   Poisoning   Scrape   Sliver   Sprain   Sting
Other _____
Location where injury occurred _____
(e.g., child-care room, bathroom, hall, playground, large muscle room, bus, car, walk)
Type of equipment involved _____
How injury happened (who, what, where, how, when) _____
_____
_____
_____

Type of treatment required _____
(e.g., first aid only in day care, visit to doctor's office or clinic, emergency room, hospitalized/ sutures,
cast, bandage, medication given)
Witnesses of injury incident _____
Signatures of witnesses _____
Name of medical professional consulted _____
Date ____ Time ____ Advice _____

Retrospectively, what would have prevented this injury?
_____
_____
_____
_____

Figure 9–1   Sample injury report form.
Source: Reprinted with permission from *Health in Day Care: A Manual for Health Professionals.* Copyright © 1987 American Academy of Pediatrics.

Directors, teachers, providers, and others caring for young children should research which materials have been most successful in preventing serious injuries from falls in their area and climate. (See *Playground Surfacing and Equipment Standards,* 1989.)

Obtaining liability insurance is another serious concern for child-care centers. For further information, see Chapter 11, Strickland and Levbarg (1990), Hayes and coworkers (1990), Reynolds and Strickland (1991), or numerous NAEYC publications.

Parental Involvement

Teachers as well as parents plan environments for children. Both should keep in mind the expectations of children of different ages, thereby using precaution in purchasing toys and equipment. Toys should be stored so children have easy access to them. Adults should avoid buying toys that are broken easily or are flammable; that cause pinches, cuts, or punctures; that have a toxic paint; that have parts small enough to be swallowed or put in noses or ears; that limit cre-

activity; or that encourage aggressive behavior or destructive play.

Adults should familiarize themselves with the growth characteristics of children: 2-year-olds like to climb, wander, explore, and defy; 3-year-olds move quickly, forget, and are curious; 4-year-olds are in constant motion and are inquisitive, social, and independent; and 5-year-olds are easily fascinated, impulsive, willing to please, and curious. Knowing what characteristics are age-consistent, teachers and parents can better plan for the safety and happiness of young children.

Adults at school or at home are in a position to help or hinder young children in the practice of safety habits. With little forethought, adults purchase and store a wide variety of items that could cause serious injury or even death to young children. Poisonous cleaning materials, pesticides, paint, and other toxic materials are often stored improperly. Poorly maintained facilities are dangerous—spilled liquids, broken fences and gates, improperly wired or secured electrical outlets, unscreened fireplaces and heaters, unreplaced light bulbs, loose boards, hazardous debris, and open ditches or pools can cause accidents. Curious about things they see adults do, children often are injured when they model adult behavior—using matches, sharp tools, ropes, sporting equipment, or playing with animals.

Discussing accidents that might happen, perhaps even role playing, helps adults focus on areas that need special supervision, children who are more accident-prone, activities that can get out-of-hand, or things that might distract adults from concentrating on the children.

SAFETY IN CHILD CARE COMPARED WITH HOME CARE

Questions have been raised about the frequency of accidents in child care versus accidents in the home. Aronson (1991) reports:

1. Medically treatable injuries occur at the same rate or less frequently in child care than in other settings.

2. Most common injuries requiring medical treatment are falls to hard surfaces, a variety of injuries on playground equipment, interactions between children with hard toys and blocks, door-related, indoor floor surfaces, and motor vehicles.

3. Most common types of wounds of children in child care are scrapes and bruises—most often to the head, face, forehead, and upper extremities.

4. Three fourths of all injuries are preventable by better supervision, removal or modification of obvious hazards (space heaters, guarding stairs, adjusting temperature of water), and better information regarding emergencies and poisons.

In addition to centers, some children are cared for in home settings, where caregivers must be just as cautious and aware of the health and safety of these children. The facility should be made "child-proof" so that the experience for the children will be on their developmental levels, rich in opportunities, and safe from harm, accident, and hazards—which include lead, pesticides, vegetation, toxins, animals, and humans.

In addition to policing their own facilities, in-home caregivers may be inspected by others. In recent surveys in several states, infractions were found such as "tripping hazards, tap water above scald temperature, exposed wiring and outlets, exposed space heaters, unguarded stairs, toxic chemicals and medications accessible to children, and lack of information for handling emergencies. Many of these hazards cannot be permanently corrected by a single action. Safety requires constant vigilance and surveillance" (Aronson, 1991, p. 106).

The age and number of children will prompt the caregiver to take certain safety precautions. Infants, for example, experience things from visual, tactile, auditory, and mouthing modes. They often roll over unexpectedly, they bury their heads, they snuggle soft objects, and they choke easily. Knowing these simple but basic facts, one should never leave children unattended (even when they are asleep) because they could roll off a bed or table, they could suffocate or choke, or they could get entangled in bedding or toys. Toddlers, for another example, are "into everything." They pull, push, taste, climb, crawl into and under objects, fall, choke, and are here-there-and-everywhere. Because of their mobility and curiosity, they must be watched constantly—their environment must be free from objects they could choke on, unsafe places to climb, hide, or get caught, and especially harmful things—cords, toxins, and climbing places. Preschoolers, a third category likely to be cared for in a home setting, are now more verbal, more mobile, more curious, and more interactive with people and things. They, too, must have careful supervision and facilities that have been checked and rechecked for safety hazards.

Children of all ages are inquisitive, and caregivers at all sites must be constantly alert for activities and materials that could cause unsafe conditions but yet satisfy the child's curiosity at her present level of ability and development. (See Chapter 8.)

SAFETY IN ROUTINES

Routines are important to children. It is often during confusion that problems, which otherwise attract little attention, occur. More individuals may congregate in a small space, causing some children and/or adults to become restless or impatient. Problems, which often involve safety, become more than casual events.

Arrival/Departure

Because individuals may arrive or depart in clusters, perhaps excited about prior or subsequent happenings or teachers and parents wanting to relay information, extra precaution needs to be focused on the safety and protection of the children. Young children have been known to wander, try unexpected things, or even steer younger siblings into dangerous situations because parents and teachers are momentarily distracted.

Set a goal to observe the children carefully so each day will begin and end with the needs of the child in mind. Often having another staff member available at this time will help children get involved in activities and in preparation for departure.

Attention must be focused on who is legally designated to pick up each child. Custody battles may cause problems; therefore, a list of authorized individuals must be at the check-out station *daily*. It is the teacher's responsibility—not the child's—to release the child to an authorized person.

Parents who are unable to park easily near the door of the center sometimes become careless due to their frustration. Safe arrival and departure of the children are considered in the design of an off-street entrance and ample parking near the building so children and adults can easily enter the building without concern for traffic or safety.

In many centers, parents stay through their child's check-in, make contact with a teacher, and say goodbye to the child as she begins the daily activities. If parents drop a child off (which is illegal in many states), (1) they have no assurance that the teachers know the child is there and (2) the child and teachers can become frustrated and anxious when the child is not well enough (physically or emotionally) to stay. Often just a nod, a smile, or a few words between a parent and teacher reassures everyone, including the child.

Transportation for Center Activities

Off-center transportation is of serious concern and must be given careful consideration when field trips or activities are planned away from the center. Local and federal regulations must be precisely followed, including review of the center's liability policy and that of the insurance company. Drivers must have a specific license to transport the children, and their attention must be on driving—not on watching the children. The vehicle must be in good repair and every effort should be taken to ensure the safety of all passengers. Drivers must be given a map with specific directions to the destination and return—with alternates *if necessary*.

Before leaving the center, rules of behavior should be reviewed with the children, parental (guardian) permission slips must be signed, and first-aid and emergency items should be checked and packed. Each child should be given a tag with her own name; the name, address, and phone number of the center; and any other information related to the field trip. The driver (whether parent or center personnel) should pick up and discharge children only at the curb. Conforming to law and for good safety practice, each child must be securely fastened with an individual seat belt, infants must be secured in car seats. Hard objects should be placed where the children will not be injured (in a trunk, on the floor, etc.). After checking for fingers and toes, doors should be tightly shut and locked (even if it requires additional safety locks). Ventilation should be enough to refresh the passengers but not wide enough for strong gusts or extended hands and arms. To make the trip more enjoyable for the children, the teacher (other than the driver) should carry on simple conversations, sing familiar songs, or call attention to points of interest and should attend to any misbehavior. Drivers, parents, and staff should *never* leave the children unattended in the car.

Walking Trips from the Center

Children should be cautioned about turning cars, crossing directly, observing lights, using pedestrian lane (when available), and facing the approaching traffic.

CURRICULUM

Regardless of whether the teacher is teaching specifically on a safety theme, safety is always of utmost concern. Modeling behavior, making appropriate comments, and providing opportunities for children to practice safety measures will help the children incorporate these principles into their daily lives. When a teacher removes a broken toy, gives reasons for a required behavior, or includes children in the elimination of a hazardous situation (e.g., unsafe climbing boards), children's awareness is encouraged. Soon the children are bringing dangerous situations to the teacher's attention!

At times, teachers will provide specific themes or lessons related to safety measures. One day the class may focus on expected behavior during a field trip, another day on protecting the body from weather, and still another day on playground safety.

Teachers must be especially alert during activities for which scissors, hammers, saws, hoes, rakes, needles, or other potentially dangerous items are used. The uses of these items should be demonstrated; the reasons for the kind of behavior that is expected when such tools are used should be given. Children should not be prohibited from using these tools. Rather, teachers should teach the children to use them effectively and safely. Safety can and should be included in specific and incidental lessons. However, if individual children are in danger, the teacher must immediately step in and divert any potential disaster. Children are not permitted to harm themselves or others, or to destroy property. Through hands-on experiences, teachers define, give reasons for, and demonstrate appropriate safety and courteous behaviors.

Children can learn about safety from those around them who value and practice safety measures without becoming unduly concerned, fearful, or authoritarian. Most routines can be taught in a positive, congenial manner in which children enjoy learning and experimenting in a safe environment. An atmosphere of fear, making mistakes, displeasing someone, or of getting hurt causes children to become distrustful, hesitant, and negative.

Behavior away from the classroom is important to discuss and model. Field trips need to be considered on an individual basis. Actions in case of emergencies (such as fire drills or disasters) should be well conceived, understood, and practiced. Alternate solutions to problems must also be considered in case planned routes or actions

Imagine each of the following situations. Brainstorm about the following: (1) What immediate action is required? (2) Why did the accident/injury/illness occur? (3) Could the situation have been predicted? (4) How could the situation be prevented in the future? (5) Explain what to do and why it is the best approach.

1. Angela has fallen down, and her front tooth has pierced her lip.

2. Jimmy complains of a sliver in his finger but will not let anyone look at it.

3. As tempers erupt in the sandbox, Randolph throws sand in Jeff's eyes.

4. Timothy pinches his finger in the shed door. It is not bleeding, but he is crying and screaming.

5. Michelle falls off the climbing gym, has a bump on her head, and wants only to sleep.

6. Rosie complains of a stomachache.

7. About an hour before time to go home, the twins become feverish and start scratching. On examination, you find small blisters erupting on their skin, and their coughing has become frequent and uncontrollable.

8. Mickey suddenly inhales the small spool he was using as a whistle.

are blocked. If your original plan is inoperable, be ready with a feasible alternate plan. Know where the center's circuit breakers and water and gas valves are located. Know where and how to turn off the fire alarm (to reduce frustration when it has been set off without proper cause!).

Meals/Snacks/Food Experiences

Perhaps a teacher wishes to introduce an experience to the child but is hesitant because of possible danger. For example, during a snack, one of the children quizzes the teacher about how the applesauce was made. Other children join the discussion. Because of continued interest, the teacher decides to make applesauce with the children and considers the following safety factors:

Cleanliness—Preparing the apples, tasting, cleaning up after the experience, hand washing

Safety—Using peelers and knives, tasting (hot) applesauce, using heat (temperature, cords)

The teacher begins the experience with some general comments about the tools and procedure. *How would you proceed from there?*

It is not uncommon for children to try to eat, talk, play, and entertain while eating. Therefore, the setting should be calm, relaxed, and unrushed.

The food should be carefully prepared, nourishing, attractive, bite size, and served family style. (See Chapter 8.) Toddlers and preschoolers should be encouraged to pour their own beverages. Preschoolers may be able to dish their own food.

Low tables and chairs (where the child's feet can rest on the floor) provide comfortable and safe seating. Dishes should be unbreakable, attractive, easily handled, and carefully sanitized. Utensils should be comfortable and appropriate for the size of the child's hands and for the type of food provided. See Figure 9–2 regarding choking of children.

Stories, Music, and Conversation

Safety features to incorporate during stories, music, language/conversation times, and so on include the following:

Sufficient space for each child to see and move (determined by the activity and number of children participating)

Things that cause choking	Precautions
Meat, hot dogs	Serve well-cooked meat; cut hot dogs in quarters lengthwise and then slice
Hard candy and marshmallows	Serve candy infrequently; cut marshmallows into quarters
Apples and carrots	Peel apples; cut into bite-sized pieces
Grapes	Remove from stems and cut in half
Unchewed food	Encourage children to take small bites, chew well, and swallow before talking or leaving table
Nuts, popcorn	Avoid nuts and popcorn until child can chew them well
Food in mouth after leaving table, or children unattended while eating	Insist that child remain at table until mouth is empty; have an adult at the table until all children have finished eating
Liquids	Sit down, drink in an upright position, and have no objects or food in mouth
Rushing while eating	Provide plenty of time for child to chew and eat
Objects in mouth at any time	Watch carefully for and remove objects that can be easily placed in mouth

Figure 9–2 Causes of choking and their precautions.
Source: Food items adapted from *Journal of American Medical Association.*

Careful supervision on the part of the teacher under unsure conditions (fragile or precious items, harmful items—sharp objects or balloons, unknown actions or reactions of children or item—pets, time restriction, etc.)

Using instruments that are not placed in the mouth (drums, shakers, bells, rhythm sticks, strings, etc.)

Monitoring time spent in activity

Cooperative Activities

Safety features to incorporate during cooperative activities include the following:

Sufficient materials for each child

Nonharmful materials (see Figure 9–3)

Enough time to satisfy the child's interest

Encouragement toward cooperative learning

Creative/Expressive Art

Teachers must be especially alert during activities for which scissors, needles, or other potentially dangerous items are used. Rather than prohibiting these items, teachers should teach the children to use them effectively and safely. Teachers should exercise caution when providing projects for young children as indicated in Figure 9–3. Art supplies for young children should always be nontoxic, nonflammable, and water based.

When buying children's art supplies remember to look for products marked with a CP (certified product), AP (approved product), or HL/NT (Health Label/Nontoxic) seal. These seals mean they have been certified by a medical expert as not containing materials in sufficient quantities to be toxic or injurious.

Warning: According to the Art and Craft Materials Institute, the word *nontoxic* on the label does not necessarily mean the product is safe. A

Media	Avoid	Use
Clay	powdered clay because of silica, which is easily inhaled and harmful to the lungs	damp clay to avoid dust inhalation
Glazes	those with lead content	poster paints
Paints	paints that require chemicals to clean brushes, etc.	water-based paints
Paint	powdered tempera because of additives	liquid tempera or any nontoxic paint
Dyes	chemical additives, cold-water or commercial dyes with chemical additives	natural dyes from vegetables, (e.g., onions)
Markers	permanent markers because of toxic solvents	water-based markers
Papier-mâché	instant papier-mâché because of lead or asbestos	newspaper (printed with black ink only) and library paste or liquid starch
Glues	epoxy, instant, or solvent-based glues because of chemical additives	water-based white glue or library paste

Figure 9–3 Safety for art activities.

Source: For additional information, contact Art Hazards Information Center, 5 Beekman St., New York, NY 10038 (212) 227–6231. Chart adapted from Kendrick and coworkers (1988) and Aronson (1991). A list of arts and crafts materials that *cannot* be purchased for use in kindergarten through grade six is available from the California Department of Health Services, Health Hazard Assessment Division, 2151 Berkeley Way, Berkeley, CA 94704.

nontoxic designation may relate only to acute or short-term adverse effects and not take into account whether the product may have adverse chronic or long-term effects on a child. The quantity of substances ingested over time is the key factor. The certified products in Figure 9–3 take this distinction into account in their assurance of safety.

Further Warning: The American Society for Testing and Materials (ASTM) has developed standards for many products, including substances intended for use in arts and crafts. ASTM D4236 is the "standard practice for labeling art materials for chronic health hazards." Art materials labeled in accordance with this voluntary standard have been assessed for their toxicity to adults. However, products labeled *nontoxic,* even with the

designation that the product complies with ASTM D4236, cannot be considered safe for use with children.

Such products that contain toxic substances may be recognized by labels such as *harmful if swallowed, use with adequate ventilation, avoid inhalation,* or *avoid skin contact.* None of these products should be used by young children or be used where young children could gain access to them. Unfortunately, no standard for toxicity of products to children exists (Aronson, 1991).

WHAT TO DO IN CASE OF EMERGENCY

Young children are often uncoordinated and lack good judgment. As a result, they get many scrapes, cuts, bumps, and bruises, and they tend to choke. Teachers and staff members at the center should know how to control bleeding, dislodge objects in the throat, and give cardiopulmonary resuscitation as well as how to treat both major and minor injuries. Centers should require their employees to have first-aid training with periodic refresher courses. Discussion and demonstrations before an accident occurs can prepare teachers to better handle the incidents. When an emergency or injury occurs, the main things for teachers to do are remain calm and think clearly. A teacher who is unable to handle a situation must get someone who can handle it without alarming the already insecure children.

Teachers should review emergency center procedures frequently. Each classroom should have a readily accessible first-aid kit (state regulations frequently list items for these kits; suggested items are given in Appendix E) and a chart dealing with minor injuries, a list of emergency phone numbers, evacuation procedures, and an emergency/health card for each child in that classroom (see Chapter 11 and Appendix E). As minor injuries occur, the teacher should administer recommended first aid and write a report including the cause of the injury and the treatment given. Parents must know this information about their children.

Each teacher should have a personal list of the children currently enrolled in the group; keep a daily attendance record; and a current list of the names of parents or guardians of each child plus their addresses, phone numbers, and other critical information about each child (allergies, custody, etc.). If these records are current and in the teacher's possession, there should be no delay in notifying parents if an emergency arises. Some centers require parents to sign a form giving the center permission to act for them when they cannot be reached. Employees must realize that any negligence on the part of the center can result in a lawsuit or license revocation.

First Aid

First aid is the immediate attention needed until more professional care is available (or needed). It does not include treatment or diagnosis.

Every child-center employee should have a basic course on first aid as it applies to young children, and at least one staff member, who has certification in emergency pediatric first-aid treatment, cardiopulmonary resuscitation techniques (CPR) for infants and children, and emergency management of choking from a licensed health professional is always present. The American Red Cross offers a course that teaches four steps:

1. Help the child—survey scene to see how many are hurt and how seriously, do a primary check of life-threatening conditions—the traditional ABCs (airway, breathing, circulation); phone the emergency medical system (if injury is serious); make a secondary survey for specific injuries.

2. Call the parent, who will be required to authorize any care other than life-saving measures. Parents also make the decision about whether further evaluation is necessary.

3. Talk with and care for the other children, who may not be injured but need comforting.

4. Complete the injury report and injury log. (Details may be difficult to recall later.)

Injuries

Known Playground Hazards. The U.S. Consumer Product Safety Commission has studied the types of hazards associated with playground injuries. Obvious sources of injury include protruding objects or obstructions in the fall zones under and around equipment; sharp edges, pinch points on moving parts, exposed bolts, open hooks, or exposed chain links or other holes sized so that they can catch a child's finger; heavy or sharp swing seats; steps made of round tubing or steps spaced more than a child's knee height apart; loosely mounted equipment or exposed mountings and supports; hard surfaces in all fall zones around equipment; maximum fall height from the head of the child on the highest part of the equipment to the surface exceeds the rating for the surface under the equipment; spaces between bars of horizontal climbing equipment

Facts and Figures

- The majority of injuries in child-care programs occur in gross-motor play areas—mainly climbers and slides. Injuries are more common when children have the least experience with the equipment (fall, or when outdoor play has been limited) (Aronson, 1989).
- Other times when injuries may occur are when a child becomes ill or injured and the routine is disrupted, staff are absent or busy, children are not involved in the activity that was planned and they are tired or hungry, hazards are too attractive, staff are not up-to-date with children's abilities, or during field trips (when safety rules may be forgotten) (Kendrick et al., 1988).
- National estimate of 185.8 playground equipment-related injuries per thousand emergency room visits in 1988: 76.1 on swings, 9.7 on seesaws, 57.2 on monkey bars, and 42.8 on slides. Studies on playground accidents by type of equipment and age of children showed that the children up to age 4 had the highest accident rate of all three groups on swings (59.8 percent), on seesaws (63 percent), on monkey bars (78.5 percent), and on slides (48.9 percent) (FYI, Young Children, May, 1989).
- Various researchers have found that educational and intervention programs can be effective in improving day-care safety practices (Snow et al., 1992; Aronson, 1991)
- Scald burns from hot liquids are the most frequent cause of nonfatal burn injuries in young children: 75 percent of scald injuries occur in children between 6 months and 3 years of age—spilling hot liquid on themselves, excessively hot water, microwave ovens to heat infant food (Aronson, 1991).
- Two common activities injure children: falling and running. Morris (1991) states the problem well: "When an object is dropped to a surface, either the surface gives to absorb the impact or the object gives. In the case of children and playgrounds, that is either the surface fallen on or the part of the child impacting the ground first" (p. 48).

"Injury, not disease, is the leading cause of death for children after the first year of life," states Aronson (1991). She believes that "breaks in safe behaviors are more likely to occur when the rationale for the desired behavior is not well understood and when the desired behavior is not reinforced on a regular basis."

Causes of injury for infants (birth until able to walk), toddlers (walking but not toilet trained), and preschoolers (toilet trained but not at age of mandatory schooling) are car related, as passengers, burns and house fires, falls, drowning, and choking. Causes of injury for young school-age children (ages 5 to 9 years) are similar: car related, as passengers, and pedestrians, burns and house fires, drowning, bicycles, and falls.

Boys are injured more frequently than girls (ratio of 1.5 to 1); increased activity level does not increase the risk of injury; and more timid children are injured more often than those who are more confident, concludes Aronson (1991).

Injuries include minor injuries, major personal injuries, individual and multiple injuries, and catastrophes. Studies done in 90 preschools in Los Angeles and in a single center in Iowa indicated that the peak period for injury was midmorning; the peak season was fall. In a national study of injuries among children ages 1 to 4, spring was the most common season (Aronson, 1989).

Disposable plastic gloves for teachers handling bleeding injuries and bandages for immediate care of minor wounds and comfort of young children should be strategically placed throughout the indoor and outdoor facilities.

exceed the easy reach of the users (14 inches for school-age children, less for preschoolers); rails and bars on equipment for preschoolers are more than 1 inch in diameter, preventing secure grasp by a child-size hand; swinging exercise rings (do not belong on young children's playgrounds); any spaces hidden or inaccessible to an adult; any toxic, irritating, or injurious materials and vegetation; metal equipment that can overheat when exposed to the sun; equipment located so that moving parts cross paths children might use to go from one activity to another; broken equipment; litter; inadequate supervision; inadequate source of drinking water; inadequate shade to protect children from excess exposure to the sun, with resultant sunburn or heat-related illness; insect nests, fruiting plants, garbage cans, and other objects that attract stinging insects; lack of barriers to prevent intrusion by animals and to keep children from wandering beyond the limits where caregivers can easily supervise them (Aronson, 1991).

Government publications are available about playground safety from the U.S. Consumer Product Safety Commission. The address and website address are given at the end of the chapter. These publications note recurring problems—aimless activity, unused areas, overcrowding, unsupervised areas, overlapping hazards because of conflicting play (trikes through quiet area, etc.), inappropriate restrictions, excessive maintenance, and storage for movable equipment—that can cause accidents and problems. They also identify areas within a center that justify rule making for safety purposes. One section deals with water safety, noting that drowning is among the leading causes of death of young children. There is a caution about unattended children swimming or playing in water, about rules of behavior (walking, not pushing or dunking), about not having objects in one's mouth when swimming, and methods of getting attention when necessary.

An important lesson for children to learn is how to play in a risk-free, productive, and creative way without being exposed to risk of serious injury. Safety does not mean that children are observers only; they need suggestions, limits, and understanding.

SAFETY FEATURES OF THE INDOOR FACILITY

Ratio

The ratio of adults to children should carefully conform to state, federal, and/or organizational recommendations for the ages of the children enrolled. Low ratios and better qualified teachers are more likely to be rated as high quality.

Space

The floor space (excluding food preparation, special uses [isolation rooms, offices, adult work areas, toileting, halls, etc.]) should meet the federal recommendations (35 square feet of clear space per child), preferably be all on one floor for ease of supervision and safety, have at least two exits in case of emergency, and be well lighted and ventilated. (Refer to state and federal requirements; see also Chapters 3 and 10.)

Personnel

Each individual working closely with young children should be carefully screened and eliminated if there is any evidence of abuse or criminal behavior.

General Facility

Doors. Doors should open in the direction of the exit, be light-weight enough for children to easily manipulate them, preferably have a slow-closure to prevent pinching, have a vision-panel when appropriate to prevent individuals from walking into them, have handles that can be manipulated by small hands, and prevent children from being entrapped in closets or other small places.

Entry from the outside should be limited to doors where there is adequate supervision; however, these same doors should be easily exited in case of emergencies inside the building.

Windows/Glass. Windows and other use of glass (mirrors) should be low enough for children to enjoy them, have safety features, be cleaned frequently, and provide light.

Electrical Outlets. Electrical outlets should be child-resistant, mounted out of the reach of young children, covered with safety plates, and conveniently placed around the room to avoid stringing cords. When used, electrical cords must be in good condition, continually and carefully supervised, and out of the traffic pattern. Guard against outlets and cords being placed near water sources.

Floors. Floors should have a nonabrasive cover, preferably one that is securely attached; be free from wear and hazards; and spills should be immediately wiped up. Floor coverings not only look nice, they absorb sound, bring color and warmth, and often encourage longer play by children. Initial cost and upkeep are important to consider. Throw rugs and runners are hazardous; rather, floors should be coated with nonskid surfaces. Open floor areas invite running; areas can be broken into smaller units by furniture, dividers, change in floor covering.

Restrooms

Toilet. There needs to be a ratio of 1 toilet for every 10 children. Portable toilets, potty chairs, and training chairs pose a sanitation hazard for centers. If the stalls are semiprivate, the doors should be easily used by children (avoid pinching, easily latched and unlatched, swing space, etc.).

Handwashing. Faucetless sinks are more sanitary. Liquid soap is recommended. Paper towels or blowers are recommended over a child's personal towel. Paper towels may cause clutter; blowers may be dangerous if the heat is not controlled carefully. Waste containers should be near by.

Water. The temperature of the water should not exceed 100°F (43°C). Water from basins or toilets should be wiped up immediately. Many toileting areas have a slick floor surface and spilled water adds to the danger.

Drinking fountains that can be operated by children should be available both indoors and outdoors.

Play Areas in General

Personal areas (lockers) easily accessible, carefully identified, and out of traffic pattern

Mats beneath all indoor climbing equipment

Areas of play carefully identified (active/quiet, solitary/group, building, wheel toys, etc.)

Toys age and interest appropriate, frequently inspected, cleaned, repaired, or replaced

Teachers always on the alert for (and quickly remove) any objects that can be put into the mouth, ears, or nose

Teachers should help and encourage children to set limits for use of toys and equipment, work cooperatively with others, and retrieve and replace items used. Helping children to know reasons, to feel a part of situations, to be equal with peers, and to have ideas and words to say will help increase safety and reduce problem behavior.

Teachers and children should be aware of toys and themes that encourage friendliness and constructive play—and avoid those that promote competition and destructive play (violence). (See "Violence" later in this chapter.)

All medications and toxic cleaning supplies at the center should be double-locked, out of the reach of children, and carefully monitored. (See discussion in Chapter 8.)

Noise Reduction. The noise level in some settings can cause frayed nerves, stress, irritation, unusual behavior, and even accidents. Awareness of annoying noise can alleviate the causes, such as floor covering under blocks reduces the loud and hollow noise created when blocks are knocked over; draperies help muffle sounds near windows; acoustical tile on the walls calms the echoing; display boards of foam, cork, fabric and other such materials increases the beauty of the things depicted and helps absorb the room sounds; padded furniture, floor covering, and soft toys in the domestic area reduce sounds made by busy feet and housekeeping equipment.

In addition to noise inside the center playrooms or playground, there are other sounds like electrical appliances, cleaning apparatuses, heating and cooling motors, construction, vehicles and motorcycles, bells, sirens, and other ones that may be outside our control. Where possible, noise should be reduced or eliminated (keeping children inside during the noisiest time of day, monitoring the volume when they listen to tapes and CDs, learning about the use and care of the ear, the danger of intense, continuous, and sudden sounds, and other measures).

Waste Disposition. The amount of waste from a child-care center could be enormous—especially if infants and toddlers are cared for (disposable diapers, food items, etc.). Without proper care, germs and odors could multiply rapidly—attracting insects, rodents, and animals. Some waste companies furnish and insist on using their receptacles, which are usually metal or nonporous to prevent animal access and leakage. Safety and health of those at the center could be at risk if receptacles are not emptied and sanitized frequently.

For a discussion on space, density, lighting, and color, see Chapter 10.

Safety in Buying Toys. Good toy selection for young children should include one or more of the characteristics shown in Figure 9–4.

Many good toys are available for children of all ages. For help, write to U.S. Consumer Product Safety Commission (CPSC), Washington, DC, 20207, and request a copy of "Which Toy for Which Child" (specify: ages birth through 5 or ages 6 through 12). This useful pamphlet includes abilities and interests of children at different ages, toys for different types of play (active, manipulative, make-believe, creative, learning), and for developmental growth of the child. Consumers are encouraged to report unsafe products to the CPSC hotline, toll free at (800) 638–2772.

If a teacher or parent believes that a toy is hazardous, Gillis and Fise (1993) suggest three options:

1. Contact the U.S. Consumer Product Safety Commission at (800) 638-CPSC to register a complaint. If you believe the product should be recalled or banned, you can also write a letter to the Commission at Consumer Product Safety Commission, Washington, DC 20207. Be sure to include information about the name of the product, manufacturer, where you purchased the product, the hazard it poses, and any injury or potential injury it was or is associated with, and state the action you wish the agency to take.

Good toy selection for young children should include one or more of the following characteristics:

- Be on the developmental level of the child but adaptable and progressive (encouraging large and small muscle development as well as eye-hand coordination)
- Promote areas of development: social, emotional, intellectual, physical
- Provide high and prolonged interest
- Require minimal adult supervision
- Encourage creativity, imagination, and social relationships
- Strengthen the child's self-concept
- Encourage constructive, nonviolent play
- Provide for both solitary and cooperative play
- Be sturdily made and easily cleaned
- Be void of negative or cultural bias
- Teach good work and play habits (getting, using, returning)
- Provide satisfaction to the child

Figure 9–4 Safety in buying toys.

2. Write or call the manufacturer to register a complaint against the product. Request a repair, a replacement, or refund for the product. You can also return the product to the place of purchase.

3. Write to CFA, Unsafe Toys, 1424 16th St., NW, #604, Washington, DC 30036. Your letter will be passed on to the government and help inform others about the toy hazard.

"Spread the word—tell others about the hazard, including your child's friends' parents, your child's day-care or school teachers, your pediatrician, and others" (Gillis & Fise, 1993, p. 266).

SAFETY FEATURES OF THE OUTDOOR ENVIRONMENT

Outdoor play is an extension of the learning that occurs indoors. It is the duty and responsibility of teachers to see that children play in a safe, inviting environment. Factors needing attention include the following:

- Type of playground enclosure (wire, wood, brick)
- Exits from the area in case of emergency
- Weathering of equipment
- Guidelines for using various types of equipment (wheeled toys, gardening utensils, climbing structures)
- Activities planned (sand area, obstacle course)
- Supervision of children
- Climate
- Vegetation (see Figures 8–2 and 8–3)

Ratio

The ratio of teachers to the number and ages of the children should conform with state, federal, or other requirements. A sufficient number of teachers should be on the playground and should be strategically placed so that all children are under surveillance—especially children near activities that might be more dangerous, such as climbing, tools, new activities, wheel toys, and so on.

All children and *all* activities must be supervised at *all* times.

Space

Generally, a minimum of 75 square feet per child for the number of children using the outdoor play area at any one time is sufficient. Different areas of the playground may have special interest to particular age groups or activities. Playground equipment should include stationary and moveable pieces to create interest and challenge as the children develop more skills.

Climate

Children must be properly dressed for the climate and amount of time they will spend outdoors.

In most climates children can, and should, play outdoors for a portion of the day. In some climates children play outdoors all or most of the day (activities usually reserved for indoors can just as easily be provided outdoors).

In climates where outdoor play is hazardous to young children (extreme cold, extreme heat, insects, pollution, etc.), some time could be spent under a covered shelter with appropriate equipment or the center could have a large room where regular outdoor activities could occur indoors.

In cold and wet weather, metal materials are cold, adherent, slippery, and dangerous; wood materials deteriorate, splinter, and weaken.

Storage

Toys and equipment should be stored nearest the areas where they are most commonly used. Children should be encouraged to get and replace toys and equipment, providing opportunities to learn independence, cooperation, decision making, responsibility, and safety as toys are used.

Doors on sheds should be tall enough and wide enough for children and teachers to comfortably remove and replace wheeled, sand, and other toys.

Water

There should be drinking fountains and other means of getting water for supervised activities (watering gardens, washing toys, painting with water, drinking, etc.). Wading pools must be closely supervised and limits defined and enforced. Sprinkler heads and watering for the landscaping should not interfere with the play of children. Uneven surfaces where water accumulates can cause slipping, attraction of insects, and unwanted play.

Repairs

Toys, equipment, and areas should be checked daily for repairs, replacements, hazards, and so on. Unsafe items should be repaired immediately. Some surfaces require less maintenance than others depending on the climate, placement of equipment, popularity, and construction.

One person could have the ongoing responsibility of checking for items needing repair, but all staff members should report items needing attention.

Permanent Equipment/Special Activities

Permanent equipment (swings, climbers, etc.) should be checked daily for needed repairs. Children should be informed about the use of equipment (taking turns, not walking into moving swings, holding on, number of children, etc.).

Sand areas should be covered nightly for protection from animals and debris. (The APHA/AAP standards recommend regular cleaning and disinfecting of sand, turning it over to a depth of 18 inches annually, and complete replacement at least every 2 years.)

When woodworking tools are used, they must be very closely supervised. Inexperienced children should be instructed in the use of the tools, where to get and replace supplies, and where to put finished products (will they be used later at the center or are they to be taken home?).

Traffic rules should be established and followed for wheel toys, running, and other mobile activities.

Types of Surfacing

There should be a variety of surfaces for the children to explore: sand, dirt, grass (where feasible), hard, soft, and others to suit local conditions and activities. Each type of surface brings similar and different conditions for safety. (Sand is for digging—not throwing; dirt is for planting; hard surfaces are for riding on or using wheel-toys; and soft surfaces are for sitting/playing on, or under climbing apparatuses.)

The CPSC and the ASTM have set standards for manufacturing and testing materials, which many companies voluntarily follow. Before ordering surfacing, the center should ask for a copy of standards and testing from the particular company. Concrete and asphalt have been found to offer no injury protection and are not recommended by the CPSC as a playground surface. Surfaces that are considered to be safer fall into three categories, each with advantages and disadvantages: organic loose material (play bark, pine bark mulch), inorganic loose materials (sand, shredded tires, pea gravel), and compact materials (rubber and foam mats). In addition to the basic cost of materials, other cost factors to consider when selecting a surface are site preparation, professional installation, ongoing maintenance, and loose material replacement (Morris, 1991).

In an internal memo, the CPSC staff reported the following findings of the hazards analysis (Aronson, 1990):

1. about 60% of all playground equipment-related injuries (for both public and home equipment) are the result of falls to the surface below the equipment;

2. 9 out of 10 of the "serious" injuries associated with both public and home playground equipment resulted from falls to the surface;

3. for both public and home playground equipment, the arm/hand areas were the body parts involved most frequently in injuries resulting from falls to the surface and the majority of these injuries were fractures;

4. natural and paved surfaces were involved in a larger proportion of the injuries, and to a

somewhat greater extent, of serious injuries than might have been expected based on the proportion of such surfaces in use in public locations; and

5. head injuries were involved in about three-fourths of the fall-related deaths reported to the Commission.

The CPSC has identified falls to surfaces as the single greatest hazard on a playground (accounting for 70 percent of all playground accidents). Likewise, in order of risk or accident potential, merry-go-rounds, slides, swings, seesaws, and climbers have also been identified as high-risk playground sites (Zeece & Graul, 1993).

Because many accidents experienced by young children are from falling, Snow and coworkers (1992) suggest the following precautions:

1. *Impact absorbing materials* (pea gravel, wood chips, sand, shredded rubber, etc.). Ten or more inches under playground equipment to reduce chances of serious injury from falls as high as 8 to 10 feet.

2. *Structure heights.* A minimum of 3 feet for children under 3 years of age and 4½ feet for ages 3 to 6. Guard rails should be installed wherever possible.

3. *Exposed or protruding parts.* Cover with impact-absorbing foam or rubber and shield moving parts that may cause pinch injuries.

4. *Placement of equipment.* To avoid collisions, leave a 9-foot minimum space between other structures and child traffic patterns.

5. *Security.* Check and tighten bolts and other fasteners.

6. *Inspections.* Check regularly for playground hazards such as nests of bees, poisonous plants, and so on.

7. *Supervision.* Encourage supervisors to remain especially alert and attentive; increase the quality and quantity of supervision when children are engaged in physical activities such as climbing, sliding, swinging, and so on. (See Figure 9–5.)

8. *Restrictions.* When important, limit the number of children using equipment at one time.

9. *Vigilance.* Conduct educational programs on outdoor safety for children and staff.

Asking the question, "Is playground safety being taken seriously?", Aronson (1992) reports that:

. . . inspectors found the surfacing under climbing equipment to be a common and critical hazard. Over half of the climbing structures four feet or more in height had earth, grass, or concrete beneath them. Only 7.1% had three or more inches of loose-fill surfacing material, although 10 to 12 inches of cushioning materials is desirable.

Playground hazards identified by the Centers for Disease Control (CDC) are as follows: inadequate surfacing material in fall zones around equipment; exposed concrete anchoring; inadequate clearance around equipment for traffic patterns; rocks in fall zones; exposed roots, concrete, rocks, nails, or other sharp objects; tripping hazards; broken equipment, sharp or splintering surfaces; open "S" hooks on swings; and rusting surfaces.

At the time of the article, Aronson (1992) reported that wood mulch was the Consumer Product Safety Council's favorite recommendation for loose fill materials. Based on their studies and the reality that loose fill materials will get scattered and compressed, they recommended 10 to 12 inches of the wood mulch in the landing zone around climbers at all times.

Landscaping

The setting should be inviting, comfortable, versatile, but safety should be at the forefront of planning. The accesses should be conveniently located for child's play as well as maintenance.

Plantings should be nontoxic (see Figures 8–2 and 8–3), nonabrasive (thorns, rough bark), and chemical free. According to a study reported in 1982 by the EPA, 84 percent of pesticides had not been adequately tested for their capacity to cause

- A teacher precedes the children to the playground.
- As more children go outside, more adults accompany them. (There is a sufficient teacher-child ratio.)
- Guidelines ("rules") are established, children are informed, and procedures are followed.
- Teachers should arrange activities for best participation and supervision.
- The outdoor area is fenced (preferably with a fence children can see through but not climb over).
- Cushions, padding, or appropriate surface is placed below equipment (swings, slide, climbers).
- Equipment is maintained in a safe condition, is clean and attractive, and is developmentally appropriate.
- A variety of equipment is provided, but may be rotated into and out of use.
- There is some protection from hot, cold, wet, or wind.
- Stationary equipment is well placed, allowing space for moveable or temporary activities (parachute, obstacle course, balls, etc.).
- At *no time* should a teacher leave her outdoor post. If help is needed, send a child to recruit another adult.
- When it is time to leave the outdoor area, assist the children in returning their toys to the proper places and in tidying up the grounds.
- An adult *must* remain near activities that could be dangerous or invite problems (high climbers, moving swings, woodworking tools, exciting activities, etc.).
- Equipment and activities should be interesting and inviting to the children and meet their developmental abilities.
- The vegetation in the playground should be nonpoisonous (see Chapter 8).
- There should be areas for quiet play (digging, etc.) and areas for active play (wheel toys, running, etc.).
- Activities and materials commonly used indoors could be brought outdoors for interest and variety (art materials, music, dramatic play, etc.).
- Adults should pay attention to the *children* and not use this time for visiting with other adults.
- Children and adults should look on outdoor time as a period of relaxation and invigoration, not punishment.
- Adults should be interested in and supportive of the activities of the children. This isn't guard duty.

Figure 9–5 Guidelines for outdoor supervision.

cancer, 90 to 93 percent had not been tested for their ability to cause genetic damage, and 60 to 70 percent had not been tested for their ability to cause birth defects. The trend had been to ban pesticides when their side effects were studied. (See Chapter 8 for a discussion on environmental hazards.)

Physical Layout

Well-designed playgrounds provide for individual differences among users disabled children are children first and disabled second (Shaw, 1987), opportunities to develop competence and a positive sense of self, a sense of security and trust and a feeling of belonging, and opportunities to optimize child growth across all developmental areas (Zeece and Graul, 1993).

The outdoor playground should be designed for utility as well as beauty with areas for quiet, undisturbed play; active play; planting and digging; and areas where children initiate their own themes.

There should be storage space for portable equipment, tools, and toys. Some items will be in the sun or partial shade so there must be provision for some shade and water for drinking and use.

The entire property should be enclosed; the type of structure depends on cost, privacy, safety, and personal preference. Administrators will need to seek bids for original and maintenance costs and for types of materials recommended and available in their particular setting.

Playground Infractions

The Centers for Disease Control, realizing that just calling infractions to the attention of child-care workers was inadequate, suggested several interventions: explicit regulations, better training of regulators, support for enforcement of regulations, more extensive training of child-care center directors, increasing parental awareness and conspicuously posting inspection reports at the center.

Legal action for playground infractions has caused concern in some states. California passed a law requiring all playgrounds to meet basic safety standards by January 1, 2000. Similar legislation is being considered in other states.

Center operators know the safety guidelines that must be followed; unfortunately, some are lax in following the guidelines. Examples of some violations include poisons and medicines accessible to children, broken glass, playground equipment in disrepair, traffic hazards, inoperable fire extinguishers, insufficient planning for emergency medical care, high water temperature, lead-based paint on walls, disregard for fire-resistant fabrics, and inadequate insurance on transportation vehicles that had faulty seat belts or none at all. Any one of these violations could result in license revocation, lawsuit, or enrollment decline.

Playgrounds for Safety

Playgrounds are designed for the types of activities that will occur there. Changing the physical environment changes children's behavior: open spaces encourage running and active play; less space increases group play; proper props and defined areas encourage dramatic play, construction play, and art; removing equipment on the playground and paving it with asphalt encourages children to fight; complex, multifaceted play structures increase language use; areas should encourage group and/or solitary play as decided by the children (Dempsey et al., 1993).

To make sure the playground is at an appropriate "managed-risk" level, there are seven critical areas to consider: a systematically organized playground, carefully selected equipment, adherence to child-care licensing standards, adherence to CPSC guidelines (available by calling 800-638-2772), carefully planned supervision and staff training, a periodic inspection and *written* service record, and a written record of actions taken after an injury (Dempsey et al., 1993). See Figure 9–6 for a list of the most common safety issues.

And last, but not least, safe playgrounds are designed to meet the needs of the children who will play there—their ages, their experience, their abilities, and their preferences. Three issues will need special attention: (1) the outdoor play of children with disabilities, chronic illnesses, or other special conditions, (2) complete and adequate insurance, and (3) well-trained, alert teachers. See Figure 9–7 for a playground safety checklist.

After all the preceding information about safety in child care, it may be well to conclude this section with the three goals of a 1996 NICHD study of positive caregiving: (1) to identify which structural characteristics of infant care (such as ratios and group size) and which caregiver qualifications (such as education and specialized training) are related to more sensitive, warm caregiving practices; (2) to find out whether different types of infant care (such as center-based care, family child care, and in-home care by sitters and relatives) have different structural characteristics and distinct caregiving practices; and (3) to provide a description of the overall quality of infant care experienced by the infants in the study.

The team followed 1,364 families at 10 sites across the United States since the birth of the children. The study found four significant predictors

Figure 9–6 Most common safety issues.
Source: Dempsey, Strickland, and Frost, 1993.

1. Falls to a nonresilient surface (grass is not acceptable)
2. Inadequate fall zone area (depth, type of cover, or size)
3. Head entrapments (spaces 3.5 to 9 inches)
4. Entanglements (catching clothing or laces on protrusions)
5. Scrapes, abrasions, and punctures or protrusions
6. Inappropriate barriers (too low or horizontal in design)
7. Crush or pinch points between moving pieces
8. Falls onto lower portions of equipment or other pieces
9. Inappropriate placement of equipment in the playground
10. Swings attached to climbing structures
11. Inappropriate slide design (sides too low, no runout/exit)
12. Inappropriate handrails or handholds
13. Developmentally inappropriate equipment

Figure 9–7 Playground safety checklist.
As a guide for evaluating play equipment and playground safety, use the Consumer Federation of America's "Report and Model Law on Public Play Equipment and Areas" (1424 16th St., NW, #604, Washington, DC 20036.) or the government's free playground publication, "A Handbook for Public Playground Safety" (Consumer Product Safety Commission, Washington, DC, 20207).

- Are there any potential entanglement hazards on which children may catch clothing or body part, especially the neck?
- Are there any exposed moving parts that may pinch or crush body parts?
- Are there any unnecessary protrusions or projections?
- What kind of maintenance is there for the yard and equipment?
- Are there any environmental hazards on which children could trip or fall?
- Is the playground enclosed for safety of children and exclusion of unwanted individuals or pets?
- Is equipment included that may cause injuries to young children, such as high slides, twirling apparatus, unpadded climbers, improper place for wheel toys, and so on?
- Have children been properly instructed in the use of the equipment and/or area (necessary limits, for example).

of sensitive, warm, responsive care: (1) child-adult ratio, (2) group size, (3) caregivers who were less authoritarian about child rearing, and (4) safe, uncluttered physical environment containing age-appropriate materials. The findings included: *Ratios* were extremely important—1:1 was extremely important in sensitive, positive caregiving. Infant care was much more likely to occur when *group size* was smaller. Caregivers who were *less authoritarian* were more likely to provide positive interactions with infants. And positive caregivers were more likely to be found in a *safe, uncluttered physical environment* containing age-appropriate materials.

The study concluded: "The results of this study show what common sense would suggest: When caregivers are responsible for large number of infants, in any setting, they are less likely to provide warm, responsive care. The findings are consistent with policies that limit the number of children in the setting and regulate the quality of the physical environment. Further research will show what effects caregiving practices may have on these infants' later development" (p. 69).

Shallcross (1999) reminds us of the reality of child care in our country:

> Regulatory guidelines for family child care facilities vary strikingly from state to state. For example, in some states there are no training requirements at all for family child care providers, while in other states family child care providers must participate in specific types of training and must also meet experiential requirements. . . . Emergencies occur! Be prepared! Have a rescue plan in place; register with the local fire/rescue department so authorities know as much as possible about the facility; take and renew proper training in the areas of health and safety; and be alert to possible problem areas. (p. 70)

In addition to the "expected" safety factors in child care, there are many others that are of extreme importance. Following are some selected ones, including facts and figures, that should be of concern to all of us—whether or not we are involved in child care.

OTHER SAFETY FACTORS

Criminal Background Checks on Staff

The National Child Protection Act of 1993 (HR 1237) established procedures for national criminal background checks for child-care providers. Passed by both the House and the Senate, the act was signed into law by President Clinton. The major provisions of the act require states to report child-abuse crime information to the national criminal history background system (maintained by the FBI) and allow states to conduct national background checks on child-care providers. The act authorized $20 million in funding for the fiscal years 1994 through 1997. No funds were appropriated for fiscal year 1994 (National Association for the Education of Young Children, 1994). Later funding was not obtained.

Sexual Abuse

"We must distinguish between prevention and detection in sexual abuse prevention programs. *Prevention*, in general, refers to efforts to do something proactively—usually with groups—to forestall problems down the road. . . . *Detection* follows reporting of the problem and leads to intervention and treatment, whereas prevention programs address the issue prior to abuse" (Jordan, 1993, p. 76).

Directors should carefully check the references, employment history, and other sources of any applicant who will be alone with a child or a group of children in child care as to prior abuse of any child in any way, or if he or she is sexually oriented to children (Fiene, n.d.).

Any educational program for young children must take developmental competencies and needs into consideration. It is difficult for young children to understand the content of sexual abuse so they must be allowed to interact with that content in order to internalize the material. Learning activities should be concrete and relevant to young children's lives.

Jordan (1993) states:

> So far, little research exists indicating that abuse prevention curricula are appropriate to young children's intellectual developmental levels. . . . Even after children had participated in a prevention program, large gaps remained in their knowledge of the material presented. . . .
>
> At a young age children must be able to trust their adult caretakers and to rely on them as safe bases from which to experiment with their budding independence and autonomy. For adults to be responsible for the care and safety of children and for children to trust those adults is developmentally

Facts and Figures

"Child abuse by those working with children violates the fundamental principle in NAEYC's *Code of Ethical Conduct* for working with young children: 'ABOVE ALL, WE SHALL NOT HARM CHILDREN' " (Feeney & Kipnis, 1992).

NAEYC's (1997a) Position Statement on Prevention of Child Abuse recommends that early childhood programs in centers, homes, and schools adopt policies consistent with the guidelines that follow. In some cases these policies will be set by a larger organizational structure, such as a school district, religious group, corporation, or community agency (pp. 42–46).

The position statement includes:

1. Program policies (for staff, environment, training, safety, supervision of staff, and abuse prevention).
2. Screening, recruitment, and retention policies for staff and others who may have access to (but not direct responsibility for) young children.
3. Policies to promote close partnerships with families.
4. Role of family members in child abuse awareness.
5. Role of public regulation.
6. Role of early childhood professionals (Feeney & Kipnis, 1992).

The source for the following information is *The State of America's Children* (1992):

1. In 1991 an estimated 2.7 million children were reported to child protection agencies as victims of maltreatment, according to the National Committee for Prevention of Child Abuse. Almost half of reported cases involve neglect; 25 percent physical abuse, 15 percent sexual abuse, and 65 percent emotional abuse.
2. Nationwide, the number of children reported abused or neglected almost tripled since 1980, increasing 40 percent between 1985 and 1991. The three most prevalent problems among families reported for abuse or neglect are economic stress, difficulties in handling parental responsibilities, and substance abuse.
3. An estimated 1,383 children (about half of them 1 year or younger) died from abuse or neglect in 1991, more than in any of the six previous years in which such data were collected.
4. More than 4.5 million women of childbearing age were current users of illegal drugs in 1990.

   - "Child abuse is any nonaccidental injury or pattern of injuries to a child for which there is no 'reasonable' explanation" (National Committee to Prevent Child Abuse, 1995).
   - "Child abuse is perpetrated by family members; 1994 figures indicate that in 90% of reported abuse, perpetrators were parents or other relatives" (U.S. Department of Health and Human Services, 1996).
   - "Estimates of the proportion of child abuse in out-of-home settings vary, ranging from 1% to 7% of reported rates of abuse" (Wells et al., 1995).

appropriate. Expecting children to shoulder the task of protecting themselves, especially from their so-called caretakers, is not appropriate. (p. 77)

Furman (1987) recommends a slow, ongoing process of teaching children "ownership" of their bodies through careful supervision and responsive and responsible interactions with adults.

Jordan encourages important societal changes in teaching young children to resist or report their attackers, by looking closely at sexual abuse prevention programs to determine their developmental appropriateness, effectiveness, and possible negative side effects. This program should be only one part of a larger community-wide effort at prevention.

One of the most serious threats to children's safety is child abuse and neglect. According to the National Committee to Prevent Child Abuse, nearly 3 million children were reported abused and neglected in 1993, of whom an estimated 1,299 died.

How is one to teach children to protect themselves from strangers, abuse, and other frightening and negative situations (being lost, being alone) and yet instill in them that this is a pretty good world in which to live? Schools can help by educating young children, by offering educational information to parents, by providing before-and-after care for latch-key children, by encouraging parents and community members to establish block parent programs, providing parent centers, and involving parents in their child's school and education (Hatkoff, 1994). It will take a family, school, community, religious, state, and federal effort to recognize and report suspected child abusers: staff members, family members, neighbors, friends, strangers, community offenders—wherever they may be. One resource that may be helpful is Hoot and Bartkowiak (1994), a valuable listing of health and safety resources for making environments a bit safer for children and youth. The authors have a two-page quad-column list of safety resources including general resources, violence (general, gun, and media), drugs/alcohol, child abuse/at-risk children, pro-

grams (parenting, community service programs, and leadership), peer counseling, conflict resolution, and safety. Such a listing of names, addresses, and telephone numbers is invaluable for each and every child-care/education center, school classroom, and home.

Violence

In the June/July 1999 CDF Reports (Voice Archives) the following questions are posed: Why are guns the only unregulated consumer product in America? Why do we regulate toy guns, but not the real guns that kill a child every two hours? What is it going to take for us to stop this senseless neglect and child carnage?

A 1993 report published by the American Psychological Association stated: "There is absolutely no doubt that the higher levels of viewing on television are correlated with increased acceptance of aggressive attitudes and increased aggressive behavior. Children's exposure to violence in the mass media, particularly at young ages, can have harmful lifelong consequences."

A recent study of students in grades 7–12 showed that teenagers who feel "connected" to their schools and families are less likely to engage in risky or violent behavior. We cannot underestimate the importance of family, teachers, and faith communities, and we must nurture that feeling of "connectedness" very early. The importance of early childhood education, both for academic and social purposes, is crucial. Studies prove that early intervention and education for preschoolers not only sparks a love of learning, but also reduces the likelihood of violent behavior later on.

Educational Needs of Children Living with Violence

Children witness violence in their neighborhoods, in the media, and in places they go. Children who experience violence within their homes are at a further disadvantage. Abusive family environments influence children's problem-defining and

Facts and Figures

NAEYC Position Statement on Violence in the lives of Children (1996): NAEYC #588. This brochure suggests *specific resources for teachers and parents to teach children prosocial, nonviolent attitudes and behaviors*—including public policy actions to reduce violence; generate public outrage; allocate sufficient resources to the prevention of violence; support every child's right to a safe, nonviolent, and nurturing society; revitalize neighborhoods by ensuring peacekeeping and comprehensive delivery of human services, job training, health care, early childhood education programs, and parenting education; limit the availability of firearms and other weapons, especially their access to children; regulate children's television programming; prohibit corporal punishment in schools and all other programs for children.

- Children in the United States watch an average of three to five hours of television daily viewing an average of five to six violent acts per hour.
- "Only 35% of three- to eight-year-old children are read to by family members on a daily basis" (FYI, 1996 p. 25).
- "Only 10% of children's viewing time is spent watching children's television. The other 90% is spent watching programs designed for adults" (NAEYC, 1998).
- Research consistently identifies six problems associated with repeated viewing of media violence by young children (Horton & Simmer, 1998). Young children: (1) more likely will behave in aggressive/harmful ways to others; (2) may become less sensitive to pain and suffering of others and see violent behavior as normal; (3) may become more fearful of the world around them; (4) may use it as models of language development; (5) may limit their imagination; and (6) may become passive about their environment.

Following are excerpts from the National Television Violence Study (1996):

1. The context in which most violence is presented on television poses risks to viewers.
2. Perpetrators go unpunished in 73 percent of all violent scenes.
3. Negative consequences of violence are not often portrayed in violent programming.
4. One out of four violent interactions on television (25 percent) involves the use of a handgun.
5. On the positive side, television violence is usually not explicit or graphic.
6. There are some notable differences in the presentation of violence across television channels and television programs.

Recommendations: (based on the findings of this study and extensive research upon which this study is based):

For Parents: Watch television *with* your child, encourage critical evaluation of television content, use child's developmental age when making viewing selections, consider risks of viewing violence (aggressive attitudes and behaviors, fear, desensitization or loss of sympathy toward victims of violence, other).

(continued)

Facts and Figures (continued)

For the television community: Mainly a plea for more programs that avoid violence, an increase of powerful nonviolent heroes and characters, scheduling high violence during late-evening hours, better advisory and content codes, and limiting time devoted to sponsor, station, or network messages.

For policy and public interest leaders: recognize and consider the violent depictions that pose the greatest concern, consider technology to restrict access to inappropriate content, provide target audiences with specific and realistic actions for resolving conflicts peacefully, and (when possible) link antiviolence *public service announcements* (PSAs) to school-based or community audiences.

The latest data released in 1999 shows that in a single year (Ward, 1999, p. 2):

- 4,205 children and teens were killed by gunfire
- 2,562 were murdered by gunfire
- 1,262 committed suicide using a firearm
- 306 died from an accidental shooting
- 2,357 were white; 1,687 were black
- 84 were under 5 years of age

---

problem-solving behaviors. "These behaviors," states Craig (1992),

in turn, can affect both social competence and school achievement. . . . Parenting styles that include verbal and physical abuse are frequently linked with reduced competence of children. . . . The majority (of authors) link this type of parenting to a variety of neurological soft sign deficits (e.g., short attention span, impulsive behavior, heightened physical activity) as well as to impairments of intellectual functioning and language development. (p. 67)

And further:

. . . The impact on the self is simple yet profound. Children living with violence learn quickly that safety is best achieved through a "sensory muting" that allows them to mirror the preference of the caregiver at any given time. The price children pay is an absence of feeling and a sense of incompetence that stem from an inability to define the boundaries of the self and thereby to experience self-control.

This lack of differentiation limits all areas of development. . . . Abused children often develop symptoms of timidity, fear of strange places, and a pervasive fear of taking risks. (p. 18)

According to Craig (1992), management and educational instruction of children living in violent environments requires educators to

infuse the current curriculum with the consistency, predictability, safety, and sense of purpose that can accommodate the cognitive style of these children. Constructivist views of education, which make children active participants in their own learning, are important to the educational needs of children who live with violence. The lack of congruence between the life experience of these children and the reality assumed by public schools cannot be left unacknowledged. Life with violence leaves children without the internal control required to engage in independent inquiry in the absence of external support. For these children to be successful, teachers must orchestrate learning environments in which the discovery of competence is possible. (p. 70)

Facts and Figures

Of course, it would be simple if sharing toys were the biggest problems of young children. Many of them face much greater daily problems: real violence to themselves and their families, impoverished conditions, life-threatening health conditions, poverty, homelessness, and others.

- An estimated 2.7 million children were reported to child-protection agencies in 1991 as victims of neglect, physical abuse, sexual abuse, or emotional maltreatment; nationwide, the number of children reported abused or neglected has tripled since 1980 (Children's Defense Fund, 1992).

- Gun-related violence takes the life of an American child at least every 3 hours and the lives of at least 25 children—the equivalent of a classroom full—every 3 days. In 1990 alone, guns were used to kill 222 children under the age of 10 and 6,795 young people under the age of 25. Another 30 children are injured every day by guns (Edelman, 1999). Every day 100,000 children carry guns to school.

- In a national survey 91 percent of the responding teachers reported increased violence among children in their classrooms as a result of cross-media marketing of violent cartoons, toys, videos, and other licensed products (Carlsson-Paige & Levin, 1992).

- Today every fifth child lives in poverty—25 percent of children under the age of 6 (Children's Defense Fund, 1992).

- "Research demonstrates that children who are frequent viewers of violence on television are less likely to show empathy toward the pain and suffering of others and more likely to behave aggressively" (National Association for the Education of Young Children, 1993, p. 81).

- "The younger the child, the greater the threat of exposure to violence is to healthy development. Individuals who experience an initial trauma before the age of 11 were three times more likely to develop psychiatric symptoms than those who experience their first trauma as teens" (Garbarino et al., 1992, p. 70).

- Chronic exposure to violence can have serious developmental consequences for children including psychological disorders, grief and loss reactions, impaired intellectual development and social problems, truncated moral development, pathological adaptation to violence, and identification with the aggressor.

It is estimated that up to 80 percent of all children exposed to powerful stressors do not sustain developmental damage. Research indicates that certain factors contribute to the resilience of these children: (1) a child's individual characteristics and early life experiences; (2) a stable, emotional relationship with at least one parent or other significant adult; (3) an open, supportive educational climate; (4) parental model of behavior that encourages constructive coping with problems; and (5) social support from persons outside the family. The most important buffer is (6) a supportive relationship with parents. Schools and child-care programs can be vitally important support systems. (National Association for the Education of Young Children, 1993, p. 81).

❖ **Stimulator**

Block building is one of the activities set out for the day. A structure catches the interest of Child 1 and Child 2. At first their play is solitary but as each one becomes more involved in the play, their interests begin to combine. Talking and laughter take place as the play becomes more involved. Child 3 watches from a distance and then moves closer to the play. Not being invited to play immediately, Child 3 begins wandering through the blocks, makes a couple of undirected comments, and joins Child 4, who is looking at books nearby. Still not being involved with any of the children, Child 3 asks Child 4 to join in playing with some animals near the structure of the first two children. Half-heartedly, they begin to interact, but they notice the full-scale play of Child 1 and Child 2. Totally dissatisfied with being excluded, Child 3 picks up a long block, points it at Child 1 and 2 and says, "You let me play or I'll shoot down your tower." Child 4 feels trouble in the air and immediately withdraws into a far-away corner. Child 1 and Child 2 jump up to guard their structure and to defend themselves.

You are the nearest teacher. What do you do? Should you referee the situation? Should you wait for the children to work out their own problems? Should you have stepped in sooner? (The participants in this Stimulator have not been identified by sex, age, culture, or body structure—would it make a difference if you knew these characteristics?) Discuss the incident from the following points:

1. Using force to solve the problem (either child or teacher)

2. Removing Child 3 without further comment

3. Ignoring the situation, hoping someone else will solve it

4. Cajoling all the children

5. Beginning the building all over, inviting all four children to participate, showing them how to cooperate rather than confront

6. Telling Child 3 that guns are not allowed at school and just leaving him "hanging." ["The superhero is reminded that guns can hurt people and aren't allowed in the classroom, as if a pretend gun were real. This confuses children: It seems okay to pretend about nice things, but aggressive, powerful pretend is viewed as if it were real and is therefore unacceptable." (Gottschall, 1992, p. 15)]

❖ **Stimulator**

Note the different steps, reactions, and solutions. What does each child (and the teacher) learn in each circumstance?

What Caregivers Can Do

Caregivers are in a position to have a significant impact on the cognitive, social, and language development of children living with violence. Child misbehaviors can lead to academic frustration—as school failure accompanies histories of family violence. Caregivers cannot witness the violence in the home, which may be severe, but they can help children through violent situations at the center by being there for support and guidance through difficult situations.

Children in violent atmospheres feel unsafe and out of control. Levin (1994a) suggests ways to build peaceable classrooms and help children feel safe in violent times: "No amount of effort on our parts could ever fully counteract the devastating effects violence is having on children and society. But we cannot close our eyes. . . . Children should not have to carry the burden of keeping themselves safe from the dangers that surround them; this should be the job of adults" (p. 270). It is important to remember that people don't learn social lessons cognitively; they learn them affectively, by emotionally processing and anchoring lessons learned from intense experiences (Clark & Clark, 1992).

Influence of Media on Violence

In their study on long-term effects of repeated exposure to media violence in childhood, Huesmann and Miller (1994) summarize: Antisocial behavior results when a number of important factors converge. (1) No one factor is sufficient to produce long-term antisocial behavior. (2) Media violence is one potential contributor to children who eventually go on to develop aggressive patterns of behavior. (3) Observing violent television scenes can teach aggression because of the acceptance and reinforcement of such patterns. (4) Experimental studies have clearly demonstrated that under well-controlled conditions, the observation of violent scenes in the media causes children to behave more aggressively. (5) The amount of violent television is positively related to the child's current aggressivity. (6) Longitudinal studies provide additional support for the hypothesis that television violence viewing leads to the development of aggressive behavior but it is not the only cause of aggressive behavior. (7) The long-term effects are likely to be a result of the child who is reinforced in her own natural environment for displaying such aggressive behavior.

In an NAEYC publication, Horton and Zimmer (1994) provide a guide for parents regarding media violence and children, reminding parents, teachers, and broadcasters that children younger than age 7 are greatly influenced by what they see on television because they are unable to distinguish between fantasy and reality. Research consistently identifies three behaviors of children who watch television. They are more likely to behave in aggressive or harmful ways toward others, become less sensitive to the pain and suffering of others, and may become more fearful of the world around them. Further effects of repeated viewing of television violence can harm children's social development, limit models of good language development, and limit children's imaginations.

Efforts are being made to improve the quality and reduce the number of commercials on children's programs, and to increase the quality and amount of programming for children. [See Kessler, 1994; American Psychological Association Commission on Violence and Youth, 1993; Donnerstein et al., 1994. Other sources include *Coalition for Quality Children's Video*, 535 Cordova Road, Suite 456, Santa Fe, NM 87501. (505) 989-8076. Fax (505) 986-8477 and *National Foundation to Improve Television*, 60 State Street, Suite 3400, Boston, MA 02109. (617) 523-6353.]

In a published and adopted position statement on media violence in children's lives, NAEYC has committed to two actions: (1) "to decrease the extent of violence in all forms in children's lives by advocating for public policies and actions at the national level," and (2) "to enhance the ability of educators to help children cope with violence, and promote children's resilience, and assist families by improving professional practice in early childhood programs" (National Association for the Education of Young Children, 1993 p. 81).

Aggressive Behavior

"Children who tend to behave aggressively may choose to associate with children similar to themselves, thus setting up a 'vicious cycle' in which aggressive patterns are perpetuated. The primary aim of this study was to examine the roles of cliques in young children's aggressive behavior (*aggression* being broadly defined to include 'any behavior intended to hurt, annoy, or harass another child or to obtain objects, territory, or privileges')" (Farver, 1996, p. 68).

Findings: (a) a minority of children (generally four or five children; highly aggressive boys in groups of three or four) in each classroom was involved in a majority of the events; (b) aggressive preschoolers were not consistently rejected by their peers; rather they seemed to gravitate toward aggressive children who reciprocated their friendship; (c) children who were highly ranked in a particular social clique were the most likely to engage in aggressive incidents.

There were strong implications for teachers of young children: "teachers who move quickly to stop aggression may sometimes prevent children from developing their own strategies for dealing with peer's aggression. Perhaps it would be more effective to observe and then to strengthen the children's efforts to deal with aggressors—teachers may unwittingly reinforce the aggressive behavior of high-status children who are looked up to by lower-ranking members of the class. Thoughtful intervention in these early social patterns may help prevent reciprocal aggressive socialization and may guide young children's relationships in a prosocial direction" (Farver, 1996, p. 69).

Teasing and Bullying

"At any age, teasing and bullying are harmful and can create a classroom climate that negatively affects children's ability to learn and the teacher's ability to teach" (Ross, 1996). Therefore, it seems critical for teachers and parents to address this behavior in early childhood before it becomes ingrained.

The early childhood curriculum ensures many occasions for using a proactive approach to reducing teaching and bullying. Familiar activities—storytime, reading, meeting-time discussions, experience charts, drawings, art projects, creative story writing or dictation, puppet plays, charting, or graphing—all are avenues for exploring the topic of behaviors within the daily curriculum (Froschl & Sprung, 1999). Here are a few examples: talking about teasing and bullying, classroom rule making, noncompetitive games, and quieting activities.

Try involving parents. Share details on how children created their own rules; send a letter home suggesting parents practice "what if. . ."; or present some situations (real and imagined) and discuss various solutions to these problems.

Anger

Anger is believed to have three components (Lewis & Michaelson, 1983), including the emotional state, the expression, and the understanding of the emotion.

Emotional state: ". . . anger is an affective or arousal state or a feeling experienced when a goal is blocked or needs are frustrated. Children are likely to experience the emotional state of anger when they encounter an obstacle to attaining any significant goal" (Lewis et al., 1990). "Even the youngest children (including infants and toddlers) seem to sense a goal blockage, and such a realization is possible long before they can consciously reflect on the feeling of anger" (Campos et al., 1983, p. 784).

"The second component of anger is its expression. This unpleasant emotion is first expressed in infancy. Children who feel that an important goal has been blocked attempt to cope by expressing anger" (Karraker et al., 1994, p. 173).

"The third component of the anger experience is understanding—interpreting and evaluating—the emotion. . . . Children need guidance from teachers and parents first in understanding and then in managing their feelings of anger" (Marion, 1997, p. 64).

Implications for guiding children's expressions of anger:

1. Create a safe emotional climate—acknowledges a child's right to feel anger while prohibiting expression in destructive or hurtful ways.

2. Model responsible anger management—adults who are most effective in helping children manage anger model responsible anger management by acknowledging, accepting, and taking responsibility for their own anger in direct and nonaggressive ways.

3. Help children develop self-regulatory skills—adults use positive child guidance strategies gradually to transfer control of the self to children so they can develop healthy self-regulatory skills.

4. Encourage children to label feelings of anger—use your own words, a little or very angry, mad, irritated, annoyed, furious, upset, sad.

5. Encourage children to talk about anger-arousing interactions—listen without judging, evaluating, or ordering them to feel differently. . . . teachers can plan activities involving discussions about anger to teach more effective anger management skills—maybe use puppets.

6. Use appropriate books and stories to help children understand and manage anger. Follow-up with child-like discussions—avoid moralizing. (Ask your school or public librarian, your local book store or preschool teachers for some appropriate suggestions.)

7. Use role playing, puppets, pictures, or use incidents as they occur in your classroom to help the children recognize and manage their frustrations.

8. Foster friendships between girls and boys often. Avoid sex stereotyped ideas in your classroom.

9. Take every opportunity to help children learn about their own feelings and how these feelings relate to those of other children and adults. (Froschl & Sprung, 1999, p. 71).

Teachers and parents need to understand frustration and anger in children and help them to find more acceptable ways of expressing themselves or solving their problems. Young children need experience in recognizing, handling, and accepting their frustrations. They can learn coping behavior through practice, experience, and assistance from a loving and kind person.

"Early childhood teachers work with children during a period of great intellectual, physical, and emotional growth and learning. As teachers, they play a critical role in the positive socialization of children and have an optimum opportunity to influence families during children's formative years. All of these factors are important in addressing teasing and bullying behavior at the beginning of a child's educational experience" (Froschl & Sprung, 1999, p. 73).

Injuries

"56% of parents in the 1992 survey believed that they could prevent three fifths or more of children's serious injuries as compared to 42% in 1987. . . . Parents expressing high interest in receiving materials on child safety declined from 39% (1987) to 24% (1992). . . . Parents' and children's reliance on health professionals and teachers as sources of child safety information decreased significantly, with firefighters and police as the groups increasingly identified in this role. Parents reporting teachers as the group their children would listen to most about injury prevention decreased from 52% (1987) to 33% (1992)" (Mickalide, 1993; FYI, 1994, p. 3).

"Why should we be concerned about playground safety? Injuries are the leading cause of death in the United States for children older than 9 months. And most playground injuries—from scraped knees or cracked teeth to broken limbs or concussions—can be prevented" (McCracken, 1999).

Other Causes

"Sudden infant death syndrome (SIDS) is one of the leading causes of death for babies one month to one year of age, and we *can* take steps to prevent it. Because many babies are in our care, we who provide family child care services should know the right thing to do" (Shallcross, 1999, p. 70). See also Chapter 8.

Playground Safety

Guidelines for outdoor play for young children: Have adequate supervision. Make the playground attractive and fun! Set reasonable and appropriate limits that the children can understand and follow. Prevent injuries—but have a first-aid kit nearby. Offer choices to promote physical development, encourage friendships, and increase enjoyment. Enlist the children's aid to keep the playground appropriately clean, the equipment maintained, the areas interesting, and the yard tidy. If some areas of the playground are less used, how many ideas could you suggest (or recruit from the children) to stimulate new and active play? Children learn responsibility when they participate in their environment: appropriate cleanup (washing tricycles and wagons for a parade or sand toys for tomorrow), maintenance, use of equipment.

Children learn responsibility when they participate in appropriate cleanup and maintenance

 **Stimulator**

Here are some of the activities and equipment available for the 2- to 4-year-olds on the playground today. Help the children to enjoy being outdoors. Help them to be observant, creative, friendly, innovative, and happy!

Digging in the sand	Wheel toys	Climbers
Water and toys	Planting	Stick horses
Few housekeeping items	Usual pets	Riding trucks and cars
Reading in the shade	Swings	Personal imagination

How many teachers will you need on the playground to ensure safe, happy, and productive play for the 15 children? Which areas require closer supervision? Which areas can the children effectively manage themselves? What do you do if most of the children congregate in one area (you decide which area)? Are there some children who need more support than others? Can you try the "buddy" system for less experienced children? Suppose this is an "unusual day" where the children are all happy, involved, and cooperating? What is your role? (Anticipate the day when children are all sad, listless, uncooperative, and negative! What is your role then?)

activities, such as gathering sticks and papers. Keep trash cans handy for routine pickups. With supervision children can rake grass and sand wood. A weekly fun wash can clean riding vehicles and sand toys.

Playgrounds must be designed and installed to be safe places for young children. Materials and toys not in present use should be stored properly (see McCracken, 1999).

Equipment

1. Hazardous equipment, such as things that pinch, crush, splinter, cut, or puncture, should be carefully supervised or stored away from children when not in use.

2. Slides and climbing equipment should have a large top deck and handrails.

3. Holes can be drilled in tires to drain out moisture and prevent insect breeding.

4. Climbing equipment should be carefully selected.

5. Outdoor equipment should be age- and skill-appropriate.

6. Children with special needs should be able to use the playground with few modifications or with some assistance.

7. Some pieces of equipment will need resilient surfaces for "landing zones" (shred-

ded pine bark, sand, wood fiber, etc.). The height of the equipment will determine the depth of the cushion.

CHAPTER SUMMARY

1. Centers take a serious responsibility in caring for children. The safety and health of the children begins before they arrive at the center and must be of prime importance, requiring cooperation of home and school.

2. The teacher has many opportunities to promote safety during a usual day—some planned, some spontaneous.

3. The center must have written and enforced safety goals for the safety of children, staff, and families based on state, local, federal, and organizational requirements.

4. Safety in child care has similarities and difference with home care.

5. Curriculum, routines, and all activities must be based on safety factors. Some activities require special monitoring (outdoor play, art and food experiences, animals, etc.).

6. Emergencies should be handled promptly, carefully, professionally, and with compassion. Each classroom should be equipped with first-aid information, a first-aid kit, and backup procedures to handle emergency situations.

7. Safety features for general indoor facilities include ratio of children to adults, supervision, arrangement of space and activities, noise reduction, lighting/heating, restrooms, proper selection of toys and activities, and other considerations specific to each room.

8. Safety features for general outdoor environment are similar to indoor facilities (ratio of children to adults, supervision, selection of toys and activities, special considerations, etc.). Differences occur because of generally increased momentum of the children, climatic changes, danger of climbing apparatus, surfacing, physical layout of the playground, and other *expected* or *unexpected* activity of the children. Children often feel more adventurous in outdoor play. This is a time when teachers need to focus completely on the children! Adult conversations and relaxation are better kept for another setting!

9. In addition to safety in child-care settings, one must be aware of, prevent, and report to proper officials, the incidence of abuse, violence, aggressive behavior, teasing and bullying, anger, injuries, and other occurrences that impair the health/safety of young children and families.

PARTICIPATORS

1. Walk through a classroom, outdoor area, or both, noting possible hazards that need immediate attention. Devise a method of reporting problems and following through on their repair or replacement. Or select one of the following:

   a. Conduct an inspection of a child-care center or family day care. Be friendly, positive, and helpful!

   b. Arrange to accompany a licensing inspector, a building/fire inspector, and a health inspector to a child-care site.

   c. Discuss how to correct safety problems in a child-care center when expense is involved.

   d. Discuss how routine surveillance for safety hazards can be maintained.

   e. Describe an emergency situation from a real experience or a scenario from the newspaper.

   f. Make a tour through your own apartment or home and determine any possible hazards regarding your safety. Make a list of things that need to be corrected *immediately, soon,* and set a schedule to correct them.

2. Observe parents as they drop off and pick up children at a center. Note the parents' safety precautions. Compare these with the policies of the center.

3. Note the safety/emergency information posted in each classroom. Is there a procedure to follow in case of emergency? Are phone numbers of fire department, police department, ambulance, paramedics, hospital, clinic, and other important places posted? Is a list of emergency numbers readily available for each child (parent at home/work, alternate person, special arrangements)?

4. Check to see that each classroom has a first-aid chart, procedure for evacuation, and procedures for treating the most common and most serious injuries.

5. Watch children playing at a center or park. Identify which areas (or activities) need closer supervision than others.

6. Ask a teacher in which cooking experiences have the children participated. Follow up by asking what guidelines or precautions were used for the safety and health of the children, how much the children participated, and how the cleanup was initiated.

7. Plan an emergency drill (fire, flood, earthquake, etc.) for young children. What precautions would you need to take so as not to frighten the children or cause them to be nonchalant when drills occur?

8. Make a checklist for each of the main topics in this chapter (routines, emergencies, indoor facilities, etc.). How many of these items are

presently in force? How could you initiate all of the items for a more safe environment for the children?

9. *Routines.* Ask yourself about the following:

   a. Safety procedures between the parking lot and the center

   b. Hand washing before eating and after using the toilet

   c. Suggesting change of pace activities (from active to quiet or vice versa)

   d. Provisions for children who become ill at the center or who are on medications

   e. Inviting children to enter group activities (for food, stories, etc.)

10. *Emergencies:* Ask yourself these questions:

   a. How frequently do incidental accidents occur?

   b. Is there a particular pattern for accidents (time of day, same children, type of play, etc.)?

   c. How should *minor* injuries be handled and what first-aid items are readily available?

   d. How should *major* injuries be handled?

   e. How should one report minor and major injuries?

   f. How adequate is the supervision of all children at all times?

   g. If an emergency occurs, what procedures are the children and staff to follow (what to do, where to go)?

   h. Where can one find a current list of emergency numbers, parental numbers, and enrolled children?

   i. Which caregivers are certified in first aid and CPR?

   j. What are the specific roles for each caregiver in case of emergency: fire, injuries, disasters? Are specific routes and routines known and practiced?

   k. Where are first-aid kits located and what do they contain?

   l. How often are smoke detectors and alarms checked?

   m. How could you prepare and present easy first-aid lessons to the children in your classroom?

   n. How can you teach children about "environmental first-aid" (refuse, reuse, recycle, and respect).

11. *Indoor facilities:* Ask yourself these questions:

   a. What is the required indoor space for the number of children currently enrolled in your center?

   b. How is the indoor area divided (for children, for staff, etc.)?

   c. What changes could be made in the traffic patterns so that areas would be more safe for children and adults?

   d. What safety features have been incorporated in the facility to protect children from unnecessary danger? Could you suggest further measures?

   e. Are exits clearly marked and free from clutter?

   f. Are the premises checked frequently to remove hazards and to note and remove items that need repair?

12. *Indoor play:* Ask yourself these questions:

   a. Are the areas arranged for the most constructive play of the children? If you were revising the indoor space, what changes would you make? Why? (See Chapter 10.)

   b. Are compatible activities placed near each other? Are incompatible activities separated from each other?

   c. In what condition are the toys and equipment that are provided for the children's use? How appropriate is the variety (too much or not enough of a certain type)?

   d. What provisions are made for children to play individually to further personal endeavors or to join cooperative play if that is their desire?

   e. Do toys and activities promote constructive rather than destructive play?

f. Is there adequate supervision—teachers neither ignoring nor consuming the children's play?

g. How easily do children have access to toys/materials for getting them out and putting them away? How is this a safety factor?

h. Why are some activities available most of the time and others only on special occasions?

i. How are seasonal, holiday, and/or special activities introduced to the children? How do they involve safety?

j. Frequently make a casual, walk-through assessment of your center (or another center) to see how well it measures up to the items discussed above. Suggest a regular *serious* periodic check. Make a checklist for a comparison of safety from one time to another.

13. *Outdoor facilities:* Ask yourself these questions:

a. How much outdoor space is required for the number of children in this center?

b. Are the activities arranged for easy supervision by teachers and easy access by children?

c. What are the safety features of the playground?

d. Is the physical layout of the playground attractive and void of dangers to children (poisonous vegetation, hazards, human and animal intruders, refuse, etc.)? There is a good chart of common poisonous vegetation in Marotz and coworkers (1993, p. 165).

e. How does the enclosure of the playground provide for safety of children as well as aesthetic beauty?

14. *Outdoor play:* Ask yourself these questions:

a. How accessible and adequate is the outdoor storage for movable items by children and adults?

b. What are the safety features of the playground?

c. How adequate of provision is there for a variety of large muscle activities?

d. Will children be stimulated to engage in private or cooperative activities as their moods direct?

e. Is there adequate supervision for all areas and all types of activities? How would the teacher respond if an emergency happened on the playground?

f. What encouragement is given for children to get out and put away their outdoor toys?

g. How do children respond to permanent equipment? To moveable equipment? Are there preferences?

h. How do teachers introduce special pieces of equipment or activities? Is this procedure too adult-oriented?

i. What seasonal, holiday, or special activities can be introduced on the playground? How do children respond?

j. Can playground gates and doors be opened easily in case of emergency but remain secure from children opening them accidentally?

15. *Curriculum:* Ask yourself these questions:

a. Are certain activities used too frequently, supervised less, and taken for granted by children? If so, what safety measures should be taken?

b. When special activities (seasonal, holiday, etc.) are used, should special instruction, supervision, or precautions be taken? Give some examples.

c. How can accidents be prevented when using wheel toys inside the classroom or on the playground?

d. What "creative" materials could be harmful to young children? What are some good substitutes?

e. What precautions would you suggest for a teacher who wanted to introduce cooking (or food preparation) in a classroom of preschool children?

f. How many science experiences can you think of that would be appropriate for young children? How can a teacher be assured that these experiences would be appropriate and nonharmful?

g. Should a teacher discourage spontaneous opportunities or eliminate planned experience because of fear of failure or danger? Outline some precautions to follow in both types of activities.

h. What are some guidelines to follow when inviting a guest into your classroom? Relate your answer to interest and education of young children as well as satisfaction for both children and guest.

i. What are some safety precautions when bringing animals into the classroom or in caring for pets?

j. How can the use of table toys (puzzles, peg boards, fitting toys, etc.) encourage safety in activities?

REFERENCES

American Psychological Association Commission on Violence and Youth. 1993. *Violence and youth: Psychology's response* (Vol. 1). Washington, DC: Author.

Aronson, S. D. 1992. Is playground safety being taken seriously? *Exchange,* 85, May, 47–48.

Aronson, S. S. 1989. Injury prone children. *Exchange,* April.

Aronson, S. S. 1990. A playground surface question for Dr. Sue. *Exchange,* 74, June, 54.

Aronson, S. S. 1991. *Health and safety in child care.* New York: HarperCollins.

Campos, J., Barrett, K., Lamb, M., Goldsmith, H., & Stenberg, C. 1983. Socio-emotional development. Infancy and developmental psycho-biology. In M. Haith & J. Campos, (Eds.) *Handbook of Child Psychology,* (pp. 783–915). New York: Wiley.

Carlsson-Paige, N., & Levin, D. B. 1992. Making peace in violent times: A constructivist approach to conflict resolution. *Young Children,* 48(1), 4–13.

Chang, A., Lugg, M., & Nebedum, A. 1989. Injuries among preschool children enrolled in day-care centers. *Pediatrics,* 83(2), 272–277.

Children's Defense Fund. 1992. 25 E Street, NW, Washington, DC 20001; (202) 628-8787.

Children's Defense Fund. 2000. Http://childrens defense.org/voice.html.

Clark, L., Dewolf, S., & Clark, C. 1992. Teaching teachers to avoid having culturally assaultive classrooms. *Young Children,* 47(5), 4–9.

Craig, S. E. 1992. The educational needs of children living with violence. *Phi Delta Kappan,* 74(1), 67–71.

Dempsey, J., Strickland, E., & Frost, J. 1993. What's going on out here? An evaluation tool for your playground? *Exchange,* 91, May, 41–45.

Donerstein, E., Slaby, R., & Eron, L. 1994. The mass media and youth violence. In L. Eron & J. Gentry (Eds.). *Violence and youth: Psychology's response* Vol 2. Washington, DC: American Psychological Association.

Edelman, M. W. 1993. *Curbing the epidemic violence.* Testimony prepared for the Joint Senate House Hearing on Keeping Children Safe, 103d Congress, first session, March 10.

Farver, J. M. 1996. Aggressive behavior in preschoolers' social networks: Do birds of a feather flock together? Today's research, tomorrow's practices. Highlights from *Early Childhood Research Quarterly,* 11(3), 533–550. *Young Children,* March, 68–69.

Feeney, S., & Kipnis, K. 1992. *Code of ethical conduct & statement of professional commitment.* Washington, DC: NAEYC.

Fiene, R. n.d. *National health & safety performance standards weighted key indicators (APHA/AAP/WICL).* Harrisburg, PA: Pennsylvania State University.

Froschl, M., & Sprung, B. 1999. On purpose: Addressing teasing and bugging in early childhood. *Young Children,* March, 70–73.

Frost, J., & Sweeney, T. B. 1996. *Causes and prevention of playground injuries and litigation.* Olney, MD: Association for Childhood Education International.

Furman, F. 1987. More protections, fewer directions. *Young Children,* 42(5), 5–7.

FYI. 1994. Parents' perceptions and practices concerning childhood injury. 1994. *Young Children,* March, p. 3.

FYI. 1996. TV-turnoff week—April 24–30, 1996. *Young Children,* March, p. 25.

Garbarino, J., Dubrow, N., Kostelney, K., & Pardo, C. 1992. *Children in danger: Coping with the effects of community violence.* San Francisco: Jossey-Bass.

Gillis, J., & Pise, M. E. 1993. *The childwise catalog: A consumer's guide to buying the safest and best products for your children* (3rd ed.). New York: HarperCollins.

Gottschall, S. M. 1992. Guns, ghosts, and monsters: menace or meaning in aggressive play? *Day Care and Early Education,* 20(2) 14–16.

Hatkoff, A. 1994. Safety and children: How schools can help. *Childhood Education,* 70(3), 283–286.

Hayes, C. D., Palmer, J. L., & Zaslow, M. J. (Eds.). 1990. *Who cares for America's children? Child-care policy for the 1990s.* Washington, DC: National Academy Press.

Health and safety tips: Emergency planning for early childhood programs. 1991a. *Young Children,* 46(4), May.

Health and safety tips: Toward safer, exciting playground environments. 1991b. Sept. *Young Children,* 46(6).

Hoot, J. L., & Bartkowiak, E. T. 1994. Safety resources. *Childhood Education,* 70(5), 287–288.

Horton, J., & Simmer, J. 1994. *Media Violence and children: A guide for parents.* NAEYC #585. Washington, DC: NAEYC.

Huesmann, L. R., & Miller, L. S. 1994. Long-term effects of repeated exposure to media violence in childhood. In L. R. Heusmann (ed.). *Aggressive behavior: Current perspectives* (pp. 153–182). New York: Plenum.

Jordan, N. H. 1993. Sexual abuse prevention programs in early childhood education: A caveat. *Young Children,* 48(6), Sept. 76–79.

Karraker, K., Lake, M., & Parry, T. 1994. Infant coping with everyday stressful events. *Merrill-Palmer Quarterly,* 40(2), 171–189.

Kendrick, A. S., Kaufmann, R., & Messenger, K. P. (Eds.). 1988. *Healthy young children: A manual for programs.* Washington, DC: National Association for the Education of Young Children.

Kessler, B. 1994, July. Coalition hopes to improve TV for kids. *Dallas Morning News.*

Kritchevsky, S., & Prescott E., with Walling, L. 1997. Planning environments for young children, physical space (2nd ed., ninth printing, 1999), NAEYC #115.

Lamorey, S., Robinson, E. B., Rowland, B. H., & Coleman, M. 1999. *Latchkey kids.* (2nd ed.). Thousand Oaks, CA: Sage Publishing.

Levin, D. E. 1994a. Annual theme. Building a peaceable classroom: Helping young children feel safe in violent times. *Childhood Education,* 70(5), 267–273.

Levin, D. E. 1994b. *Teaching young children in violent times: Building a peaceable classroom.* Cambridge, MA: Educators for Social Responsibility.

Levin, R. 1991, your center needs an emergency/crisis plan! *Exchange,* 78, May/June, 34–37.

Lewis, M., & Michalson, L. 1983. *Children's emotions and moods.* New York: Plenum.

Marion, M. 1997. Guiding young children's understanding and management of anger. Research in Review. *Young Children,* Nov., 62–67.

Marotz, L. R., Cross, M. Z., & Rush, J. M. 1993. *Health, safety & nutrition for the young child* (3rd ed.). Albany, NY: Delmar.

Mccracken, J. B. 1999. Playgrounds: Safe and sound. NAEYC #552. Washington, DC: NAEYC.

Mickalide, A. D. 1993. Parents' perception and practices concerning childhood injury: 1987 versus 1992. *Childhood Injury Prevention Quarterly,* 4(4), 29–32. Washington DC: Children's National Medical Center, National SAFE KIDS Campaign.

Morris, S. 1991. Indoor climbing structure buying guide. *Exchange,* 79, May/June, 55–58.

NAEYC. 1991. *Accreditation criteria and procedures of the National Academy of Early Programs,* (rev. ed.). Washington, DC: Author.

NAEYC. 1993. NAEYC position statement on violence in the lives of children. *Young Children,* 48(6), 80–84.

NAEYC. 1994. Washington Update: President moves closer to a detailed welfare reform plan, while congress takes action on legislation affecting children's programs. *Young Children,* 49(2), 19.

NAEYC. 1997a. NAEYC position statement on the prevention of child abuse in early childhood programs and the responsibilities of early childhood professionals to prevent child abuse. *Young Children,* March, 42–46.

NAEYC. 1997b. *Preparing for illness: A joint responsibility for parents and caregivers* (rev.)

NAEYC. 1998. Media violence and children: A guide for parents. NAEYC #585. Washington, DC: Author.

National Committee to Prevent Child Abuse. 1995. *Annual survey of incidence of child abuse.* Chicago: Author.

National Television Violence Study. 1996: Key findings and recommendations. *Young Children,* March, 54–55.

NICHD. 1996. Characteristics of infant child care: Factors contributing to positive caregiving. NICHD Early Childhood Care Research Network. *ECQR,* 11(3), 269–306.

Playground surfacing and equipment standards. 1989. American Society for Testing Materials Committee F-08, 1916 Race St., Philadelphia, PA 19103.

Reynolds, S. W., & Strickland, J. 1991. Buyer's guide to child care liability: Discover what's under the cover! *Exchange,* 77, Jan./Feb., 56–58.

Ross, D. M. (1996). *Childhood bullying and teasing: What school personnel, other professionals, and parents can do.* Alexandria, VA: American Counseling Association.

Shallcross, M. A. 1999. Family child care homes need health and safety training and an emergency rescue system. *Young Children,* Sept. 70–73.

Shaw, L. 1987. Designing playgrounds for able and disabled children. In C. Weinstein & T. David (Eds.), *Spaces for children. The built environment and child development* (pp. 187–216). New York: Plenum.

Slaby, R. G., Roedell, W. D. Arezzo, A. & Hendrix, K. 1995. *Early violence prevention. tools for teachers of young children.* NAEYC #325. Washington, DC: National Association for the Education of Young Children.

Snow, C. W., Teleki, J. K., Cline, D. M., & Dunn, K. 1992. Is day care safe? A review of research on accidental injuries. *Day Care and Early Education,* 19(3), 28–31.

Strickland, J., & Levbarg, M. 1990, Teacher aides and other dangerous instruments. *Exchange,* 73, June, 37–43.

U. S. Department of Health and Human Services. 1996 National Center on Child Abuse and Neglect. *Child maltreatment 1994: Reports from the states to the National Center on Child Abuse and Neglect.* Washington, DC: Government Printing Office.

Ward, J. M. 1999. Children and guns: A Children's Defense Fund report on children dying from gunfire in America. Children's Defense Fund, 25 E Street, NW, Washington, DC 20001. Phone: (202) 628–8787. Fax: (202) 662–3550. *www.childrensdefense.org.*

Weiser, M. G. 1982. *Group care and education of infants and toddlers.* St. Louis: C. V. Mosby.

Wells, S., Davis, N., Dennis, K., Chipman, R., Sandt, C., & Liss, M. 1995. *Effective screening of child care and youth service workers.* Washington, DC: American Bar Association Center on Children and the Law.

Zeece, P. D., & Graul, S. K. 1993, Play, grounds for play: Sound, safe, and sensational. *Day Care and Early Education,* 20(4), 23–27.

Resources

For further information contact:

American Alliance for Health, Physical Education, Recreation, and Dance
1900 Association Drive
Reston, VA 22091
http://www.aahperd.org

The Arts & Crafts Materials Institute, Inc.
715 Boylston Street
Boston, MA 02116
(617) 266-6800

Back to Sleep Campaign
For free material, contact Ruth Dubois
National Institute of Child Health and Human Development
Phone 301-435-3457
or call the campaign's toll-free number,
800-505-CRIB;
or check the website
http://www.nih.gov/nichd.

Center for Safety in the Arts
5 Beckman Street
New York, NY 10038
(212) 227-6220

Center for Workforce Preparation. *On target: Effective parent involvement programs.*
U. S. Chamber of Commerce
P. O. Box 1200
Washington, DC 20013
$14.00. This report of the center identifies 21 promising initiatives reflecting a new-found appreciation for linking the well-being of children to the success of business.

Centers for Disease Control and Prevention.
1600 Clifton Road, NE
Atlanta, GA 30333.
(404) 639–3311

Children's Safety Network
38th & R Streets, NW
Washington, DC 20057
(202) 625-8400

The National Center on Accessibility
5020 State Road 67 North
Martinsville, IN 46151
http://www.indiana.edu/_nca/

National Foundation to Improve Television
60 State Street, Suite 3400
Boston, MA 020109
(617) 523-6365

The National Program for Playground Safety
University of Northern Iowa
School for Health, Physical Education, and Leisure Services
Cedar Falls, IA 50614-0618
http://www.uni.edu/playground

National SAFE KIDS Campaign
111 Michigan Avenue, NW
Washington, DC 20016
(202) 939-4993

National Safety Council
444 N. Michigan Avenue
Chicago, IL 60611
http:www.nsc.org/lrs/lib/fs/home/plgrdgen.htm

Pennsylvania Chapter of the American Academy of Pediatrics & Early Childhood Education Linkage System. 1997. *Model child care health policies* (rev. ed.), Washington, DC: NAEYC.

U.S. Consumer Product Safety Commission (CPSC)
Washington, DC 20207
800-638-2772
http://www.cpsc.gov/cpscpub/pubs/rec_sfy.html

1992. C. C. Tower. U.S. Department of Health and Human Services, National Center on Child Abuse, and Neglect. *The role of educators in the prevention and treatment of child abuse and neglect: The user manual series.* DHHS publication No. (ACF) 92-30172.

U. S. Department of Education. *Employers, families, and education: Promoting family involvement in learning.* Information Resource Center
Room 2421, 600 Independence Avenue, S.W.
Washington DC 20013-1200.

Chapter 10

Planning Space and Purchasing Equipment

Guide for Readers

❖ *Good planning of space contributes to the child's ability to develop good personal characteristics and habits.*

❖ *Careful attention should be paid to the indoor environment, such as density, lighting, color, texture, size, storage, and type of space.*

❖ *Indoor space must be provided for teaching, support areas, administration, and auxiliary areas.*

❖ *Outdoor areas must consider different types of play, storage, and weather.*

❖ *Guidelines for selecting toys, materials, and equipment for young children can save money, provide versatility, and increase children's safety, health, and imagination.*

❖ *There are safety checks for equipping a center.*

❖ *The environment should be appropriate for children with and without disabilities.*

❖ *Proper maintenance of indoor and outdoor facilities can help reduce accidents and costs.*

What catches the eye of a child and pulls him into an activity? Does it change from day to day—and child to child? The amount, placement, and use of equipment gives children clues as to what they are to do and how they are to do it. Is it a quiet or solitary involvement—or is it group and language oriented?

This chapter has five main sections: (1) general principles, (2) indoor space, (3) outdoor space, (4) criteria for selecting toys, materials, and equipment, and (5) use of computers (technology) with young children. These categories are subdivided as appropriate to discuss the center's needs, planning, design, use of space, and individual characteristics of the children.

In planning the efficient use of space, include total indoor and outdoor center property; classrooms, supporting areas, administrative space, auxiliary space, outdoor play areas, storage, parking, and additional areas. Some areas are used mostly by children, some only by adults, and some are shared by children and adults.

The selection, variety, and upkeep of toys and equipment are a vital part of space planning. The purchase of equipment is generally based on philosophical, goal orientation, financial, geographical, and personal considerations.

GENERAL PRINCIPLES

Space needs must be analyzed carefully. In addition to personal preference, one must consider regulations related to zoning, fencing, safety, and health of all involved. The director should carefully review the philosophy and guidelines of the program to determine what space and equipment is needed to fulfill these requirements, a point reiterated by Rambusch (1982, p. 72): "the more all-embracing the program's goals, the more complex the planning and execution of an appropriate physical environment become." The center should provide an environment that helps children develop appropriately, brings contentment to the parents, and fulfills the staff. There must also be consideration for their health and safety, the flow of traffic, opportunities for independence

and growth, and the overall aesthetic character of the center. The facilities should always serve the purpose of the program and people—not an adaptation of the program to the physical properties of the building. To a great extent housing determines the quality of an early childhood program and needs to encompass the whole of the center: (1) transitions to and from the home, (2) children's activity rooms, (3) supporting spaces (lockers, resource rooms, changing areas/restrooms, feeding/dining areas, resting areas, isolation), (4) adult areas (parent reception area and lounge; staff working and resting areas), and (5) the outdoor space. Careful attention needs to be given to each individual area and how working/playing at the center is an overlapping and coordinating function.

Whether considering indoor or outdoor space, keep in mind the Americans with Disabilities Act (ADA), signed into law on July 26, 1990, which prohibits discrimination on the basis of disability in employment, public services, transportation, public accommodations—including many services operated by private entities. Title III of the legislation includes within the definition of public accommodation: "a park, zoo, amusement park, or other place of recreation"; a school, including nursery schools; a day-care center; and a gymnasium, health spa, or "other places of exercise or recreation" (Tinsworth & Kramer, 1990, p. 21). For young children, it means being educated in the least restrictive environment. Guidelines are provided for facilities, playgrounds, curriculum, and teaching. For additional information, refer to federal or state guidelines, organizations who support young children [National Association for the Education of Young Children (NAEYC), Association for Childhood Education International (ACEI), etc.], or other available sources.

To a great extent and without careful attention of adults, the housing can determine the center program—what activities can be done, how people will interact with each other, the traffic pattern, and unforseen consequences. This must not happen! The philosophy of the program and the ages/number of the children should be the first consideration. Programs and activities should not be dictated by the size, location, floor plan, or other aspects of the building! Before land or a building is purchased, leased, or renovated, it must be determined whether it meets regulations (or can be brought into compliance) and whether it meets the needs of children and families. Such things as building materials, surrounding areas (industrial or commercial), and traffic flow can enhance the site as a center for young children or discourage its consideration. According to Hayes and coworkers (1990), "Research raises the possi-

bility that more adequate space and physical design in child-care settings may be linked with positive caregiver and child behaviors. However, further research is needed to examine the casual directions of these findings."

Directors and administrators will be involved in acquiring, arranging, decorating, remodeling, distributing, maintaining, evaluating, and perhaps trading or disposing of space. In order to address these tasks effectively, one needs a combination of education, psychology, architecture, interior decoration, finance, and personal characteristics of patience and cooperation.

❖ Stimulator

Using the floor plan below, identify how you would modify an "old" existing house into a workable facility for 3- to 5-year-olds attending a part-day play group. Label the activities to be used in each of the rooms. How will you provide for safety, supervision, and freedom? How many children would this facility accommodate?

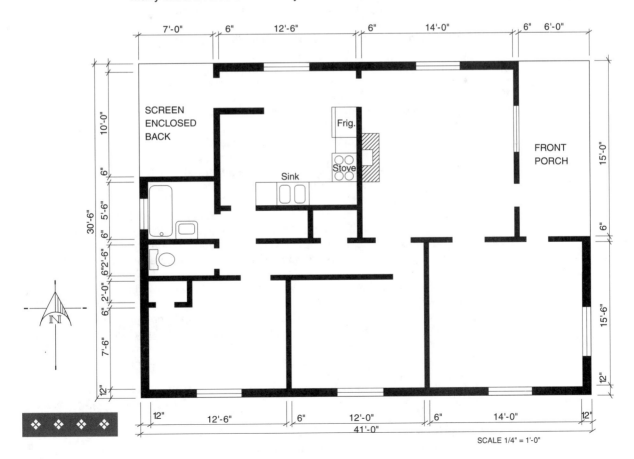

The type of program, ages of the children, how much time they spend in the center, the needs and abilities of the children (infants and toddlers have different needs than preschoolers), and other factors will dictate what areas and spaces are needed. Although builder-planners can make suggestions and perform the work, directors must remember that it is they—not interior designers or architects—who know the needs of children and what is important in making a care facility functional. An architect, designing a preschool for a university in the western United States, insisted that the aesthetics of the outdoor sheds was more important than their function.

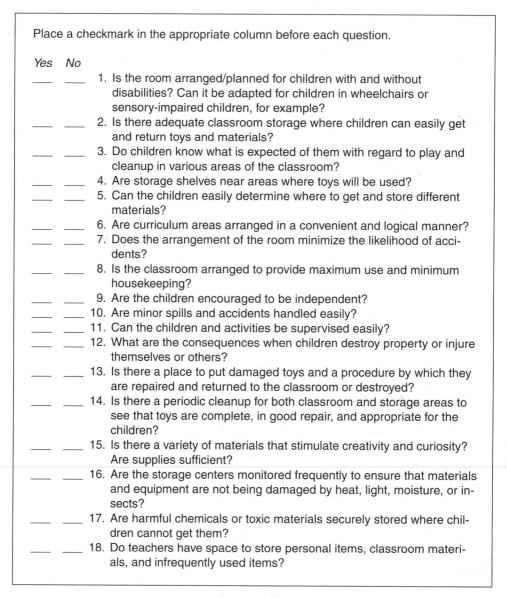

Place a checkmark in the appropriate column before each question.

Yes   No

_____ _____ 1. Is the room arranged/planned for children with and without disabilities? Can it be adapted for children in wheelchairs or sensory-impaired children, for example?

_____ _____ 2. Is there adequate classroom storage where children can easily get and return toys and materials?

_____ _____ 3. Do children know what is expected of them with regard to play and cleanup in various areas of the classroom?

_____ _____ 4. Are storage shelves near areas where toys will be used?

_____ _____ 5. Can the children easily determine where to get and store different materials?

_____ _____ 6. Are curriculum areas arranged in a convenient and logical manner?

_____ _____ 7. Does the arrangement of the room minimize the likelihood of accidents?

_____ _____ 8. Is the classroom arranged to provide maximum use and minimum housekeeping?

_____ _____ 9. Are the children encouraged to be independent?

_____ _____ 10. Are minor spills and accidents handled easily?

_____ _____ 11. Can the children and activities be supervised easily?

_____ _____ 12. What are the consequences when children destroy property or injure themselves or others?

_____ _____ 13. Is there a place to put damaged toys and a procedure by which they are repaired and returned to the classroom or destroyed?

_____ _____ 14. Is there a periodic cleanup for both classroom and storage areas to see that toys are complete, in good repair, and appropriate for the children?

_____ _____ 15. Is there a variety of materials that stimulate creativity and curiosity? Are supplies sufficient?

_____ _____ 16. Are the storage centers monitored frequently to ensure that materials and equipment are not being damaged by heat, light, moisture, or insects?

_____ _____ 17. Are harmful chemicals or toxic materials securely stored where children cannot get them?

_____ _____ 18. Do teachers have space to store personal items, classroom materials, and infrequently used items?

Figure 10–1 Checklist for indoor equipment and materials.

He insisted the sheds be no higher than the brick wall surrounding the playground. Now every time an adult goes into or out of the sheds, it is necessary to crouch down. How much better it would have been to locate the sheds where adults could walk into and out of them. And some interior designers may insist on certain color or pattern combinations—even those that detract from the functional use of the space.

Good planning of space contributes to (1) children becoming independent, competent, dependable, supportive, and educated; (2) security for both children and adults; (3) self-discipline; (4) a positive atmosphere; (5) tasks being accomplished easily; and (6) a peaceful and aesthetic environment. Keep in mind how children are expected to behave; the traffic patterns; whether play is to be cooperative or individual (group or private); how materials and areas are to be set up and cleaned up, and by whom; the format of the daily schedule; whether the children's projects are to be displayed; where children store daily projects and personal items (change of clothing); and the types of play (imitative, explorative, constructive, social).

The National Association for the Education of Young Children (1991) addresses minimum footage; activity definitions; space for infants, toddlers, and preschoolers; age-appropriate materials and equipment; individual and private spaces for children; sound-absorbing materials; and outdoor surfaces.

Physical properties of the facilities that require attention include density, lighting, color, texture, and size, with consideration of the different requirements for teaching, support-area, and administrative space (see Figure 10–1).

DENSITY

Density refers to the number of people and the size of the space they occupy. It can be high (many people in a crowded space) or low (few people in a spacious setting). In child care, the goal is to have sufficient space for a specific number of people, taking into account the ages of the people, their particular use of the space, and the reasons for which they gather.

Inasmuch as physical environments affect mood and work habits, the total design of the center will influence attitude and productivity. Jorde (1982) warned: "Arrangements that are stressful, harmful, or otherwise unpleasant can result in costly management problems as well as excessive absenteeism, employee turnover, and job burnout" (p. 149). Too little space, or high density causes children to "engage in more acts of aggressive behavior. But it is possible to have too much space. When the density is too low, more than 50 square feet per child, children wander aimlessly, supervision is poorer, and accidents happen," continues Jorde (p. 167). High-quality space use encourages children and teachers to be sensitive, friendly, cooperative, respectful, helpful, and congenial. Low-quality space use increases noise level, disruptive behavior, tiredness, irritability, and arbitrary management procedures of teachers (Kritchevsky et al., 1969). A well-designed classroom decreases aggressive behavior, wasted motion, confusion, and frustration. Researchers have found, and child-care workers agree, that there is a correlation between density and behavior.

While many states use 35 square feet per child as the *minimum* square footage in licensing regulations (NAEYC Information Service, 1989), it is considered adequate for infants and toddlers (Lally et al., 1986), but for older children in programs that require extra activity places, 40 to 60 square feet per child would be more adequate (NAEYC Information Service, 1989). Note that the minimum square footage of the room should be *exclusive* of sinks, lockers, storage cabinets, and other permanent fixtures.

Prescott and David (1977) report a marked increase of negative and idle behavior in situations with a high density of children and few resources. They further report positive and constructive behavior in day-care centers with low density (of at least 48 square feet per child) and plenty of resources. The quality and quantity of resources should be increased if high density is unavoidable. In addition, Shapiro (1975) found that some lower density centers (over 50 square feet per child) used space ineffectively.

The National Association for the Education of Young Children (1991) also notes: "Small group sizes and lower staff-child ratios have been found to be strong predictors of compliance with indicators of quality such as positive interactions among staff and children and developmentally appropriate curriculum" (p. 41). Thus, high density and overcrowding are viewed as negative effects on behavior. Researchers indicate that scale or density is particularly relevant in a child development center. Teachers have discovered that when space is arranged so that children are actually working in small groups, the goals for the group and individuals are further facilitated. As reported by Hildebrand (1994), "social psychologists also indicate that group unity decreases as the size of the group increases. They find that when there is a high 'goal achievement' in a group, the group is stronger and more unified. . . . Thus, the freedom necessary in a person-centered child development center is facilitated by small groups. . . . Density applies not only to the total space for the whole group, but to smaller spaces within the playroom" (pp. 233–234).

The National Day Care Study compared groups of 12 children and 24 children, respectively, and found that small groups fostered positive behaviors such as cooperation, reflection, and innovation in the children. In smaller groups children were more verbal, giving opinions and making spontaneous comments; they were also more involved in tasks and were less frequently seen wandering aimlessly than were children in larger groups (Ruopp et al., 1979). However, compliance with staff standards does not guarantee quality for children.

Refer to the discussion on burnout in Chapter 6 and surmise how it might be related to density.

LIGHTING

To be most effective, space should be beautiful, orderly, and clean. These characteristics impress young children and therefore aid in their learning. Special attention should be given to lighting, color, and other factors, as discussed later in this chapter.

Lighting has a psychological, aesthetic, and physical impact on the individuals in an environment. Lighting may have a powerful influence on the physiology of humans, and it alters the attention span and behavior of children (Ott, 1976). Many teachers find they can calm children by using lighting with manual dimmer controls; others rely on natural light when it is sufficient. Jorde (1982) proposed: "A general rule is to use lower illumination levels for activities that are less active and require concentration and higher illumination for more active areas that do not require as much concentration" (pp. 159–160).

The size and number of windows in a center affect the lighting. It is recommended that window areas equal approximately one fifth of the floor area, with approximately 50 percent of the windows openable but screened. A good sill height is 22 to 24 inches above floor level. A pleasant view of outdoor greenery has a calming effect on children.

Regulatory agencies frequently specify the minimum amount of light intensity for various parts of the facility. Fluorescent bulbs above plastic diffusing panels (diffused light) should be considered for use in a child-care center. It gives off little heat, provides nonglare lighting, and is less expensive to operate (but is more expensive to install) than incandescent lighting. Incandescent light is recommended for highlighting learning/activity areas. Lighting should be appropriate for the area and the needs of the children and can have dimming controls. For example, Osmond (1971) states that "the art area could have sun-free directional light from skylights or windows, the reading area could have soft incandescent light and a view of the window, and the plant area could be a small greenhouse" (p. 97).

Window size and location should be considered for the particular location, aesthetics, and building codes. Attention should be focused on safety glass, screening, and whether windows are stationary or openable.

Young children spend a quantity of time on visual tasks, making illumination highly important for physical well-being and psychological and aesthetic impact. Also, approximately one fifth of the enrolled children will have below-normal vision (Decker & Decker, 1997).

The directional orientation of the room is also an important consideration in lighting. Southern or eastern exposure is generally preferred to western. Northern exposure is not recommended by most building planners unless it is in a hot climate and there is no air conditioning. Climate, topographical setting, and costs will be considered factors in the placement of the building.

As in all areas of the center, the health and safety needs of the children should apply in lighting and ventilation—screens over open windows, electrical outlets covered, secure floor coverings, well-lighted stairways with secure handrails, proper lumination in play areas, and other situations that apply to specific centers and settings.

COLOR

The directional facing of the building will influence the colors used within the rooms. Sunny rooms (southern or western exposure) may be painted with soft pastels, and cooler rooms (northern exposure) may need a stronger color, such as a light-reflecting yellow.

Color has been found to influence academic achievement. For example, red is a good choice for areas planned for gross motor activities and

concept development activities; yellow is good for music and art activities; and green, blue, and purple are effective in reading areas. The use of various colors may be most important in infant and toddler programs, because children have a perception of color over form until 4 years of age (Environmental Criteria, 1971). Equipment, art work, and the children themselves add to the room's brightness.

Coverings other than paint may be used to decorate rooms. The space can contain tackboards for displaying items, soft porous materials to deaden sound, mirrors to encourage activities, fabrics for aesthetics, and artwork of children and famous painters for self-worth and cultural encouragement. Vinyl and other decorative coverings can add interest and color to classrooms. Figure 10–2 shows the basic principles of color.

Because color can be the single most powerful visual cue in attracting the attention of young children, it should be chosen with special care. Inappropriate use of color can actually produce unintended behavior, thereby causing problems in classroom management.

Mahnke and Mahnke (1987) report that

many cases of nervousness, irritability, lack of interest, and behavioral problems can be attributed directly to incorrect environmental conditions

Figure 10–2   Basic principles of color.

- Light colors make rooms appear larger; dark colors make rooms look smaller.
- Cool colors (blue, green, purple) give the appearance of height (ceilings seem higher).
- Mildly contrasting colors effectively separate work spaces.
- Neutral colors (white, cream, pale gray) make good backgrounds for bulletin boards and displaying artwork.
- Warm colors (red, orange, yellow) stimulate individuals and are more appropriate where activity and interaction are expected and encouraged.
- Cool colors tend to calm individuals and are appropriate in quiet areas such as reading, concentrating, or napping.

involving poorly planned light and color. Studies have shown that a functionally and thoughtfully planned school interior facilitates learning new subject matter and improves scholastic performance.

Because of the mostly extroverted nature of preschool and kindergarten children, Mahnke and Mahnke (1987) recommend a warm, bright color scheme that

> compliments this tendency, thereby reducing tension, nervousness, and anxiety. Good colors are light salmon, soft warm yellow, pale yellow-orange, coral, and peach. A kindergarten room could have light salmon as the dominant color on walls, with a moss-green floor and olive-green tables. (p. 83)

Color has a decisive influence on children's academic performance. Ertel (1973) found that blue, yellow, yellow-green, and orange stimulate alertness and creativity, and white, black, and brown make children duller; thus, he concluded that bright colors in children's environments affect children's IQs. Maria Montessori purposefully decorated walls and shelves in light colors to contrast with, and emphasize, her colorful teaching materials. Teacher-directed programs use light or dull room colors to focus children's attention on materials, programs, and activities rather than on the environment. Many child-centered programs use warm, stimulating colors to instill productive and sociable attitudes.

TEXTURE

Use of texture should be considered in conjunction with lighting and color. Because young children are very sensory oriented, they need richly tactile environments. Soft and cuddly objects are favorites (blankets, fabrics, rugs, pillows, stuffed toys, and dress-up clothes), as are soft, smooth, malleable, and inviting art materials (finger paint, dough clay, sand, and water). Children frequently get cues for appropriate activities from the textures provided in certain areas; for example, "soft environments are good for low-activity

area; hard surfaces (tile, wood, asphalt) encourage louder, more active participation. Keying activities appropriately helps with managing the space over-all" (Jorde, 1982, p. 163).

SIZE AND LOCATION

It is crucial that a facility meet the needs of the individuals it serves and not attempt to adapt the children, adults, and program to the facility. Size and location of the center should be early considerations. Whether the center is an ongoing one that is currently housed or a new program to be housed in an existing, renovated, or new structure, certain factors must be addressed, such as zoning, federal and state regulations, philosophy, and financial limitations.

Although it is not uncommon for spaces that originally were designed for adults or older children to be used for young children, such space needs to be rescaled. Electrical outlets, door knobs, heaters, and other dangerous apparatus may need to be raised, removed, or covered to prevent injury to young children. Windows, doors, cupboards, and shelves may need to be realigned with the height and independence of the children in mind.

In the National Day Care study, Ruopp and coworkers (1973) found that the way space was used was more important than the amount of space:

> Our centers ranged from those with shiny new facilities and plenty of room to those housed in old and crowded buildings, in factories, churches, storefronts, and even trailers. Interestingly enough, shiny new centers may have as many problems in using their space as do programs with fewer resources and smaller facilities. (p. 68)

Boguslawski (1968) reported similar findings and concluded that the condition of the building (makeshift or luxurious) is more important than the building itself. Moreover, "if economy is necessary, it is better to economize on the building rather than on the staff." Other program requirements that affect planning of the facility include the length of time children spend at the center (whether there is napping, for example), parents' involvement, children's age span, whether children have special needs or are mainstreamed into the group, and factors that may be unique to a center, such as climate or religious education. The climate and the lot shape, size, and orientation have a strong influence on the building. Whenever possible, planners should take advantage of exposures that enhance the facility in terms of light, heat, and view.

TYPES OF SPACE

There are four categories of child-care center space: (1) teaching, (2) support, (3) administrative, and (4) auxiliary.

1. *Teaching space* is the area used by teachers and children, both indoors and outdoors. Individual needs should be balanced with environmental concerns. Area use is planned to accommodate a variety of activities; for example, individual/ cooperative, sound/silent, softness/hardness (pliability of materials), active/quiet, tidy/messy, open/closed (single or shared use of toys or areas), and gross/fine muscle activities. Arrangement takes into account the different curriculum areas and interest centers.

To start up a new center, consideration will need to be made for furniture and toys, based on the goals of the center. An ongoing program will add new toys and equipment as needed and affordable. Probably the two largest areas to equip will be the indoor playroom, considering each curriculum area, and the outdoor play yard.

Directors and teachers should constantly be aware of space and area arrangement for children with special needs (physical handicap, temporary problems, etc.).

2. *Support space* for staff and/or support personnel includes rest rooms, kitchen and laundry facilities, halls, storage, entries, and so on. For teachers, it includes the above areas plus prepa-

ration rooms, isolation space for ill children, file for center records, personal space, conference room, lounge, and other areas as needed. It will require comfortable adult-size furniture. Additional office equipment may include a word processor, a copy machine, a typewriter, adding machine, and so on.

It is hoped there will be a professional library that contains journals, newsletters, special publications, instructional manuals, curriculum guides, guidelines by state boards of education and other governmental agencies, professional books and audiovisuals related to early childhood education, equipment catalogs, brochures, course offerings by junior colleges and universities, community resources, current topics on child development, care and education, and parenting skills. Ideally, the library will be available for parents to browse, borrow, and learn.

3. *Administrative space* includes offices, storage, workrooms, and other space needed by nonteaching adults.

4. *Auxiliary space* is provided for adults and purposes not available in other areas. It adds to the professional yet homey atmosphere of the center.

Space that is well organized and designed will contribute to the children's learning, their feelings of independence and competence, both children's and adults' security, teachers' positive methods of guidance, accomplishment of required tasks, and order and beauty for all the individuals involved (Hildebrand, 1994).

Whatever the arrangement of the center and its location, it must serve the needs of the community and its clientele. Commercial or industrial areas are generally poor locations for centers due to their limited outdoor play space, noise pollution, congested traffic, high cost, and potential danger.

Indoor Space

For Adults. The center must meet the space needs of both children and adults. Jones (1983) observed that if administrators have been teachers previously, they tend to slight the learning needs of the adults they supervise in favor of those of the children. However, adults, too, need to

> be safe; they need to have enough resources to work with; and they need to be encouraged to play. . . . If you want people to stay excited about their jobs, there has to be some opportunity for them to explore, to be decision-makers, to say, "This is what I want to do next." That's playful in the very best sense. Children become active learners through play; and so do adults.

Adults need places to get away from the hustle and bustle of the center, to relax quietly, and to meet confidentially with center personnel, parents, and others. They need private places to keep personal belongings and teaching materials and curriculum storage space and a desk to make their work easier. Administrators also need private spaces in which to work, train, and consult. Secretaries, bookkeepers, and food handlers need space to perform their tasks of running the center. Parents should have designated waiting, studying, observing, and meeting spaces.

There should be an area where adults can care for their personal needs (toileting, relaxing, quiet meditation, etc.) without the noise or interference of anyone else. A place where one can sit comfortably and quietly, perhaps with feet elevated, for a few moments of contemplation and rejuvenation.

For Children

The Classroom Floor Plan. Space allocation must be consistent with the goals of the center, philosophy of guidance or behavior control, type of program, ages of the children, number of adults in the room, local climate, changeable equipment, traffic flow, support areas and their location, children's health and safety, and teachers' experience and skills. Teachers should plan carefully for children with physical disabilities, such as those using wheelchairs or crutches and those with vision problems. Traffic patterns, the amount of space around activities, ramps, and

easily opened doors should all be considered to help these children negotiate space more easily.

Typically, the classroom space can be divided into three categories: activity space for children (where daily activities occur), support space within the classroom (food preparation area, cubbies, rest rooms, napping areas), and nonusable space (walls, partitions, mechanical equipment). If the philosophy is that children are sources of knowledge and that they learn from one another, the setting should be informal. Traffic patterns should encourage walking indoors and running outdoors. Proper design and use of space and materials will encourage cooperation. Include some isolated spaces for children to go for relief from vigorous activity and to meet in small groups. Whenever the children gather into one group, there should be sufficient space to provide comfort (good-fitting chairs, soft and warm floors) and freedom from distractions (stimulating toys, noise). Furniture arrangement encourages verbalization, eye contact, and interaction, which can be maintained by periodic rotation.

If the center's philosophy is that the teacher is the source of knowledge, however, the spatial arrangement should allow a minimum of distractions. The classroom is more formal. Furniture is arranged for individual or group purposes, depending on the activities the teacher plans.

As teachers design and place equipment and furniture and set up activities, they should consider their expectations of children's behavior. Children feel competent when they can work independently of adults, for example, prepare for an activity and clean up afterwards. They can do this when shelves are low, water supply is convenient, and materials are accessible. Inasmuch as the number of children at a particular activity can be limited by the number of cover-ups or chairs, allowing the children to get additional cover-ups and chairs from nearby rooms will give them the freedom to join ongoing activities. Activities that require concentration should be separated from traffic and noise by low dividers, buffer activities, or open space. See Figure 10–3.

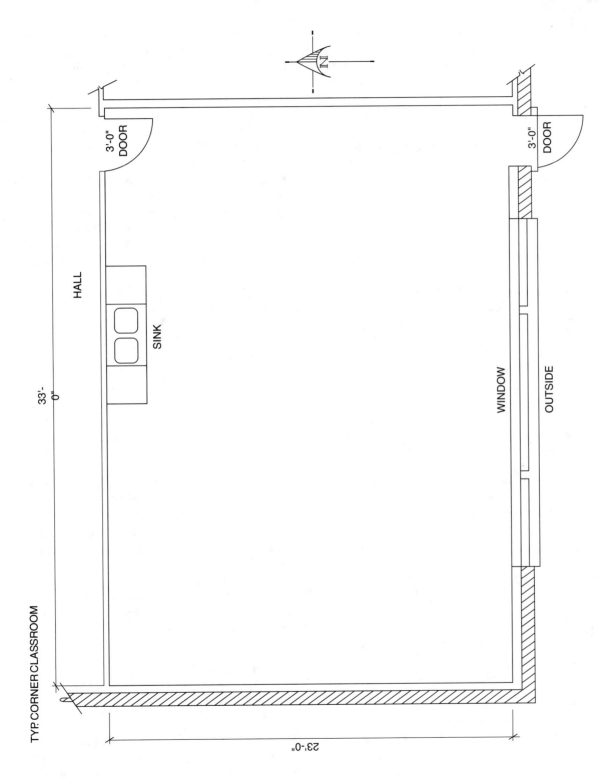

TYP. CORNER CLASSROOM

HALL

SINK

WINDOW

OUTSIDE

3'-0"
DOOR

3'-0"
DOOR

33'-0"

23'-0"

N

Figure 10–3 Floor plan 2. *Note:* Provide security checks.

373

Effective layout calls for experimentation and flexibility. A layout for one age or season may be inappropriate for another, for example. At times, activities may be expanded or reduced because of the number of children interested or due to safety measures. Periodically changing the environment can increase children's interest, exploration, and involvement. (One teacher replaced the housekeeping equipment with large building blocks. At first, the children were frustrated and avoided the area, which had been a favorite. Then, still wanting to play there, the children joined forces and built needed items out of the blocks. The play was especially creative that day.) Portable furniture, suitable storage, and teacher perception help make the classroom appropriate and comfortable. Variable features can be modified to suit the program or situation.

Rooms should be large enough to provide sufficient space for all who participate (children, teachers, staff, and parents). The division of space and the size and location of rooms will greatly affect program management, goal achievement, and satisfaction of children's needs. Room arrangements depend on the room's fixed features, such as immovable columns, supportive walls, plumbing, electrical outlets, windows, doors, stairways, and so on. A room that is slightly longer than it is wide is less formal looking and easier to arrange, in addition to allowing adequate teacher supervision.

Acoustics are better controlled in a nearly square room than in a long, narrow one. There are, however, a number of noise-reducing techniques: cloths on tables, area rugs, padded furniture legs, drapes, fabric or carpeting on walls, room dividers, wall hangings, low voices, soft music, and concentration of activity types (quiet activities clustered near each other; boisterous ones grouped together). Acoustical absorption materials on floors are more effective and more economical than similar materials on ceilings and walls. One or the other (floor or ceiling) should be treated; treating both produces a deadening effect (Jorde, 1982). Curtains, drapes, blinds, pictures, and wall hangings should be included in a room plan to reduce both noise and stress.

Beginning at the entrance, the center should appear warm and friendly. Teachers and children respond best to a homelike, inviting, comfortable setting—one that is friendly and safe. "Children will not internalize a sense of order unless they are in an orderly environment" (Jorde, 1982, p. 172). For children to feel successful, the environment must be structured in ways that encourage them to participate and take pride in the center.

Areas should be arranged so they clearly portray the activities that should occur there. Materials and activities that can be used cooperatively should be placed near each other. However, water or art materials placed near books give the erroneous impression that books can be colored or washed. One mixing of water and beans will convince teachers that sensory tables are sometimes incompatible with other activities.

Rambusch (1982) encouraged the use of the one-way street principle—mazelike patterns of identifiable pathways that lead to specific places and activities. Such an approach provides clear space delineation and clear behavioral expectations, which go hand in hand; it "becomes the exemplar for appropriate behavior in the space" (p. 77). Through it, the child gains control of the space while gaining self-control.

Children learn not only through teachers but also through the environment. They can gain new insights when supportive activities are placed side by side, such as blocks and vehicles or replicas of animals. Spatial arrangement encourages child participation through interesting placement of materials. It can invite or discourage interaction among peers or provide welcome solace. Children need to be free to move around, to integrate their senses, to sequence their activities, and to pay attention to people and materials.

Space and Facilities

According to the National Research Council reported by Hayes and coworkers (1990):

Research and professional standards agree that children's experiences in child care are generally more positive when the space is well organized, differentiated, orderly, and designed for children's use. The adequacy of space as a qualitative dimension differs for family day care and center care. In family day care, the issue is whether children are cared for in a space that remains designed primarily for adults or whether adaptations have been made to orient the space for children. In center care, where space is oriented for children, the relevant issues are sufficiency and organization of space and equipment. When family day care space is not child oriented (for example, children are in a family's unadapted living room or kitchen), care-givers tend to be more restrictive and less responsive to children, and positive emotional climates and positive social relations are more difficult to achieve. In centers, some research indicates that children's social problem-solving skills are influenced by whether the center has a variety of age-appropriate materials and is arranged to accommodate groups of varying sizes. Children demonstrate better cognitive and social skills in orderly centers with more varied and stimulating materials and with space organized into activity areas. (p. 31)

Part of the classroom space must be allotted for rest rooms; they should be located so children can care for their own bodily needs, but receive immediate assistance if necessary. State laws regulate the size and number of toilets and wash basins (generally one toilet and one wash basin for every 8 to 10 children).

First-aid materials should be placed conspicuously and be readily available in the classroom. Also, a quiet, warm place should be set aside for ill or injured children. The following are guidelines for using space in a center for young children, including the safety of everyone at the center:

1. The classroom supports the philosophy of the center, whether child- or teacher-centered, through size and arrangement of furniture, placement of materials and toys, and compatibility of activities, traffic patterns, and storage.

2. Maximum importance is given to the safety of both children and teachers.

   a. Supervision is adequate; necessary limits are set and enforced.
   b. Dangerous and toxic items are removed.
   c. The center complies with all fire, sanitation, and safety laws.
   d. Equipment and toys are maintained.
   e. Children's arrivals and departures are carefully supervised.
   f. Children and teachers are insured.
   g. Special precautions are taken with regard to safety features of the particular facility: windows/doors, electrical outlets, heating units, floors, handrails,

---

❖ Stimulator

Carefully look over the following list of items and areas in a center for young children.

- large building blocks
- science area
- table toys
- books
- sensory table
- workbooks
- balls
- sound/texture boxes
- counting boards
- dolls
- musical instruments

- puzzles
- housekeeping area
- finger paints
- records and player
- easels
- pull toys
- food preparation area
- scales
- animal cage
- dress-up clothes
- woodworking bench

Select the items, areas, or activities from the list that would be more common in a child-centered classroom and those that would be more common in a teacher-centered classroom. Discuss selections and justify them. What difference does age make in the kinds of items and activities provided (e.g., toddlers vs. kindergartners, or mixed-age classes vs. chronological-age classes)?

water (drinking and temperature), food handlers, storage of unused food, first-aid, emergency procedures, repairs, and any other possible hazardous situations.

3. All areas and children can be supervised easily. Areas should be arranged to reduce fatigue and strain on children and teachers.

4. Floor space throughout the center is designed with the occupants in mind—some for adults, some for children, and some for both. There is sufficient space for freedom of movement and for necessary furnishings.

5. The number of children per group is determined by the ages of children and the space. Extra precaution is taken so that large groups are not housed together just because space permits it. Large classrooms may excite or frighten young children.

6. Developmental needs of children (ages, abilities, handicaps, and interests) must be taken into account. Focuses of interest are rotated frequently.

7. There must be individual space for each child (i.e., a box or locker) for personal items, things to take home, and "treasures."

8. There should be variety in space and materials: in placement of objects in space (high, eye-level, and low), in size of areas (large areas for movement and small areas for privacy), in sound levels (noisy and quiet places), and in kinds of play (solitary and cooperative).

9. Careful attention should be given to aesthetics and decoration—color, texture, acoustics, and lighting.

10. Adequate storage must be provided and, when possible, items should be stored where they will be used.

11. If at all possible, classrooms are on one level—the ground floor—and open directly onto the play yard. There is easy access for pickup and delivery of children.

Climbing equipment is not limited to outdoor areas; some centers use climbers inside the facil-

ity because of better supervision, weather/climate, and change of pace. As with outdoor climbers, there must be a protective mat under the climbers when they are used indoors. Safety is of great importance. The Consumer Product Safety Commission (CPSC) (1990) has guidelines for outdoor climbing equipment, but there are no specific safety guidelines for indoor climbing equipment. Teachers can anticipate the same kinds of problems indoors and see that precautions are taken. Morris (1991) provides a list of manufacturers or distributors of indoor climbing equipment.

Storage

Two types of storage are needed: short-range and long-range. Short-range storage items include daily-use or in-use toys and materials and materials that will be consumed quickly. Long-range space is needed for items that are rotated into the classroom periodically and for quantity materials that are consumed over a long period of time.

So that children can help retrieve and replace toys and materials, items should be placed on low, open shelves near the area in which they are used. Carts on wheels are handy for transporting items between storage and classrooms. Heavy items, in particular, should be placed where they are to be used so that lifting and moving are reduced.

Daily materials that require special cleanup should be used near water supplies, waste containers, and on surfaces that can be easily cleaned. Brushes of all kinds can be washed and rinsed easily if sinks or tubs are placed conveniently. Jars, containers, and tables can be cleaned with warm, soapy water and sponges. Cleaning up should be treated as a part of the activity, and children should be involved. Raw materials for art activities, such as paint, flour, salt, and soap flakes, should also be close at hand. Encourage frugality, as budgets become quickly unbalanced if materials are stored or used improperly.

Support Space

Indoor support space should be convenient to the classroom and is generally used for the preparation and storage of classroom materials. A limited amount of each item should be available for current use, with a reserve supply stored elsewhere. Materials that can be damaged by moisture, insects, or time, should be stored carefully. For example, flour should be stored in a metal can on a shelf—not on the floor. Glass, plastic, or metal containers are easily stored on shelves. Brushes, scissors, and other small items can be kept in drawers or in silverware trays. Cupboards with doors can be attractive and are a convenient place to store items like paper, newspapers, magazines, paint jars, dishes for dramatic play, and other classroom items. A sink, water, and easily cleaned surfaces (including the floor) are necessary in messy areas. Regardless of the way materials are stored, labeling is essential to locating and returning materials easily. Cupboards containing caustic or harmful materials must be locked and out of the reach of children.

Teachers may or may not be responsible for cleaning rest room, kitchen, and laundry facilities. Regardless of who maintains them, all personnel should be involved in keeping them neat and sanitary at all times.

Administrative Space

Administrative areas (offices, storage areas, workrooms, lounge) may or may not be used by teachers and children; however, it is still important to design and arrange the space with their needs in mind. Room arrangement, color, lighting, noise level, and so on (as discussed in use of space for children) can cause negative adult reactions such as losing interest in their work, fatigue, or carelessness.

Auxiliary Space

Auxiliary space is provided for adults (parents, visitors, prospective enrollees/employees, media personnel, community leaders, etc.) who may need a place to wait for children, to conference with the director, hold a small group meeting, or other purposes not included in the support space category. It adds a note of friendliness and provides for the needs of persons not directly connected to the center. See Figure 10–4 for a list of how to use classroom indoor space and equipment jointly.

Large and small muscle development, eye-hand coordination, sensorimotor, and other growth-promoting activities are included in many of the above curriculum areas. Activities and opportunities vary from center to center based on the philosophy of the center, ages of children, number and training of teachers, length of the day, and so on.

OUTDOOR SPACE

Outdoor play opportunities develop muscles, skills, knowledge, and relationships. Unfortunately, too many of our young children are exposed to outdoor space that may be dangerous to their health and safety. Some inner-city playgrounds, although fenced for protection and supervision, are in neighborhoods rife with gangs, violence, substance abuse, poverty, toxic waste, and other conditions from which we would like to protect our children. These same playgrounds may have limited equipment, often in need of repair or replacement. But what can teachers (and parents) do under these adverse conditions? Each situation must be dealt with according to its unique initiative, people resources, and financial and social constraints. Often the children can be involved in a beautification campaign—picking up litter, planting here and there, rearranging toys and equipment for new play or from less appealing areas. Teachers can and need to teach children about their environment in ways that are meaningful. Playgrounds serve important functions for a child-care center. They can be useful and beautiful, limiting and ugly, or somewhere in between. They should be designed to meet the needs of the children and be an extension of the classroom. Outdoor play emphasizes exercise, especially that of the gross (large) muscles. Outdoor play lets the children enjoy fresh air, sunlight, and the beauties of nature. Appealing play areas invite use. Good planning makes them safe, easy to maintain, suited to a variety of uses, and conveniently located.

 **Stimulator**   When planning space for young children, one concentrates on the indoor floor plan. As an exercise in seeing the relationship between indoor and outdoor play, use the property plan below and suggest outdoor activities for the same group of children (see Stimulator on page 365 and Fig. 10-3 on page 373). Note traffic patterns, vegetation, and relationship between areas.

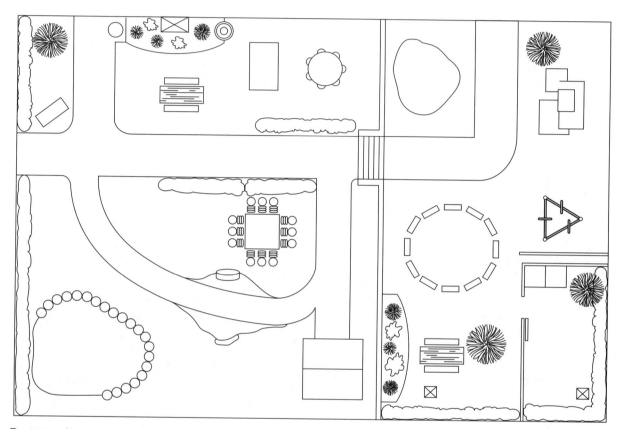

Property plan. *Note:* Provide security checks.

Several considerations should be made in planning the outdoor areas. The placement of the playground depends on the climate and ground space. Generally, play areas with southern exposures are recommended because they will get optimum sunlight throughout the day. In hot climates, however, children may need to be protected from heat and direct sunlight. All playgrounds should have both sunny and shady areas for different types of activities. Although opportunities for activities similar to those conducted indoors should be provided, outdoor play areas should challenge the children's mental, social, and physical abilities. Attention should be given to children with disabilities in any area of development, with consideration of equipment, toys, access, and activities. [See Lovell and Harris, (1985) for a playground rat-

Center	Types of Toys/Equipment
Locker area	Cubbies for coats and personal items
Art (creative)	Paper, paints, brushes, collage materials, glue, clay, fingerpaint, rolling pins, cookie cutters, etc.
Block	Various sizes and shapes of blocks; supporting items like small vehicles, animals, people, etc.
Dramatic play	Dress-ups, household props, dolls, kitchen utensils, costumes, shoes, hats, wigs, ties
Hygiene	Low toilets and basins, water and soap, toilet paper, paper towels, drinking fountain
Language development	Books, pictures, visual/audio materials, puppets, dress-up clothes, interesting objects, games, songs, new activities
Manipulatives (table toys)	Puzzles, peg boards, small blocks, lacing frames
Music	Rhythm instruments, tapes and recorders, records and players, scarves, streamers, pictures and books about music, piano
Microcomputer (if used)	Computers, programs
Pets/plants (if used)	Small pets, feed and water, housing; indoor plants, watering can
Resting	Cribs and changing area for infants; quiet places for toddlers and preschoolers (perhaps cots, bedding)
Sensory	Sand, water, flour, cornmeal, rice, etc.; cups, sifters, toys
Water play (for cooking, art, snack, playing, cleaning)	Measuring cups and spoons, aprons, sponges, water toys, water wheels, drinking fountain

Figure 10–4 Using classroom indoor space and equipment jointly.

ing scale.] Easy access between classroom and playground is important because children often need to go indoors to get toys and drinks or to use the toilet. Doors that are heavy or that block vision can be troublesome.

Children need space in which to release their energy and curiosity. Most states require 75 to 100 square feet of outdoor space per child (some individuals recommend up to 200 square feet per child). One third of the space should be used for passive play such as sand, art, and blocks; two thirds should be allocated for such activities as running, climbing, and riding. Spaces should allow freedom of movement, lounging, shelter, enjoyment of nature, sociodramatic play, interaction with peers, and sensory and skill development.

The surface of playgrounds for young children should receive careful attention; some areas should be smooth, some hard, some soft, and some varied. Play areas should have good drainage and be easy to maintain, safe, and attractive. One half to two thirds of the total area should be covered with grass, part of the area should be sand, and the rest concrete or asphalt. Children enjoy places where they can climb (jungle gyms, ropes, manufactured hills), slide, crawl (tunnels), ride, walk, run, jump, swing, dig, plant, and explore. (See Chapter 9 for safety precautions.)

The playground must be enclosed by a fence to keep children in and animals or intruders out. The type of fence depends on the director, the cost, and the location. Wire fences provide protection and allow for visibility. Brick or wood fences appear more secure but have other problems, such as high initial cost, expensive repair, limited visibility, and injury risk.

Landscaping should be carefully planned to include only nontoxic and thorn-free bushes, trees, and plants; color and texture variety; and planting and digging ground. Landscaping should make the playground an inviting and a safe place to play. Relief from sun, wind, rain, and snow can be provided by covered areas, buildings, trees, and shrubs. Children need fresh air, even in inclement weather. A covered walkway from the classroom to certain outdoor areas is convenient in all kinds of weather.

For a sand area serving 20 children, Decker and Decker (1992) recommend approximately 250 square feet of space, plus a border for closure.

Traditionally playgrounds have been level. A hill or slope could be made without too much cost and would add interest and variety for the children. Caution should be taken to place the mound away from walls or fences, and traffic patterns. It should be covered with grass for ease in running, rolling, and other things children like to do.

Outdoor Storage

Outdoor toys and equipment should be stored where they will be used, and the children should be able to take them out and replace them without help from adults. For example, toys stored near the sand should include shovels, buckets, molds, and other props. Nails on which to hang toys can be hammered into the walls of a nearby shed at a height convenient for the children. Other toys and props can be placed on low shelves. Trikes and wheeled toys can be stored near a hard-surfaced area. A ramp is helpful for getting and returning the wheeled toys; a raised floor can prevent moisture from getting into the shed. Sheds should be free from insects, rodents, extreme temperature, and access by animals or intruders.

Sometimes it is more convenient to have storage in different parts of the playground; some-

times it is mandatory that all storage be in one location. Whichever condition exists, items should be stored as close to their place of use as possible. Dragging heavy equipment for a distance, trying to get wheel toys from a shed to a hard surface, misusing equipment, or refusing to replace used items can cause accidents or friction. When possible, a slightly raised or sloped floor aids in getting large toys in and out of the shed and helps remove water from the shed.

Doors to storage units should be easily manipulated by children, avoiding hardware that pinches or is difficult for young fingers. We have two sets of double-opening, hinged doors for our sheds so openings can accommodate one to four doors at one time. There is no center post for each set of doors; however, there is a post between the two sets of doors. Tilt- or roll-a-door garage-type openings can be used with a different set of safety conditions.

The size and placement of outdoor storage sheds may or may not be within the control of the director—sometimes architects, builders, or owners may propose sites and sizes for reasons entirely different from the purpose for which the sheds will exist. When it is important, and being understanding but firm, directors (or teachers) should present a valid case for changes.

Long-range storage is often needed for large pieces of equipment used only in certain seasons, activities, or special play. Storage may also be needed to protect outdoor equipment from the elements, even if such equipment is used frequently.

In addition to the previously mentioned factors of outdoor area design, toys, equipment, and landscaping, the administrator must keep items of cost-efficiency, durability, safety, and maintenance in mind.

Outdoor Play

The Consumer Product Safety Council, writing (1991) about public playground safety and children of many ages, believes that guidelines, rather than mandatory rules, are more appropriate in discussing playground safety of children. It knows

 **Stimulator**   Visit any public park and also a preschool playground setting. Be sure to take a pencil, paper, measuring tape, and so on. Make a list of the areas of play (sand, climbing, open). For each area list three or more specific things to check for playground safety, such as general upkeep (debris, litter), missing garbage cans, broken or missing equipment parts, guardrails, height of stairs, damage to fences or benches, and so on. Compare differences between the two settings. Use the following checklist. To whom would you refer your suggested actions?

Area	Items for Attention	Suggested Action
General playground		
Variety of equipment		
Age span		
Surfacing		
Equipment hazards (entrapment, pinching, entanglement, etc.)		
Equipment deterioration		
Hardware		
Drainage/water		
Traffic		
Cleanliness		
Other (list)		
Other (list)		
Other (list)		

General playground maintenance checklist.

that children can be expected to use equipment in unintended and unanticipated ways, that playgrounds should allow children to develop progressively and test their skills so that challenges should be appropriate for age-related abilities, and that children will choose which activities they are ready for and which ones exceed their present abilities.

Many of the injuries cited in Chapter 9 were a result of outdoor equipment. The CPSC recognizes the potential hazards that exist with the use of public playground equipment. A commission study (Tinsworth & Kramer, 1990) of playground equipment-related injuries treated in U.S. hospital emergency rooms indicated that the majority resulted from falls from equipment to the ground surface below, impact by swings and other moving equipment, hazards such as protrusions, pinch points, sharp edges, hot surfaces, and playground debris. Fatal injuries involved falls, entanglement of clothing or other items on equipment such as slides, entanglement in ropes tied to or caught on equipment, head entrapment in openings, impact from equipment tipover or structural failure, and impact by moving swings (Tinsworth & Kramer, 1990).

The CPSC also recommends that ferrous metals be painted (with CPSC regulation for lead), galvanized, or otherwise treated to prevent rust; wood (sanding, sawing, sawdust disposal) conform to a consumer information sheet often available at the point of sale (American Wood Preservers Institute, n.d.); guardrails or protective barriers at elevated surface more than 20 inches above the underlying surface should have a guardrail or protective barrier to prevent falls; and protective barriers should always be used for platforms that exceed 30 inches in height. Surfacing can reduce the impact of a fall—the more shock absorbing the surface can be made, the more is the likelihood that the severity of the injury will be reduced. However, it should be recognized that all injuries due to falls cannot be prevented no matter what playground surfacing material is used (see Collantes, 1990). Surfacing materials such as asphalt or concrete are unsuitable for use unless they are required as a base for a shock absorbing unitary material such as a rubber mat.

Other surfaces not recommended are soils, hard-packed dirt, grass, and turf. Acceptable playground surfacing materials are available in two basic types: unitary (generally rubber mats or a combination of rubberlike materials held in place by a binder that may be poured in place at the playground site and cures to form a unitary shock-absorbing surface) or loose-fill (installed at a sufficient depth, they include but are not limited to sand, gravel, and shredded-wood products). Loose-fill materials should not be installed over hard surfaces such as asphalt.

CRITERIA FOR SELECTING TOYS, MATERIALS, AND EQUIPMENT FOR YOUNG CHILDREN

General Principles

Costs of equipping a center are high. Unwise planning depletes precious funds; purchases must be carefully assessed and evaluated before they are made. In this text, *toys* will be categorized as objects used in indoor and outdoor play (table games, blocks, sociodrama, wheeled toys, balls, and so on). *Materials* include consumables that will be combined for use in art activities, science experiences, and food activities. *Equipment* includes tables, chairs, cubbies, portable storage carts, audiovisual items, large climbing and outdoor pieces, and other similar items. The cost of equipment items is generally higher than that of toys or materials.

Emphasis in this chapter is that material bought and activities planned for the classroom should be nonsexist, nondiscriminatory, nonviolent, and nontoxic. Items should meet the criterion on which the center is based, be developmentally appropriate for the ages of the children served, but allow for individual interest, abilities, and possibility of the child to extend the item in new and constructive ways. Teacher-directed programs will use program-unique materials as well as materials similar to those of child-centered programs. Attention should be given to items that have multiple uses, whether they are toys, materials, or equipment. However, single-purpose items should not be eliminated when they are appropriate. Beginning with the inventory, the director must anticipate the current and future needs of the center, including repairs, replacements, and additions.

Clutter can be distracting and disorienting for children, so proper storage of in-use and seldom-used items is very important. There should be a variety of play options—manipulative toys, blocks, science equipment, and specific materials (puzzles, for example)—for children to practice their skills and develop new ones. Items should be selected for the ages and developmental skills of the children for whom they are intended. They should slightly challenge the children.

After referring to Chapter 11 and Appendix H, and *before* making purchases, the purchasing agent should *budget carefully and spend wisely* by doing the following:

1. Check the amount of money available (overspending, spending before funds have been appropriated, and impulse buying can create financial problems); do comparative buying; buy the appropriate quantity (not too much or too little); consider the life expectancy of the item (storage, spoilage, deterioration, popularity). Is it better to buy more expensive items and expect them to last longer? Could an item be made, repaired from other pieces, or donated?

2. Refer to a perpetual inventory list to see what items need to be added or replaced (see "Inventories" in Chapter 11).

3. Check for safety standards of item (toxic, flammable, removable parts that can be swallowed, sharp edges or splinters, sanitary).

4. Purchase from reputable dealer (guarantees, replacement).

5. Select items with the idea that they may be used equally by all children; reflect many cultures and roles; avoid sex stereotyping; and depict the culturally pluralistic society in which the children live.

6. Ask dealers about discounts, perks, guarantees, and so on.

When soliciting donations, request specific items and give the criteria for their condition. Avoid items that are inappropriate, damaged beyond repair, costly to repair, or harmful. Accept only usable items. Cost must be considered even when items are made instead of purchased. A general rule of thumb is to figure the cost of raw materials and then allow the same amount (or a slightly higher amount) for labor. Making things has hidden costs: Even though cash outlay is small, considerable time and effort are expended.

Comparative buying (checking local vendors, catalogs, and other centers; making rather than purchasing items) takes time but usually saves money. Purchasing agents are encouraged to price items from at least three sources to determine if there is a best vendor. Alternative sources include surplus stores, second-hand stores, sales outlets, discount stores, garage sales, and families. Large centers might put items out for bid or contact a local establishment for a discount. In some states, nonprofit centers are exempt from sales tax. Remember that freight or shipping charges are added to an item's original cost—a cost often forgotten until the bill arrives. Buy from a reputable firm that will stand behind its merchandise; better still, get equipment and materials on a trial basis before paying for them.

Buying from toy and equipment catalogs is one option for centers. Leasing it is another (see Smith, 1987; Stephens, 1987), and trading with other centers or checking it out from a central storehouse are others. Some directors prefer actually seeing and checking equipment before buying. That is one drawback of catalog buying; others may be assembly of items or unclear information; but if catalog buying is selected, exercise the precautions identified in Figure 10–5.

Teachers will sometimes want to include in their curriculum some potentially dangerous items, such as balloons, saws and hammers, scissors, and knives for food preparation. These items can be used in the classroom if proper precautions are taken, limits are defined, and children are supervised carefully. Under no condition should teachers allow situations in which children could injure themselves or someone else or destroy property. Teachers must be particularly alert whenever dangerous items are being used.

Whereas teachers are responsible for classroom safety, they should encourage children to develop responsibility for their own safety. It is easier for children to follow rules that they help make. Teachers should not expect blind obedience; explanations should be given, including why or why not. Young children can understand limitations and help form rules related to safety.

- Keep a wish list handy—with items, quantities, colors, sizes, vendors, and other important information. Then when funds are available you are ready to order—no time wasted wondering "What do we need?"
- Get a number of *current* catalogs from which to order (this also helps in comparison buying). *Study their policies carefully regarding:*
   costs: credit, discount, freight/handling, fees
   performance: returns, warranties, promptness, customer satisfaction, dependability, etc.
  Several catalogs may feature the exact same item but at a different price!
- When shipping is involved, check for the nearest location of the vendor selected and note how items are shipped (truck, UPS, train, etc.) to keep costs down.
- When placing an order, include your telephone number (in case of questions) and keep a copy of your order. This helps in checking off the order when it arrives, gives you a record of what you ordered and when, and the current price paid.
- Order in quantity if the price is lower, your budget can accommodate it, and storage is available. It may be possible to combine your order with another center to take advantage of discounts.
- Immediately on receipt of the goods, check for quantity ordered, damage, back orders, or discrepancies. If there is a problem, notify the company immediately for instructions. Check any warranties and record them in a location where they can be easily found.
- If the order is large (over $1,000), consider getting at least three bids (catalogs and local).
- Pay close attention to when the bill is due. Pay it on time to retain a good credit rating. If you have any problems, contact the company from which you ordered.
- If all considerations are equal, you may wish to split your order between several vendors to check their service and also to establish your center's account.
- Order in ample time. Remember it is your responsibility to order items in a timely manner. During busy seasons for equipment suppliers, your order may be delayed or back-ordered.
- After receiving your order (and before reordering) make notations on the form to help in future buying—items liked/disliked, workmanship and quality, longevity of items, and storage problems. Also note items that were unsatisfactory (easily broken, difficult to use, disliked by children/teachers, stereotyped, required extra supervision, etc.). Note when items should be reordered and place this information in a tickler file for later budgeting and ordering.

Figure 10–5   Checklist for catalog buying.

If they are to develop responsibility and self-control, children need practice under loving and accepting conditions.

The director should arrange for a wide variety of materials to provide different kinds of play and opportunities not offered within the home. Attention also should be given to toys and materials that encourage use of both large and small muscles. Children are attracted to activities that have eye appeal and that stimulate curiosity. Aesthetically pleasing toys invite children to approach them. Texture, form, size, odor, temperature, sound, versatility, and shareability are as important as brightness and color.

Items and activities should give good sex-role and cultural-role models. Sociocultural, ethnic, or racial toys (puppets, books, pictures, puzzles) and materials may be of special interest. Materials in the past often stereotyped little girls as passive, dependent, quiet, shy, and obedient and little boys as active, aggressive, independent, and boisterous. Directors must make conscious efforts to correct and amend misrepresentations in sex roles and racial and ethnic stereotyping in materials (toys, games, picture books, photographs) and in activities (games, traditions, costumes, and other items) presented at the center. Stevens and King (1976) reported: "The impressions children receive in these first years of life are crucial, not only for what is expected and accepted practice, but also for what is omitted and missing (i.e., women are never seen doing physical labor, minorities of color are never portrayed as professionals—doctors and lawyers)" (p. 180). Although many story books, visual aids, and other classroom materials have been changed in recent years, directors need to watch for any stereotyping of persons due to race, color, ethnic background, dress, or traditions. Children's books that portray males and females in a realistic, sensitive way with males entering occupations generally considered by females, and vice versa, are appropriate for today's classroom. Young children can and should be taught to value the culture and traditions of others as well as their own.

Often, the acid test of the value of toys and equipment is appeal over time. Young children frequently spend time and energy on items not especially valued by adults, such as boxes, kitchen utensils, clothing items, and old clocks. If children can be actively involved with the item—if it challenges creativity—the item is a success!

Safety Checks

There are safety standards when purchasing equipment and materials that are partially regulated by the Child Protection and Toy Safety Act (1969, 1982), the Child Safety Committee of the National Safety Council, and the Toy Manufacturers of America. Electrical equipment and materials should have the Underwriters' Laboratories (UL) seal. Fabric products should be labeled nonflammable, flame retardant, or flame resistant. Stuffed toys should be filled with hygienic, washable, and nonflammable materials. Painted items should have nontoxic paints.

The *Consumer's Report* can also be a helpful guide.

Consider the health and safety of every child. (Some art materials and coatings are hazardous to one's health. See Chapters 8 and 9.)

Essential items to avoid for young children include sharp edges and protrusions; breakable parts; removable parts small enough to be placed in mouths, noses, ears; and ropes, strings that entangle or entrap. For placement of toys or room layouts, see pages 365, 373, and 393.

To report a product one believes to be unsafe, write to the following:

Standards Development Service Section
National Bureau of Standards
Washington, DC 20234

or

U.S. Consumer Product Safety Commission
Washington, DC 20207
(800) 638-2772
Maryland residents only, (800) 492-2937

To request information about a product, call Consumer Product Safety Hot Line (800) 638-2666 (Maryland residents only, 800-492-2937).

Children with Disabilities

Children with less severe disabilities use many of the same materials and equipment as do children without disabilities; some children may require special consideration. (See Chapter 3.)

In checking suppliers' catalogs, many early childhood and special education equipment and materials are listed in the same section.

YOUNG CHILDREN AND TECHNOLOGY

Perhaps the conflict to use or not to use computers in the classroom for young children has heated up, perhaps it has subsided. Whichever the direction, or stagnation, administrators and teachers should carefully consider the individual children, the teacher interest/support, and the rationale for computer addition to the classroom and curriculum.

An example of appropriate cognitive development for 4- and 5-year-olds follows:

Children develop understanding of concepts about themselves, others, and the world around them through observation, interacting with people and real objects, and seeking solutions to concrete problems. Learning about math, science, social studies, health, and other content areas are all integrated through meaningful activities such as those when children build with blocks; measure sand, water, or ingredients for cooking; observe changes in the environment; work with wood and tools; sort objects for a purpose; explore animals, plants, water, wheels and gears; sing and listen to music from various cultures; and draw, paint, and work with clay. Routines are followed that help children keep themselves healthy and safe. (Bredekamp, 1987, p. 56)

Do computers and software have a place in the young classroom?

Personally, I think computers are the best invention since the wheel. Work is completed faster, is frequently more accurate, has amazing capabilities, and simplifies human work. The question seems to be: when, where, and under what circumstances should it be introduced and promoted? Children can be just as hypnotized as adults. Surely there is a way for them to use computers without interfering with normal growth and development. But the way must be carefully, thoughtfully, and progressively considered.

Haugland (1993a) states:

When used wisely, they can have a dramatic impact on children's learning. In fact, research suggests that, when computers are placed in a central location in a classroom and developmentally appropriate software is used, children make significant gains in key developmental areas. Children in a research study who used a computer for one year showed significant gains in intelligence, non-verbal skills, structural knowledge, long-term memory, complex manual dexterity, and self-esteem. When the computer software was supplemented with activities that reinforced the main objectives of the software,

---

Facts and Figures

Of the people who own home computers and have young children, 70 percent have purchased educational software for their children to use (SPA *Consumer Market Report,* 1996). While many new titles are good contributions to the field, an even larger number are not (Haugland & Shade, 1994).

"It is my recommendation (and that of some of my colleagues) (Elkind, 1998; Hohman, 1998) that computers be introduced to young children when they are about three years of age, no younger. . . . Children younger than age three learn through their bodies: their eyes, ears, mouths, hands, and legs. . . . Unfortunately, all too often computers are used in ways that are developmentally *inappropriate*" (Haugland, 1999, p. 27).

"Research has shown that three- and four-year-old children who use computers with supporting activities that reinforce the major objectives of the programs have significantly greater developmental gains when compared to children without computer experiences in similar classrooms—gains in intelligence (mean score increases were 6 points), nonverbal skills, structural knowledge, long-term memory, manual dexterity, verbal skills, problem solving, abstraction, and conceptual skills" (Haugland, 1992, p. 28).

children had these same gains as well as significant gains in verbal skills, problem solving, abstraction, and conceptual skills. (The study referred to above was not identified in the article.) (p. 45)

Cautions about Using Computers with Young Children

When "teachers and parents replace rich experiences such as blocks, dramatic play props, art media, manipulatives, and so on" with computers, or when they "pressure children to perform tasks and achieve skills that they are simply not ready to acquire," they run a risk of inhibiting or destroying children's creativity, writes Haugland (1993a, p. 30).

Suggestion: When using computers, provide activities and software that fit into the regularly scheduled activities of interest, and encourage children to think and act individually and collectively when there are many possible responses and the topics are stimulating and expanding. Rather than "schedule" a child or children, let computer use and length be determined by their present interests. (Some basic guidelines can prevent many squabbles.) If possible, move the computer to different curriculum areas of the room, thereby stimulating new interest and participation. Socialization, thinking, and interaction should be part of the computer time.

Many adults prefer uninterrupted computer use; young children want and need attention—not social isolation. When a young child is sent to the computer, often in a quiet or secluded part of the room and often by himself, it discourages language exchange and cognitive development.

Suggestion: Software should encourage thinking, language and social interaction, and exploration of ideas.

Concerns about Software and Computer Use

1. *Developmentally appropriate.* "Only about 20 percent of the available software is developmentally appropriate. Inappropriate software can indeed have a significant negative impact on creativity and can place totally unrealistic demands and pressures on young children" (Haugland, 1992).

2. *Selection.* Software should be selected for individual children or purposes—not because they're on special, they're someone else's preference, or they're "popular"—using the best rationale for selecting any curriculum materials.

3. *Sources.* Two tools are available: *Developmental evaluations of software for young children* and *Survey of early childhood software* (Buckleitner, 1993; Haugland, 1993a).

"Some of the problems associated with 'educational' software," write Gillis and Fise (1993),

include the simple transfer of workbook exercises to a computer program; programs that don't give an explanation of mistakes; confusing directions; and, programs that fail to keep records of progress. Finally, because software manufacturers seek the largest possible market, programs suited to a small group (grades six to eight, for example) may be mislabeled for a wide grade range (kindergarten to nine). The best programs are those that teach problem-solving strategies, rather than giving only drills.

According to High/Scope Educational Research Foundation, the following are a few hints to help sharpen computer software buying skills: quick beginning after being turned on; frequent reactions, decisions, or creative input with no delays; easy to use by small fingers; simple and easy-to-follow menus; clear direction on the program; and activities that will get and hold the interest of young children.

Quality software meets the challenges of diversity by reflecting diverse backgrounds, cultures, and experiences of young children. The following characteristics are important to reflect an antibiased curriculum: multiple languages, universal focus, gender equity, heterogeneous races, different ages/abilities, and diverse family styles (Haugland, 1993b). Haugland, after evaluating current software, states: ". . . 6 percent meet the criteria for anti-bias, 65 percent meet half or more of the characteristics (but not all), and 29 percent meet fewer than half the characteristics . . ." (p. 45) (English

only, males or humanized male animals as leading figures, Euro-American culture, limited abilities, ages, and diverse family styles).

Awards are given for early childhood software, but these can be poor indicators due to the lack of a standard of evaluation. Shade (1992) concludes that "inappropriate software (drill-and-practice) receives three times as many awards as appropriate software" (p. 42). Shade also cautions teachers to "learn to evaluate software yourself; order software only from companies and/or catalogs that offer a thirty-day trial; and use the software with a few children alone or together to evaluate its value for your classroom. Use the same criteria for evaluating software as you do other activities and materials for young children" (p. 43).

If, and when, computers are used in the classroom, they should be featured like any other activity—not a pressure to use but for learning enrichment. Their placement in the classroom will influence young children to use them or ignore them. The placement of teachers will be important (there to help and encourage, but not to force or control).

Costs will be another factor as to whether or not computers are available in classrooms for young children. If there has to be a choice, it might be more economical to get computers for office personnel and the best types of toys and equipment for the classroom.

In Part 1 of her two-part article Haugland (1999) makes some points that need to be carefully considered by parents and teachers, such as:

Many of my colleagues (Elkind, 1998; Hohman, 1998) and I do not recommend computer use for children younger than three. Computers simply do not match their bodies. . . computers are not a good choice for the developmental skills these children are learning to master: crawling, walking, babbling, talking, toilet training, and making friends, to name just a few. . . they are active doers, gaining control of their bodies and making things happen in a fascinating world of possibilities . . . manipulating a wide variety of objects . . . learning about themselves and their environment. . . . My recommenda-

tion is that computers be introduced to young children when they are about three years of age. . . . Unfortunately, computers are used all too often in ways that are developmentally inappropriate. (p. 26)

Thus the statement of several child development/computer people that "too often computers are used in ways that are developmentally *in*appropriate" (p. 28). Haugland continues: "What we as early childhood educators are presently doing most often with computers is what research and NAEYC guidelines say we should be doing least often" (p. 33).

In Part 2 of her article Haugland (2000), asks: "What role should technology play in young children's learning?" (pp. 12–18). She states that computers empower young children to enable them to become totally immersed in the joys of learning. It is the *how* they are used to that is important. She states: "As computers are connected with young children and integrated into their curriculum, the benefits to children come clear. If computer experiences are not developmentally appropriate, the child would be better served with no computer access." And further: "As children explore developmentally appropriate software and Websites, important issues emerge, such as access, availability, and parent collaboration. Our goals should be to have multiple computers in classrooms (five or more) so that children can easily access these tremendous learning tools and teachers can effectively integrate computers into their curriculum. Parent collaboration provides an important opportunity to increase computer access and provide children empowering learning experiences, at home and at school" (p. 18).

In 1995 there was a comprehensive federal study (U.S. Congress, Office of Technology Assessment, 1995) about teachers and technology making a "connection." The study found that while "schools are steadily increasing their access to new technologies . . . most teachers use these technologies in traditional ways, including drills in basic skills and instructional games" (p. 103) rather than developing problem-solving or creative skills.

Papert (1998) stresses that computers have an impact on children when they provide concrete experiences, children have free access, children and teachers learn together, peer tutoring is encouraged, children control the learning experience, and the computers are used to teach powerful ideas. For a more detailed description of developmentally appropriate and inappropriate computer experiences, see "Young Children and Technology: A World of Discovery" (Haugland & Wright, 1997).

The location of computers in the classroom is very important. If it is tucked away in a corner, children will be less likely to use it. Its visibility "stimulates peer mentoring, social interaction, language development, cooperative play and easy monitoring for the teacher" (Haugland, 1999, p. 27).

Gatewood and Conrad (1997) report that only a few teachers in a relatively small number of schools have been trained to maximize technology use in their classrooms. Because of this fact, some schools make teacher training their first step before computers are purchased.

Computers will indeed change the ways teachers teach. "Many of us agreed that teaching at all levels should follow the early childhood model" states Elkind (1996), who believes that children often can display a level of computer competence that masks a much lower level of cognitive understanding. Rather than being dispensers of information "teachers become guides to the learning process as facilitators and organizers of learning activities; they are free to focus on small groups and individuals who need more specialized attention, helping them to make choices and validate their learning" (Van Dusen & Worthen, 1995, p. 32). "And just because young children can operate the computer, some teachers choose software programs that emphasize building reading skills through text rather than programs that are musical and animated—those which children actually prefer" (Miller & Olson, 1995).

Further cautions are issued by Elkind (1996), such as: "It is important to recognize that a young child's ability to click a mouse and manipulate computer icons is probably far in advance of his or her logical comprehension of these actions and symbols." And

the danger is that the young child's proficiency with the computer may tempt us to ignore what we know about cognitive development. Despite their skill with computers, many kindergarten children have yet to attain the concrete operations described by Piaget. Concrete operations, as you will recall, enable children to reason syllogistically, to follow rules, and to grasp that one and the same thing can be two things at once. We forget how time consuming and effortful the path to these attainments is, and if we rate a child's intellectual competence by his or her performance on a computer, then we will have lost what we have been working so hard to attain, a broad appreciation of developmentally appropriate practice. (p. 23)

Elkind concludes his article with: "I had the opportunity to preview the 'NAEYC Position Statement on Technology and Young Children—Ages Three through Eight.' It was so much in keeping with my own views. . . . It really is a very thoughtful, balanced approach to technology and young children that I am sure will prove a very useful guideline for early childhood educators."

The NAEYC position statement to which Elkind (1996) refers (adopted in April 1996) contains the following:

Early childhood educators must take responsibility to influence events that are transforming the daily lives of children and families. This statement addresses several issues related to technology's use with young children:

1. the essential role of the teacher in evaluating appropriate uses of technology; (NAEYC believes that in any given situation, a professional judgment by the teacher is required to determine if a specific use of technology is age, individual, and culturally appropriate) (NAEYC & NAECS/SDE, 1992);

2. the potential benefits of appropriate use of technology in early childhood programs;

3. the integration of technology into the typical learning environment;

4. equitable access to technology, including children with special needs;

5. stereotyping and violence in software;

6. the role of teachers and parents as advocates; and

7. the implications of technology for professional development. (p. 11)

Others have voiced opinions about using computers/software with preschool children. For example, "the central role teachers must take to ensure that the potential benefits of technology for young children are realized" (Wright & Shade, 1994). Also consider: "The most critical decision a teacher can make is that of software selection. After all, a computer is little more than plastic and electronic circuitry until software is loaded. Just how crayons are used depends on whether children are given blank paper or coloring books (Elkind, 1987), the use of a computer is determined by the developmental appropriateness of the software selected" (p. 17).

Shade (1996) lists three features to consider in evaluating software for young children:

Child features

1. Can the child make decisions about what he wants to do and operate the software to accomplish that task, with minimum help from adults?

2. Can the child manipulate the screen to make concrete representations?

3. Can the child manipulate the graphics on the screen (is the child the "change agent")?

4. Can the child expand the complexity of the computer to meet his own knowledge and skills?

Teacher features

1. Is the program suitable across the curriculum?

2. Does the program empower the children to learn through self-directed exploration?

3. Is the program representative of diversity within the classroom?

4. Does the program expand with the interests and abilities of individual children?

Technical features

1. Are the capabilities of your computer powerful enough to run the software well?

2. How are you influenced to buy a certain piece of software?—Look carefully beyond the bright packaging and wonderful graphics to see what the software is really doing. ["Look for software that three-year-olds can access, yet seven-year-olds can benefit from because of the more complex knowledge and skills the same software teaches" (Shade, 1996, p. 21)].

In a current article, Anderson (2000) draws some thoughtful conclusions:

1. There are not enough computers to go around, but more important is learning to cooperate and solve problems with one's peers.

2. Computers offer young children a rich curriculum; however, it was not unusual to find six children in the reading center and but one or two at the computers.

3. Children who rarely spoke in other centers of the classroom verbalized more freely at the computers.

4. Computers supported the rest of the curriculum in facilitating children's acquisition of skills, knowledge, and dispositions to a higher level (such as cooperation and independence) with minimal adult supervision.

CHAPTER SUMMARY

1. Of prime importance to space use are the goals and philosophy on which the program is based. Toys, materials, and equipment should enhance and support these objectives. Zoning and state and federal regulations determine some of the physical conditions of the center.

2. This chapter has five main sections: (1) general principles, (2) indoor space,

(3) outdoor space, (4) criteria for selecting toys, materials, and equipment, and (5) use of computers.

3. The local, state, and federal laws must be followed when providing out-of-home care for young children. Some facilities can be remodeled for child-care use but must adhere to all laws.

4. The Americans with Disabilities Act (ADA) applies to preschools and day-care centers.

5. The type of program, the ages of the children, the time spent at the center, the different needs of children, and other factors will determine the kinds and amount of space needed.

6. Good planning of space contributes to individual growth, security, independence, and so forth.

7. The type of program, the ages of the children, the time spent at the center, the different needs of children, and other factors will determine the kinds and amounts of space needed.

8. Of particular concern to indoor space are density, lighting, color, texture, and size and location of activities.

9. The four categories of space are: teaching, support, administrative, and auxiliary.

10. A checklist regarding indoor equipment and materials is helpful (see Figure 10–1).

11. Criteria for outdoor space include meeting the needs of the children; challenging their mental, social, and physical abilities; providing a release for their energy and curiosity; being safe; and being cost efficient.

12. Items having multiple uses are desirable at the center; they should be selected for the ages and developmental skills of the children who will use them.

13. Proper storage increases the life span of items used at the center.

14. Initial cost, repair, replacement, and additions to the curriculum are important considerations.

15. Purchasing agents or directors should practice comparative buying—including catalogs, local vendors, leasing, and sharing.

16. Teachers and children should keep the classroom and playground safe; children can learn responsibility for toys and behavior.

17. Items and activities should give good sex- and cultural-role models. Attention should be given to diversity in people, cultures, abilities, and ideas. (See Chapter 3.)

18. Safety, health, and attractiveness should be considered when buying items for young children; durability reduces replacement costs.

19. Safety checks regarding use of equipment and material (especially with children with disabilities) is essential.

20. It is desirable that children over the age of 3 years have opportunities to explore technology (computers); however, the ways they are used should be *developmentally appropriate* for each child.

21. Computers have an impact on children when they provide concrete experiences, children have free access, children and teachers learn together, peer tutoring is involved, the children control the experience, and the computers are used to teach powerful ideas.

22. The most important consideration of computers in the classroom is *the selection of the software*—Is it developmentally appropriate for the children who will use it?

23. Evaluation of software should include the child features, the teacher features, and the technical features.

PARTICIPATORS

1. Arrange a classroom to represent a teacher-centered program. Discuss the floor plan, equipment, role of the teacher, and expected behavior of the children. (Alternate: Using the scale drawing provided earlier in this chapter or a scale drawing of a classroom and equipment in Participator 5, design the space and equipment placement for a teacher-centered program. Discuss the teacher's role and expected behavior of the children.)

2. Physically set up a classroom to represent a developmental, discovery, or whole-child program. Discuss the floor plan, equipment, teacher role, and expected behavior of the children. (Alternate: Using the scale drawing provided earlier in this chapter or a scale drawing of a classroom and equipment, design the floor plan and equipment placement for a developmental, discovery, or whole-child program. Discuss the teacher's role and expected behavior of the children.)

3. Set up a classroom to represent a behavioral model. Discuss the floor plan, equipment, teacher's role, and expected behavior of the children. (Alternate: Using a scale drawing of a classroom and equipment, design the floor plan and equipment placement for a behavioral model. Discuss the teacher's role and expected behavior of the children.)

4. Using one of the scale and equipment drawings provided, make a floor plan for a one-room classroom or an existing house for each of the following programs: academic, developmental, and behavioral. Compare and contrast the differences.

5. Now that you have learned about space utilization, purchasing toys and equipment, etc., using the floor plans on pp. 393–394, try your skills at planning for:

   a. The first floor for infants, toddlers, and preschool children, and children with special needs (p. 393);
   b. the second floor for school-age children who need care before and after school, who are "off track," whose parents are ill or absent, or who have other special child or family needs (p. 394),
   c. Note the elevations of the building as you plan indoor/outdoor activities that may need more or less direct sunlight (p. 395).
   d. Consider how staffing changes with the expanded space.
   e. Do state and/or local regulations change with additional space and number of children?

6. Determine the following:

   a. Calculate the number of square feet in a room 20 × 30 feet. Using the minimum standard of 35 square feet per child for indoor space, how many children could legally be in this room? How many children could be in this room if the area were increased to 40 square feet per child? To 50?
   b. Calculate the number of square feet in adjoining rooms that are 20 × 20 feet each. Should the rooms be figured separately and then the footage added together or should it be considered one large room? Should there be a deduction for wall space? How many children can be accommodated at 35 square feet each? at 40 square feet? at 50 square feet?
   c. Calculate the area of a playground that is 50 × 75 feet and has a 6 × 12 foot storage shed. Using a minimum requirement of 50 square feet for each child, how many children could be on the playground at one time? How many children could be there if the required square footage was increased to 75 per child? to 100?
   d. Calculate the footage of the playground shown in Figure 10–6. Determine the number of children who could play here using the ratios of 50, 75, and 100 square feet per child.

7. Make a list of types of equipment desired in an outdoor play yard for children between the ages of 2 and 6. Place this equipment on the plot plan (Figure 10–6).

8. Visit a preschool or child-care center. Note the size and shape of the classrooms and play areas. Mentally determine traffic flow patterns. How could the furniture and equipment be rearranged? Give rationale.

9. While visiting a preschool or child-care center, note the relationship between teaching areas and supporting areas. Make constructive notes for better use of the space.

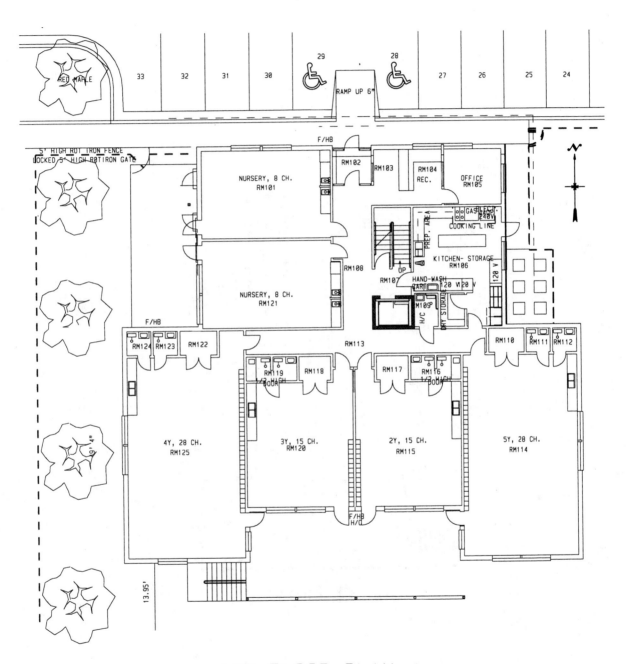

1ST FLOOR PLAN

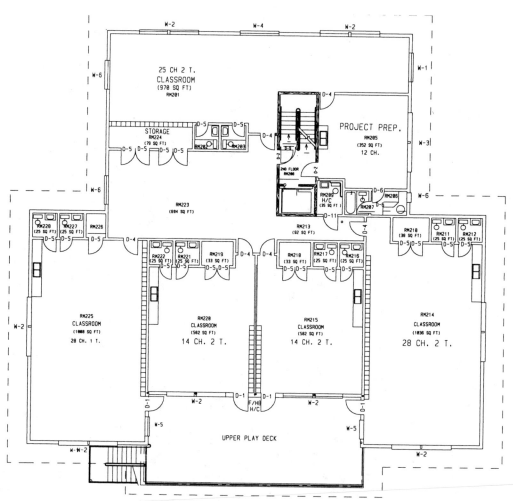

2ND FLOOR PLAN

NORTH ELEVATION

SOUTH ELEVATION

EAST ELEVATION

WEST ELEVATION

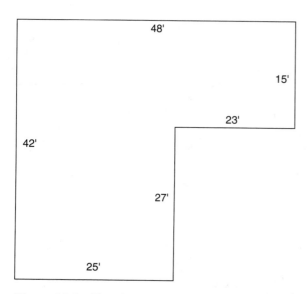

Figure 10-6   Planning space and purchasing equipment.

10. Using a floor plan of your choice or one of the floor plans provided in Participator 5, design (on paper) room changes to meet the needs of (a) toddlers, (b) 3- to 5-year-olds, and (c) school-age children. Note the different needs for each age group.

11. Make a list of precautions to consider when placing furniture and equipment in a classroom.

12. With the consent of the instructor or supervising teacher, remove part or all of the furniture and work with the children in improvising equipment and areas (for example, use blocks for housekeeping equipment, section off a quiet reading area, use shelves and portable equipment).

13. Sketch three different floor plans for a current classroom. Try one plan for a week.

14. Identify the type and amount of supporting space a teacher would need for personal items, work-related materials, preparation space, and relaxation.

15. Sketch a room arrangement for the director's office. Justify the changes.

16. Give the rationale for providing or excluding space for parents (auxiliary space)—discuss amount of space, equipment needed, frequency of use, and whether it could include use of the center's library and materials.

17. Using a floor plan provided, or an original one, practice interior decorating skills. Include samples of wall and floor coverings, window treatments, and other materials. Pay particular attention to color, texture, acoustics, lighting, eye level of children, durability, maintenance, usefulness, and effect on people using the room. Indicate whether the room has a northern, southern, eastern, or western exposure, and other pertinent facts (e.g., climate, children's ages, geographic location, ethnic population).

18. Design an outdoor playground for a group of children between the ages of 2 and 6.

19. Design outdoor storage for the items in number 18.

20. Discuss an approach to buying equipment and toys for a new center from the following points: (a) merely going through catalogs or visiting appropriate wholesalers or vendors; (b) looking only at a center or floor plan; (c) consulting catalogs and vendors concurrently with consideration of floor space and the center's philosophy.

21. Prepare a budget for toys, materials, and equipment for a new center that will enroll 20 children. Assume the budget will allow only $2,000 for these items. What items are most important? What ones could be reduced or eliminated? What allowance has been made for the balance of items in curriculum areas, the developmental skills of the children, and variety?

22. Look for and write about selecting toys from a director's, a child's, a teacher's, and a par-

ent's point of view. Ask about discounts, perks, guarantees, shipping.

23. For experience in using toy and equipment catalogs, make headings of the following types of toys: creative (art), outdoor, table, consumables, floor, and large muscle. Obtain a commercial catalog, list items appropriate for children (you specify the ages), record the quantity needed, and the cost.

REFERENCES

American Wood Preservers Institute. n.d. *Consumer information sheet: Inorganic arsenical pressure-treated wood.* Vienna, VA: Author.

Anderson, G. T. 2000. Computers in a developmentally appropriate curriculum. *Young Children,* March, 90–93.

Boguslawski, D. B. 1968. *Guide for establishing and operating day care centers for young children.* New York: Child Welfare League of America.

Bredekamp, S. (Ed.) 1987. *Developmentally appropriate practices in early childhood programs serving children from birth through age 8 (expanded edition).* Washington, DC: NAEYC.

Buckleitner, W. 1993. *Survey of early childhood software.* Upsilanti, MI: High Scope Press.

Collantes, M. 1990, Oct. *Evaluation of the importance of using head injury criterion (HIC) to estimate the likelihood of head impact injury as a result of a fall onto playground surface materials.* Washington, DC: U.S. Consumer Product Safety Commission.

Consumer Product Safety Commission. 1991. *Public playground handbook for safety.* Washington, DC: Author.

Consumer Product Safety Commission. 1990. Guidelines for outdoor climbing equipment. *Exchange,* Aug.

Decker, C. A., & Decker, J. R. 1992. *Planning and administering early childhood programs.* Upper Saddle River, NJ: Prentice Hall/Merrill.

Elkind, D. 1998. Computers for infants and young children. *Child Care Information Exchange,* 123, 44–46.

Elkind, D. 1996, Sept. Young children and technology: A cautionary note. *Young Children.*

Elkind, D. 1987. *Miseducation: Preschoolers at risk.* New York: Knoff.

Environmental criteria: Mentally retarded preschool daycare facilities. 1971. College Station, TX: Texas A & M.

Ertel, H. 1973. Blue is beautiful. *Time Magazine,* Sept. 17.

Gatewood, T., & Conrad, S. 1997. Is your school's technology up to date? A practical guide for assessing technology in elementary schools. *Childhood Education,* 2(2), 13–15.

Gillis, J., & Fise, M. E. 1993. *The childwise catalog.* New York: HarperCollins.

Haugland, S. W. 1992. Effects of computer software on preschool children's developmental gains. *Journal of Computing in Childhood Education,* 2(2), 3–15.

Haugland, S. 1993a. Computers and young children: Are computers an important learning resource? *Day Care & Early Education,* 20(3), 44–45.

Haugland, S. 1993b, Winter. Computers and young children: Mainstreaming an anti-bias curriculum. *Day Care & Early Education,* 20(3), 44–45.

Haugland, S. W. 1999. What role should technology play in young children's learning? Part I. *Young Children,* Nov., 26–31.

Haugland, S. W. 2000. Early childhood classrooms in the 21st century. Using computers to maximize learning. What role should technology play in young children's learning? Part 2. *Young Children,* Jan., 12–18.

Haugland, S. W., & Shade, D. D. 1994. Software evaluation for young children. In J. L. Wright & D. D. Share (Eds.). *Young Children: Active learners in a technological age* (pp. 63–76). Pamphlet #341. Washington, DC: NAEYC.

Haugland, S., & Wright, J. 1997. *Young children and technology: A world of discovery.* New York: Allyn & Bacon.

Hayes, C. D., Palmer, J. L., & Zaslow, M. J. (Eds.). 1990. *Who cares for America's children? Child care policy for the 1990s.* Washington, DC: National Academy Press.

Healy, J. M. 1998. *Failure to connect: How computers affect our children's minds—For better or worse.* New York: Simon & Shuster.

Hildebrand, V. 1994. *Management of child development centers* (4th ed). Upper Saddle River, NJ: Prentice Hall/Merrill.

Hohman, C. 1998. Evaluating and selecting software for children. *Child Care Information Exchange,* 123, 60–62.

Jones, E. 1983. Creating environments where teachers, like children, learn through play. *Child Care Information Exchange.*

Jorde, P. 1982. *Avoiding burnout: Strategies for managing time, space, and people in early childhood education.* Washington, DC: Acropolis Books.

Kritchevsky, S., Prescott, E., & Walling, L. 1969. *Planning environments for young children: Physical space.* Washington, DC: National Association for the Education of Young Children.

Lally, R., Provence, S., Szanton, E., & Weissbourd, B. 1986. Developmentally appropriate care for children from birth to age 3. In S. Bredekamp (Ed.). *Developmentally appropriate practice in early childhood programs serving children from birth through age eight* (expanded ed.). Washington, DC: National Association for the Education of Young Children.

Lovell, P., & Harris, T. 1985. How can playgrounds be improved? *Young Children,* Mar., 3–8.

Mahnke, F. H., & Mahnke, R. G. 1987. *Color and light in man-made environments.* New York: Van Nostrand Reinhold.

Miller, L., & Olson, J. 1995. How computers live in schools. *Educational Leadership,* 53(2), 74–77.

Morris, S. 1991. Indoor climbing structure buying guide. *Exchange,* 79, May/June, 55–58.

NAEYC & NAECS/SDE (National Association of Early Childhood Specialists in State Departments of Education). 1992. Guidelines for appropriate curriculum content and assessment in programs serving children ages 3 through 8. In S. Bredekamp & T. Rosegrant (Eds.). *Reaching potentials: Appropriate curriculum and assessment for young children,* Vol. 1 (pp. 9–27). Washington, DC: NAEYC.

NAEYC. 1999. *Accreditation criteria & procedures of the National Academy of Early Childhood Programs* (rev.). Washington, DC: Author.

NAEYC. 1996. NAEYC position statement: Technology and young children—Ages three through eight. *Young Children,* 51(6), 11–16.

NAEYC Information Service, 1989. *Facility design for early childhood programs* (pp. 2, 13–16). Washington, DC: Author.

NAEYC 1991. *Accreditation criteria & procedures of the National Academy of Early Childhood Programs* (rev.). Washington, DC: Author.

O'Riordan, K. 1999. Report view current research on education technology. Available online at *http://www.milkenexchange.org/,* click on Articles.

Osmond, F. 1971. *Patterns for designing children's centers* (p. 97). New York: Educational Facilities Laboratories.

Ott, J. 1976. Influences of fluorescent lights on hyperactivity and learning disabilities. *Journal of Learning Disabilities,* Aug./Sept.

Papert, S. 1998, Sept. 1. Technology in schools: To support the system or render it obsolete? Milken Exchange on Education Technology (online serial). Available at: *www.milkenexchange.org/feature/papert.html.*

Papert, S. 1999. *Child power: Keys to the new learning of the digital century* (See "Education's 19th Century Thinking in a 21st Century World"). Available online at *http://www.connectedfamily.com/.*

Prescott, E., & David, T. G. 1977, April. *Effects of physical environments in child care systems.* New York: Paper presented at the annual meeting of the American Education Research Association. (ERIC ED 142–284)

Rambusch, N. M. 1982. The organization of environment. In D. T. Streets (Ed.), *Administering day care and preschool programs* (pp. 71–85). Boston: Allyn & Bacon.

Ruopp, R., O'Farrell, B., Warner, D., Rowe, M., & Freedman, R. 1973. *A day care guide for administrators, teachers, and parents.* Cambridge, MA: MIT Press.

Ruopp, R., O'Farrell, B., Warner, D., Rowe, M., & Freedman, R. 1979. *Children at the center. Final report of the National Day Care Study* (Vol. 1). Washington, DC: Department of Health, Education, and Welfare.

Shade, D. D. 1992, Fall. Computers and young children: A developmental look at award-winning software. *Day Care & Early Education,* 20(1), 41–43.

Shade, D. D. 1996. Software evaluation. *Young Children,* Sept., 17–21.

Shapiro, S. 1975. Preschool ecology: A study of three environmental variables. *Reading Improvement,* 12, 236–241.

Smith, D. G. 1987. Have you explored leasing a vehicle for equipping your center? *Exchange,* Sept., 29–30.

SPA *consumer market report.* 1996. Washington, DC: Software Publishers Association (SPA).

Stephens, K. 1987. Leasing commercial space for your child-care program. *Exchange,* Nov., 15–18.

Stevens, J. H., Jr., & King, E. W. 1976. *Administering early childhood education programs.* Boston: Little, Brown.

Tinsworth, D. K., & Kramer, J. T. 1990, April. *Playground equipment-related injuries and deaths.* Washington, DC: U.S. Consumer Product Safety Commission.

U.S. Congress, Office of Technology Assessment. 1995. *Teachers and technology: Making the connection,* OTA-EHR-616. Washington, DC: Government Printing Office.

U.S. Consumer Product Safety Commission. 1981a. *A handbook for public playground safety,* Vol. 1. *General guidelines for new and existing playgrounds.* Washington, DC: U.S. Government Printing Office.

U.S. Consumer Product Safety Commission. 1981b. *A handbook for public playground safety*, Vol. 2. *Technical guidelines for equipment and surfacing.* Washington, DC: U.S. Government Printing Office.

U.S. Consumer Product Safety Commission. 1991, Nov. *Public playground handbook for safety.* Washington, DC: Author.

Van Dusen, L. M., & Worthen, B. R. 1995. Can integrated instructional technology transform the classroom? *Educational Leadership,* 53(2), 28–33.

Wright, J. L., & Shade, D. D. (Eds.). 1994. *Young Children: Active learners in a technological age.* Pamphlet #341. Washington, DC: NAEYC.

Chapter 11

Record Keeping

Guide for Readers

❖ *Some records are mandated, some are optional; some are useful, some are useless.*

❖ *Attitudes toward record keeping influence the type of information taken, the way it is used and kept, and its value.*

❖ *Records about the center—its program, people, participants, financial transactions, inventories— are essential.*

❖ *Suggested records on children include applications, personal and family data sheets, health information, and records of progress at the center.*

❖ *Suggested records on employees include applications, job descriptions, performance appraisals and goals, payroll information, health records, emergency data sheets, and other personal items.*

❖ *Records can be maintained manually or by computer.*

INTRODUCTION

Keeping accurate and complete records is essential in any business. What records to keep, how to keep them, and for how long depend on laws, policies, and the director's personal preference and attitude. This chapter deals with records for children, personnel, inventories, and so on and computer-assisted record keeping.

Record keeping can be tedious, time-consuming, and frustrating. It can also be valuable or valueless.

Someone at the center will be hired for or assigned to the responsibility of keeping records—of all kinds. This person should understand the importance of accurate and current records in all areas—it's a professional skill! The employee may come with different amounts of skill in record keeping (fundamentals and/or experience and training in finance, personnel and child records, etc.), but some specialized training for the center's needs will be necessary. The management of the center (board or director) must determine in advance (1) whether or not an accounting service or tax advisor will be used, (2) the information needed and use of personal records, and (3) operational records (office supplies, classroom needs, inventories, etc.). Monthly, quarterly, or annual reports will be generated from these records. Sound accounting procedures are essential in profit and nonprofit centers and should be seriously considered and maintained.

Centers operated by a larger body (corporation, chain, university, government agency, etc.) will keep and forward records and receipts as required by that body. It is very different to forward insurance premium notices, for example, to an accounting department rather than pay them out of center funds.

Regardless of inventory and financial control, situations arise when there is need for small and/or immediate purchases. Centers that have petty cash funds must maintain them meticulously—justification for purchasing with cash, the amount used, proper receipts kept, and payment authorized by only one person to see that the fund is not misused.

ATTITUDE

The success or failure of record keeping depends largely on the attitude of the personnel. Butler (1974) wrote:

> Some teachers see records as an end unto themselves; they do not use the records of other teachers, and they do not see the records they keep as valuable to other teachers. For this type of teacher, record-keeping is another form of red tape, and their records are as routine and minimal as possible. . . . Others see records as tools to help them meet some of the complex problems of teaching. They are able to handle the mechanics of record-keeping and may be able to offer constructive suggestions to other teachers. A relatively simple record-keeping system, used intelligently, can be an asset to the school and to individual teachers. (p. 168)

Records should be kept for the right reasons—for teachers, parents, and board members to make and accurately measure goals and progress of adults, children, and programs; to meet individual and group needs; to have a tool for constructive comparison; and to reveal the value of the collected information. Examples of the way good records can save time and money for individuals and the center will convince nonbelievers of the importance of record keeping—budgets may be increased, lawsuits may be won, salaries may be increased, and items may be efficiently purchased or replaced, to name a few.

IMPORTANCE OF RECORDS

Before deciding how to keep records, decide what information is pertinent to record. Decisions are often made on what records to keep without analyzing the significance of the information or the ways it will be collected, interpreted, and used. Certain information might be useful, but attempts to collect or use it can fall short of expectations. If information is unusable or insignificant, why collect it?

Consider overall management principles (e.g., goals and philosophy of the center, type of management, use of time, personnel interac-

Facts and Figures

"The 1998 revision of NAEYC's *Accreditation Criteria and Procedures* includes a greater emphasis on creating support systems that contribute to teachers' and administrators' professional development and retention in a program. These support systems include improved work environment, enhanced roles in decisionmaking, more collegial relationships among staff, and, especially, improved compensation. Several new resources can help centers that are seeking to achieve or maintain accreditation meet these criteria" (*Young Children,* March, 1999, p. 68):

Washington Update, February 10, 1999: Highlights to President Clinton's FY 2000 budget submitted to Congress on Feb. 1, 1999 seeking, among other things, new funds for the Department of Health and Human Services-administered Child Care and Development Block Grant, proposing a $1.2 billion increase over the FY 1999 funding level. To help improve child care quality and safety over the next five years, Clinton proposes the creation of an Early Learning Fund to be funded at $600 million for FY 2000. In addition, the president has requested $607 million increase for Head Start and Early Head Start programs (*Young Children,* March, 1999, p. 69).

Researchers at the National Institute of Child Health and Human Development (NICHD) and 14 universities recently reported on child care quality, concluding that child care in the United States is 'fair,' although 'high-quality' child care is beneficial for children's cognitive and language development. The research also shows that parents have a greater influence on children's development than does the child care setting and that child care has no discernible influence on children's attachment to their mothers by age three (*Young Children,* March, 1999, p. 69). A news alert on the study results may be found on NICHDS's Website, *http://www.nih.gov/nichd/html/news.html.*

Washington Update, October 12, 1999: The House and Senate cut funding for Goals 2000. Overall funding for education was significantly cut (*Young Children,* p. 55).

Presidential candidates for year 2000 presented different strategies for improving children's school readiness through early childhood education: Gore's proposal would have provided federal funding for prekindergarten programs; Bush proposed making Head Start more education focused.

The Senate Appropriations Committee jeopardized funding for children by level-funding the Child Care and Development Block Grant (CCDBG) and cutting Title XX funds by 45%. However, an amendment was introduced to increase the CCDBG appropriations by $818 million to $2 billion and was passed by a narrow margin.

The Head Start program was funded with a $100 million increase in the House and a $150 million increase in the Senate but was one of several programs that was 'forwarded funded.' This means that some funds are not available until October 2000 and do not count against the year 2000 spending caps. This political tactic essentially creates a gap in program funding that is likely to have negative impact on the services children and families receive in the next year.

tion, enrollment of children, parent involvement, funding policies, etc.) and relate them directly to record keeping. This should strengthen each area and produce a cohesive result for your center.

Record keeping does not always have a positive effect. Kontos and Fiene (1985) found that the more time spent on record keeping, the lower the quality of the child-care center. Teachers or directors sometimes use record keeping in

The following may sound like a fairy tale, but it has happened and, without careful attention, could happen again.

Once upon a time there was an ambitious secretary. She wanted to do her job quickly, accurately, and as infrequently as possible. She decided to order supplies and food items only once a year. Not being familiar with the children's likes or the center's required quantities, she made some guesstimates. Some were mild and some were wild! She encountered problems with the budget, inadequate storage, spoilage, and inappropriate items. Three items were especially problemsome: crackers, cleanser, and stainless-steel pads. The children disliked the strong-flavored crackers, and other crackers were invaded by weevils or became stale. The custodial staff forbade the use of cleansers on the stainless-steel sinks and the tabletops. Nobody could figure out the intended use of the stainless-steel pads.

What to do! The director tried a storage sale that was unsuccessful, then a campaign to encourage staff members to help reduce the stockpile, and, finally, super bargains and a trip to the dump with the crackers.

Moral of this story: For a long, happy life, keep an eye on inventories, oversee expenditures, keep good records, and use those records.

Outline a record procedure for a center to avoid experiencing this situation.

lieu of planning and working with children to occupy their time. Records can positively or negatively prejudice teachers toward a particular child or suggest that all children of a particular chronological age should behave in a certain way. Information may be inaccurate, inappropriate, misleading, or irrelevant. Ineffective use of data can render records meaningless.

If directors could choose, they probably would maintain some records differently than they currently do. However, certain records and forms are required by regulatory agencies or by boards. Funded programs may be required to record information that gives evidence that those programs operate within contractual agreements or provide research data. Records that are easily kept up-to-date, require minimal time and money, can be delegated, and have specific value for children, adults, and the program have the most value for centers. The way records are collected and kept should be of concern to the director. Records that are difficult to use have little value for the staff; but when they help employees accomplish their jobs, they are used more often.

Records will be kept for varying lengths of time, depending on the reasons for collecting the information. Funded programs may require that the records be returned to the respective funding agencies for further use. Centers may want to keep records for longitudinal studies of children who were previously in their programs. How long employee records are maintained may be dictated by the center policies, by board decisions, by funding agencies, or by law. Former employees seeking references from centers benefit if directors can call on actual records rather than on recollection.

Several categories of records should be considered for collection and retention: those of children, employees, inventories, and finance (see Chapter 12). Thoughtfully gathered and carefully interpreted information gives teachers and parents a better understanding of individual children in comparison with growth norms. Such information also allows independent evaluation by more than one adult and can be a basis for parent conferences. It assists teachers with personal development by identifying personal strengths and weaknesses, by indicating a need for more education or training, or for use in personal appraisals, salary reviews, and promotions.

COMPUTER-ASSISTED RECORD KEEPING

The discussion in this chapter will be limited to the use of a computer in maintaining and facilitating the operational function of a facility for young children. Other texts deal with children using computers as part of the curriculum. See Chapter 10. Most centers find it inconvenient and costly to share a computer between staff and children.

Some centers have less need for computers than others. Small centers, those on very limited budgets, those who have use of computers through other channels (chains, corporations, public funded centers), or those who have their records and finances handled through existing channels may not need computers for record keeping. Money should go *first* to directly benefit the children: increased staff, better trained staff, appropriate toys and materials, safety and health measures, and so on before it is spent on a computer. Directors of centers must determine whether a computer could save them time, effort, and money. Each director must carefully consider her center's needs when answering this question.

There is the legitimate question asked by many directors: Why would we consider the expenditure for a computer when other things are of a higher priority? This question deserves careful consideration, for many centers operate on a shoe-string budget. Wouldn't it be more cost effective (and morale boosting) to consider employees first? This question needs to be answered for each individual center. In some cases, the cost of keeping records and budgets may actually be reduced through computer use (fewer employees, less time), and staff could be shifted to work directly with the children. In other cases though, centers generate additional (but not necessary) reports to justify the purchase of a computer. Small centers may be able to handle their record keeping more easily without a computer; large centers may find a computer well worth the

money. Additional benefits of a computer may be increased accuracy and availability, and applications to planning, word processing, and so on. An initial introduction to the computer can be slow, tedious, and uncertain.

In evaluating whether or not to get a computer, one of the first steps should be to determine all the ways a computer could be used:

Keeping records on children and personnel

Maintaining material and equipment inventories

Planning snacks/meals

Monitoring financial transactions (budget, income and expenses, tuition records, payroll, tax records, etc.)

Word processing (agendas, parent education, employee information, job descriptions, announcements, records, inventories, work schedules, etc.)

Printing (making copies of computer information)

Education (new skills and information, new jargon, keeping current, etc.)

Internet and e-mail may be great additions to some centers and of little value to others due to size of organization, costs, training, time, and access to computers, and so on.

Before purchasing computer hardware, center needs and available programs (software) must be examined. Being specific, creative, and exhaustive will help make the distinction between *needs* and *wants*. Keeping *your* priorities in mind, talk with people in and out of the child-care field who have computers. See if (and how) they use computers. Contact reliable sources that promote

❖ Stimulator

Make a list of information you feel would be important to have on file about each child in the center.

Design a form using this information.

Indicate why the information is important and how to use it in meeting the child's needs or in counseling with staff or parents. Compare the form with those in Appendix E and Chapter 8.

good child-care practices (local and national day-care and child-care organizations). Don't rely on the local software dealer or advertisements without checking with someone who actually uses that brand of software. Are their needs similar enough to yours to make a good comparison (funding, size, etc.)?

If the decision is made to invest in a computer and software, ask the vendor to supply you with a list of current software users in your area. Call directors and compare programs. When you find a program similar to yours, ask about their experience with the software. Ask other directors what they like and dislike about the software. Then decide if the expense and the particular program meet your needs (see Neugebauer, 1990, and Morris, 1991).

Many types of computers are on the market; they become outdated quickly but are becoming more and more affordable. Focus on your present and future needs. Software is usually updated periodically so you will probably not be stuck with an outdated program, but you could get one that does not meet your needs.

A computer can be inexpensive or expensive, easy or difficult to master, an aid or a hindrance, a necessity or a luxury. There are a number of programs written specifically for child-care management. They need to be carefully matched with the needs of each individual center. (See the references at the end of this chapter and numerous NAEYC publications or contact centers that are pleased/displeased with computer use.)

When a software program has been selected, the computer operator must study it carefully in order to record information accurately and to get the most use out of the program. In each instance (for word processing, records, inventories, etc.) the center's own records will need to be typed into the appropriate categories. Unfortunately, computers and software don't come ready to use.

CHILDREN

If serious consideration was originally given to intake information on children and if program philosophy was clear, directors have already decided what information will be collected and whether it will be used only during the children's time at the center, passed on to the next teacher, or retained for various reasons. (See also Chapter 8 and Appendix C.) Retaining children's records may influence the intake information requested. What information is truly valuable for the present and future? How will it be useful in 3, 5, or 10 years? How are confidentiality and the Freedom of Information Act handled? How can important information be retained permanently? Children's records are protected under the Family Educational Rights and Privacy Act of 1974, PL 93-380.

Parents should always be informed of what information will be confidential and what will be available to all staff. For example, income, past medical history, and other pertinent information will be available only to the director and lead teachers. Emergency numbers, authorized persons to pick up the child, and general medical information (allergies, medications, etc.) will be available to directors, lead teachers, and office staff. Parents decide how much detail they release; however, the information must be accurate and complete.

One way this can be done efficiently is to have enrollment pages that will be viewed by the director and lead teachers only; other information, on separate pages, will be viewed and used by staff members in completion of center records.

Some teachers may prefer to collect additional information about each child, such as anecdotal records, progress reports, samples of work, and special interests or behavior. This information would be compiled in the child's individual folder and may have no interest or value to anyone other than the child's present teacher. While children participate in the center program, records of attendance, experiences, illnesses and accidents, interactions with peers and adults, family situations, and self-confidence can be helpful in meeting their needs, upgrading their experiences, and noting their progress.

Written reports are seldom meaningful to parents of preschoolers. Most written reports are for teacher use in noting children's progress. Parents may misinterpret them owing to inexperience or lack of knowledge of what to look for. A conference shared by parents and teachers is much more valuable, being less easily misinterpreted, inhibiting broad generalizations, and relaying less trivial information.

Butler (1974) identified three important policies on records: (1) records should protect children on whom the records are kept, (2) the teacher should objectively respond to the information before making any professional decisions, and (3) the time of record reading should be considered carefully. Butler concluded, "One of the first professional lessons a teacher should learn is use of good judgment regarding sensitive information about children" (p. 181). Whereas some records should be readily available, others should be strictly confidential; however, parents may request access to confidential records of their children.

Teachers need to carefully evaluate their opinions of records in relation to their responses to children, and then develop styles that will help them be objective, friendly, and perceptive. Some teachers argue that reading children's records before becoming familiar with the children personally will cause prejudice toward certain children. Others maintain that if a teacher reads children's records before they come into her class, the teacher will be better prepared to deal with each of the children as individuals. Some teachers refer to records only when problems develop. None of these attitudes is completely justifiable. It seems desirable for teachers to become familiar with children and their records at the same time. Records will need to be examined throughout the year, with reference to specific information that might have had no significance at other times of the year. Teachers can function independently of records yet use them in their work with individual children. See Figure 11–1 for a description of the privacy rights for children—PL 93-380.

As long as a child remains in school, information will be added to her records, including school accidents, contagious diseases, illness, teachers' observations and anecdotal records, major points from parent conferences and conversations, notes from home, staff discussions regarding the child, and any information to make the records current and more useful.

Enrollment

Application forms are generally state regulated; therefore, some items on them are required. In designing these forms, directors should consider the time and effort the parents must spend to furnish the requested information and the value of such information to those working with the children. (Sample forms can be found in Appendix C.)

Some centers can place a child immediately; however, if the center's quota is full, a waiting period ensues during which parents may elect to enroll their child at another center. When an opening occurs, a child is selected according to center policy, parents are notified, and arrangements are made to enroll and orient the child and parents. A brochure or handbook with pertinent information about the center may be given to the parents. (See sample handbook in Appendix A.)

Personal Information

It is important for staff members at the center to have access to personal information about each child to meet the child's individual needs and build a personal relationship. (See also Appendix C.) If a center must determine eligibility of families for service, very detailed financial information is required.

Each entry on the form should be relevant and have value for the center. Information used in research projects or for funding must be precise. Some centers require specialized information (circumstances surrounding the child's birth, early feeding patterns, general health of family members and relatives), and other centers ask only for basic information, for example, name and birth date of child, name and address of parents, names and ages of siblings, and other information. Care should be taken to protect the family's privacy; ask only for information that is vital to the

---

This law says the following:

1. Parents of children who attend a school receiving federal assistance may see information in the school's official files. This information includes test scores, grade averages, class rank, intelligence quotient, health records, psychological reports, notes on behavioral problems, family background items, attendance records, and all other records except personal notes made by a staff member solely for his own use.

2. Records must be made available for review within 45 days of the request.

3. Parents may challenge information irrelevant to education, such as religious preference, or unsubstantiated opinions.

4. Contents of records may be challenged in a hearing. If the school refuses to remove material challenged by parents as inaccurate, misleading, or inappropriate, the parent may insert a written rebuttal.

5. With some exceptions (e.g., other officials in the same school, officials in another school to which the student has applied for transfer, some accrediting associations, state educational officials, some financial aid organizations, and the courts), written consent of parents is required before school officials may release records. Schools must keep a written record as to who has seen, or requested to see, the child's records.

6. Parents have the right to know where records are kept and which school officials are responsible for them.

7. Unless a divorced parent is prohibited by law from having any contact with the child, divorced parents have equal access to official records.

8. Most of the foregoing rights pass from parent to child when the child is 18 years of age.

9. School districts must notify parents (and the 18-year-olds) of their rights.

Figure 11–1   Privacy rights for children—PL 93-380, later revised as PL 93-579, Title V, Section 522a, 1997. Source: Decker & Decker, 1992, pp. 344–345.

progress and welfare of the child. For example, questions about socioeconomic status can provide range choices (between ____ and ____) rather than a specific dollar amount. (Some programs require a more precise family income amount for funding purposes; actual figures must be provided.) If there is a question as to whether the family can afford center care, discuss it privately with the parents.

Health Record

Self-image, diseases, malnutrition, disabilities, and accidents can affect a child's interaction with others, her response to her environment, and her ability to absorb experiences. (See also Chapter 8 and Appendixes A and C.) Many diseases and disabilities can be reduced or prevented through education and attention at the center and in the home.

Many crippling and dangerous diseases previously controlled have been reappearing—in some cases, in epidemic proportions. For personal or religious reasons, parents sometimes do not have their children properly immunized. Not only can diseases be harmful, but also secondary conditions (damage to ears or eyes, for example) affect children in irreparable ways. For these reasons, certain public and private schools refuse to admit children without proof of current immunization. Parents should check with their physician or clinic for information about communicable diseases and their prevention.

Most health records ask for information about illnesses, operations or hospitalizations, and dates of the following immunizations:

- DPT and/or Td (diphtheria, tetanus, pertussis or whooping cough; or tetanus–diphtheria toxoid)
- Polio
- Measles (rubella—10-day, red measles)
- Rubella (German measles—3-day measles)
- Mumps
- Hemophilus influenza type B (Hib)

See examples of health records in Appendices C and D.

Emergency and Illness Procedure

Accidents and illnesses do happen even when caution is practiced, and the center must be prepared to handle them. Staff members should be periodically updated in procedures to follow when such incidents occur. Employees may be required to have current first-aid and CPR training.

Not only does it make sense to be prepared, but Fiene (1984) reported that emergency contact information and procedures are key factors of the overall quality of a program. Near the telephone and in other obvious places, post a list of emergency numbers (police, fire station, ambulance, and hospitals) and some basic procedures for handling the most common and most serious accidents. (Refer to Chapter 9 on Safety.)

The center may choose to have emergency information on separate cards for each of the children, but it should also be available in other places in case the one source is not immediately accessible. Whenever children go on field trips (or on a center-sponsored outing), each child should wear a tag that includes her name and the center's name, address, and phone number. Emergency information should be taken for every child at the center in case of accident or illness. The information should include the following:

Child: name, address, and phone number

Each parent (or guardian): name, home address, and phone number; business name, address, and phone number

Additional people to contact if parent is not available: name, home address, home phone number, relationship to child, and parental permission to authorize treatment

Child's doctor: name, address, and phone number (include an alternate, if possible)

Hospital or clinic: name, address, and phone number (include an alternate, if possible)

Family insurance company: name, address, phone number, and policy number

Center insurance company: name, address, and phone number

As soon as possible after an accident, a complete report should be written, including time and date, circumstances, witnesses, procedure followed, treatment, and outcome. Accurate and complete information should be recorded for the files, for the insurance company, and in case of any legal action. Be prepared! See Chapter 8 for more information and Appendix C for sample forms.

Physical Examination

Pre-enrollment physical examinations are recommended by some centers, required by others, and ignored by yet others. (See also Chapter 8.) There are several advantages to requiring physical examinations: Early detection of abnormalities or problems can be vital to a child's health; parents and teachers can be informed of the growth and development of each child and whether the child is within normal range for her age; the child gets experience apart from illness and injury with medical persons; and immunizations can be updated. If the cost of an examination is a problem for any parents, a number of referral agencies can be contacted.

Information from a doctor or clinic is valuable to a center. It should be reported on a simple form or note showing the doctor's or clinic's name. The information should be meaningful and thorough, verifying the date of the exam and including anything that would assist staff members who are working with the child.

The examination should be conducted within 30 days of the child's enrollment. Centers may also require a physical each year that the child is enrolled and request that parents report any new information to the center to maintain up-to-date records.

Few centers are fortunate enough to have a physician or registered nurse on their staff. The major responsibilities of the physician are to oversee the general health of the staff and children, to handle emergencies, and to counsel the staff. The major responsibility of the nurse is the routine daily checking for changes in the children's physical appearances. Many parents enjoy and appreciate interactions with the nurse and often ask for guidance in dealing with personal health and safety. In the event that having a medical person on the staff is not affordable, the local public health department can be used as a health resource.

Referral Records

At times child-care workers come in contact with families who need specialized child care. Where this occurs frequently, a center may assign a full- or part-time employee who has training in the medical, psychometric, guidance, remedial, speech, or other related areas. When this situation occurs infrequently, the center should develop a resource directory, if one is not presently available in the community, through the local Chamber of Commerce, the United Fund, the Community Council, the State Department of Social Services, or other recognized agency.

Helpful information compiled by the center should include the following:

1. The name, address, phone number, hours, and contact person
2. A description of the basic service (physical health, mental health, etc.)
3. Eligibility requirements
4. A form, based on referral needs, for the specific type of referral
5. A permission signature of parent/guardian
6. Name of person to whom referral is made (if different than number one)
7. Name of referring person, date, telephone number, and reason for referral
8. Any supporting information or records for referral, including information about behavior (length of time, intensity, child's response, parental response, procedures taken at center and results, etc.)
9. A section for the agency to report back to the center as to evaluation or disposition
10. A copy of the referral form should be retained by the center

Reporting to Parents

A method of periodic interchange between parents and center is provided in "Parent Conferences" (see Appendix A). Teachers who keep open communication with parents about center events find it easier to communicate with parents about their individual children when specific situations arise.

When a child is referred to a special agency, the contact person for the child may be the parents or the center. At any rate, both parties must be informed about diagnosis, treatment, and future action if the child is to benefit in both the home and center setting.

In advance of need to report to parents, the center should initiate a procedure based on program objectives and for the good of those involved. The purpose of reporting to parents, unambiguous concepts, best method of feedback (written, oral, private or group input), and different responses of parents to different types of situations and different methods of feedback should be considered.

Progress

Many centers keep running accounts of children's progress. Personal information is kept in each child's record and is available to those who have contact with the child. The progress record is sometimes used in parent conferences. (See Chapter 4.)

Possible Computer Application. Important personal information about children can easily be coded and typed into the computer. When information is needed (such as emergency information, health record, personal history, center record, etc.), it is quickly retrieved for viewing or printing. Additional information or corrections can be added easily. Many personal files can be typed on a single disk for easy storage and can be kept confidential by restricting access to them through a special code. Caution: Computers are not infallible—they can and will go down. Information may also be inadvertently erased; the more people accessing the records, the greater the chance of error or elimination. For security, the computer operator should make hard (printed) copies and back up all information and records on other disks.

PERSONNEL

Records on employees must conform to state laws and the policies of the organization. They must include pertinent personal, education, experiential information, and must be accessible to authorized persons while being protected by federal privacy legislation.

Personnel records usually include current personal information such as name, birth date, address, phone number, and social security number and marital status. Additional information may include (but not be a factor of employment) one's sex, age, limitations, and nationality. Frequently the original application for employment listing one's education and experience along with names, addresses, and recommendations of references may be included in this file. (See Figure 11–2.)

Records showing past and present mental and physical health of the employee is included, with results of physical examinations or health impairments that would hinder their working with young children. An annual TB test is required by most programs. Employees are cautioned about their use of mood-altering substances. Smoking should not be permitted in the presence of young children.

For information suggested for an application form, emergency information (which should be easily accessible, current, and contain information regarding any allergies or health conditions), a checklist for each employee's personal records, job descriptions, and job announcements, see Appendix C, Figure C–1, and Appendixes D and E.

Emergency information should be easily accessible and always current. This includes any allergies or conditions that could be critical in an emergency.

Centers should keep information about the service of each employee—present title and job description, ages of children cared for/taught, absences incurred or leaves taken, professional participation (in-service education, conference attendance, workshop participation, committee service), salary increases, job advancement, and termination (when it occurs).

Payroll records will include the employee's social security number, marital status, number of dependents for tax purposes, descriptions of deductions, insurance, present job classification and salary, dates of job advancement/change, and other financial information.

When personnel records are no longer needed, they must be stored in accordance with state and federal regulations.

An important consideration to employees is the confidentiality of their records. The Privacy Act of 1974 (PL 93-579) requires federal agencies to take certain steps to safeguard the accuracy,

---

EMPLOYEE'S PERSONAL RECORD

The center should provide and maintain a file for each individual employee. Most centers have a preferred way of doing this; however, some suggestions follow:

1. Keep together all records of a particular individual.
2. File information such as:
   a. Original job application (Figure G-1), job description, advancements, or changes
   b. Performance appraisals, including goals, attendance record, additional training or experience, and professional participation
   c. Payroll information (starting salary, dates and amounts of increases, social security number, number of deductions, etc.)
   d. Health records, emergency information (Figure G-2)
   e. Specific information about this particular employee
3. Have a checklist of included forms for quick and easy reference on the outside of each individual folder (Figure G-3).
4. Specific information about this particular job.

As a prospective employer, look for these key items:

1. If employed, has applicant allowed for notice to present employer?
2. Are there gaps in employment that would indicate health problems or instability of the applicant?
3. Are there frequent job changes that indicate dissatisfaction or job hopping?
4. Does the applicant give clear information (position held, responsibilities, reason for leaving)?
5. Is the applicant neat and logical?
6. Does the applicant have the required skills/experience to fill the available job?
7. How well would this applicant work with present staff?
8. What special contributions could this applicant bring to the center, children, and/or families?
9. Would you want your own child associated with this person?

The Equal Opportunity Act of 1972 and the Affirmative Action Guidelines prohibit the asking of certain types of questions.

Figure 11–2   Screening information regarding new employees.

---

currentness, and security of records concerning individuals and limit record keeping to necessary and lawful purposes. Individuals also have a right to examine federal records containing such information and to challenge the accuracy of data with which they disagree (*Title v. section 522a U.S. code 1976 edition: Containing the general and perma-* *nent laws of the U.S., in force on January 3, 1977,* 1977). There are procedures whereby an individual can obtain further information on any record system covered by The Privacy Act (Office of the Federal Register, 1977).

For protection of children, employees at the center, parents, and others, a criminal check and an abuse check must be made on each potential employee *before* final consideration. (See Chapter 6.)

Personnel records should be current and complete, as all records should. They should contain the original application, social security number, number of tax exemptions, health record form and records, performance appraisals (including goals, center assignments), wage increases, contracts, time sheets, center assignments (leadership, promotion, training received or conducted), and any other miscellaneous information pertaining to the individual's performance at the center.

Possible Computer Application. Important personal information about employees can easily be coded and entered into the computer. When information is needed (such as emergency information, health record, personal history, center record, etc.), it is quickly retrieved for viewing or printing. Additional information or corrections can be added easily. Many personal files can be on a single disk for easy storage and can be kept confidential by restricting access to them through a special code. A further use of the center's computer is to make employee work schedules for posting or handing to each employee.

INVENTORIES

Inventories that should be recorded and updated periodically include teaching materials of all kinds, toys and equipment, classroom and office supplies, food, and other records pertinent to the efficiency of the individual center. Without such inventories, it is difficult to plan programs, prioritize needs, and distribute funds.

Accurate inventory records permit teachers to check beforehand what materials, toys, books, and other items are available and where to locate them quickly. This saves much time and effort and increases planning and teaching efficiency.

Because of storage space, availability of materials, number of persons involved, budget, and philosophy, each center is encouraged to develop a usable check-in and check-out procedure to fit its particular needs. Following are some suggested methods.

Books

Most centers have at least a small library for children and teachers (and sometimes parents) that is supplemented with books from the local public library. This increases selection and reduces costs—but does require someone's time to pick up and return books to the library. Many public libraries also lend flannelboard stories, records, tapes, pictures, equipment, and other items.

For books to be usable, they must be easy to locate and shelve. The versatility of any of various methods to organize and store book information will determine the information's value to the users. Books could be organized by author's name, title (omitting articles *a, an, the*), subject matter, or an agreed-on center method. Information could be stored on index cards, alphabetically in a three-ring binder, on removable strips inserted in a frame, in manila envelopes, or by other convenient methods. All teaching staff need to know the system. See Figure 11–3 to visualize book location information as it would appear on index cards and arranged alphabetically in a three-ring binder.

Teaching personnel may wish to obtain a book on a certain subject. Centers who use the subject method can make broad categories with appropriate headings and subheadings as the need arises; however, too many categories or too specific subheadings make the system cumbersome and useless. For example:

Families		*Families*	
Parents	Mothers		Fathers
Children	Infants	School-Agers	Teens
Extended	Grandparents		Other relatives

The list on the left gives general categories and is often enough information for most centers. The list on the right has subdivided each category in the left column and may be so specific that few

Index Cards:
    By Author:

Author	Title	Subject	Call #
Publisher, year		Condition or Use	Copies
Vendor (place of purchase)			
Cook, B.	*The Curious Little Kitten*	1, 5	C 17
Young Scott Books, 1956		3	3
Knowledge Book Store (local)			

    By Title:

Title	Author	Subject
Call #		
Publisher (and date):	Condition	Copies
Vendor (place of purchase)		

    By Subject:

ANIMALS		
Author	Title	Call #
Publisher (and date):	Condition	Copies
Vendor (place of purchase)		

Binder or Individual Sheet:
    By Author:

Author	Title	Subject	Publisher	Condition	Call #
Aldis, D.	*Everything & Anything*	6	2	7	A 04
Cook, B.	*The Curious Little Kitten*	1, 5	17	3	C 17

Figure 11–3   Arrangements of book location information.
Note: For each letter of the alphabet there is a separate page or section on which to add new books easily. Loose-leaf sheets can be filed by author, title, or subject, just as file cards can.

books would be listed under each topic. If a subject method is going to be implemented at the center, it may be wise to brainstorm subheadings, allow a mellowing period, make a trial run, and then make revisions. Also, books may cover more than one category, which requires their double (or triple) listing. For example, for the book *The Curious Little Kitten* (Cook, 1956), *kittens* is the primary listing and *turtles* the second. Further listings (such as *water* and *curiosity*) would be pointless.

For ease in reordering, keep full publication information on file: the author, the book's correct title, address of the publisher, and the publication date.

The condition or use of a book is important when budgets are tight or show a surplus. In either case, books that need to be replaced or purchased

Author	Title	Primary Subject	Secondary Subjects			Publisher	Vendor	Book Cond.	# of Copies	Call Number

Figure 11–4 Sample computer-made book inventory form.

could be coded to be identified easily. Rather than using words (*good, needs repair or replacement, need multiple copies,* etc.), a code could be identified, such as a numerical code (for computer recording) or color code (for visual use), as follows:

Condition/use	Numerical code	Color code
All in good condition	1	Red
Multiple copies, some need repair/replacement	2	Yellow
All need replacement	3	Green
Need additional copies	4	Blue
Get from public library	5	
Other appropriate category	6	Orange

Making an inventory of books may seem like an enormous task, but once it is done, new books can be added or reordered efficiently, provided the records are maintained. Regardless of the inventory method, a master list should be kept in a safe place. All entries should include author, title, subject(s), call number (or location), publisher name and date, number of copies, and place of purchase (vendor).

Possible Computer Application.   A form for keeping the book inventory can be the same whether the record is kept manually or on the computer; in fact, the form can easily be computer-made. (See Figure 11–4 for an example.)

Through the use of an appropriate computer software program, the computer operator should be able to add new books, change information about a previously listed book, or display on the screen all books in the collection by titles, authors, subjects, publishers, or vendors. Software programs should provide for a printout of the books in the different categories just listed. The program should also allow for adding information. See Appendix H for more information.

Pictures

Pictures can be categorized by a subject code that is similar to the one used for books. Pictures are often of different shapes and sizes, making them more difficult to store, and they are easily torn. When possible, they should be laminated and filed in large boxes, in envelopes, in drawers, or on shelves where they are readily available, but also protected.

Topic: Plants Description	# of Copies	Condition/Use	Other Topics	Call #/Place
Boy in garden	3	2	2, 5, 17	P-27

Figure 11–5   Sample picture index entry.

Pictures have multiple uses and should be crosslisted on a master list. Those that are easy to find and easy to refile will be in constant use. The conditions of the pictures and requests for new or duplicate ones could be recorded on the master list to facilitate their purchases at ordering time. Figure 11–5 suggests a form for indexing pictures.

The example in Figure 11–5 indicates that there are three copies of a picture of a boy planting a garden; some need repair or replacement; the picture is cross-referenced with subjects 2, 5, and 17 (i.e., *boy*, *spring*, and *vegetables*); and the picture is #27 in the *Plants* folder. Consistent coding across books, pictures, cassette tapes, filmstrips, videos, slide sets, phonograph records, and other teaching materials (e.g., *P-27* for the file and picture location in Figure 11–5) can greatly simplify all teaching material inventories, especially when the code is memorized.

Possible Computer Application. As with book inventories, picture inventories that are kept in a computer increase usability and reduce time and frustration for the person recording the information and those using it. Forms for picture inventories can be made on the computer much faster than by other methods. The information for manual or computer picture inventories could be identical: subject(s), condition, description, requests, location, and so on.

To be most valuable, information must be accurate and current, an easy task with a computer. This method has several advantages: a permanent record is maintained, items can be added or deleted easily, additional copies of the inventory can be made quickly and inexpensively, and record-keeping time is reduced.

A software program for picture inventories should have the same capabilities as the one for the book inventory, for example, adding new pictures, displaying or changing information about a picture, listing all pictures, listing pictures in a specific category (subject), listing purchasing sources used, and giving additional commands for the full use of the program. It excludes information that is inappropriate for pictures, such as author and publisher. It should also include a computer command to print all the information stored on its disks.

For additional information about picture inventories, see Appendix H.

Audio Media

CDs or tapes can be listed on a single sheet or index card, numbered as they are acquired, and identified by topic or curriculum area. Coding depends on the number and variety of tapes and the frequency of their use. Popular tapes should be bought in multiple copies or scheduled in advance.

Some centers require that only teachers handle the loading and unloading of tapes because of high replacement costs. However, some centers believe that the children's experiencing complete use of the tapes is well worth the replacement costs.

Figure 11–6 shows a method of inventorying tapes. The interpretation of the entry could be as follows: This cassette tape has stories with music; there is one copy; it can be used by the children; it is about family life; the recording company is #7 on the code and the company's number of the tape is #782; it is in good condition; and it is #29

Description	# of Copies	Used by T or C	Curriculum Subject	Order #	Condition/ Use	Call #/ Place
Stories/music	1	C	Family	7-782	1	CT29

Figure 11–6   Sample tape inventory entry.

in the box of cassette tapes. Filmstrips, videos, CDs, and slide sets could be categorized in the same way as this cassette.

Copies of cassette tapes can be made under certain conditions without violating the copyright law. However, the use of such a copy should be carefully checked to be in conformance with the law.

Possible Computer Application. Additions and changes in audio and video inventories are simple and forms can be easily kept on computer. See the information on picture inventories.

Phonograph Records[1]

Records can be easily damaged or destroyed; they need special care when used and stored. For longevity, they should have individual jackets or covers, should be filed upright rather than stacked, and should have enough space between them so that teachers can see the numbers and can remove and replace the records easily. If children are permitted to handle the records, they should be taught to hold and use them properly.

Records can be listed by use (e.g., listening, participating, singing, instrumental), by music type (e.g., classical, jazz, contemporary), or by any other method that is convenient for the staff.

They can also be crosslisted in different combinations to make them more useful to teachers.

[1] The availability of records is diminishing rapidly; however, some centers are fortunate enough to have a good supply of a variety of types of records. Therefore, this section is retained in this edition although this option may soon be obsolete.

Figure 11–7 shows an outline and an example of listing records on index cards.

The record in the example in Figure 11–7 is a participation record; its name is "Stretch, Move, and Wiggle"; and it is filed on the participation shelf under #304. Specific songs and the vocalist are listed, as are the number of copies, the recording company (or code), multiple copies with those needing replacement, the company from whom they were last ordered (Greenleaf Record Company catalog), the company's number for identification and ordering (PA-227), and teacher use only.

The individual record number should appear on the jacket and on the corresponding record. It can be recorded easily with a felt-tip pen or by applying a matching adhesive label to the jacket and record. The number should be conspicuous, easily read, and consistently in the same location on each record.

It may be helpful to center personnel if the records are filed by category or use rather than by record title or company. For example, all classical records are given the first number of 3, followed by the individual record numbers. When there are multiple copies, the copy number follows: 3-117-2. Subsequent records take on the next available number in the category into which they fit. Cross referencing facilitates the search for a particular type of music or a particular song—thumbing through cards or sheets is easier than handling each record.

Inventories that list each record's recording company and reference number simplify reordering whenever records are lost or damaged or additional copies are desired (as long as they are available).

Figure 11–7   Sample record index card.

Index card:	
Type of record:	Call #
Record name:	
Song Title(s):	
Recording artist(s):	# of copies:
Recording company:	Condition or use:
Recording company number:	Used by T or C:
Vendor or place of purchase:	
[example]	
Participation	
"Stretch, Move, and Wiggle"	PR-304
"See Me Stretch"	
"Move Like Me"	
"Wiggle, Wiggle, Wiggle"	
(list each song)	
Byrd Van Tract	4
Foothill Associates (or #84)	2
Greenleaf Record Company (catalogue) PA-227	T

Possible Computer Application. Similar to other media listed.

Toys and Play Equipment

Toys and play equipment are used, abused, lost, and damaged; they also become obsolete. Budgets should provide funds for these items by allotting a specified yearly amount or by allotting larger amounts for 3- and 5-year periods.

Some directors know in advance the amounts they can afford to spend on toys and play equip-ment; others must wait until the end of the fiscal year to decide. Regardless of the purchasing method or time, inventories that are kept current allow ease in prioritizing needs and allocating funds where they will give the most return. The method of keeping toy and equipment records will, therefore, depend on the director and the center. Some suggestions include the following:

1. Keep a file folder for each type of equip-ment. Record pertinent information as listed in Figure 11–8. One center preferred

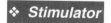

Regarding the storage and use of cassette tapes, CDs, and phonograph records at the center, do three things:

1. Evaluate the way the media is presently stored, checked in and out, and used

2. Brainstorm for various ways to keep each media (in topical boxes, by musician, by size, etc.)

3. Ask audio users outside the center how they keep their personal records

Combine the three ideas above and present your findings in a 5-minute report in the next staff meeting regarding confirmation to retain the current inventory system or make some specific modifications.

certain shovels and buckets over others. This was noted in the *Sand Toy* folder. When purchasing these items, the director was able to order them quickly from a known vendor.

2. Use a three-ring binder to add additional pages or remove unnecessary ones easily. Individual sheets in a file folder are also acceptable.

3. File index cards for each category in a box where they will be readily available for notations or requests. Cards can be removed for ordering or prioritizing and then easily replaced.

All employees (and even children) can watch for and practice ways to recycle, repair, and reduce costs of toys and equipment. The director (or designated person) should keep current information as to replacement dates of items, the best sources from which to purchase them, and their most recent purchase costs. The center personnel should give input about how to catalog or group items, the present condition of the items, and the popularity of each of the items from the standpoints of both teachers and children.

Wise directors do two things in regard to toys and equipment: (1) They provide a very convenient place for teachers to record needs, wants, or dreams, but request specific information as to sources, required quantities, costs, and classroom uses; (2) they check the list periodically, prioritize it, and attempt to purchase items as frequently as funds allow. Teachers take the responsibility of recording items; the director orders them as funds are available.

There are many ways to categorize toy and equipment inventories. A few examples include the way materials are used (small- or large-muscle, indoor or outdoor, cooperatively or independently), where they are stored, related curriculum topic (music, art, science), and alphabetically. Obviously, many materials fit into more than one category. Staff members who use the materials most frequently can suggest a convenient way—but remember that individuals have differing ideas. Try the consensus method—and if this fails, try logic!

Possible Computer Application. Keeping track of toys and equipment with a computer is simple. Repairs, additions, receipts, and other information can be noted and handled. Changes on records can be made frequently and with little effort. When it is time to reorder, a computerized inventory can be invaluable. A computer program might include the information shown in Figure 11–8.

Supplies

This section covers consumables for creative experiences, craft projects, and classroom activities. Food items will be considered in the following section.

It is very frustrating to plan to use certain materials for a lesson and, on the day of the lesson, find that they are unavailable. This problem can be reduced by keeping inventory records current and by reordering at specified times.

Name of item:		Quantity:
Location:		Type:
Condition:	Popularity: adults _____ children _____	
Replace:		
Vendor:	Cost:	Date:
Check-out method:		
Other:		

Figure 11–8 Sample toy inventory card.

Name of commodity:	Amount on hand:
Purchase size preferred:	Estimated user per _____:
Storage life:	Reorder level:
Preferred vendor:	Replacement time:
Cost last:	Most common uses:
Preferred colors, materials:	
Comments:	

Figure 11–9   Sample supplies inventory card.

Besides money, factors that determine the supplies that are on hand are storage space, popularity, shelf life, replacement time, season, and versatility. For inventory purposes a supply form (of index cards, a three-ring binder, or other method) should include the information listed in Figure 11–9.

Each center has different needs and must make different decisions as to how much, when, what, and how to order and store its supplies. But *every* center has a need to count and organize the supplies on hand and to anticipate future needs.

Purchasing and storing are important for reducing costs and increasing availability. Some items can be bought in large quantities and stored without spoilage; others may be damaged by moisture or insects. Without an accurate inventory, both purchasing and storing can be frustrating and expensive.

Items commonly classed as supplies include materials used for the following:

Creative and craft projects: Paper, paint, paste, glue, soap flakes, flour, salt, cornstarch, liquid starch, food coloring, straws, pasta, brushes, scissors, wood, nails, bowls, pans, utensils (egg beaters, spoons, graters), etc.

Snack: Napkins, glasses, dishes, utensils, trays, etc.

General use: Paper towels, sponges, dish towels, hot pads, washing and cleaning compounds, brooms, dust pans, mops, etc.

Sensory table: Rice, wheat, beans, sawdust, etc.

Possible Computer Application.   It's a laborious job to have to personally check items before ordering or planning. Using a computer adds an element of interest and challenge to the task. Manual and computer lists can and should be kept current. After checking these lists, a quick eye-ball of storage can confirm items for reorder.

As supplies are consumed and new purchases are made, records must be updated or the computer will not be able to perform its job. Inaccurate information can alter amounts, affect reordering, distort costs, and reduce availability of items.

Because this procedure is similar to food inventorying, an example will not be included here.

Food

Food purchases must be considered carefully. Some items have a long shelf life; others do not. Storage type and required space also need attention. Whether centers serve meals and snacks or only snacks, each food item should be considered as to nutritive value, amount needed, cost per child, availability, and storage life.

Most centers that serve meals are regulated by state, federal, and funding agency requirements. These requirements regard the ages of the children, their length of time in the center, and other pertinent factors. Because these regulations are well established, this chapter will discuss only snack programs; however, the same principles apply to meal programs. See Chapter 8 for nutrition information.

❖ Stimulator

To cut down on workload and expedite needed snack menus, you (as the director) delegate a staff member to plan snacks for a month. Unfortunately, the delegatee has had no classroom experience; knows little of children's likes and dislikes; and does not take quantities, combinations, or preparation time into consideration. He searches his own ideas, asks fellow employees, and finally calls roommates and friends for ideas. He has no awareness of the amount of time he has spent, the inappropriateness of some items on his list, or the increased acquisition and preparation time of the items. His final plan is unusable—and both of you are frustrated.

As the director, what do you do?

1. Tell him it was a waste of time and a poor attempt.

2. Thank him for trying, throw it away, and redo it.

3. Go over it carefully with him, pointing out the good and bad menus and helping him correct errors.

4. Make note of inappropriate menus, give him an inventory list, and ask him to make substitutions.

5. Have him calculate the cost of each day's menu and reduce it to a certain dollar amount, then send him shopping.

6. All of the above.

7. None of the above.

Explain your reasoning.

This was really a loaded stimulator. Why was the person asked to do the task in the first place? Was it to save you (the director) time? The best answer isn't listed—but you might rationalize with 3 (teaching) or 7 (admitting your error)—but that doesn't schedule the meals! Before you get too involved, consider these possible expediters and frustration releasers: preparation (prevention) is far better than treatment! Without adequate preparation, both director and delegatee will waste time and experience frustration!

1. Determine beforehand what experience the delegatee has had with children and meal planning for them; the willingness of this person to attempt such a task; the limits (dollar amounts, preparation time, availability of commodities); your willingness to coach this person; and other unforseen problems.

2. Ask the delegatee to observe meal/snack times for a reasonable period of time. Then observe together, pointing out individual observations.

3. Request the delegatee to discuss with the cook: food preferences and dislikes of the children, ways to get children to eat new foods, amounts of food consumed by the children, appetizing ways to serve food (family style, ready-dished, color combinations, etc.).

4. Now you and the delegatee are ready for his first attempt at meal planning. It may take both of you to come up with the finished plan.

❖ ❖ ❖ ❖

Snack planning can be routine, or it can be tedious and frustrating. Consideration needs to be given to nutritious snack items that can be purchased in quantity, are easily accessible, nonseasonal, nonperishable, inexpensive, and/or used for only special occasions. The major factor of planning is to provide nutritional foods for the children. Also, it is important to determine the quantity per child, ways to use leftovers, and possible opportunities for the children to help prepare and serve the food. The director should gather information to achieve these goals and note the children's likes, availability of foods, and allowable costs (per child per day). Staff members can give valuable suggestions about food items to include, which foods their children could benefit from helping to prepare, and general organization for both meals and snacks.

It is the director's responsibility to organize a system of planning and purchasing snack items that will best meet the center's needs. Grouping similar items under broad categories, such as the following, might be convenient (see also Appendix H).

Juices (or beverages other than milk)

Dairy products

Vegetables: fresh, frozen, canned, and dried

Fruit: fresh, frozen, canned, and dried

Cookies/crackers

Meat and meat products (lean cuts; avoid additives)

Grains

Baking needs

Miscellaneous items

As purchases are made, current costs should be recorded for comparison with previous costs, determining the cost of snack per child, and selecting the best source of specific items. This helps reduce the amount of time spent in purchasing food. It can also help the director be alert for sales and seasonal foods to save money.

To determine the quantity consumed per child (or group of children of a certain size), the director can make a guesstimate and try it out, observe snack periods to determine the exact amount, or predetermine the quantity to be used. Some programs (e.g., government-funded) mandate the quantities and nutritional contents children are to receive daily in snacks and/or meals (see Chapter 8). (Note: Children usually drink more in the summer; they eat less regular food, but more seasonal items, near a holiday.) Because purchasing and scheduling the right amount of food per snack is sometimes difficult, allow some flexibility for using leftover food. Food dollars can be wasted when there is no control over the amount of food served or allowance for using leftovers.

The typical juice-and-cracker snack need not be the only menu. Many juices and crackers are high in sugar and fat content, costly, and uninteresting to children. So a note of caution to the planner to avoid preservatives, cholesterol, sugars, and fats may be in order. A well-developed planning approach gives a director not only ease in planning, but also a challenge to provide nutritional items and to involve the children.

As items are used from the food inventory, the appropriate quantities should be reduced from the current list and a notation made so that items can be reordered at the proper time. (Delegate this important but director-consuming task.) If the list is kept current, snacks can be scheduled from the inventory list rather than by checking the actual supplies.

A form may include the categories shown in Figure 11–10.

Figure 11–11 is a printed copy of snack menus for a 4-day week. Do not be overly concerned if the sample menu has variety, if the amounts don't fit your group, or the prices are out-of-line with your community costs. This is merely an exercise to show how menus can be made, how

Figure 11–10 Sample food order form.

Name of item: _____ Quantity on hand: _____ Best size to order and store (pounds, cases, sizes): _____ Most recent price: _____ Most recent place of purchase: _____ Preferred place of purchase (if any): _____ Estimated use (time in days, weeks, etc.): _____ Storage required (freezer, refrigerator, shelf): _____ When to reorder (when quantity gets how low?): _____ Replacement time (days, weeks): _____ Preferred brands or kinds: _____ Comments: _____

daily/weekly/per child totals can be calculated, and if spending is too much or too little on snacks.

Before making a snack schedule, check with the teachers to see if they have any special requests, planned food experiences, or dates for certain items. Teachers should be aware of the possibility of ordering special food items and of the center's method of doing so. Avoiding changes in the schedule after it has been prepared ensures that food will be used wisely (and promotes efficient time use).

The period of time to schedule and post snacks will vary from one center to another; however, if snacks are posted a week or two in advance, teachers can use snack preparation as an important part of their lesson plans. Old snack menus can be valuable—especially if notations have been made about quantity, combination of items, ways to use leftovers, favorites or dislikes, and ease or difficulty in preparation.

Possible Computer Application. Basic information must first be recorded onto the computer disk (even if it has to be changed later). It should include items used, prices, vendors, quantities per child, quantities on hand, nutritive values, and reorder levels. Once this information has been compiled, snack and meal planning can begin, and additions to the disk or changes in food schedules can be made with little effort—and no eraser!

A computer software program for snacks or meals should include the names of items, quantities added or subtracted from stock, instructions on ways to create or change menus, amounts of food required to complete the menus, a shopping list, a complete food inventory, and planned menus. This information can be viewed on the screen or printed.

OTHER RECORDS

Records that should be maintained, in addition to those mentioned, include work schedule, finance, and payroll records. Other information deemed important to the operation of the center may include a current list of acceptable substitute teachers, meeting minutes, policies and procedures, repair requests, current equipment catalogs, handbooks, newsletters, snack and meal menus, and brochures and manuals. All records should be organized, current, and accessible.

A correspondence file should include copies of each transaction, whether it be letters, invoices, bills, or other items. A record of outgoing correspondence can save hours of searching. For example, make a notation in a ledger for each letter—including date, to whom it is sent, a brief notation about its content, and where the letter is filed—such as:

Snack Menus for a 4-Day Week for 25 Children

Day 1

Item No.*	Item Name	Amount	Total Cost	Cost/Child
40	Apple slices	10 ea.	1.25	0.05
47	Banana slices	8 ea.	0.75	0.03
29	Fruit yogurt dip	12 oz	0.69	0.03
		Totals	$2.69	$0.11

Day 2

Item No.	Item Name	Amount	Total Cost	Cost/Child
134	Bran muffins	50 ea.	1.75	0.07
52	Grapes	2 lb	1.29	0.05
		Totals	$3.04	$0.12

Day 3

Item No.	Item Name	Amount	Total Cost	Cost/Child
114	Carrots	2 lb	0.98	0.04
115	Cauliflower	1.25 lb	0.75	0.03
116	Celery	1.25 lb	0.49	0.02
73	W/W Crackers	1 box	0.98	0.04
		Totals	$3.20	$0.13

Day 4

Item No.	Item Name	Amount	Total Cost	Cost/Child
22	Saltines	1 box	0.89	0.04
61	Cheese	1 lb	1.72	0.07
2	Grape juice froz.	2 cans	1.39	0.06
		Totals	$4.00	$0.16
		Weekly Total	$12.93	$0.52

Figure 11–11 Sample snack menu and costs.
*Some centers list food items by number for ease in planning.

Date	To Whom	Content	Filed
6-5-02	Friendly Insurance Co.	Insurance renewal	Insurance

Financial Transactions

Computer software saves administrative time, allowing directors to spend more time with their staff and the children. Computer applications relevant to financial transactions are determining budgets, figuring payrolls, writing checks, recording daily transactions, locating entries, and summing figures. For detailed information, see Chapter 12.

OTHER COMPUTER USES

Word Processing

Even though computers save time and work in financial transactions, the most common use of computers is word processing. Although a child-care center can benefit from the myriad other uses of the computer, the computer's value in word processing is not to be minimized. Word processors are ideal for preparing reports, memos, form letters, manuals, handbooks, newsletters, and routine materials. They address letters and envelopes and prepare individual tuition billings for children. They make convenient rough drafts and final copies quickly. They have the following advantages over typewriters:

- Processors are faster.
- Entire words, sentences, and paragraphs can be updated, deleted, and moved without retyping the whole page, etc.
- Corrections can be viewed on the screen or from a printed copy.
- Many pages of material can be stored on a single disk.
- Some processors offer color screens and a capability of making forms or designs.
- The screen is at eye level.

An invaluable aid in word processing is the spelling check, which is much faster and more accurate than proofreading. However, the speller determines only misspelled words, not incorrectly used words; for example, it could identify *neu* as misspelled, but not *now* incorrectly used for *not*.

Printer

Printers add versatility and value to computers. They are used to print documents from computer disks and are not like photocopy printers. In other words, they cannot be used to make copies of documents that have not previously been recorded on an internal computer disk.

CHAPTER SUMMARY

1. Record keeping is an important function of a child-care center; it should be accurate and complete.
2. It is necessary to decide on pertinent information to record, how to record it, how to use it, and how it is to be retained.
3. Records should be consistent with the philosophy and goals of the center.
4. Important center records include information about children and personnel, inventories of teaching materials and supplies, food planning, finances and budgeting, and other center-specific categories.
5. Attitude is very important when collecting, using, and retaining information.
6. Records can be kept manually or with computers.
7. Center tasks can be simplified and time, effort, and money can be saved through appropriate use of computers.
8. Before a computer is purchased, the specific needs of the center must be identified.
9. Computers can promote accuracy in record keeping.

PARTICIPATORS

Read the following suggestions, then select and complete those items that would be growth promoting to you.

Record Keeping

1. Discuss your opinion about the importance of record keeping.
2. What records do you think are important to keep on
   a. Children?
   b. Personnel?

   Why? How will they be used? How and when should they be destroyed?
3. Turn to the forms suggested for children, parents, and personnel in Appendices B, C, and G or those used in the center. Go over the items carefully to determine their importance, use, and validity. Propose changes, additions, or deletions.
4. Visit a preschool, child-care center, or kindergarten. Ask for copies of required forms, and ask about the ways information is used and the treatment of old records.
5. Using the following categories, make an inventory of 10 items each for (a) books, (b) pictures, (c) audiovisual materials, and (d) supplies. Or suggest changes for inventory forms presented in this chapter.
6. Prepare a work schedule for four full-time and six part-time employees. Assign jobs and classrooms.
7. Prepare a 1-week snack schedule for a group in your center (or assume the number and ages of the children). Check with a cook or director to see what the reasonable quantity would be for the items you have selected. Price the items at a local store. Record the daily cost and per child cost for the week. If possible, try your snack schedule with preschool children.

Computer Use

1. Specifically outline the computer needs or desires of a child-care center.
2. Visit child-care centers that use computer programs in their administrations. If possible, ask for demonstrations and feedback. Is their software a commercial program or was it written for their center? Talk directly to the person who enters the information and the person who uses printed records (may be the same person).
3. Visit a computer dealer and become more knowledgeable about available programs and machines. Ask about some of the ideas suggested in this chapter (such as warranty, service, instruction, financing, specifically written programs, available software, etc.).
4. Check with at least two different sources involved in child care (a center, state or national organizations, local support groups, etc.). In a nonoffensive way, discuss whether computers would aid or detract from operation of a child-care center.
5. Practice using a word processor if one is available. Allow plenty of time to become familiar with the machine; proficiency will come! Try to construct some computer forms that would be assets to a child-care program.
6. Describe the advantages of using computers to gather, store, and use records at the center.

REFERENCES

Butler, A. L. 1974. *Early childhood education: Planning and administering programs.* New York: Van Nostrand.

Cook, B. 1956. *The curious little kitten.* New York: Young Scott Books.

Fiene, R. J. 1984. *Child development program evaluation scale.* Washington, DC: Children's Services Monitoring Consortium.

Kontos, S., & Fiene, R. 1985. *Pennsylvania State University and Office of Children, Youth, and Families outcome study*. Harrisburg: Pennsylvania Office of Children, Youth, and Families.

Morris, S. 1991. Child care center management software buying guide #6. *Exchange*, 82, Nov./Dec., 37–40. (Vendor supplied information only.)

Neugebauer, R. 1990. Fifth annual child care center management software buying guide. *Exchange*, 76, Nov./Dec., 53–55.

Office of the Federal Register. 1977. *Protecting your right to privacy—Digest of systems of records, agency rules, and research aids*. Washington, DC: U.S. Government Printing Office.

Title v. section 522a U.S. code 1976 edition: Containing the general and permanent laws of the U.S., in force on January 3, 1977 (Vol. 1). 1977. Washington, DC: U.S. Government Printing Office.

Chapter 12

Finance and Budgeting

Guide for Readers

- ❖ *Unless they are well trained in financial matters, center directors are encouraged to record basic information and then get an accountant or financial consultant to prepare tax and other reports.*
- ❖ *Cost-cutting measures are important considerations; however, all costs must be included and all measures or safety must be followed.*
- ❖ *Preparing budgets can be frustrating and time-consuming; however, accurate planning and careful spending determine the financial success of a child-care program.*
- ❖ *Basic accounting procedures can be learned in various ways (self-improvement courses, junior colleges, financial management at colleges, professional services, etc.).*
- ❖ *Financial transactions can be done manually or by computer.*

Facts and Figures

- In 1986, child care in the United States was a $12 billion industry. By 1991, child care had grown to a $15.3 billion industry, and it is expected to rise to $48 billion before the turn of the century (Perreault, 1991).

- In 1986 child care cost a family $1500 to $15,000 per year—the average cost was $3000 (Friedman, 1986).

- A quality program will cost $5000 or more per year per child. . . . For many families, quality early childhood programs are simply not affordable (Decker & Decker, 1997, p. 218).

- The U.S. General Accounting Office (1990) estimated the full cost for preschoolers in a center was $5000 per child year (Decker & Decker, 1997, p. 206).

- Willer (1990) estimated the full cost of high-quality center care was $8000 per child year for children under age 5.

- "In last year's debates over federal child-care legislation, advocates frequently asserted that quality child care costs $3,000 per year. It is not clear where this claim originated, but it is clear that it is dangerously misleading. . . . In fact, our survey indicates, there are very few places where you can buy any form of child care for $3,000 per year. Child care for a 4-year-old costs anywhere from $3,120 to $7,176 per year. Infant care costs range from $3,640 to $10,920 per year" (Child Care Fees on the Rise Nationwide, 1990, p. 24).

- A report from the U.S. Department of Labor stated that yearly infant care costs were about $5000, preschoolers' care $3000, and before- and after-school care $2000 per child (U.S. Department of Labor, 1988). Custodial care is less expensive than educational or developmental programs, but it may also be less valuable to both children and families.

- "In our annual survey of fees charged by child care centers, we found that fees increased by an average of 9% from March 15, 1989, to March 15, 1990 . . . . Not surprisingly, fees are highest in states that have the most stringent licensing requirements . . . . Increases in fees help centers survive and pay marginally higher salaries. But they also make child care unaffordable for larger numbers of America's families" (Child Care Fees on the Rise Nationwide, 1990, p. 24).

- The best single predictor of teacher effectiveness was salary (Whitebook et al., 1990).

- The National Association for the Education of Young Children (NAEYC) has stated that the crisis facing early childhood programs is rooted in this nation's failure to recognize the antinomy of three basic needs: (a) children's need for services, (b) staff's need for adequate compensation, and (c) parents' need for affordable care (NAEYC, 1987).

Facts and Figures

- The Cost, Quality, and Outcomes Study team (1995) found that:
  - (a) *Cash costs* (the amount charged/paid for services) for centers meeting minimal standards (but not those with good to excellent ratings) was $2.11 per child hour ($95 per child week, or $4940 per child year). Geographic differences vary.
  - (b) The difference in today's cash (not full) costs of going from minimal-quality services was 10 percent (from $4940 to $5434 per child year).
  - (c) For-profit and not-for-profit centers charge similar fees per child hour and receive similar (3.7 percent) profit (in for-profit programs) or surplus (in not-for-profit programs).
  - (d) Dual-earner households paid 8 percent of the 1993 median before-tax income on child care, and full-time employed single parents paid 23 percent of the average before-tax income (Reported in Decker & Decker, 1997, 208).
- "If families took the federal child-care tax credit available to them, their estimated full tuition would be $1.72 per child hour or 82 percent of center revenue and 61 percent of full center cost" (Decker & Decker, 1997, 205, 207).
- Child care represents the fourth largest expense for the working family after housing, food, and taxes (LaFleur & Newsom, 1988).
- Parents report difficulty in finding high-quality care. However, once care is found, these parents report satisfaction with the arrangements. This satisfaction seemed to be based on parents' needs for convenient and low-cost care and not on their children's needs for quality services (Decker & Decker, 1997, p. 206).
- "Labor is the most expensive aspect of early childhood programs. In the highest quality programs, about 70% of the budget is in salaries/benefits. The easiest way to make a program more affordable and to ensure profit/surplus is to decrease wages and increase the number of children per staff member" (Decker & Decker, 1997, p. 206).
- "Quality child care is labor intensive and expensive. When adjusted for inflation, program costs have not risen much since the mid-1970s" (Willer, 1990).
- For-profit centers had almost half the operating budgets as federally funded centers, paid lower wages to personnel, and gave fewer supplemental services to families (Ruopp et al., 1978).

INTRODUCTION

This chapter is not a course in accounting; the three main purposes are (1) to outline a tentative budget of elements unique to a child-care center, (2) to touch on accounting procedures with emphasis on recording daily, weekly, or monthly income and expenses at the center, with an accountant doing the bookkeeping, tax, and other reports, and (3) to indicate that using a computer may help the center with reports, payroll, check writing, and other administrative financial tasks. The chapter concludes with references for use in solving individual centers' problems. Local accountants, universities, or government agencies can give invaluable assistance in setting up new books or maintaining ongoing accounts.

Many preschools and child-care centers have been established and run successfully by individuals who have been trained in child development, in management, and in business. Many individuals who establish and run centers have had training in one or two of these areas—or no formal training in any of them. Training can be very helpful, but it does not guarantee success. Nor does lack of training guarantee failure.

The center administrator should know the direct effect of budget on policy and vice versa. Cash-flow analysis and break-even point must be addressed. If the center operates on a sliding-fee program, what are the conditions and how are they administered? Is fund raising appropriate? Does the center qualify for government funds? If so, what are the major sources and the proper procedures? How much and what kinds of insurance are mandatory or desirable? In the event of a lawsuit, what recourse does the center have?

NAEYC accreditation standards require that centers maintain a sound fiscal policy to meet their obligations to children and their families. Written policies and procedures are required to keep decision making consistent and fair. A formula for expenditures for materials, equipment, space, and human energy (MESH) must be developed. Funding sources are private, community, state and national, churches, cooperatives, businesses trying to attract top employees, and others.

Fiscal records are kept with evidence of long-range budgeting and sound financial planning. Operating budgets, prepared annually, show quarterly reconciliation of expenses to budgets.

It is easy to feel rich when fees have been collected and poor as disbursements are made and financial obligations are met.

Certain prescribed factors influence the allocation and total amount spent by the center, such as number and ages of children (including those with special needs), teacher-child ratio, training of and number of staff, type and size of housing, availability of equipment, the philosophy of the program (including services offered), physical location and climate of the center, community prosperity, amount and kind of in-kind contributions, and other factors related to the specific community.

COST-CUTTING MEASURES

When possible, the director (or purchasing agent) should strive to keep costs down by competitive bidding (for supplies, materials, equipment, insurance, maintenance, financial services, and other necessary items and procedures) or consolidating vendors (all food items from the same source, all insurance from one carrier, all toys from one vendor, etc.); however, if this is more costly, break up your purchases to get the most value for your dollar.

Apply for a tax-exempt status for your center. If you qualify, it saves on sales tax. Small purchases made over-the-counter cost time and money (you do pay sales tax on these items).

Look for a bank where you can avoid paying monthly service charges on your checking account and where your money will earn interest until it is needed. Credit is expensive. Pay your bills on time and monitor your income and expenses carefully.

BASIC ACCOUNTING PROCEDURES

Most people have had experience managing money; even their allowances when they were children brought choices, problems, possessions, and varying amounts of satisfaction. Handling the finances of a business is complex; goals must be achieved, boards and clients must be satisfied, local and federal regulations must be met, and the venture must be successful. Although owning or directing a child-care center or preschool may appear easy and prestigious, its many hidden demands can cause frustration and anxiety.

A director of a child-care center chain frequently uses preplanned forms for financial matters. The novice would be wise to visit bookstores, office suppliers, colleges or universities, or private management companies to become familiar with the different types of available forms before attempting to set up the center's books or visiting an accountant. Receipt books, payroll forms, billing sheets, requisitions or purchase orders, and other printed materials—staples in keeping the center's financial records—can be purchased at nominal costs.

Directors who have had little or no experience with bookkeeping should contact a local accounting firm, read books, take classes, or become knowledgeable in financial management of the center. They will be accountable to the board, the owner, or themselves for collecting fees and seeing that funds are disbursed efficiently. Even when bookkeepers are used, directors should be familiar with basic accounting methods and jargon. [Example: What are the differences between *cost-beneficial*, *cost-efficient*, and *cost-effective?* Halpern (1982) defined *cost-beneficial* as "income exceeds costs," or "good return on investment"; *cost-efficient* as "well managed," or "getting the most out of funds"; and *cost-effective* as "reflecting low cost to achieve goals" (p. 25).]

The director should know about debits (expenses) and credits (income), discounts on invoices; the high cost of borrowing, waste, the use and abuse of petty cash; the importance of salary and wage rates; pay periods (for employees and patrons); preventing and collecting delinquent accounts; stretching dollars and anticipating expenses; recording income and expense; allocating supplies and money to cover an allotted period of time; and meeting the needs of personnel and children with a limited budget.

Pay attention to depreciation, amortization (writing off expenditures by prorating over a fixed period), tax requirements, savings, insurance needs, and availability and cost of services. If a director selects a firm or individual to help with financial records, certain information

should be given—the duties of the center versus the duties of the accountant, the procedures of drawing up and signing a contract, and joint responsibility in setting up the center's books to make them current, accurate, and complete.

Accounting entries recorded at the center should include all income and expenditures, regardless of the source or use. The entries reflect all financial transactions and should be recorded at appropriate intervals (daily, weekly, or immediately). Intermittent recording may cause errors or deletions. Sloppy accounting records may result in inability to borrow funds or substantiate tax records, inaccurate reports, confusion about the center's financial standing, and poor work habits. As an aid, the director can obtain a simple how-to book for basic information.

BUDGET FORMATION

There are two types of budgets: (1) the start-up, or initial, funds and (2) in-kind contributions.

Start-up funds cover major equipment, housing, advertising, all salaries, deposits and charges, renovations, and loans (if received). Some individuals use their own money rather than borrowing funds, but these funds must also be considered as costs.

In-kind contributions involve costs that are not received in cash—donations, contributions, and so on. An organization, individual, church, corporation or other entity may permit use of facilities with small or no cost or individuals may volunteer their services. These must be considered as costs.

At a prescribed time, generally prior to the end of the financial period (fiscal or calendar year), involved individuals meet to go over the past financial records (income and expense records must balance) and to prepare for the next financial period (see Figure 12–1).

Although programs for young children are costly, the cost varies according to the type of program and the general economic conditions of the location/country. Comprehensive programs of day

The operating budget consists of a plan of income and expenses for either a fiscal or calendar year. If there is a board, its approval is required before hiring or purchasing is begun. The budget becomes the working financial plan and the director has responsibility for its implementation.

Salaries (major component—will spend major part of budget here)	Salaries for full- and part-time staff (director, teachers, staff, cooks, janitors, and substitutes). Include personnel costs over and above salaries and wages to employees (percentages of these wages that are imposed as taxes that the employer is required to pay). Bookkeeping and record-keeping costs. Benefits such as health insurance, substitute staff who work when regular employees are sick, and vacation leave.
Consultants (Both the center and the consultant should agree in writing on all financial arrangements in advance of any serv-ices rendered.)	Contract services for specified services for the center or its clients—medical, dental, social workers, educational consultants, etc.
Plant and equipment (largest cost is in rental or mortgage payments)	Purchase of, maintenance of, repairs to building and grounds. Difficult to pre-dict needs—provide a lump sum. Also utilities (heat, electricity, gas, water, garbage removal—when utilities are not included in rent payments). Provide start-up budget and then yearly allowance (perhaps $50 per child enrolled), computer purchase or rental.
Supplies (Consumable supplies can be ordered in large quantities when economical; watch for overuse, waste, or dete-rioration.)	*Office and general:* Usual items, pencils, stationery, toilet paper and paper towels, cleaning agents, brooms, etc. *Classroom:* Art materials: paper, paint, crayons, glue, scissors, pet food, doll clothes, misc. items. *Food:* All items available for human consumption—sufficient so teachers can eat with the children. Costs depend both on the availability of federal food subsidies and on factors in the economy. Some centers provide food for teachers and some do not.

Figure 12–1 Budget categories.

care were estimated to cost from $2,000 to $3,000 per child per year by Keyserling (1971), about $2,000 per child in 1980 (Ruopp & Travers, 1982), close to $2,000 per year in 1984 dollars by the Brookline Early Education Project (Pierson et al., 1986), and $3,000 per year for good-quality full-day programs (Decker & Decker, 1992). Olenick (1986) reported overall ratings of quality related to cost: "the annual per child cost was $2,038 for low qual-ity centers and $3,300 for high quality centers."

Capital for programs may come from privately supported endowments; philanthropic sources; grants from state, federal, or public agencies; churches; community chests; fund-raising events; special gifts; employer participation; and school funds. However, the most common source is (par-tial or total) tuition paid by parents.

A Census Bureau release of child-care costs for 1993 reports the following:

- Families with working mothers spent an average of $74 a week, or about 8 percent of their income, to care for preschool chil-dren in 1993.

Transportation (must be equipped with child safety seats or seat belts, depending on the size of the child, and other regulations)	May include purchase or lease of vans to transport children to and from school, for field trips, etc. Include gas, insurance, maintenance, and license fees. Consider renting a bus for special occasions. Many centers require that parents provide the child's transportation to and from school. Cost of travel to professional meetings, home visits, etc.
Miscellaneous	Telephones: Number and placement Insurance: Get quotes from insurance agents on fire, theft, and liability. Read policies *carefully* and ask questions. Postage: For payments, advertising, etc. Send notes home with children instead of mailing. Advertising: Usually higher during initial start-up and to fill vacancies. Licensing: Obtain from licensing agent; professional fees. Auditing: At least annually.

In kind contributions: Budget items not received nor paid in cash are called *in-kind* and should be shown in the budget so that the true cost of center operation will be known. For example, center space may be donated by a church, individual, or organization. To assess the value of the space, *add* the square footage and *multiply* it times the fair rental cost *times* the length of time of the rental (example: # of square feet 2 fair rental cost 2 length = amount of in-kind donation).

Figure 12–1   *Continued*

- A total of 9.9 million children under age 5 were in need of child care in 1993 while their mothers were at work. The principal child-care arrangements were family members, 41 percent; organized child-care facilities, 30 percent; family day-care settings, 17 percent.

- Families with two or more preschool children paid $110 per week for child care, or about 11 percent of their monthly family income. Poor families paid a much larger portion of their incomes—about 18%—on such care.

- Poor families paid about $25 a week less for child care than families who were not poor.

- As a double check to see that matters are handled in a timely manner, make a tickler file to remind oneself of budget milestones.

Further divisions can be made for a major category. See the categories for an ongoing budget in Figure 12–3.

A budget checklist may include assigning one person the central authority for the budget; listing goals for the coming year (or specified period); getting input from colleagues, requesting justification for additions/deletions; setting a deadline for the preliminary budget; discussing the preliminary budget; getting approval from appropriate source (government-sponsored programs may require that the budget be presented to licensing and/or funding agencies prior to approval); formalizing the budget; and beginning the new budget on time. Once the budget has been approved, it should be binding; emergency items or justified trade-offs may or may not be considered for this budget period. Making adjustments may nullify the entire budget.

Expenses	Approx. %	Income	Approx. %
Initial building (down payment, cost of remodeling, rent)		Funds available (cash, loan, grant, etc.)	
Licensing and related costs		Advanced tuition (if any)	
Purchase of major equipment		Donations (if any)	
Office and classroom furniture		Other (specify)	
Telephone and utility hook-up			
Publicity, advertising			
Director's salary (several months)			
Salaries for additional personnel			
Toys, materials, and equipment for children			
Office supplies			
Food and cooking utensils			
First-aid supplies			
Items specified by law			
Items of strong concern by director/owner			
Other (specify)			

Figure 12–2   Categories for a start-up budget.

An outline for a start-up and an ongoing budget is shown in Figures 12–2 and 12–3 respectively.

Figure 12–4 shows hints to use in scrutinizing your budget.

In preparing the budget, check carefully to see that expenditures are in keeping with program goals; there is adequate staff compensation; that benefits exceed costs; and that it shows fiscal responsibility to funders, clients, employees, children, and so on. [Industries use 10 percent of their capital outlay for structures and 90 percent for equipment, and schools spend 90 percent of their capital outlay for buildings and 10 percent for equipment (Boles, 1965)]. Decker and Decker (1992) state: "Most early childhood programs, whether federal, public school, or private, have similar procedures for purchasing. However, publicly funded programs are subject to more restrictions than privately owned programs, and early childhood programs with large enrollments follow a more formal procedure for purchasing than programs with small enrollments."

The purpose of this section is to impress on readers that there are different ways to organize the finances of a child-care center and that different types of programs require different amounts of money. The complexities in bookkeeping procedures for a small business are many. The most basic rule of budget formulation is that planned expenditures *cannot* exceed projected income.

Recent estimates of operating costs for the various components of an early childhood program are unavailable. *Care and teaching* include salaries of caregivers and substitutes, laundry personnel, consumable supplies, insurance, paper and cloth goods, teaching supplies, equipment that costs less than $300, and depreciation on equipment that costs more than $300. *Administration* includes such items as office supplies, telephone, printing, and salaries of administrators, bookkeepers, and secretaries. *Feeding* includes the cost of the food,

Expenses	Approx. %	Income	Approx. %

Personnel
    Administration
    Teaching
    Office
    Meals/planning
    Others
    Benefits
    TOTAL
		Tuition
		Fees (if any)
		Additional:
		    grant, loan, gift, in-kind, donations,
		        subsidies, registration, etc. (if any)
		Use of facility
		Ancillary sources
		Interest
		TOTAL	

Variable (controllable)
    Rent, loan payment
    Building maintenance
    Equipment maintenance
    Office supplies
    Classroom supplies
    Publicity
    Food
    Parent information
    Telephone
    Utilities
    Contingency
    Vehicle costs (if any)
    Professional development
    TOTAL			

Fixed
    Building rent
    Interest/depreciation
    Insurance
    Property tax
    State income
    Absentee credit
    Fees
    Others
    TOTAL			

Total of all expenses Total income Total expenses Balance (+ or −)		Total of all income Total income less personnel expenses less controllable expenses less fixed expenses equals an operating profit	

Figure 12–3   Categories for an ongoing budget.

Figure 12–4 Hints to use in scrutinizing your budget. (Condensed and adapted from Click & Click, 1990, p. 220.)

- Is every item necessary to meet the goals of the school?
- Has every cost been included?
- If there are marked differences between this budget and last year's (or between schools of similar size), are the changes fully justified? Have objectives changed?
- Was there great difficulty in reconciling differences between Income and Expenditure? If so, maintenance, or other items may have to be postponed.
- Is everyone reasonably satisfied with the final budget? No one gets everything; everyone should get a little bit.

the salary of the cook, depreciation of kitchen equipment, utilities, and paper goods. *Health* services are available to all centers through the health department. *Occupancy* includes building and land costs, salary of custodians, utilities, cleaning supplies, and minor repairs. *Other* includes transportation, social services and other uses.

- Is every item necessary to meet the goals of the school?
- Has every cost been included?
- If there are marked differences between this budget and last year's (or between schools of similar size), are the changes fully justified? Have objectives changed?
- Was there great difficulty in reconciling differences between Income and Expenditure? If so, maintenance, or other items may have to be postponed.
- Is everyone reasonably satisfied with the final budget? No one gets everything; everyone should get a little bit.

BUDGET PROCEDURE

Too often, directors do not take budgeting seriously. As long as money is coming in, orders are made regularly, and the checkbook is balanced, directors think finances are no real problem. They may divert their attention to other matters, only to realize too late that money is running dangerously low even though the fiscal year is just beginning.

To establish fees, the director should have some ideas about the costs of operating the proposed center, the need for such a center, the community factors (current wage and salary rates, cost of living, types of industry or employment, frequency and dates of paychecks), due dates of fees, multiple enrollments per family, delinquent accounts, allowances for children's absences, and retention of center money until depositing it in the bank. Funds must be handled in a businesslike manner: Receipts should be promptly written, with a copy for the parent and one for the center. The policy and procedure regarding tuition and fees should be outlined in the center's organizational structure. Sometimes these fees are determined by the director, sometimes by the board of directors, sometimes by corporate headquarters (in the case of franchised care), and sometimes by the owner. (See Chapter 5.)

The budget, showing close correlation between the goals of the center and the expenditures listed, should be prioritized to ensure allotting enough money for the most important or most desired purposes—with provision for emergency costs and overlapping categories. A small, but often overlooked, expense is upkeep and repair of toys and equipment. From your past records of replacement and repairs, determine a realistic figure for this expense item.

Income and Expenditures

To formulate the budget for a new center, the director should make a list of all anticipated sources of income and expenditures. The following headings and subcategories may be helpful:

Income	Fixed Costs	Variable Costs
Fees	Initial	Wages
Subsidies	investment	Food
Donations	Physical	Certain
Grants	facility	supplies
In-kind gifts	Start-up	In-service
Miscellaneous	Certain	training
	salaries	Benefits
	Certain	Toys,
	supplies	equipment
	Insurance	Upkeep,
	Taxes	repairs
		Miscellaneous

However straightforward or divided, comparisons of costs must be made in a similar manner; cost analyses must include all costs to be accurate. It has been suggested that a two-column cost list be expanded as follows: (1) *fixed* (program planning that does not vary with the number of children served) *and variable costs* (which do vary with the number of children served, the size of the building, teacher salaries, etc.), (2) *marginal costs* (which may decrease to a given point and then increase with additional size and staff), (3) *capital* (one-time costs) *versus operating costs* (recurring costs such as salaries, consumable materials), (4) *hidden costs* (in-kind contributions), *joint costs* (such as sharing space, equipment, etc.), and *foregone income costs* (services or goods provided) (Decker & Decker, 1992).

Using Petty Cash

Having a petty cash fund can be useful or it can be problemsome. The director (funding agency or board) must determine *if* there will be such a fund, *who* will authorize, reimburse, and have access to it, *what* dollar amount or purchases can be made from it, *how* frequently it can be used, and other important issues. It should be used for emergency, low dollar amount purposes only. The fund should be a small dollar amount to prevent loss, theft, and carelessness.

If the fund is allowed, a specific procedure must be established, followed, and not abused. Usually a designated person receives the specified amount, and disburses it as policy allows and in return for an appropriate receipt. Some centers use petty cash for all unexpected small needs. The director keeps a sum of cash on hand and gives it to staff members who present legitimate requests. For example, if the milk has not been delivered in time for snack, petty cash may be used to purchase enough for snack. Petty cash should be used as little as possible to avoid substantial program expenditures under the heading *petty cash*, which may be called into question by the auditor, and certainly will not be reflected in the proper budget category.

Insurance

All financial items require forethought. One item needing extra scrutiny is insurance, a fixed cost. Not knowing what to insure and for how much may cause undue frustration for a novice. Whether or not the property is owned by the center, insurance will be needed on the building and personal property (furniture, equipment, supplies, etc.). Liability insurance will be needed for employees, children, and others while they are on the premises.

Note that there are different kinds of insurance: health, accident, automobile, building, contents, and so on. Adequate coverage is expensive but essential. Some types of insurance and retirement plans may be mandated by state or federal laws, whereas other types may be voluntary.

Outdoor climbing structures and other outdoor equipment present a special problem. Property insurance typically covers items inside the building, and building insurance covers the building and equipment, or structures appurtenant to the building. Consequently, outdoor equipment may not be covered unless a special endorsement is purchased. (Murray & Stevenson, 1981, pp. 10–13)

Health and accident insurance is available for employees and children. Insurance for center-owned vehicles is an absolute necessity, especially if children are transported. [See Chapter 8 for new children's health insurance program (CHIP), passed by Congress in 1997.]

> Programs sometimes attempt to shift this risk to others, for example through the use of parent or volunteer cars. However, if an accident occurs, it is highly likely that the program itself will be named as a defendant along with the driver. Therefore, it is extremely important for programs to recognize the risks they run in carrying children in vehicles, and to develop ways in which they can protect themselves from potential liability. (Murray & Stevenson, 1981, pp. 10–13)

Coverage for center-owned vehicles includes bodily injury liability, property-damage liability, collision, comprehensive, medical payments, uninsured-motorist protection, and underinsured-motorist protection. As to the amount of insurance for bodily injury and property damage,

> experts suggest that a bare minimum coverage is $300,000. However, a program which regularly transports numbers of children will probably wish to increase its coverage substantially . . . for example, $1,000,000 worth of coverage costs only about 25% more than does $300,000 worth of coverage. (Murray & Stevenson, 1981, p. 13)

Employees' and parents' cars may be used to transport children. The center, however, could be responsible in the case of serious accident if (1) there was evidence of negligence—driver distraction due to the number of children or inadequate supervision, (2) the center was named as a codefendant in a lawsuit, and (3) the center was the employer of the driver or owner. Using public transportation places the liability on the transit provider (this means of transportation may not be available to all centers).

There should be adequate insurance coverage for the facility and its contents, including mortgaged buildings and contents of rented buildings. Read a policy carefully to see whether it covers for fire, lightning, and extended coverage for such things as wind, hail, explosion, vandalism, civil commotion, aircraft, vehicles, smoke, and malicious mischief. In order to have adequate fire insurance (basic or extended coverage endorsement), the administrator must maintain up-to-date property records that reflect current values. The administrator is encouraged to seek three bids before securing a policy and must make sure that the policy suits the center—not just a general overall policy that may be more expensive or not cover the center's needs. For example, theft or malicious mischief may be so high in some areas that it is unobtainable. To reduce rates, the federal government and some states have initiated a crime insurance program sold through regular insurance agents.

"Liability insurance does not protect the health and safety of children; only staff members following sound procedures can do that. Insurance simply protects the owners and operators from financial devastation. Most charges of liability will come as a result of problems in the health and safety arena" states Hildebrand (1993, p. 254).

In recent years escalating expense of property and liability insurance has been phenomenal. Some policies that had been in effect for long periods of time were even canceled—child-care industry was among the casualties, even if they had filed no claims. Some centers had their fees raised out of reach. When centers are a part of a larger organization (church, industry, educational institution, etc.), the parent organization maintained their coverage.

When NAEYC surveyed its members in 1985, it found that 90 percent of the programs had never filed on their liability insurance policy. Of the remaining 10 percent, those who had filed claims, 80 percent were for less than $500, with the highest being $15,000.

To help members with their property and center liability coverage, optimal automobile, worker's

- There are some "musts" in running a business: employees expect to be paid on time and in full; suppliers expect the same. If you expect the same from your patrons (in full and on time), matters will flow more smoothly. You can devote more of your time and attention to the children.

- "Both the scope and the quality of services are related to the financial status of a program although programs with similar hourly costs range in quality from poor to excellent. . . . Good programs cannot operate effectively for long depending on donations and volunteers without weakening the quality and quantity of their services and without damaging the morale of those involved" (Decker & Decker, 1997, p. 204).

- In an earlier writing, Olenick (1986) found a positive relationship between program quality and budget allocations for teacher salaries and benefits (programs that spent approximately two-thirds of their budgets on salaries and staff benefits tended to be of high quality, and quality diminished considerably in programs spending less than one-half of their budgets on salaries and staff benefits).

- Decker and Decker (1997) offer these clarifications: "Cost-effectiveness analysis compares the costs of two or more programs that have the same or similar goals to find the least-cost method of reaching a particular goal. . . . Cost efficiency analysis usually follows cost-effectiveness analysis. Cost-effective programs can further reduce costs by developing a least-cost, within-program management. Cost efficiency is achieved when all program components are optimally used (e.g., staffing patterns, curriculum, scheduling)" (pp. 208–209).

- Costs to operate the various components of early childhood programs vary from program to program. The estimated costs are as follows: personnel—69% to 73%; housing, space, and utilities—10% to 12%; equipment—2% to 3%, supplies, excluding food—2% to 3.5%; food—11% to 15.5%; and miscellaneous—the remainder (ABT Associates, 1980; Keener & Sebestyen, 1981; Seaver & Cartwright, 1986; Willer, 1990).

- For-profit centers making the most profit spend a lower percentage of their revenues on salaries (53.7 percent) than do centers making the least profits (62.4 percent) (Stephens, 1991).

- Early childhood programs can be financed in a number of ways, including government (local, state, and/or federal — block grants) and private funds. (See earlier discussion in this chapter and also Chapter 3.) However, each funding agent will have rules and regulations that must be adhered to before funds are allocated or continued. Those interested in funding early childhood education programs are encouraged to consult government agencies and brochures, private lending institutions, legal advisors, and other sources to determine the best way(s) to finance the venture. Caution should be exercised to avoid misunderstandings and misuse of resources.

- Dates and amounts of fees should be discussed and understood by all parties (those owing money and those lending money). Late or missed payments can lead to serious consequences. For example, fees owed to the center are expected for paying commitments (teachers, vendors). Fees for absent children or staff must be carefully defined. It is highly recommended that new centers contact financial advisors for establishing a budget and guidelines to manage money matters in a professional and acceptable manner.

compensation, and student accident medical coverage, NAEYC initiated an insurance program through MarketDyne, a division of CIGNA Corporation. Information regarding these policies and other insurance matters is available from NAEYC at (800) 424–2460.

In an effort to assist centers in getting insurance, the Child Care Action Campaign has provided a list of insurance providers who write child-care liability insurance. (Write to CCA Campaign, 330 Seventh Avenue, 18th Floor, New York, NY 10001.) Ask the insurers about the number of child-care centers they presently insure, how long current policies have been marketed, and the average premium amount per child-care account.

Purchasers of liability insurance need to be cautious about negligence:

> The failure to use the degree of care that a person of reasonable prudence would use under given or similar circumstances. *Child care providers may be sued based on a theory of negligence—such as negligent supervision, negligent training, and negligent or wrongful hiring. Problems of negligence may be minimized through modern risk management practices and effective training.* (Reynolds & Strickland, 1991, p. 57)

Although insurance may seem a high cost for some centers, it is necessary and must be kept current.

FEDERAL PROGRAMS

New Federal Dollars/Tax Breaks for Parents Using Child Care

Each director should know how to apply for federal funds for child-care centers and be aware of child-care tax credits for parents. Because this information changes periodically, directors should contact their accountant and/or local/federal tax authorities for updated information. The 1990 tax law has financial penalties for those not in conformance. Consult a competent tax professional about how this law affects your center (Lukaszewski, 1991).

There are new or expanded sources of federal funds that may help parents pay for services or help programs make quality improvements. These include the following. (See also Chapter 3.)

Child Care and Development Block Grant (CCDBG). This program is one of the major child-care programs administered by the Administration for Children and Families. CCDBG serves low-income families that need child care either because a parent is working, attending a training or educational program, or because the family receives or needs to receive protective services. This block grant focuses on increasing the availability, affordability, and quality of child-care services. Funds are available to provide grants, contracts, and certificates for child care and related services. In addition, CCDBG provides funds to increase the availability of early childhood development and before- and after-school care services.

For fiscal year 1993, Congress appropriated nearly $893 million for the CCDBG program. Grantees must spend 75 percent of the CCDBG funds on child-care services and activities to improve the availability and quality of child care. To ensure that the majority of funds are targeted to services, grantees must spend at least 85 percent of the 75 percent portion to purchase child-care services. The remaining 25 percent of CCDBG funds is set aside as follows: (1) three fourths of that amount is earmarked for early childhood development services and before- and after-school care; (2) 20 percent is targeted for quality improvement activities in the following areas: (a) resource and referral programs, (b) grants or loans to assist providers in meeting state or local standards, (c) monitoring compliance with licensing and regulator requirements, (d) training for caregivers, and (e) improving salaries for child-care staff; and (3) the remaining 5 percent may be used either for early childhood development services and before- and after-school care or for quality improvement activities.

Proposed rule changes for the CCDBG, Aid to Families with Dependent Children (AFDC) Child Care, Transitional Child Care, and At-Risk Child Care programs were announced in the *Federal Register* on May 11, 1994. (See Chapter 3.) Key changes include amended payment rates that permit accessibility to higher-quality care; adaptation of payment policies to comply with the Americans with Disabilities Act (ADA), the Fair Labor Standards Act (FLSA), and federal and state statutes on in-home care; the deletion of the effects test that may have minimized regulator protection for children in state implementation of health and safety standards; the addition of an immunization requirement for children receiving funds under the CCDBG; and other technical amendments (*Public policy alert!*, 1994).

Title IVA At-Risk Child Care Funds.

Three billion dollars was appropriated for fiscal year 1991. This title provides child-care funds for families receiving AFDC who are working or in approved education or training programs, as well as 1 year of transitional child-care assistance for those moving off AFDC due to increased earnings. This new amendment will provide additional funds for non-AFDC families who would be at risk of becoming eligible for AFDC if it were not for child-care assistance.

Title IVA Licensing, Monitoring, and Improvement Funds.

Thirteen million dollars were appropriated for fiscal year 1991. These funds are for states to make improvements in their child-care system, including licensing, monitoring, and training. At least half of these funds must now be used for child-care training.

CDA Scholarship Funds.

These funds have been available since 1986 to provide scholarships to pay for CDA credentialing. Although no additional dollars have been appropriated, a portion of the funds can now be used for training. In addition, eligibility has been significantly expanded.

For answers to questions regarding eligibility for funds, reimbursement rates, sliding fee scales, vouchers or grants, contracts, licensing or registration, resource and referral, available training, compensation issues, how funds are coordinated, and information for consumers, contact your local or state licensing office, your governor's office, or the district office of your local legislator.

It will be important for parents and providers to monitor implementation of these funds in the states and communities.

Insurance and retirement plans for employees include the following:

Federal Insurance Contributions Act (FICA)

Worker's compensation insurance

State unemployment insurance

Liability insurance

Health insurance and hospital-medical insurance

Crime coverage

Retirement programs

Taxes

Taxes, another fixed cost, must be prepared accurately. Help can be obtained from an accountant, from the IRS, or from state agencies. Federal forms required are consistent throughout the country; state forms, however, vary as to their content, due date, percentage of tax, and other items. The current tax bill should be reviewed carefully. Federal and state publications, self-help books, accountants, or other sources used in tax preparation and submittal provide assistance with current interpretations.

Payroll taxes must be withheld from each employee's pay check. The employer is required to match FICA and Medicare funds. For current information for your state and area, check with a certified public accountant or federal tax offices.

Costs to Families

Half or more than half of families with young children cannot afford to pay for child care. For higher-income families, child care is less than 5 percent of their budgets; for middle-income families, child care is 10 percent of their family budgets (comparable to food), but for low-income families, child care is 20 to 26 percent of their family budgets (comparable to housing costs) (Hofferth, 1989; Decker & Decker, 1992). Day care is the fourth largest expenditure for working families after food, clothing, and taxes (Winget, 1982). It is estimated that only 1 percent of families can afford quality day-care program costs for one child, and even fewer can afford quality programs for more than one child (Stephen, 1973; Decker & Decker, 1992).

Costs to families may differ from absolute program costs because of direct subsidies. There are several types of direct subsidies, including the following:

1. *Aid to Families with Dependent Children (AFDC).* In October 1988 Congress passed the Family Support Act. The act significantly expands the federal funds available for AFDC parents who are working or in school or training, and for parents leaving AFDC for employment (Blank, 1989).

2. *Project Head Start for families who qualify.* Currently Head Start serves only one fifth of all eligible 4-year-old children and even fewer eligible younger children. Since 1994 there has been authorization for full funding of Head Start for all eligible 3- to 5-year-old children (101st Congress: The Children's Congress, 1991).

3. *Federal income tax deduction allowed for day-care services (IRS Form 2441).* Child-care tax credit can also now be claimed on Form 1040A, the short income tax form. Families can deduct 20 to 30 percent of their annual child-care expenses, but this cannot exceed $2,400 for one child or $4,800 for more than one child from their income tax bill. There are three problems with this subsidy. First, this subsidy does not address the quality of early childhood programs. Second, poor families may not earn sufficient income to take advantage of this bill. And third, dependent care tax credit is not reimbursable; thus, poor families with little or no tax liability are unable to recoup any of their expenditures for child care (Decker & Decker, 1992).

Many parents pay full costs of child care, others receive public and philanthropic assistance. Hildebrand (1993) states:

It is outlandish that a professional couple who both are making large salaries and living an affluent lifestyle should receive subsidized child care services—subsidized at the expense of staff members who cannot even live securely and comfortably on their meager salary. In most cases, if child care services did not exist, one partner would have to quit work and face the reality of the opportunity costs of having a child. Obviously, the availability of high-quality child development services makes it possible for both parents to work. . . . Parents may be frustrated with raises in fees; some may not be able to handle higher costs. Sources of partial and full scholarships and other funds should be explored. Frustrations must be reported to government officials by parents and child advocates. (p. 205)

For answers to questions regarding eligibility for funds, reimbursement rates, sliding fee scales, vouchers or grants, contracts, licensing or registration, resource and referral, available training, compensation issues, how funds are coordinated, and information for consumers, contact your local or state licensing office, your governor's office, or the district office of your local legislator.

It will be important for parents and providers to monitor implementation of these funds in the states and communities.

Child-Care Licensing and Monitoring

State officials view the monitoring of child-care programs as the most essential activity for ensuring quality, according to a recent study by the U.S. General Accounting Office (1992). At least 40 states have used block grant money to improve licensing and monitoring activities.

Twenty-two states have used block grant money to provide grants and loans to help child-care providers meet licensing or registration requirements and to help with start-up costs.

Resource and Referral Services

Resource and referral services (R&Rs) are an essential component of a strong child-care system. They counsel families about their child-care options and help families locate appropriate services. In some locations, R&Rs administer child-care voucher or certificate programs, gather data concerning their community's child-care needs, and provide various types of assistance to child-care providers.

Child Care for Infants, School-Agers, and Children with Special Needs

In general, parents have difficulty finding appropriate care for infants, school-age children, and children with special needs because these types of care are in short supply.

Virtually all (46) states put block grant money into developing school-age programs or training providers serving school-age children; expand child-care services for teen parents; expand or improve the quality of child-care services for children with special needs. The state of Washington will fund each of its counties to pay for comprehensive child care for homeless children.

Block Grants Provide Child Care for Low-Income Families and Training for Care Providers

Low state reimbursement rates in public child-care programs historically have discouraged providers from serving low-income families. Block grants can raise reimbursement rates and thereby increase the supply and improve the quality of providers serving low-income children.

Block grants ensure that children's health-care needs are met and that parents receive support to help them nurture their children and become involved in their learning.

Training for Providers

Since 1990 every state but one has invested some block grant money in training—special training for providers serving low-income children, the use of mobile vans bringing training programs to rural providers, or helping child-care workers pay for coursework toward early childhood credentials or degrees.

Only nine states have used block grant funds for specific compensation-related projects. These states are using a variety of approaches, including

establishing commissions, conducting surveys or studies about ways to improve salaries and benefits for providers, and linking increased training and credentialing to salary improvements.

Although federal entitlement money is available for Family Support Act (FSA) child care, states must provide matching funds to receive the entitlement. By using block grant money for FSA child care, states have avoided the cost of the state match.

Federal Financing and Foundation Support

In addition to programs receiving some federal fiscal support, such as the public schools, the federal government remains the primary source of support for comprehensive early childhood programs for low-income children through Head Start programs . . . . The purpose of most federal assistance programs is to accomplish particular educational objectives or meet the needs of specific groups. Most federal assistance programs have these characteristics: (1) require early childhood programs to meet specified standards; (2) give priority or restrict services to certain client groups; (3) require state and/or local support in varying amounts; and (4) specify funds to be used for certain purposes (e.g., food, program supplies), which in turn curtail a program's flexibility. (Decker & Decker, 1992)

FINANCES

Inexperienced (and sometimes not so inexperienced) child-care providers try to operate on a minimal budget, only to experience frustration and problems. Stephens (1990) has outlined seven deadly financial pitfalls: (1) being out of money without knowing why, (2) committing to costs that can't be supported by income, (3) not seeing a total financial picture, (4) not charging high enough fees, (5) not being realistic about stagnated or declining revenues, (6) being lax about collecting delinquent fees, and (7) permitting the credit ratio to get out of balance.

Categorizing Items

Expenses and incomes are categorized differently at various centers; examples include

Category	Possible computer codes
EXPENSES—Personnel	
Administration	100–199
Teaching	100+
Supplementary	120+
Benefits (federal and state taxes, disability and health insurance, pension, vacation, etc.)	170+
Other	190+
EXPENSES—Variable (controllable)	200–299
Building (repairs, renovations, maintenance)	200+
Equipment (repairs, rental, maintenance)	210+
Supplies (educational, office, other)	220+
Food (including equipment and supplies)	230+
Utilities (including telephone and postage)	240+
Debt (payments and interest)	250+
Publicity	260+
Transportation	270+
Professional development	280+
Other	290+
EXPENSES—Fixed	300–399
Building (loan or rental including depreciation, interest)	300+
Insurance (liability, fire, building, vehicle)	310+
Taxes (property, vehicle, payroll)	320+
Fees (accountant, consultant)	330+
Other	390+
INCOME	500–599
Tuition from parents (also tuition waivers)	500+
Subsidies for children	510+
Registration	515+
Use of facility	520+
Ancillary sources (fundraisers, products, services)	530+
Donations/gifts	540+
Grants	550+
In-kind	560+
Sales of equipment, etc.	570+
Interest	580+
Other	590+

Figure 12–5 Child-care center expense categories and possible computer codes.

alphabetically, personal and personnel, variable and fixed, and by budget percentage divisions. Figure 12–5 lists typical child-care center expenses, income categories, and possible codes for computer recording.

The symbol + indicates a main code or possible subcodes, depending on how finely the expenses are to be identified.

Each category could be broken down further according to the needs and desires of the center. For example, Expenses—Variable: Utilities could be 240 for gas or heating; 242 for electricity; 244 for telephone; 246 for postage; and so on. The breakdown for Income: Subsidies could be 510 for state or federal allowances; 512 for church or other sources; 514 for scholarship grants, and so on. A manual ledger could show *Utilities* as the main heading, with Gas, Electricity, Telephone, Postage, Other as subheadings. Income entries could be similarly labeled. If a computer is used, the proper coding is entered with the information. Each category should be given a code number to facilitate bookkeeping and posting. Skipping numbers allows for new kinds of deductions or income to be added as needed.

Trimming payroll costs may reduce the quality of the program. Economizing should be done in other areas, unless the adult-child ratio is excessive. It should also be noted that increasing payroll and other expenditures does not necessarily mean a higher-quality program. Goals and finance should be considered jointly.

Monies owed should be paid in a timely manner—payrolls must be met on time. Directors can avoid some money problems if they estimate the amount and timing of income realistically, equip the center cautiously, hire staff in a proper ratio to enrolled children, expect times of high and low enrollment, allocate funds for specific purchases and expenses, and keep inventories of classroom supplies that will last for approximately 2 months of operation. New centers must allow for start-up and continuing costs; ongoing centers must allow for continuing and replacement costs.

Possible Computer Application

Many computer software programs can help keep finances organized: preparing the budget, recording transactions, preparing the payroll, maintaining individual payroll records, preparing tax records (monthly, quarterly, annually), totaling amounts for individual categories (either income or expense), reviewing cash flow, writing checks, and making receipts.

CHAPTER SUMMARY

1. Financial decisions must be based on the policies and procedures of the center.
2. Every director should have a basic knowledge of accounting procedure and jargon.
3. Financial records must be meticulously maintained.
4. Managers with little or no training in financial matters should seek help from accountants, libraries, periodicals, agencies (private, public, governmental), universities, and other sources.
5. Accounting forms can be purchased at an office supply store or designed by the center.
6. Accounting entries include all income and expenditures, regardless of the source or use. Common groupings are *income, fixed costs,* and *variable costs.*
7. Budgets must be prepared carefully, monitored frequently, and modified cautiously.
8. Funds must be handled in a businesslike manner: records kept, receipts given, payments made in a timely manner, and all transactions recorded.
9. Income and expense items can be categorized in various ways. The director (perhaps with the assistance of a board member or accountant) should determine the best means for the individual center.
10. Types of insurance that are needed include building, personal property, health, accident, and center-owned-vehicle, among others.
11. The percentage of money allocated to different needs is based on center size, teacher-child

ratio, philosophy, services rendered, and other center-specific components.

12. Accounting can be done manually or by computer.

13. Computers can either save or cost the center money, depending on the efficiency of their use.

14. Computer software is available for general accounting. Individual programs can be designed for the specific needs of the center.

PARTICIPATORS

For Directors/Managers of an Ongoing Center

1. Review the center's budget for the current year; compare it with the categories and percentages presented in this chapter. How close are your proposed income and expenses at the present time? Are modifications appropriate?

2. If the center does not have a budget, prepare one using categories that are appropriate to its operation. Determine the sources and amounts of income, compile projected expenditures, and determine the percentage of funds that can be allotted to each category. If possible, prepare a tentative budget and review it with board or staff members before adopting it.

3. Contact directors or administrators who hold similar jobs and discuss problems and solutions to financial problems. Be professional—keep confidences!

4. Review your center's method of budgeting, making financial transactions, and record keeping. Which, if any, changes would be beneficial? Consider consultation or accounting services; contemplate purchasing a computer; redesign forms or procedures.

5. On the basis of past experience and projected needs, determine whether or not the center has adequate insurance to cover all required areas. Check with at least three insurance agencies for advice.

6. Determine the steps necessary to increase tuition and fees with the goal of giving every employee a 5 percent wage or salary increase.

7. Explain the way tuition fees were set in the center for children who attend a full-day program and for those who attend a half-day or part-time program. How equitable are the fees for services rendered?

8. List and describe the kinds of financial services that are available for small businesses in your community. Estimate the cost for you to subscribe to a service.

9. Review the federal programs that are available. For which ones would your center be eligible? How do you decide whether or not to apply for funds?

For the Student

1. Develop a budget for an ongoing half-day program that enrolls 20 children in three different groups, or a total of 60 preschool children. Include monthly figures and a yearly total. Indicate the type of program offered, the facility used, the teacher-child ratio, and other information.

2. Develop a budget for an ongoing full-day child-care center. Include monthly figures and a yearly total. Indicate the age and number of children enrolled, type of program, kind of facility, services offered, teacher-child ratio, and other aspects of the center's plan.

3. Brainstorm about the sources of income and expenditures for establishing both half-day and full-day programs (as in number 1 and number 2).

4. Using the budgets from number 1 and number 2, determine the percentages of total cost for each category.

5. Formulate policies on wages and salaries, benefits, sick leave, vacation, overtime, pay periods, insurance, and so on. How do center policies increase or decrease costs?

6. Check the pay scale for directors, teachers, and supporting staff in both preschools and child-care centers in the community. How do these scales compare with those for public school teachers? How do teacher qualifications differ with each classroom type?

7. Check with centers about their systems of financial budgeting—(a) categories used, (b) percentage of budget allocated to each category, (c) use of bookkeepers or accountants, (d) use of computers, and (e) other pertinent information.

8. Without violating confidences, check local centers to determine current tuition for full- or part-time enrollment of children. Record high, low, and average fees. What is the licensed occupancy for each center? Explain methods of setting tuition fees for children who attend full-day and half-day programs.

9. If the centers in number 1 and number 2 are new, what additional costs need to be added to the budget? Determine the cost per child.

10. Make a list of the kinds of insurance that are needed by the center. Check with three different agents about insurance availability, coverage, and cost.

11. Identify 20 items needed at the center (e.g., toys, supplies, food). Using three different sources, compare the prices of each item. Also compare quality, quantity, availability, and payment. (See Chapter 10.)

12. Investigate community practices of paying employees (i.e., weekly or monthly; wages or salary, dates). Write a plan for paying employees at a child-care center.

13. Propose a method of using petty cash at the center (how much would be available, how it could be used, how often it would be turned in).

REFERENCES

ABT Associates. 1980. *Day care centers in the U.S.: A national profile, 1966–77.* Washington, DC: U.S. Department of HEW, Administration for Children, Youth and Families.

Blank, H. 1989. Child care and welfare reform: New opportunities for families. *Young Children,* 44(4), 28–30.

Boles, H. 1965. *Step by step to better school facilities* (p. 190). New York: Holt, Rinehart and Winston.

Child care fees on the rise nationwide. 1990, April. *Exchange,* 72, 24.

Click, P. M., & Click, D. W. 1990. *Administration of schools for young children* (3rd ed.). Albany, NY: Delmar.

Cost, Quality, and Outcomes Study Team. (1995). Cost, quality, and child outcomes in child care centers: Key findings and recommendations. *Young Children,* 50(4), 40–44.

Decker, C. A., & Decker, J. R. 1992. *Planning and administering early childhood programs* (5th ed.). Upper Saddle River, NJ: Merrill/Prentice Hall.

Decker, C. A., & Decker, J. R. 1997. *Planning and administering early childhood programs* (6th ed.) Upper Saddle River, NJ: Merrill Prentice Hall.

Friedman, D. 1986. Child care for employees' kids. *Harvard Business Review,* March/April, 28–34.

Halpern, R. 1982. Surviving the competition: Economic skills and arguments for program directors. *Young Children,* July, 25–32, 49–50.

Hildebrand, V. 1993. *Management of child development centers* (3rd ed.). Upper Saddle River, NJ: Merrill/Prentice Hall.

Hofferth, S. L. 1989. What is the demand for and supply of child care in the United States? *Young Children,* 44(5), 28–33.

Keener, T., & Sebestyen, D. 1981. A cost-analysis of selected Dallas day-care centers. *Child Welfare,* 60, 87–88.

Keyserling, M. D. 1971. Day care: Crisis and challenge. *Childhood Education.* 8(62).

LaFleur, E. K., & Newsom, W. B. 1988. Opportunities for child care. *Personnel Administrator,* 12, 146–154.

Lukaszewski, T. E. 1991. The tax man cometh: Protecting your resources. *Exchange,* 77, Jan./Feb., 19–20.

Murray, K., & Stevenson, C. 1981. Insuring your program—property and vehicle insurance. *Exchange,* Sept./Oct. 10–13.

National Association for the Education of Young Children. 1987. NAEYC position statement on quality, compensation, and affordability in early childhood programs. *Young Children,* 43(1), 31.

Olenick, M. 1986. The relationship between daycare quality and selected social policy variables. Unpublished doctoral dissertation, University of California, Los Angeles.

101st Congress: The children's Congress. 1991. *Young Children,* 46(2), 78–80.

Perreault, J. (1991). Society as extended family: Giving a childhood to every child. *Dimensions,* 19(4), 3–8, 31.

Pierson, D. E., Walker, D. K., & Tivnan, T. 1986. A school-based program for infancy to kindergarten for children and parents. In F. M. Hechinger (Ed.), *A better start: New choices for early learning* (pp. 73–92). New York: Walker.

Public policy alert! 1994, May 31. Washington, DC: National Association for the Education of Young Children.

Reynolds, S. W., & Strickland, J. 1991. Buyer's guide to child care liability: Discover what's under the cover. *Exchange,* 77, 56–58.

Ruopp, R., O'Farrell, B., Warner, D., Rowe, M., & Freedman, R. 1978. *Children at the Center: Final Report of the National Day Care Study* (Vol. 1). Washington, DC: U.S. Department of Health, Education and Welfare.

Ruopp, R., & Travers, J. 1982. Janus faces day care: Perspectives on quality and cost. In E. Zigler & E. Gordon (Eds.), *Day care: Scientific and social policy issues* (pp. 72–101). Boston: Auburn House.

Seaver, J. W., & Cartwright C. A. 1986. *Child-care administration.* Belmont, CA: Wadsworth.

Stephen, M. 1973. *Policy issues in early childhood education.* Menlo Park, CA: Stanford Research Institute. (ERIC ED 008 59530)

Stephens, K. 1990. Minding your business: How to avoid the seven deadly financial pitfalls. *Exchange,* 74, 9–12.

Stephens, K. (1991). *Confronting your bottom line: Financial guide for child care centers.* Redmond, WA: Exchange Press.

U.S. Department of Labor, Bureau of Labor Statistics. 1988. *Child care: A workforce issue.* Washington, DC: U.S. Government Printing Office.

U.S. General Accounting Office (GAO). 1990. *Early childhood education: What are the costs of high-quality programs?* (GAO/HRD-90-43BR). Washington, DC: Author.

U.S. General Accounting Office, 1992, Nov. Child care: States face difficulties in enforcing standards promoting quality. Gaithersburg, MD: author.

Whitebook, M., Howes, C., & Phillips, D. A. 1990. *Who cares: Child care teachers and the quality of care in America* (Final report of the National Child Care Staffing Study). Oakland, CA: Child Care Employee Project.

Willer, B. (1990). Estimating the full cost of quality. In B. Willer (Ed.), *Reaching the full cost of quality in early childhood programs* (pp. 1–8). Washington, DC: National Association for the Education of Young Children.

Winget, W. 19822. The dilemma of affordable child care. In E. Zigler & E. Gordon (eds.), *Day-care: Scientific & social policy issues.* Boston: Auburn House.

Appendix A

Handbook for Parents

Figure A–1 is a sample handbook written for a half-day preschool program. Because policies differ from program to program, any assumptions made are for example purposes only.

[Logo]
[Center name, Address, Telephone]
[printing date]
HANDBOOK FOR PARENTS

Preschool Group

Introduction
The director and staff welcome your child and family to our center. We look forward to having a pleasant association with you. For convenience only, the masculine pronoun will be used in this handbook when referring to children; however, both males and females are admitted to our program.

We have prepared this handbook so that you know what you can expect from us and what we will expect of you. If you have questions or concerns, please contact us. We will be happy to assist you.

Center Personnel
Gloria Orton, Director
    Center phone number: 000-000-0000
    Home phone number: (give number or specify calls at the center only, except in case of emergency)

Juanita Hernaldo, Head Teacher
    Center phone number: 000-000-0000
    Home phone number: (give number or specify calls at the center only, except in case of emergency)

Note: List this information for key staff members, such as the head teacher, nutritionist, or custodian. Because other staff members may not be permanent, insert a sheet with their names and phone numbers, if appropriate.

Center's Main Goals
We believe that children are the most important part of any center or group experience; the program and facilities must be built around the children and not vice versa. We also believe that each area of development (physical, social, emotional, intellectual, and spiritual) must be acknowledged and provided for. We believe in the individuality of children and adults, but that there are appropriate times and places for these individuals to participate in small or large groups. We believe that children need, expect, and deserve to be guided in ways that will help them be safe, healthy, happy, and well adjusted.

Figure A–1 Sample handbook.

Policy on Health and Safety

When discipline is necessary, we use measures that show love and kindness, but also firmness and consistency. We attempt to help children gain the confidence and knowledge that will develop their self-control. We do not allow children to hurt themselves or others or to destroy property.

It is our desire to keep the children and adults at the center as healthy and safe as possible. We need your cooperation.

If your child has symptoms of illness (runny nose, red or runny eyes, fever, vomiting, diarrhea, etc.), we ask that you keep him home. You may want to check with his doctor. Home rest will prevent spreading of the illness and help the child regain his health.

When a child becomes ill at the center, he will be isolated, as much as possible, and the parents will be called. If it is impossible for parents to pick up the child within 1 hour's time, they will be assessed a special fee for having someone attend to the child.

Parents will be notified of any communicable or serious illness of children or adults at the center. We are required to report children's immunizations as part of our licensing. Before a child returns to the center after having a communicable disease, the parent must check with a doctor to assure that return is safe for the child and others.

The center will make every attempt to serve wholesome and nourishing foods to the children. Parents are asked to report allergies, cultural restrictions, and strong dislikes to the director.

The children will be outside each day and should be properly dressed to avoid their becoming sunburned, wet, too hot, or too cold, depending on the weather. In inclement weather, children play in our covered area. We believe children who are well enough to be at the center are well enough to be outside a portion of the time.

The children are supervised in their indoor and outdoor activities; however, accidents may occur. In any case, parent (guardians) will be notified of any accident and its circumstances. If the accident is minor, the center staff will handle it and either call to report the incident or report it when the child is picked up. The parent or staff member or both can then decide if the child needs medical attention. When a serious accident occurs and the child needs immediate medical attention, our first action will be to obtain the needed help. The second action will be to notify the parents. The center will refer to the child's "Emergency and Health Procedure" form.

Parents should notify the center of the times (1) when the child is not to be at the center and (2) when the parents will not be at their regular address or phone number, so that they can be reached at all times, not just in case of emergency.

The tuition fee covers accidents and injuries that occur while the child is at the center. *(Note: Give specific details about the insurance policy and what it covers. Do not let yourself or the parents be misled!)*

Delivery and Pickup of Children

We have a special off-the-street driveway, parking, and entrance for our center. We encourage you to use them for safety and convenience.

The adult accompanying the child to the center *must come into the classroom with him and wait while he is checked in and accepted into his group.* If for any reason the child is not permitted to stay at the center, this adult *is responsible for either returning the child home or making other arrangements for his care.*

Figure A–1   *Continued*

Group times are as follows:

MORNING:
    Arrival   between 8:45 and 9:00 a.m.
    Departure between 11:15 and 11:30 a.m.
AFTERNOON:
    Arrival   between 12:45 and 1:00 p.m.
    Departure between 3:15 and 3:30 p.m.

Please bring and pick up your child during the indicated times. Because our staff members have responsibilities in addition to being in the classroom, they will be unable to be with the children during times other than their scheduled times. If you cannot meet the indicated times, please arrange for another person to do so. Paying a late fee is not an acceptable alternative.

Please leave with us the names and relationships of persons authorized to pick up your child. If you must make emergency changes, please phone the center to inform us of the change and to allow us to prepare the child for it. Because of safety and liability, we will release a child only to authorized persons.

Carpools

Parents are responsible for transporting their children to and from the center. We will be happy to provide the addresses and phone numbers of children who attend simultaneously, but we do not accept the cost or legal responsibility of transporting children, except on authorized field trips.

(Note: If your center does form and maintain carpools or offer limousine services, state the particulars of each service; for example, cost, liability, and schedule.)

Basic Daily Program

Because we are concerned about the well-being of the total child, we plan daily experiences to enhance the child's physical, mental, social, and emotional development. An overemphasis on one developmental area could result in a deficiency in another area. In our curriculum, we provide for each child's individual and group needs: opportunities for creative and expressive arts, music, science, literature, excursions, food experiences, mathematics, and play.

Our qualified and caring teachers carefully plan each day's activities on the developmental level of the children in the group. We believe in encouraging children to participate, in stimulating their curiosity, in following their interests, and in increasing their abilities and skills; but we do not believe in pressuring or pushing children beyond their capabilities.

Basically, each (half-) day is divided into four periods; however, gathering or activity times may be used more than once during a session:

Opening time: This is a period of time when the child makes the transition from home to center. He is checked in and welcomed into the group. Children choose activities at this time from among the toys set out by the teachers—such as large building blocks; transportation vehicles; table toys like puzzles, pegs and boards, or small interlocking blocks—or they engage in dramatic play with props in a quiet place.

Figure A–1   *Continued*

Gathering time:	All children participate as a group. Although individual differences may be apparent, the focus is on the group. Some activities that may take place are theme setting for the day, stories, music, snack, or specific demonstrations or interactions.
Activity time:	Children are free to move among preselected activities such as art or craft materials, sensory table, easel and paint, science experiences, food preparation, and others.
Closing time:	Children are helped to finish activities, get their things together, and make the transition back to their homes. One teacher remains with the children, reading stories, talking informally, or perhaps singing songs. A second teacher helps the children gather their belongings and leave for home.

Activities during these four periods may be inside or outside; they may vary from day to day or last several days, depending on the children's interest. The length of each period is determined by the children's interests and activities. As a period draws to a close, the children help put toys and materials away in preparation for the next activity.

Snacks (and/or Meals) Served

A snack is served during each morning and afternoon session. We use healthful and nourishing foods of low sugar content and, when possible, involve the children in preparing and serving the food. We provide many finger foods, use seasonal produce, and encourage the children to at least taste everything served.

Snack is a group experience. We encourage the children to practice good manners, converse freely, eat at the table, serve themselves, and use their utensils properly.

If your child has food allergies, strong dislikes, or cultural restrictions, we would appreciate knowing about them.

Parents who wish to bring a food treat should make prior arrangements with the teacher. We suggest such things as fresh or dried fruit, nuts, or other nutritious foods. Sugar, chocolate, and food colorings (punch, for example) are discouraged.

Toys from Home

The center has many appropriate play materials for the age groups served. These materials can help the children learn to share, trade, initiate activities, and plan ahead. We therefore request that toys not be brought from home. They cause problems, such as becoming lost or broken.

On very special occasions, a child may bring a toy or object to show to the teachers and children, with the understanding that it will be taken home after he has shown it. If it is brought by an adult at departure time, the child may show it to those present and then take it back home. Advance arrangements should be made with the teacher as to the best time and way to show an item.

When a new child joins an intact group, this child may need the security of something from home. This situation should be discussed with the teacher so that appropriate arrangements can be made (what the child should bring, how it will be used at school, for what length of time he can bring it, etc.).

Absence from the Center

We would appreciate being notified when the child will be absent from the center, in addition to the reason and duration of the absence. In case of a communicable disease, we need to notify other parents to watch for symptoms in their children. Children can become disturbed by the absence of their friends unless they are reassured with the reason for the child's absence and the approximate time of his return. Parents of children returning to the center following a communicable disease should contact the director for any specific instructions. (Students are referred to Chapter 7.)

There will be no reduction in fee because of absence. In the event of an extended absence, the parent and director should decide if the child's place should be retained (and paid for) or released to another child.

Figure A–1   *Continued*

Dress Code for Children

The children will play freely, be more independent, and be happier in clothing that is modest, comfortable, and easily laundered.

Children should wear clothing that protects them from the sun in summer, from the cold in winter, and from moisture during wet weather. Mittens, boots, and coverings for legs are a must for cold weather, because the children play outside daily—even in inclement weather.

We provide cover-ups (aprons) for each child and see that clothes are protected during messy or wet activities. In anticipation of those times, however, when clothes do get wet or soiled, to prevent the child's distress and embarrassment, we require a change of clothing that is kept in his personal locker or box. Clothes needing to be laundered will be sent home with the request that they (or others) be returned the next day.

Please mark your child's name in all of his clothing. Without the marking, it is difficult for us to know the owner because most of the children wear similar sizes and some have similar articles of clothing. We will notify you when activities (such as swimming or excursions) require special clothing.

While at the center, children are required to wear shoes to protect their feet from injuries and cold. Shoes should fit well and be comfortable. Thongs are not permitted: they impede walking, make running and climbing dangerous, and do not stay on. We request that children do not wear fabric shoes when it is cold or wet unless they also bring or wear boots. Weather boots have recently become popular. If your child wears such boots to school, please send a pair of shoes that he can wear inside the classroom. Continuous wearing of weather boots can cause foot problems.

Holidays and Birthdays

Some holidays are beyond the understanding of young children. When we celebrate a holiday at the center, we design concepts and activities that give the children more experience with and understanding of the holiday. We will notify you of the times and formats of our celebrations. Generally, there will be no special requirements of parents.

The most important occasion for a child is his own birthday. We will honor him at this time by doing something special—perhaps a favorite activity or snack. Parents who wish to send a special food treat at this time are referred to important information under "Snacks."

We feel it is important for our young children to become familiar with the values, beliefs, and cultural traditions of different people and the ways they celebrate special occasions. From time to time, we will provide such opportunities. We would appreciate knowing if, and how, any of the parents could assist us.

We will attempt to highlight holidays and special occasions as close to their actual dates as possible.

Gift Giving

We regret that we must mention such a personal thing as bringing gifts to our staff members. By calling it to your attention, we hope to avoid embarrassing situations for children, parents, and staff members. We discourage gift giving, because it tends to put financial and emotional pressure on other families and on teachers. If it is important to you to show love and appreciation with a gift, could we suggest that the child be involved as much as possible, that the cost be nominal, and that it be presented in a private place other than the center?

At times, we help the children prepare gifts for others. These are items that are especially chosen to provide children with the pleasure of knowing they made the gifts themselves. We talk about love and sharing. It may sound as if we teach one thing, but discourage its practice (through gift giving). Thoughtfulness and caring, however, can be meaningfully shown through a hug, a smile, a comment, or something personally created.

Figure A–1   *Continued*

Parent Conferences

At least twice each year, or more often if deemed necessary by parents or teachers, parents may make an appointment to meet with the director or head teacher. This is an opportunity for parents and teachers to share ideas, impressions, and information about the children's total environment—both home and school.

Parent Education

We have found that parents/guardians and center staff interact favorably in parent education when both parents/guardians are fully involved. We have an excellent program outlined for this year and would encourage parents to make arrangements now to attend and participate with us. The meetings will be the second Thursday of each month, 7:30 to 9:00 P.M., as follows:

September	Get-acquainted social for families
October	Growth Patterns of Young Children (presented by the director and applied to age groupings at the center; includes handouts)
November	Discipline (presented by a guest; includes a practice session)
December	Customs, traditions, and beliefs of different cultural groups (presented by parents or community members using appropriate costumes, foods, displays, and so on; selected presentations will be planned on the children's developmental levels and used in the classrooms periodically throughout the school year)
January	Health and Safety of Children (presented by a local pediatrician)
February	Self-Concept Development (workshop including activities and role playing)
March	Parents and Families (presentation by a marriage counselor followed by small-group discussion; parents may suggest topics to the director before February 15)
April	Open (please submit ideas to the director by March 15)
May	Family picnic at the center.

Visitors to the Center

We welcome parents to our center. We would appreciate their reporting to the office before going to the classroom, except when they are bringing or picking up children. Although we do not now have observation facilities, we will attempt to provide a place for inconspicuous observation.

Siblings, young friends, and relatives of enrolled children cannot participate in the group without the director's special consent.

Calendar of Events

Each parent will be given a calendar of important center events.

(Note: Calendar divisions should coincide with payment schedules, for example, monthly, quarterly, or semester. Rather than printing the calendar as part of the handbook, printing it separately for periodic distribution may be more current and economical. Items of special note include days the center is closed (holidays, workshops or training for teachers, vacations, etc.), parent/family involvement (e.g., meetings, conferences, socials, fund-raising events, volunteering, etc.), and community events (e.g., concerts, outings, celebrations, and other events of interest and value to families with young children).

Additional Services for Families

Parents wishing to consult about their child or other family matters may schedule an appointment with the director. The director will refer parents to an appropriate agency or source in matters that are outside the expertise of the center.

Periodically, the center will provide meetings, workshops, guest speakers, and socials as a regular part of our ongoing parent education program.

Figure A–1   *Continued*

Request for Parental Input

We aim to be current, perceptive, and thorough in the services we provide at the center. Parents are encouraged to discuss concerns with the teachers or director. Suggestions will be thoughtfully considered and implemented whenever appropriate or possible.

(Note: This section should be used for constructive input from parents about the services at the center. Grievances should be handled immediately on a personal basis.)

This invitation to respond should not be viewed as an opportunity for parents to dictate the goals, policies, procedures, philosophy, or management of the center. Rather, it should be regarded as a time of constructive evaluation. Parents who have major disagreements with our center might be happier if their child were enrolled in a program that more closely resembled parental philosophy and desires.

(Note: Some centers include a short form or card that parents must sign and return, indicating their awareness of the policies and willingness to support them.)

Figure A–1   *Continued*

The preceding sample handbook works well for half-day programs. For a full-day program, the handbook should be more extensive, covering the needs of the children of out-of-home parents, such as meals, naps, toilet training, care of sick children, and other matters. Also, certain local, state, and federal regulations must be met.

In addition to the handbook and required forms, other information may help the center personnel better understand and work with the children. Parents may feel it is intruding on the family's privacy. Consider the following questions:

- Are the children ever left in anyone else's care?
- What are the rules for children in your home?
- What is your attitude toward discipline? Can you give examples of when you use discipline?
- Is there a back-up plan for the days you are ill? On vacation?
- Do you belong to any professional child-care organizations?
- May I have several references to call of people who have recently been in your program?
- What are the qualifications for substitute teachers? Will it always be the same substitute?

Appendix B

Child-Care Applications

Office use only: Placed: _____   Option: _____

[Logo, Center name, Address, Telephone]

Application Form for Part-Day Preschool Attendance

Child's name (first, middle, last) _____   Sex _____

Birth date _____   Today's date _____   Nickname _____

Parent/guardian name _____

    Address _____

    Phone (home and work) _____

Person to notify if parent/guardian is not immediately available:

    Name and relationship _____

    Address _____

    Phone number _____

Specify child's native language if other than English _____

Names and birth dates of siblings (oldest to youngest) _____

_____

_____

(circle names of siblings who have attended our center)

Child's previous group experience (name and address of group, dates) _____

_____

Important medical information about child (allergies, disabilities, diseases) _____

_____

Options for which you are applying (check one):

Summer (June through August) _____   Fall/Winter (September through May) _____

Indicate first (1) and second (2) choice below:

    _____ Tues., Wed., Thurs. 9:00–11:30 A.M.   _____ Mon. thru Fri. 9:00–11:30 A.M.

    _____ Tues., Wed., Thurs. 1:00–3:30 P.M.   _____ Mon. thru Fri. 1:00–3:30 P.M.

Fee schedule:

    Three half-days per week $ _____ per month

    Five half-days per week $ _____ per month

    Monthly fees are due by the   _____ of each month.

Parental expectations of center (or reasons for applying at this center): _____

_____

A nonrefundable fee of $ _____ must accompany applications. Make check payable to (enter

information). _____

Deadline for applications for _____ year is _____ .

Included in the monthly fee is an accident insurance policy for injuries that may be incurred while the child is engaged in activities sponsored by the center.

If parent/guardian would like additional information please specify: _____

_____

_____

Signature of parent/guardian

Figure B–1   Information on children, part day.

Office use only: Placed: _____   Option: _____

[Logo, Center name, Address, Telephone]

Application Form for Full-Day Preschool Attendance

Child's name (first, middle, last) _____   Sex _____

Birth date _____   Today's date _____   Nickname _____

Parent/guardian name _____

    Address _____

    Phone (home and work) _____

Person to notify if parent/guardian is not immediately available:

    Name and relationship _____

    Address _____

    Phone number _____

Specify child's native language if other than English _____

Names and birth dates of siblings (oldest to youngest) _____

_____

_____

(circle names of siblings who have attended our center)

Child's previous group experience (name and address of group, dates) _____

_____

Important medical information about child (allergies, disabilities, diseases) _____

_____

Parental expectations of center (or reasons for applying at this center): _____

_____

_____

_____

A nonrefundable fee of $ _____ must accompany applications. Make check payable to (enter
information). _____

(Make specific statements about fees, hours for arrival and departure of the children, philosophy of program, transportation, or any other information that may help parents evaluate whether or not this program
would fit their needs.)

Included in the monthly fee is an accident insurance policy for injuries that may be incurred while the child
is engaged in activities sponsored by the center.

If parent/guardian would like additional information please specify: _____

_____

_____

_____

_____

_____

Signature of parent/guardian

Figure B–2   Information on children, full day.

[Logo, Center name, Address, Telephone, Date]

[Name and address of parent/guardian]

Dear _____

It is a pleasure to inform you that we can place _____(child's name)_____ in our Center beginning _____ . Our Center policy requires that a deposit of _____ be paid by _____ . This
deposit will apply toward the first month's tuition; the balance is to be paid the first day of attendance.

We are enclosing the following forms and request that you fill them out and bring them when you and
your child come for orientation on _____(date)_____ at _____(time)_____ .

1. Personal information about your child

2. Health record and dates of immunization

3. Emergency and medical information

4. Evidence of the child's recent physical examination

5. Parent resource questionnaire

We are also enclosing a copy of our Parent/Guardian Handbook and request you review it before the
orientation so we can answer your questions about our Center. You will be asked to signify your awareness of the information in the Handbook before your child is enrolled.

If you have any questions before your scheduled orientation, please call so we can assist you.

We look forward to having your child and your family participate in our program.

Sincerely,

Director

Enclosures

Figure B–3 Letter of acceptance.

[Logo, Center name, Address, Telephone, Date]

[Name and address of parent/guardian]

Dear _____ ,

We are sorry that we are unable to place your child in our Center at this time.

Your application will be held in our replacement file. We will notify you as soon as we have an opening
for your child.

If you decide to withdraw your application, or if you have a change of address or phone number,
please notify us so our records will be current.

Thank you for your interest in our Center.

Sincerely,

Director

Figure B–4 Letter of inability to place a child.

Appendix C

Children's Records

```
                                           (Today's date) _____
Name of child _____  Date of birth_____
Parent/guardian _____
Address _____
Home phone # _____  Work phone # _____
Family doctor _____  Phone # _____
Address _____
Name of clinic _____
Alternate doctor _____  Phone # _____
Address _____
Name of clinic _____

Person to notify if parent/guardian is not immediately available (name, relationship, address, phone #).
_____

In case of serious illness or accident, paramedics will be contacted and the child taken to (list hospital or
clinic name) _____
_____

Please check any health problems the child has and explain below:
_____ Asthma                              _____ Limited foods
_____ Hay fever or allergies             _____ Receiving any medication
_____ Limited activity                   _____ Frequent colds, diarrhea, earaches, or
_____ Disabilities                              skin eruptions
          List _____    Extent _____

          _____         _____

Insurance information:
Insurance company name and address _____
Family's ID number _____
Name on policy _____
Employer _____

Necessary explanations _____
_____
_____

Persons authorized to pick up your child _____
Persons not authorized to pick up your child _____
```

Figure C–1   Emergency/health card.

Date _____

I. Identification Information

Name _____ Boy ____ Girl ____

　　　　　　　last　　　　　first　　　middle　　nickname _____

Date of birth _____ Place of birth _____

Parents'/guardian's name _____

Parents'/guardian's address _____

Home telephone _____ Business telephone _____

II. Family History

Members of household: List adults first, then children in order of age, then other household members; star those who take responsibility for child.

Name	Relationship to Child	Age
1.		
2.		
3.		
4.		
5.		
6.		
7.		
8.		

List any ways in which your family varies from the usual, for example, foster or stepparents, separated or divorced parents.

Does family live in: ____ House ____ Apartment ____ Duplex ____ Other

Education: Check appropriate category:

Mother ____ High School ____ 1–3 yrs college ____ 4+ yrs college ____ Other _____

Father ____ High School ____ 1–3 yrs college ____ 4+ yrs college ____ Other _____

Occupation:

Mother/guardian (if employed) _____

Father/guardian (if employed) _____

Figure C–2　Personal information.

III. Physical Regime

Does your child enjoy his/her food? _____ What meal does (s)he enjoy most? _____

Is there anything unusual about his/her eating that would be important for us to know (allergies, dislikes, etc.)?

_____

What is your child's usual bedtime? _____ Usual waking time? _____

Does (s)he take a nap regularly? _____ How long is nap? _____

What is your child's attitude toward going to bed? _____

_____

Toward taking a nap? _____

When did your child walk? _____ talk? _____

At what age was your child toilet-trained? _____ Bladder _____ Bowel

How does (s)he state this need? _____

How dependable is (s)he? _____

Any special information _____

IV. Time with Children

On the average, how much time do you spend per week interacting with your preschool child? (Just you and the child, do not include other family members.) This does not include time watching TV, eating, or sleeping.

Mother/guardian _____ Father/guardian _____

Approximately how much time per week do you spend interacting with your child and other family members together? (Do not include time watching TV, eating, or sleeping.)

Mother/guardian _____ Father/guardian _____

V. Play and sociability

What kinds of physical activities do you engage in with your preschool child? (e.g., walking, playing ball, wrestling)

Mother/guardian: _____

Father/guardian: _____

What other activities do you usually participate in just with your preschool child?

Mother/guardian: _____

Father/guardian: _____

Does your child play alone? Always _____ Often _____ Seldom _____ Never _____

Does (s)he like to play alone? _____

Are playmates girls? _____ boys? _____ younger? _____ older? _____

What play materials does (s)he use most indoors? _____

_____

What play materials does (s)he use most outdoors? _____

_____

What experiences with music does (s)he have at home? _____

_____

What opportunities for hearing stories are offered? _____

_____

Figure C–2   *Continued*

VI. Personality and Emotional Development

Do you regard your child as affectionate? _____

To whom? _____

Does (s)he accept new people easily? _____

Does (s)he seek adult attention? _____ Whose? _____

How? _____

Has (s)he any fears? _____ Of what? _____

Is (s)he usually happy? _____

What does your child do to indicate his/her feeling of self-worth? (e.g., shows what (s)he can do, tells feelings about self, etc.) _____

What do you do to enhance your child's feelings of self-worth?

Mother/guardian: _____

Father/guardian: _____

VII. Intellectual Development

Would you say your child is superior _____, average _____, or less than average _____ in his/her thinking ability?

What kind of activities do you do with your preschool child to stimulate his/her thinking and expression?

Mother/guardian: _____

Father/guardian: _____

VIII. Discipline

When you find it necessary to exert authority over your child, what do you usually do?

Mother/guardian: _____

Father/guardian: _____

IX. Additional Information

Write below any further information about your child or your family that you believe will be helpful to us in understanding your child's behavior.

Figure C–2   *Continued*

Appendix D

Contagious Diseases and Immunizations

Recommended Ages for Administration of Currently Licensed Childhood Vaccines, August 1995

Vaccines are listed under the routinely recommended ages. Solid bars indicate range of acceptable ages for vaccination. Shaded bars indicate new recommendations or vaccines licensed since publication of the Recommended Childhood Immunization Schedule in January 1995. Hepatitis B vaccine is recommended at 11–12 years of age for children not previously vaccinated. Varicella Zoster Virus vaccine is recommended at 11–12 years of age for children not previously vaccinated, and lack a reliable history of chickenpox.

Age ▶ Vaccine ▼	Birth	2 mos.	4 mos.	6 mos.	12[1] mos.	15 mos.	18 mos.	4–6 yrs.	11–12 yrs.	14–16 yrs.
Hepatitis B[2,3]	Hep B–1	Hep B–2		Hep B–3					Hep B–3[3]	
Diphtheria, Tetanus, Pertussis[4]		DTP	DTP	DTP	DTP[1,4] DTaP at 15+ m			DTP or DtaP	Td	
H. influenzae type b[5]		Hib	Hib	Hib[5]	Hib[1,5]					
Polio		OPV	OPV	OPV				OPV		
Measles, Mumps, Rubella[6]					MMR[1,6]			MMR	or [6] MMR	
Varicella Zoster[7]					VZV[7]				VZV[7]	

Figure D–1 Immunization chart.

Source: Reprinted with permission from "Immunization Protects Children." Copyright © 1991 Amercian Academy of Pediatrics.

Disease	Incubation Period	Period of Communicability	Associated Symptoms	Rash
Adenovirus	6–9 days	First few days of illness	Runny nose, red eyes, sore throat	Flat and raised pink dots
Chicken pox	11–20 days	1–2 days before and 4–6 days after rash appears	Fever, loss of appetite, headache, malaise	Red ringed blisters that progress to scabs
Fifth disease	6–14 days	Unknown	Low fever, rarely sore throat, runny nose, headache	Flushed, red cheeks, slapped face appearance, pink dots on extremities
German measles (rubella)	14–21 days	Few days before and few days after rash	Runny nose, sore throats, mild fever	Flat and raised pink dots that begin on head and neck and spread downward
Hand, foot and mouth disease (some coxsackie viruses)	2–5 days	Several weeks after onset of infection	Fever, malaise	Rash fades in 3 days. Small red bumps and blisters especially on palms and soles and mucous membranes
Herpes simplex virus	2–12 days	Unknown	Fever, sore mouth and gums, cold sores	Blisters
Impetigo	2–5 days	As long as crusts persist or 24 hours after start of antibiotics	None	Blisters, pus containing and honey-colored crusted sores
Infectious mononucleosis	2–7 weeks	Unknown	Fever, lymph node swelling, sore throat	Flat and raised pink dots
Measles (rubeola)	10–12 days	4 days before and 4 days after onset of rash	Fever, runny nose and eyes, cough	Flat and raised pink dots, begins on head and neck, spreads downward, peels
Roseola	5–14 days	Unknown	3–5 days of high fever	Flat and raised pink dots appear on and chest trunk, then spread to face as fever breaks
Scarlet fever (strep throat with rash)	2–5 days	24 hours after start of antibiotic	Malaise, sore throat, fever, vomiting	Pinpoint, raised red dots all over body, especially on neck, axilla, groin skin folds, hands and feet peel afterward

Figure D–2   Rashes of common infectious diseases.

Source: Reprinted with permission from *Child Care Information Exchange,* P.O. Box 2890, Redmond, WA 98073, (800)221-2864.

Appendix E

First Aid

FIRST AID is the immediate temporary care given in cases of accident or sudden illness before the services of a physician can be secured. It includes procedures that can be applied by nonmedical persons to prevent further injury and reduce suffering.

Emergency Only: 911 personnel can walk you through the skills over the phone.

Poison Control: 1-800-456-7707 Ask A Nurse _____ Ambulance _____ Doctor _____ Police _____ Fire

BITES, ANIMAL AND HUMAN
Control bleeding. Clean thoroughly with soap and water. Apply sterile dressing or bandage. Notify parent.

BITES, SNAKE
DO NOT try to suck venom out. Call 911. Call parent. Keep victim calm and lying down. Keep bite area below the heart if possible.

BLEEDING AND OPEN WOUNDS
Abrasion or Scraped Skin
Wash with soap and water. Remove all debris. Dry well with sterile gauze and apply sterile dressing or bandage.

Cuts and Lacerations (tearing)
Control bleeding. Wash wound. Dry well with sterile gauze and apply sterile dressing or bandage. If bleeding persists, seek emergency care.

Puncture Wounds
Minor puncture wounds: Remove object. Control bleeding. Wash with soap and water. Dry well with sterile gauze and apply sterile dressing or bandage.

Severe puncture wounds: **DO NOT** remove impaled objects. Control bleeding. Call 911 immediately. Call parent.

Amputations
Control bleeding and follow procedures as directed above. Care for the amputated body part by:
— Wrapping the amputated part in moist sterile gauze and place in plastic bag.
— Transport with victim or take to hospital immediately.

BURNS
First Degree (a small reddened area, no blister formation): hold burned area under cold running water until pain stops (5–10 minutes).

Second Degree (blisters develop): immerse in cold water until pain stops (5–10 minutes). Blot dry with sterile cloth and cover with dry sterile dressing. Obtain medical attention if severe. Call parent.

Third Degree (deep burn, skin layers destroyed): cover with sterile cloth to protect. Call 911. Call parent. **DO NOT** pop blisters. **DO NOT** apply ointments, butter, or petroleum jelly to **ANY** burn. **DO NOT PULL CLOTHING FROM BURNED AREAS.**

CHOKING
If the infant or child is coughing forcefully, crying, or can speak **DO NOT** hit on the back, encourage to cough. If the infant or child is making a high pitched squeaky noise the airway is blocked.

Figure E–1 A guide for first aid and emergency care for young children.

CHOKING CHILD (over one year) Call 911. Heimlich Maneuver—Stand behind the child and wrap your arms around the child's waist. Make a fist with one hand. Place the fist's thumb side against the child's abdomen, slightly above the navel and well below the tip of breastbone. Grasp your fist with the other hand. Press the fist into the child's abdomen with a quick upward thrust. Repeat until the object is dislodged or the child becomes unconscious.

IF YOU HAVE TO USE THE HEIMLICH MANEUVER, OR ANY KIND OF CHEST OR ABDOMINAL THRUSTS, THE CHILD SHOULD BE CHECKED BY A PHYSICIAN IN CASE AN ABDOMINAL INJURY MAY HAVE OCCURRED.

ADVISE PARENTS TO HAVE THE CHILD SEEN BY A DOCTOR.

UNCONSCIOUS—Call 911. Place the victim on his/her back with the face up. Straddle the child's thighs. Place the heel of one hand against the child's abdomen, slightly above the navel and well below the tip of the breastbone. Place the outer hand directly on top of the first hand. Press into the abdomen with a quick, upward thrust 6–10 times. Finger sweep, breathe, reposition head. Repeat if unsuccessful. Call parent.

CHOKING INFANT (child less than one year) Call 911. The Heimlich Maneuver can also be performed successfully on infants. Sit the infant on your lap. Using the pads of the index and middle fingers, gently press against the baby's abdomen, above the navel and below the tip of breastbone, with quick, upward motion. Repeat until the object is dislodged or the infant becomes unconscious.

Please note: Organizations such as the American Red Cross and the American Heart Association recommend the following procedure for infants: Call 911, report facts:

1. Place the baby on your forearm, face down and with his/her head below baby's trunk. Rest your forearm on your thigh for support.
2. Using the heel of your hand, hit the baby four times on the back high between the shoulder blades. If he/she is not breathing, support the head and neck and place him/her on the thigh with the head lower than the trunk and give four chest thrusts (one finger width below the nipple line).
3. Repeat this sequence of back blows and chest compressions until the airway opens or medical help arrives.
4. Attempt rescue breathing, check airway, position head, breathe 2 puffs.

COLDS & COUGHS

DO NOT provide treatment for children with obvious symptoms of colds/coughs (runny nose and eyes, sore throat, coughing, sneezing, and/or fever). Isolate all children with these symptoms and notify the parents to exclude the children from the center and urge parents to obtain medical care.

COMMUNICABLE DISEASES

DO NOT provide treatment for children with apparent communicable diseases. Isolate children with signs and symptoms (cold symptoms, rash, nausea, vomiting, diarrhea, yellow eyes and skin, fatigue and malaise). Notify parents and exclude children from center and urge parents to obtain medical care.

CONVULSIONS AND SEIZURES

DO NOT restrain the convulsive movements or try to move child during the seizure. **DO NOT** put anything in child's mouth. Move everything out of the area so that child will not strike objects. **KEEP THE OTHER CHILDREN AWAY**. Following any convulsion the child should be allowed to rest. Keep quiet, loosen clothing. Notify parent and urge parents to seek medical care. Seizures may continue.

DIABETIC EMERGENCIES

INSULIN SHOCK: Results when the child has taken too much insulin and has not eaten.

FIRST AID: If the child is **CONSCIOUS** and can swallow give a drink containing sugar (orange juice). If the child does not improve in 10 to 15 minutes, call 911. Call parent. If child is UNCONSCIOUS call 911 immediately. Call parent.

Figure E–1 *Continued*
Source: Utah Department of Health Services, 1993.

DIABETIC COMA: Results when the blood sugar level becomes too high because there is too little insulin in the blood; these conditions can be fatal unless something is done to reverse them.

FIRST AID: If child is **UNCONSCIOUS** call 911 immediately. Call parent.

EARS

A child with discharge from the ear(s) should be under medical care. Other than comfort, do not give treatment for earache. Notify parents and urge them to seek medical care.

Foreign body in external canal: **DO NOT** attempt to remove. Notify parent and urge parent to seek medical care.

EYES

Eye injuries may result in permanent loss of sight. Early treatment of injuries may prevent permanent damage or loss of sight. If the injury is severe or if you are concerned about an eye injury, call 911.

Blunt injury apply an ice cold compress immediately for about 15 minutes. Keep child quiet. If there is redness or persistent pain, call 911. Call parent. If pupil of eye appears cloudy, call 911 immediately.

Foreign body: **DO NOT** permit child to rub eye. Try to flush object out by rinsing eye gently with warm water. If object does not flush out, notify parent and urge parents to seek medical care.

Injury: In all injuries, cover both eyes loosely with sterile dressing. Notify parent. Urge parent to seek medical care.

FAINTING

If child looks pale, feels dizzy, is nauseated, sweating, and/or seeing spots, have him lie down and elevate the legs. Loosen tight clothing, and look for injuries. Apply cold compresses to forehead. Watch breathing and pulse. Notify parent and urge parent to seek medical care.

FALLS

After a serious fall **DO NOT** move a child if you suspect a neck or back injury. Assume that all unconscious victims have a spinal or neck injury. Watch breathing. Call 911. Call parent. If the child can get up by himself, have the child rest. Observe for headache, vomiting, or drowsiness. Notify parent and urge parent to seek medical care.

GASTROINTESTINAL

Nausea and vomiting: Isolate child and have child lie on his/her side. Give nothing by mouth except sips of water. Use appropriate hand washing. Notify parent to exclude child from center. Encourage parent to seek medical care.

Diarrhea: Isolate child and have child lie down and rest. Use appropriate hand washing. Notify parent to exclude child from center. Encourage parent to seek medical care.

HEADACHE

Have child lie down and rest in a quiet environment. Apply cold wet cloth to forehead. Notify parent and encourage parent to seek medical care.

HEAD INJURIES

Complete rest until medical evaluation can be made. Consult physician, ASK-A-NURSE, or call 911. Notify parent. Call 911 immediately if:

1. There is loss of consciousness at the time of the injury or at any time thereafter.
2. You are unable to arouse the child from sleep. You may allow the child to sleep after injury but check frequently to see whether child can be aroused. Check at least every one or two hours during the day, and two to three times during the night.
3. There is persistent vomiting. Many children vomit immediately from fright, but the vomiting usually does not persist unless head injury is severe. If a child continues to vomit after 30 minutes, call 911.
4. Inability to move a limb.
5. Oozing of blood or watery fluid from the ear or nose.
6. Persistent headache lasting over one hour. The headache will be severe enough to interfere with activity and normal sleep.
7. Persistent dizziness for one hour after the injury.
8. Unequal pupils.
9. Pale color that does not return to normal in a short time.

Figure E–1 *Continued*

NOSE INJURIES

Nosebleeds: Have child sit up with head slightly forward so that blood will not run back into the throat. Hold nostrils together with pressure over middle part of nose for about 5 minutes with a cool cloth or gauze. **DO NOT** allow to blow or pick nose. Keep child quiet. If bleeding cannot be controlled, call 911. Call parent.

Foreign body: **DO NOT** attempt to remove. Notify parent and urge parent to seek medical care.

PEDICULOSIS (bugs or head lice)

Isolate the child from the other children. Notify parent and urge them to seek medical care. Examine all other children and follow the same directive. Before re-admitting any child that has had lice, make certain that the child has had adequate treatment.

POISONING

Call 911 or the Poison Control Center immediately. **DO NOT** give antidotes or induce vomiting unless you are directed to by 911 or Poison Control. Follow their instructions.

SKIN INFECTIONS

Some skin conditions are highly communicable. The diagnosis and treatment of a skin condition should be made by a physician. **DO NOT** admit any child with skin condition until a physician declares in writing the condition is noncommunicable.

SPLINTERS

Slight: If superficial, remove with tweezers. After removal, wash area with soap and water. Cover with sterile gauze or bandage. Deeply imbedded or under finger nail, **DO NOT** attempt to remove. Notify parent, and encourage parent to seek medical care.

SPRAINS

Keep limb at rest. Apply ice pack for 20 to 30 minutes. Urge parent to seek medical care.

SUSPECTED FRACTURES AND DISLOCATIONS

Avoid manipulation and movement of affected parts. Protect, support, and cover skin loosely with sterile dressing. Notify parent. Call 911.

STINGS AND INSECT BITES

Normal reaction: Momentary pain, redness around sting site, itching, heat. First aid for normal reactions: remove stinger by scraping the sack away with a credit card or similar object. Apply ice pack over the sting site to relieve pain. Observe victim for at least 30 minutes for signs of excessive swelling or difficulty breathing. If this should start to occur, call 911 immediately. Call parent.

More severe reactions: skin flush, hives, localized swelling of lips or tongue, "tickle" in throat, wheezing abdominal cramps, diarrhea. Call 911. Call parent.

Life Threatening Reactions: Bluish or grayish skin, seizures, unconsciousness, inability to breathe due to swelling of vocal cords. Call 911 immediately. Call parent.

TEETH

Toothache: notify parent and encourage they obtain dental care.

Tooth injury: control bleeding by having child bite on a sterile gauze. If tooth is knocked out, find tooth (if possible). **DO NOT** wash tooth. Wrap it in sterile gauze. Notify parents and urge they seek immediate dental care and send the child and the tooth to the dentist.

CONTENTS OF FIRST AID KIT

A quick reference first aid manual
Sterile gauze pads, 3″ 2 3″, 2″ 2 2″
Bandage, 1″ rolls, 2″ rolls
Medical bandage, assorted sizes
Absorbent cotton
Adhesive bandage tape
Alcohol (70%) or alcohol-based wipes
Cotton-tipped applicators
Tongue depressors
Triangle bandage (for sling) 30″ or 40″
Tweezers
Scissors (bandage)
Disposable tissue or tissue wipes
Soap
Syrup of ipecac to induce vomiting
Ice bag
Safety pins
Ace bandage
Latex gloves
Thermometer

Figure E–1 *Continued*

Appendix F

Job Descriptions and Announcements

JOB ANNOUNCEMENTS

The announcement should clearly state the title, primary and secondary duties of each position (job description), personal and professional qualifications required, contract period, salary range, brief statement of qualifications, the name of person to contact, the application process, the deadline for applying, and the starting date. The hours may or may not be specified.

In an interview, the name or title of the administrative person to whom the candidate will be responsible (or titles of employees for whom he will be responsible if the position includes leadership) will be discussed.

The announcement should be distributed as widely as possible so as to attract the most qualified applicants. Suggested locations include public and private schools, employment offices, college and university placement offices, civic groups, clubs, special-interest groups, professional organizations, churches, local newspaper ads, flyers on public bulletin boards, and so on.

PLEASE POST   PLEASE POST   PLEASE POST

[Logo, Center name, Address, Telephone]

Position available:	Head teacher for 3-year-old group
Responsible to:	Preschool program director
Calendar:	September 1 through May 31, full-time. June through August, as needed. Two-week vacation during summer.
Qualifications:	Baccalaureate degree with specialization in early childhood education, special education, or equivalent. Minimum: two years preschool experience. Experience in parent education. Good mental and physical condition. Congenial with adults and children.
Desirable (not mandatory):	Special talent in music, art, or science for young children. Skill in conducting curriculum workshops. Current state teaching credential.
Duties:	Plan and implement a program for 3-year-olds that meets their individual and group needs in all developmental areas. Keep accurate records of individual children; evaluate curriculum and personal needs of the children. Supervise aids and trainees. Assist with and participate in professional growth of staff and in parent education.
Salary:	Depends on experience and personal qualifications. Negotiable.
Fringe benefits:	Semiannual review for pay increases and promotion (when available). Health insurance, retirement, and paid 2-week vacation.
Application deadline:	July 1, 20—. Please bring application and vita in person between 1:00 and 5:00 p.m., weekdays, to: Frances Featherstone, Director Featherstone's Preschool 6682 Southwest Main Street Anywhere, UT 88888
Interviews:	Applicant will be briefly interviewed when the application is submitted. Those who meet requirements will be notified by phone of a further interview to be held one week after the deadline. Final selection will be made by July 20. All candidates having the second interview will be notified of the outcome by mail or phone by July 21.

Equal Opportunity Employer

Figure F–1   Sample job announcement number one.

PLEASE POST   PLEASE POST   PLEASE POST

[Logo, Center name, Address, Telephone]

Position available:	Child-care aid
Responsible to:	Preschool classroom teacher
Assignment:	To assist teacher in working with 4-year-old children.
Calendar:	40-hour week, variable scheduling. September 1 through May 31. May be opportunity for part-time summer employment.
Qualifications:	High school graduation. One year training beyond high school (community college, university, special) with courses in child development or 2 years full-time experience working with preschoolers in a supervised setting. Good mental and physical health. Congenial and teachable. Desire for further education and experience with children and parents.
Desirable (not mandatory):	Two or more years in educational and professional training. Artistic talent. Able to play a musical instrument.
Duties:	Support lead teacher in classroom with curriculum planning and implementation. Lead various areas of program at specified times. Assist in preparing visual aids for bulletin boards, stories, songs, etc. Build a warm, sincere relationship with each child and parent. Participate in staff meetings, workshops, and other educational opportunities. Help keep records and prepare physical environment for the children. Assist with center maintenance.
Salary:	Negotiable, but depends on experience. Employees are considered for promotion based on performance and attitude.
Application deadline:	February 7, 20— Application must be submitted in person between 8:00 A.M. and 5:00 P.M., weekdays, to: Lorenzo Ludwig, Director 145 North Arlington Boulevard, SW Mathersville, IN 22222
Interviews:	Interviews for all eligible applicants will be scheduled during the week of February 10 to 14. Applicants will be notified of interview time by phone. Final selection will be made February 18. Each applicant will be notified of results by phone or mail by February 20. Job begins March 15.

Equal Opportunity Employer

Figure F–2 Sample job announcement number two.

PLEASE POST   PLEASE POST   PLEASE POST

[Logo, Center name, Address, Telephone]

Position available:	Nutritionist
Responsible to:	Director of child-care center
Position:	Plan, prepare, and serve meals for 40 children between the ages of 2 and 5. Weekdays only.
Qualifications:	Baccalaureate degree in food science from reputable university or college. At least 15 semester hours in basic child development or early childhood education. One year (or more) of food planning and preparing experience with young children. Familiarity with local, state, and federal food requirements. Budgeting skills. Ability to work well with children and adults. Good mental and physical health.
Desirable (not mandatory):	Written evidence of experience with feeding young children (food preferences and dislikes, amounts consumed per child, foods high in nutritive value, a variety of snack and lunch menus, etc.).
Duties:	Plan, purchase, prepare, and serve nourishing snacks and lunches for preschool children. At times, assist teachers and children in food experiences, possibly using the kitchen. Prepare file of favorite, inexpensive, and seasonal foods and easy recipes for children to make. Supervise kitchen staff. Oversee food storage, inventory, and use. Assist staff in food preparation for special events: holidays, parent meetings, etc.
Salary:	Negotiable.
Application deadline:	June 10, 20—.
Interviews:	For an interview, please call Mr. LaVell at 427-627-2727 (Lakewood Child Care Center, 726 Florida Avenue, Lakewood, CA 12345). Bring to the interview a résumé of experience, three personal and three professional references, and doctor's certificate of state of health. Job begins on July 2, 20—.

Equal Opportunity Employer

Figure F–3 Sample job announcement number three.

Appendix G

Employee Records

EMPLOYEES' PERSONAL RECORDS

The center should provide and maintain a file for each individual employee. Most centers have a preferred way of doing this; however, some suggestions follow:

1. Keep together all records of a particular individual
2. File information such as:
   a. Original job application (Figure G–1), job description, advancements or changes
   b. Performance appraisals, including goals, attendance record, additional training or experience, and professional participation
   c. Payroll information (starting salary, dates and amounts of increases, social security number, number of deductions)
   d. Health records, emergency information (Figure G–2)
3. Have a checklist of included forms for quick and easy reference on the outside of each individual folder (Figure G–3)

As a prospective employer, look for these key items:

1. If employed, has applicant allowed for notice to present employer?
2. Are there gaps in employment that would indicate health problems or instability of the applicant?
3. Are there frequent job changes that indicate dissatisfaction or job hopping?
4. Does the applicant give clear information (position held, responsibilities, reason for leaving)?
5. Is the application neat and logical?
6. Does the applicant have the required skills/experience to fill the available job?
7. How well would this applicant work with present staff?
8. What special contribution could this applicant bring to the center?
9. Would you want your own child associated with this person?

The Equal Opportunity Act of 1972 and the Affirmative Action Guidelines prohibit the asking of certain types of questions.

[Name and address of center]

Applicant _____ Date _____

Current address _____

Home phone _____ Other phone _____

Title of position for which you are applying _____

Present position _____

If presently employed, have you given notice? _____ Can we contact employer? ___

When could you start? _____

FORMER EMPLOYERS—List last four employers, starting with most current job:

Month & Year	Employer Name & Address	Start/ End Salary	Position	Responsibilities	Reason Left
From To					
From To					
From To					
From To					

EDUCATION/TRAINING

Check highest grade completed:

_____ High school   _____ Community college/trade school
_____ University   _____ Graduate school

List dates and school(s) where education/training was received:

_____

_____

REFERENCES

List the names, addresses, and phone numbers of two professional (work) references:

1. _____
2. _____

List the names, addresses, and phone numbers of two personal references:

1. _____
2. _____

Figure G–1   Application for employment.

Name _____

Address _____

Telephone _____

Soc. sec. no. _____ Date of birth _____

In case of emergency please contact

(1)   Name _____ Telephone _____

       Relationship to employee _____

(2)   Name _____ Telephone _____

       Relationship to employee _____

Doctor _____ Health plan no. _____

Hospital _____

Doctor's telephone _____

Any allergies or special health problems _____

_____

Company insurance policy # _____

Other Insurance:

      Company name and address _____

      Policy # _____

Figure G–2   Employee emergency information.

Forms and Reports

_____Original job application
_____Original job description
_____Date and description of subsequent assignment
_____Date and description of subsequent assignment
_____Date and description of subsequent assignment
_____Date and description of subsequent assignment
_____Date and evaluation of performance appraisal
_____Date and evaluation of performance appraisal
_____Date and evaluation of performance appraisal

Payroll information

Social Security # _____

_____Base salary   Date _____
_____Increase amount   Date _____
_____Increase amount   Date _____
_____Increase amount   Date _____
_____Increase amount   Date _____
_____No. of deductions   Date _____
_____Deduction changes   Date _____
_____Deduction changes   Date _____

Health Record

_____Date submitted   Physical exam:
_____Updated   date:
_____Updated   results:
                              T.B. test:
                                  date:
                                  results:

Emergency Information

_____Date submitted
_____Updated
_____Updated

Special Information

Have you ever been arrested or convicted of
  1. child abuse or crimes against children? Yes _____ No _____
  2. any criminal offenses?   Yes _____ No _____

Figure G–3 Checklist of forms to keep with employee's personal records.

Appendix H

Inventories

Pertinent center information must be typed into the computer before it can be retrieved and used. Refer to Chapters 11 and 12.

BOOKS

When using a computer program for book inventories, consider the following items:

1. *Recording present books or adding future books.* The following information is important:
   - Author's surname and given name or initials
   - Book title
   - Subject classifications (center-defined)
   - Publisher and year of publication
   - Vendor (where book was purchased)
   - Number of copies
   - Condition of copies
   - Call number (assigned by center)

   Example

   a. Author: Adelson, Leone
   b. Title: *All Ready for Summer*
   c. Subject(s): Summer
   d. Publisher and year: David McKay Co., 1955
   e. Vendor: Local bookstore
   f. Number of copies: 3
   g. Condition of copies: 2 good, 1 needs repair
   h. Call #: A-3

2. *Displaying a book entry.* The computer program should be easy to access, easy to record, easy to use, and easy to change or delete. In addition to screen viewing, center employees will want to use the information in various ways.

Example: For the inventory to be most useful, it should be flexible. Sometimes it is needed in one form, sometimes in another. Suppose the possible options are by author, by subject, by publisher, by vendor, and by condition.

Focus: What are the values of each option?

Author: The writing style or illustrations of a particular author may be popular. Knowing which books in the center were written by this author could be very helpful. Sometimes it is easier to remember an author's name than the book title.

Subject: When teaching on a particular subject, it is helpful to have a list of available books on that subject. Sometimes just reading through the topics gives teachers refreshing ideas. The following suggested book subjects are useful as listed or subdivided.

alphabet	families	pets
animals, farm	farms	poetry
animals, wild	flowers	school
animals, zoo	food	science
babies	friends	seasons
birds	fruits	senses
children	horses	sounds
cooking	mountains	space
desert	names	transportation
emotions	numbers	vegetables
energy	people	water

Publisher or vendor: Knowing where books are published is of greatest value when ordering them. Sometimes publishers or vendors have sales (or give discounts), and it is important to know which books are printed or sold by them.

Condition and number: When budgets are low and demands are high, it is important to know which books need to be replaced before new ones are ordered. Also, because of increased demand at certain times of year, employees will want to know the number of available copies of certain books. Awareness of the conditions of books helps in planning for their replacement.

3. *Changing a book entry.* Recording information carelessly or in duplicate can cause problems. Computers facilitate corrections and updates.

Example: Suppose an author's name is recorded incorrectly, the copy number is increased, or a book needs to be classified under a second subject. By completing the appropriate steps, current information appears on the screen; the operator then replaces, deletes, or adds the correct information.

4. *Deleting the information.* When information is no longer accurate or useful, it should be deleted. Computer programs without this option clutter the computer files. The change option can be used to write over outdated information to conserve file space.

Example: Suppose a book has gone out of print and is totally unavailable. When the center's copy is no longer repairable or usable, the entry needs to be deleted.

5. *Printing the information.* In considering computer software, ascertain that it prints data as well as displaying it on the screen. The center must have access to a printer that is compatible with its computer. Printed lists of the center's books can be invaluable—especially when the power is out, the computer is down, and someone wants a copy of your book list. In such an event, it would be a simple matter to refer to a printed (hard) copy of books listed by author, by subject, by publisher, or by condition.

Example: The book lists that can be printed are the same as those that can be viewed, provided appropriate information has been recorded in the

computer: author, subject, publisher, vendor, condition, or simply, title.

PICTURES

A picture inventory should include the same items as a book inventory and is used similarly. (See the preceding discussion of computer-assisted book inventories.) One additional bookkeeping item should be included for pictures. Because they come in different sizes and are used in different ways, their locations in center storage should be recorded in the inventory.

Example

How will large pictures, flannelboard figures, bulletin board cutouts, and three-dimensional aids be stored? Suppose there is a shelf for oversized pictures, a large envelope for regular-sized pictures, a wooden box for objects, and a drawer for multisubject pictures. How would a teacher know where to look for *any* oversized visual aids about horses, let alone know what kinds of aids are available at the center? The center records need to include where items can be found, if they are stored in different locations.

Using the same subject categories as those used for books helps teachers locate various aids on specific topics (e.g., books, pictures, or replicas).

AUDIO/VISUAL MEDIA

The software used should provide the same information as that of book inventorying software. (See the previous sections on book and picture inventories.)

Audio tapes and visual materials (filmstrips, videos,) will be fewer in number than books and pictures; however, there may be more than one copy and items may be stored in different places. Teachers need to know where to locate items (including large equipment) and may need to reserve them in advance. The inventory should provide a means by which a teacher can reserve equipment and materials for a particular time.

TOY AND CLASSROOM EQUIPMENT

An inventory program for toys and classroom equipment follows the basic format of that for other inventories. Continuity and ease in recording and using all inventory information will be valuable to the input operator and the center. One additional record-keeping item must be added to the toy and equipment category for emphasis, but is considered in all other inventories—replacement (or repair). Based on an item's popularity among teachers and children and its possible uses, duplicates, or even one for each child, may be needed.

The toy inventory will probably be the most extensive of the center's inventories, due to the multitude of items that are included. Some items may be categorized (large-muscle, scientific, dramatic-play) for convenience in using, ordering, and locating. Recording current costs of items and the purchase date gives a running account of price changes, durability, and longevity. (See Figure 11–8.)

SUPPLIES—CLASSROOM AND FOOD

The center needs to determine whether the classroom and general center food needs will be combined. As similar information is needed for both, they are discussed jointly here.

The similarities between supply inventories and other inventories are as follows:

1. Recording present items and future purchases
2. Using the computer information in

a. displaying (screen viewing) the information
b. changing the information
c. deleting the information
d. printing the information
e. locating items
f. replacing items

Differences occur in the frequency of purchasing, quantities purchased, methods of storage, kinds of items (perishable, multiuse), and amount of record keeping required.

The following information is necessary:

Name of item

Units in which ordered (ounces, pounds, packages)

Quantity in which ordered (sack, case)

Reorder level (when, at what quantity, delivery time)

Amount in stock

How and how much is used per usage

Unit price

Similarly to toy inventories, supply inventories can be conveniently subdivided into categories such as the following:

A number can be attached to each entry so that items could be ordered by code number instead of name in a computer program. Codes should allow extra numbers for new items, or new items could replace unused items.

Fresh Vegetables
avocado
bean sprouts
broccoli
cabbage
carrots
cauliflower
celery
lettuce
peas
peppers
potatoes
tomatoes
turnips

Juices
apple
grape
lemonade
orange
pear/grape
pineapple/grapefruit
tomato
V8 cocktail
other

Processed Fruits
applesauce
fruit cocktail
peaches
pears
pineapple

Cookies/Crackers
animal
butter
Fig Newtons
grahams
oatmeal
oyster
pretzels
Ritz
saltines
sugar
Town House
Triscuit
vanilla wafers
wheat thins
Wheatsworth
windmill

Grains
biscuits
bread—wheat
bread—white
bread sticks
cones, ice cream
croutons
mix—cake
mix—muffins
mix—pancakes

Dairy Products
butter
cheese
cheese spread
cottage cheese
cream
cream cheese
curd
eggs
ice cream
milk—canned
milk—dry
milk—fresh
sherbet
yogurt

Baking Needs
baking powder
flour
salt
shortening
soda
sugar—brown
sugar—powdered
sugar—white
vanilla
yeast

Meat
lean
avoid additives

Fresh Fruits
apples
bananas
berries
cantaloupe
grapes
lemons
melons
nectarines
oranges
pineapples
plums
strawberries
watermelon

Miscellaneous
catsup
Chinese noodles
gelatin
honey
mayonnaise
nuts
popcorn
prunes
pudding
raisins
soup—chicken
    noodle
soup—tomato
soup—vegetable

Glossary

Administrator: The person most responsible for the onsite, ongoing, daily supervision of the program and staff. The terms *administrator* and *director* are used interchangeably. (National Association for the Education of Young Children, 1984).

Adult- (Teacher) centered program: One in which the program is initiated, conducted, and evaluated from an adult point of view.

Assistant teacher: An adult with less training or experience who assists the head (or lead) teacher. Works in the classroom, under supervision, and is sometimes called a *support teacher.*

Associate's degree: The degree awarded from a postsecondary, 2-year program, generally equivalent to 60 to 64 college credits. May be offered as an Associate of Arts (A.A.), Associate of Science (A.S.), or Associate of Applied Science (A.A.S.) (Morgan et al., 1993).

At-risk children and families: This term includes families who experience poverty, unemployment, the presence of HIV, medical problems, substance abuse, teen-age parents, domestic violence, and other problems that limit their probability of success.

Authority: The power to judge, act, or command legally or as an agent. The person overseeing programs for young children may have dual roles or responsibilities and generally has the title of *director, coordinator, supervisor,* or *operator.* The term will be used interchangeably regardless of whether the person is an owner or an employee. The term also applies to some person or agency who presides over programs or people and has the responsibility of leadership and accountability.

Bachelor's degree: The degree awarded after completion of a 4-year postsecondary program of study, generally including general education courses, and a concentration or major in a liberal arts area or a career; it may be issued as a Bachelor of Arts (B.A.) or a Bachelor of Science (B.S.) (Morgan et al., 1993).

Board of directors: A set number of individuals who govern the financial and administrative workings of the organization.

Budget: A financial plan with goals for a specified time period.

Caregiver: An adult who oversees the care of a child or children in their home(s) or other settings. Usually a person who has a license or training, depending on state requirements. May also be called a *provider.*

Center-based care: Also referred to as child-care centers, or centers, it provides group experiences for children under school age. It consists of private care purchased by parents, government, private charity, or employers; Head Start; and public school programs. Center-based care includes for-profit, nonprofit, full-day, part-day, nursery schools, church-sponsored, employer-sponsored, day nurseries, and other child development programs.

Certificate: A document that is granted by a state for teachers, administrators, and related professional staff to indicate that an individual has met specific state training standards (Morgan et al., 1993).

Certification requirements: Requirements specifying the amount of training and education a prospective teacher must complete before employment. Requirements vary from state to state (Morgan et al., 1993).

Child Care and Development Block Grant (CCDBG): Comprehensive federal legislation passed in 1990 that provides funds to subsidize and enhance the quality of child-care services. The U.S. Department of Health and Human Services, through its Administration for Children and Families, disburses funds to the state agencies, designated by each governor, who further disburse funds (Morgan et al., 1993).

Child-care center: The child has interests, abilities, and needs that, when followed, lead the child to activities, time periods, and individuals with whom to be involved; has more responsibility for personal behavior. The program can be financed by private, religious, community, government, or other groups.

Child-centered program: One in which the curriculum and program are based on developmentally appropriate activities. The children have choices in activities, length of time spent, playmates, and in retrieving and replacing toys, and so on.

Child Development Associate Credential (CDA): A federally funded early childhood credential administered by the National Academy of Early Childhood

Programs, a division of the National Association for the Education of Young Children (NAEYC).

Children with special needs: Children whose developmental progress is deficient or delayed and need specific accommodation in education settings to help them reach their potential. Special needs are usually identified according to Public Law 91–142 (Morgan et al., 1993).

Classroom aide: A person without specialized experience or education who is hired provisionally and who may be promoted to assistant teacher after supervised experience and training.

Competency demonstration: A process through which practitioners gain college credit (or CDA experience) by demonstrating their knowledge and skills.

Developmentally appropriate practices: See *Child-centered program.*

Director: See *Administrator.*

Early care and education: All types of education and care for children from birth through age 5 and programs for school-age children before and after school and during vacations. *Care* and *education* cannot be separated. When one is caring for a child, one is also educating the child, and vice versa.

Early childhood education: See *Early care and education.*

Early childhood group: Birth through age 8. "The children assigned to a staff member or team of staff members, occupying an individual classroom or well-defined physical space within a larger room" (National Association for the Education of Young Children, 1984).

Endorsement: Additional information added to a teaching certificate indicating the services the endorsed individual can perform because of special training.

Facilities: Refers to the building, the equipment and supplies, the program of activities, and the people who work in the facility (Morgan et al., 1993).

Family child-care provider: Practitioners in charge of the care and education of six or fewer children in their own homes (Morgan et al., 1993).

Group child-care provider: Practitioners who generally provide care and education in their own homes for seven or more children with one or more paid assistants (Morgan et al., 1993).

Head Start: The federally funded, comprehensive early childhood education and enrichment program for low-income children and their families, originally created as one of the War on Poverty programs established in 1965 (Morgan et al., 1993).

Head teacher: See *Master teacher.*

Home-based care and education: Care and education that takes place in the home of the practitioner. See *Family child-care provider* and *Group child-care home provider* (Morgan et al., 1993).

Infants: Children from birth to 12 months of age.

In-service training: Ongoing training after the person is employed at a center or in a program.

Lead teacher: A trained or experienced adult who takes the leadership role planning for and working in the classroom with children. See *Master teacher.*

License: Permission by the licensing agent to operate a child-care center or home.

Management: Provides cohesiveness and continuity working with and through individuals to accomplish goals of the center. The following terms will be used interchangeably in this text: *management, administration,* and *leadership.*

Master teacher: A teacher who meets specified higher qualifications than those required of other classroom teachers. A person who plans for and works with young children in the classroom.

Mentor: A well-trained, experienced person, such as a supervisor, advisor, or teacher, who is willing to share knowledge, experiences, and time about a career with someone less experienced.

National Association for the Education of Young Children (NAEYC):   "The NAEYC is a nonprofit membership organization representing over 90,000 early childhood educators, policy makers, researchers, practitioners, and parents dedicated to improving the quality of services provided to young children and their families. The Association strives to promote the professional development of those who work with young children and to increase public understanding and support for high quality early childhood programs" (National Association for the Education of Young Children, 1984). Because of the high quality of publications, performance of staff, and other offerings (conferences, position statements, leadership, etc.), NAEYC has been used as a reliable source of information in this text.

Noncredit training: Includes workshops, conferences, and other kinds of experiences that are neither offered for college credit nor part of a recognized credentialing/accreditation system (Morgan et al., 1993).

Nonteaching staff: Individuals who are necessary in the operation of the program in roles other than teaching the children (secretarial, custodial, nutritional, etc.).

Owner: "Person legally responsible for the business operation of the program. This person may or may not be the same person who directs the daily implementation of the program including the supervision of staff and curriculum" (National Association for the Education of Young Children. 1984).

Performance appraisal: A two-way negotiation in which the supervisor and supervisee have input into goals, are working toward accomplishment, and is intended to be a positive, growth-promoting experience.

Practitioner: Individuals who work in early care and education.

Preschool children: Children from ages of 3 through 5 years.

Preservice training: The training (and experience) that is required to qualify for employment in a given role in early care training.

Program: A certain teaching style or philosophy adopted in a particular setting. This may also include vertical or horizontal age grouping as identified by a center.

Purchase of service: The arrangement of purchasing early care and eduction from private centers (both nonprofit and for-profit) and family child-care providers; the system includes both part- and full-day programs. Arrangements may be made by parents, employers, organizations, government agencies, or others.

Provider: The person in charge of a group of children in a home-based program.

Quality: "In terms of early care and education, high quality has the following features: low adult/child ratio, relatively small group size, age-appropriate activities, a safe environment, and access to comprehensive services, as needed, such as health and nutrition and parent involvement" (Morgan et al., 1993).

Resource and referral (R&R): "Agencies that help parents find suitable early care and education programs, provide training and technical assistance to practitioners, and develop and recruit practitioners to meet community needs. Child care resource and referral agencies also play a policy role at the local, state, and national level. A resource and referral agency can serve a community, a county, or a regional area" (Morgan et al., 1993).

Roles: Positions held by practitioners in early care and education.

School-age children: Children attending kindergarten or beyond.

Sponsor: An individual or group who underwrites a child-care center or group experience for young children. Most common examples are private franchise or independent (profit or nonprofit), church, federal, or local government, school, administration, industry, individual (in-home, rotating, foster, or day-care), university, and trade tech.

Staff: Paid adults who have nonteaching assignments in the center (secretary, custodian, cook).

Support person: Any less-trained or less-experienced adult working in the classroom with the children or an adult who upholds (backs up, aids, and bolsters) the lead teacher. This person is commonly called an *aide;* however, because of the responsibility given this role in this text, the person will also be called a *support teacher.*

Teacher: A paid adult who has direct responsibilities for the care and education of children; may also be called a *caregiver.*

Teacher- (Adult) centered program: One in which the program is initiated, conducted, and evaluated from an adult point of view.

Tickler file: A method of filing to remind the filer of things that need to be done in a certain order, or at a certain time.

Time management: The effective use of personal time.

Toddlers: Children between the ages of 13 and 36 months.

Training: "We use the term training generically to cover all specialized preparation for work in early care and education, from non-credit workshops, vocational education, and all levels of higher education degrees. We believe that early care and education training should be designed to transform beliefs, perspectives, and behaviors, and to contribute to personal growth" (Morgan et al., 1993).

REFERENCES

Morgan, G., Azer, S. L., Costley, J. B., Benser, A., Goodman, I. P., Lombardi, J., & McGimsey, B. 1993. *Making a career of it: The state of the states report on career development in early care and education.* Boston: Wheelock College.

National Association for the Education of Young Children. 1984. *Accreditation criteria and procedures of the National Academy of Early Childhood Programs.* Washington DC: Author.

Index